Stanley Gibb
Commonwealth Stan

Indian Ocean

3rd edition 2016

STANLEY GIBBONS LTD
London and Ringwood

By Appointment to
Her Majesty The Queen
Philatelists
Stanley Gibbons Ltd,
London

Published by Stanley Gibbons Ltd
Editorial, Publications Sales Offices
and Distribution Centre:
7 Parkside, Christchurch Road, Ringwood,
Hants BH24 3SH

1st Edition – 2006
2nd Edition – 2012
3rd Edition – 2016

British Library Cataloguing in
Publication Data.
A catalogue record for this book is available
from the British Library.

Errors and omissions excepted
the colour reproduction of stamps is only as
accurate as the printing process will allow.

ISBN-10: 0-85259-968-4
ISBN-13: 978-0-85259-968-6

Item No. R2986-16

Printed by
Latimer Trend & Company Ltd, Plymouth

Contents

Stanley Gibbons Holdings Plc

Stanley Gibbons Limited, Stanley Gibbons Auctions
399 Strand, London WC2R 0LX
Tel: +44 (0)207 836 8444
Fax: +44 (0)207 836 7342
E-mail: help@stanleygibbons.com
Website: www.stanleygibbons.com
for all departments, Auction and Specialist Stamp Departments.

Open Monday–Friday 9.30 a.m. to 5 p.m. Shop. Open Monday–Friday 9 a.m. to 5.30 p.m. and Saturday 9.30 a.m. to 5.30 p.m.

Stanley Gibbons Publications Gibbons Stamp Monthly and Philatelic Exporter
7 Parkside, Christchurch Road, Ringwood, Hampshire BH24 3SH.
Tel: +44 (0)1425 472363
Fax: +44 (0)1425 470247
E-mail: help@stanleygibbons.com
Publications Mail Order.
FREEPHONE 0800 611622

Monday–Friday 8.30 a.m. to 5 p.m.

Stanley Gibbons (Guernsey) Limited
18–20 Le Bordage, St Peter Port, Guernsey GY1 1DE.
Tel: +44 (0)1481 708270
Fax: +44 (0)1481 708279
E-mail: investment@stanleygibbons.com

Stanley Gibbons (Jersey) Limited
18 Hill Street, St Helier, Jersey, Channel Islands JE2 4UA.
Tel: +44 (0)1534 766711
Fax: +44 (0)1534 766177
E-mail: investment@stanleygibbons.com

Stanley Gibbons (Asia) Limited
Room 618, 6/F,
100 Queen's Road Central
Central,
Hong Kong
Tel: +852 3180 9370
E-mail: elee@stanleygibbons.com

Stanley Gibbons Publications Overseas Representation
Stanley Gibbons Publications are represented overseas by the following

Australia *Renniks Publications PTY LTD*
Unit 3 37-39 Green Street, Banksmeadow, NSW 2019, Australia
Tel: +612 9695 7055
Website: www.renniks.com

Canada *Unitrade Associates*
99 Floral Parkway, Toronto, Ontario M6L 2C4, Canada
Tel: +1 416 242 5900
Website: www.unitradeassoc.com

Germany *Schaubek Verlag Leipzig*
Am Glaeschen 23, D-04420 Markranstaedt, Germany
Tel: +49 34 205 67823
Website: www.schaubek.de

Italy *Ernesto Marini S.R.L.*
V. Struppa, 300, Genova, 16165, Italy
Tel: +3901 0247-3530
Website: www.ernestomarini.it

Japan *Japan Philatelic*
PO Box 2, Suginami-Minami, Tokyo 168-8081, Japan
Tel: +81 3330 41641
Website: www.yushu.co.jp

Netherlands also covers Belgium Denmark, Finland & France
Uitgeverij Davo BV
PO Box 411, Ak Deventer, 7400 Netherlands
Tel: +315 7050 2700
Website: www.davo.nl

New Zealand *House of Stamps*
PO Box 12, Paraparaumu, New Zealand
Tel: +61 6364 8270
Website: www.houseofstamps.co.nz

New Zealand *Philatelic Distributors*
PO Box 863
15 Mount Edgecumbe Street
New Plymouth 4615, New Zealand
Tel: +6 46 758 65 68
Website: www.stampcollecta.com

Norway *SKANFIL A/S*
SPANAV. 52 / BOKS 2030
N-5504 HAUGESUND, Norway
Tel: +47-52703940
E-mail: magne@skanfil.no

Singapore *C S Philatelic Agency*
Peninsula Shopping Centre #04-29
3 Coleman Street, 179804, Singapore
Tel: +65 6337-1859
Website: www.cs.com.sg

South Africa *Mr. Thematic*
737 Redwood Street
Randparkridge Ext 14
Gauteng, South Africa
Tel: +1606 553107
E-mail: ianfrith146@gmail.com, chrisb@asapcc.co.za

Sweden *Chr Winther Sorensen AB*
Box 43, S-310 20 Knaered, Sweden
Tel: +46 43050743
Website: www.collectia.se

USA *Regency Superior Ltd*
229 North Euclid Avenue
Saint Louis, Missouri 63108, USA

PO Box 8277, St Louis,
MO 63156-8277, USA
Toll Free Tel: (800) 782-0066
Tel: (314) 361-5699
Website: www.RegencySuperior.com
Email: info@regencysuperior.com

General Philatelic Information and Guidelines to the Scope of Stanley Gibbons Commonwealth Catalogues

These notes reflect current practice in compiling the Stanley Gibbons Commonwealth Catalogues.

The Stanley Gibbons Stamp Catalogue has a very long history and the vast quantity of information it contains has been carefully built up by successive generations through the work of countless individuals. Philately is never static and the Catalogue has evolved and developed over the years. These notes relate to the current criteria upon which a stamp may be listed or priced. These criteria have developed over time and may have differed somewhat in the early years of this catalogue. These notes are not intended to suggest that we plan to make wholesale changes to the listing of classic issues in order to bring them into line with today's listing policy, they are designed to inform catalogue users as to the policies currently in operation.

PRICES

The prices quoted in this Catalogue are the estimated selling prices of Stanley Gibbons Ltd at the time of publication. They are, unless it is specifically stated otherwise, for examples in fine condition for the issue concerned. Superb examples are worth more; those of a lower quality considerably less.

All prices are subject to change without prior notice and Stanley Gibbons Ltd may from time to time offer stamps below catalogue price. Individual low value stamps sold at 399 Strand are liable to an additional handling charge. Purchasers of new issues should note the prices charged for them contain an element for the service rendered and so may exceed the prices shown when the stamps are subsequently catalogued. Postage and handling charges are extra.

No guarantee is given to supply all stamps priced, since it is not possible to keep every catalogued item in stock. Commemorative issues may, at times, only be available in complete sets and not as individual values.

Quotation of prices. The prices in the left-hand column are for unused stamps and those in the right-hand column are for used.

A dagger (†) denotes that the item listed does not exist in that condition and a blank, or dash, that it exists, or may exist, but we are unable to quote a price.

Prices are expressed in pounds and pence sterling. One pound comprises 100 pence (£1 = 100p).

The method of notation is as follows: pence in numerals (e.g. 10 denotes ten pence); pounds and pence, up to £100, in numerals (e.g. 4.25 denotes four pounds and twenty-five pence); prices above £100 are expressed in whole pounds with the '£' sign shown.

Unused stamps. Great Britain and Commonwealth: the prices for unused stamps of Queen Victoria to King George V are for lightly hinged examples. Unused prices for King Edward VIII, King George VI and Queen Elizabeth issues are for unmounted mint.

Some stamps from the King George VI period are often difficult to find in unmounted mint condition. In such instances we would expect that collectors would

need to pay a high proportion of the price quoted to obtain mounted mint examples. Generally speaking lightly mounted mint stamps from this reign, issued before 1945, are in considerable demand.

Used stamps. The used prices are normally for fine postally used stamps, but may be for stamps cancelled-to-order where this practice exists.

A pen-cancellation on early issues can sometimes correctly denote postal use. Instances are individually noted in the Catalogue in explanation of the used price given.

Prices quoted for bisects on cover or large piece are for those dated during the period officially authorised.

Stamps not sold unused to the public (e.g. some official stamps) are priced used only.

The use of 'unified' designs, that is stamps inscribed for both postal and fiscal purposes, results in a number of stamps of very high face value. In some instances these may not have been primarily intended for postal purposes, but if they are so inscribed we include them. We only price such items used, however, where there is evidence of normal postal usage.

Cover prices. To assist collectors, cover prices are quoted for issues up to 1945 at the beginning of each country.

The system gives a general guide in the form of a factor by which the corresponding used price of the basic loose stamp should be multiplied when found in fine average condition on cover.

Care is needed in applying the factors and they relate to a cover which bears a single of the denomination listed; if more than one denomination is present the most highly priced attracts the multiplier and the remainder are priced at the simple figure for used singles in arriving at a total.

The cover should be of non-philatelic origin; bearing the correct postal rate for the period and distance involved and cancelled with the markings normal to the offices concerned. Purely philatelic items have a cover value only slightly greater than the catalogue value for the corresponding used stamps. This applies generally to those high-value stamps used philatelically rather than in the normal course of commerce. Low-value stamps, e.g. ¼d. and ½d., are desirable when used as a single rate on cover and merit an increase in 'multiplier' value.

First day covers in the period up to 1945 are not within the scope of the system and the multiplier should not be used. As a special category of philatelic usage, with wide variations in valuation according to scarcity, they require separate treatment.

Oversized covers, difficult to accommodate on an album page, should be reckoned as worth little more than the corresponding value of the used stamps. The condition of a cover also affects its value. Except for 'wreck covers', serious damage or soiling reduce the value where the postal markings and stamps are ordinary ones. Conversely, visual appeal adds to the value and this can include freshness of appearance, important addresses, old-fashioned but legible hand-writing, historic town-names, etc.

The multipliers are a base on which further value would be added to take account of the cover's postal historical importance in demonstrating such things as unusual, scarce or emergency cancels, interesting routes, significant postal markings, combination usage, the development of postal rates, and so on.

Minimum price. The minimum catalogue price quoted is 10p. For individual stamps prices between 10p. and 95p. are provided as a guide for catalogue users. The lowest price charged for individual stamps or sets purchased from Stanley Gibbons Ltd is £1

Set prices. Set prices are generally for one of each value, excluding shades and varieties, but including major colour changes. Where there are alternative shades, etc., the cheapest is usually included. The number of stamps in the set is always stated for clarity. The prices for sets containing *se-tenant* pieces are based on the prices quoted for such combinations, and not on those for the individual stamps.

Varieties. Where plate or cylinder varieties are priced in used condition the price quoted is for a fine used example with the cancellation well clear of the listed flaw.

Specimen stamps. The pricing of these items is explained under that heading.

Stamp booklets. Prices are for complete assembled booklets in fine condition with those issued before 1945 showing normal wear and tear. Incomplete booklets and those which have been 'exploded' will, in general, be worth less than the figure quoted.

Repricing. Collectors will be aware that the market factors of supply and demand directly influence the prices quoted in this Catalogue. Whatever the scarcity of a particular stamp, if there is no one in the market who wishes to buy it cannot be expected to achieve a high price. Conversely, the same item actively sought by numerous potential buyers may cause the price to rise.

All the prices in this Catalogue are examined during the preparation of each new edition by the expert staff of Stanley Gibbons and repriced as necessary. They take many factors into account, including supply and demand, and are in close touch with the international stamp market and the auction world.

Commonwealth cover prices and advice on postal history material originally provided by Edward B Proud.

GUARANTEE

All stamps are guaranteed originals in the following terms:

If not as described, and returned by the purchaser, we undertake to refund the price paid to us in the original transaction. If any stamp is certified as genuine by the Expert Committee of the Royal Philatelic Society, London, or by BPA Expertising Ltd, the purchaser shall not be entitled to make any claim against us for any error, omission or mistake in such certificate.

Consumers' statutory rights are not affected by the above guarantee.

The recognised Expert Committees in this country are those of the Royal Philatelic Society, 41 Devonshire Place, London W1G, 6JY, and BPA Expertising Ltd, PO Box 1141, Guildford, Surrey GU5 0WR. They do not undertake valuations under any circumstances and fees are payable for their services.

MARGINS ON IMPERFORATE STAMPS

| Superb | Very fine | Fine | Average | Poor |

GUM

| Unmounted | Very lightly mounted | Lightly mounted | Mounted/ large part original gum (o.g.). | Heavily mounted small part o.g. |

CENTRING

| Superb | Very fine | Fine | Average | Poor |

CANCELLATIONS

| Superb | Very fine | Fine | Average | Poor |

| Superb | Very fine |

| Fine | Average | Poor |

CONDITION GUIDE

To assist collectors in assessing the true value of items they are considering buying or in reviewing stamps already in their collections, we now offer a more detailed guide to the condition of stamps on which this catalogue's prices are based.

For a stamp to be described as 'Fine', it should be sound in all respects, without creases, bends, wrinkles, pin holes, thins or tears. If perforated, all perforation 'teeth' should be intact, it should not suffer from fading, rubbing or toning and it should be of clean, fresh appearance.

Margins on imperforate stamps: These should be even on all sides and should be at least as wide as half the distance between that stamp and the next. To have one or more margins of less than this width, would normally preclude a stamp from being described as 'Fine'. Some early stamps were positioned very close together on the printing plate and in such cases 'Fine' margins would necessarily be narrow. On the other hand, some plates were laid down to give a substantial gap between individual stamps and in such cases margins would be expected to be much wider.

An 'average' four-margin example would have a narrower margin on one or more sides and should be priced accordingly, while a stamp with wider, yet even, margins than 'Fine' would merit the description 'Very Fine' or 'Superb' and, if available, would command a price in excess of that quoted in the catalogue.

Gum: Since the prices for stamps of King Edward VIII, King George VI and Queen Elizabeth are for 'unmounted' or 'never hinged' mint, even stamps from these reigns which have been very lightly mounted should be available at a discount from catalogue price, the more obvious the hinge marks, the greater the discount.

Catalogue prices for stamps issued prior to King Edward VIII's reign are for mounted mint, so unmounted examples would be worth a premium. Hinge marks on 20th century stamps should not be too obtrusive, and should be at least in the lightly mounted category. For 19th century stamps more obvious hinging would be acceptable, but stamps should still carry a large part of their original gum—'Large part o.g.'—in order to be described as 'Fine'.

Centring: Ideally, the stamp's image should appear in the exact centre of the perforated area, giving equal margins on all sides. 'Fine' centring would be close to this ideal with any deviation having an effect on the value of the stamp. As in the case of the margins on imperforate stamps, it should be borne in mind that the space between some early stamps was very narrow, so it was very difficult to achieve accurate perforation, especially when the technology was in its infancy. Thus, poor centring would have a less damaging effect on the value of a 19th century stamp than on a 20th century example, but the premium put on a perfectly centred specimen would be greater.

Cancellations: Early cancellation devices were designed to 'obliterate' the stamp in order to prevent it being reused and this is still an important objective for today's postal administrations. Stamp collectors, on the other hand, prefer postmarks to be lightly applied, clear, and to leave as much as possible of the design visible. Dated, circular cancellations have long been 'the postmark of choice', but the definition of a 'Fine' cancellation will depend upon the types of cancellation in use at the time a stamp was current—it is clearly illogical to seek a circular datestamp on a Penny Black.

'Fine', by definition, will be superior to 'Average', so, in terms of cancellation quality, if one begins by identifying what 'Average' looks like, then one will be half way to identifying 'Fine'. The illustrations will give some guidance on mid-19th century and mid-20th century cancellations of Great Britain, but types of cancellation in general use in each country and in each period will determine the appearance of 'Fine'.

As for the factors discussed above, anything less than 'Fine' will result in a downgrading of the stamp concerned, while a very fine or superb cancellation will be worth a premium.

Combining the factors: To merit the description 'Fine', a stamp should be fine in every respect, but a small deficiency in one area might be made up for in another by a factor meriting an 'Extremely Fine' description.

Some early issues are so seldom found in what would normally be considered to be 'Fine' condition, the catalogue prices are for a slightly lower grade, with 'Fine' examples being worth a premium. In such cases a note to this effect is given in the catalogue, while elsewhere premiums are given for well-centred, lightly cancelled examples.

Stamps graded at less than fine remain collectable and, in the case of more highly priced stamps, will continue to hold a value. Nevertheless, buyers should always bear condition in mind.

The Catalogue in General

Contents. The Catalogue is confined to adhesive postage stamps, including miniature sheets. For particular categories the rules are:

(a) Revenue (fiscal) stamps are listed only where they have been expressly authorised for postal duty.

(b) Stamps issued only precancelled are included, but normally issued stamps available additionally with precancel have no separate precancel listing unless the face value is changed.

(c) Stamps prepared for use but not issued, hitherto accorded full listing, are nowadays foot-noted with a price (where possible).

(d) Bisects (trisects, etc.) are only listed where such usage was officially authorised.

(e) Stamps issued only on first day covers or in presentation packs and not available separately are not listed but may be priced in a footnote.

(f) New printings are only included in this Catalogue where they show a major philatelic variety, such as a change in shade, watermark or paper. Stamps which exist with or without imprint dates are listed separately; changes in imprint dates are mentioned in footnotes.

(g) Official and unofficial reprints are dealt with by footnote.

(h) Stamps from imperforate printings of modern issues which occur perforated are covered by footnotes, but are listed where widely available for postal use.

Exclusions. The following are excluded:

(a) non-postal revenue or fiscal stamps;

(b) postage stamps used fiscally (although prices are now given for some fiscally used high values);

(c) local carriage labels and private local issues;

(d) bogus or phantom stamps;

(e) railway or airline letter fee stamps, bus or road transport company labels or the stamps of private postal companies operating under licence from the national authority;

(f) cut-outs;

(g) all types of non-postal labels and souvenirs;

(h) documentary labels for the postal service, e.g. registration, recorded delivery, air-mail etiquettes, etc.;

(i) privately applied embellishments to official issues and privately commissioned items generally;

(j) stamps for training postal officers.

Full listing. 'Full listing' confers our recognition and implies allotting a catalogue number and (wherever possible) a price quotation.

In judging status for inclusion in the catalogue broad considerations are applied to stamps. They must be issued by a legitimate postal authority, recognised by the government concerned, and must be adhesives valid for proper postal use in the class of service for which they are inscribed. Stamps, with the exception of such categories as postage dues and officials, must be available to the general public, at face value, in reasonable quantities without any artificial restrictions being imposed on their distribution.

For errors and varieties the criterion is legitimate (albeit inadvertent) sale through a postal administration in the normal course of business. Details of provenance are always important; printers' waste and deliberately manufactured material are excluded.

Certificates. In assessing unlisted items due weight is given to Certificates from recognised Expert Committees and, where appropriate, we will usually ask to see them.

Date of issue. Where local issue dates differ from dates of release by agencies, 'date of issue' is the local date. Fortuitous stray usage before the officially intended date is disregarded in listing.

Catalogue numbers. Stamps of each country are catalogued chronologically by date of issue. Subsidiary classes are placed at the end of the country, as separate lists, with a distinguishing letter prefix to the catalogue number, e.g. D for postage due, O for official and E for express delivery stamps.

The catalogue number appears in the extreme left-column. The boldface Type numbers in the next column are merely cross-references to illustrations.

Once published in the Catalogue, numbers are changed as little as possible; really serious renumbering is reserved for the occasions when a complete country or an entire issue is being rewritten. The edition first affected includes cross-reference tables of old and new numbers.

Our catalogue numbers are universally recognised in specifying stamps and as a hallmark of status.

Illustrations. Stamps are illustrated at three-quarters linear size. Stamps not illustrated are the same size and format as the value shown, unless otherwise indicated. Stamps issued only as miniature sheets have the stamp alone illustrated but sheet size is also quoted. Overprints, surcharges, watermarks and postmarks are normally actual size. Illustrations of varieties are often enlarged to show the detail. Stamp booklet covers are illustrated half-size, unless otherwise indicated.

Designers. Designers' names are quoted where known, though space precludes naming every individual concerned in the production of a set. In particular, photographers supplying material are usually named only where they also make an active contribution in the design stage; posed photographs of reigning monarchs are, however, an exception to this rule.

CONTACTING THE CATALOGUE EDITOR

The editor is always interested in hearing from people who have new information which will improve or correct the Catalogue. As a general rule he must see and examine the actual stamps before they can be considered for listing; photographs or photocopies are insufficient evidence.

Submissions should be made in writing to the Catalogue Editor, Stanley Gibbons Publications at the Ringwood office. The cost of return postage for items submitted is appreciated, and this should include the registration fee if required.

Where information is solicited purely for the benefit of the enquirer, the editor cannot undertake to reply if the answer is already contained in these published notes or if return postage is omitted. Written communications are greatly preferred to enquiries by telephone or e-mail and the editor regrets that he or his staff cannot see personal callers without a prior appointment being made. Correspondence may be subject to delay during the production period of each new edition.

The editor welcomes close contact with study circles and is interested, too, in finding reliable local correspondents who will verify and supplement official information in countries where this is deficient.

We regret we do not give opinions as to the genuineness of stamps, nor do we identify stamps or number them by our Catalogue.

TECHNICAL MATTERS

The meanings of the technical terms used in the catalogue will be found in our *Philatelic Terms Illustrated*.

References below to (more specialised) listings are to be taken to indicate, as appropriate, the Stanley Gibbons *Great Britain Specialised Catalogue* in five volumes or the *Great Britain Concise Catalogue*.

1. Printing

Printing errors. Errors in printing are of major interest to the Catalogue. Authenticated items meriting consideration would include: background, centre or frame inverted or omitted; centre or subject transposed; error of colour; error or omission of value; double prints and impressions; printed both sides; and so on. Designs *tête-bêche*, whether intentionally or by accident, are listable. *Se-tenant* arrangements of stamps are recognised in the listings or footnotes. Gutter pairs (a pair of stamps separated by blank margin) are not included in this volume. Colours only partially omitted are not listed. Stamps with embossing omitted are reserved for our more specialised listings.

Printing varieties. Listing is accorded to major changes in the printing base which lead to completely new types. In recess-printing this could be a design re-engraved; in photogravure or photolithography a screen altered in whole or in part. It can also encompass flat-bed and rotary printing if the results are readily distinguishable.

To be considered at all, varieties must be constant.

Early stamps, produced by primitive methods, were prone to numerous imperfections; the lists reflect this, recognising re-entries, retouches, broken frames, misshapen letters, and so on. Printing technology has, however, radically improved over the years, during which time photogravure and lithography have become predominant. Varieties nowadays are more in the nature of flaws and these, being too specialised for this general catalogue, are almost always outside the scope.

In no catalogue, however, do we list such items as: dry prints, kiss prints, doctor-blade flaws, colour shifts or registration flaws (unless they lead to the complete omission of a colour from an individual stamp), lithographic ring flaws, and so on. Neither do we recognise fortuitous happenings like paper creases or confetti flaws.

Varieties of varieties. We no longer provide individual listings for combinations of two or more varieties; thus a plate variety or overprinting error will not be listed for different watermark orientations.

Overprints (and surcharges). Overprints of different types qualify for separate listing. These include overprints in different colours; overprints from different printing processes such as litho and typo; overprints in totally different typefaces, etc. Major errors in machine-printed overprints are important and listable. They include: overprint inverted or omitted; overprint double (treble, etc.); overprint diagonal; overprint double, one inverted; pairs with one overprint omitted, e.g. from a radical shift to an adjoining stamp; error of colour; error of type fount; letters inverted or omitted, etc. If the overprint is handstamped, few of these would qualify and a distinction is drawn. We continue, however, to list pairs of stamps where one has a handstamped overprint and the other has not.

Albino prints or double prints, one of them being albino (i.e. showing an uninked impression of the printing plate) are listable unless they are particularly common in this form (see the note below Travancore No. 32fa, for example). We do not, however, normally list reversed albino overprints, caused by the accidental or deliberate folding of sheets prior to overprinting (British Levant Nos. 51/8).

Varieties occurring in overprints will often take the form of broken letters, slight differences in spacing, rising spaces, etc. Only the most important would be considered for listing or footnote mention.

Sheet positions. If space permits we quote sheet positions of listed varieties and authenticated data is solicited for this purpose.

De La Rue plates. The Catalogue classifies the general plates used by De La Rue for printing British Colonial stamps as follows:

VICTORIAN KEY TYPE

Die I

1. The ball of decoration on the second point of the crown appears as a dark mass of lines.
2. Dark vertical shading separates the front hair from the bun.
3. The vertical line of colour outlining the front of the throat stops at the sixth line of shading on the neck.
4. The white space in the coil of the hair above the curl is roughly the shape of a pin's head.

Die II

1. There are very few lines of colour in the ball and it appears almost white.
2. A white vertical strand of hair appears in place of the dark shading.
3. The line stops at the eighth line of shading.
4. The white space is oblong, with a line of colour partially dividing it at the left end.

Plates numbered 1 and 2 are both Die I. Plates 3 and 4 are Die II.

GEORGIAN KEY TYPE

Die I

A. The second (thick) line below the name of the country is cut slanting, conforming roughly to the shape of the crown on each side.
B. The labels of solid colour bearing the words "POSTAGE" and "& REVENUE" are square at the inner top corners.
C. There is a projecting "bud" on the outer spiral of the ornament in each of the lower corners.

Die II

A. The second line is cut vertically on each side of the crown.
B. The labels curve inwards at the top.
C. There is no "bud" in this position.

Unless otherwise stated in the lists, all stamps with watermark Multiple Crown CA (w **8**) are Die I while those with watermark Multiple Crown Script CA (w **9**) are Die II. The Georgian Die II was introduced in April 1921 and was used for Plates 10 to 22 and 26 to 28. Plates 23 to 25 were made from Die I by mistake.

2. Paper

All stamps listed are deemed to be on (ordinary) paper of the wove type and white in colour; only departures from this are normally mentioned.

Types. Where classification so requires we distinguish such other types of paper as, for example, vertically and horizontally laid; wove and laid bâtonné; card(board); carton; cartridge; glazed; granite; native; pelure; porous; quadrillé; ribbed; rice; and silk thread.

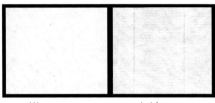

Wove paper   Laid paper

Granite paper   Quadrillé paper

Burelé band

The various makeshifts for normal paper are listed as appropriate. The varieties of double paper and joined paper are recognised. The security device of a printed burelé band on the back of a stamp, as in early Queensland, qualifies for listing.

Descriptive terms. The fact that a paper is handmade (and thus probably of uneven thickness) is mentioned where necessary. Such descriptive terms as "hard" and "soft"; "smooth" and "rough"; "thick", "medium" and "thin" are applied where there is philatelic merit in classifying papers.

Coloured, very white and toned papers. A coloured paper is one that is coloured right through (front and back of the stamp). In the Catalogue the colour of the paper is given in italics, thus:

black/*rose* = black design on rose paper.

Papers have been made specially white in recent years by, for example, a very heavy coating of chalk. We do not classify shades of whiteness of paper as distinct varieties. There does exist, however, a type of paper from early days called toned. This is off-white, often brownish or buffish, but it cannot be assigned any definite colour. A toning effect brought on by climate, incorrect storage or gum staining is disregarded here, as this was not the state of the paper when issued.

"Ordinary" and "Chalk-surfaced" papers. The availability of many postage stamps for revenue purposes made necessary some safeguard against the illegitimate re-use of stamps with removable cancellations. This was at first secured by using fugitive inks and later by printing on paper surfaced by coatings containing either chalk or china clay, both of which made it difficult to remove any form of obliteration without damaging the stamp design.

This catalogue lists these chalk-surfaced paper varieties from their introduction in 1905. Where no indication is given, the paper is "ordinary".

The "traditional" method of indentifying chalk-surfaced papers has been that, when touched with a silver wire, a black mark is left on the paper, and the listings in this catalogue are based on that test. However, the test itself is now largely discredited, for, although the mark can be removed by a soft rubber, some damage to the stamp will result from its use.

The difference between chalk-surfaced and pre-war ordinary papers is fairly clear: chalk-surfaced papers being smoother to the touch and showing a characteristic sheen when light is reflected off their surface. Under good magnification tiny bubbles or pock marks can be seen on the surface of the stamp and at the tips of the perforations the surfacing appears "broken". Traces of paper fibres are evident on the surface of ordinary paper and the ink shows a degree of absorption into it.

Initial chalk-surfaced paper printings by De La Rue had a thinner coating than subsequently became the norm. The characteristics described above are less pronounced in these printings.

During and after the Second World War, substitute papers replaced the chalk-surfaced papers, these do not react to the silver test and are therefore classed as "ordinary", although differentiating them without recourse to it is more difficult, for, although the characteristics of the chalk-surfaced paper remained the same, some of the ordinary papers appear much smoother than earlier papers and many do not show the watermark clearly. Experience is the only solution to identifying these, and comparison with stamps whose paper type is without question will be of great help.

Another type of paper, known as "thin striated" was used only for the Bahamas 1s. and 5s. (Nos. 155a, 156a, 171 and 174) and for several stamps of the Malayan states. Hitherto these have been described as "chalk-surfaced" since they gave some reaction to the silver test, but they are much thinner than usual chalk-surfaced papers, with the watermark showing clearly. Stamps on this paper show a slightly 'ribbed' effect when the stamp is held up to the light. Again, comparison with a known striated paper stamp, such as the 1941 Straits Settlements Die II 2c. orange (No. 294) will prove invaluable in separating these papers.

Glazed paper. In 1969 the Crown Agents introduced a new general-purpose paper for use in conjunction with all current printing processes. It generally has a marked glossy surface but the degree varies according to the process used, being more marked in recess-printing stamps. As it does not respond to the silver test this presents a further test where previous printings were on chalky paper. A change of paper to the glazed variety merits separate listing.

Green and yellow papers. Issues of the First World War and immediate postwar period occur on green and yellow papers and these are given separate Catalogue listing. The original coloured papers (coloured throughout) gave way to surface-coloured papers, the stamps having "white backs"; other stamps show one colour on the front and a different one at the back. Because of the numerous variations a grouping of colours is adopted as follows:

Yellow papers

(1) The original *yellow* paper (throughout), usually bright in colour. The gum is often sparse, of harsh consistency and dull-looking. Used 1912–1920.

(2) The *white-backs*. Used 1913–1914.

(3) A bright lemon paper. The colour must have a pronounced greenish tinge, different from the "yellow" in (1). As a rule, the gum on stamps using this lemon paper is plentiful, smooth and shiny, and the watermark shows distinctly. Care is needed with stamps printed in green on yellow paper (1) as it may appear that the paper is this lemon. Used 1914–1916.

(4) An experimental *orange-buff* paper. The colour must have a distinct brownish tinge. It is not to be confused with a muddy yellow (1) nor the misleading appearance (on the surface) of stamps printed in red on yellow paper where an engraved plate has been insufficiently wiped. Used 1918–1921.

(5) An experimental *buff* paper. This lacks the brownish tinge of (4) and the brightness of the yellow shades. The gum is shiny when compared with the matt type used on (4). Used 1919–1920.

(6) A *pale yellow* paper that has a creamy tone to the yellow. Used from 1920 onwards.

Green papers

(7) The original "green" paper, varying considerably through shades of blue-green and yellow-green, the front and back sometimes differing. Used 1912–1916.

(8) The *white backs*. Used 1913–1914.

(9) A paper blue-green on the surface with *pale olive* back. The back must be markedly paler than the front and this and the pronounced olive tinge to the back distinguish it from (7). Used 1916–1920.

(10) Paper with a vivid green surface, commonly called *emerald-green*; it has the olive back of (9). Used 1920.

(11) Paper with *emerald-green* both back and front. Used from 1920 onwards.

3. Perforation and Rouletting

Perforation gauge. The gauge of a perforation is the number of holes in a length of 2 cm. For correct classification the size of the holes (large or small) may need to be distinguished; in a few cases the actual number of holes on each edge of the stamp needs to be quoted.

Measurement. The Gibbons *Instanta* gauge is the standard for measuring perforations. The stamp is viewed against a dark background with the transparent gauge put on top of it. Though the gauge measures to decimal accuracy, perforations read from it are generally quoted in the Catalogue to the nearest half. For example:

Just over perf 12¾ to just under 13¼ = perf 13
Perf 13¼ exactly, rounded up   = perf 13½
Just over perf 13¼ to just under 13¾ = perf 13½
Perf 13¾ exactly, rounded up   = perf 14

However, where classification depends on it, actual quarter-perforations are quoted.

Notation. Where no perforation is quoted for an issue it is imperforate. Perforations are usually abbreviated (and spoken) as follows, though sometimes they may be spelled out for clarity. This notation for rectangular stamps (the majority) applies to diamond shapes if "top" is read as the edge to the top right.

P 14: perforated alike on all sides (read: "perf 14").

P 14×15: the first figure refers to top and bottom, the second to left and right sides (read: "perf 14 by 15"). This is a compound perforation. For an upright triangular stamp the first figure refers to the two sloping sides and second to the base. In inverted triangulars the base is first and the second figure to the sloping sides.

P 14–15: perforation measuring anything between 14 and 15: the holes are irregularly spaced, thus the gauge may vary along a single line or even along a single edge of the stamp (read: "perf 14 to 15").

P 14 *irregular*: perforated 14 from a worn perforator, giving badly aligned holes irregularly spaced (read: "irregular perf 14").

P *comp(ound)* 14×15: two gauges in use but not necessarily on opposite sides of the stamp. It could be one side in one gauge and three in the other; or two adjacent sides with the same gauge. (Read: "perf compound of 14 and 15".) For three gauges or more, abbreviated as "P 12, 14½, 15 *or compound*" for example.

P 14, 14½: perforated approximately 14¼ (read: "perf 14 or 14½"). It does *not* mean two stamps, one perf 14 and the other perf 14½. This obsolescent notation is gradually being replaced in the Catalogue.

Imperf: imperforate (not perforated)

Imperf×P 14: imperforate at top ad bottom and perf 14 at sides.

P 14×*imperf*: perf 14 at top and bottom and imperforate at sides.

Such headings as "P 13×14 (*vert*) and P 14×13 (*horiz*)" indicate which perforations apply to which stamp format—vertical or horizontal.

Some stamps are additionally perforated so that a label or tab is detachable; others have been perforated for use as two halves. Listings are normally for whole stamps, unless stated otherwise.

Imperf×perf

Other terms. Perforation almost always gives circular holes; where other shapes have been used they are specified, e.g. square holes; lozenge perf. Interrupted perfs are brought about by the omission of pins at regular intervals. Perforations merely simulated by being printed as part of the design are of course ignored. With few exceptions, privately applied perforations are not listed.

In the 19th century perforations are often described as clean cut (clean, sharply incised holes), intermediate or rough (rough holes, imperfectly cut, often the result of blunt pins).

Perforation errors and varieties. Authenticated errors, where a stamp normally perforated is accidentally issued imperforate, are listed provided no traces of perforation (blind holes or indentations) remain. They must be provided as pairs, both stamps wholly imperforate, and are only priced in that form.

Stamps imperforate between stamp and sheet margin are not listed in this catalogue, but such errors on Great Britain stamps will be found in the *Great Britain Specialised Catalogue*.

Pairs described as "imperforate between" have the line of perforations between the two stamps omitted.

Imperf between (horiz pair): a horizontal pair of stamps with perfs all around the edges but none between the stamps.

Imperf between (vert pair): a vertical pair of stamps with perfs all around the edges but none between the stamps.

Imperf between   Imperf horizontally
(vertical pair)   (vertical pair)

Where several of the rows have escaped perforation the resulting varieties are listable. Thus:

Imperf vert (horiz pair): a horizontal pair of stamps perforated top and bottom; all three vertical directions are imperf—the two outer edges and between the stamps.

Imperf horiz (vert pair): a vertical pair perforated at left and right edges; all three horizontal directions are imperf—the top, bottom and between the stamps.

Straight edges. Large sheets cut up before issue to post offices can cause stamps with straight edges, i.e. imperf on one side or on two sides at right angles. They are not usually listable in this condition and are worth less than corresponding stamps properly perforated all round. This does not, however, apply to certain stamps, mainly from coils and booklets, where straight edges on various sides are the manufacturing norm affecting every stamp. The listings and notes make clear which sides are correctly imperf.

Malfunction. Varieties of double, misplaced or partial perforation caused by error or machine malfunction are not listable, neither are freaks, such as perforations placed diagonally from paper folds, nor missing holes caused by broken pins.

Types of perforating. Where necessary for classification, perforation types are distinguished.

These include:

Line perforation from one line of pins punching single rows of holes at a time.

Comb perforation from pins disposed across the sheet in comb formation, punching out holes at three sides of the stamp a row at a time.

Harrow perforation applied to a whole pane or sheet at one stroke.

Rotary perforation from toothed wheels operating across a sheet, then crosswise.

Sewing machine perforation. The resultant condition, clean-cut or rough, is distinguished where required.

Pin-perforation is the commonly applied term for pin-roulette in which, instead of being punched out, round holes are pricked by sharp-pointed pins and no paper is removed.

Mixed perforation occurs when stamps with defective perforations are re-perforated in a different gauge.

Punctured stamps. Perforation holes can be punched into the face of the stamp. Patterns of small holes, often in the shape of initial letters, are privately applied devices against pilferage. These (perfins) are outside the scope except for Australia, Canada, Cape of Good Hope, Papua and Sudan where they were used as official stamps by the national administration. Identification devices, when officially inspired, are listed or noted; they can be shapes, or letters or words formed from holes, sometimes converting one class of stamp into another.

Rouletting. In rouletting the paper is cut, for ease of separation, but none is removed. The gauge is measured, when needed, as for perforations. Traditional French terms descriptive of the type of cut are often used and types include:

Arc roulette (percé en arc). Cuts are minute, spaced arcs, each roughly a semicircle.

Cross roulette (percé en croix). Cuts are tiny diagonal crosses.

Line roulette (percé en ligne or *en ligne droite).* Short straight cuts parallel to the frame of the stamp. The commonest basic roulette. Where not further described, "roulette" means this type.

Rouletted in colour or coloured roulette (percé en lignes colorées or *en lignes de coleur).* Cuts with coloured edges, arising from notched rule inked simultaneously with the printing plate.

Saw-tooth roulette (percé en scie). Cuts applied zigzag fashion to resemble the teeth of a saw.

Serpentine roulette (percé en serpentin). Cuts as sharply wavy lines.

Zigzag roulette (percé en zigzags). Short straight cuts at angles in alternate directions, producing sharp points on separation. US usage favours "serrate(d) roulette" for this type.

Pin-roulette (originally *percé en points* and now *perforés trous d'epingle*) is commonly called pin-perforation in English.

4. Gum

All stamps listed are assumed to have gum of some kind; if they were issued without gum this is stated. Original gum (o.g.) means that which was present on the stamp as issued to the public. Deleterious climates and the presence of certain chemicals can cause gum to crack and, with early stamps, even make the paper deteriorate. Unscrupulous fakers are adept in removing it and regumming the stamp to meet the unreasoning demand often made for "full o.g." in cases where such a thing is virtually impossible.

The gum normally used on stamps has been gum arabic until the late 1960s when synthetic adhesives were introduced. Harrison and Sons Ltd for instance use *polyvinyl alcohol,* known to philatelists as PVA. This is almost invisible except for a slight yellowish tinge which was incorporated to make it possible to see that the stamps have been gummed. It has advantages in hot countries, as stamps do not curl and sheets are less likely to stick together. Gum arabic and PVA are not distinguished in the lists except that where a stamp exists with both forms this is indicated in footnotes. Our more specialised catalogues provide separate listing of gums for Great Britain.

Self-adhesive stamps are issued on backing paper, from which they are peeled before affixing to mail. Unused examples are priced as for backing paper intact, in which condition they are recommended to be kept. Used examples are best collected on cover or on piece.

5. Watermarks

Stamps are on unwatermarked paper except where the heading to the set says otherwise.

Detection. Watermarks are detected for Catalogue description by one of four methods: (1) holding stamps to the light; (2) laying stamps face down on a dark background; (3) adding a few drops of petroleum ether 40/60 to the stamp laid face down in a watermark tray; (4) by use of the Stanley Gibbons Detectamark, or other equipment, which work by revealing the thinning of the paper at the watermark. (Note that petroleum ether is highly inflammable in use and can damage photogravure stamps.)

Listable types. Stamps occurring on both watermarked and unwatermarked papers are different types and both receive full listing.

Single watermarks (devices occurring once on every stamp) can be modified in size and shape as between different issues; the types are noted but not usually separately listed. Fortuitous absence of watermark from a single stamp or its gross displacement would not be listable.

To overcome registration difficulties the device may be repeated at close intervals *(a multiple watermark),* single stamps thus showing parts of several devices. Similarly, a *large sheet watermark* (or *all-over watermark*) covering numerous stamps can be used. We give informative notes and illustrations for them. The designs may be such that numbers of stamps in the sheet automatically lack watermark: this is not a listable variety. Multiple and all-over watermarks sometimes undergo modifications, but if the various types are difficult to distinguish from single stamps notes are given but not separate listings.

Papermakers' watermarks are noted where known but not listed separately, since most stamps in the sheet will lack them. Sheet watermarks which are nothing more than officially adopted papermakers' watermarks are, however, given normal listing.

Marginal watermarks, falling outside the pane of stamps, are ignored except where misplacement caused the adjoining row to be affected, in which case they may be footnoted. They usually consist of straight or angled lines and double-lined capital letters, they are particularly prevalent on some Crown CC and Crown CA watermarked stamps.

Watermark errors and varieties. Watermark errors are recognised as of major importance. They comprise stamps intended to be on unwatermarked paper but issued watermarked by mistake, or stamps printed on paper with the wrong watermark. Varieties showing letters omitted from the watermark are also included, but broken or deformed bits on the dandy roll are not listed unless they represent repairs.

Watermark positions. The diagram shows how watermark position is described in the Catalogue. Paper has a side intended for printing and watermarks are usually impressed so that they read normally when looked through from that printed side. However, since philatelists customarily detect watermarks by looking at the back of the stamp the watermark diagram also makes clear what is actually seen.

Illustrations in the Catalogue are of watermarks in normal positions (from the front of the stamps) and are actual size where possible.

Differences in watermark position are collectable varieties. This Catalogue now lists inverted, sideways inverted and reversed watermark varieties on Commonwealth stamps from the 1860s onwards except where the watermark position is completely haphazard.

Great Britain inverted and sideways inverted watermarks can be found in the *Great Britain Specialised Catalogue* and the *Great Britain Concise Catalogue*.

Where a watermark comes indiscriminately in various positions our policy is to cover this by a general note: we do not give separate listings because the watermark position in these circumstances has no particular philatelic importance.

As shown in the table, a watermark described as "sideways" will normally show the top of the letters or device (as shown in its illustration), pointing to the left of the stamp, as seen from the front and to the right as seen from the back.

For clarification, or in cases where the "normal" watermark is "sideways inverted", a note is generally provided at the foot of the relevant listing, particularly where sideways and sideways inverted varieties exist.

AS DESCRIBED (Read through front of stamp)		AS SEEN DURING WATERMARK DETECTION (Stamp face down and back examined
GvR	Normal	ЯvƆ
ЯʌƆ	Inverted	ƆʌЯ
ЯvƆ	Reversed	GvR
ƆʌЯ	Reversed and Inverted	ЯʌƆ
GvR (sideways, rotated)	Sideways	ƆʌЯ (sideways, rotated)
GvR (sideways inverted)	Sideways Inverted	ЯʌƆ (sideways inverted)

Standard types of watermark. Some watermarks have been used generally for various British possessions rather than exclusively for a single colony. To avoid repetition the Catalogue classifies 11 general types, as under, with references in the headings throughout the listings being given either in words or in the form ("W w **9**") (meaning "watermark type w **9**"). In those cases where watermark illustrations appear in the listings themselves, the respective reference reads, for example, W **153**, thus indicating that the watermark will be found in the normal sequence of illustrations as (type) **153**.

The general types are as follows, with an example of each quoted.

W	Description	Example
w 1	Large Star	St. Helena No. 1
w 2	Small Star	Turks Is. No. 4
w 3	Broad (pointed) Star	Grenada No. 24
w 4	Crown (over) CC, small stamp	Antigua No. 13
w 5	Crown (over) CC, large stamp	Antigua No. 31
w 6	Crown (over) CA, small stamp	Antigua No. 21
w 7	Crown CA (CA over Crown), large stamp	Sierra Leone No. 54
w 8	Multiple Crown CA	Antigua No. 41
w 9	Multiple Script CA	Seychelles No. 158
w 9a	do. Error	Seychelles No. 158a
w 9b	do. Error	Seychelles No. 158b
w 10	V over Crown	N.S.W. No. 327
w 11	Crown over A	N.S.W. No. 347

CC in these watermarks is an abbreviation for "Crown Colonies" and CA for "Crown Agents". Watermarks w **1**, w **2** and w **3** are on stamps printed by Perkins, Bacon; w **4** onwards on stamps from De La Rue and other printers.

w **1**
Large Star

w **2**
Small Star

w **3**
Broad-pointed Star

Watermark w **1**, *Large Star*, measures 15 to 16 mm across the star from point to point and about 27 mm from centre to centre vertically between stars in the sheet. It was made for long stamps like Ceylon 1857 and St. Helena 1856.

Watermark w **2**, *Small Star* is of similar design but measures 12 to 13½mm from point to point and 24 mm from centre to centre vertically. It was for use with ordinary-size stamps such as Grenada 1863–71.

When the Large Star watermark was used with the smaller stamps it only occasionally comes in the centre of the paper. It is frequently so misplaced as to show portions of two stars above and below and this eccentricity will very often help in determining the watermark.

Watermark w **3**, *Broad-pointed Star*, resembles w **1** but the points are broader.

| w **4** | w **5** |
| Crown (over) CC | Crown (over) CC |

Two *Crown (over) CC* watermarks were used: w **4** was for stamps of ordinary size and w **5** for those of larger size.

| w **6** | w **7** |
| Crown (over) CA | CA over Crown |

Two watermarks of *Crown CA* type were used, w **6** being for stamps of ordinary size. The other, w **7**, is properly described as *CA over Crown*. It was specially made for paper on which it was intended to print long fiscal stamps: that some were used postally accounts for the appearance of w **7** in the Catalogue. The watermark occupies twice the space of the ordinary Crown CA watermark, w **6**. Stamps of normal size printed on paper with w **7** watermark show it *sideways*; it takes a horizontal pair of stamps to show the entire watermark.

| w **8** | w **9** |
| Multiple Crown CA | Multiple Script CA |

Multiple watermarks began in 1904 with w **8**, *Multiple Crown CA*, changed from 1921 to w **9**, *Multiple Script CA*. On stamps of ordinary size portions of two or three watermarks appear and on the large-sized stamps a greater number can be observed. The change to letters in script character with w **9** was accompanied by a Crown of distinctly different shape.

It seems likely that there were at least two dandy rolls for each Crown Agents watermark in use at any one time with a reserve roll being employed when the normal one was withdrawn for maintenance or repair.

Both the Mult Crown CA and the Mult Script CA types exist with one or other of the letters omitted from individual impressions. It is possible that most of these occur from the reserve rolls as they have only been found on certain issues. The MCA watermark experienced such problems during the early 1920s and the Script over a longer period from the early 1940s until 1951.

During the 1920s damage must also have occurred on one of the Crowns as a substituted Crown has been found on certain issues. This is smaller than the normal and consists of an oval base joined to two upright ovals with a circle positioned between their upper ends. The upper line of the Crown's base is omitted, as are the left and right-hand circles at the top and also the cross over the centre circle.

Substituted Crown

The *Multiple Script CA* watermark, w **9**, is known with two errors, recurring among the 1950–52 printings of several territories. In the first a crown has fallen away from the dandy-roll that impresses the watermark into the paper pulp. It gives **9a**, *Crown missing*, but this omission has been found in both "Crown only" (*illustrated*) and "Crown CA" rows. The resulting faulty paper was used for Bahamas, Johore, Seychelles and the postage due stamps of nine colonies

w **9a**:
Error, Crown missing

w **9b**:
Error, St. Edward's Crown

When the omission was noticed a second mishap occurred, which was to insert a wrong crown in the space, giving w **9b**, St. Edward's Crown. This produced varieties in Bahamas, Perlis, St. Kitts-Nevis and Singapore and the incorrect crown likewise occurs in (Crown only) and (Crown CA) rows.

w 10
V over Crown

w 11
Crown over A

Resuming the general types, two watermarks found in issues of several Australian States are: w **10**, *V over Crown*, and w **11**, *Crown over A*.

w 12
Multiple St. Edward's
Crown Block CA

w 13
Multiple PTM

The *Multiple St. Edward's Crown Block CA* watermark, w **12**, was introduced in 1957 and besides the change in the Crown (from that used in Multiple Crown Script CA, w **9**) the letters reverted to block capitals. The new watermark began to appear sideways in 1966 and these stamps are generally listed as separate sets.

The watermark w **13**, *Multiple PTM*, was introduced for new Malaysian issues in November 1961.

w 14
Multiple Crown CA Diagonal

By 1974 the two dandy-rolls the "upright" and the "sideways" for w **12** were wearing out; the Crown Agents therefore discontinued using the sideways watermark one and retained the other only as a stand-by. A new dandy-roll with the pattern of w **14**, *Multiple Crown CA Diagonal*, was introduced and first saw use with some Churchill Centenary issues.

The new watermark had the design arranged in gradually spiralling rows. It is improved in design to allow smooth passage over the paper (the gaps between letters and rows had caused jolts in previous dandy-rolls) and the sharp corners and angles, where fibres used to accumulate, have been eliminated by rounding.

This watermark had no "normal" sideways position amongst the different printers using it. To avoid confusion our more specialised listings do not rely on such terms as "sideways inverted" but describe the direction in which the watermark points.

w 15
Multiple POST OFFICE

During 1981 w **15**, *Multiple POST OFFICE* was introduced for certain issues prepared by Philatelists Ltd, acting for various countries in the Indian Ocean, Pacific and West Indies.

w 16
Multiple Crown Script CA Diagonal

A new Crown Agents watermark was introduced during 1985, w **16**, *Multiple Crown Script CA Diagonal*. This was very similar to the previous w **14**, but showed "CA" in script rather than block letters. It was first used on the omnibus series of stamps commemorating the Life and Times of Queen Elizabeth the Queen Mother.

w 17
Multiple CARTOR

Watermark w **17**, *Multiple CARTOR*, was used from 1985 for issues printed by this French firm for countries which did not normally use the Crown Agents watermark.

w **18**

In 2008, following the closure of the Crown Agents Stamp Bureau, a new Multiple Crowns watermark, w **18** was introduced

In recent years the use of watermarks has, to a small extent, been superseded by fluorescent security markings. These are often more visible from the reverse of the stamp (Cook Islands from 1970 onwards), but have occurred printed over the design (Hong Kong Nos. 415/30). In 1982 the Crown Agents introduced a new stock paper, without watermark, known as "C-Kurity" on which a fluorescent pattern of blue rosettes is visible on the reverse, beneath the gum. This paper was used for issues from Gambia and Norfolk Island.

6. Colours

Stamps in two or three colours have these named in order of appearance, from the centre moving outwards. Four colours or more are usually listed as multicoloured.

In compound colour names the second is the predominant one, thus:

orange-red = a red tending towards orange;
red-orange = an orange containing more red than usual.

Standard colours used. The 200 colours most used for stamp identification are given in the Stanley Gibbons Stamp Colour Key. The Catalogue has used the Stamp Colour Key as standard for describing new issues for some years. The names are also introduced as lists are rewritten, though exceptions are made for those early issues where traditional names have become universally established.

Determining colours. When comparing actual stamps with colour samples in the Stamp Colour Key, view in a good north daylight (or its best substitute; fluorescent "colour matching" light). Sunshine is not recommended. Choose a solid portion of the stamp design; if available, marginal markings such as solid bars of colour or colour check dots are helpful. Shading lines in the design can be misleading as they appear lighter than solid colour. Postmarked portions of a stamp appear darker than normal. If more than one colour is present, mask off the extraneous ones as the eye tends to mix them.

Errors of colour. Major colour errors in stamps or overprints which qualify for listing are: wrong colours; one colour inverted in relation to the rest; albinos (colourless impressions), where these have Expert Committee certificates; colours completely omitted, but only on unused stamps (if found on used stamps the information is footnoted) and with good credentials, missing colours being frequently faked.

Colours only partially omitted are not recognised, Colour shifts, however spectacular, are not listed.

Shades. Shades in philately refer to variations in the intensity of a colour or the presence of differing amounts of other colours. They are particularly significant when they can be linked to specific printings. In general, shades need to be quite marked to fall within the scope of this Catalogue; it does not favour nowadays listing the often numerous shades of a stamp, but chooses a single applicable colour name which will indicate particular groups of outstanding shades. Furthermore, the listings refer to colours as issued; they may deteriorate into something different through the passage of time.

Modern colour printing by lithography is prone to marked differences of shade, even within a single run, and variations can occur within the same sheet. Such shades are not listed.

Aniline colours. An aniline colour meant originally one derived from coal-tar; it now refers more widely to colour of a particular brightness suffused on the surface of a stamp and showing through clearly on the back.

Colours of overprints and surcharges. All overprints and surcharges are in black unless stated otherwise in the heading or after the description of the stamp.

7. Specimen Stamps

Originally, stamps overprinted SPECIMEN were circulated to postmasters or kept in official records, but after the establishment of the Universal Postal Union supplies were sent to Berne for distribution to the postal administrations of member countries.

During the period 1884 to 1928 most of the stamps of British Crown Colonies required for this purpose were overprinted SPECIMEN in various shapes and sizes by their printers from typeset formes. Some locally produced provisionals were handstamped locally, as were sets prepared for presentation. From 1928 stamps were punched with holes forming the word SPECIMEN, each firm of printers using a different machine or machines. From 1948 the stamps supplied for UPU distribution were no longer punctured.

Stamps of some other Commonwealth territories were overprinted or handstamped locally, while stamps of Great Britain and those overprinted for use in overseas postal agencies (mostly of the higher denominations) bore SPECIMEN overprints and handstamps applied by the Inland Revenue or the Post Office.

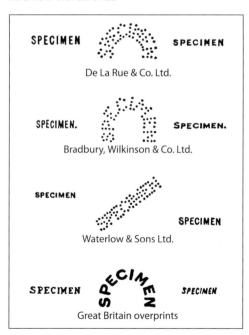

Some of the commoner types of overprints or punctures are illustrated here. Collectors are warned that dangerous forgeries of the punctured type exist.

The *Stanley Gibbons Commonwealth Catalogues* record those Specimen overprints or perforations intended for distribution by the UPU to member countries. In addition the Specimen overprints of Australia and its dependent territories, which were sold to collectors by the Post Office, are also included.

Various Perkins Bacon issues exist obliterated with a "CANCELLED" within an oval of bars handstamp.

Perkins Bacon "CANCELLED"
Handstamp

This was applied to six examples of those issues available in 1861 which were then given to members of Sir Rowland Hill's family. 75 different stamps (including four from Chile) are recorded with this handstamp although others may possibly exist. The unauthorised gift of these "CANCELLED" stamps to the Hill family was a major factor in the loss of the Agent General for the Crown Colonies (the forerunner of the Crown Agents) contracts by Perkins Bacon in the following year. Where examples of these scarce items are known to be in private hands the catalogue provides a price.

For full details of these stamps see *CANCELLED by Perkins Bacon* by Peter Jaffé (published by Spink in 1998).

All other Specimens are outside the scope of this volume.

Specimens are not quoted in Great Britain as they are fully listed in the Stanley Gibbons *Great Britain Specialised Catalogue*.

In specifying type of specimen for individual high-value stamps, "H/S" means handstamped, "Optd" is overprinted and "Perf" is punctured. Some sets occur mixed, e.g. "Optd/Perf". If unspecified, the type is apparent from the date or it is the same as for the lower values quoted as a set.

Prices. Prices for stamps up to £1 are quoted in sets; higher values are priced singly. Where specimens exist in more than one type the price quoted is for the cheapest. Specimen stamps have rarely survived even as pairs; these and strips of three, four or five are worth considerably more than singles.

8. Luminescence

Machines which sort mail electronically have been introduced in recent years. In consequence some countries have issued stamps on fluorescent or phosphorescent papers, while others have marked their stamps with phosphor bands.

The various papers can only be distinguished by ultraviolet lamps emitting particular wavelengths. They are separately listed only when the stamps have some other means of distinguishing them, visible without the use of these lamps. Where this is not so, the papers are recorded in footnotes or headings.

For this catalogue we do not consider it appropriate that collectors be compelled to have the use of an ultraviolet lamp before being able to identify stamps by our listings. Some experience will also be found necessary in interpreting the results given by ultraviolet. Collectors using the lamps, nevertheless, should exercise great care in their use as exposure to their light is potentially dangerous to the eyes.

Phosphor bands are listable, since they are visible to the naked eye (by holding stamps at an angle to the light and looking along them, the bands appear dark). Stamps existing with or without phosphor bands or with differing numbers of bands are given separate listings. Varieties such as double bands, bands omitted, misplaced or printed on the back are not listed.

Detailed descriptions appear at appropriate places in the listings in explanation of luminescent papers; see, for example, Australia above No. 363, Canada above Nos. 472 and 611, Cook Is. above 249, etc.

For Great Britain, where since 1959 phosphors have played a prominent and intricate part in stamp issues, the main notes above Nos. 599 and 723 should be studied, as well as the footnotes to individual listings where appropriate. In general the classification is as follows.

Stamps with phosphor bands are those where a separate cylinder applies the phosphor after the stamps are printed. Issues with "all-over" phosphor have the "band" covering the entire stamp. Parts of the stamp covered by phosphor bands, or the entire surface for "all-over" phosphor versions, appear matt. Stamps on phosphorised paper have the phosphor added to the paper coating before the stamps are printed. Issues on this paper have a completely shiny surface.

Further particularisation of phosphor – their methods of printing and the colours they exhibit under ultraviolet – is outside the scope. The more specialised listings should be consulted for this information.

9. Coil Stamps

Stamps issued only in coil form are given full listing. If stamps are issued in both sheets and coils the coil stamps are listed separately only where there is some feature (e.g. perforation or watermark sideways) by which singles can be distinguished. Coil stamps containing different stamps *se-tenant* are also listed.

Coil join pairs are too random and too easily faked to permit of listing; similarly ignored are coil stamps which have accidentally suffered an extra row of perforations from the claw mechanism in a malfunctioning vending machine.

10. Stamp Booklets

Stamp booklets are now listed in this catalogue.

Single stamps from booklets are listed if they are distinguishable in some way (such as watermark or perforation) from similar sheet stamps.

Booklet panes are listed where they contain stamps of different denominations *se-tenant*, where stamp-size labels are included, or where such panes are otherwise identifiable. Booklet panes are placed in the listing under the lowest denomination present.

Particular perforations (straight edges) are covered by appropriate notes.

The majority of booklets were made up from normal sheets and panes may be bound upright or inverted and booklets may be stapled or stitched at either the left or right-hand side. Unless specifically mentioned in the listings, such variations do not command a price premium.

11. Miniature Sheets and Sheetlets

We distinguish between "miniature sheets" and "sheetlets" and this affects the catalogue numbering. An item in sheet form that is postally valid, containing a single stamp, pair, block or set of stamps, with wide, inscribed and/or decorative margins, is a miniature sheet if it is sold at post offices as an indivisable entity. As such the Catalogue allots a single MS number and describes what stamps make it up. The sheetlet or small sheet differs in that the individual stamps are intended to be purchased separately for postal purposes. For sheetlets, all the component postage stamps are numbered individually and the composition explained in a footnote. Note that the definitions refer to post office sale—not how items may be subsequently offered by stamp dealers.

12. Forgeries and Fakes

Forgeries. Where space permits, notes are considered if they can give a concise description that will permit unequivocal detection of a forgery. Generalised warnings, lacking detail, are not nowadays inserted, since their value to the collector is problematic.

Forged cancellations have also been applied to genuine stamps. This catalogue includes notes regarding those manufactured by "Madame Joseph", together with the cancellation dates known to exist. It should be remembered that these dates also exist as genuine cancellations.

For full details of these see *Madame Joseph Forged Postmarks* by Derek Worboys (published by the Royal Philatelic Society London and the British Philatelic Trust in 1994) or *Madame Joseph Revisited* by Brian Cartwright (published by the Royal Philatelic Society London in 2005).

Fakes. Unwitting fakes are numerous, particularly "new shades" which are colour changelings brought about by exposure to sunlight, soaking in water contaminated with dyes from adherent paper, contact with oil and dirt from a pocketbook, and so on. Fraudulent operators, in addition, can offer to arrange: removal of hinge marks; repairs of thins on white or coloured papers; replacement of missing margins or perforations; reperforating in true or false gauges; removal of fiscal cancellations; rejoining of severed pairs, strips and blocks; and (a major hazard) regumming. Collectors can only be urged to purchase from reputable sources and to insist upon Expert Committee certification where there is any kind of doubt.

The Catalogue can consider footnotes about fakes where these are specific enough to assist in detection.

ACKNOWLEDGEMENTS

We are grateful to individual collectors, members of the philatelic trade and specialist societies and study circles for their assistance in improving and extending the Stanley Gibbons range of catalogues. The address of the study circle relevant to this volume is:

Indian Ocean Study Circle
Secretary — Mrs S. Hopson
Field Acre, Hoe Benham
Newbury,
Berkshire RG20 8PD

Abbreviations

Printers

A.B.N. Co.	American Bank Note Co, New York.
B.A.B.N.	British American Bank Note Co. Ottawa
B.D.T.	B.D.T. International Security Printing Ltd, Dublin, Ireland
B.W.	Bradbury Wilkinson & Co, Ltd.
Cartor	Cartor S.A., La Loupe, France
C.B.N.	Canadian Bank Note Co, Ottawa.
Continental	Continental Bank Note Co. B.N. Co.
Courvoisier	Imprimerie Courvoisier S.A., La-Chaux-de-Fonds, Switzerland.
D.L.R.	De La Rue & Co, Ltd, London.
Enschedé	Joh. Enschedé en Zonen, Haarlem, Netherlands.
Format	Format International Security Printers Ltd., London
Harrison	Harrison & Sons, Ltd. London
J.W.	John Waddington Security Print Ltd., Leeds
P.B.	Perkins Bacon Ltd, London.
Questa	Questa Colour Security Printers Ltd, London
Walsall	Walsall Security Printers Ltd
Waterlow	Waterlow & Sons, Ltd, London.

General Abbreviations

Alph	Alphabet
Anniv	Anniversary
Comp	Compound (perforation)
Des	Designer; designed
Diag	Diagonal; diagonally
Eng	Engraver; engraved
F.C.	Fiscal Cancellation
H/S	Handstamped
Horiz	Horizontal; horizontally
Imp, Imperf	Imperforate
Inscr	Inscribed
L	Left
Litho	Lithographed
mm	Millimetres
MS	Miniature sheet
N.Y.	New York
Opt(d)	Overprint(ed)
P or P-c	Pen-cancelled
P, Pf or Perf	Perforated
Photo	Photogravure
Pl	Plate
Pr	Pair
Ptd	Printed
Ptg	Printing
R	Right
R.	Row

Recess	Recess-printed
Roto	Rotogravure
Roul	Rouletted
S	Specimen (overprint)
Surch	Surcharge(d)
T.C.	Telegraph Cancellation
T	Type
Typo	Typographed
Un	Unused
Us	Used
Vert	Vertical; vertically
W or wmk	Watermark
Wmk s	Watermark sideways

(†) = Does not exist

(–) (or blank price column) = Exists, or may exist, but no market price is known.

/ between colours means "on" and the colour following is that of the paper on which the stamp is printed.

Colours of Stamps

Bl (blue); blk (black); brn (brown); car, carm (carmine); choc (chocolate); clar (claret); emer (emerald); grn (green); ind (indigo); mag (magenta); mar (maroon); mult (multicoloured); mve (mauve); ol (olive); orge (orange); pk (pink); pur (purple); scar (scarlet); sep (sepia); turq (turquoise); ultram (ultramarine); verm (vermilion); vio (violet); yell (yellow).

Colour of Overprints and Surcharges

(B.) = blue, (Blk.) = black, (Br.) = brown, (C.) = carmine, (G.) = green, (Mag.) = magenta, (Mve.) = mauve, (Ol.) = olive, (O.) = orange, (P.) = purple, (Pk.) = pink, (R.) = red, (Sil.) = silver, (V.) = violet, (Vm.) or (Verm.) = vermilion, (W.) = white, (Y.) = yellow.

Arabic Numerals

As in the case of European figures, the details of the Arabic numerals vary in different stamp designs, but they should be readily recognised with the aid of this illustration.

٠	١	٢	٣	٤	٥	٦	٧	٨	٩
0	1	2	3	4	5	6	7	8	9

Features Listing

An at-a-glance guide to what's in the Stanley Gibbons catalogues

Area	Feature	Collect British Stamps	Stamps of the World	Thematic Catalogues	Comprehensive Catalogue, Parts 1-22 (including Commonwealth and British Empire Stamps and country catalogues)	Great Britain Concise	Specialised catalogues
General	SG number	√	√	√	√	√	√
General	Specialised Catalogue number						√
General	Year of issue of first stamp in design	√	√	√	√	√	√
General	Exact date of issue of each design				√	√	√
General	Face value information	√	√	√	√	√	√
General	Historical and geographical information	√	√	√	√	√	√
General	General currency information, including dates used	√	√	√	√	√	√
General	Country name	√	√	√		√	√
General	Booklet panes				√	√	√
General	Coil stamps				√		
General	First Day Covers	√				√	√
General	Brief footnotes on key areas of note	√	√	√		√	√
General	Detailed footnotes on key areas of note				√	√	√
General	Extra background information				√	√	√
General	Miniature sheet information (including size in mm)	√	√	√	√	√	√
General	Sheetlets				√		
General	Stamp booklets				√	√	√
General	Perkins Bacon "Cancelled"				√		
General	PHQ Cards	√				√	√
General	Post Office Label Sheets				√		
General	Post Office Yearbooks	√				√	√
General	Presentation and Souvenir Packs	√				√	√
General	Se-tenant pairs	√			√	√	√
General	Watermark details - errors, varieties, positions				√	√	√
General	Watermark illustrations	√			√	√	√
General	Watermark types	√			√	√	√
General	Forgeries noted				√		√
General	Surcharges and overprint information	√	√	√	√	√	√
Design and Description	Colour description, simplified		√	√			
Design and Description	Colour description, extended	√			√	√	√
Design and Description	Set design summary information	√	√	√	√	√	√
Design and Description	Designer name				√	√	√
Design and Description	Short design description	√	√	√	√	√	√

Area	Feature	Collect British Stamps	Stamps of the World	Thematic Catalogues	Commonwealth and British Empire Stamps and country catalogues)	Comprehensive Catalogue, Parts 1-22 (including Commonwealth catalogues)	Great Britain Concise	Specialised catalogues
Design and Description	Shade varieties					√	√	√
Design and Description	Type number	√	√			√	√	√
Illustrations	Multiple stamps from set illustrated	√				√	√	√
Illustrations	A Stamp from each set illustrated in full colour (where possible, otherwise mono)	√	√	√		√	√	√
Price	Catalogue used price	√	√	√		√	√	√
Price	Catalogue unused price	√	√	√		√	√	√
Price	Price - booklet panes					√	√	√
Price	Price - shade varieties					√	√	√
Price	On cover and on piece price					√	√	√
Price	Detailed GB pricing breakdown	√				√	√	√
Print and Paper	Basic printing process information	√	√	√		√	√	√
Print and Paper	Detailed printing process information, e.g. Mill sheets					√		√
Print and Paper	Paper information					√		√
Print and Paper	Detailed perforation information	√				√	√	√
Print and Paper	Details of research findings relating to printing processes and history							√
Print and Paper	Paper colour	√	√			√	√	√
Print and Paper	Paper description to aid identification					√		√
Print and Paper	Paper type					√		√
Print and Paper	Ordinary or chalk-surfaced paper					√	√	√
Print and Paper	Embossing omitted note							√
Print and Paper	Essays, Die Proofs, Plate Descriptions and Proofs, Colour Trials information							√
Print and Paper	Glazed paper					√	√	√
Print and Paper	Gum details					√		√
Print and Paper	Luminescence/Phosphor bands - general coverage	√				√	√	√
Print and Paper	Luminescence/Phosphor bands - specialised coverage							√
Print and Paper	Overprints and surcharges - including colour information	√	√	√		√	√	√
Print and Paper	Perforation/Imperforate information	√	√			√	√	√
Print and Paper	Perforation errors and varieties					√	√	√
Print and Paper	Print quantities							√
Print and Paper	Printing errors					√	√	√
Print and Paper	Printing flaws							√
Print and Paper	Printing varieties					√	√	√
Print and Paper	Punctured stamps - where official					√		
Print and Paper	Sheet positions					√	√	√
Print and Paper	Specialised plate number information							√
Print and Paper	Specimen overprints (only for Commonwealth & GB)					√	√	√
Print and Paper	Underprints						√	√
Print and Paper	Visible Plate numbers	√				√	√	√
Print and Paper	Yellow and Green paper listings					√		√
Index	Design index	√				√	√	

International Philatelic Glossary

English	French	German	Spanish	Italian
Agate	Agate	Achat	Agata	Agata
Air stamp	Timbre de la poste aérienne	Flugpostmarke	Sello de correo aéreo	Francobollo per posta aerea
Apple Green	Vert-pomme	Apfelgrün	Verde manzana	Verde mela
Barred	Annulé par barres	Balkenentwertung	Anulado con barras	Sbarrato
Bisected	Timbre coupé	Halbiert	Partido en dos	Frazionato
Bistre	Bistre	Bister	Bistre	Bistro
Bistre-brown	Brun-bistre	Bisterbraun	Castaño bistre	Bruno-bistro
Black	Noir	Schwarz	Negro	Nero
Blackish Brown	Brun-noir	Schwärzlichbraun	Castaño negruzco	Bruno nerastro
Blackish Green	Vert foncé	Schwärzlichgrün	Verde negruzco	Verde nerastro
Blackish Olive	Olive foncé	Schwärzlicholiv	Oliva negruzco	Oliva nerastro
Block of four	Bloc de quatre	Viererblock	Bloque de cuatro	Bloco di quattro
Blue	Bleu	Blau	Azul	Azzurro
Blue-green	Vert-bleu	Blaugrün	Verde azul	Verde azzuro
Bluish Violet	Violet bleuâtre	Bläulichviolett	Violeta azulado	Violtto azzurrastro
Booklet	Carnet	Heft	Cuadernillo	Libretto
Bright Blue	Bleu vif	Lebhaftblau	Azul vivo	Azzurro vivo
Bright Green	Vert vif	Lebhaftgrün	Verde vivo	Verde vivo
Bright Purple	Mauve vif	Lebhaftpurpur	Púrpura vivo	Porpora vivo
Bronze Green	Vert-bronze	Bronzegrün	Verde bronce	Verde bronzo
Brown	Brun	Braun	Castaño	Bruno
Brown-lake	Carmin-brun	Braunlack	Laca castaño	Lacca bruno
Brown-purple	Pourpre-brun	Braunpurpur	Púrpura castaño	Porpora bruno
Brown-red	Rouge-brun	Braunrot	Rojo castaño	Rosso bruno
Buff	Chamois	Sämisch	Anteado	Camoscio
Cancellation	Oblitération	Entwertung	Cancelación	Annullamento
Cancelled	Annulé	Gestempelt	Cancelado	Annullato
Carmine	Carmin	Karmin	Carmín	Carminio
Carmine-red	Rouge-carmin	Karminrot	Rojo carmín	Rosso carminio
Centred	Centré	Zentriert	Centrado	Centrato
Cerise	Rouge-cerise	Kirschrot	Color de ceresa	Color Ciliegia
Chalk-surfaced paper	Papier couché	Kreidepapier	Papel estucado	Carta gessata
Chalky Blue	Bleu terne	Kreideblau	Azul turbio	Azzurro smorto
Charity stamp	Timbre de bienfaisance	Wohltätigkeitsmarke	Sello de beneficenza	Francobollo di beneficenza
Chestnut	Marron	Kastanienbraun	Castaño rojo	Marrone
Chocolate	Chocolat	Schokolade	Chocolate	Cioccolato
Cinnamon	Cannelle	Zimtbraun	Canela	Cannella
Claret	Grenat	Weinrot	Rojo vinoso	Vinaccia
Cobalt	Cobalt	Kobalt	Cobalto	Cobalto
Colour	Couleur	Farbe	Color	Colore
Comb-perforation	Dentelure en peigne	Kammzähnung, Reihenzähnung	Dentado de peine	Dentellatura e pettine
Commemorative stamp	Timbre commémoratif	Gedenkmarke	Sello conmemorativo	Francobollo commemorativo
Crimson	Cramoisi	Karmesin	Carmesí	Cremisi
Deep Blue	Blue foncé	Dunkelblau	Azul oscuro	Azzurro scuro
Deep bluish Green	Vert-bleu foncé	Dunkelbläulichgrün	Verde azulado oscuro	Verde azzurro scuro
Design	Dessin	Markenbild	Diseño	Disegno

English	French	German	Spanish	Italian
Die	Matrice	Urstempel. Type, Platte	Cuño	Conio, Matrice
Double	Double	Doppelt	Doble	Doppio
Drab	Olive terne	Trüboliv	Oliva turbio	Oliva smorto
Dull Green	Vert terne	Trübgrün	Verde turbio	Verde smorto
Dull purple	Mauve terne	Trübpurpur	Púrpura turbio	Porpora smorto
Embossing	Impression en relief	Prägedruck	Impresión en relieve	Impressione a relievo
Emerald	Vert-eméraude	Smaragdgrün	Esmeralda	Smeraldo
Engraved	Gravé	Graviert	Grabado	Inciso
Error	Erreur	Fehler, Fehldruck	Error	Errore
Essay	Essai	Probedruck	Ensayo	Saggio
Express letter stamp	Timbre pour lettres par exprès	Eilmarke	Sello de urgencia	Francobollo per espresso
Fiscal stamp	Timbre fiscal	Stempelmarke	Sello fiscal	Francobollo fiscale
Flesh	Chair	Fleischfarben	Carne	Carnicino
Forgery	Faux, Falsification	Fälschung	Falsificación	Falso, Falsificazione
Frame	Cadre	Rahmen	Marco	Cornice
Granite paper	Papier avec fragments de fils de soie	Faserpapier	Papel con filamentos	Carto con fili di seta
Green	Vert	Grün	Verde	Verde
Greenish Blue	Bleu verdâtre	Grünlichblau	Azul verdoso	Azzurro verdastro
Greenish Yellow	Jaune-vert	Grünlichgelb	Amarillo verdoso	Giallo verdastro
Grey	Gris	Grau	Gris	Grigio
Grey-blue	Bleu-gris	Graublau	Azul gris	Azzurro grigio
Grey-green	Vert gris	Graugrün	Verde gris	Verde grigio
Gum	Gomme	Gummi	Goma	Gomma
Gutter	Interpanneau	Zwischensteg	Espacio blanco entre dos grupos	Ponte
Imperforate	Non-dentelé	Geschnitten	Sin dentar	Non dentellato
Indigo	Indigo	Indigo	Azul indigo	Indaco
Inscription	Inscription	Inschrift	Inscripción	Dicitura
Inverted	Renversé	Kopfstehend	Invertido	Capovolto
Issue	Émission	Ausgabe	Emisión	Emissione
Laid	Vergé	Gestreift	Listado	Vergato
Lake	Lie de vin	Lackfarbe	Laca	Lacca
Lake-brown	Brun-carmin	Lackbraun	Castaño laca	Bruno lacca
Lavender	Bleu-lavande	Lavendel	Color de alhucema	Lavanda
Lemon	Jaune-citron	Zitrongelb	Limón	Limone
Light Blue	Bleu clair	Hellblau	Azul claro	Azzurro chiaro
Lilac	Lilas	Lila	Lila	Lilla
Line perforation	Dentelure en lignes	Linienzähnung	Dentado en linea	Dentellatura lineare
Lithography	Lithographie	Steindruck	Litografía	Litografia
Local	Timbre de poste locale	Lokalpostmarke	Emisión local	Emissione locale
Lozenge roulette	Percé en losanges	Rautenförmiger Durchstich	Picadura en rombos	Perforazione a losanghe
Magenta	Magenta	Magentarot	Magenta	Magenta
Margin	Marge	Rand	Borde	Margine
Maroon	Marron pourpré	Dunkelrotpurpur	Púrpura rojo oscuro	Marrone rossastro
Mauve	Mauve	Malvenfarbe	Malva	Malva
Multicoloured	Polychrome	Mehrfarbig	Multicolores	Policromo
Myrtle Green	Vert myrte	Myrtengrün	Verde mirto	Verde mirto
New Blue	Bleu ciel vif	Neublau	Azul nuevo	Azzurro nuovo
Newspaper stamp	Timbre pour journaux	Zeitungsmarke	Sello para periódicos	Francobollo per giornali
Obliteration	Oblitération	Abstempelung	Matasello	Annullamento
Obsolete	Hors (de) cours	Ausser Kurs	Fuera de curso	Fuori corso

English	French	German	Spanish	Italian
Ochre	Ocre	Ocker	Ocre	Ocra
Official stamp	Timbre de service	Dienstmarke	Sello de servicio	Francobollo di
Olive-brown	Brun-olive	Olivbraun	Castaño oliva	Bruno oliva
Olive-green	Vert-olive	Olivgrün	Verde oliva	Verde oliva
Olive-grey	Gris-olive	Olivgrau	Gris oliva	Grigio oliva
Olive-yellow	Jaune-olive	Olivgelb	Amarillo oliva	Giallo oliva
Orange	Orange	Orange	Naranja	Arancio
Orange-brown	Brun-orange	Orangebraun	Castaño naranja	Bruno arancio
Orange-red	Rouge-orange	Orangerot	Rojo naranja	Rosso arancio
Orange-yellow	Jaune-orange	Orangegelb	Amarillo naranja	Giallo arancio
Overprint	Surcharge	Aufdruck	Sobrecarga	Soprastampa
Pair	Paire	Paar	Pareja	Coppia
Pale	Pâle	Blass	Pálido	Pallido
Pane	Panneau	Gruppe	Grupo	Gruppo
Paper	Papier	Papier	Papel	Carta
Parcel post stamp	Timbre pour colis postaux	Paketmarke	Sello para paquete postal	Francobollo per pacchi postali
Pen-cancelled	Oblitéré à plume	Federzugentwertung	Cancelado a pluma	Annullato a penna
Percé en arc	Percé en arc	Bogenförmiger Durchstich	Picadura en forma de arco	Perforazione ad arco
Percé en scie	Percé en scie	Bogenförmiger Durchstich	Picado en sierra	Foratura a sega
Perforated	Dentelé	Gezähnt	Dentado	Dentellato
Perforation	Dentelure	Zähnung	Dentar	Dentellatura
Photogravure	Photogravure, Heliogravure	Rastertiefdruck	Fotograbado	Rotocalco
Pin perforation	Percé en points	In Punkten durchstochen	Horadado con alfileres	Perforato a punti
Plate	Planche	Platte	Plancha	Lastra, Tavola
Plum	Prune	Pflaumenfarbe	Color de ciruela	Prugna
Postage Due stamp	Timbre-taxe	Portomarke	Sello de tasa	Segnatasse
Postage stamp	Timbre-poste	Briefmarke, Freimarke, Postmarke	Sello de correos	Francobollo postale
Postal fiscal stamp	Timbre fiscal-postal	Stempelmarke als Postmarke verwendet	Sello fiscal-postal	Fiscale postale
Postmark	Oblitération postale	Poststempel	Matasello	Bollo
Printing	Impression, Tirage	Druck	Impresión	Stampa, Tiratura
Proof	Épreuve	Druckprobe	Prueba de impresión	Prova
Provisionals	Timbres provisoires	Provisorische Marken. Provisorien	Provisionales	Provvisori
Prussian Blue	Bleu de Prusse	Preussischblau	Azul de Prusia	Azzurro di Prussia
Purple	Pourpre	Purpur	Púrpura	Porpora
Purple-brown	Brun-pourpre	Purpurbraun	Castaño púrpura	Bruno porpora
Recess-printing	Impression en taille douce	Tiefdruck	Grabado	Incisione
Red	Rouge	Rot	Rojo	Rosso
Red-brown	Brun-rouge	Rotbraun	Castaño rojizo	Bruno rosso
Reddish Lilac	Lilas rougeâtre	Rötlichlila	Lila rojizo	Lilla rossastro
Reddish Purple	Poupre-rouge	Rötlichpurpur	Púrpura rojizo	Porpora rossastro
Reddish Violet	Violet rougeâtre	Rötlichviolett	Violeta rojizo	Violetto rossastro
Red-orange	Orange rougeâtre	Rotorange	Naranja rojizo	Arancio rosso
Registration stamp	Timbre pour lettre chargée (recommandée)	Einschreibemarke	Sello de certificado lettere	Francobollo per raccomandate
Reprint	Réimpression	Neudruck	Reimpresión	Ristampa
Reversed	Retourné	Umgekehrt	Invertido	Rovesciato
Rose	Rose	Rosa	Rosa	Rosa
Rose-red	Rouge rosé	Rosarot	Rojo rosado	Rosso rosa
Rosine	Rose vif	Lebhaftrosa	Rosa vivo	Rosa vivo
Roulette	Percage	Durchstich	Picadura	Foratura
Rouletted	Percé	Durchstochen	Picado	Forato
Royal Blue	Bleu-roi	Königblau	Azul real	Azzurro reale

English	French	German	Spanish	Italian
Sage green	Vert-sauge	Salbeigrün	Verde salvia	Verde salvia
Salmon	Saumon	Lachs	Salmón	Salmone
Scarlet	Écarlate	Scharlach	Escarlata	Scarlatto
Sepia	Sépia	Sepia	Sepia	Seppia
Serpentine roulette	Percé en serpentin	Schlangenliniger Durchstich	Picado a serpentina	Perforazione a serpentina
Shade	Nuance	Tönung	Tono	Gradazione de colore
Sheet	Feuille	Bogen	Hoja	Foglio
Slate	Ardoise	Schiefer	Pizarra	Ardesia
Slate-blue	Bleu-ardoise	Schieferblau	Azul pizarra	Azzurro ardesia
Slate-green	Vert-ardoise	Schiefergrün	Verde pizarra	Verde ardesia
Slate-lilac	Lilas-gris	Schierferlila	Lila pizarra	Lilla ardesia
Slate-purple	Mauve-gris	Schieferpurpur	Púrpura pizarra	Porpora ardesia
Slate-violet	Violet-gris	Schieferviolett	Violeta pizarra	Violetto ardesia
Special delivery stamp	Timbre pour exprès	Eilmarke	Sello de urgencia	Francobollo per espressi
Specimen	Spécimen	Muster	Muestra	Saggio
Steel Blue	Bleu acier	Stahlblau	Azul acero	Azzurro acciaio
Strip	Bande	Streifen	Tira	Striscia
Surcharge	Surcharge	Aufdruck	Sobrecarga	Soprastampa
Tête-bêche	Tête-bêche	Kehrdruck	Tête-bêche	Tête-bêche
Tinted paper	Papier teinté	Getöntes Papier	Papel coloreado	Carta tinta
Too-late stamp	Timbre pour lettres en retard	Verspätungsmarke	Sello para cartas retardadas	Francobollo per le lettere in ritardo
Turquoise-blue	Bleu-turquoise	Türkisblau	Azul turquesa	Azzurro turchese
Turquoise-green	Vert-turquoise	Türkisgrün	Verde turquesa	Verde turchese
Typography	Typographie	Buchdruck	Tipografia	Tipografia
Ultramarine	Outremer	Ultramarin	Ultramar	Oltremare
Unused	Neuf	Ungebraucht	Nuevo	Nuovo
Used	Oblitéré, Usé	Gebraucht	Usado	Usato
Venetian Red	Rouge-brun terne	Venezianischrot	Rojo veneciano	Rosso veneziano
Vermilion	Vermillon	Zinnober	Cinabrio	Vermiglione
Violet	Violet	Violett	Violeta	Violetto
Violet-blue	Bleu-violet	Violettblau	Azul violeta	Azzurro violetto
Watermark	Filigrane	Wasserzeichen	Filigrana	Filigrana
Watermark sideways	Filigrane couché	Wasserzeichen liegend	Filigrana acostado	Filigrana coricata
Wove paper	Papier ordinaire, Papier uni	Einfaches Papier	Papel avitelado	Carta unita
Yellow	Jaune	Gelb	Amarillo	Giallo
Yellow-brown	Brun-jaune	Gelbbraun	Castaño amarillo	Bruno giallo
Yellow-green	Vert-jaune	Gelbgrün	Verde amarillo	Verde giallo
Yellow-olive	Olive-jaunâtre	Gelboliv	Oliva amarillo	Oliva giallastro
Yellow-orange	Orange jaunâtre	Gelborange	Naranja amarillo	Arancio giallastro
Zig-zag roulette	Percé en zigzag	Sägezahnartiger Durchstich	Picado en zigzag	Perforazione a zigzag

Guide to Entries

Ⓐ Country of Issue – When a country changes its name, the catalogue listing changes to reflect the name change, for example Namibia was formerly known as South West Africa, the stamps in Southern Africa are all listed under Namibia, but split into South West Africa and then Namibia.

Ⓑ Country Information – Brief geographical and historical details for the issuing country.

Ⓒ Currency – Details of the currency, and dates of earliest use where applicable, on the face value of the stamps.

Ⓓ Illustration – Generally, the first stamp in the set. Stamp illustrations are reduced to 75%, with overprints and surcharges shown actual size.

Ⓔ Illustration or Type Number – These numbers are used to help identify stamps, either in the listing, type column, design line or footnote, usually the first value in a set. These type numbers are in a bold type face – **123**; when bracketed (**123**) an overprint or a surcharge is indicated. Some type numbers include a lower-case letter – **123a**, this indicates they have been added to an existing set.

Ⓕ Date of issue – This is the date that the stamp/set of stamps was issued by the post office and was available for purchase. When a set of definitive stamps has been issued over several years the Year Date given is for the earliest issue. Commemorative sets are listed in chronological order. Stamps of the same design, or issue are usually grouped together, for example some of the New Zealand landscapes definitive series were first issued in 2003 but the set includes stamps issued to May 2007.

Ⓖ Number Prefix – Stamps other than definitives and commemoratives have a prefix letter before the catalogue number.
Their use is explained in the text: some examples are A for airmail, D for postage due and O for official stamps.

Ⓗ Footnote – Further information on background or key facts on issues.

Ⓘ Stanley Gibbons Catalogue number – This is a unique number for each stamp to help the collector identify stamps in the listing. The Stanley Gibbons numbering system is universally recognized as definitive.
Where insufficient numbers have been left to provide for additional stamps to a listing, some stamps will have a suffix letter after the catalogue number (for example 214a). If numbers have been left for additions to a set and not used they will be left vacant.
The separate type numbers (in bold) refer to illustrations (see **E**).

Ⓙ Colour – If a stamp is printed in three or fewer colours then the colours are listed, working from the centre of the stamp outwards (see **R**).

Ⓚ Design line – Further details on design variations

Ⓛ Key Type – Indicates a design type on which the stamp is based. These are the bold figures found below each illustration, for example listed in Cameroon, in the West Africa catalogue, is the Key type A and B showing the ex-Kaiser's yacht *Hohenzollern*. The type numbers are also given in bold in the second column of figures alongside the stamp description to indicate the design of each stamp. Where an issue comprises stamps of similar design, the corresponding type number should be taken as indicating the general design. Where there are blanks in the type number column it means that the type of the corresponding stamp

is that shown by the number in the type column of the same issue. A dash (–) in the type column means that the stamp is not illustrated. Where type numbers refer to stamps of another country, e.g. where stamps of one country are overprinted for use in another, this is always made clear in the text.

Ⓜ Coloured Papers – Stamps printed on coloured paper are shown – e.g. "brown/*yellow*" indicates brown printed on yellow paper.

Ⓝ Surcharges and Overprints – Usually described in the headings. Any actual wordings are shown in bold type. Descriptions clarify words and figures used in the overprint. Stamps with the same overprints in different colours are not listed separately. Numbers in brackets after the descriptions are the catalogue numbers of the non-overprinted stamps. The words "inscribed" or "inscription" refer to the wording incorporated in the design of a stamp and not surcharges or overprints.

Ⓞ Face value – This refers to the value of each stamp and is the price it was sold for at the Post Office when issued. Some modern stamps do not have their values in figures but instead it is shown as a letter, for example Great Britain use 1st or 2nd on their stamps as opposed to the actual value.

Ⓟ Catalogue Value – Mint/Unused. Prices quoted for Queen Victoria to King George V stamps are for lightly hinged examples.

Ⓠ Catalogue Value – Used. Prices generally refer to fine postally used examples. For certain issues they are for cancelled-to-order.

Prices
Prices are given in pence and pounds. Stamps worth £100 and over are shown in whole pounds:

Shown in Catalogue as	Explanation
10	10 pence
1.75	£1.75
15.00	£15
£150	£150
£2300	£2300

Prices assume stamps are in 'fine condition'; we may ask more for superb and less for those of lower quality. The minimum catalogue price quoted is 10p and is intended as a guide for catalogue users. The lowest price for individual stamps purchased from Stanley Gibbons is £1.

Prices quoted are for the cheapest variety of that particular stamp. Differences of watermark, perforation, or other details, often increase the value. Prices quoted for mint issues are for single examples, unless otherwise stated. Those in *se-tenant* pairs, strips, blocks or sheets may be worth more. Where no prices are listed it is either because the stamps are not known to exist (usually shown by a †) in that particular condition, or, more usually, because there is no reliable information on which to base their value.

All prices are subject to change without prior notice and we cannot guarantee to supply all stamps as priced. Prices quoted in advertisements are also subject to change without prior notice.

Ⓡ Multicoloured – Nearly all modern stamps are multicoloured (more than three colours); this is indicated in the heading, with a description of the stamp given in the listing.

Ⓢ Perforations – Please see page xiii for a detailed explanation of perforations.

A Country of issue ────•

Bangladesh

B Country Information

In elections during December 1970 the Awami League party won all but two of the seats in the East Pakistan province and, in consequence, held a majority in the National Assembly. On 1 March 1971 the Federal Government postponed the sitting of the Assembly with the result that unrest spread throughout the eastern province. Pakistan army operations against the dissidents forced the leaders of the League to flee to India from where East Pakistan was proclaimed independent as Bangladesh. In early December the Indian army moved against Pakistan troops in Bangladesh and civilian government was re-established on 22 December 1971.

From 20 December 1971 various Pakistan issues were overprinted by local postmasters, mainly using handstamps. Their use was permitted until 30 April 1973. These are of philatelic interest, but are outside the scope of the catalogue.

C Currency ────────•**(Currency. 100 paisa = 1 rupee)**

D Illustration

5c
N.Z. GOVERNMENT LIFE INSURANCE OFFICE

L 17 •

E Illustration or Type number

F Date of issue ────•**1978** (8 Mar). No. *L* 57 surch with Type *L* **16**. Chalky paper.

L63	*L* **14**	25c. on 2½c. ultramarine, green and buff	75	1·75

(Des A. G. Mitchell. Litho Harrison)

G Number prefix ────•

1981 (3 June). P 14½.

L64	*L* **17**	5c. multicoloured	10	10
L65		10c. multicoloured	10	10
L66		20c. multicoloured	15	15
L67		30c. multicoloured	25	25
L68		40c. multicoloured	30	30
L69		50c. multicoloured	30	45
L64/9 *Set of 6*			1·00	1·25

H Footnote ────• Issues for the Government Life Insurance Department were withdrawn on 1 December 1989 when it became the privatised Tower Corporation.

(Des G. R. Bull and G. R. Smith. Photo Harrison)

I Stanley Gibbons catalogue number ────•

1959 (2 Mar). Centenary of Marlborough Province. T **198** and similar horiz designs. W **98** (sideways). P 14½×14.

772		2d. green	30	10
773		3d. deep blue	30	10
774		8d. light brown	1·25	2·25
772/4 *Set of 3*			1·60	2·25

J Colour

K Design line ────• Designs:—3d. Shipping wool, Wairau Bar, 1857; 8d. Salt industry, Grasmere.

1915 (12 July). Stamps of German Kamerun. Types *A* and *B*, surch as T **1** (Nos. B1/9) or **2**. (Nos. B10/13) in black or blue.

L Key type column ────•

B1	*A*	1½d. on 3pf. (No. k7) (B.)	13·00	42·00
		a. Different fount "d"	£150	£350

340	**41**	2d. purple (1903)	£350	£325
341	**28**	3d. bistre-brown (1906)	£700	£600
342	**37**	4d. blue and chestnut/*bluish* (1904)..	£300	£350
		a. Blue and yellow-brown/*bluish*	£300	£350

M Coloured papers

N Surcharges and overprints ────

1913 (1 Dec). Auckland Industrial Exhibition. Nos. 387aa, 389, 392 and 405 optd with T **59** by Govt Printer, Wellington.

412	**51**	½d. deep green	20·00	55·00
413	**53**	1d. carmine	25·00	48·00
		a. "Feather" flaw	£225	
414	**52**	3d. chestnut	£130	£250
415		6d. carmine	£160	£300
412/15 *Set of 4*			£300	£600

O Face value ────

P Catalogue value – Mint

Q Catalogue value – Used

These overprinted stamps were only available for letters in New Zealand and to Australia.

(Des Martin Bailey. Litho Southern Colour Print)

R Multicoloured stamp ────

2008 (2 July). Olympic Games, Beijing. T **685** and similar diamond-shaped designs. Multicoloured. Phosphorised paper. P 14½.

3056	50c. Type **685**	1·00	85

S Perforations

Stanley Gibbons
Stamp Catalogues

Stamps of the World 1
Simplified Catalogue 2016 Edition

2016 Stanley Gibbons Stamp Catalogue
COMMONWEALTH & BRITISH EMPIRE STAMPS 1840-1970

The vital reference work for Commonwealth collectors
Many thousands of price increases
Hundreds of new items listed

We have catalogues to suit every aspect of stamp collecting

Our catalogues cover stamps issued from across the globe - from the Penny Black to the latest issues. Whether you're a specialist in a certain reign or a thematic collector, we should have something to suit your needs. All catalogues include the famous SG numbering system, making it as easy as possible to find the stamp you're looking for.

Commonwealth & British Empire Stamps 1840-1970 (118th edition, 2016)

Commonwealth Country Catalogues

Australia & Dependencies (9th Edition, 2014)
Bangladesh, Pakistan & Sri Lanka (3rd edition, 2015)
Belize, Guyana, Trinidad & Tobago (2nd edition, 2013)
Brunei, Malaysia & Singapore (4th edition, 2013)
Canada (5th edition, 2014)
Central Africa (2nd edition, 2008)
Cyprus, Gibraltar & Malta (4th edition, 2014)
East Africa with Egypt & Sudan (3rd edition, 2014)
Eastern Pacific (3rd edition, 2015)
Falkland Islands (7th edition, 2016)
Hong Kong (5th edition, 2015)
India (including Convention & Feudatory States) (4th edition, 2013)
Indian Ocean (3rd edition, 2016)
Ireland (6th edition, 2015)
Leeward Islands (2nd edition, 2012)
New Zealand (5th edition, 2014)
Northern Caribbean, Bahamas & Bermuda (4th edition, 2016)
St. Helena & Dependencies (5th edition, 2014)
Southern Africa (2nd edition, 2008)
Southern & Central Africa (2nd edition, 2014)
West Africa (2nd edition, 2012)
Western Pacific (3rd edition, 2014)
Windward Islands & Barbados (3rd edition, 2015)

Stamps of the World 2016

Volume 1 Abu Dhabi – Charkhari
Volume 2 Chile – Georgia
Volume 3 German Commands – Jasdan
Volume 4 Jersey – New Republic
Volume 5 New South Wales – Singapore
Volume 6 Sirmoor – Zululand

Great Britain Catalogues

Collect British Stamps (67th edition, 2016)
Collect Channel Islands & Isle of Man (30th edition, 2016)
Great Britain Concise Stamp Catalogue (30th edition, 2015)

Great Britain Specialised

Volume 1   Queen Victoria (16th edition, 2012)
Volume 2   King Edward VII to King George VI (14th edition, 2015)
Volume 3   Queen Elizabeth II Pre-decimal issues (12th edition, 2011)
Volume 4   Queen Elizabeth II Decimal Definitive Issues – Part 1 (10th edition, 2008)
Queen Elizabeth II Decimal Definitive Issues – Part 2 (10th edition, 2010)

Foreign Countries

Arabia (1st edition, 2016)
Austria & Hungary (8th edition, 2014)
Balkans (5th edition, 2009)
Belgium & Luxembourg (1st edition, 2015)
Central America (3rd edition, 2007)
Central Asia (4th edition, 2006)
China (11th edition, 2015)
Czech Republic, Slovakia & Poland (7th edition, 2012)
France, Andorra and Monaco (1st edition, May 2015)
Germany (11th edition, 2014)
Italy & Switzerland (8th edition, 2013)
Japan & Korea (5th edition, 2008)
Middle East (7th edition, 2009)
Portugal & Spain (6th edition, 2011)
Poland (1st edition, 2015)
Russia (7th edition, 2014)
Scandinavia (7th edition, 2013)
South America (4th edition, 2008)
South-East Asia (5th edition, 2012)
United States of America (8th edition, 2015)

To order, call **01425 472 363** or for our full range of catalogues, **visit www.stanleygibbons.com**

Est 1856
STANLEY GIBBONS

Stanley Gibbons Limited
7 Parkside, Christchurch Road, Ringwood, Hants, BH24 3SH
+44 (0)1425 472 363
www.stanleygibbons.com

British Indian Ocean Territory

This Crown Colony was created on 8 November 1965 when it comprised the Chagos Archipelago, previously administered by Mauritius, together with the islands of Aldabra, Farquhar and Desroches, previously administered by Seychelles.

(Currency. 100 cents = 1 rupee).

B.I.O.T.

(1)

1968 (17 Jan). As Nos. 196/200, 202/4 and 206/12 of Seychelles, optd with T **1**. W w **12** (sideways* on 5, 10, 15, 20, 25, 50, 75c. and 10r.).

1	5c. multicoloured	1·00	1·50
	a. No stop after "I"	18·00	21·00
	b. No stop after "O"	6·50	10·00
	w. Wmk Crown to right of CA	75·00	
2	10c. multicoloured	10	15
	a. No stop after "I"	32·00	32·00
	b. No stop after "O"	5·50	12·00
3	15c. multicoloured	25	20
	a. No stop after "I"	16·00	19·00
	b. No stop after "O"	5·50	9·50
4	20c. multicoloured	20	15
	a. No stop after "I"	17·00	17·00
	b. No stop after "O"	7·00	8·50
5	25c. multicoloured	20	15
	a. No stop after "I"	12·00	17·00
	b. No stop after "O"	5·50	10·00
6	40c. multicoloured	20	20
	a. No stop after "I"	20·00	20·00
	b. No stop after "O"	8·50	13·00
7	45c. multicoloured	20	30
	a. No stop after "I"	24·00	18·00
	b. No stop after "B"	40·00	27·00
	c. No stop after "O"	75·00	55·00
8	50c. multicoloured	20	30
	a. No stop after "I"	19·00	19·00
	b. No stop after "O"	7·50	9·50
9	75c. multicoloured	3·00	35
10	1r. multicoloured	2·00	35
	a. No stop after "I"	27·00	24·00
	b. No stop after "O"	8·00	11·00
11	1r.50 multicoloured	2·00	1·50
	a. No stop after "I"	50·00	50·00
	b. No stop after "O"	26·00	17·00
12	2r.25 multicoloured	3·00	3·75
	a. No stop after "I"	£110	£120
	b. No stop after "O"	80·00	80·00
13	3r.50 multicoloured	3·00	4·50
	a. No stop after "1"	£100	£100
	b. No stop after "O"	45·00	42·00
14	5r. multicoloured	10·00	6·50
	a. No stop after "I"	£150	£140
	b. No stop after "O"	60·00	55·00
15	10r. multicoloured	20·00	15·00
	a. No stop after "B"	£190	£180
	b. No stop after "I"	£250	£250
	c. No stop after "O"	£110	£110
1/15	*Set of 15*	40·00	30·00

*The normal sideways watermark shows Crown to left of CA, *as seen from the back of the stamp.*

These were issued by the Crown Agents on 15 January but owing to shipping delays they were not put on sale locally until 17 January.

The positions of the "no stop" varieties are as follows:

After "I": R. 2/4 on horiz stamps except 45c. where it occurs on R. 3/3, and R. 8/5 on vert stamps except 10r. where it occurs on R. 4/3.

After "O": R. 3/2 and 5/1 on vert stamps, R. 2/1 and 4/4 on horiz stamps (only occurs on R. 2/1 for 45c.), and R. 2/7 and 5/9 on 10r. value.

After "B": R. 10/4 (45c.) or R. 1/8 (10r.).

As sheets of all values from 5c. to 50c. are known with all stops in place the no stop varieties either developed during printing or their omission was discovered and replacements inserted.

2 Lascar

(Des G. Drummond, based on drawings by Mrs. W. Veevers-Cartor. Litho D.L.R.)

1968 (23 Oct)–**70**. Marine Life. Multicoloured designs as T **2**. White paper (Nos. 20a, 23a, 24a) or cream paper (others). W w **12** (sideways on horiz, inverted on vert designs). P 14.

16	5c. Type **2**	1·00	2·50
17	10c. Smooth Hammerhead (*vert*)	30	1·25
18	15c. Tiger Shark	30	1·75
19	20c. Spotted Eagle Ray ("Bat Ray")	30	1·00
20	25c. Yellow-finned Butterflyfish and Earspotted Angelfish (*vert*)	80	1·00
20a	30c. Robber Crab (7.12.70)	3·50	2·75
21	40c. Blue-finned Trevally ("Caranx")	2·25	40
22	45c. Crocodile Needlefish ("Garfish") (*vert*)	2·25	2·50
23	50c. Pickhandle Barracuda	2·25	30
23a	60c. Spotted Pebble Crab (7.12.70)	3·50	4·00
24	75c. Indian Ocean Steep-headed Parrotfish	2·50	2·25
24a	85c. Rainbow Runner ("Dorado") (7.12.70)	4·50	3·00
	b. Magenta omitted	£1100	
25	1r. Giant Hermit Crab	1·75	35
26	1r.50 Parrotfish ("Humphead")	2·50	3·00
27	2r.25 Yellow-edged Lyretail and Areolate Grouper ("Rock Cod")	10·00	10·00
28	3r.50 Black Marlin	4·00	3·75
29	5r. black, blue-green and greenish blue (Whale Shark) (*vert*)	24·00	16·00
30	10r. Lionfish	6·00	6·50
	a. Imperf (pair)	£1100	
16/30	*Set of 18*	65·00	50·00

The 5c. was re-issued in 1973 on white paper with watermark w **12** upright.

3 Sacred Ibis and Aldabra Coral Atoll

(Des and litho D.L.R.)

1969 (10 July). *Coral Atolls.* W w **12** (sideways). P 13½×13.

31	**3**	2r.25 multicoloured	1·75	1·00

4 Outrigger Canoe

(Des Mrs. M. Hayward adapted by V. Whiteley. Litho D.L.R.)

1969 (15 Dec). Ships of the Islands. T **4** and similar horiz designs. Multicoloured. W w **12** (sideways). P 13½×14.

32	45c. Type **4**	55	75
33	75c. Pirogue	55	80
34	1r. M. V. *Nordvaer*	60	90
35	1r.50 *Isle of Farquhar*	65	1·00
32/5	*Set of 4*	2·10	3·00

5 Giant Land Tortoise

(Des G. Drummond. Litho Format)

1971 (1 Feb). Aldabra Nature Reserve. T **5** and similar horiz designs. Multicoloured. W w **12** (sideways). P 13½.

36	45c. Type **5**	2·50	2·50
37	75c. Aldabra Lily	3·00	2·50
38	1r. Aldabra Tree Snail (*Rhachis aldabrae*)	3·50	2·75
39	1r.50 Western Reef Herons	12·00	10·00
36/39	*Set of 4*	19·00	16·00

6 Arms of Royal Society and White-throated
Rail

(Des V. Whiteley. Litho J. W.)

1971 (30 June). Opening of Royal Society Research Station on
Aldabra. W w **12** (sideways). P 13½.

40	**6**	3r.50 multicoloured	15·00	11·00

7 Staghorn Coral

(Des V. Whiteley. Litho A. & M.)

1972 (1 Mar). Coral. T **7** and similar horiz designs. Multicoloured.
W w **12** (sideways*). P 13½.

41		40c. Type **7**	3·50	4·00
		w. Wmk Crown to left of CA	22·00	
42		60c. Brain coral	4·00	4·25
		w. Wmk Crown to left of CA	9·50	
43		1r. Mushroom coral	4·00	4·25
		w. Wmk Crown to left of CA	5·50	
44		1r.75 Organ Pipe coral	5·00	6·50
		w. Wmk Crown to left of CA	14·00	
41/44		Set of 4	15·00	17·00

*The normal sideways watermark shows Crown to right of CA, *as
seen from the back of the stamp.*
On some sheets of No. 43 the inks have been applied in a different
order, resulting in an almost total absence of blue.

8 White-throated Rail and Sacred Ibis   **9** "Christ on the
Cross"

(Des (from photograph by D. Groves) and photo Harrison)

1972 (20 Nov). Royal Silver Wedding. Multicoloured; background
colour given. W w **12**. P 14×14½.

45	**8**	95c. deep dull green	50	40
		a. Silver (frame and inset) ptd double	£550	
		b. *Slate-green*	2·00	2·00
46		1r.50 bright bluish violet	50	40

(Des Jennifer Toombs. Litho Questa)

1973 (9 Apr). Easter. T **9** and similar vert design showing illustrations
from 17th-century Ethiopian manuscript. Multicoloured. W w **12**
(sideways). P 14.

47		45c. Type **9**	20	40
48		75c. Joseph and Nicodemus burying Jesus	30	55
49		1r. Type **9**	30	60
50		1r.50 As 75c	30	70
47/50		Set of 4	1·00	2·00
MS51		126×110 mm. Nos. 47/50	1·00	4·00

1973 (2 Oct). As No. 16 but white paper and wmk upright.

52		5c. Type **2**	1·00	4·00

No. 52 differs in shade from No. 16 because of the change of
paper.

10 Upsidedown   **11** M.V. *Nordvaer*
Jellyfish

(Des G. Drummond. Litho Walsall)

1973 (12 Nov). Wildlife (1st series). T **10** and similar vert designs.
Multicoloured. W w **12** (sideways*). P 14.

53		50c. Type **10**	3·50	3·00
54		1r. *Hypolimnas misippus* and *Belenois aldabrensis* (butterflies)	4·00	3·00
55		1r.50 *Nephila madagascariensis* (spider)	4·25	3·00
		w. Wmk Crown to right of CA	4·50	
53/55		Set of 3	10·50	8·00

*The normal sideways watermark shows Crown to left of CA, *as seen
from the back of the stamp.*
See also Nos. 58/61, 77/80 and 86/9.

(Des C. Abbott. Litho Walsall)

1974 (14 July). Fifth Anniv of "*Nordvaer*" Travelling Post Office. T **11**
and similar vert design. Multicoloured. W w **12** (sideways). P 14.

56		85c. Type **11**	85	75
57		2r.50 *Nordvaer* offshore	1·40	1·25

12 Red-cloud Auger (*Terebra nebulosa*)
and Subulate Auger (*Terebra subulata*)

(Des PAD Studio. Litho J. W.)

1974 (12 Nov). Wildlife (2nd series). T **12** and similar horiz designs
showing shells. Multicoloured. W w **12**. P 13½×14.

58		45c. Type **12**	1·75	1·25
59		75c. Great Green Turbo (*Turbo marmoratus*)	2·00	1·50
60		1r. Strawberry Drupe (*Drupa rubusidaeus*)	2·25	1·75
61		1r.50 Bull-mouth Helmet (*Cypraecassis rufa*)	2·25	2·00
58/61		Set of 4	7·50	6·00

13 Aldabra Drongo   **14** *Grewia salicifolia*

(Des R. Granger Barrett. Litho Questa)

1975 (28 Feb). Birds. Multicoloured designs as T **13**. W w **12**
(sideways* on horiz designs). P 14.

62		5c. Type **13**	1·25	2·75
63		10c. Black Coucal	1·25	2·75
64		20c. Mascarene Fody	1·25	2·75
		w. Wmk inverted	£130	
65		25c. White Tern	1·25	2·75
66		30c. Crested Tern	1·25	2·75
67		40c. Brown Booby	1·25	2·75
68		50c. Common Noddy (*horiz*)	1·25	3·00
69		60c. Grey Heron	1·25	3·00
70		65c. Blue-faced Booby (*horiz*)	1·25	3·00
71		95c. Madagascar White Eye (*horiz*)	1·25	3·00
		w. Wmk Crown to right of CA	£100	
72		1r. Green Heron (*horiz*)	1·25	3·00
73		1r.75 Lesser Frigate Bird (*horiz*)	2·00	5·00
74		3r.50 White-tailed Tropic Bird (*horiz*)	3·75	6·00

75	5r. Souimanga Sunbird (*horiz*)	3·00	5·00
76	10r. Madagascar Turtle Dove (*horiz*)	4·50	9·00
62/76	Set of 15	24·00	55·00

The normal sideways watermark shows Crown to left of CA, as seen from the back of the stamp.

(Des Sylvia Goaman. Litho Questa)

1975 (10 July). Wildlife (3rd series). T **14** and similar vert designs showing seashore plants. Multicoloured. W w **12** (sideways). P 14.

77	50c. Type **14**	40	1·10
78	65c. *Cassia aldabrensis*	45	1·25
79	1r. *Hypoestes aldabrensis*	55	1·40
80	1r.60 *Euphorbia pyrifolia*	60	1·50
77/80	Set of 4	1·75	4·75

15 Map of Aldabra

(Des L. Curtis. Litho Questa)

1975 (8 Nov). Tenth Anniv of Territory. Maps. T **15** and similar horiz designs. Multicoloured. W w **12**. P 13½.

81	50c. Type **15**	70	65
82	1r. Desroches	85	85
83	1r.50 Farquhar	90	1·00
84	2r. Diego Garcia	1·00	1·25
81/84	Set of 4	3·00	3·25
MS85	147×147 mm. Nos. 81/84 (wmk sideways)	7·00	14·00

16 *Utetheisa pulchella* (moth)

(Des PAD Studio. Litho Questa)

1976 (22 Mar). Wildlife (4th series). T **16** and similar horiz designs. Multicoloured. W w **12** (sideways). P 13½.

86	65c. Type **16**	50	75
87	1r.20 *Dysdercus fasciatus* (bug)	65	1·00
88	1r.50 *Sphex torridus* (wasp)	65	1·10
89	2r. *Oryetes rhinoceros* (beetle)	70	1·10
86/89	Set of 4	2·25	3·50

When the Seychelles achieved independence on 29 June 1976 the islands of Aldabra, Farquhar and Desroches reverted to its administration so that British Indian Ocean Territory from that date consisted of the Chagos Archipelago, an island group, the largest of whose five main atolls is Diego Garcia. The indigenous population was resettled on Mauritius and Diego Garcia was developed as a U.S. Navy base while remaining under British administration.

Nos. 62/76 were withdrawn in August 1979 and, until May 1990, base personnel used British and American forces mail facilities routed via the Philippines and San Francisco. From 1987 British mails were routed via Singapore. The growing number of civilian workers eventually led to the re-introduction of a postal service in May 1990 using stamps with face values in sterling. The only post office is at the Diego Garcia base.

(New Currency. Sterling)

17 White-tailed Tropic Bird

18 1974 Wildlife 1r.50 Stamp

(Des N. Arlott. Litho Questa)

1990 (3 May). Birds. T **17** and similar vert designs. Multicoloured. W w **16** (sideways). P 14.

90	15p. Type **17**	1·10	2·00
91	20p. Madagascar Turtle Dove	1·25	2·00
92	24p. Great Frigate Bird	1·40	2·00
93	30p. Green Heron	1·50	2·25
94	34p. Great Sand Plover	1·60	2·25
95	41p. Crab Plover	1·75	2·50
96	45p. Crested Tern	4·50	2·50
97	54p. Lesser Crested Tern	2·25	3·00
98	62p. White Tern	2·25	3·00
99	71p. Red-footed Booby	2·25	3·00
100	80p. Common Mynah	2·50	3·25
101	£1 Madagascar Red Fody	3·25	3·50
90/101	Set of 12	23·00	28·00

(Des D. Miller. Litho Walsall)

1990 (3 May). "Stamp World London '90" International Stamp Exhibition. T **18** and similar horiz designs showing stamps. Multicoloured. W w **14** (sideways). P 14.

102	15p. Type **18**	4·50	3·25
103	20p. 1976 Wildlife 2r.	5·00	3·50
104	34p. 1975 Diego Garcia map 2r.	8·50	5·50
105	54p. 1969 Nordvaer 1r.	10·00	7·50
102/5	Set of 4	25·00	18·00

18a Lady Elizabeth Bowes-Lyon, 1923

18b Queen Elizabeth and her Daughters, 1940

(Des D. Miller. Litho Questa)

1990 (4 Aug). 90th Birthday of Queen Elizabeth the Queen Mother. W w **16**. P 14×15 (24p.) or 14½ (£1).

| 106 | **18a** | 24p. multicoloured | 3·00 | 3·50 |
| 107 | **18b** | £1 brownish black and purple-brown | 4·50 | 6·50 |

19 Territory Flag

20 Postman emptying Pillar Box

(Des D. Miller. Litho Questa)

1990 (8 Nov). 25th Anniv of British Indian Ocean Territory. T **19** and similar vert designs. Multicoloured. W w **14**. P 14×13½.

108	20p. Type **19**	4·00	4·50
109	24p. Coat of arms	4·00	4·50
MS110	63×99 mm. £1 Map of Chagos Archipelago	9·50	12·00

(Des O. Bell. Litho Walsall)

1991 (3 June). British Indian Ocean Territory Administration. T **20** and similar horiz designs. Multicoloured. W w **14** (sideways). P 14.

111	20p. Type **20**	1·50	2·50
112	24p. Commissioner inspecting guard of Royal Marines	1·75	2·50
113	34p. Policemen outside station	3·50	4·50
114	54p. Customs officers boarding yacht	4·25	6·00
111/14	Set of 4	10·00	14·00

21 *Experiment* (E.I.C. survey brig), 1786

(Des E. Nisbet. Litho Walsall)

1991 (8 Nov). Visiting Ships. T **21** and similar horiz designs. Multicoloured. W w **14** (sideways). P 14.

115	20p. Type **21**	2·00	3·00
116	24p. *Pickering* (American brig), 1819	2·25	3·25
117	34p. *Emden* (German cruiser), 1914	3·00	4·25
118	54p. H.M.S. *Edinburgh* (destroyer), 1988	3·75	5·50
115/18 *Set of 4*		10·00	14·50

21a Catholic Chapel, Diego Garcia

(Des D. Miller. Litho Questa (54p.), Walsall (others))

1992 (6 Feb). 40th Anniv of Queen Elizabeth II's Accession. T **21a** and similar horiz designs. Multicoloured. W w **14** (sideways). P 14.

119	15p. Type **21a**	1·75	1·40
120	20p. Planter's house, Diego Garcia	2·00	1·60
121	24p. Railway tracks on wharf, Diego Garcia	4·50	2·25
122	34p. Three portraits of Queen Elizabeth	3·50	2·50
123	54p. Queen Elizabeth II	3·50	2·75
119/23 *Set of 5*		14·00	9·50

22 R.A.F. Consolidated PBY-5 Catalina (flying boat)

(Des A. Theobald. Litho Walsall)

1992 (23 Oct). Visiting Aircraft. T **22** and similar horiz designs. Multicoloured. W w **16** (sideways). P 14.

124	20p. Type **22**	1·50	2·50
125	24p. R.A.F. Hawker Siddeley H.S.801 Nimrod M.R.2 (maritime reconnaissance aircraft)	1·75	2·50
126	34p. Lockheed P-3 Orion (transport aircraft)	2·50	3·25
127	54p. U.S.A.A.F. Boeing B-52 Stratofortress (heavy bomber)	3·00	4·50
124/27 *Set of 4*		8·00	11·50

23 "The Mystical Marriage of St. Catherine" (Correggio)

24 Coconut Crab and Rock

(Des D. Miller. Litho Walsall)

1992 (27 Nov). Christmas. Religious Paintings. T **23** and similar vert designs. Multicoloured. W w **16**. P 14½×14.

128	5p. Type **23**	70	80
129	24p. "Madonna" (anon)	1·25	1·60
130	34p. "Madonna" (anon) (*different*)	1·40	2·25
131	54p. "The Birth of Jesus" (Kaspar Jele)	1·75	3·50
128/31 *Set of 4*		4·50	7·50

(Des G. Vasarhelyi. Litho Questa)

1993 (5 Mar). Endangered Species. Coconut Crab. T **24** and similar horiz designs. Multicoloured. W w **16** (sideways). P 14.

132	10p. Type **24**	1·25	1·25
133	10p. Crab on beach	1·25	1·25
134	10p. Two crabs	1·25	1·25
135	15p. Crab climbing coconut tree	1·50	1·50
132/35 *Set of 4*		4·75	4·75

24a Vickers Virginia Mk X

25 *Stachytarpheta urticifolia*

(Des A. Theobald. Litho Questa)

1993 (1 Apr). 75th Anniv of Royal Air Force. T **24a** and similar horiz designs. Multicoloured. W w **14** (sideways). P 14.

136	20p. Type **24a**	1·10	1·50
137	24p. Bristol Bulldog IIA	1·25	1·50
138	34p. Short S.25 Sunderland Mk III	1·40	2·00
139	54p. Bristol Type **142** Blenheim Mk IV	2·00	3·25
136/39 *Set of 4*		5·25	7·50
MS140 110×77 mm. 20p. Douglas DC-3 Dakota; 20p. Gloster G.41 Javelin; 20p. Blackburn Beverley C1; 20p. Vickers VC-10		6·50	8·00

(Des N. Shewring. Litho Questa)

1993 (22 Nov). Christmas. Flowers. T **25** and similar vert designs. Multicoloured. W w **14**. P 14½.

141	20p. Type **25**	80	1·50
142	24p. *Ipomea pes-caprae*	80	1·50
143	34p. *Sida pusilla*	1·10	2·25
144	54p. *Catharanthus roseus*	1·75	3·50
141/44 *Set of 4*		4·00	8·00

(25a)

1994 (18 Feb). "Hong Kong '94" International Stamp Exhibition. Nos. 92 and 101 optd with T **25a**.

145	24p. Great Frigate Bird	4·00	3·00
146	£1 Madagascar Red Fody	5·50	7·50

26 Forrest's Map of Diego Garcia, 1778

27 *Junonia villida*

(Des D. Miller. Litho Questa)

1994 (1 June). 18th-century Maps. T **26** and similar vert designs. Each black and cobalt. W w **14**. P 14½.

147	20p. Type **26**	70	1·50
	a. Horiz strip of 5. Nos. 147/51	3·75	7·75
148	24p. Blair's plan of Diego Garcia harbour, 1786–87	75	1·60
149	34p. Blair's chart of Chagos Archipelago, 1786–87	80	1·75
150	44p. Plan of part of Diego Garcia, 1774	90	1·90
151	54p. Fontaine's plan of Diego Garcia, 1770	1·10	2·00
147/51 *Set of 5*		3·75	7·75

Nos. 147/51 were printed together, *se-tenant*, in horizontal strips of five throughout the sheet.

(Des I. Loe. Litho Walsall)

1994 (16 Aug). Butterflies. T **27** and similar vert designs. Multicoloured. W w **16**. P 14½×14.

152	24p. Type **27**	1·50	1·75
153	30p. *Petrelaea dance*	1·75	2·50
154	56p. *Hypolimnas misippus*	2·75	4·00
152/54 *Set of 3*		5·50	7·50

28 Short-tailed Nurse Sharks   **28a** Military Cemetery

(Des N. Shewring. Litho Walsall)

1994 (1 Nov). Sharks. T **28** and similar horiz designs. Multicoloured. W w **14** (sideways). P 14.

155	15p. Type **28**	4·50	3·50
156	20p. Silver-tipped Sharks	4·50	3·50
157	24p. Black-finned Reef Shark	4·50	3·50
158	30p. Oceanic White-tipped Sharks	5·00	4·00
159	35p. Black-tipped Shark	5·50	4·50
160	41p. Smooth Hammerhead	5·50	4·50
161	46p. Sickle-finned Lemon Shark	5·50	4·50
162	55p. White-tipped Reef Shark	6·50	5·50
163	65p. Tiger Sharks	7·00	5·50
164	74p. Indian Sand Tiger	7·00	6·00
165	80p. Great Hammerhead	7·00	6·00
166	£1 Great White Shark	8·00	7·00
155/66 *Set of 12*		60·00	50·00

For miniature sheets containing the 65p. or 74p. (with "1997" imprint date) see Nos. **MS**193/4.

(Des R. Watton. Litho Walsall (Nos. 167/70) or Questa (No. **MS**171))

1995 (8 May). 50th Anniv of End of Second World War. T **28a** and similar horiz designs. Multicoloured. W w **14** (sideways). P 14.

167	20p. Type **28a**	1·75	1·75
168	24p. Rusty 6-inch naval gun at Cannon Point	2·00	1·75
169	30p. Short S.25 Sunderland flying boat	2·25	2·25
170	56p. H.M.I.S. *Clive* (sloop)	3·50	3·75
167/70 *Set of 4*		8·50	8·50
MS171 75×85 mm. £1 Reverse of 1939–45 War Medal (*vert*). Wmk upright		2·00	3·00

29 Dolphin (fish)   **30** *Terebra crenulata*

(Des K. McGee. Litho B.D.T.)

1995 (6 Oct). Gamefish. T **29** and similar horiz designs. Multicoloured. W w **16** (sideways). P 14.

172	20p. Type **29**	1·75	1·60
173	24p. Sailfish	1·90	1·60
174	30p. Wahoo	2·50	2·50
175	56p. Striped Marlin	3·50	3·75
172/75 *Set of 4*		8·75	8·50

(Des G. Drummond. Litho Walsall)

1996 (8 Jan). Sea Shells. T **30** and similar horiz designs. Multicoloured. W w **14** (sideways). P 14½.

176	20p. Type **30**	1·25	1·50
177	24p. *Bursa bufonia*	1·25	1·50
178	30p. *Nassarius papillosus*	1·75	2·00
179	56p. *Lopha cristagalli*	3·00	3·25
176/79 *Set of 4*		6·50	7·50

30a View of Lagoon from South   **31** Loggerhead Turtle

(Des D. Miller. Litho Walsall)

1996 (22 Apr). 70th Birthday of Queen Elizabeth II. T **30a** and similar horiz designs. Each incorporating a different photograph of the Queen. Multicoloured. W w **16**. P 14½.

180	20p. Type **30a**	70	85

181	24p. Manager's House, Peros Banhos	75	85
182	30p. Wireless Hut, Peros Banhos	80	1·10
183	56p. Sunset	1·10	1·75
180/83 *Set of 4*		3·00	4·00
MS184 64×66 mm. £1 Queen Elizabeth II		3·25	3·50

(Des O. Bell. Litho Questa)

1996 (2 Sept). Turtles. T **31** and similar horiz designs. Muiticoloured. W w **14** (sideways). P 14×14½.

185	20p. Type **31**	1·00	1·25
186	24p. Leatherback Turtle	1·10	1·25
187	30p. Hawksbill Turtle	1·40	1·60
188	56p. Green Turtle	2·00	2·50
185/88 *Set of 4*		5·00	6·50

32 Commissioner's Representative (naval officer)   **32a** Queen Elizabeth at Bristol, 1994

(Des R. Walton. Litho Questa)

1996 (16 Dec). Uniforms. T **32** and similar vert designs. Multicoloured. W w **14**. P 14.

189	20p. Type **32**	1·00	1·10
190	24p. Royal Marine officer	1·10	1·10
191	30p. Royal Marine in battledress	1·50	1·75
192	56p. Police officers	2·25	2·75
189/92 *Set of 4*		5·25	6·00

(Des D. Miller. Litho Questa)

1997 (3 Feb). "HONG KONG '97" International Stamp Exhibition. Sheet 130×90 mm, containing design as No. 163. Multicoloured. W w **14**. P 14.

MS193 65p. Tiger Sharks		2·00	2·75

(Des N. Shewring. Litho Walsall)

1997 (20 June). Return of Hong Kong to China. Sheet 130×90 mm containing design as No. 164, but with "1997" imprint date.

MS194 74p. Indian Sand Tiger		2·75	3·50

(Des N. Shewring (No. **MS**201), D. Miller (others). Litho Questa)

1997 (10 July). Golden Wedding of Queen Elizabeth and Prince Philip. T **32a** and similar horiz designs. Multicoloured. W w **14**. P 14½.

195	20p. Type **32a**	1·60	1·75
	a. Horiz pair. Nos. 195/6	3·25	3·50
196	20p. Prince Philip competing in Royal Windsor Horse Show, 1996	1·60	1·75
197	24p. Queen Elizabeth in phaeton, Trooping the Colour, 1987	1·60	1·75
	a. Horiz pair. Nos. 197/8	3·25	3·50
198	24p. Prince Philip	1·60	1·75
199	30p. Queen Elizabeth and Prince Philip with Land Rover	1·60	1·75
	a. Horiz pair. Nos. 199/200	3·25	3·50
200	30p. Queen Elizabeth at Balmoral	1·60	1·75
195/200 *Set of 6*		8·75	9·50
MS201 110×71 mm. £1.50 Queen Elizabeth and Prince Philip in landau (*horiz*). Wmk sideways. P 14×14½		9·00	9·50

Nos. 195/6 197/8 and 199/200 were each printed together, *se-tenant*, in horizontal pairs throughout the sheets with the backgrounds forming composite designs.

33 H.M.S. *Richmond* (frigate) and H.M.S. *Beaver* (frigate)   **33a** Wearing Patterned Jacket, 1993

(Litho Questa)

1997 (1 Dec). Exercise Ocean Wave. T **33** and similar horiz designs. Multicoloured. W w **14** (sideways). P 14×14½.

202	24p. Type **33**	2·25	1·75
	a. Sheetlet of 12. Nos. 202/13	24·00	19·00
203	24p. H.M.S. *Illustrious* (aircraft carrier) launching aircraft	2·25	1·75
204	24p. H.M.S. *Beaver*	2·25	1·75
205	24p. Royal Yacht *Britannia*, R.F.A. *Sir Percival* and H.M.S. *Beaver*	2·25	1·75
206	24p. Royal Yacht *Britannia*	2·25	1·75
207	24p. H.M.S. *Richmond*, H.M.S. *Beaver* and H.M.S. *Gloucester* (destroyer)	2·25	1·75
208	24p. H.M.S. *Richmond*	2·25	1·75
209	24p. Aerial view of H.M.S. *Illustrious*	2·25	1·75
210	24p. H.M.S. *Gloucester*	2·25	1·75
211	24p. H.M.S. *Trenchant* (submarine) and R.F.A. *Diligence*	2·25	1·75
212	24p. R.F.A. *Fort George* replenishing H.M.S. *Illustrious* and H.M.S. *Gloucester*	2·25	1·75
213	24p. Aerial view of H.M.S. *Richmond*, H.M.S. *Beaver* and H.M.S. *Gloucester*	2·25	1·75
202/13 *Set of 12*		24·00	19·00

Nos. 202/13 were printed together, *se-tenant*, in sheetlets of 12. No. 210 is inscribed "HMS Sheffield" in error.

(Des D. Miller. Litho Questa)

1998 (31 Mar). Diana, Princess of Wales Commemoration. Sheet 145×70 mm, containing vert designs as T **33a**. Multicoloured. W w **14** (sideways). P 14½×14.

MS214 26p. Type **33a**; 26p. Wearing heart-shaped earrings, 1988; 34p. Wearing cream jacket, 1993; 60p. Wearing blue blouse, 1982 (sold at £1·46+20p. charity premium) .... 2·00 3·25

33b Blackburn Iris

(Des A. Theobald. Litho Questa)

1998 (1 Apr). 80th Anniv of the Royal Air Force. T **33b** and similar horiz designs. Multicoloured. W w **16** (sideways). P 14.

215	26p. Type **33b**	1·25	1·10
216	34p. Gloster Gamecock	1·50	1·40
217	60p. North American Sabre F.4	2·50	2·50
218	80p. Avro Lincoln	3·00	3·00
215/18 *Set of 4*		7·50	7·25

MS219 110×77 mm. 34p. Sopwith Baby (seaplane); 34p. Martinsyde Elephant; 34p. de Havilland Tiger Moth; 34p. North American Mustang III .... 6·00 7·50

34 Bryde's Whale

(Des N. Shewring. Litho Walsall)

1998 (7 Dec). International Year of the Ocean. T **34** and similar horiz designs. W w **14** (sideways). P 13½×14.

220	26p. Type **34**	2·50	2·50
221	26p. Striped Dolphin	2·50	2·50
222	34p. Pilot Whale	2·50	2·50
223	34p. Spinner Dolphin	2·50	2·50
220/23 *Set of 4*		9·00	9·00

35 *Westminster* (East Indiaman), 1837

(Des J. Batchelor. Litho Walsall)

1999 (1 Feb). Ships. T **35** and similar horiz designs. Multicoloured. W w 14 (sideways). P 13½×14.

224	2p. Type **35**	60	1·25
225	15p. *Sao Cristovao* (Spanish galleon), 1589	1·75	1·50
226	20p. *Sea Witch* (U.S. clipper), 1849	1·75	1·50
227	26p. H.M.S. *Royal George* (ship of the line), 1778	2·00	1·50
228	34p. *Cutty Sark* (clipper), 1883	3·00	2·00
229	60p. *Mentor* (East Indiaman), 1789	3·75	3·75
230	80p. H.M.S. *Trincula* (brig), 1809	4·00	4·25
231	£1 *Enterprise* (paddle-steamer), 1825	5·00	5·50
232	£1.15 *Confiance* (French privateer), 1800	5·50	6·00
233	£2 *Kent* (East Indiaman), 1820	8·50	9·50
224/33 *Set of 10*		32·00	32·00

36 *Cutty Sark* (clipper) **37** Field Vole (Colin Sargent)

(Des J. Batchelor. Litho Questa)

1999 (19 Mar). "Australia '99" World Stamp Exhibition, Melbourne. Sheet 150×75 mm, containing T **36** and similar horiz design. Multicoloured. W w **16** (sideways). P 13½×14.

MS234 60p. Type **36**; 60p. *Thermopylae* (clipper) .... 6·00 8·00

(Litho Walsall)

2000 (22 May). "The Stamp Show 2000", International Stamp Exhibition, London. "Shoot a Stamp" Competition Winners. Sheet 150×100 mm, containing T **37** and similar vert designs. Multicoloured. W w **14**. P 14½.

MS235 26p. Type **37**; 34p. Puffin (P. J. Royal); 55p. Red Fox (Jim Wilson); £1 Robin (Harry Smith) .... 11·00 11·00

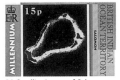

38 Satellite Image of Salomon Island

(Litho Questa)

2000 (3 July). New Millennium. Satellite Images of Islands. T **38** and similar horiz designs. Multicoloured. W w **14** (sideways). P 14.

236	15p. Type **38**	1·75	1·60
237	20p. Egmont	2·00	1·75
238	60p. Blenheim Reef	3·00	3·00
239	80p. Diego Garcia	3·00	3·25
236/39 *Set of 4*		8·75	8·75

39 Queen Elizabeth the **40** *Delonix regia*
Queen Mother

(Litho Questa)

2000 (4 Aug). Queen Elizabeth the Queen Mother's 100th Birthday. T **39** and similar vert designs. Multicoloured. W w **14**. P 14.

240	26p. Type **39**	1·40	1·40
241	34p. Wearing green hat and outfit	1·40	1·40

MS242 113×88 mm. 55p. In blue hat and outfit; £1 In yellow hat and outfit .... 4·75 5·50

(Des I. Loe. Litho Questa)

2000 (4 Dec). Christmas. Flowers. T **40** and similar vert designs. Multicoloured. W w **14**. P 14½.

243	26p. Type **40**	1·75	1·75
244	34p. *Barringtonia asiatica*	2·00	2·00
245	60p. *Zephyranthes roses*	3·50	4·00
243/45	Set of 3	6·50	7·00

41 *Precis orithya* (butterfly)

(Des T. Thackeray and A. Robinson. Litho Questa)

2000 (1 Feb). "HONG KONG 2001" Stamp Exhibition. Sheet 150×90 mm, containing T **41** and similar horiz design showing butterfly. Multicoloured. W w **14** (sideways). P 14.

MS246	26p. Type **41**; 34p. *Junonia villida chagoensis*	3·00	3·50

42 HMS *Turbulent*   **43** Cushion Star

(Litho Questa)

2001 (28 May). Centenary of Royal Navy Submarine Service. T **42** and similar horiz designs. Multicoloured (except Nos. 248 and 252). W w **14**. P 14×14½.

247	26p. Type **42**	1·75	2·00
	a. Sheetlet of 6. Nos. 247/52	11·00	13·00
248	26p. HMS *Churchill* (grey and black)	1·75	2·00
249	34p. HMS *Resolution*	2·00	2·50
250	34p. HMS *Vanguard*	2·00	2·50
251	60p. HMS *Otter* (73×27 mm)	2·50	3·00
252	60p. HMS *Oberon* (73×27 mm) (grey and black)	2·50	3·00
247/52	Set of 6	11·00	13·00

Nos. 247/52 were printed together, *se-tenant*, in sheetlets of 6.

(Des A. Robinson. Litho B.D.T.)

2001 (1 Aug). Endangered Species. Seastars. T **43** and similar horiz designs. Multicoloured. W w **14** (sideways). P 13½.

253	15p. Type **43**	1·25	1·25
	a. Strip of 4. Nos. 253/6	7·00	7·25
254	26p. Azure Sea Star	1·75	1·50
255	34p. Crown-of-Thorns	1·90	1·75
256	56p. Banded Bubble Star	3·00	3·50
253/6	Set of 4	7·00	7·25

Nos. 253/6 were printed in separate sheets of 50 and also in sheets of 16 with the four values *se-tenant* in horizontal or vertical strips.

44 *Scadoxus multiflora*   **45** Crab Plovers on Beach

(Des I. Loe. Litho Questa)

2001 (24 Sept). Plants. Flowers. T **44** and similar multicoloured designs. W w **14** (sideways). P 14.

257	26p. Type **44**	1·75	1·75
258	34p. *Striga asiatica*	2·00	2·00
MS259	173×78 mm. Nos. 257/8 and 10p. *Catharanthus roseus* (horiz); 60p. *Argusia argentea* (horiz); 70p. *Euphorbia cyathophora* (horiz)	5·50	6·50

In No. **MS259** the 60p. is inscribed "argentia" in error.

(Des N. Arlott. Litho Questa)

2001 (1 Oct). Birdlife World Bird Festival. Crab Plovers. Sheet, 175×80 mm, containing T **45** and similar multicoloured designs. W w **14** (sideways). P 14.

MS260	50p. Type **45**; 50p. Crab Plover catching crab (*vert*); 50p. Head of Crab Plover (*vert*); 50p. Crab Plovers in flight; 50p. Crab Plover standing on one leg.	8·50	9·50

45a Princess Elizabeth in Pantomime, Windsor, 1943   **46** Adult Red-footed Booby

(Des A. Robinson. Litho Questa)

2002 (6 Feb). Golden Jubilee. T **45a** and similar designs. W w **14** (sideways). P 14½.

261	10p. blackish brown, new blue and gold	1·00	1·00
262	25p. multicoloured	1·50	1·50
263	35p. grey-black, new blue and gold	1·75	1·75
264	55p. multicoloured	2·50	2·75
261/4	Set of 4	6·00	6·25
MS265	162×95 mm. Nos. 261/4 and 75p. multicoloured. P 13½ (75p.) or 14½ (others)	6·50	7·00

Designs as Nos. 261/4 in No. **MS265** omit the gold frame around each stamp and the "Golden Jubilee 1952–2002" inscription.

Designs: Horiz—25p. Queen Elizabeth in floral hat, 1967; 35p. Princess Elizabeth and Prince Philip on their engagement, 1947; 55p. Queen Elizabeth in evening dress. Vert (38×51 *mm*)—75p. Queen Elizabeth after Annigoni.

2002 (17 June). BirdLife International. Red-footed Booby. Sheet, 175×80 mm, containing T **46** and similar multicoloured designs. W w **14** (sideways). P 14.

MS266	50p. Type **46**; 50p. Head of dark morph Red-footed Booby; 50p. Adult bird in flight (*vert*); 50p. Dark morph on nest (*vert*); 50p. Fledgling on nest	9·00	11·00

46a Lady Elizabeth Bowes-Lyon, 1921   **47** Microgoby

(Des A. Robinson. Litho Questa)

2002 (5 Aug). Queen Elizabeth the Queen Mother Commemoration. T **46a** and similar designs. W w **14**. P 14½×14.

267	26p. blackish brown, gold and purple	1·25	1·00
268	£1 multicoloured	2·75	3·00
MS269	145×70 mm. £1 brownish black and gold; £1 multicoloured. Wmk sideways	6·00	8·00

Designs in No. **MS269** omit the "1900–2002" inscription and the coloured frame.

Designs:—£1 (No. 268) Queen Mother, 1986; £1 brownish black and gold (No. **MS269**) Queen Elizabeth at garden party, 1951; £1 multicoloured (No. **MS269**) Queen Mother at Cheltenham Races, 1994.

(Litho Walsall)

2002 (3 Oct). Tenth Anniv of Friends of Chagos (conservation association). Reef Fish. T **47** and similar horiz designs. Multicoloured. W w **14** (sideways). P 14×14½.

270	2p. Type **47**	45	70
271	15p. Angelfish	1·25	1·25
272	26p. Surgeonfish	1·50	1·50
273	34p. Trunkfish	1·75	1·75
274	58p. Soldierfish	2·75	3·25
275	£1 Chagos Anemonefish	5·00	6·00
270/75	Set of 6	11·50	13·00

The miniature sheet which accompanied Nos. 270/75 is inscribed "PARCEL POST" and is listed separately as No. PMS1.

48 *Halgerda tesselata*

(Des A. Robinson. Litho B.D.T.)

2003 (17 Mar). Sea Slugs. T **48** and similar horiz designs. Multicoloured. W w **14**. P 13.

276	2p. Type **48**	40	70
277	15p. *Notodoris minor*	90	90
278	26p. *Nembrotha lineolata*	1·10	1·10
279	50p. *Chromodoris quadricolor*	2·00	2·50
280	76p. *Glossodoris cincta*	2·75	3·50
281	£1.10 *Chromodoris cf leopardus*	3·50	4·50
276/81	*Set of 6*	9·50	12·00

48a Queen Elizabeth II wearing Imperial State Crown in Coronation Coach

(Des A. Robinson. Litho D.L.R.)

2003 (2 June). 50th Anniv of Coronation. T **48a** and similar horiz designs. Multicoloured. W w **14** (sideways). P 14×14½.

282	£1 Type **48a**	2·50	3·50
283	£2 Queen with members of Royal Family in Coronation robes	4·50	6·00
MS284	95×115 mm. £1 As No. 282; £2 As No. 283	7·00	10·00

Nos. 282/3 have scarlet frame; stamps from **MS**284 have no frame and country name in mauve panel.

48b Queen Elizabeth II   **48c** Prince William at Cirencester Polo Club

(Des CASB Studio. Litho B.D.T.)

2003 (2 June). W w **14**. P 13½.

285	**48b** £2.50 grey-black, rose-pink and brown-lake	5·50	7·50

(Des A. Robinson. Litho D.L.R.)

2003 (21 June). 21st Birthday of Prince William of Wales. T **48c** and similar horiz designs. Multicoloured. W w **14** (sideways). P 14½.

286	50p. Type **48c**	1·75	2·25
	a. Horiz pair. Nos. 286/7	4·25	5·25
287	£1 With Prince Charles on skiing holiday and at Cirencester Polo Club	2·50	3·00

Nos. 286/7 were printed together, *se-tenant*, as horizontal pairs in sheets of ten (2×5) with enlarged illustrated left-hand margins.

48d Avro Type 683 Lancaster

(Des R. Hutchins. Litho D.L.R.)

2003 (18 July). Centenary of Powered Flight. T **48d** and similar horiz designs. Multicoloured. W w **14**. P 14.

288	34p. Type **48d**	2·00	2·00
289	34p. de Havilland DH. 98 Mosquito	2·00	2·00
290	58p. Hawker Hurricane	3·00	3·00
291	58p. Supermarine Spitfire	3·00	3·00
292	76p. Vickers-Armstrong Wellington	3·50	3·50
293	76p. Lockheed C-130 Hercules	3·50	3·50
288/93	*Set of 6*	15·00	15·00

MS294 233×85 mm. 26p. Boeing E-3A Sentry AWACS; 26p. Boeing B-17 Flying Fortress; 26p. Lockheed P-3 Orion; 26p. Consolidated B-24 Liberator; 26p. Lockheed C-141 StarLifter; 26p. Supermarine Walrus; 26p. Short S.25 Sunderland (flying boat); 26p. Supermarine Stranraer; 26p. PBY Catalina; 26p. Supermarine Sea Otter. Wmk sideways .... 10·00   12·00

Nos. 288/93 were each printed in sheets containing vertical rows of stamps alternated with rows of illustrated half stamp-size labels.

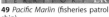

49 *Pacific Marlin* (fisheries patrol ship)   **50** Madagascar Red Fody ("Madagascar Fody")

(Des A. Robinson. Litho D.L.R.)

2004 (16 Feb). Fisheries Patrol. T **49** and similar horiz designs. Multicoloured. W w **14** (sideways). P 14½×14.

MS295 150×110 mm. 34p. Type **49**; 34p. Marlin; 58p. Skipjack Tuna; 58p. Yellowfin Tuna; 76p. Swordfish; 76p. Bigeye Tuna .... 12·00   13·00

(Des A. Robinson. Litho B.D.T.)

2004 (21 June). Birds. T **50** and similar horiz designs. Multicoloured. W w **14** (sideways). P 14.

296	2p. Type **50**	60	1·00
297	14p. Zebra Dove ("Barred Ground Dove")	1·50	1·50
298	20p. Common Mynah ("Indian Mynah")	1·75	1·50
299	26p. Cattle Egret	2·00	1·50
300	34p. White Tern ("Fairy Tern")	2·25	1·60
301	58p. Blue-Faced Booby ("Masked Booby")	3·00	3·00
302	76p. Great Frigate Bird	4·25	4·25
303	80p. White-tailed Tropic Bird	4·25	4·25
304	£1·10 Green-backed Heron ("Little Green Heron")	5·50	6·00
305	£1·34 Pacific Golden Plover	6·50	7·50
306	£1·48 Garganey ("Garganey Teal")	7·00	8·00
307	£2·50 Bar-tailed Godwit	10·00	12·00
296/307	*Set of 12*	45·00	48·00

51 Coconut Crab   **52** Two Hawksbill Turtle Babies

(Des A. Robinson. Litho B.D.T.)

2004 (20 Dec). Crabs. T **51** and similar horiz designs. Multicoloured. W w **14** (sideways). P 14.

308	26p. Type **51**	1·25	90
309	34p. Land crab	1·60	1·10
310	76p. Rock crab	3·25	3·50
311	£1·10 Ghost crab	4·25	5·50
308/11	*Set of 4*	9·50	10·00

(Des R. Watton. Litho B.D.T.)

2005 (13 Feb). Turtles. T **52** and similar horiz designs. Multicoloured. W w **14** (sideways). P 14.

312	26p. Type **52**	1·75	1·75
313	26p. Baby Green turtle	1·75	1·75
314	34p. Adult Hawksbill turtle	2·25	2·25
315	34p. Adult Green turtle	2·25	2·25
316	76p. Hawksbill turtle swimming	3·50	3·50
317	£1·10 Green turtle swimming	4·50	4·50
312/17	*Set of 6*	14·50	14·50
MS318	90×63 mm. £1·70 As No. 317	6·50	7·50

No. **MS**318 commemorates the Turtle Cove Clean-up operation sponsored by Cable and Wireless.

52a Tower Sea Service Pistol, 1796   **53** HMAS *Wollongong*, September 1942

(Des J. Batchelor. Litho Cartor)

2005 (6 May). Bicentenary of Battle of Trafalgar (1st issue). T **52a** and similar multicoloured designs. W w **14** (inverted on Nos. 319/20, 323) or no wmk (No. 324). P 13½.

319	26p. Type **52a**	1·75	1·75
320	26p. HMS *Phoebe*	1·75	1·75
321	34p. *Boatswain RN, 1805*	2·00	2·00
322	34p. HMS *Harrier*	2·00	2·00
323	76p. Portrait of Admiral Nelson	3·50	4·00
324	76p. HMS *Victory* (*horiz*)	3·50	4·00
319/24	*Set of 6*	13·00	14·00
MS325	120×79 mm. £1·10 HMS *Minotaur*; £1·10 HMS *Spartiate*	7·50	8·50

Nos. 319/24 were each printed in sheetlets of six with illustrated margins. No. 324 contains traces of powdered wood from HMS *Victory*. See also Nos. 344/6.

(Des R. Watton. Litho B.D.T.)

2005 (26 June). 60th Anniv of the End of World War II. "Route to Victory". Horiz designs as T **53**. Multicoloured. W w **14** (sideways). P 14.

326	26p. Type **53**	1·25	1·25
	a. Sheetlet of 10. Nos. 326/35	13·00	13·00
327	26p. *Ondina* (Dutch tanker) and HMIS *Bengal* attacked by Japanese surface raiders, 11 November 1942	1·25	1·25
328	26p. HMS *Pathfinder* (arrived at Diego Garcia, 4 April 1944)	1·25	1·25
329	26p. HMS *Lossie* (rescued survivors from Australian freighter *Nellore*, 29 June 1944)	1·25	1·25
330	26p. US Liberty Ship *Jean Nicolet* (sunk by Japanese, 2 July 1944)	1·25	1·25
331	34p. General Douglas MacArthur and landing party wading ashore	1·60	1·60
332	34p. General Bernard Montgomery and tanks in North African desert	1·60	1·60
333	34p. General George Patton and tanks	1·60	1·60
334	34p. Winston Churchill and St. Paul's Cathedral	1·60	1·60
335	34p. US Pres. Franklin Roosevelt and steelworks	1·60	1·60
326/35	*Set of 10*	13·00	13·00

Nos. 326/35 were printed together, *se-tenant*, in sheetlets of ten stamps.

54 Blacktip Reef Shark

(Des N. Shewring. Litho B.D.T.)

2005 (15 Aug). Sharks and Rays. T **54** and similar horiz designs. Multicoloured. W w **14** (sideways). P 13½×14.

336	26p. Type **54**	1·00	1·00
337	26p. Grey Reef Shark	1·00	1·00
338	34p. Silvertip Shark	1·40	1·40
339	34p. Tawny Nurse Shark	1·40	1·40
340	34p. Spotted Eagle Ray	1·40	1·40
341	34p. Manta Ray	1·40	1·40
342	76p. Porcupine Ray	2·75	3·00
343	£2 Feathertail Stingray	7·00	8·00
336/43	*Set of 8*	16·00	17·00

54a HMS *Victory*

55 Crab on Beach

(Des J. Batchelor (26p) or Pauline Gyles (£2). Litho Cartor)

2005 (18 Oct). Bicentenary of the Battle of Trafalgar (2nd issue). T **54a** and similar horiz designs. Multicoloured.

344	26p. Type **54a**	1·25	1·00
345	34p. Ships engaged in battle (*horiz*)	1·75	1·50
346	£2 Admiral Lord Nelson	7·00	8·50
344/46	*Set of 3*	9·00	10·00

(Des D. Miller. Litho B.D.T.)

2005 (8 Nov). 40th Anniv of British Indian Ocean Territory. T **55** and similar vert designs. Multicoloured. W w **14**. P 15×14.

MS347	205×129 mm. 34p. Type **55**; 34p. Two Hermit Crabs on beach; 34p. Blue-faced Boobies at nest; 34p. Outline map of Indian Ocean and Lesser Frigate Bird; 34p. Pair of Imperial Angelfish; 34p. Pair of Racoon Butterflyfish; 34p. Moorish Idol (fish); 34p. Outline map of British Indian Ocean Territory and turtle	14·00	15·00

The stamps within No. **MS**347 form a composite background design showing a beach and coral reef.

55a Princess Elizabeth

(Litho B.D.T.)

2006 (21 Apr). 80th Birthday of Queen Elizabeth II. T **55a** and similar horiz designs. Multicoloured. W w **14** (sideways). P 14.

348	26p. Type **55a**	1·25	1·00
349	34p. Queen Elizabeth II, c. 1952	1·75	1·50
350	76p. Wearing tiara	3·00	3·50
351	£1·10 Wearing headscarf	3·50	4·00
348/51	*Set of 4*	8·50	9·00
MS352	144×75 mm. £1 As No. 349; £1 As No. 350	7·00	8·00

56 Dusky Angelfish

57 Great Frigatebird

(Des A. Robinson. Litho B.D.T.)

2006 (29 May). Marine Life (1st series). Angelfish. Sheet 205×129 mm containing T **56** and similar horiz designs. Multicoloured. W w **14** (sideways). P 14.

MS353	26p. Type **56**; 26p. Two-spined Angelfish; 26p. Bicolour Angelfish; 34p. Orangeback Angelfish; 34p. Emperor Angelfish; £2 Threespot Angelfish	14·00	15·00

The stamps and margins of No. **MS**353 form a composite design showing a coral reef.

See also Nos. **MS**354, **MS**356 and **MS**372.

(Des A. Robinson. Litho B.D.T.)

2006 (31 July). Marine Life (2nd series). Butterflyfish. Sheet 205×129 mm containing horiz designs as T **56**. Multicoloured. W w **14** (sideways). P 14.

MS354	26p. Melon Butterflyfish; 26p. Raccoon Butterflyfish; 26p. Scrawled Butterflyfish; 34p. Longnose Butterflyfish; 34p. Threadfin Butterflyfish; £2 Masked Bannerfish	14·00	15·00

The stamps and margins of No. **MS**354 form a composite design showing a coral reef.

(Des N. Shewring. Litho B.D.T.)

2006 (6 Oct). BirdLife International. Barton Point Nature Reserve. Sheet 170×85 mm containing T **57** and similar horiz designs. Multicoloured. W w **14** (sideways). P 14.

MS355	26p. Type **57**; 26p. Black-naped Tern; 26p. Yellow-billed Tropicbird; 26p. White Tern; 26p. Brown Noddy; £2 Red-footed Booby	15·00	15·00

The stamps within No. **MS**355 form a composite design.

(Des A. Robinson. Litho B.D.T.)

2007 (29 Mar). Marine Life (3rd series). Parrotfish. Sheet 205×129 mm containing horiz designs as T **56**. Multicoloured. W w **14** (sideways). P 14.

MS356	54p. Common Parrotfish; 54p. Daisy Parrotfish; 54p. Bicolour Parrotfish; 54p. Bridled Parrotfish; 90p. Indian Ocean Steephead Parrotfish; 90p. Ember Parrotfish	14·00	16·00

The stamps and margins of No. **MS**356 form a composite design showing a coral reef.

58 Princess Elizabeth and Lt. Philip Mountbatten, c. 1947

59 Charles Darwin and Beach with Tropic Bird, Terns and Turtle

(Litho B.D.T.)

2007 (1 June). Diamond Wedding of Queen Elizabeth II and Duke of Edinburgh. T **58** and similar vert designs. Multicoloured. W w **14**. P 14.

357	54p. Type **58**	1·60	1·60
358	54p. Wedding procession and crowds, 1949	1·60	1·60
359	90p. Princess Elizabeth and Lt. Philip Mountbatten in arm, c. 1947	3·00	3·00
360	90p. Wedding ceremony, 1949	3·00	3·00
357/60	Set of 4	8·25	8·25

MS361 125×85 mm. £2·14 Princess Elizabeth and Lt. Philip Mountbatten, c. 1947 (42×56 mm) ..... 8·00 8·50

Nos. 357/60 were each printed in sheetlets of six stamps with enlarged illustrated margins.

(Des Derek Miller. Litho B.D.T.)

2007 (23 July). 125th Death Anniv of Charles Darwin. T **59** and similar square designs. Multicoloured. W w **14** (sideways). P 13½.

362	54p. Type **59**	2·50	2·50
363	54p. HMS Beagle	2·50	2·50
364	90p. Turtles	4·50	4·50
365	90p. Coral reef	4·50	4·50
362/65	Set of 4	12·50	12·50

60 Pomarine Skua pursuing Tropic Bird

61 Royal Marines

(Des Alan Harris. Litho Lowe-Martin, Canada)

2007 (1 Oct). BirdLife International. Pomarine Skua (Stercorarius pomarinus). T **60** and similar horiz designs. Multicoloured. W w **14** (sideways). P 12½×13.

366	54p. Type **60**	2·50	2·50
367	54p. Pomarine Skua Pursuing Booby	2·50	2·50
368	54p. Pair of Pomarine Skuas in flight	2·50	2·50
369	54p. Pair of Pomarine Skuas on beach	2·50	2·50
370	90p. Pomarine Skua pursuing Terns	4·50	4·50
371	90p. Pomarine Skua on sea	4·50	4·50
366/71	Set of 6	17·00	17·00

(Des Andrew Robinson. Litho B.D.T.)

2008 (30 Jan). Marine Life (4th series). Damselfish. Sheet 205×129 mm containing horiz designs as T **56**. Multicoloured. W w **14**. P 14.

MS372 54p. Chrysiptera unimaculata (Onespot Demoiselle); 54p. Abudefduf septemfasciatus (Banded Sergeant); 54p. Plectroglyphidodon johnstonianus (Johnston Island Damsel); 54p. Amphiprion chagosensis (Chagos Anemonefish); 90p. Chromis atripectoralis (Black-axil Chromis); 90p. Pomacentrus caeruleus (Caerulean Damsel) ..... 9·50 10·00

The stamps and margins of No. **MS**372 form a composite design showing a coral reef.

(Des Ross Watton. Litho B.D.T.)

2008 (3 Mar). Military Uniforms. T **61** and similar multicoloured designs. W w **14**. P 14.

373	27p. Type **61**	1·40	1·40
374	27p. Royal Engineers	1·40	1·40
375	54p. Sepoys, East India Company Army	2·25	2·25
376	54p. Officer, East India Company Army	2·25	2·25
377	54p. Artillery Corps	2·25	2·25
378	54p. Sergeant, Royal Military Police	2·25	2·25
373/8	Set of 6	10·50	10·50

Nos. 373/8 were each printed in sheetlets of six stamps with enlarged illustrated margins.

62 Avro 504

(Litho B.D.T.)

2008 (1 Apr). 90th Anniv of the Royal Air Force. T **62** and similar multicoloured designs. W w **14** (sideways). P 14.

379	27p. Type **62**	1·25	1·25
380	27p. Short Sunderland	1·25	1·25
381	27p. de Havilland Mosquito	1·25	1·25
382	27p. Vickers VC10	1·25	1·25
383	54p. English Electric Canberra	2·00	2·00
379/83	Set of 5	6·25	6·25

MS384 70×110 mm. £1·72 King George V, Marshal of the RAF (vert). Wmk inverted ..... 11·00 12·00

Nos. 379/83 were each printed in sheetlets of eight stamps with a central label showing anniversary emblem and enlarged illustrated margins.

 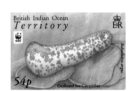

63 Pte Harry Lamin, 1918

64 Bohadschia argus (Ocellated Sea Cucumber)

(Litho B.D.T.)

2008 (16 Sept). 90th Anniv of the End of World War I. T **63** and similar vert designs showing soldiers and their letters home. Multicoloured. W w **18** (inverted). P 14.

385	50p. Type **63**	2·00	2·25
386	50p. Second Lt. Eric Heaton, 1916	2·00	2·25
387	50p. Pte Dennis Harry Wilson, 1917	2·00	2·25
388	50p. Second Lt. Eric Rose, 1917	2·00	2·25
389	50p. Sgt-Major Francis Proud, 1915	2·00	2·25
390	50p. Second Lt. Charles Roberts, 1917	2·00	2·25
385/90	Set of 6	11·00	12·00

MS391 110×70 mm. £1 UK Overseas Territories Wreath of Remembrance ..... 4·25 4·75

Nos. 385/90 were each printed in sheetlets of six stamps with enlarged illustrated bottom margins.

(Des Ian Loe. Litho B.D.T.)

2008 (1 Dec). Endangered Species. Sea Cucumbers. T **64** and similar horiz designs. Multicoloured. W w **14** (sideways). P 14.

392	54p. Type **64**	2·75	2·75
	a. Strip of 4. Nos. 392/5	12·00	12·00
393	54p. Thelenota ananas (Pineapple Sea Cucumber)	2·75	2·75
394	90p. Pearsonothuria graeffei (Graeffe's Sea Cucumber)	4·00	4·00
395	90p. Stichopus chloronotus (Dark Green Sea Cucumber)	4·00	4·00
392/5	Set of 4	12·00	12·00

Nos. 392/5 were printed together, se-tenant, as horizontal and vertical strips of four in sheetlets of 16, and also in separate sheets.

65 HMS Endeavour (Cook)

65a Short S.38

(Litho B.D.T.)

2009 (9 Mar). Seafaring and Exploration. T **65** and similar multicoloured designs. W w **18**. P 14.

396	54p. Type **65**	3·00	3·00
397	54p. HMS Victory (Nelson)	3·00	3·00
398	54p. HMS Beagle (Darwin)	3·00	3·00
399	54p. SS Windsor Castle (landing of Captain Raymond, Diego Garcia, 1884)	3·00	3·00
400	54p. SMS Fürst Bismarck (German armoured cruiser, 1900)	3·00	3·00

401	54p. HMS *Edinburgh* (1983)	3·00	3·00
396/401	*Set of 6*	16·00	16·00

MS402 110×70 mm. £1·30 Vasco da Gama (Portuguese navigator, sighted Chagos Archipelago, early 16th-century) (*vert*). Wmk inverted .... 6·50 7·00

Nos. 396/401 were each printed in sheetlets of six stamps with enlarged illustrated margins.

(Des Tim O'Brien. Litho B.D.T.)

2009 (17 Apr). Centenary of Naval Aviation. T **65a** and similar multicoloured designs Multicoloured (except **MS**407). W w **18** (sideways). P 14.

403	27p. Type **65a**	2·00	2·00
404	27p. Sopwith Pup	2·00	2·00
405	54p. Supermarine Scimitar	3·25	3·25
406	54p. Westland Wessex helicopter	3·25	3·25
403/6	*Set of 4*	9·50	9·50

MS407 110×70 mm. £1·72 Sqn. Cdr. E. H. Dunning landing aircraft on HMS *Furious*, 1917 (black, deep ultramarine and rosine) .... 11·00 12·00

Nos. 403/6 were each printed in sheetlets of eight stamps with a central label and enlarged illustrated bottom margins.

65b Development of early rockets *Corporal* and *Private*

66 Two Band Anemonefish (*Amphiprion bicinctus*)

2009 (20 July). International Year of Astronomy. 40th Anniv of First Moon Landing. T **65b** and similar multicoloured designs. W w **18** (sideways). P 13.

408	54p. Type **65b**	2·50	2·50
409	54p. *Flying Bedstead*, 1964	2·50	2·50
410	54p. Apollo Launch Site, 1969	2·50	2·50
411	54p. Space Transportation System 71 launch, 1995	2·50	2·50
412	90p. ESA *Columbus* Laboratory STS 122, 2008.	4·00	4·00
408/12	*Set of 5*	12·50	12·50

MS413 100×80 mm. £1·50 *Savoring the Moment* (astronaut Jack Schmitt on Moon) (Alan Bean) (39×59 *mm*). Wmk upright .... 6·50 7·00

Nos. 408/12 were printed in separate sheetlets of six stamps with enlarged illustrated margins.

(Litho B.D.T.)

2009 (5 Oct). T **66** and similar vert designs. Multicoloured. W w **18**. P 13½.

414	1p. Type **66**	10	10
415	2p. Angelfish (*Centropyge bicolor*)	15	15
416	5p. Royal poinciana (*Delonix regia*)	25	25
417	12p. Beach morning glory (*Ipomoea pes-caprae*)	55	55
418	27p. Bay cedar (*Suriana maritima*)	1·25	1·25
419	45p. Scaevola bush (*Scaevola taccada*)	2·00	2·00
420	54p. Madagascan Red Fody (*Foudia madagascariensis*)	2·50	2·50
421	90p. Greater Frigatebird (*Fregata minor*)	4·00	4·00
422	£1·30 Sharks Cove	5·00	5·00
423	£1·72 Turtle Cove	6·25	6·25
424	£2·64 Hawksbill Turtle	8·75	8·75
425	£3·02 Sicklefin Lemon Shark (*Negaprion acutidens*)	11·00	11·00
414/25	*Set of 12*	38·00	38·00

MS426 194×134 mm. Nos. 414/25 .... 38·00 38·00

67 *Lentinus* sp.

(Des Andrew Robinson. Litho B.D.T.)

2009 (7 Dec). Fungi. T **67** and similar square designs. Multicoloured. W w **18** (sideways). P 13½.

427	54p. Type **67**	2·50	2·50
428	54p. *Entoloma* sp.	2·50	2·50
429	90p. *Leucocoprinus* sp.	4·00	4·00

430	90p. *Pycnoporus* sp.	4·00	4·00
427/30	*Set of 4*	12·00	12·00

68 Hugh Dowding

69 Great Britain George V 1934 1½d. Stamp

(Litho Lowe-Martin Group)

2010 (18 Mar). 70th Anniv of the Battle of Britain. Aces and Leaders. T **68** and similar horiz designs. Multicoloured. W w **18** (inverted). P 13.

431	50p. Type **68**	2·50	2·50
432	50p. Bob Stanford-Tuck	2·50	2·50
433	50p. Ginger Lacey	2·50	2·50
434	50p. Eric Lock	2·50	2·50
435	50p. Mike Crossley	2·50	2·50
436	50p. Bob Doe	2·50	2·50
431/36	*Set of 6*	13·50	13·50

MS437 110×70 mm. £1·50 Sir Douglas Bader. Wmk upright .... 6·00 6·50

(Litho B.D.T.)

2010 (8 May). London 2010 Festival of Stamps and Centenary of Accession of King George V. Sheet 110×70 mm. W w **18**. P 14.

MS438 **69** £1·50 multicoloured .... 7·50 8·00

70 Archer and Mounted Knight, Battle of Hastings, 1066

(Litho Lowe-Martin Group)

2010 (30 Sept). Great Battles. T **70** and similar square designs. Multicoloured. P 13½.

439	50p. Type **70**	2·25	2·25
440	50p. Mounted knight carrying standard and archers, Battle of Agincourt, 1415	2·25	2·25
441	50p. Mounted knights, Battle of Bosworth, 1485	2·25	2·25
442	50p. Cavalry, Battle of Naseby, 1645	2·25	2·25
443	50p. Soldiers, Battle of Culloden, 1746	2·25	2·25
444	50p. Duke of Wellington on horseback and soldiers, Battle of Waterloo, 1815	2·25	2·25
445	50p. Soldiers and cavalryman, Battle of Alma, 1854	2·25	2·25
446	50p. British soldiers, Battle of Rorke's Drift, 1879.	2·25	2·25
447	50p. Soldiers, Siege of Mafeking, 1899	2·25	2·25
448	50p. Soldiers, Battle of the Somme, 1916	2·25	2·25
449	50p. Soldiers, Battle of El Alamein, 1942	2·25	2·25
450	50p. Normandy Landings, 1944	2·25	2·25
439/50	*Set of 12*	24·00	24·00

Nos. 439/50 were each printed in sheetlets of six stamps with enlarged illustrated margins.

70a Queen Elizabeth II, c. 1952

(Litho B.D.T.)

2011 (1 Mar). Queen Elizabeth II and Prince Philip 'A Lifetime of Service'. Diamond-shaped designs as T **70a**. Multicoloured. P 13½.

451	54p. Type **70a**		1·80	1·80
452	54p. Queen Elizabeth II and Prince Philip (black/white photo), c. 1972		1·80	1·80
453	54p. Queen Elizabeth II and Prince Philip, c. 1955		1·80	1·80
454	54p. Queen Elizabeth II and Prince Philip (seen in profile) , c. 2010		1·80	1·80
455	54p. Queen Elizabeth II and Prince Philip, c. 1970		1·80	1·80
456	54p. Prince Philip, c. 1955		1·80	1·80
451/6 Set of 6			9·75	9·75
MS457 174×163 mm. Nos. 451/6 and three stamp-size labels			10·50	11·50
MS458 110×70 mm. £3·02 Queen Elizabeth II and Prince Philip, c. 2007			10·50	11·50

Nos. 451/6 were printed in separate sheetlets of eight stamps.

No. **MS**457 forms a diamond shape but with the left, right and top corners removed.

71 Prince William and Miss Catherine Middleton

(Litho B.D.T.)

2011 (29 Apr). Royal Wedding (1st issue). Sheet 118×90 mm. W w **18** (sideways). P 14½×14.

MS459 **71** £3 multicoloured		11·00	11·00

71a Duke and Duchess of Cambridge waving from State Landau

72 Field of Poppies, Flanders

(Litho Lowe-Martin Group)

2011 (1 Aug). Royal Wedding (2nd issue). Multicoloured designs as T **71a**. W w **18** (sideways on horiz designs). P 12½.

460	54p. Type **71a**		2·25	2·25
461	54p. Duke and Duchess of Cambridge kissing on Buckingham Palace balcony (vert)		2·25	2·25
462	90p. Duke and Duchess of Cambridge at Westminster Abbey after wedding ceremony (vert)		3·00	3·00
463	90p. Leaving Buckingham Palace in car with 'JUST WED' numberplate		3·00	3·00
460/63 Set of 4			9·50	9·50

(Litho Lowe-Martin Group)

2011 (11 Nov). 90th Anniv of the Royal British Legion. T **72** and similar horiz designs, each showing poppy at lower left. Multicoloured. W w **18** (sideways). P 13½.

464	50p. Type **72**		2·25	2·25
465	50p. Silhouette of soldier and war memorials		2·25	2·25
466	50p. War graves		2·25	2·25
467	50p. Poppy Appeal		2·25	2·25
468	50p. Aircraft dropping poppies		2·25	2·25
469	50p. Ex-servicemen wearing medals		2·25	2·25
470	50p. Wooden remembrance crosses with poppies		2·25	2·25
471	50p. Festival of Remembrance		2·25	2·25
464/71 Set of 8			16·00	16·00
MS472 94×64 mm. £1·50 Remembrance Day service			7·00	7·00

Nos. 464/71 were each printed in sheetlets of six stamps with enlarged margins showing wooden remembrance cross with poppy and silhouette of soldier.

73 Queen Elizabeth II, c. 1970

(Litho B.D.T.)

2012 (6 Feb). Diamond Jubilee. T **73** and similar diamond-shaped designs. Multicoloured. P 13½.

473	54p. Type **73**		2·00	2·00
474	54p. Queen Elizabeth II wearing blue hat, c. 1975		2·00	2·00
475	54p. Queen Elizabeth II wearing red, c. 1980		2·00	2·00
476	54p. Queen Elizabeth II wearing tiara, pendant and pearl earrings. c. 1955 (colour photo)		2·00	2·00
477	54p. Queen Elizabeth II wearing tiara, c. 1955 (black/white photo)		2·00	2·00
478	54p. Queen Elizabeth II, c. 2005		2·00	2·00
473/8 Set of 6			11·00	11·00
MS479 174×164 mm. Nos. 473/8 and three stamp-size labels			11·00	11·50
MS480 110×70 mm. £3·02 Queen Elizabeth II wearing red cardigan and pearl necklace, c. 1975			17·00	18·00

Nos. 473/8 were printed in separate sheetlets of eight stamps.

No. **MS**479 forms a diamond-shape but with the left, right and top corners removed.

74 Queen Elizabeth II   **75** Crest (left)

(Litho Cartor)

2013 (2 Dec). 60th Anniv of the Coronation. T **74** and similar vert designs. Multicoloured. W w **18**. P 13½×13.

481	34p. Type **74**		1·00	1·00
482	54p. Coronation portrait of Queen Elizabeth II and Duke of Edinburgh		1·90	1·90
483	90p. Queen Elizabeth II wearing diadem, c. 1952 (black/white photo)		2·75	2·75
484	£1·10 Queen Elizabeth II wearing diadem, c. 1952 (colour photo)		3·25	3·25
481/484 Set of 4			8·00	8·00

(Litho Cartor)

2014 (9 June). Crest. T **75** and similar multicoloured designs. W w **18**. P 13½.

485	54p. Type **75**		1·90	1·90
	a. Horiz pair. Nos. 485/6		3·75	3·75
486	54p. Crest (right portion)		1·90	1·90
MS487 118×72 mm. £2 Crest (45×45 mm)			7·00	7·00

Nos. 485/6 were printed together, se-tenant, forming a composite design showing the complete crest.

PARCEL POST STAMP

2002 (3 Oct). Tenth Anniv of Friends of Chagos (conservation association). Reef Fish. Sheet, 115×95 mm, containing horiz design as T **47**. Multicoloured. W w **14**. P 14×14½.

PMS1	£1·90 Parrotfish	10·00	13·00

Madagascar

BRITISH CONSULAR MAIL

After May 1883 mail from the British community at Antananarivo, the capital, was sent by runner to the British Consulate at Tamatave for forwarding via the French Post Office.

In March of the following year the British Vice-Consul at Antananarivo, Mr. W. C. Pickersgill, reorganised this service and issued stamps for use on both local and overseas mail. Such stamps were only gummed at one of the top corners. This was to facilitate their removal from overseas mail where they were replaced by Mauritius stamps (at Port Louis) or by French issues (at the Vice-Consulate) for transmission via Tamatave and Réunion. Local mail usually had the stamps removed also, being marked with a "PAID" or a Vice-Consular handstamp, although a few covers have survived intact.

CONDITION. Due to the type of paper used, stamps of the British Consular Mail are usually found with slight faults, especially thins and creases. Our prices are for fine examples.

USED STAMPS. Postmarks are not usually found on these issues. Cancellations usually take the form of a manuscript line or cross in crayon, ink or pencil or as five parallel horizontal bars in black, red or violet, approximately 15 mm long. Examples of Nos. 1/3, 5/8 and 11 showing a red diagonal line may have been pre-cancelled for accounting purposes.

1

2

1884 (Mar). Typo British Mission at Antananarivo. Rouletted vertically in colour. No gum, except on one upper corner. With circular consular handstamp reading "BRITISH VICE-CONSULATE ANTANANARIVO" around Royal arms in black.

(a) Inscr "LETTER"

1	**1**	6d. (½ oz) magenta	£475	£475
		a. Violet handstamp	£2750	

2		1s. (1 oz) magenta	£500	£450
3		1s.6d. (1½ oz) magenta	£500	£500
4		2s. (2 oz) magenta	£850	£900

(b) Inscr "POSTAL PACKET"

5	**1**	1d. (1 oz) magenta	£550	£425
		a. Without handstamp	£10000	£10000
6		2d. (2 oz) magenta	£375	£300
7		3d. (3 oz) magenta	£400	£325
8		4d. (1 oz amended in ms to "4 oz") magenta	£1000	£700
		a. Without manuscript amendment	£6000	£5000
		ab. Violet handstamp	£1800	
		ac. Without handstamp	£9000	£9000

Nos. 1/8 were printed in horizontal strips of four, each strip containing two impressions of the setting. Each strip usually contained two stamps with normal stops after "B.C.M." and two with a hollow stop after "B" (1d., 2d., 3d., 4d., 6d. and 2s.) or after "M" (1s. and 1s.6d.), although the 2d. and 3d. have also been seen with a hollow stop after "M" and the 6d. with hollow stops after both "B" and "C".

Several values are known with the handstamp either inverted or double.

1886. Manuscript provisionals.

(a) No. 2 with "SHILLING" erased and "PENNY" written above in red ink

9	**1**	1d. on 1s. (1 oz) magenta	†	—

(b) No. 2 surch "4½d." and "W.C.P." in red ink with a line through the original value

10	**1**	4½d. on 1s. (1 oz) magenta	†	—

1886. As No. 1, but colour changed. Handstamped with circular "BRITISH VICE-CONSULATE ANTANANARIVO" in black.

11	**1**	6d. (½ oz) rose-red	£1400	£800

1886. As No. 8a, but handstamped "BRITISH CONSULAR MAIL ANTANANARIVO" in black.

12	**1**	4d. (1 oz) magenta	£1600	
		a. Violet handstamp	£7500	

1886. Typo British Mission at Antananarivo. "POSTAGE" and value in words printed in black. Rouletted vertically in colour. No gum, except on one upper corner.

I. "POSTAGE" 29½ mm long. Stops after "POSTAGE" and value

(a) Handstamped "BRITISH VICE-CONSULATE ANTANANARIVO" in black

14	**2**	1d. rose	£140	£275
		a. Violet handstamp	£400	
15		1½d. rose	£3000	£1300
		a. Violet handstamp	£1500	£850
16		2d. rose	£200	
		a. Violet handstamp	£400	
17		3d. rose	£4000	£1400
		a. Violet handstamp	£550	£375
18		4½d. rose	£3750	£550
		a. Violet handstamp	£700	£325
19		8d. rose	£5000	£3000
		a. Violet handstamp	£2750	£1800
20		9d. rose	£4750	£2750
		a. Violet handstamp	£1300	

(b) Handstamped "BRITISH CONSULAR MAIL ANTANANARIVO" in black.

21	**2**	1d. rose	£130	
22		1½d. rose	£160	£275
23		2d. rose	£190	
24		3d. rose	£160	£250
		a. Handstamp in red	†	£20000
25		4½d. rose	£180	£225
		a. Handstamp in red	†	£12000
26		8d. rose	£200	
		a. Handstamp in violet	£1700	
27		9d. rose	£225	£350
		a. Without handstamp	£8500	
		b. Handstamp in violet	£450	

II. "POSTAGE" 29½ mm long. No stops after "POSTAGE" or value.

(a) Handstamped "BRITISH VICE-CONSULATE ANTANANARIVO" in violet

28	**2**	1d. rose	£1300	
29		1½d. rose	£3000	
30		3d. rose	£1300	
31		4½d. rose	£2250	
32		6d. rose	£1700	

(b) Handstamped "BRITISH CONSULAR MAIL ANTANANARIVO" in black

33	**2**	1d. rose	£130	£225
		a. Without handstamp	£4750	
		b. Violet handstamp	£170	
34		1½d. rose	£140	£200
		a. Without handstamp	£5000	
		b. Violet handstamp	£275	
35		2d. rose	£150	£200
		b. Violet handstamp	£325	
36		3d. rose	£160	£225
		a. Without handstamp	£8000	
		b. Violet handstamp	£200	

37		4½d. rose	£150	£200
		a. Without handstamp	£9000	
		b. Violet handstamp	£225	
38		6d. rose	£160	£275
		a. Without handstamp	£9500	
		b. Violet handstamp	£500	

III. "POSTAGE" 24½ mm long. No stop after "POSTAGE", but stop after value

(a) Handstamped "BRITISH VICE-CONSULATE ANTANANARIVO" in violet

39	**2**	4d. rose	£500
40		8d. rose	£700
40*a*		1s. rose	£22000
41		1s.6d. rose	£12000
42		2s. rose	£6500
		a. Handstamp in black	£18000

(b) Handstamped "BRITISH CONSULAR MAIL ANTANANARIVO" in black

43	**2**	4d. rose	£375
		a. Without handstamp	£6000
		b. Violet handstamp	£450
44		8d. rose	£2250
		a. Without handstamp	£6000
		b. Violet handstamp	£1400
45		1s. rose	£600
		a. Without handstamp	£8500
		b. Violet handstamp	£1700
46		1s.6d. rose	£750
		a. Without handstamp	£7500
		b. Violet handstamp	£1700
47		2s. rose	£750
		a. Without handstamp	£8500
		b. Violet handstamp	£1700

Nos. 14/47 were also printed in horizontal strips of four.

The stamps of the British Consular Mail were suppressed in 1887, but the postal service continued with the charges paid in cash.

BRITISH INLAND MAIL

In January 1895 the Malagasy government agreed that a syndicate of British merchants at Antananarivo, including the Vice-Consul, should operate an inland postal service during the war with France. Mail was sent by runner to the port of Vatomandry and forwarded via Durban where Natal stamps were added.

Nos. 50/62 were cancelled with dated circular postmarks inscribed "BRITISH MAIL".

4   **5** Malagasy Runners

(Typeset London Missionary Society Press, Antananarivo)

1895 (1 Jan). Rouletted in black.

(a) Thick laid paper

50	**4**	4d. black	65·00	22·00
		a. "FUOR" for "FOUR" (R. 3/2)	—	£1200

(b) In black on coloured wove paper

51	**4**	1d. *blue-grey*	50·00	13·00
52		6d. *pale yellow*	50·00	13·00
53		8d. *salmon*	50·00	13·00
54		1s. *fawn*	60·00	13·00
55		2s. *bright rose*	75·00	30·00
		a. Italic "2" at left (R. 1/2)	£150	65·00
56		4s. *grey*	75·00	13·00
50/6	*Set of 7*		£375	£100

There are six types of each value, printed in blocks of six (2×3) separated by gutters, four times on each sheet; the upper and lower blocks being *tête-bêche*.

Nos. 51/6 have been reported on paper showing a sheet watermark in four lines, including a date and the words "Tinted", "Tul..." and "Austria".

(Typo John Haddon & Co, London)

1895 (Mar). The inscription in the lower label varies for each value. P 12.

57	**5**	2d. blue	14·00	60·00
		a. Imperf between (horiz pair)	£450	
		b. Imperf between (vert pair)	£750	
58		4d. rose	14·00	60·00
		a. Imperf between (horiz pair)	£250	
		b. Imperf between (vert pair)	£300	
		c. Imperf vert (horiz pair)	£275	
59		6d. green	14·00	75·00
		a. Imperf between (horiz pair)	£950	
60		1s. slate-blue	14·00	£120
		a. Imperf between (horiz pair)	£550	

61		2s. chocolate	32·00	£160
		a. Imperf between (horiz pair)	£700	
		b. Imperf between (vert pair)	£1000	
62		4s. bright purple	55·00	£225
		a. Imperf between (horiz pair)	£2250	
57/62	*Set of 6*		£130	£650

This post was suppressed when the French entered Antananarivo on 30 September 1895.

Maldive Islands

BRITISH PROTECTORATE

(Currency. 100 cents = 1 Ceylon rupee)

MALDIVES
(1)

2 Minaret,
Juma Mosque,
Malé

3

1906 (9 Sept). Nos. 277/9, 280a and 283/4 of Ceylon optd with T **1**.
Wmk Mult Crown CA. P 14.

1	**44**	2c. red-brown	24·00	50·00
2	**45**	3c. green	38·00	55·00
3		4c. orange and ultramarine	55·00	90·00
4	**46**	5c. dull purple	4·00	6·50
5	**48**	15c. blue	£110	£180
6		25c. bistre	£120	£225
1/6 Set of 6			£300	£550

The T **1** opt has been extensively forged.

Supplies of Nos. 1/6 were exhausted by March 1907 and the stamps of CEYLON were used until 1909.

(Recess D.L.R.)

1909 (May). T **2** (18½×22½ mm). W **3**. P 14×13½ (2c., 5c.) or 13½×14 (3c., 10c.).

7	**2**	2c. orange-brown	2·25	4·50
		a. Perf 13½×14	2·50	90
8		3c. deep myrtle	50	70
9		5c. purple	50	35
10		10c. carmine	7·50	80
7/10 Set of 4			9·50	2·50

These stamps perforated 14×13½ (14×13.7) are from a line machine and those perforated 13½×14 (13.7×13.9) from a comb machine.

4

(Photo Harrison)
1933. T **2** redrawn (reduced to 18×21½ mm). W **4**. P 15×14.

A. Wmk upright

11A	**2**	2c. grey	2·75	2·00
12A		3c. red-brown	70	2·75
14A		5c. mauve	55·00	10·00
15A		6c. scarlet	1·50	5·50
16A		10c. green	85	55
17A		15c. black	8·50	28·00
18A		25c. brown	8·50	28·00
19A		50c. purple	8·50	35·00
20A		1r. deep blue	15·00	28·00
11A/20A Set of 9			90·00	£130

B. Wmk sideways

11B	**2**	2c. grey	9·00	5·50
12B		3c. red-brown	5·00	1·75
13B		5c. claret	40·00	32·00
15B		6c. scarlet	10·00	8·50
16B		10c. green	3·75	11·00
17B		15c. black	15·00	28·00
18B		25c. brown	11·00	23·00
19B		50c. purple	16·00	27·00
20B		1r. deep blue	16·00	4·50
11B/20B Set of 9			£110	£130

(New Currency. 100 larees = 1 rupee)

5 Palm Tree and Dhow

(Recess B.W.)

1950 (24 Dec)–**52**. P 13.

21	**5**	2l. olive-green	4·50	5·50
		a. Olive-brown (1952)	12·00	12·00
22		3l. blue	17·00	3·00
23		5l. emerald-green	17·00	3·00
24		6l. red-brown	1·25	1·75
25		10l. scarlet	1·25	1·00
26		15l. orange	1·25	1·00
27		25l. purple	1·25	4·00
28		50l. violet	1·50	6·00
29		1r. chocolate	14·00	42·00
21/9 Set of 9			55·00	65·00

7 Fish   **8** Native Products

1952. P 13.

30	**7**	3l. blue	2·00	60
31	**8**	5l. emerald	1·00	2·00

SULTANATE
Sultan Mohammed Fareed Didi
20 November 1953–10 November 1968

The Maldive Islands became a republic on 1 January 1953, but reverted to a sultanate on 29 November 1953.

9 Malé Harbour   **10** Fort and Building

(Recess B.W.)

1956 (1 Feb). P 13½ (T **9**) or 11½×11 (T **10**).

32	**9**	2l. purple	10	10
33		3l. slate	10	10
34		5l. red-brown	10	10
35		6l. blackish violet	10	10
36		10l. emerald	10	10
37		15l. chocolate	10	85
38		25l. rose-red	10	10
39		50l. orange	10	10
40	**10**	1r. bluish green	15	10
41		5r. blue	2·00	30
42		10r. magenta	2·75	1·25
32/42 Set of 11			5·00	2·75

11 Cycling   **12** Basketball

(Des C. Bottiau. Recess and typo B.W.)

1960 (20 Aug). Olympic Games. P 11½×11 (T **11**) or 11×11½ (T **12**).

43	**11**	2l. purple and green	15	90
44		3l. greenish slate and purple	15	90
45		5l. red-brown and ultramarine	15	25
46		10l. emerald-green and brown	15	25
47		15l. sepia and blue	15	25
48	**12**	25l. rose-red and olive	15	25
49		50l. orange and violet	20	40
50		1r. emerald and purple	40	1·25
43/50 Set of 8			1·40	4·00

13 Tomb of Sultan

14 Custom House

15 Cowrie Shells

16 Old Royal Palace

17 Road to Junin Mosque, Malé

18 Council House

19 New Government Secretariat

20 Prime Minister's Office

21 Old Ruler's Tomb

22 Old Ruler's Tomb (distant view)

23 Maldivian Port

(Recess B.W.)

1960 (15 Oct). T **13/23**. P 11½×11.

51	**13**	2l. purple	10	10
52	**14**	3l. emerald-green	10	10
53	**15**	5l. orange-brown	3·75	4·00
54	**16**	6l. bright blue	10	10
55	**17**	10l. carmine	10	10
56	**18**	15l. sepia	10	10
57	**19**	25l. deep violet	10	10
58	**20**	50l. slate-grey	10	10
59	**21**	1r. orange	15	10
60	**22**	5r. deep ultramarine	9·00	60
61	**23**	10r. grey-green	15·00	1·25
51/61 *Set of 11*			25·00	6·00

Higher values were also issued, intended mainly for fiscal use.

24 "Care of Refugees"

(Recess B.W.)

1960 (15 Oct). World Refugee Year. P 11½×11.

62	**24**	2l. deep violet, orange and green	10	15
63		3l. brown, green and red	10	15
64		5l. deep green, sepia and red	10	10
65		10l. bluish green, reddish violet and red	10	10
66		15l. reddish violet, grey-green and red	10	10
67		25l. blue, red-brown and bronze-green	10	10
68		50l. yellow-olive, rose-red and blue	10	10
69		1r. carmine, slate and violet	15	35
62/9 *Set of 8*			60	1·00

25 Coconuts

26 Map of Malé

(Photo Harrison)

1961 (20 Apr). P 14×14½ (Nos. 70/74) or 14½×14 (others).

70	**25**	2l. yellow-brown and deep green	10	85
71		3l. yellow-brown and bright blue	10	85
72		5l. yellow-brown and magenta	10	10
73		10l. yellow-brown and red-orange	15	10
74		15l. yellow-brown and black	20	15
75	**26**	25l. multicoloured	45	20
76		50l. multicoloured	45	40
77		1r. multicoloured	50	70
70/7 *Set of 8*			1·75	3·00

27 5c. Stamp of 1906

(Des M. Shamir. Photo Harrison)

1961 (9 Sept). 55th Anniv of First Maldivian Stamp. T **27** and similar horiz designs. P 14½×14.

78		2l. brown-purple, ultramarine and light green	10	1·10
79		3l. brown-purple, ultramarine and light green	10	1·10
80		5l. brown-purple, ultramarine and light green	10	15
81		6l. brown-purple, ultramarine and light green	10	1·40
82		10l. green, claret and maroon	10	15
83		15l. green, claret and maroon	15	15
84		20l. green, claret and maroon	15	20
85		25l. claret, green and black	15	20
86		50l. claret, green and black	25	80
87		1r. claret, green and black	40	2·00
78/87 *Set of 10*			1·40	6·50
MS87*a* 114×88 mm. No. 87 (block of four). Imperf.			1·50	7·00

Designs:—2 to 6l. Type **27**; 10 to 20l. 1906 3c. and posthorn; 25l. to 1r. 1906 2c. and olive sprig.

30 Malaria Eradication Emblem

31 Children of Europe and America

(Recess B.W.)

1962 (7 Apr). Malaria Eradication. P 13½×13.

88	**30**	2l. chestnut	10	1·50
89		3l. emerald	10	1·50
90		5l. turquoise-blue	10	15
91		10l. red	10	15
92	–	15l. deep purple-brown	15	15
93	–	25l. deep blue	20	20
94	–	50l. deep green	25	55
95	–	1r. purple	55	80
88/95 *Set of 8*			1·40	4·50

Nos. 92/5 are as T **30**, but have English inscriptions at the side.

(Des C. Bottiau. Photo Harrison)

1962 (9 Sept). 15th Anniv of U.N.I.C.E.F. T **31** and similar horiz design. Multicoloured. P 14½×14.

96		2l. Type **31**	10	1·50
97		6l. Type **31**	10	1·50
98		10l. Type **31**	10	15
99		15l. Type **31**	10	15
100		25l. Children of Middle East and Far East...	15	15
101		50l. As 25l.	20	15
102		1r. As 25l.	25	20
103		5r. As 25l.	1·25	5·00
96/103 *Set of 8*			2·00	8·00

33 Sultan Mohammed Fareed Didi   **34** Royal Angelfish

(Photo Harrison)

1962 (29 Nov). Ninth Anniv of Enthronement of Sultan. P 14×14½.

104	**33**	3l. orange-brown and bluish green....	10	1·50
105		5l. orange-brown and indigo...	15	20
106		10l. orange-brown and blue...	20	20
107		20l. orange-brown and olive-green...	30	25
108		50l. orange-brown and deep magenta	35	45
109		1r. orange-brown and slate-lilac...	45	65
104/9 *Set of 6*			1·40	3·00

(Des R. Hegeman. Photo Enschedé)

1963 (2 Feb). Tropical Fish. T **34** and similar triangular designs. Multicoloured. P 13½.

110		2l. Type **34**	10	1·50
111		3l. Type **34**	10	1·50
112		5l. Type **34**	15	55
113		10l. Moorish Idol...	35	55
114		25l. As 10l.	75	55
115		50l. Diadem Soldierfish...	1·25	70
116		1r. Powder-blue Surgeonfish...	1·50	75
117		5r. Racoon Butterflyfish...	6·25	12·00
110/17 *Set of 8*			9·25	16·00

39 Fish in Net   **40** Handful of Grain

(Photo State Ptg Wks, Vienna)

1963 (21 Mar). Freedom from Hunger. P 12.

118	**39**	2l. brown and deep bluish green...	35	3·25
119	**40**	5l. brown and orange-red...	55	1·75
120	**39**	7l. brown and turquoise...	75	1·75
121	**40**	10l. brown and blue...	90	1·75
122	**39**	25l. brown and brown-red...	2·75	4·00
123	**40**	50l. brown and violet...	4·00	8·00
124	**39**	1r. brown and deep magenta...	6·50	12·00
118/24 *Set of 7*			14·00	29·00

41 Centenary Emblem   **42** Maldivian Scout Badge

(Photo Harrison)

1963 (1 Oct). Centenary of Red Cross. P 14×14½.

125	**41**	2l. red and deep purple...	30	2·00
126		15l. red and deep bluish green...	1·00	1·00
127		50l. red and deep brown...	1·75	1·75
128		1r. red and indigo...	2·50	2·00
129		4r. red and deep brown-olive...	5·00	21·00
125/9 *Set of 5*			9·50	25·00

(Photo Enschedé)

1964. World Scout Jamboree, Marathon (1963). P 13½.

130	**42**	2l. green and violet...	10	65
131		3l. green and bistre-brown...	10	65
132		25l. green and blue...	15	15
133		1r. green and crimson...	55	1·50
130/3 *Set of 4*			80	2·50

43 Mosque, Malé   **44** Putting the Shot

(Recess B.W.)

1964 (10 Aug). "Maldives Embrace Islam". W w **12**. P 11½.

134	**43**	2l. purple...	10	60
135		3l. emerald-green...	10	60
136		10l. carmine...	10	10
137		40l. deep dull purple...	30	25
138		60l. blue...	50	40
139		85l. orange-brown...	60	60
134/9 *Set of 6*			1·50	2·25

(Litho Enschedé)

1964 (1 Oct). Olympic Games, Tokyo. T **44** and similar horiz design. W w **12**. P 14×13½.

140		2l. deep maroon and turquoise-blue...	10	1·75
141		3l. crimson and chestnut...	10	1·75
142		5l. bronze-green and deep green...	15	35
143		10l. slate-violet and reddish purple...	20	35
144		15l. sepia and yellow-brown...	30	35
145		25l. indigo and deep blue...	50	35
146		50l. deep olive-green and yellow-olive...	75	40
147		1r. deep maroon and olive-grey...	1·25	75
140/7 *Set of 8*			3·00	5·50
MS147*a* 126×140 mm. Nos. 145/7. Imperf...			2·25	4·50

Designs:—2 to 10l. Type **44**; 15l. to 1r. Running.

46 Telecommunications Satellite

(Des M. Shamir. Photo Harrison)

1965 (1 July). International Quiet Sun Years. P 14½.

148	**46**	5l. blue...	20	75
149		10l. brown...	25	75
150		25l. green...	50	75
151		1r. deep magenta...	1·00	1·25
148/51 *Set of 4*			1·75	3·25

On 26 July 1965, Maldive Islands became independent and left the Commonwealth, rejoining the organisation on 9 July 1982.

47 Isis (wall carving, Abu Simbel)   **48** President Kennedy and Doves

(Des M. and G. Shamir. Litho Harrison)

1965 (1 Sept). Nubian Monuments Preservation. T **47** and similar vert design. W w **12**. P 14½.

152	**47**	2l. bluish green and brown-purple	15	1·00
153	–	3l. lake and deep green	15	1·00
154	**47**	5l. dull green and brown-purple	20	15
155	–	10l. steel-blue and orange..................	35	15
156	**47**	15l. red-brown and deep violet	60	15
		w. Wmk inverted............................	—	†
157	–	25l. reddish purple and deep blue.......	90	15
158	**47**	50l. yellow-green and sepia................	1·10	45
159	–	1r. ochre and myrtle-green................	1·50	55
152/9	*Set of 8*		4·50	3·25

Design:—3, 10, 25l., 1r. Rameses II on throne (wall carving, Abu Simbel).

(Photo State Ptg Wks, Vienna)

1965 (10 Oct). Second Death Anniv of President Kennedy. T **48** and similar horiz design. P 12.

160	**48**	2l. black and mauve	10	1·00
161		5l. bistre-brown and mauve..............	10	10
162		25l. indigo and mauve	20	10
163	–	1r. bright reddish purple, yellow and blue-green	35	25
164	–	2r. bronze-green, yellow and blue-green	50	1·10
160/4	*Set of 5*		1·00	2·25
MS164*a*	150×130 mm. No. 164 in block of four. Imperf..		2·75	3·25

Design:—1r., 2r. Pres. Kennedy and hands holding olive-branch.

49 "XX" and U.N. Flag

50 I.C.Y. Emblem

(Des O. Adler. Photo State Ptg Wks, Vienna)

1965 (24 Nov). 20th Anniv of U.N. P 12.

165	**49**	3l. turquoise-blue and red-brown	15	50
166		10l. turquoise-blue and violet..............	40	10
167		1r. turquoise-blue and bronze-green .	1·25	35
165/7	*Set of 3*		1·60	85

(Des M. and G. Shamir. Photo State Ptg Wks, Vienna)

1965 (20 Dec). International Co-operation Year. P 12.

168	**50**	5l. brown and yellow-bistre................	25	20
169		15l. brown and slate-lilac....................	40	20
170		50l. brown and yellow-olive	85	30
171		1r. brown and orange-red...................	1·50	1·50
172		2r. brown and new blue	2·00	4·50
168/72	*Set of 5*		4·50	6·00
MS173	101×126 mm. Nos. 170/2. Imperf..........		6·50	9·50

51 Princely Cone Shells

(Des M. and G. Shamir. Photo State Ptg Wks, Vienna)

1966 (1 June). T **51** and similar multicoloured designs. P 12.

174		2l. Type **51**	20	1·75
175		3l. Yellow flowers	20	1·75
176		5l. Reticulate Distorsio and Leopard Cone shells...	30	15
177		7l. Camellias	30	15
178		10l. Type **51**	1·00	15
179		15l. Crab Plover and Seagull	3·75	30
180		20l. As 3l...	80	30
181		30l. Type **51**	2·75	35
182		50l. As 15l.	6·00	55
183		1r. Type **51**	4·00	70
184		1r. As 7l.	3·50	70
185		1r.50 As 3l..	3·75	3·75
186		2r. As 7l.	5·00	4·25
187		5r. As 15l.	23·00	17·00
188		10r. As 5l.	23·00	25·00

174/88	*Set of 15*		70·00	50·00

The 3l., 7l., 20l., 1r. (No. 184), 1r.50 and 2r. are diamond-shaped (43½×43½ mm); the others are horizontal designs as T **51**.

52 Maldivian Flag

(Des M. and G. Shamir. Litho Harrison)

1966 (26 July). First Anniv of Independence. P 14×14½.

189	**52**	10l. green, red and turquoise................	4·00	75
190		1r. green, red, brown orange-yellow ..	10·00	1·25

53 "Luna 9" on Moon

(Des M. and G. Shamir. Litho Harrison)

1966 (1 Nov). Space Rendezvous and Moon Landing. T **53** and similar horiz designs. W w **12**. P 15×14.

191		10l. light brown, grey-blue and bright blue	40	10
192		25l. green and carmine........................	60	10
193		50l. orange-brown and green...............	90	15
194		1r. turquoise-blue and chestnut..........	1·50	35
195		2r. green and violet..........................	2·00	65
196		5r. rose-pink and deep turquoise-blue	3·00	1·60
191/6	*Set of 6*		7·50	2·50
MS197	108×126 mm. Nos. 194/6. Imperf........		3·75	6·00

Designs:—25l., 1r., 5r. "Gemini 6" and '7" rendezvous in space; 2r. "Gemini" spaceship as seen from the other spaceship; 50l. Type **53**.

54 U.N.E.S.C.O. Emblem, and Owl on Book

55 Sir Winston Churchill and Cortège

(Litho Harrison)

1966 (15 Nov). 20th Anniv of U.N.E.S.C.O. T **54** and similar vert designs. W w **12**. Multicoloured. P 15×14.

198		1l. Type **54**	40	2·00
199		3l. U.N.E.S.C.O. emblem, and globe and microscope...............................	40	2·00
200		5l. U.N.E.S.C.O. emblem, and mask, violin and palette.................................	80	40
201		50l. Type **54**	7·00	65
202		1r. Design as 3l...............................	8·00	90
203		5r. Design as 5l...............................	22·00	24·00
198/203	*Set of 6*		35·00	27·00

(Des M. and G. Shamir. Litho Harrison)

1967 (1 Jan). Churchill Commemoration. T **55** and similar horiz design. Flag in red and blue. P 14½×13½.

204	**55**	2l. olive-brown	40	3·50
205	–	10l. turquoise-blue.............................	2·75	60
206	**55**	15l. green	3·50	60
207	–	25l. violet	5·00	70
208	–	1r. brown	13·00	1·50
209	**55**	2r.50 crimson	22·00	23·00
204/9	*Set of 6*		42·00	27·00

Design:—10l., 25l.,1r. Churchill and catafalque.

IMPERFORATE STAMPS. From No. 210 onwards some sets and perforated miniature sheets exist imperforate from limited printings.

56 Footballers and Jules Rimet Cup

(Des M. and G. Shamir. Photo Govt Printer, Israel)

1967 (22 Mar). England's Victory in World Cup Football Championship. T **56** and similar horiz designs. Multicoloured. P 14×13½.

210	2l. Type **56**	30	2·00
211	3l. Player in red shirt kicking ball	30	2·00
212	5l. Scoring goal	30	50
213	25l. As 3l.	2·00	50
	a. Emerald (face value and inscr) omitted	£450	
214	50l. Making a tackle	2·75	50
215	1r. Type **56**	4·50	80
216	2r. Emblem on Union Jack	7·00	7·00
210/16	Set of 7	15·00	12·00
MS217	100×121 mm. Nos. 214/16. Imperf	15·00	12·00

57 Ornate Butterflyfish

(Des M. and G. Shamir. Photo Govt Printer, Israel)

1967 (1 May). Tropical Fish. T **57** and similar horiz designs. Multicoloured. P 14.

218	2l. Type **57**	15	1·25
219	3l. Black-saddled Pufferfish	20	1·25
220	5l. Blue Boxfish	40	30
221	6l. Picasso Triggerfish	40	40
222	50l. Semicircle Angelfish	4·00	50
223	1r. As 3l.	6·00	90
224	2r. As 50l.	10·00	9·00
218/24	Set of 7	19·00	12·00

58 Hawker Siddeley H.S.748 over Hulule Airport Building

(Des M. and G. Shamir. Photo Govt Printer, Israel)

1967 (26 July). Inauguration of Hulule Airport. T **58** and similar horiz design. P 14×13½.

225	2l. reddish violet and yellow-olive	25	75
226	5l. deep green and lavender	50	10
227	10l. reddish violet and light turquoise-green	65	10
228	15l. deep green and yellow-ochre	1·00	10
229	30l. deep ultramarine and light blue	1·75	10
230	50l. deep brown and magenta	2·50	20
231	5r. deep ultramarine and yellow-orange	6·00	5·50
232	10r. deep brown and blue	8·00	9·00
225/32	Set of 8	18·00	14·00

Designs:—2l., 10l., 30l., 5r. T **58**; 5l., 15l., 50l., 10r. Airport building and Hawker Siddeley H.S.748. Higher values were also issued, intended mainly for fiscal use.

59 "Man and Music" Pavilion **(60)**

(Des M. and G. Shamir. Photo Govt Printer, Israel)

1967 (1 Sept). World Fair Montreal. T **59** and similar horiz design. Multicoloured. P 14×13½.

233	2l. Type **59**	10	1·00
234	5l. "Man and His Community" Pavilion	10	10
235	10l. Type **59**	10	10
236	50l. As 5l.	50	30
237	1r. Type **59**	85	50
238	2r. As 5l.	2·00	2·25
233/8	Set of 6	3·25	3·75
MS239	102×137 mm. Nos. 237/8. Imperf	2·50	4·25

1967 (1 Dec). International Tourist Year. Nos. 225/32 optd as T **60** (in one or three lines), in gold.

240	2l. reddish violet and yellow-olive	20	1·00
241	5l. deep green and lavender	40	25
242	10l. reddish violet and light turquoise-green	55	25
243	15l. deep green and yellow-ochre	60	25
244	30l. deep ultramarine and light blue	80	30
245	50l. deep brown and magenta	1·00	35
246	5r. deep ultramarine and yellow-orange	4·50	5·00
247	10r. deep brown and blue	5·50	7·50
240/7	Set of 8	12·00	13·50

61 Cub signalling and Lord Baden-Powell

62 French Satellite "A 1"

(Litho Harrison)

1968 (1 Jan). Maldivian Scouts and Cubs. T **61** and similar vert design. P 14×14½.

248	**61**	2l. brown, green and yellow	10	1·00
249	–	3l. carmine, bright blue and light blue	10	1·00
250	**61**	25l. bluish violet, lake and orange-red	1·50	40
251	–	1r. blackish green, chestnut and apple-green	3·50	1·60
248/51		Set of 4	4·50	3·50

Design:—3l., 1r. Scouts and Lord Baden-Powell.

(Des M. and G. Shamir. Photo Govt Printer, Israel)

1968 (27 Jan). Space Martyrs. Triangular designs as T **62**. P 14.

252	2l. magenta and ultramarine	20	1·00
253	3l. violet and yellow-brown	20	1·00
254	7l. olive-brown and lake	40	1·00
255	10l. deep blue, pale drab and black	45	20
256	25l. bright emerald and reddish violet	1·00	20
257	50l. blue and orange-brown	1·40	30
258	1r. purple-brown and deep bluish green	2·00	50
259	2r. deep brown, pale blue and black	2·50	2·50
260	5r. magenta, light drab and black	3·50	4·00
252/60	Set of 9	10·50	9·50
MS261	110×155 mm. Nos. 258/9. Imperf	6·00	7·00

Designs:—2l., 50l. Type **62**; 3l., 25l. "Luna 10"; 7l.,1r. "Orbiter" and "Mariner"; 10l., 2r. Astronauts White, Grissom and Chaffee; 5r. Cosmonaut V. M. Komarov.

63 Putting the Shot

64 "Adriatic Seascape" (Bonington)

(Des M. Shamir. Litho Harrison)

1968 (1 Feb). Olympic Games, Mexico (1st issue). T **63** and similar vert design. Multicoloured. P 14½.

262	2l. Type **63**	10	90
263	6l. Throwing the discus	25	90
264	10l. Type **63**	40	15
265	15l. As 6l.	55	15
266	1r. Type **63**	1·00	35
267	2r.50 As 6l.	2·25	2·50
262/7	Set of 6	4·00	4·50

See also Nos. 294/7.

(Des M. Shamir. Litho Govt Printer, Israel)

1968 (1 Apr). Paintings. T **64** and similar horiz designs. Multicoloured. P 14.

268	50l. Type **64**	2·25	30
269	1r. "Ulysses deriding Polyphemus" (Turner)	2·75	45
270	2r. "Sailing Boat at Argenteuil" (Monet)	3·50	2·75
271	5r. "Fishing Boats at Les Saintes-Maries" (Van Gogh)	6·00	7·00
268/71 Set of 4		13·00	9·50

65 LZ-130 *Graf Zeppelin II* and Montgolfier's Balloon

(Des M. Shamir. Photo Govt Printer, Israel)

1968 (1 June). Development of Civil Aviation. T **65** and similar horiz designs. P 14×13½.

272	2l. orange-brown, yellow-green and ultramarine	20	1·25
273	3l. turquoise-blue, violet and orange-brown	20	1·25
274	5l. slate-green, crimson and turquoise-blue	20	20
275	7l. bright blue, purple and red-orange	4·00	1·75
276	10l. brown, turquoise-blue and bright purple	45	20
277	50l. crimson, slate-green and yellow-olive	1·50	30
278	1r. emerald, blue and vermilion	3·25	60
279	2r. maroon, bistre and bright blue	22·00	12·00
272/9 Set of 8		28·00	16·00

Designs:—3l., 1r. Boeing 707-420 and Douglas DC-3; 5l., 50l. Wright Type A and Lilienthal's glider; 7l., 2r. Projected Boeing 733 and Concorde; 10l. Type **65**.

66 W.H.O. Building, Geneva

International Boy Scout Jamboree, Farragut Park, Idaho, U.S.A. August 1-9, 1967

(67)

(Litho Harrison)

1968 (15 July). 20th Anniv of World Health Organisation. P 14½×13½.

280	**66**	10l. violet, turquoise-blue and light greenish blue	1·00	30
281		25l. bronze-green, yellow-brown and orange-yellow	1·50	30
282		1r. deep brown, emerald and bright green	4·00	90
283		2r. bluish violet, magenta and mauve	6·50	7·00
280/3 Set of 4			11·50	7·75

1968 (1 Aug). First Anniv of Scout Jamboree, Idaho. Nos. 248/51 optd with T **67**.

284	2l. brown, green and yellow	10	75
285	3l. carmine, bright blue and light blue	10	75
286	25l. bluish violet, lake and orange-red	1·50	55
287	1r. blackish green, chestnut and apple-green	4·50	2·10
284/7 Set of 4		5·50	3·75

68 Curlew and Redshank

1968 (24 Sept). T **68** and similar horiz designs. Photo. Multicoloured. P 14×13½.

288	2l. Type **68**	50	1·25
289	10l. Pacific Grinning Tun and Papal Mitre shells	1·25	20
290	25l. Oriental Angel Wing and Tapestry Turban shells	1·75	25
291	50l. Type **68**	9·50	1·10
292	1r. As 25l.	4·50	1·10
293	2r. As 10l.	5·50	5·00
288/93 Set of 6		21·00	8·00

69 Throwing the Discus

(Des M. Shamir. Photo Govt Printer, Israel)

1968 (12 Oct). Olympic Games, Mexico (2nd issue). T **69** and similar multicoloured designs. P 14.

294	10l. Type **69**	10	10
295	50l. Running	20	20
296	1r. Cycling	5·50	1·25
297	2r. Basketball	7·50	4·00
294/7 Set of 4		12·00	5·00

INDEPENDENT REPUBLIC

11 November 1968

70 Fishing Dhow

(Photo Harrison)

1968 (11 Nov). Republic Day. T **70** and similar horiz design. P 14×14½.

298	10l. brown, ultramarine and light yellow-green	1·50	50
299	1r. green, red and bright blue	11·00	2·00

Design:—1r. National flag, crest and map.

71 "The Thinker" (Rodin)

72 Module nearing Moon's Surface

(Des M. Shamir. Litho Rosenbaum Brothers, Vienna)

1969 (10 Apr). U.N.E.S.C.O. "Human Rights". T **71** and similar vert designs, showing sculptures by Rodin. Multicoloured. P 13½.

300	6l. Type **71**	75	60
301	10l. "Hands"	75	20
302	1r.50 "Eve"	3·75	3·75
303	2r.50 "Adam"	4·00	4·00
300/3 Set of 4		8·25	7·75
MS304 112×130 mm. Nos. 302/3. Imperf		13·00	13·00

(Des M. Shamir. Litho Govt Printer, Israel)

1969 (25 Sept). First Man on the Moon. T **72** and similar square designs. Multicoloured. P 14.

305	6l. Type **72**	50	35
306	10l. Astronaut with hatchet	50	20
307	1r.50 Astronaut and module	3·25	2·25
308	2r.50 Astronaut using camera	3·50	2·75
305/8 Set of 4		7·00	5·00
MS309 101×130 mm. Nos. 305/8. Imperf		6·50	7·50

*Gold Medal Winner
Mohamed Gammoudi
5000 m. run
Tunisia*

REPUBLIC OF MALDIVES

(73)

1969 (1 Dec). Gold-medal Winners, Olympic Games, Mexico (1968). Nos. 295/6 optd with T **73**, or similar inscr honouring P. Trentin (cycling) of France.

310	50l. multicoloured	60	60
311	1r. multicoloured	1·40	90

74 Racoon Butterflyfish

(Des M. Shamir. Litho)

1970 (1 Jan). Tropical Fish. T **74** and similar diamond-shaped designs. Multicoloured. P 10½.

312	2l. Type **74**	40	70
313	5l. Clown Triggerfish	65	40
314	25l. Broad-barred Lionfish	1·25	40
315	50l. Long-nosed Butterflyfish	1·50	1·00
316	1r. Emperor Angelfish	1·75	1·00
317	2r. Royal Angelfish	2·25	6·50
312/17	Set of 6	7·00	9·00

75 Columbia Dauman Victoria, 1899

(Des M. Shamir. Litho)

1970 (1 Feb). 75 Years of the Automobile. T **75** and similar horiz designs. Multicoloured. P 12.

318	2l. Type **75**	25	50
319	5l. Duryea Phaeton, 1902	30	30
320	7l. Packard S-24, 1906	40	30
321	10l. Autocar Runabout, 1907	45	30
322	25l. Type **75**	1·25	30
323	50l. As 5l	1·50	55
324	1r. As 7l	1·75	90
325	2r. As 10l	1·90	5·50
318/25	Set of 8	7·00	7·75
MS326	95×143 mm. Nos. 324/5. P 11½	3·25	7·50

76 U.N. Headquarters, New York **77** Ship and Light Buoy

(Des M. Shamir. Litho Rosenbaum Brothers, Vienna)

1970 (26 June). 25th Anniv of United Nations. T **76** and similar horiz designs. Multicoloured. P 13½.

327	2l. Type **76**	10	1·00
328	10l. Surgical operation (W.H.O.)	2·25	40
329	25l. Student, actress and musician (U.N.E.S.C.O.)	3·75	50
330	50l. Children at work and play (U.N.I.C.E.F.)	2·00	70
331	1r. Fish, corn and farm animals (F.A.O.)	2·00	1·00
332	2r. Miner hewing coal (I.L.O.)	7·50	7·50
327/32	Set of 6	16·00	10·00

(Des M. Shamir. Litho)

1970 (26 July). Tenth Anniv of Inter-governmental Maritime Consultative Organization. T **77** and similar vert design. Multicoloured. P 13½.

333	50l. Type **77**	1·25	50
334	1r. Ship and lighthouse	6·50	1·50

78 "Guitar-player and Masqueraders" (A. Watteau) **79** Australian Pavilion

(Des M. Shamir. Litho Govt Printer, Israel)

1970 (1 Aug). Famous Paintings showing the Guitar. T **78** and similar vert designs. Multicoloured. P 14.

335	3l. Type **78**	15	80
336	7l. "Spanish Guitarist" (E. Manet)	25	80
337	50l. "Costumed Player" (Watteau)	1·25	40
338	1r. "Mandolins-player" (Roberti)	2·00	55
339	2r.50 "Guitar-player and Lady" (Watteau)	3·50	4·00
340	5r. "Mandolins-player" (Frans Hals)	6·50	7·50
335/40	Set of 6	12·00	12·50
MS341	132×80 mm. Nos. 339/40. Roul	9·00	11·00

(Des M. Shamir. Litho Rosenbaum Brothers, Vienna)

1970 (1 Aug). EXPO 70 World Fair, Osaka, Japan. T **79** and similar vert designs. Multicoloured. P 13½.

342	2l. Type **79**	15	1·00
343	3l. West German Pavilion	15	1·00
344	10l. U.S.A. Pavilion	65	10
345	25l. British Pavilion	2·00	15
346	50l. Soviet Pavilion	2·50	45
347	1r. Japanese Pavilion	2·75	65
342/7	Set of 6	7·25	3·00

80 Learning the Alphabet

(Des M. Shamir. Litho Govt Printer, Israel)

1970 (7 Sept). International Education Year. T **80** and similar horiz designs. Multicoloured. P 14.

348	5l. Type **80**	50	60
349	10l. Training teachers	60	40
350	25l. Geography lesson	2·75	60
351	50l. School inspector	2·75	80
352	1r. Education by television	3·00	1·00
348/52	Set of 5	8·75	3·00

Philympia

London 1970

(**81**)

1970 (18 Sep). Philympia 1970 Stamp Exhibition, London. Nos. 306/ **MS**309 optd with T **81**, in silver.

353	10l. multicoloured	20	10
354	1r.50 multicoloured	1·25	1·00
355	2r.50 multicoloured	1·25	1·50
353/5	Set of 3	2·40	2·25
MS356	101×130 mm. Nos. 305/8 optd. Imperf	6·50	8·50

82 Footballers

83 Little Boy and U.N.I.C.E.F. Flag

(Des M. Shamir. Litho Rosenbaum Brothers, Vienna)

1970 (1 Dec). World Cup Football Championship, Mexico. T **82** and similar vert designs, each showing football scenes and outline of the Jules Rimet Trophy. P 13½.

357	3l. multicoloured	15	1·00
358	6l. multicoloured	20	65
359	7l. multicoloured	20	40
360	25l. multicoloured	90	20
361	1r. multicoloured	2·50	90
357/61	*Set of 5*	3·50	2·75

(Des M. Shamir. Litho State Printing Works, Budapest)

1971 (1 Apr). 25th Anniv of U.N.I.C.E.F. T **83** and similar vert design. Multicoloured. P 12.

362	5l. Type **83**	10	15
363	10l. Little girl with U.N.I.C.E.F. balloon	10	15
364	1r. Type **83**	2·00	85
365	2r. As 10l.	3·00	3·00
362/65	*Set of 4*	4·50	3·75

84 Astronauts Lovell, Haise and Swigert

85 "Multiracial Flower"

(Des M. Shamir. Litho Govt Printer, Israel)

1971 (27 Apr). Safe Return of "Apollo 13". T **84** and similar vert designs. Multicoloured. P 14.

366	5l. Type **84**	35	35
367	20l. Explosion in Space	65	25
368	1r. Splashdown	1·40	50
366/68	*Set of 3*	2·25	1·00

(Des M. Shamir. Litho)

1971 (3 May). Racial Equality Year. P 14.

369	**85**	10l. multicoloured	15	15
370		25l. multicoloured	20	15

86 "Mme. Charpentier and her Children" (Renoir)

87 Alan Shepard

1971 (1 Aug). Famous Paintings showing "Mother and Child". T **86** and similar vert designs. Multicoloured. Litho. P 12.

371	5l. Type **86**	30	20

372	7l. Susanna van Collen and her Daughter" (Rembrandt)	35	20
373	10l. Madonna nursing the Child" (Titian)	45	20
374	20l. "Baroness Belleli and her Children" (Degas)	1·25	20
375	25l. "The Cradle" (Morisot)	1·25	20
376	1r. "Helena Fourment and her Children" (Rubens)	3·25	85
377	3r. "On the Terrace" (Renoir)	5·50	6·50
371/77	*Set of 7*	11·00	7·50

(Photo State Ptg Works, Vienna)

1971 (11 Nov). Moon Flight of "Apollo 14". T **87** and similar vert designs. Multicoloured. P 12½.

378	6l. Type **87**	40	40
379	10l. Stuart Roosa	45	30
380	1r.50 Edgar Mitchell	5·50	3·50
381	5r. Mission insignia	11·00	11·00
378/81	*Set of 4*	16·00	14·00

88 "Ballerina" (Degas)   (**89**)

(Litho Rosenbaum Brothers, Vienna)

1971 (19 Nov). Famous Paintings showing "Dancers". T **88** and similar vert designs. Multicoloured. P 14.

382	5l. Type **88**	25	20
383	10l. "Dancing Couple" (Renoir)	30	20
384	2r. "Spanish Dancer" (Manet)	3·00	2·50
385	5r. "Ballerinas" (Degas)	5·50	5·00
386	10r. "La Goulue at the Moulin Rouge" (Toulouse-Lautrec)	7·50	8·00
382/86	*Set of 5*	15·00	14·00

1972 (13 Mar). Visit of Queen Elizabeth II and Prince Philip. Nos. 382/6 optd with T **89**.

387	5l. multicoloured	20	10
388	10l. multicoloured	25	10
389	2r. multicoloured	5·00	4·00
390	5r. multicoloured	9·00	8·00
391	10r. multicoloured	10·00	10·00
387/91	*Set of 5*	22·00	20·00

90 Book Year Emblem

91 Scottish Costume

(Des M. Shamir. Litho Bradbury Wilkinson)

1972 (1 May). International Book Year. P 13×13½.

392	**90**	25l. multicoloured	15	15
393		5r. multicoloured	1·60	2·25

(Des M. Shamir. Litho State Printing Works, Budapest)

1972 (15 May). National Costumes of the World. T **91** and similar vert designs. Multicoloured. P 12.

394	10l. Type **91**	1·25	10
395	15l. Netherlands	1·50	15
396	25l. Norway	2·50	15
397	50l. Hungary	3·25	55
398	1r. Austria	3·75	80
399	2r. Spain	4·75	3·50
394/99	*Set of 6*	15·00	4·75

REPUBLIC of MALDIVES
92 Stegosaurus

(Des M. Shamir. Litho Rosenbaum Brothers, Vienna)

1972 (31 May). Prehistoric Animals. T **92** and similar horiz designs. Multicoloured. P 14.

400	2l. Type **92**	75	75
401	7l. Dimetrodon (inscr "Edaphosaurus")	1·50	60
402	25l. Diplodocus	2·25	50
403	50l. Triceratops	2·50	75
404	2r. Pteranodon	5·50	5·00
405	5r. Tyrannosaurus	9·50	9·50
400/5 *Set of 6*		20·00	15·00

An imperforate miniature sheet containing Nos. 404/5 also exists, but was never freely available.

(Des M. Shamir. Litho Rosenbaum Brothers, Vienna)

93 Cross-country Skiing

1972 (1 June). Winter Olympic Games, Sapporo, Japan. T **93** and similar vert designs. Multicoloured. P 14.

406	3l. Type **93**	10	50
407	6l. Bob sleighing	10	50
408	15l. Speed-skating	20	20
409	50l. Ski jumping	1·00	45
410	1r. Figure-skating (pair)	1·75	70
411	2r.50 Ice-hockey	5·50	3·25
406/11 *Set of 6*		7·50	5·00

94 Scout Saluting

95 Cycling

(Des M. Shamir. Litho Govt Printer, Israel)

1972 (1 Aug). 13th World Scout Jamboree, Asagiri, Japan (1971). T **94** and similar vert designs. Multicoloured. P 14.

412	10l. Type **92**	75	20
413	15l. Scout signalling	95	20
414	50l. Scout blowing bugle	3·25	1·25
415	1r. Scout beating drum	4·50	2·25
412/15 *Set of 4*		8·50	3·50

PRINTERS AND PROCESS. *Unless otherwise stated,* all the following issues to No. 1277 were lithographed by Format International Security Printers Ltd, London.

1972 (30 Oct). Olympic Games, Munich. T **95** and similar vert designs. Multicoloured. P 14½×14.

416	5l. Type **95**	1·25	30
417	10l. Running	20	20

418	25l. Wrestling	30	20
419	50l. Hurdling	50	35
420	2r. Boxing	1·50	2·00
421	5r. Volleyball	3·00	3·75
416/21 *Set of 6*		6·00	6·00
MS422 92×120 mm. 3r. As 50l.; 4r. As 10l. P 15		5·75	8·00

96 Globe and Conference Emblem

97 "Flowers" (Van Gogh)

(Litho Harrison)

1972 (15 Nov). U.N. Environmental Conservation Conference, Stockholm. P 14½.

423	**96**	2l. multicoloured	10	40
424		3l. multicoloured	10	40
425		15l. multicoloured	30	15
426		50l. multicoloured	75	45
427		2r.50 multicoloured	3·25	4·25
423/27 *Set of 5*			4·00	5·00

(Des M. Shamir)

1973 (1 Mar). Floral Paintings. T **97** and similar vert designs. Multicoloured. P 13½.

428	1l. Type **97**	10	60
429	2l. "Flowers in Jug" (Renoir)	10	60
430	3l. "Chrysanthemums" (Renoir)	10	60
431	50l. "Mixed Bouquet" (Bosschaert)	1·50	30
432	1r. As 3l.	2·00	40
433	5r. As 2l.	4·25	5·50
428/33 *Set of 6*		7·25	7·25
MS434 120×94 mm. 2r. as 50l.; 3r. Type **97**. P 15		7·00	8·50

LEMECHEV MIDDLE-WEIGHT GOLD MEDALLIST
(98)

1973 (1 Apr). Gold-medal Winners, Munich Olympic Games. Nos. 420/ **MS**422 optd with T **98** or similar commemorative inscr, in blue.

435	2r. multicoloured	3·25	2·50
436	5r. multicoloured	4·25	3·75
MS437 92×120 mm. 3r. multicoloured; 4r. multicoloured		7·50	8·50

Overprints:—2r. Type **98**; 5r. "JAPAN GOLD MEDAL WINNERS" (volleyball). Miniature sheet:—3r. "EHRHARDT 100 METER HURDLES GOLD MEDALLIST"; 4r. "SHORTER MARATHON GOLD MEDALLIST".

99 Animal Care

100 Blue Marlin

(Des M. Shamir)

1973 (1 Aug). International Scouting Congress, Nairobi and Addis Ababa. T **99** and similar horiz designs. Multicoloured. P 14½.

438	1l. Type **99**	10	30
439	2l. Lifesaving	10	30
440	3l. Agricultural training	10	30
441	4l. Carpentry	10	30
442	5l. Playing leapfrog	10	30
443	1r. As 2l.	2·75	75
444	2r. As 4l.	4·00	4·75
445	3r. Type **99**	4·50	7·00
438/45 *Set of 8*		10·00	12·50
MS446 101×79 mm. 5r. As 3l.		8·00	14·00

1973 (1 Aug). Fish. T **100** and similar horiz designs. Multicoloured. P 14½.

447	1l. Type **100**	10	40

448	2l. Skipjack Tuna	10	40
449	3l. Blue-finned Tuna	10	40
450	5l. Dolphin (fish)	10	40
451	60l. Humpbacked Snapper	80	40
452	75l. As 60l.	1·00	40
453	1r.50 Yellow-edged Lyretail	1·75	2·00
454	2r.50 As 5l.	2·00	3·00
455	3r. Spotted Coral Grouper	2·00	3·25
456	10r. Spanish Mackerel	4·00	8·00
447/56 Set of 10		10·50	17·00
MS457 119×123 mm. 4r. As 2l.; 5r. Type **100**		17·00	20·00

Nos. 451/2 are smaller, size 29×22 mm.

101 Golden-fronted Leafbird

102 *Lantana camara*

(Des M. Shamir)

1973 (1 Oct). Fauna. T **101** and similar diamond-shaped designs. Multicoloured. P 14½.

458	1l. Type **101**	10	50
459	2l. Indian Flying Fox	10	50
460	3l. Land tortoise	10	50
461	4l. *Kallima inachus* (butterfly)	30	50
462	50l. As 3l.	60	40
463	2r. Type **101**	5·50	4·50
464	3r. As 2l.	3·50	4·50
458/64 Set of 7		9·25	10·00
MS465 66×74 mm. 5r. As 4l.		16·00	20·00

(Litho Questa)

1973 (19 Dec). Flowers of the Maldive Islands. T **102** and similar vert designs. Multicoloured. P 14.

466	1l. Type **102**	10	50
467	2l. *Nerium oleander*	10	50
468	3l. *Rosa polyantha*	10	50
469	4l. *Hibiscus manihot*	10	50
470	5l. *Bougainvillea glabra*	10	20
471	10l. *Plumera alba*	15	20
472	50l. *Poinsettia pulcherrima*	70	30
473	5r. *Orionis natrix*	3·75	5·50
466/73 Set of 8		4·50	7·50
MS474 110×100 mm. 2r. As 3l.; 3r. As 10l.		3·25	5·25

103 "Tiros" Weather Satellite

104 "Apollo" Spacecraft and Pres. Kennedy

(Des M. Shamir)

1974 (10 Jan). Centenary of World Meteorological Organization. T **103** and similar horiz designs. Multicoloured. P 14½.

475	1l. Type **103**	10	30
476	2l. "Nimbus" satellite	10	30
477	3l. *Nomad* (weather ship)	10	30
478	4l. Scanner, APT Instant Weather Picture equipment	10	30
479	5l. Richard's wind-speed recorder	10	20
480	2r. Type **103**	3·50	3·75
481	3r. As 3l.	3·75	4·00
475/81 Set of 7		7·00	8·25
MS482 110×79 mm. 10r. As 2l.		8·50	14·00

(Des M. Shamir)

1974 (1 Feb). American and Russian Space Exploration Projects. T **104** and similar horiz designs. Multicoloured. P 14½.

483	1l. Type **104**	10	35
484	2l. "Mercury" capsule and John Glenn	10	35
485	3l. "Vostok 1" and Yuri Gagarin	10	35
486	4l. "Vostok 6" and Valentina Tereshkova	10	35
487	5l. "Soyuz 11" and "Salyut" space-station	10	25
488	2r. "Skylab" space laboratory	3·75	3·75
489	3r. As 2l.	4·25	4·25

483/89 Set of 7		7·75	8·75
MS490 103×80 mm. 10r. Type **104**		13·00	15·00

105 Copernicus and "Skylab" Space Laboratory

106 "Maternity" (Picasso)

(Des G. Vasarhelyi)

1974 (10 Apr). 500th Birth Anniv of Nicholas Copernicus (astronomer). T **105** and similar horiz designs. Multicoloured. P 14½.

491	1l. Type **105**	10	35
492	2l. Orbital space-station of the future	10	35
493	3l. Proposed "Space-shuttle" craft	10	35
494	4l. "Mariner 2" Venus probe	10	35
495	5l. "Mariner 4" Mars probe	10	20
496	25l. Type **105**	1·25	80
497	1r.50 As 2l.	2·75	3·25
498	5r. As 3l.	4·50	11·00
491/98 Set of 8		8·00	14·50
MS499 106×80 mm. 10r. "Copernicus" orbital observatory		15·00	18·00

(Des M. Shamir. Litho Questa)

1974 (1 May). Paintings by Picasso. T **106** and similar vert designs. Multicoloured. P 14.

500	1l. Type **106**	10	40
501	2l. "Harlequin and Friend"	10	40
502	3l. "Pierrot Sitting"	10	40
503	20l. "Three Musicians"	50	20
504	75l. "L'Aficionado"	1·25	80
505	5r. "Still Life"	4·75	6·50
500/5 Set of 6		6·00	7·75
MS506 100×101 mm. 2r. As 20l.; 3r. As 5r.		8·50	11·00

107 U.P.U. Emblem, Steam and Diesel Locomotives

108 Footballers

(Des M. Shamir)

1974 (1 May). Centenary of Universal Postal Union. T **107** and similar horiz designs. Multicoloured. P 14½.

507	1l. Type **107**	10	30
508	2l. Paddle-steamer and modern mailboat	10	30
509	3l. Airship LZ-127 *Graf Zeppelin* and Boeing 747 airliner	10	30
510	1r.50 Mailcoach and motor van	1·40	1·10
511	2r.50 As 2l.	1·50	1·75
512	5r. Type **107**	2·00	3·25
507/12 Set of 6		4·50	6·00
MS513 126×105 mm. 4r. Type **107**		6·00	7·00

Nos. 507/12 were first issued in sheets of 50, but were later released in small sheets of five stamps and one label. These small sheets were perforated 13½.

(Des M. Shamir)

1974 (1 June). World Cup Football Championship, West Germany. T **108** and similar vert designs, showing football scenes. P 14½.

514	1l. multicoloured	15	20
515	2l. multicoloured	15	20
516	3l. multicoloured	15	20
517	4l. multicoloured	15	20
518	75l. multicoloured	1·00	75
519	4r. multicoloured	2·00	4·00
520	5r. multicoloured	2·00	4·00
514/20 Set of 7		5·00	8·50
MS521 88×95 mm. 10r. multicoloured		10·00	12·00

109 "Capricorn"

110 Churchill and Avro Type 683 Lancaster

(Des G. Vasarhelyi)

1974 (3 July). Signs of the Zodiac. T **109** and similar horiz designs. Multicoloured. P 14½.

522	1l. Type **109**	25	50
523	2l. "Aquarius"	25	50
524	3l. "Pisces"	25	50
525	4l. "Aries"	25	50
526	5l. "Taurus"	25	50
527	6l. "Gemini"	25	50
528	7l. "Cancer"	25	50
529	10l. "Leo"	40	50
530	15l. "Virgo"	40	50
531	20l. "Libra"	40	50
532	25l. "Scorpio"	40	50
533	5r. "Sagittarius"	6·50	12·00
522/33 Set of 12		8·75	16·00
MS534 119×99 mm. 10r. "The Sun" (49×37 mm). P 13½		22·00	23·00

(Des M. Shamir)

1974 (30 Nov). Birth Centenary of Sir Winston Churchill. T **110** and similar horiz designs. Multicoloured. P 14½.

535	1l. Type **110**	40	70
536	2l. Churchill as pilot	40	70
537	3l. Churchill as First Lord of the Admiralty	40	70
538	4l. Churchill and H.M.S. *Eagle* (aircraft carrier)	40	70
539	5l. Churchill and de Havilland DH.98 Mosquito bombers	40	45
540	60l. Churchill and anti-aircraft battery	3·75	2·00
541	75l. Churchill and tank in desert	4·00	2·00
542	5r. Churchill and Short S.25 Sunderland flying boat	15·00	15·00
535/42 Set of 8		22·00	20·00
MS543 113×83 mm. 10r. As 4l.		22·00	23·00

111 Bullmouth Helmet (*Cypraecassis rufa*)

112 Royal Throne

113 Guavas

(Des M. Shamir)

1975 (25 Jan). Sea Shells and Cowries. T **111** and similar multicoloured designs. P 14×13½ (60l., 75l.) or 14½ (others).

544	1l. Type **111**	10	30
545	2l. Venus Comb Murex (*Murex pecten*)	10	30
546	3l. Common or Major Harp (*Harpa major*)	10	30
547	4l. Chiragra Spider Conch (*Lambis chiragra chiragra*)	10	30
548	5l. Geography Cone (*Conus geographus*)	10	30
549	60l. Dawn Cowrie (*Cypraea diluculum*) (22×30 mm)	3·00	2·00
550	75l. Purplish Clanculus (*Clanculus puniceus*) (22×30 mm)	3·50	2·00
551	5r. Ramose Murex (*Murex ramosus*)	8·50	11·00
544/51 Set of 8		14·00	15·00
MS552 152×126 mm. 2r. As 3l.; 3r. As 2l.		14·00	17·00

(Des M. Shamir. Litho Questa)

1975 (22 Feb). Historical Relics and Monuments. T **112** and similar multicoloured designs. P 14.

553	1l. Type **112**	10	10
554	10l. Candlesticks	10	10
555	25l. Lamp-tree	15	10
556	60l. Royal umbrellas	30	30
557	75l. Eid-Miskith Mosque (*horiz*)	35	35
558	3r. Tomb of Al-Hafiz Abu-al Barakath-al Barubari (*horiz*)	1·60	2·75
553/58 Set of 6		2·25	3·25

(Des M. Shamir)

1975 (1 Mar). Fruits. T **113** and similar vert designs. Multicoloured. P 14½.

559	2l. Type **113**	10	40
560	4l. Maldive mulberry	15	40
561	5l. Mountain apples	15	40
562	10l. Bananas	20	15
563	20l. Mangoes	40	25
564	50l. Papaya	1·00	60
565	1r. Pomegranates	1·75	70
566	5r. Coconut	5·50	11·00
559/66 Set of 8		8·00	12·00
MS567 136×102 mm. 2r. As 10l.; 3r. As 2l.		12·00	16·00

114 *Phyllangia*

(Des M. Shamir)

1975 (6 June). Marine Life. T **114** and similar triangular designs. Multicoloured. P 14½.

568	1l. Type **114**	10	40
569	2l. *Madreporo oculata*	10	40
570	3l. *Acropora gravida*	10	40
571	4l. *Stylotella*	10	40
572	5l. *Acrophoro cervicornis*	10	40
573	60l. *Strongylocentrotus purpuratus*	75	65
574	75l. *Pisaster ochraceus*	85	75
575	5r. *Marthasterias glacialis*	5·00	6·50
568/75 Set of 8		6·00	9·00
MS576 155×98 mm. 4r. As 1l. Imperf		11·00	14·00

115 Clock Tower and Customs Building within "10"

14th Boy Scout Jamboree July 29 – August 7, 1975
(**116**)

(Des M. Shamir)

1975 (26 July). Tenth Anniv of Independence. T **115** and similar horiz designs. Multicoloured. P 14½.

577	4l. Type **115**	10	30
578	5l. Government Offices	10	15
579	7l. Waterfront	10	20
580	15l. Mosque and minaret	10	15
581	10r. Sultan Park and museum	2·25	6·00
577/81 Set of 5		2·25	6·00

1975 (26 July). "Nordjamb 75" World Scout Jamboree, Norway. Nos. 443/5 and **MS446** optd with T **116**.

582	1r. multicoloured	85	60
583	2r. multicoloured	1·25	80
584	3r. multicoloured	1·75	1·60
582/84 Set of 3		3·50	2·75
MS585 101×79 mm. 5r. multicoloured		7·00	8·00

117 Madura Prau

118 *Brahmophthalma wallichi* (moth)

(Des M. Shamir)

1975 (1 Aug). Ships. T **117** and similar multicoloured designs. P 14½.

586	1l. Type **117**	10	20
587	2l. Ganges patela	10	20
588	3l. Indian palla (*vert*)	10	20
589	4l. Odhi (dhow) (*vert*)	10	20
590	5l. Maldivian schooner	10	20
591	25l. *Cutty Sark*	1·50	40
592	1r. Maldivian baggala (*vert*)	1·75	70
593	5r. Freighter *Maldive Courage*	3·00	6·00
586/93 Set of 8		6·00	7·25
MS594 99×85 mm. 10r. As 1r.		10·00	14·00

(Des M. Shamir)

1975 (7 Sept). Butterflies and Moth. T **118** and similar horiz designs. Multicoloured. P 14½.

595	1l. Type **118**	15	30
596	2l. *Teinopalpus imperialis*	15	30
597	3l. *Cethosia biblis*	15	30
598	4l. *Idea jasonia*	15	30
599	5l. *Apatura ilia*	15	30
600	25l. *Kallima horsfieldi*	1·25	35
601	1r.50 *Hebomoia leucippe*	3·50	3·75
602	5r. *Papilio memnon*	8·00	10·00
595/602 *Set of 8*		12·00	14·00
MS603 134×97 mm. 10r. As 25l.		20·00	20·00

119 "The Dying Captive"

120 Beaker and Vase

1975 (9 Oct). 500th Birth Anniv of Michelangelo. T **119** and similar vert designs. Multicoloured. P 14½.

604	1l. Type **119**	10	20
605	2l. Detail of "The Last Judgement"	10	20
606	3l. "Apollo"	10	20
607	4l. Detail of Sistine Chapel ceiling	10	20
608	5l. "Bacchus"	10	20
609	1r. Detail of "The Last Judgement" (*different*)	1·25	30
610	2r. "David"	1·50	2·00
611	5r. "Cumaean Sibyl"	2·25	5·00
604/11 *Set of 8*		5·00	7·50
MS612 123×113 mm. 10r. As 2r.		5·00	11·00

The 1, 3, 5l. and 2, 10r. are sculptures; the other values show details of the frescoes in the Sistine Chapel.

(Des M. Shamir. Litho Questa)

1975 (1 Dec). Maldivian Lacquerware. T **120** and similar vert designs. Multicoloured. P 14.

613	2l. Type **120**	10	50
614	4l. Boxes	10	50
615	50l. Jar with lid	30	20
616	75l. Bowls with covers	40	30
617	1r. Craftsman at work	50	40
613/17 *Set of 5*		1·10	1·75

REPUBLIC OF MALDIVES

121 Map of Maldives

(Des M. Shamir. Litho Questa)

1975 (25 Dec). Tourism. T **121** and similar horiz designs. Multicoloured. P 14.

618	4l. Type **121**	40	50
619	5l. Motor launch and small craft	40	50
620	7l. Sailing boats	40	50
621	15l. Underwater fishing	40	40
622	3r. Hulule Airport	5·00	3·00
623	10r. Motor cruisers	7·00	8·50
618/23 *Set of 6*		12·00	12·00

REPUBLIC OF MALDIVES

122 Cross-country Skiing

REPUBLIC OF MALDIVES

123 "General Burgoyne" (Reynolds)

(Des M. Shamir)

1976 (10 Jan). Winter Olympic Games, Innsbruck, Austria. T **122** and similar vert designs. Multicoloured. P 15.

624	1l. Type **122**	10	20
625	2l. Speed ice-skating	10	20
626	3l. Pairs figure-skating	10	20
627	4l. Four-man bobsleigh	10	20
628	5l. Ski jumping	10	20
629	25l. Women's figure-skating	35	20
630	1r.15 Slalom skiing	90	1·25
631	4r. Ice-hockey	1·50	4·00
624/31 *Set of 8*		2·50	5·50
MS632 93×117 mm. 10r. Downhill skiing		7·00	13·00

Nos. 624/31 exist imperforate from stock dispersed by the liquidator of Format International Security Printers Ltd.

1976 (15 Feb). Bicentenary of American Revolution. T **123** and similar multicoloured designs. P 15.

633	1l. Type **123**	15	20
634	2l. "John Hancock" (Copley)	15	20
635	3l. "Death of General Montgomery" (Trumbull) (*horiz*)	15	20
636	4l. "Paul Revere" (Copley)	15	20
637	5l. "Battle of Bunker Hill" (Trumbull) (*horiz*).	15	20
638	2r. "The Crossing of the Delaware" (Sully) (*horiz*)	2·00	2·75
639	3r. "Samuel Adams" (Copley)	2·25	3·25
640	5r. "Surrender of Cornwallis" (Trumbull) (*horiz*).	2·50	3·50
633/40 *Set of 8*		6·75	9·50
MS641 147×95 mm. 10r. "Washington at Dorchester Heights" (Stuart)		17·00	20·00

REPUBLIC OF MALDIVES

124 Thomas Edison

MAY 29TH–JUNE 6TH "INTERPHIL" 1976

(**125**)

1976 (10 Mar). Telephone Centenary. T **124** and similar horiz designs. Multicoloured. P 15.

642	1l. Type **124**	10	40
643	2l. Alexander Graham Bell	10	40
644	3l. Telephones of 1919, 1937 and 1972	10	40
645	10l. Cable entrance into station	20	20
646	20l. Equaliser circuit assembly	30	20
647	1r. *Salernum* (cable ship)	2·25	55
648	10r. "Intelsat IV-A" and Earth Station	4·75	8·00
642/48 *Set of 7*		7·00	9·00
MS649 156×105 mm. 4r. Early telephones		7·50	9·00

1976 (29 May). "Interphil 76" International Stamp Exhibition, Philadelphia. Nos. 638/**MS**641 optd with T **125**, in blue (5r.) or silver (others).

650	2r. multicoloured	1·50	1·75
651	3r. multicoloured	2·00	2·25
652	5r. multicoloured	2·50	2·75
650/52 *Set of 3*		5·50	6·00
MS653 147×95 mm. 10r. multicoloured		10·00	12·00

REPUBLIC OF MALDIVES

126 Wrestling

Republic of Maldives

127 *Dolichos lablab*

(Des M. Shamir)

1976 (1 June). Olympic Games, Montreal. T **126** and similar vert designs. Multicoloured. P 15.

654	1l. Type **126**	10	20
655	2l. Putting the shot	10	20
656	3l. Hurdling	10	20
657	4l. Hockey	10	20
658	5l. Running	10	20
659	6l. Javelin-throwing	10	20
660	1r.50 Discus-throwing	1·25	1·75
661	5r. Volleyball	2·75	5·25
654/61 *Set of 8*		4·00	7·25
MS662 135×106 mm. 10r. Throwing the hammer		8·50	12·00

Nos. 654/61 exist imperforate from stock dispersed by the liquidator of Format International Security Printers Ltd.

(Des M. Shamir. Litho Questa)

1976 (26 July)–**77**. Vegetables. T **127** and similar vert designs. Multicoloured. P 14.

663	2l. Type **127**	10	40
664	4l. *Moringa pterygosperma*	10	40
665	10l. *Solanum melongena*	15	15
666	20l. *Moringa pterygosperma* (1977)	3·25	2·25
667	50l. *Cucumis sativus*	50	65
668	75l. *Trichosanthes anguina*	55	75
669	1r. *Momordica charantia*	65	85
670	2r. *Trichosanthes anguina* (1977)	4·75	8·00
663/70 *Set of 8*		9·00	12·00

128 "Viking" approaching Mars

1976 (2 Dec). "Viking" Space Mission. T **128** and similar horiz design. Multicoloured. P 14.

671	5r. Type **128**	1·90	2·75
MS672	121×89 mm. 20r. Landing module on Mars	10·00	14·00

129 Coronation Ceremony

1977 (6 Feb). Silver Jubilee of Queen Elizabeth II. T **129** and similar horiz designs. Multicoloured. P 14×13½.

673	1l. Type **129**	10	30
674	2l. Queen and Prince Philip	10	30
675	3l. Royal couple with Princes Andrew and Edward	10	30
676	1r.15 Queen with Archbishops	65	35
677	3r. State coach in procession	1·25	75
678	4r. Royal couple with Prince Charles and Princess Anne	1·25	1·25
673/78 *Set of 6*		3·00	3·00
MS679	120×77 mm. 10r. Queen and Prince Charles	5·00	3·75

Nos. 673/8 also exist perf 12 (*Price per set of 6* £1·50 *mint or used*) from additional sheetlets of five stamps and one label in changed colours.

 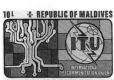

130 Beethoven and Organ   **131** Printed Circuit and I.T.U. Emblem

(Des M. Shamir)

1977 (26 Mar). 150th Death Anniv of Ludwig van Beethoven (composer). T **130** and similar horiz designs. Multicoloured. P 14.

680	1l. Type **130**	25	30
681	2l. Portrait and manuscript of *Moonlight Sonata*	25	30
682	3l. With Goethe at Teplitz	25	30
683	4l. Portrait and string instruments	25	30
684	5l. Beethoven's home, Heiligenstadt	25	30
685	25l. Hands and gold medals	1·50	20
686	2r. Portrait and part of *Missa solemnis*	4·00	3·75
687	5r. Portrait and hearing-aids	6·50	7·00
680/87 *Set of 8*		12·00	11·00
MS688	121×92 mm. 4r. Death mask and room where composer died	9·50	11·00

(Des M. Shamir. Litho Questa)

1977 (17 May). Inauguration of Satellite Earth Station. T **131** and similar horiz designs. Multicoloured. P 14.

689	10l. Type **131**	10	10
690	90l. Central telegraph office	45	45
691	10r. Satellite Earth station	3·00	6·00
689/91 *Set of 3*		3·25	6·00
MS692	100×85 mm. 5r. "Intelsat IV-A" satellite over Maldives	4·50	5·50

132 "Miss Anne Ford" (Gainsborough)   **133** Lesser Frigate Birds   **134** Charles Lindbergh

(Des M. Shamir. Litho Questa)

1977 (20 May). Artists' Birth Anniversaries. T **132** and similar vert designs. Multicoloured. P 14.

693	1l. Type **132** (250th anniv)	10	30
694	2l. Group painting by Rubens (400th anniv)	10	30
695	3l. "Girl with Dog" (Titian) (500th anniv)	10	30
696	4l. "Mrs. Thomas Graham" (Gainsborough)	10	30
697	5l. "Artist with Isabella Brant" (Rubens)	10	30
698	95l. Portrait by Titian	1·25	30
699	1r. Portrait by Gainsborough	1·25	30
700	10r. "Isabella Brant" (Rubens)	4·50	7·00
693/700 *Set of 8*		6·50	8·25
MS701	152×116 mm. 5r. "Self-portrait" (Titian)	3·75	5·50

(Des M. Shamir)

1977 (26 July). Birds. T **133** and similar vert designs. Multicoloured. P 14½.

702	1l. Type **133**	20	40
703	2l. Crab Plover	20	40
704	3l. White-tailed Tropic Bird	20	40
705	4l. Wedge-tailed Shearwater	20	40
706	5l. Grey Heron	20	40
707	20l. White Tern	90	30
708	95l. Cattle Egret	2·25	1·60
709	1r.25 Black-naped Tern	2·50	2·50
710	5r. Pheasant Coucal	6·50	8·00
702/10 *Set of 9*		12·00	12·50
MS711	124×117 mm. 10r. Green Heron	26·00	26·00

(Des M. Shamir)

1977 (31 Oct). 50th Anniv of Lindbergh's Transatlantic Flight and 75th Anniv of First Navigable Airships. T **134** and similar multicoloured designs. P 14½.

712	1l. Type **134**	25	30
713	2l. Lindbergh and Ryan NYP Special *Spirit of St. Louis*	25	30
714	3l. Lindbergh's Miles Mohawk aircraft (*horiz*)	25	30
715	4l. Lebaudy-Juillot airship *Morning Post* (*horiz*)	25	30
716	5l. Airship LZ-127 *Graf Zeppelin* and portrait of Zeppelin	25	30
717	1r. Airship ZR-3 *Los Angeles* (*horiz*)	1·25	30
718	3r. Lindbergh and Henry Ford	2·00	2·00
719	10r. Vickers airship R-23	2·75	6·00
712/19 *Set of 8*		6·50	8·50
MS720	148×114 mm. 5r. Ryan NYP Special *Spirit of St. Louis*, Statue of Liberty and Eiffel Tower; 7r.50, Airship L-31 over *Ostfriesland* (German battleship)	13·00	18·00

No. 715 is inscr "Lebaudy I built by H. Juillot 1902".

135 Boat Building   **136** Rheumatic Heart

(Des M. Shamir. Litho J. W.)

1977 (11 Nov). Occupations. T **135** and similar multicoloured designs. P 13½×13 (2r.) or 13×13½ (others).

721	6l. Type **135**	75	45
722	15l. Fishing	1·25	20
723	20l. Cadjan weaving	1·50	20
724	90l. Mat weaving	3·50	1·60
725	2r. Lace making (*vert*)	5·50	4·75
721/25 *Set of 5*		11·00	6·50

(Des M. Shamir. Litho Questa)

1977 (1 Dec). World Rheumatism Year. T **136** and similar vert designs. Multicoloured. P 14.

726	1l. Type **136**	10	30
727	50l. Rheumatic shoulder	40	20
728	2r. Rheumatic fingers	75	1·25
729	3r. Rheumatic knee	85	1·40
726/29 *Set of 4*		1·75	2·75

137 Lilienthal's Biplane Glider

(Des M. Shamir. Litho Questa)

1978 (27 Feb). 75th Anniv of First Powered Aircraft. T **137** and similar horiz designs. Multicoloured. P 13×13½.

730	1l. Type **137**	25	40
731	2l. Chanute's glider	25	40
732	3l. Wright testing *glider No. II*, 1900	25	40
733	4l. Roe's Triplane I aircraft	25	40
734	5l. Wright demonstrating Wright Type A aircraft to King Alfonso of Spain	25	40
735	10l. Roe's second Avro Type D biplane	80	40
736	20l. Wright Brothers and A.G. Bell	2·25	40
737	95l. Hadley's triplane	5·50	2·25
738	5r. Royal Aircraft Factory B.E.2A biplanes at Upavon, 1914	11·50	11·00
730/38 *Set of 9*		19·00	14·50
MS739 98×82 mm. 10r. Wright Brothers' Wright Type A		14·00	16·00

No. 732 is wrongly dated "1900".

138 Newgate Prison   **139** Television Set

1978 (15 Mar). World Eradication of Smallpox. T **138** and similar multicoloured designs. P 14.

740	15l. Foundling Hospital, London (*horiz*)	50	30
741	50l. Type **138**	1·25	60
742	2r. Edward Jenner	2·25	4·00
740/42 *Set of 3*		3·50	4·50

(Des M. Shamir. Litho J. W.)

1978 (29 Mar). Inauguration of Television in Maldives. T **139** and similar multicoloured designs. P 13×13½ (1r.50) or 13½×13 (others).

743	15l. Type **139**	40	30
744	25l. Television aerials	55	30
745	1r.50 Control desk (*horiz*)	2·25	2·75
743/45 *Set of 3*		2·75	3·00

140 Mas Odi

(Des M. Shamir)

1978 (27 Apr). Ships. T **140** and similar multicoloured designs. P 14½.

746	1l. Type **140**	10	35
747	2l. Battela	10	35
748	3l. Bandu odi (*vert*)	10	35
749	5l. *Maldive Trader* (freighter)	20	35
750	1r. *Fath-hul Baaree* (brigantine) (*vert*)	65	30
751	1r.25 Mas dhoni	85	1·00
752	3r. Baggala (*vert*)	1·10	1·75
753	4r. As No. 751	1·10	1·75

746/53 *Set of 8*	3·50	5·50
MS754 152×138 mm. 1r. As No. 747; 4r. As No. 751	2·00	3·75

Nos. 746/8, 750 and 752/4 exist imperforate from stock dispersed by the liquidator of Format International Security Printers Ltd.

141 Ampulla   **142** Capt. Cook

(Des M. Shamir. Litho Questa)

1978 (15 May). 25th Anniv of Coronation of Queen Elizabeth II. T **141** and similar vert designs. Multicoloured. P 14.

755	1l. Type **141**	10	20
756	2l. Sceptre with dove	10	20
757	3l. Golden orb	10	20
758	1r.15 St. Edward's Crown	30	20
759	2r. Sceptre with cross	40	35
760	5r. Queen Elizabeth II	60	80
755/60 *Set of 6*		1·40	1·75
MS761 108×106 mm. 10r. Anointing spoon		1·75	2·25

Nos. 755/60 were also each issued in small sheets of three stamps and one label, perf 12, in changed colours.

(Des M. Shamir)

1978 (15 July). 250th Anniv of Capt. James Cook and Bicentenary of Discovery of Hawaii. T **142** and similar multicoloured designs. P 14½.

762	1l. Type **142**	10	25
763	2l. Statue of Kamehameha I of Hawaii	10	25
764	3l. H.M.S. *Endeavour*	10	25
765	25l. Route of Cook's third voyage	45	45
766	75l. H.M.S. *Resolution*, H.M.S. *Discovery* and map of Hawaiian Islands (*horiz*)	1·25	1·25
767	1r.50 Cook meeting Hawaiian islanders on ship (*horiz*)	2·00	2·25
768	10r. Death of Cook (*horiz*)	3·50	10·00
762/68 *Set of 7*		6·50	13·00
MS769 100×92 mm. 5r. H.M.S. *Endeavour* (different)		13·00	20·00

Nos. 763/4 exist imperforate from stock dispersed by the liquidator of Format International Security Printers Ltd.

143 *Schizophrys aspera*

1978 (30 Aug). Crustaceans. T **143** and similar multicoloured designs. P 14.

770	1l. Type **143**	10	25
771	2l. *Atergatis floridus*	10	25
772	3l. *Perenon planissimum*	10	25
773	90l. *Portunus granulatus*	50	40
774	1r. *Carpilius maculatus*	50	40
775	2r. *Huenia proteus*	1·00	1·40
776	25r. *Etisus laevimanus*	4·50	13·00
770/76 *Set of 7*		6·00	14·00
MS777 147×146 mm. 2r. *Panulirus longipes* (*vert*)		2·00	2·50

144 "Four Apostles"   **145** T.V. Tower and Building

(Des BG Studio. Litho Questa)

1978 (28 Oct). 450th Death Anniv of Albrecht Dürer (artist). T **144** and similar designs. P 14.

778	10l. multicoloured	10	10
779	20l. multicoloured	15	10
780	55l. multicoloured	20	20
781	1r. black, cinnamon and brown	30	30
782	1r.80 multicoloured	45	60
783	3r. multicoloured	70	1·25
778/83	*Set of 6*	1·60	2·25
MS784	141×122 mm. 10r. multicoloured	4·00	6·00

Designs: Vert—20l. "Self-portrait at 27", 55l. "Madonna and Child with a Pear"; 1r.80, "Hare"; 3r. "Great Piece of Turf"; 10r. "Columbine". Horiz—1r. "Rhinoceros".

(Des M. Shamir)

1978 (11 Nov). Tenth Anniv of Republic. T **145** and similar horiz designs. Multicoloured. P 14½.

785	1l. Fishing boat	10	60
786	5l. Montessori School	10	40
787	10l. Type **145**	10	10
788	25l. Islet	20	15
789	50l. Boeing "737"	80	25
790	95l. Beach scene	60	30
791	1r.25 Dhow at night	75	55
792	2r. President's official residence	80	1·25
793	5r. Masjidh Afeefuddin (mosque)	1·00	3·00
785/93	*Set of 9*	4·00	6·00
MS794	119×88 mm. 3r. Fisherman casting net	2·25	4·00

146 Human Rights Emblem

1978 (10 Dec). 30th Anniv of Declaration of Human Rights. P 14.

795	**146**	30l. pale magenta, deep mauve and green	15	15
796		90l. yellow-ochre, red-brown and green	40	60
797		1r.80 lt greenish blue, deep blue and green	70	1·00
795/97	*Set of 3*		1·10	1·60

147 Great Spotted or Rare Spotted Cowrie (*Cypraea guttata*)

148 Delivery by Bellman

(Des M. Shamir. Litho Questa)

1979 (1 Jan). Shells. T **147** and similar vert designs. Multicoloured. P 14.

798	1l. Type **147**	10	20
799	2l. Imperial Cone (*Conus imperialis*)	10	20
800	3l. Great Green Turban (*Turbo marmoratus*)	10	20
801	10l. Giant Spider Conch (*Lambis truncata*)	45	10
802	1r. White-toothed Cowrie (*Cypraea leucodon*)	2·00	40
803	1r.80 Fig Cone (*Conus figulinus*)	3·00	2·50
804	3r. Glory of the Sea Cone (*Conus gloriamaris*)	4·50	3·75
798/804	*Set of 7*	9·00	6·50
MS805	141×110 mm. 5r. Common Pacific Vase (*Vasum turbinellus*)	14·00	12·00

(Des M. Shamir. Litho Questa)

1979 (28 Feb). Death Centenary of Sir Rowland Hill. T **148** and similar multicoloured designs. P 14.

806	1l. Type **148**	10	20
807	2l. Mail coach, 1840 (*horiz*)	10	20
808	3l. First London letter box, 1855	10	20
809	1r.55 Penny Black stamps and posthorn	40	50
810	5r. Maldives 15c. stamp, 1906, and carrier pigeon	70	1·25
806/10	*Set of 5*	1·00	2·00

MS811	132×107 mm. 10r. Sir Rowland Hill	1·25	3·00

Nos. 806/10 were also each issued in small sheets of five stamps and one label, perf 12, in changed colours.

149 Girl with Teddy Bear

150 "White Feathers"

(Des M. Sharmir. Litho Questa)

1979 (10 May). International Year of the Child (1st issue). T **149** and similar vert designs. Multicoloured. P 14.

812	5l. Type **149**	10	10
813	1r.25 Boy with model sailing boat	40	50
814	2r. Boy with toy rocket	45	55
815	3r. Boy with toy airship	60	75
812/15	*Set of 4*	1·40	1·60
MS816	108×109 mm. 5r. Boy with toy train	1·25	2·00

See also Nos. 838/**MS**847.

(Des M. Shamir)

1979 (25 June). 25th Death Anniv of Henri Matisse (artist). T **150** and similar horiz designs. Multicoloured. P 14.

817	20l. Type **150**	15	15
818	25l. "Joy of Life"	15	15
819	30l. "Eggplants"	15	15
820	1r.50 Harmony in Red"	45	65
821	5r. "Still-life"	70	2·25
817/21	*Set of 5*	1·40	3·00
MS822	135×95 mm. 4r. "Water Pitcher"	4·25	4·50

151 Sari with Overdress

152 *Gloriosa superba*

(Des M. Shamir. Litho Questa)

1979 (22 Aug). National Costumes. T **151** and similar vert designs. Multicoloured. P 14.

823	50l. Type **151**	20	15
824	75l. Sashed apron dress	25	20
825	90l. Serape	30	25
826	95l. Ankle-length printed dress	35	30
823/26	*Set of 4*	1·00	80

(Des M. Shamir. Litho Questa)

1979 (29 Oct). Flowers. T **152** and similar vert designs. Multicoloured. P 14.

827	1l. Type **152**	10	10
828	3l. *Hibiscus tiliaceus*	10	10
829	50l. *Barringtonia asiatica*	20	15
830	1r. *Abutilon indicum*	40	25
831	5r. *Guettarda speciosa*	1·00	2·00
827/31	*Set of 5*	1·50	2·25
MS832	94×85 mm. 4r. *Pandanus odoratissimus*	1·75	2·75

153 Weaving

(Litho Questa)

1979 (11 Nov). Handicraft Exhibition. T **153** and similar horiz designs. Multicoloured. P 14.

833	5l. Type **153**	10	10
834	10l. Lacquer work	10	10
835	1r.30 Tortoiseshell jewellery	45	55
836	2r. Carved woodwork	60	90
833/36 Set of 4		1·00	1·40
MS837 125×85 mm. 5r. Gold and silver jewellery		1·25	2·25

154 Mickey Mouse attacked by Bird

(Des Walt Disney Productions)

1979 (10 Dec). International Year of the Child (2nd issue). T **154** and similar multicoloured designs. P 11.

838	1l. Goofy delivering parcel on motor-scooter (vert)	10	10
839	2l. Type **154**	10	10
840	3l. Goofy half-covered with letters	10	10
841	4l. Pluto licking Minnie Mouse's envelopes.	10	10
842	5l. Mickey Mouse delivering letters on roller skates (vert)	10	10
843	10l. Donald Duck placing letter in mail-box	10	10
844	15l. Chip and Dale carrying letter	10	10
845	1r.50 Donald Duck on monocycle (vert)	75	95
846	5r. Donald Duck with ostrich in crate (vert)	2·25	3·25
838/46 Set of 9		3·00	4·00
MS847 127×102 mm. 4r. Pluto putting parcel in mail-box. P 13½		5·00	7·00

155 Post-Ramadan Dancing

(Litho Questa)

1980 (19 Jan). National Day. T **155** and similar horiz designs. Multicoloured. P 14.

848	5l. Type **155**	10	10
849	15l. Musicians and dancer, Eeduu Festival ...	10	10
850	95l. Sultan's ceremonial band	35	30
851	2r. Dancer and drummers, Circumcision Festival	60	85
848/51 Set of 4		1·00	1·25
MS852 131×99 mm. 5r. Swordsmen		1·90	2·50

156 Leatherback Turtle
(Dermochelys coriacea)

157 Paul Harris
(founder)

(Des M. Shamir. Litho Questa)

1980 (17 Feb). Turtle Conservation Campaign. T **156** and similar horiz designs. Multicoloured. P 14.

853	1l. Type **156**	20	30
854	2l. Flatback Turtle (Chelonia depressa)	20	30
855	5l. Hawksbill Turtle (Eretmochelys imbricata)	25	30
856	10l. Loggerhead Turtle (Caretta caretta)	35	30
857	75l. Olive Ridley Turtle (Lepidochelys olivacea)	1·00	45
858	10r. Atlantic Ridley Turtle (Lepidochelys kempii)	3·00	4·25

853/58 Set of 6		4·50	5·50
MS859 85×107 mm. 4r. Green turtle (Chelonia mydas)		2·00	2·75

(Des J.W. Litho Questa)

1980 (7 Apr). 75th Anniv of Rotary International. T **157** and similar vert designs. Multicoloured. P 14.

860	75l. Type **157**	45	10
861	90l. Family (Humanity)	50	20
862	1r. Wheat (Hunger)	50	25
863	10r. Caduceus of Hermes (Health)	2·75	4·50
860/63 Set of 4		3·75	4·50
MS864 109×85 mm. 5r. Globe		1·75	2·50

(**158**)   **159** Swimming

1980 (6 May). "London 1980" International Stamp Exhibition. Nos. 809/**MS**811 optd with T **158**.

865	1r.55 multicoloured	2·50	1·00
866	5r. multicoloured	4·00	2·75
MS867 132×107 mm. 10r. multicoloured		7·50	8·00
On No. **MS**867 the overprint is horizontal.			

(Des J.W. Litho Questa)

1980 (4 June). Olympic Games, Moscow. T **159** and similar horiz designs. Multicoloured. P 14.

868	10l. Type **159**	10	10
869	50l. Running	20	20
870	3r. Putting the shot	70	1·10
871	4r. High jump	80	1·40
868/71 Set of 4		1·60	2·50
MS872 105×85 mm. 5r. Weightlifting		1·25	2·25

160 White-tailed Tropic Bird

(Des A. Abbas. Litho Questa)

1980 (10 July). Birds. T **160** and similar horiz designs. Multicoloured. P 14.

873	75l. Type **160**	25	15
874	95l. Sooty Tern	35	30
875	1r. Common Noddy	35	30
876	1r.55 Curlew	50	70
877	2r. Wilson's Petrel	60	85
878	4r. Caspian Tern	1·10	1·60
873/78 Set of 6		2·75	3·50
MS879 124×85 mm. 5r. Red-footed Booby and Brown Booby		8·00	9·00

161 Seal of Ibrahim II   **162** Queen Elizabeth the Queen Mother

(Litho Questa)

1980 (26 July). Seals of the Sultans. T **161** and similar horiz designs. Each purple-brown and black. P 14.

880	1l. Type **161**	10	10
881	2l.11 Muhammed Imaduddin II	10	10
882	5l. Bin Haji Ali	10	10
883	1r. Kuda Mohammed Rasgefaanu	40	30
884	2r. Ibrahim Iskander I	50	70
880/84 Set of 5		1·00	1·00
MS885 131×95 mm. 3r. Ibrahim Iskander I (different)		85	1·60

(Des and litho Questa)

1980 (29 Sept). Queen Mother's 80th Birthday. P 14.

886	**162** 4r. multicoloured	1·00	1·25
MS887 85×110 mm. **162** 5r. multicoloured		1·60	2·00
Imperforate examples of **MS**887 are known, but status is unclear.			

163 Munnaru

(Des A. Abbas and M. Hassan)

1980 (9 Nov). 1400th Anniv of Hegira. T **163** and similar horiz designs. Multicoloured. P 15.

888	5l. Type **163**	20	10
889	10l. Hukuru Miskiiy mosque	25	10
890	30l. Medhuziyaaraiy (shrine of saint)	30	30
891	55l. Writing tablets with verses of Koran	40	35
892	90l. Mother teaching child Koran	60	70
888/92 *Set of 5*		1·60	1·40
MS893 124×101 mm. 2r. Map of Maldives and coat of arms		80	1·60

164 Malaria Eradication

(Des J. W. Litho Questa)

1980 (30 Nov). World Health Day. T **164** and similar horiz designs. P 14.

894	15l. black, yellow and vermilion	20	10
895	25l. multicoloured	20	10
896	1r.50 orange-brown, yellow-ochre and black	2·00	1·00
897	5r. multicoloured	3·25	3·00
894/97 *Set of 4*		5·00	3·75
MS898 68×85 mm. 4r. black, greenish blue and azure..		1·25	2·50

Designs:—25l. Food (Nutrition); 1r.50, Molar and toothbrush (Dental health); 4, 5r. People and medical equipment (Clinics).

165 White Rabbit

(Des Walt Disney Productions)

1980 (22 Dec). Scenes from film "Alice in Wonderland". T **165** and similar horiz designs. Multicoloured. P 11.

899	1l. Type **165**	10	10
900	2l. Alice falling into Wonderland	10	10
901	3l. Alice too big to go through door	10	10
902	4l. Alice and Tweedledum and Tweedledee..	10	10
903	5l. Alice and the caterpillar	10	10
904	10l. Cheshire cat	10	10
905	15l. Alice painting the roses	10	10
906	2r.50 Alice and the Queen of Hearts	2·25	2·50
907	4r. Alice on trial	2·50	2·75
899/907 *Set of 9*		4·75	5·25
MS908 126×101 mm. 5r. Alice at the Mad Hatter's tea-party. P 13½		4·50	6·50

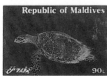

166 Indian Ocean Ridley Turtle

(Des A. Abbas and Maniku. Litho Questa)

1980 (29 Dec). Marine Life. T **166** and similar horiz designs. Multicoloured. P 14.

909	90l. Type **166**	2·25	60
910	1r.25 Pennant Coralfish	2·75	1·25
911	2r. Spiny Lobster	3·25	1·75
909/11 *Set of 3*		7·50	3·25
MS912 140×94 mm. 4r. Oriental Sweetlips and Scarlet-finned Squirrelfish		3·00	3·25

167 Pendant Lamp   **168** Prince Charles and Lady Diana Spencer

1981 (7 Jan). National Day. T **167** and similar multicoloured designs. P 14½.

913	10l. Tomb of Ghaazee Muhammad Thakurufaanu (*horiz*)	15	10
914	20l. Type **167**	20	10
915	30l. Chair used by Muhammad Thakurufaanu	25	10
916	95l. Muhammad Thakurufaanu's palace (*horiz*)	60	30
917	10r. Cushioned divan	2·75	4·50
913/17 *Set of 5*		3·50	4·50

(Des and litho J. W.)

1981 (22 June). Royal Wedding. T **168** and similar vert designs. Multicoloured. P 14.

918	1r. Type **168**	15	15
919	2r. Buckingham Palace	25	25
920	5r. Prince Charles, polo player	40	50
918/20 *Set of 3*		70	80
MS921 95×83 mm. 10r. State coach		75	1·10

Nos. 918/20 also exist perforated 12 (*Price for set of 3 £1 mint or used*) from additional sheets of five stamps and one label. These stamps have changed background colours.

Nos. 918/21 also exist imperforate from a restricted printing.

169 First Majlis Chamber   **170** "Self-portrait with a Palette"

(Des I. Azeez)

1981 (27 June). 50th Anniv of Citizens' Majlis (grievance rights). T **169** and similar multicoloured designs. P 14½.

922	95l. Type **169**	30	30
923	1r. Sultan Muhammed Shamsuddin III..	35	35
MS924 137×94 mm. 4r. First written constitution (*horiz*)		2·25	4·00

(Des J.W. Litho Questa)

1981 (1 July). Birth Centenary of Pablo Picasso. T **170** and similar vert designs. Multicoloured. P 13½×14.

925	5l. Type **170**	15	10
926	10l. "Woman in Blue"	20	10
927	25l. "Boy with Pipe"	30	10
928	30l. "Card Player"	30	10
929	90l. "Sailor"	50	40
930	3r. "Self-portrait"	80	1·00
931	5r. "Harlequin"	1·00	1·25
925/31 *Set of 7*		3·00	2·75
MS932 106×130 mm. 10r. "Child holding a Dove". Imperf		2·50	3·50

171 Airmail Envelope   **172** Boeing 737 taking off

(Des and litho Questa)

1981 (9 Sept). 75th Anniv of Postal Service. P 14.

933	**171**	25l. multicoloured	15	10
934		75l. multicoloured	25	25
935		5r. multicoloured	70	1·25
933/35 *Set of 3*			1·00	1·40

(Des A. Abbas. Litho Questa)

1981 (11 Nov). Malé International Airport. T **172** and similar horiz designs. Multicoloured. P 14.

936	5l. Type **172**	30	20
937	20l. Passengers leaving Boeing 737	55	20
938	1r.80 Refuelling	90	1·25
939	4r. Plan of airport	1·10	2·25
936/39 *Set of 4*		2·50	3·50
MS940 106×79 mm. 5r. Aerial view of airport		2·50	3·00

173 Homer

174 Preparation of Maldive Fish

(Des J. W.)

1981 (18 Nov). International Year of Disabled People. T **173** and similar vert designs. Multicoloured. P 14½.

941	2l. Type **173**	10	10
942	5l. Miguel Cervantes	10	10
943	1r. Beethoven	2·75	85
944	5r. Van Gogh	3·25	5·00
941/44 *Set of 4*		5·50	5·50
MS945 116×91 mm. 4r. Helen Keller and Anne Sullivan		3·25	5·50

(Des Central Art Palace. Litho Questa)

1981 (25 Nov). Decade for Women. T **174** and similar vert designs. Multicoloured. P 14.

946	20l. Type **174**	10	10
947	90l. 16th century Maldive women	25	25
948	1r. Farming	30	30
949	2r. Coir rope making	55	1·10
946/49 *Set of 4*		1·10	1·60

175 Collecting Bait

(Des I. Azeez. Litho Questa)

1981 (10 Dec). Fishermen's Day. T **175** and similar horiz designs. Multicoloured. P 14.

950	5l. Type **175**	45	15
951	15l. Fishing boats	85	25
952	90l. Fisherman with catch	1·60	60
953	1r.30 Sorting fish	2·00	1·10
950/53 *Set of 4*		4·50	1·90
MS954 147×101 mm. 3r. Loading fish for export		1·50	2·50

176 Bread Fruit

(Des Design Images. Litho Questa)

1981 (30 Dec). World Food Day. T **176** and similar horiz designs. Multicoloured. P 14.

955	10l. Type **176**	40	10
956	25l. Hen with chicks	80	15
957	30l. Maize	80	20
958	75l. Skipjack Tuna	2·50	65
959	1r. Pumpkin	3·00	70
960	2r. Coconuts	3·25	3·25
955/60 *Set of 6*		9·50	4·50
MS961 110×85 mm. 5r. Eggplant		2·50	3·50

177 Pluto and Cat

178 Balmoral

(Des Walt Disney Productions)

1982 (29 Mar). 50th Anniv of Pluto (Walt Disney cartoon character). T **177** and similar multicoloured design. P 13½.

962	4r. Type **177**	1·60	2·50
MS963 127×101 mm. 6r. Pluto (scene from *The Pointer*)		2·50	4·00

(Des PAD Studio. Litho Questa)

1982 (1 July). 21st Birthday of Princess of Wales. T **178** and similar vert designs. Multicoloured. P 14½×14.

964	95l. Type **178**	50	20
965	3r. Prince and Princess of Wales	1·25	65
966	6r. Princess on aircraft steps	1·75	95
964/66 *Set of 3*		3·25	1·60
MS967 103×75 mm. 8r. Princess of Wales		1·75	1·75

Nos. 964/6 also exist in sheetlets of five stamps and one label.

Nos. 964/7 and the sheetlets exist imperforate from a restricted printing.

COMMONWEALTH MEMBER
9 July 1982

179 Scout saluting and Camp-site   **180** Footballer

(Des D. Miller. Litho Questa)

1982 (9 Aug). 75th Anniv of Boy Scout Movement. T **179** and similar horiz designs. Multicoloured. P 14.

968	1r.30 Type **179**	40	45
969	1r.80 Lighting a fire	50	60
970	4r. Life-saving	1·10	1·40
971	5r. Map-reading	1·40	1·75
968/71 *Set of 4*		3·00	3·75
MS972 128×66 mm. 10r. Scout emblem and flag of the Maldives		2·00	3·00

(Des M. and S. Gerber Studio. Litho Questa)

1982 (4 Oct). World Cup Football Championship, Spain. T **180** and similar square designs. P 13½.

973	90l. multicoloured	1·25	60
974	1r.50 multicoloured	1·75	1·10
975	3r. multicoloured	2·50	1·75
976	5r. multicoloured	2·75	2·50
973/76 *Set of 4*		7·50	5·50
MS977 94×63 mm. 10r. multicoloured		4·50	6·00

ROYAL BABY
21 6 82

(180a)

1982 (18 Oct). Birth of Prince William of Wales. Nos. 964/7 optd supplied with T **180a**.

978	95l. Type **178**	30	20
979	3r. Prince and Princess of Wales	75	65
980	5r. Princess on aircraft steps	75	95
978/80 *Set of 3*		1·60	1·60
MS981 103×75 mm. 8r. Princess of Wales		3·50	2·50

Nos. 978/80 also exist in sheetlets of five stamps and one label.

Nos. 978/81 and the sheetlets exist imperforate from a restricted printing.

181 Basic Education Scheme

182 Koch isolates the Bacillus

(Des and litho Harrison)

1982 (15 Nov). National Education. T **181** and similar horiz designs. Multicoloured. P 14.

982	90l. Type **181**	20	30
983	95l. Primary education	20	30
984	1r.30 Teacher training	25	30
985	2r.50 Printing educational material	45	75
982/85	Set of 4	1·00	1·50
MS986	100×70 mm. 6r. Thaana typewriter keyboard	1·00	2·00

(Des Artists International)

1982 (22 Nov). Centenary of Robert Koch's Discovery of Tubercle Bacillus. T **182** and similar multicoloured designs. P 14.

987	5l. Type **182**	20	20
988	15l. Micro-organism and microscope	25	20
989	95l. Dr. Robert Koch in 1905	55	45
990	3r. Dr. Koch and plates from publication	95	1·75
987/90	Set of 4	1·75	2·40
MS991	77×61 mm. 5r. Koch in his laboratory (horiz)	1·00	2·00

No. **MS**991 exists imperforate from stock dispersed by the liquidator of Format International Security Printers Ltd.

183 Blohm and Voss HA 139A Seaplane *Nordsee*

184 "Curved Dash" Oldsmobile, 1902

(Des W. Wright. Litho Questa)

1983 (28 July). Bicentenary of Manned Flight. T **183** and similar horiz designs. Multicoloured. P 14.

992	90l. Type **183**	2·25	70
993	1r.45 Macchi Castoldi MC-72 seaplane	2·75	1·75
994	4r. Boeing F4B-3 biplane fighter	4·50	3·25
995	5r. Renard and Kreb's airship *La France*	4·50	3·50
992/95	Set of 4	12·50	8·25
MS996	110×85 mm. 10r. Nadar's balloon *Le Geant*	3·00	4·00

(Des Publishers Graphics Inc.)

1983 (1 Aug). Classic Motor Cars. T **184** and similar horiz designs. Multicoloured. P 14½.

997	5l. Type **184**	20	40
998	30l. Aston Martin "Tourer", 1932	60	40
999	40l. Lamborghini "Muira", 1966	60	45
1000	1r. Mercedes-Benz "300SL", 1945	1·00	70
1001	1r.45 Stutz "Bearcat", 1913	1·25	2·00
1002	5r. Lotus "Elite", 1958	2·00	4·25
997/1002	Set of 6	5·00	7·50
MS1003	132×103 mm. 10r. Grand Prix "Sunbeam", 1924. P 14½	5·50	10·00

Nos. 997/1002 were each issued in sheets of nine, including one se-tenant label.

185 Rough-toothed Dolphin

186 Dish Aerial

(Des D. Miller. Litho Questa)

1983 (6 Sept). Marine Mammals. T **185** and similar horiz designs. Multicoloured. P 14.

1004	30l. Type **185**	1·60	60
1005	40l. Indo-Pacific Hump-backed Dolphin	1·60	65
1006	4r. Finless Porpoise	5·00	4·00
1007	6r. Pygmy Sperm Whale	10·00	7·00
1004/7	Set of 4	16·00	11·00
MS1008	82×90 mm. 5r. Striped Dolphin	6·00	5·50

(Des PAD Studio. Litho Questa)

1983 (9 Oct). World Communications Year. T **188** and similar horiz designs. Multicoloured. P 14.

1009	50l. Type **186**	50	20
1010	1r. Land, sea and air communications	1·75	60
1011	2r. Ship-to-shore communication	2·50	1·75
1012	10r. Air traffic controller	4·75	7·50
1009/12	Set of 4	8·50	9·00
MS1013	91×76 mm. 20r. Telecommunications	3·75	4·75

187 "La Donna Gravida"

(Des M. Diamond)

1983 (25 Oct). 500th Birth Anniv of Raphael. T **187** and similar vert designs showing paintings. Multicoloured. P 13½.

1014	90l. Type **187**	25	25
1015	3r. Giovanna d'Aragona" (detail)	75	1·40
1016	4r. "Woman with Unicorn"	75	1·90
1017	6r. "La Muta"	1·00	2·50
1014/17	Set of 4	2·50	5·50
MS1018	121×97 mm. 10r. "The Knight's Dream" (detail)	2·50	5·50

Nos. 1014/18 exist imperforate from stock dispersed by the liquidator of Format International Security Printers Ltd.

188 Refugee Camp

(Litho Questa)

1983 (29 Nov). Solidarity with the Palestinians. T **188** and similar horiz designs each showing the Dome of the Rock, Jerusalem. Multicoloured. P 13½×14.

1019	4r. Type **188**	2·50	2·00
1020	5r. Refugee holding dead child	2·50	2·00
1021	6r. Child carrying food	2·75	2·50
1019/21	Set of 3	7·00	6·00

189 Education Facilities

190 Baseball

(Des I. Azeez. Litho Questa)

1983 (10 Dec). National Development Programme. T **189** and similar horiz designs. Multicoloured. P 13½.

1022	7l. Type **189**	20	10
1023	10l. Health service and education	50	10
1024	5r. Growing more food	1·50	1·25
1025	6r. Fisheries development	2·25	1·50
1022/25	Set of 4	4·00	2·50
MS1026	134×93 mm. 10r. Air transport	2·25	2·75

(Des PAD Studio. Litho Questa)

1984 (10 Mar). Olympic Games, Los Angeles. T **190** and similar vert designs. Multicoloured. P 14.

1027	50l. Type **190**	30	15
1028	1r.55 Backstroke swimming	65	40
1029	3r. Judo	1·40	90
1030	4r. Shot-putting	1·60	1·40
1027/30 *Set of 4*		3·50	2·50
MS1031 85×105 mm. 10r. Team Handball		2·40	2·75

Rf 1.45

19th UPU
CONGRESS HAMBURG
(**191**) (**192**)

1984 (19 June). Universal Postal Union Congress, Hamburg. Nos. 994/**MS**996 optd as T **191**.

1032	4r. Boeing "F4B-3"	1·75	1·40
1033	5r. *La France* airship	1·75	1·60
MS1034 110×85 mm. 10r. Nadar's *Le Geant*		2·75	4·50

1984 (20 Aug). Surch as T **192** in black or gold (same prices either colour).

(a) On Nos. 964/7

1035	1r.45 on 95l. Type **178**	2·00	1·50
1036	1r.45 on 3r. Prince and Princess of Wales	2·00	1·50
1037	1r.45 on 5r. Princess on aircraft steps	2·00	1·50
1035/37 *Set of 3*		5·50	4·00
MS1038 103×75 mm. 1r.45 on 8r. Princess of Wales		2·00	3·75

(b) On Nos. 978/81

1039	1r.45 on 95l. Type **178**	2·00	1·50
1040	1r.45 on 3r. Prince and Princess of Wales	2·00	1·50
1041	1r.45 on 5r. Princess on aircraft steps	2·00	1·50
1039/41 *Set of 3*		5·50	4·00
MS1042 103×75 mm. 1r.45 on 8r. Princess of Wales		2·00	3·75

Nos. 1039/42 exist imperforate from a restricted printing.
Stamps from the sheetlets of five plus one label were also surcharged, either in black or gold using a slightly different type.

193 Hands breaking Manacles

1984 (26 Aug). Namibia Day. T **193** and similar horiz designs. Multicoloured. P 15.

1043	6r. Type **193**	1·00	1·25
1044	8r. Namibia family	1·00	1·75
MS1045 129×104 mm. 10r. Map of Namibia		1·75	2·50

194 Island Resort and Common Terns
195 Frangipani

(Litho Questa)

1984 (12 Sept). Tourism. T **194** and similar vert designs. Multicoloured. P 14.

1046	7l. Type **194**	2·25	80
1047	15l. Dhow	1·00	15
1048	20l. Snorkelling	80	15
1049	2r. Wind-surfing	2·25	50

1050	4r. Aqualung diving	2·75	1·10
1051	6r. Night fishing	3·75	1·75
1052	8r. Game fishing	4·25	2·00
1053	10r. Turtle on beach	4·75	2·25
1046/53 *Set of 8*		20·00	8·00

1984 (21 Sept). 'Ausipex' International Stamp Exhibition, Melbourne. T **195** and similar horiz designs showing flowers. Multicoloured. P 15.

1054	5r. Type **195**	2·25	1·75
1055	10r. Cooktown Orchid	4·75	3·75
MS1056 105×77 mm. 15r. Sun Orchid		10·00	5·50

Nos. 1054/5 exist imperforate from stock dispersed by the liquidator of Format International Security Printers Ltd.

196 Façade of the Malé Mosque   197 Air Maldives Boeing 737

1984 (11 Nov). Opening of Islamic Centre. T **196** and similar multicoloured design. P 15.

1057	2r. Type **196**	45	50
1058	5r. Malé Mosque and minaret (*vert*)	1·10	1·25

(Des G. Drummond. Litho Questa)

1984 (19 Nov). 40th Anniv of International Civil Aviation Authority. T **197** and similar horiz designs. Multicoloured. P 14.

1059	7l. Type **197**	85	45
1060	4r. Air Lanka Lockheed L-1011 TriStar	3·25	2·00
1061	6r. Alitalia Douglas DC-10-30	4·00	3·50
1062	8r. L.T.U. Lockheed L-1011 TriStar	4·25	4·50
1059/62 *Set of 4*		11·00	9·50
MS1063 110×92 mm. 15r. Air Maldives Short S.7 Skyvan		3·75	4·00

198 Daisy Duck

(Litho Questa)

1984 (26 Nov–1 Dec). 50th Anniv of Donald Duck (Walt Disney cartoon character). T **198** and similar horiz designs. Multicoloured. P 12 (5r.) or 14×13½ (others).

1064	3l. Type **198**	10	10
1065	4l. Huey, Dewey and Louie	10	10
1066	5l. Ludwig von Drake	10	10
1067	10l. Gyro Gearloose	10	10
1068	15l. Uncle Scrooge painting self portrait	15	10
1069	25l. Donald Duck with camera	15	10
1070	5r. Donald Duck and Gus Goose (1.12)	2·25	1·25
1071	8r. Gladstone Gander	2·50	2·00
1072	10r. Grandma Duck	3·00	2·50
1064/72 *Set of 9*		7·50	5·50
MS1073 102×126 mm. 15r. Uncle Scrooge and Donald Duck in front of camera		4·75	5·00
MS1074 126×102 mm. 15r. Uncle Scrooge (1.12)		4·75	5·00

No. 1070 was printed in sheetlets of eight stamps.

199 "The Day"
(detail)
200 "Edmond Iduranty" (Degas)
201 Pale-footed Shearwater

(Litho Questa)

1984 (10 Dec). 450th Death Anniv of Correggio (artist). T **199** and similar vert designs. Multicoloured. P 14.

1075	5r. Type **199**	1·00	1·50
1076	10r. "The Night" (detail)	1·50	1·75
MS1077	60×80 mm. 15r. "Portrait of a Man"	3·50	3·25

(Litho Questa)

1984 (15 Dec). 150th Birth Anniv of Edgar Degas (artist). T **200** and similar vert designs. P 14.

1078	75l. Type **200**	20	20
1079	2r. "James Tissot"	50	50
1080	5r. "Achille de Gas in Uniform"	1·00	1·00
1081	10r. "Lady with Chrysanthemums"	1·75	2·00
1078/81	Set of 4	3·00	3·25
MS1082	100×90 mm. 15r. "Self-portrait"	3·25	3·75

(Des I. MacLaury. Litho Questa)

1985 (9 Mar). Birth Bicentenary of John J. Audubon (ornithologist) (1st issue). T **201** and similar multicoloured designs showing original paintings. P 14.

1083	3r. Type **201**	1·75	80
1084	3r.50 Little Grebe (horiz)	2·00	90
1085	4r. Common Cormorant	2·00	1·00
1086	4r.50 White-faced Storm Petrel (horiz)	2·00	1·10
1083/86	Set of 4	7·00	3·50
MS1087	108×80 mm. 15r. Red-necked Phalarope (horiz)	4·50	4·50

See also Nos. 1192/**MS**1200.

202 Squad Drilling

(Des and litho Questa)

1985 (6 June). National Security Service. T **202** and similar multicoloured designs. P 13½×14 (No. 1092) or 14×13½ (others).

1088	15l. Type **202**	50	10
1089	20l. Combat patrol	50	10
1090	1r. Fire fighting	2·00	40
1091	2r. Coastguard cutter	2·50	1·00
1092	10r. Independence Day Parade (vert)	3·25	3·50
1088/92	Set of 5	8·00	4·50
MS1093	128×85 mm. 10r. Cannon on saluting base and National Security Service badge	2·25	2·25

GOLD MEDALIST
THERESA ANDREWS
USA
(203)

1985 (17 July). Olympic Games Gold Medal Winners, Los Angeles. Nos. 1027/**MS**1031 optd as T **203** or in larger capitals (50l., 10r.).

1094	50l. Type **190** (optd "JAPAN")	30	15
1095	1r.55 Backstroke swimming (opt T **203**)	60	55
1096	3r. Judo (Optd "GOLD MEDALIST FRANK WIENEKE USA")	1·25	1·25
1097	4r. Shot Putting (optd "GOLD MEDALIST CLAUDIA LOCH WEST GERMANY")	1·25	1·40
1094/97	Set of 4	3·00	3·00
MS1098	85×105 mm. 10r. Team Handball (opt "U.S.A.")	1·90	2·00

204 Queen Elizabeth the Queen Mother, 1981

204a Liro da Braccio

(Des J. W. Litho Questa)

1985 (20 Aug). Life and Times of Queen Elizabeth the Queen Mother. T **204** and similar multicoloured designs. P 14.

1099	3r. Type **204**	45	60
1100	5r. Visiting the Middlesex Hospital (horiz)	65	1·00
1101	7r. The Queen Mother	85	1·25
1099/101	Set of 3	1·75	2·50
MS1102	56×85 mm. 15r. With Prince Charles at Garter Ceremony	4·25	3·25

Stamps as Nos. 1099/1101, but with face values of 1r., 4r. and 10r., exist from additional sheetlets of five plus a label issued 4 January 1986. These also have changed background colours and are perforated 12½×12 (4r.) or 12×12½ (others) (*Price for set of 3 stamps £2·50 mint*).

(Des Susan David. Litho Questa)

1985 (3 Sept). 300th Birth Anniv of Johann Sebastian Bach (composer). T **204a** and similar vert designs. P 14.

1103	15l. multicoloured	10	10
1104	2r. multicoloured	50	45
1105	4r. multicoloured	90	85
1106	10r. multicoloured	1·90	2·25
1103/6	Set of 4	3·00	3·25
MS1107	104×75 mm. 15r. black and reddish orange	3·00	3·50

Designs:—2r. Tenor oboe; 4r. Serpent; 10r. Table organ; 15r. Johann Sebastian Bach.

205 Mas Odi (fishing boat)　　　**206** Windsurfing

(Des H. Afeef. Litho Questa)

1985 (23 Sept). Maldives Ships and Boats. T **205** and similar horiz designs. Multicoloured. P 14.

1108	3l. Type **205**	15	30
1109	5l. Battela (dhow)	15	30
1110	10l. Addu odi (dhow)	15	30
1111	2r.60 Modern dhoni (fishing boat)	2·25	1·75
1112	2r.70 Mas dhoni (fishing boat)	2·25	1·75
1113	3r. Baththeli dhoni	2·50	1·75
1114	5r. Inter 1 (inter-island vessel)	3·75	3·50
1115	10r. Dhoni-style yacht	5·50	6·00
1108/15	Set of 8	15·00	13·50

(Des H. Afeef. Litho Questa)

1985 (2 Oct). Tenth Anniv of World Tourism Organization. T **206** and similar horiz designs. Multicoloured. P 14.

1116	6r. Type **206**	3·00	2·75
1117	8r. Scuba diving	3·25	3·00
MS1118	171×114 mm. 15r. Kuda Hithi Resort	2·75	3·00

207 United Nations Building, New York

208 Maldivian Delegate voting in U.N. General Assembly

(Litho Questa)

1985 (24 Oct). 40th Anniv of United Nations Organization and International Year of Peace. T **207** and similar multicoloured designs. P 14.

1119	15l. Type **207**	10	10
1120	2r. Hands releasing peace dove	40	45
1121	4r. U.N. Security Council meeting (horiz)	70	85
1122	10r. Lion and lamb	1·25	2·00
1119/22	Set of 4	2·25	3·00
MS1123	76×92 mm. 15r. U.N. Building and peace dove	2·25	2·75

(Des BG Studio. Litho Questa)

1985 (24 Oct). 20th Anniv of United Nations Membership. T **208** and similar horiz design. Multicoloured. P 14.

1124	20l. Type **208**	10	10
1125	15r. U.N. and Maldivian flags, and U.N. Building, New York	2·00	3·00

209 Youths playing Drums

(Des BG Studio)

1985 (20 Nov). International Youth Year. T 209 and similar multicoloured designs. P 15.

1126	90l. Type 209	15	20
1127	6r. Tug-of-war	80	1·10
1128	10r. Community service (vert)	1·25	2·00
1126/28 Set of 3		2·00	3·00
MS1129 85×84 mm. 15r. Raising the flag at youth camp (vert)		2·25	3·00

210 Quotation and Flags of Members

211 Frigate Mackerel

(Litho Questa)

1985 (8 Dec). First Summit Meeting of South Asian Association for Regional Co-operation, Dhaka, Bangladesh. P 14.

1130	210	3r. multicoloured	1·50	1·50

(Litho Questa)

1985 (10 Dec). Fishermen's Day. Species of Tuna. T 211 and similar horiz designs. Multicoloured. P 14.

1131	25l. Type 211	35	10
1132	75l. Kawakawa ("Little Tuna")	65	15
1133	3r. Dog-toothed Tuna	2·00	1·00
1134	5r. Yellow-finned Tuna	2·50	1·50
1131/34 Set of 4		5·00	2·50
MS1135 130×90 mm. 15r. Skipjack Tuna		3·50	3·50

211a Winnie the Pooh

(Des Walt Disney Productions. Litho Questa)

1985 (21 Dec). 150th Birth Anniv of Mark Twain. as T 211a showing Walt Disney cartoon characters illustrating various Mark Twain quotations. Multicoloured. P 12 (4r.) or 13½×14 (others).

1136	2l. Type 211a	10	20
1137	3l. Gepetto and Figaro the cat	10	20
1138	4l. Goofy and basket of broken eggs	10	20
1139	20l. Goofy as doctor scolding Donald Duck	25	10
1140	4r. Mowgli and King Louis	1·40	1·75
1141	13r. The wicked Queen and mirror	5·00	7·00
1136/41 Set of 6		6·00	8·50
MS1142 126×101 mm. 15r. Mickey Mouse as Tom Sawyer on comet's tail		6·50	7·00

No. 1140 was issued in sheetlets of eight stamps.

211b Donald Duck as Crabb driving oxcart

(Des Walt Disney Productions. Litho Questa)

1985 (21 Dec). Birth Bicentenaries of Grimm Brothers (folklorists). Multicoloured designs as T 211b showing Walt Disney cartoon characters in scenes from "Dr. Knowall". P 12 (3r.) or 14×13½ (others).

1143	1l. Type 211b	10	10
1144	5l. Donald Duck as Dr. Knowall	10	10
1145	10l. Dr. Knowall in surgery	10	10
1146	15l. Dr. Knowall with Uncle Scrooge as a lord	10	10
1147	3r. Dr. and Mrs. Knowall in pony trap	1·10	1·50
1148	14r. Dr. Knowall and thief	5·50	7·00
1143/48 Set of 6		6·00	8·00
MS1149 126×101 mm. 15r. Donald and Daisy Duck as Dr. and Mrs. Knowall		6·50	7·00

No. 1147 was printed in sheetlets of eight stamps.

211c Weapons on Road Sign

1986 (10 Feb). World Disarmament Day. T 211c and similar horiz design. Multicoloured. Litho. P 14.

1149a	1r.50 Type 211c	25·00	10·00
1149b	10r. Peace dove	30·00	30·00

211d N.A.S.A. Space Telescope and Comet

(Des W. Hanson. Litho Questa)

1986 (29 Apr). Appearance of Halley's Comet (1st issue). As T 211d and similar horiz designs. Multicoloured. P 14.

1150	20l. Type 211d	50	25
1151	1r.50 E.S.A. Giotto spacecraft and Comet	1·25	1·50
1152	2r. Japanese Planet A spacecraft and Comet	1·25	1·75
1153	4r. Edmond Halley and Stonehenge	2·00	3·00
1154	5r. Russian Vega spacecraft and Comet	2·00	3·00
1150/54 Set of 5		6·25	8·50
MS1155 101×70 mm. 15r. Halley's Comet		8·00	10·00

See also Nos. 1206/11.

211e Walter Gropius (architect)

(Des J. Iskowitz. Litho Questa)

1986 (5 May). Centenary of Statue of Liberty. Multicoloured designs as T 211e, showing the Statue of Liberty and immigrants to the U.S.A. P 14.

1156	50l. Type 211e	40	30
1157	70l. John Lennon (musician)	2·00	1·25
1158	1r. George Balanchine (choreographer)	2·00	1·25
1159	10r. Franz Werfel (writer)	4·00	7·00
1156/59 Set of 4		7·50	8·75
MS1160 100×72 mm. 15r. Statue of Liberty (vert)		8·00	8·50

211f Johnny Appleseed and 1966 Johnny Appleseed stamp

(Des Walt Disney Productions)

1986 (22 May). "Ameripex" International Stamp Exhibition, Chicago. As T **211f** and similar horiz designs, showing Walt Disney cartoon characters and U.S.A. stamps. Multicoloured. P 11.

1161	3l. Type **211f**	10	10
1162	4l. Paul Bunyan and 1958 Forest Conservation stamp	10	10
1163	5l. Casey and 1969 Professional Baseball Centenary stamp	10	10
1164	10l. Ichabod Crane and 1974 "Legend of Sleepy Hollow" stamp	10	10
1165	15l. John Henry and 1944 75th anniv of completion of First Transcontinental Railroad stamp	15	15
1166	20l. Windwagon Smith and 1954 Kansas Territory Centenary stamp	15	15
1167	13r. Mike Fink and 1970 Great Northwest stamp	7·00	7·00
1168	14r. Casey Jones and 1950 Railroad Engineers stamp	8·00	8·00
1161/68	Set of 8	14·00	14·00

MS1169 Two sheets, each 127×101 mm. (a) 15r. Davy Crockett and 1967 Davy Crockett stamp. (b) 15r. Daisy Duck as Pocahontas saving Captain John Smith (Donald Duck). P 14×13½. Set of 2 sheets...... 13·00 16·00

211g Royal Family at Girl Guides Rally, 1938

212 Player running with ball

(Litho Questa)

1986 (29 May). 60th Birthday of Queen Elizabeth II. P 14.

1170	1r. black and chrome-yellow	30	25
1171	2r. multicoloured	40	55
1172	12r. multicoloured	1·50	2·50
1170/72	Set of 3	2·00	3·00

MS1173 120×85 mm. 15r. black and grey-brown .... 4·00 4·25

Nos. 1170/2 were each issued in sheetlets of five stamps and one stamp-size label.

Designs:—1r. Type **211g**; 2r. Queen in Canada; 12r. At Sandringham, 1970; 15r. Princesses Elizabeth and Margaret at Royal Lodge, Windsor, 1940.

(Des BG Studio. Litho Questa)

1986 (8 June). World Cup Football Championship, Mexico. T **212** and similar vert designs. Multicoloured. P 14.

1174	15l. Type **212**	75	30
1175	2r. Player gaining control of ball	2·50	1·75
1176	4r. Two players competing for ball	4·00	3·50
1177	10r. Player bouncing ball on knee	7·50	8·00
1174/77	Set of 4	13·00	12·00

MS1178 95×114 mm. 15r. Player kicking ball .... 5·00 6·00

212a Prince Andrew and Miss Sarah Ferguson

213 Moorish Idol and Sea Fan

(Litho Questa)

1986 (1 July). Royal, Wedding. As T **212a** and similar vert designs. Multicoloured. P 14.

1179	10l. Type **212a**	20	10
1180	2r. Prince Andrew	85	70
1181	12r. Prince Andrew in naval uniform	3·75	3·75
1179/81	Set of 3	4·25	4·00

MS1182 88×88 mm. 15r. Prince Andrew and Miss Sarah Ferguson (different) .... 5·00 4·75

(Des Mary Walters)

1986 (22 Sept). Marine Wildlife. T **213** and similar horiz designs. Multicoloured. P 15.

1183	50l. Type **213**	1·50	40
1184	90l. Regal Angelfish	2·00	55
1185	1r. Maldive Anemonefish	2·00	55
1186	2r. Tiger Cowrie (*Cypraea tigris*) and Stinging Coral	2·50	1·60
1187	3r. Emperor Angelfish and Staghorn Coral	2·50	2·00
1188	4r. Black–naped Tern	3·00	3·00
1189	5r. Fiddler Crab and Staghorn Coral	2·50	3·00
1190	10r. Hawksbill Turtle	3·00	5·00
1183/90	Set of 8	17·00	14·00

MS1191 Two sheets, each 107×76 mm. (a) 15r. Long-nosed Butterflyfish. (b) 15r. Oriental Trumpetfish Set of 2 sheets .... 12·00 15·00

Nos. 1183/**MS**1191 exist imperforate from stock dispersed by the liquidator of Format International Security Printers Ltd.

(Litho Questa)

1986 (9 Oct). Birth Bicentenary of John J. Audubon (ornithologist) (1985) (2nd issue). Multicoloured designs as T **201** showing original paintings. P 14.

1192	3l. Little Blue Heron (*horiz*)	40	60
1193	4l. White-tailed Kite	40	60
1194	5l. Greater Shearwater (*horiz*)	40	60
1195	10l. Magnificent Frigate Bird	45	40
1196	15l. Black-necked Grebe	85	40
1197	20l. Goosander	90	40
1198	13r. Peregrine Falcon (*horiz*)	7·50	7·50
1199	14r. Prairie Chicken (*horiz*)	7·50	7·50
1192/9	Set of 8	16·00	16·00

MS1200 Two sheets, each 74×104 mm. (a) 15r. Fulmer. (b) 15r. White-fronted Goose (*horiz*) Set of 2 sheets .... 24·00 21·00

Nos. 1192/9 were each issued in sheetlets of five stamps and one stamp-size label, which appears in the centre of the bottom row.

WINNERS
Argentina 3
W.Germany 2
(213a)

(213b)

1986 (25 Oct). World Cup Football Championship Winners, Mexico. Nos. 1174/**MS**1178 optd with T **213a** in gold.

1201	15l. Type **212**	40	30
1202	2r. Player gaining control of ball	1·25	1·10
1203	4r. Two players competing for ball	2·00	2·00
1204	10r. Player bouncing ball on knee	2·75	4·25
1201/4	Set of 4	5·75	7·00

MS1205 95×114 mm. 15r. Player kicking ball .... 3·00 4·25

1986 (30 Oct). Appearance of Halley's Comet (2nd issue). Nos. 1150/**MS**1155 optd with T **213b** in silver.

1206	20l. N.A.S.A. space telescope and Comet......	65	40
1207	1r.50 E.S.A. *Giotto* spacecraft and Comet......	1·25	1·25
1208	2r. Japanese *Planet A* spacecraft and Comet......	1·50	1·50
1209	4r. Edmond Halley and Stonehenge	2·00	2·50
1210	5r. Russian *Vega* spacecraft and Comet......	2·00	2·50
1206/10	Set of 5	6·75	7·25

MS1211 101×70 mm. 15r. Halley's Comet .... 6·00 7·00

214 Servicing Aircraft

215 *Hypholoma fasciculare*

(Des BG Studio)

1986 (4 Nov). 40th Anniv of U.N.E.S.C.O. T **214** and similar vert designs. Multicoloured. P 15.

1212	1r. Type **214**	80	30
1213	2r. Boat building	90	1·00
1214	3r. Children in classroom	1·00	1·40
1215	5r. Student in laboratory	1·10	2·50
1212/15	Set of 4	3·25	4·75

MS1216 77×100 mm. 15r. Diving bell on sea bed .... 2·75 4·25

Nos. 1212/**MS**1216 exist imperforate from stock dispersed by the liquidator of Format International Security Printers Ltd.

(Des Mary Walters)

1986 (31 Dec). Fungi of the Maldives. T **215** and similar multicoloured designs. P 15.

1217	15l. Type **215**	80	25
1218	50l. *Kuehneromyces mutabalis* (vert)	1·50	45
1219	1r. *Amanita muscaria* (vert)	1·75	60
1220	2r. *Agaricus campestris*	2·00	1·50
1221	3r. *Amanita pantherina* (vert)	2·00	1·75
1222	4r. *Coprinus comatus* (vert)	2·00	2·25
1223	5r. *Gymnopilus junonias* ("*Pholiota spectabilis*")	2·00	2·75
1224	10r. *Pluteus cervinus*	2·50	4·50
1217/24	*Set of 8*	13·00	12·50

MS1225 Two sheets, each 100×70 mm. (a) 15r. *Armillaria mellea.* (b) 15r. *Stropharia aeruginosa* (vert) *Set of 2 sheets* ... 13·00 14·00

Nos. 1217/**MS**1225 exist imperforate from stock dispersed by the liquidator of Format International Security Printers Ltd.

216 Ixora

217 Guides studying Wild Flowers

(Des Mary Walters)

1987 (29 Jan). Flowers. T **216** and similar vert designs. Multicoloured. P 15.

1226	10l. Type **216**	10	10
1227	20l. Frangipani	10	10
1228	50l. Crinum	2·00	60
1229	2r. Pink Rose	40	80
1230	4r. Flamboyant Flower	60	1·50
1231	10r. Ground Orchid	6·00	8·00
1226/31	*Set of 6*	8·25	10·00

MS1232 Two sheets, each 100×70 mm. (a) 15r. Gardenia. (b) 15r. Oleander *Set of 2 sheets* ... 4·75 6·50

Similar 1, 7 and 12r. stamps were prepared but not issued. They exist from stock dispersed by the liquidator of Format International Security Printers Ltd as do Nos. 1226/**MS**1232 imperforate.

(Des R. Vigurs)

1987 (4 Apr). 75th Anniv of Girl Guide Movement (1985). T **217** and similar horiz designs. Multicoloured. P 15.

1233	15l. Type **217**	30	20
1234	2r. Guides with pet rabbits	50	80
1235	4r. Guide observing White Spoonbill	2·50	2·25
1236	12r. Lady Baden-Powell and Guide flag	2·50	6·50
1233/36	*Set of 4*	5·25	8·75

MS1237 104×78 mm. 15r. Guide. in sailing dinghy ... 2·25 3·75

Nos. 1233/**MS**1237 exist imperforate from stock dispersed by the liquidator of Format International Security Printers Ltd.

218 Thespesia populnea

218a Intrepid, 1970

(Litho Questa)

1987 (22 Apr). Trees and Plants. T **218** and similar multicoloured designs. P 14.

1238	50l. Type **218**	15	10
1239	1r. *Cocos nucifera*	25	20
1240	2r. *Calophyllum mophyllum*	40	40
1241	3r. *Xanthosoma indica* (horiz)	60	65
1242	5r. *Ipomoea batatas* (horiz)	1·00	1·40
1243	7r. *Artocarpus altilis*	1·25	2·25
1238/43	*Set of 6*	3·25	4·50

MS1244 75×109 mm. 15r. *Cocos nucifera* (different) ... 2·25 3·25

No. 1241 is inscribed "*Xyanthosoma indica*" in error.

(Des J. Iskowitz)

1987 (4 May). America's Cup Yachting Championship. T **218a** and similar multicoloured designs. P 15.

1245	15l. Type **218a**	10	10
1246	1r. *France II*, 1974	20	20
1247	2r. *Gretel*, 1962	40	60
1248	12r. *Volunteer*, 1887	2·00	3·00
1245/48	*Set of 4*	2·40	3·50

MS1249 113×83 mm. 15r. Helmsman and crew on deck of *Defender*, 1895 (horiz) ... 2·25 3·25

Nos. 1245/**MS**1249 exist imperforate from stock dispersed by the liquidator of Format International Security Printers Ltd.

219 Precis octavia

220 Isaac Newton experimenting with Spectrum

1987 (16 Dec). Butterflies. T **219** and similar vert designs. Multicoloured. P 15.

1250	15l. Type **219**	45	30
1251	20l. *Atrophaneura hector*	45	30
1252	50l. *Teinopalpus imperialis*	75	40
1253	1r. *Kallima horsfieldi*	1·00	45
1254	2r. *Cethosia biblis*	1·40	1·25
1255	4r. *Idea jasonia*	2·25	2·25
1256	7r. *Papilio memnon*	2·75	4·00
1257	10r. *Aeropetes tulbaghia*	3·25	5·00
1250/57	*Set of 8*	11·00	12·50

MS1258 Two sheets each 135×102 mm. (a) 15r. *Acraea violae.* (b) 15r. *Hebomoia leucippe Set of 2 sheets* ... 7·50 11·00

(Des J. Martin. Litho Questa)

1988 (10 Jan). Great Scientific Discoveries. T **220** and similar multicoloured designs. P 14.

1259	1r.50 Type **220**	1·25	1·00
1260	3r. Euclid composing *Principles of Geometry* (vert)	1·60	1·75
1261	4r. Mendel formulating theory of Genetic Evolution (vert)	1·75	2·00
1262	5r. Galileo and moons of Jupiter	3·00	3·00
1259/62	*Set of 4*	7·00	7·00

MS1263 102×72 mm. 15r. "Apollo" lunar module (vert) ... 4·50 5·50

221 Donald Duck and Weather Satellite

(Des Walt Disney Co. Litho Questa)

1988 (15 Feb). Space Exploration. T **221** and similar multicoloured designs showing Walt Disney cartoon characters. P 14×13½ (horiz) or 13½×14 (vert).

1264	3l. Type **221**	10	10
1265	4l. Minnie Mouse and navigation satellite.	10	10
1266	5l. Mickey Mouse's nephews talking via communication satellite	10	10
1267	10l. Goofy in lunar rover (vert)	10	10
1268	20l. Minnie Mouse delivering pizza to flying saucer (vert)	10	10
1269	13r. Mickey Mouse directing spacecraft docking (vert)	5·00	5·00
1270	14r. Mickey Mouse and "Voyager 2"	5·00	5·00
1264/70	*Set of 7*	9·00	9·00

MS1271 Two sheets, each 127×102 mm. (a) 15r. Mickey Mouse at first Moon landing, 1969. (b) 15r. Mickey Mouse and nephews in space station swimming pool (vert) *Set of 2 sheets* ... 13·00 13·00

222 Syringe and Bacterium
("Immunization")

223 Water Droplet and Atoll

(Des Mary Walters. Litho Questa)

1988 (7 Apr). 40th Anniv of World Health Organization. T **222** and similar horiz design. Multicoloured. P 14.

1272	2r. Type **222**	40	40
1273	4r. Tap ("Clean Water")	60	85

(Des I. Rasheed)

1988 (9 May). World Environment Day (1987). T **223** and similar multicoloured designs. P 15.

1274	15l. Type **223**	10	10
1275	75l. Coral reef	20	40
1276	2r. Audubon's Shearwaters in flight	85	1·40
1274/76 Set of 3		1·00	1·75
MS1277 105×76 mm. 15r. Banyan Tree (vert)		4·25	5·50

224 Globe, Carrier Pigeon and Letter

40TH WEDDING ANNIVERSARY

H.M.QUEEN ELIZABETH II

H.R.H. THE DUKE OF EDINBURGH

(225)

(Litho Questa)

1988 (31 May). Transport and Telecommunications Decade. T **224** and similar horiz designs, each showing central globe. Multicoloured. P 14.

1278	2r. Type **224**	75	65
1279	3r. Dish aerial and girl using telephone	1·25	1·10
1280	5r. Satellite, television, telephone and antenna tower	2·00	2·00
1281	10r. Car, ship and Lockheed L-1011 TriStar airliner	11·00	6·50
1278/81 Set of 4		13·50	11·00

1988 (7 July). Royal Ruby Wedding. Nos. 1170/**MS**1173 optd with T **225** in gold.

1282	1r. black and chrome-yellow	50	25
1283	2r. multicoloured	75	60
1284	12r. multicoloured	3·00	3·50
1282/84 Set of 3		3·75	4·00
MS1285 120×85 mm. 15r. black and grey-brown		4·50	4·50

226 Discus-throwing

227 Immunization at Clinic

(Des B. Bundock. Litho Questa)

1988 (16 July). Olympic Games, Seoul. T **226** and similar multicoloured designs. P 14.

1286	15l. Type **226**	10	10
1287	2r. 100 metres race	40	40
1288	4r. Gymnastics (horiz)	70	80
1289	12r. Three-day equestrian event (horiz)	2·25	3·25
1286/89 Set of 4		3·00	4·00
MS1290 106×76 mm. 20r. Tennis (horiz)		4·00	4·75

(Des A. DiLorenzo. Litho Questa)

1988 (20 July). International Year of Shelter for the Homeless. T **227** and similar vert designs. Multicoloured. P 14.

1291	50l. Type **227**	30	30
1292	3r. Prefab housing estate	1·10	1·40
MS1293 63×105 mm. 15r. Building site		1·75	2·50

228 Breadfruit

(229)

(Des G. Watkins. Litho Questa)

1988 (30 July). Tenth Anniv of International Fund for Agricultural Development. T **228** and similar multicoloured designs. P 14.

1294	7r. Type **228**	1·00	1·40
1295	10r. Mangos (vert)	1·50	1·90
MS1296 103×74 mm. 15r. Coconut palm, fishing boat and Yellowtail Tuna		2·75	3·00

1988 (1 Dec). World Aids Day. Nos. 1272/3 optd with T **229**.

1297	2r. Type **222**	35	45
1298	4r. Tap ("Clean Water")	65	80

230 Pres. Kennedy and Launch of "Apollo" Spacecraft

J. SCHULT
DDR
(231)

(Des A. Nahigian. Litho Questa)

1989 (13 Feb). 25th Death Anniv of John F. Kennedy (American statesman) (1988). U.S. Space Achievements. T **230** and similar vert designs. Multicoloured. P 14.

1299	5r. Type **230**	2·50	2·75
	a. Horiz strip of 4. Nos. 1299/1302	9·00	10·00
1300	5r. Lunar module and astronaut on Moon	2·50	2·75
1301	5r. Astronaut and buggy on Moon	2·50	2·75
1302	5r. President Kennedy and spacecraft	2·50	2·75
1299/1302 Set of 4		9·00	10·00
MS1303 108×77 mm. 15r. President Kennedy making speech		4·00	5·00

Nos. 1299/1302 were printed together, se-tenant, in horizontal strips of four throughout the sheet.

1989 (29 Apr). Olympic Medal Winners, Seoul. Nos. 1286/**MS**1290 optd as T **231**.

1304	15l. Type **226** (optd with T **231**)	20	20
1305	2r. 100 metres race (optd "C. LEWIS USA")	65	65
1306	4r. Gymnastics (horiz) (optd "MEN'S ALL AROUND V. ARTEMOV USSR")	1·40	1·40
1307	12r. Three-day equestrian event (horiz) (optd "TEAM SHOW JUMPING W. GERMANY")	4·00	5·50
1304/7 Set of 4		5·50	7·00
MS1308 106×76 mm. 20r. Tennis (horiz) (optd "OLYMPIC WINNERS MEN'S SINGLES GOLD M. MECIR CZECH. SILVER T. MAYOTTE USA BRONZE B. GILBERT USA")		6·50	7·50

On No. **MS**1308 the overprint appears on the sheet margin and not the 20r. stamp.

231a "Benedetto Varchi"

(Litho Questa)

1989 (20 May). 500th Birth Anniv of Titian (artist). As T **231a** and similar vert designs, showing paintings. Multicoloured. P 13½×14.

1309	15l. Type **231a**	10	10
1310	1r. "Portrait of a Young Man"	20	15
1311	2r. "King Francis I of France"	40	40
1312	5r. "Pietro Aretino"	1·10	1·25
1313	15r. "The Bravo"	3·50	5·50
1314	20r. "The Concert" (detail)	3·50	6·00
1309/14	Set of 6	8·00	12·00

MS1315 Two sheets. (a) 112×96 mm. 20r. "An Allegory of Prudence" (detail). (b) 96×110 mm. 20r. "Francesco Maria della Rovere" Set of 2 sheets .... 8·50 11·00

ASIA-PACIFIC TELECOMMUNITY 10 YEARS
(232)

1989 (10 July). Tenth Anniv of Asia-Pacific Telecommunity. Nos. 1279/80 optd with T **232** in silver.

1316	3r. Dish aerial and girl using telephone	1·25	1·50
1317	5r. Satellite, television, telephone and antenna tower	1·75	2·00

MALDIVES 15L

232a "Fuji from Hodogaya"

(Litho Questa)

1989 (2 Sept–16 Oct). Japanese Art Paintings by Hokusai. As T **232a** and similar horiz designs. Multicoloured. P 14×13½.

1318	15l. Type **232a**	10	10
1319	50l. "Fuji from Lake Kawaguchi"	15	15
1320	1r. "Fuji from Owari"	25	15
1321	2r. "Fuji from Tsukudajima in Edo"	50	40
1322	4r. "Fuji from a Teahouse at Yoshida"	80	90
1323	6r. "Fuji from Tagonoura"	90	1·25
1324	10r. "Fuji from Mishima-gee"	2·25	2·75
1325	12r. "Fuji from the Sumida River in Edo"	2·25	2·75
1318/25	Set of 8	6·50	7·50

MS1326 Two sheets, each 101×77 mm. (a) 18r. "Fuji from Inume Pass" (2 Sept). (b) 18r. "Fuji from Fukagawa in Edo" (16 Oct) Set of 2 sheets .... 8·50 9·00

Nos. 1318/25 were each printed in sheetlets of ten containing two horizontal strips of five stamps separated by printed labels commemorating Emperor Hirohito.

233 Clown Triggerfish

(Des L. Birmingham. Litho Questa)

1989 (16 Oct). Tropical Fish. T **233** and similar horiz designs. Multicoloured. P 14.

1327	20l. Type **233**	25	20
1328	50l. Blue-striped Snapper	35	25
1329	1r. Powder-blue Surgeonfish	45	30
1330	2r. Oriental Sweetlips	65	65
1331	3r. Six-barred Wrasse	80	85
1332	8r. Thread-finned Butterflyfish	1·50	2·50
1333	10r. Bicoloured Parrotfish	1·75	2·75
1334	12r. Scarlet-finned Squirrelfish	1·75	2·75
1327/34	Set of 8	6·75	9·25

MS1335 Two sheets, each 101×73 mm. (a) 15r. Butterfly Perch. (b) 15r. Semicircle Angelfish Set of 2 sheets .... 13·00 12·00

234 Goofy, Mickey and Minnie Mouse with Takuri "Type 3", 1907

(Des Walt Disney Co. Litho Questa)

1989 (17 Nov). "World Stamp Expo '89" International Stamp Exhibition, Washington (1st issue). T **234** and similar horiz designs showing Walt Disney cartoon characters with Japanese cars. Multicoloured. P 14×13½.

1336	15l. Type **234**	20	15
1337	50l. Donald and Daisy Duck in Mitsubishi "Model A", 1917	40	30
1338	1r. Goofy in Datsun "Roadstar", 1935	70	50
1339	2r. Donald and Daisy Duck with Mazda, 1940.	1·00	75
1340	4r. Donald Duck with Nissan "Bluebird 310", 1959	1·50	1·25
1341	6r. Donald and Daisy Duck with Subaru "360", 1958	1·75	1·75
1342	10r. Mickey Mouse and Pluto in Honda "5800", 1966	3·25	3·75
1343	12r. Mickey Mouse and Goofy in Daihatsu "Fellow", 1966	3·75	4·25
1336/43	Set of 8	11·50	11·50

MS1344 Two sheets, each 127×102 mm. (a) 20r. Daisy Duck with Chip n' Dale and Isuzu "Trooper II", 1981 (b) 20r. Mickey Mouse with tortoise and Toyota "Supra", 1985 Set of 2 sheets .... 11·00 13·00

234a Marine Corps Memorial, Arlington National Cemetery

235 Lunar Module *Eagle*

(Des Design Element. Litho Questa)

1989 (17 Nov). "World Stamp Expo '89" International Stamp Exhibition, Washington (2nd issue). Landmarks of Washington. Sheet 62×78 mm. P 14.

MS1345 8r. **234a** multicoloured .... 2·75 3·00

(Des W. Hanson Studio. Litho Questa)

1989 (24 Nov). 20th Anniv of First Manned Landing on Moon. T **235** and similar multicoloured designs. P 14.

1346	1r. Type **235**	30	20
1347	2r. Astronaut Aldrin collecting dust samples	50	60
1348	6r. Aldrin setting up seismometer	1·25	1·75
1349	10r. Pres Nixon congratulating "Apollo 11" astronauts	1·90	2·50
1346/49	Set of 4	3·50	4·50

MS1350 107×75 mm. 18r. Television picture of Armstrong about to step onto Moon (34×47 mm). P 13½×14.......... 7·50 8·00

236 Jawaharlal Nehru with Mahatma Gandhi

237 Sir William van Horne (Chairman of Canadian Pacific), Locomotive and Map, 1894

(Des Design Element. Litho B.D.T.)

1989 (20 Dec)–**90**. Anniversaries and Events. T **236** and similar multicoloured designs. P 14.

1351	20l. Type **236** (birth centenary)	4·25	1·50
1352	50l. Opium poppies and logo (anti-drugs campaign) (*vert*)	1·50	45
1353	1r. William Shakespeare (425th birth anniv) (15.2.90)	1·25	45
1354	2r. Storming the Bastille (bicent of French Revolution) (*vert*) (15.2.90)	1·25	1·25
1355	3r. Concorde (20th anniv of first flight) (15.2.90)	5·50	4·25
1356	8r. George Washington (bicent of inauguration)	2·00	3·00
1357	10r. William Bligh (bicent of mutiny on the *Bounty*)	9·00	6·00
1358	12r. Hamburg Harbour (800th anniv) (*vert*) (15.2.90)	4·50	5·50
1351/58 *Set of 8*		26·00	20·00

MS1359 Two sheets. (a) 115×85 mm. 18r. Baseball players (50th anniv of first televised game) (*vert*). (b) 110×80 mm. 18r. Franz von Taxis (500th anniv of regular European postal services) (*vert*) (15.2.90) *Set of 2 sheets* ..... 14·00 16·00

(Des A. Fagbohun. Litho Questa)

1989 (26 Dec). Railway Pioneers. T **237** and similar vert designs. Multicoloured. P 14.

1360	10l. Type **237**	25	15
1361	25l. Matthew Murray (engineer) with Blenkinsop and Murray's rack locomotive, 1810	35	20
1362	50l. Louis Favre (railway engineer) and steam locomotive entering tunnel	40	25
1363	2r. George Stephenson (engineer) and *Locomotion*, 1825	75	55
1364	6r. Richard Trevithick and *Catch-Me-Who-Can*, 1808	1·50	1·50
1365	8r. George Nagelmackers and "Orient Express" dining car	1·75	1·75
1366	10r. William Jessop and horse-drawn wagon, Surrey Iron Railway, 1770	2·50	2·50
1367	12r. Isambard Brunel (engineer) and G.W.R. steam locomotive, 1833	3·00	3·00
1360/67 *Set of 8*		9·50	9·00

MS1368 Two sheets, each 71×103 mm. (a) 18r. George Pullman (inventor of sleeping cars), 1864. (b) 18r. Rudolf Diesel (engineer) and first oil engine *Set of 2 sheets* ..... 11·00 12·00

238 Bodu Thakurufaanu Memorial Centre, Utheemu

239 "Louis XVI in Coronation Robes" (Duplesis)

(Litho B.D.T.)

1990 (1 Jan). 25th Anniv of Independence. T **238** and similar horiz dessgns. Multicoloured. P 14.

1369	20l. Type **238**	10	10
1370	25l. Islamic Centre, Malé	10	10
1371	50l. National flag and logos of international organizations	10	10
1372	2r. Presidential Palace, Malé	30	40
1373	5r. National Security Service	85	1·25
1369/73 *Set of 5*		1·25	1·75

MS1374 128×90 mm. 10r. National emblem ..... 5·00 5·50

(Litho Questa)

1990 (11 Jan). Bicentenary of French Revolution and "Philexfrance 89" International Stamp Exhibition, Paris. French Paintings. T **239** and similar multicoloured designs. P 13½×14.

1375	15l. Type **239**	20	15
1376	50l. "Monsieur Lavoisier and his Wife" (David)	45	25
1377	1r. "Madame Pastoret" (David)	65	35
1378	2r. "Oath of Lafayette, 14 July 1790" (anon)	1·00	70
1379	4r. Madame Trudaine" (David)	1·75	1·50

1380	6r. "Chenard celebrating the Liberation of Savoy" (Boilly)	2·50	2·50
1381	10r. "An Officer swears Allegiance to the Constitution" (anon)	4·00	4·50
1382	12r. "Self Portrait" (David)	4·00	4·75
1375/82 *Set of 8*		13·00	13·00

MS1383 Two sheets. (a) 104×79 mm. 20r. "The Oath of the Tennis Court, 20 June 1789" (David) (*horiz*). P 14×13½. (b) 79×104 mm. 20r. "Rousseau and Symbols of the Revolution" (Jeaurat). P 13½×14 *Set of 2 sheets* ..... 13·00 14·00

239a Donald Duck, Mickey Mouse and Goofy playing Rugby

(Des Walt Disney Co. Litho Questa)

1990 (3 May). "Stamp World London 90" International Stamp Exhibition. T **239a** and similar horiz designs showing Walt Disney cartoon characters playing British sports. Multicoloured. P 14×13½.

1384	15l. Type **239a**	30	15
1385	50l. Donald Duck and Chip-n-Dale curling	45	25
1386	1r. Goofy playing polo	65	40
1387	2r. Mickey Mouse and nephews playing soccer	90	70
1388	4r. Mickey Mouse playing cricket	1·75	1·50
1389	6r. Minnie and Mickey Mouse at Ascot races	2·25	1·90
1390	10r. Mickey Mouse and Goofy playing tennis	3·50	3·50
1391	12r. Donald Duck and Mickey Mouse playing bowls	3·50	3·50
1384/91 *Set of 8*		12·00	10·50

MS1392 Two sheets, each 126×101 mm. (a) 20r. Minnie Mouse fox-hunting. (b) 20r. Mickey Mouse playing golf *Set of 2 sheets* ..... 15·00 15·00

240 Silhouettes of Queen Elizabeth II and Queen Victoria

240a Lady Elizabeth Bowes-Lyon

(Des S. Pollard. Litho B.D.T.)

1990 (6 May). 150th Anniv of the Penny Black. T **240** and similar horiz designs. P 15×14.

1393	8r. black and olive-green	3·00	3·00
1394	12r. black and deep dull blue	3·50	3·50

MS1395 109×84 mm. 18r. black and yellow-brown ..... 6·00 7·00

Designs:—12r. As Type **240**, but with position of silhouettes reversed; 18r. Penny Black.

(Des Young Phillips Studio. Litho Questa)

1990 (8 July). 90th Birthday of Queen Elizabeth the Queen Mother. As T **240a** showing portraits, 1920–29. P 14.

1396	6r. Type **240a**	1·10	1·40
	a. Strip of 3. Nos. 1396/8	3·00	3·75
1397	6r. brownish blk, brt mag & turquoise-bl	1·10	1·40
1398	6r. brownish blk, brt mag & turquoise-bl	1·10	1·40
1396/98 *Set of 3*		3·00	3·75

MS1399 90×75 mm. 18r. multicoloured ..... 3·25 3·50

Designs:—No. 1396, Type **240a**; No. 1397, Lady Elizabeth Bowes-Lyon wearing headband; No. 1398 Lady Elizabeth Bowes-Lyon leaving for her wedding; No. **MS**1399, Lady Elizabeth Bowes-Lyon wearing wedding dress.

Nos. 1396/8 were printed together, horizontally and vertically se-tenant, in sheetlets of nine (3×3).

241 Sultan's Tomb　　　　**242** Defence of Wake Island, 1941

(Litho Questa)

1990 (21 July). Islamic Heritage Year. T **241** and similar horiz designs, each black and light cobalt. P 14.

1400	1r. Type **241**	35	45
	a. Block of 6. Nos. 1400/5	2·25	2·75
1401	1r. Thakurufaanu's Palace	35	45
1402	1r. Malé Mosque	35	45
1403	2r. Veranda of Friday Mosque	45	55
1404	2r. Interior of Friday Mosque	45	55
1405	2r. Friday Mosque and Monument	45	55
1400/5	Set of 6	2·25	2·75

Nos. 1400/5 were printed together, *se-tenant*, in blocks of six (3×2) within the sheet of 36.

(Des W. Wright. Litho Questa)

1990 (9 Aug). 50th Anniv of Second World War. T **242** and similar horiz designs. Multicoloured. P 14.

1406	15l. Type **242**	25	20
1407	25l. Stilwell's army in Burma, 1944	30	20
1408	50l. Normandy offensive, 1944	40	25
1409	1r. Capture of Saipan, 1944	55	40
1410	2r.50 D-Day landings, 1944	90	80
1411	3r.50 Allied landings in Norway, 1940	1·10	1·10
1412	4r. Lord Mountbatten, Head of Combined Operations, 1943	1·40	1·40
1413	6r. Japanese surrender, Tokyo Bay, 1945	2·75	3·25
1414	10r. Potsdam Conference, 1945	2·75	3·00
1415	12r. Allied invasion of Sicily, 1943	3·00	3·25
1406/15	Set of 10	11·00	11·50
MS1416	115×87 mm. 18r. Atlantic convoy	5·50	6·50

243 Crested Tern　　　　**244** Emblem, Dish Aerial and Sailboards

(Des Mary Walters. Litho Questa)

1990 (9 Aug). Birds. T **243** and similar horiz designs. Multicoloured. P 14.

1417	25l. Type **243**	15	15
1418	50l. Keel	25	25
1419	1r. White Tern	35	35
1420	3r.50 Cinnamon Bittern	90	1·00
1421	6r. Sooty Tern	1·40	1·60
1422	8r. Audubon's Shearwater	1·60	2·00
1423	12r. Common Noddy	2·50	3·00
1424	15r. Lesser Frigate Bird	2·75	3·25
1417/24	Set of 8	9·00	10·50
MS1425	Two sheets, each 100×69 mm. (a) 18r. Grey Heron. (b) 18r. White-tailed Tropic Bird *Set of 2 sheets*.	8·00	10·00

(Litho Questa)

1990 (21 Nov). Fifth South Asian Association for Regional Co-operation Summit. T **244** and similar horiz designs. P 14.

1426	75l. black and brown-orange	30	25
1427	3r.50 multicoloured	2·25	1·50
MS1428	112×82 mm. 20r. multicoloured	5·50	6·50

Designs:—3r.50, Flags of member nations; 20r. Global warming diagram.

245 Spathoglottis plicata　　　**246** The Hare and the Tortoise

(Des Dot Barlowe. Litho Questa)

1990 (9 Dec). "EXPO '90" International Garden and Greenery Exhibition, Osaka. Flowers. T **245** and similar multicoloured designs. P 14.

1429	20l. Type **245**	1·25	40
1430	75l. Hippeastrum puniceum	1·50	50
1431	2r. Tecoma stans (horiz)	1·60	90
1432	3r.50 Catharanthus roseus (horiz)	1·60	1·60
1433	10r. Ixora coccinea (horiz)	3·00	3·25
1434	12r. Clitorea ternatea (horiz)	3·25	3·50
1435	15r. Caesalpinia pulcherrima	3·25	3·75
1429/35	Set of 7	14·00	12·50
MS1436	Four sheets, each 111×79 mm. (a) 20r. Plumeria obtusa (horiz). (b) 20r. Jasminum grandiflorum (horiz). (c) 20r. Rosa sp (horiz). (d) 20r. Hibiscus tiliaceous (horiz) Set of 4 sheets	13·00	13·00

(Des Walt Disney Co. Litho Questa)

1990 (11 Dec). International Literacy Year. T **246** and similar multicoloured designs showing Walt Disney cartoon characters illustrating fables by Aesop. P 14×13½.

1437	15l. Type **246**	35	15
1438	50l. The Town Mouse and the Country Mouse	60	25
1439	1r. The Fox and the Crow	90	35
1440	3r.50 The Travellers and the Bear	1·75	1·60
1441	4r. The Fox and the Lion	1·90	1·75
1442	6r. The Mice Meeting	2·50	2·50
1443	10r. The Fox and the Goat	3·00	3·00
1444	12r. The Dog in the Manger	3·00	3·50
1437/44	Set of 8	12·50	12·00
MS1445	Two sheets, each 127×102 mm. (a) 20r. The Miller, his Son and the Ass (vert). (b) 20r. The Miser's Gold (vert). P 13½×14 Set of 2 sheets	13·00	13·00

247 East African Railways Class 31 Steam Locomotive　　　**248** Ruud Gullit of Holland

(Des T. Agans. Litho Questa)

1990 (15 Dec). Railway Steam Locomotives. T **247** and similar vert designs. Multicoloured. P 14.

1446	20l. Type **247**	85	30
1447	50l. Steam locomotive, Sudan	1·10	45
1448	1r. Class GM Garratt, South Africa	1·60	60
1449	3r. 7th Class, Rhodesia	2·50	2·00
1450	5r. No. 229, Central Pacific Class, U.S.A.	3·00	2·25
1451	8r. Reading Railroad No. 415, U.S.A.	3·50	3·00
1452	10r. Porter narrow gauge, Canada	3·50	3·00
1453	12r. Great Northern Railway No. 515, U.S.A.	3·50	3·50
1446/53	Set of 8	17·00	13·50
MS1454	Two sheets, each 90×65 mm. (a) 20r. 19th-century standard American locomotive No. 315. (b) 20r. East African Railways Garratt locomotive No. 5950 Set of 2 sheets	17·00	16·00

(Des Young Phillips Studio. Litho Questa)

1990 (27 Dec). World Cup Football Championship, Italy. T **248** and similar multicoloured designs. P 14.

1455	1r. Type **248**	1·50	50
1456	2r.50 Paul Gascoigne of England	2·25	1·25
1457	3r.50 Brazilian challenging Argentine player	2·25	1·60
1458	5r. Brazilian taking control of ball	2·50	2·00
1459	7r. Italian and Austrian jumping for header	3·25	3·25
1460	10r. Russian being chased by Turkish player	3·50	3·50
1461	15r. Andres Brehme of West Germany	4·00	4·50
1455/61	Set of 7	17·00	15·00
MS1462	Four sheets, each 77×92 mm. (a) 18r. Head of an Austrian player (horiz). (b) 18r. Head of a South Korean player (horiz). (c) 20r. Diego Maradonna of Argentina (horiz). (d) 20r. Schilacci of Italy (horiz) Set of 4 sheets	17·00	17·00

249 Winged
Euonymus

250 "Summer" (Rubens)

(Des N. Waldman. Litho Questa)

1991 (29 Jan). Bonsai Trees and Shrubs. T **249** and similar vert designs. Multicoloured. P 14.

1463	20l. Type **249**	50	20
1464	50l. Japanese Black Pine	65	35
1465	1r. Japanese Five Needle Pine	90	55
1466	3r.50 Flowering Quince	2·00	1·75
1467	5r. Chinese Elm	2·50	2·50
1468	8r. Japanese Persimmon	2·75	3·00
1469	10r. Japanese Wisteria	2·75	3·00
1470	12r. Satsuki Azalea	2·75	3·25
1463/70 *Set of 8*		13·50	13·00

MS1471 Two sheets, each 89×88 mm. (a) 20r. Trident Maple. (b) 20r. Sargent Juniper *Set of 2 sheets* .... 12·00 14·00

(Litho Questa)

1991 (7 Feb). 350th Death Anniv of Rubens. T **250** and similar horiz designs. Multicoloured. P 14×13½.

1472	20l. Type **250**	25	15
1473	50l. "Landscape with Rainbow" (detail)	40	25
1474	1r. "Wreck of Aeneas"	65	40
1475	2r.50 "Chateau de Steen" (detail)	1·25	1·00
1476	3r.50 "Landscape with Herd of Cows"	1·50	1·25
1477	7r. "Ruins on the Palantine"	2·50	2·75
1478	10r. "Landscape with Peasants and Cows"	2·75	3·00
1479	12r. "Wagon fording Stream"	3·00	3·50
1472/79 *Set of 8*		11·00	11·00

MS1480 Four sheets, each 100×71 mm. (a) 20r. "Landscape at Sunset". (b) 20r. "Peasants with Cattle by a Stream". (c) 20r. "Shepherd with Flock". (d) 20r. "Wagon in Stream" *Set of 4 sheets*..................... 15·00 16·00

251 Greek Messenger
from Marathon, 490
BC (2480th anniv)

252 Arctic Iceberg and Maldives
Dhoni

(Des W. Wright. Litho Questa)

1991 (11 Mar). Anniversaries and Events (1990). T **251** and similar multicoloured designs. P 14.

1481	50l. Type **251**	45	25
1482	1r. Anthony Fokker in Haarlem Spin monoplane (birth cent).	1·00	45
1483	3r.50 "Early Bird" satellite (25th anniv)	1·50	1·50
1484	7r. Signing Reunification of Germany agreement (*horiz*)	1·75	2·50
1485	8r. King John signing *Magna Carta* (775th anniv)	2·75	2·50
1486	10r. Dwight D. Eisenhower (birth cent)	2·25	2·75
1487	12r. Sir Winston Churchill (25th death anniv)	5·00	4·50
1488	15r. Pres. Reagan at Berlin Wall (German reunification) (*horiz*)	3·00	4·50
1481/88 *Set of 8*		16·00	17·00

MS1489 Two sheets. (a) 180×81 mm. 20r. German Junkers Ju88 bomber (50th anniv of Battle of Britain) (*horiz*). (b) 160×73 mm. 20r. Brandenburg Gate (German reunification) (*horiz*) *Set of 2 sheets* ... 14·00 14·00

(Litho Questa)

1991 (10 Apr). Global Warming. T **252** and similar horiz design. Multicoloured. P 14.

1490	3r.50 Type **252**	2·00	1·25
1491	7r. Antarctic iceberg and *Maldive Trader* (freighter)	4·50	4·25

253 S.A.A.R.C.
Emblem and Medal

254 Children on Beach

(Litho Questa)

1991 (10 Apr). Year of the Girl Child. P 14.

1492	**253**	7r. multicoloured	1·75	2·00

(Litho Questa)

1991 (14 Apr). Year of the Maldivian Child. Children's Paintings. T **254** and similar horiz designs. Multicoloured. P 14.

1493	3r.50 Type **254**	2·25	1·40
1494	5r. Children in a park	2·75	2·25
1495	10r. Hungry child dreaming of food	3·75	4·25
1496	25r. Scuba diver	7·00	12·00
1493/96 *Set of 4*		14·00	18·00

255 "Still Life: Japanese Vase
with Roses and Anemones"
(Van Gogh)

255a Queen at Trooping the
Colour, 1990

(Litho Walsall)

1991 (6 June). Death Centenary of Vincent van Gogh (artist) (1990). T **255** and similar multicoloured designs. P 13½.

1497	15l. Type **255**	60	25
1498	20l. "Still Life: Red Poppies and Daisies"	60	25
1499	2r. "Vincent's Bedroom in Arles" (*horiz*)	2·00	90
1500	3r.50 "The Mulberry Tree" (*horiz*)	2·25	1·25
1501	7r. "Blossoming Chestnut Branches" (*horiz*)	3·25	3·25
1502	10r. "Peasant Couple going to Work" (*horiz*)	3·75	3·75
1503	12r. "Still Life: Pink Roses" (*horiz*)	4·00	4·25
1504	15r. "Child with Orange"	4·25	4·75
1497/1504 *Set of 8*		19·00	17·00

MS1505 Two sheets. (a) 77×101 mm. 25r. "Houses in Anvers" (70×94 *mm*). (b) 101×77 mm. 25r. "The Courtyard of the Hospital at Arles" (94×70 *mm*). Imperf. *Set of 2 sheets* .... 13·00 14·00

(Des D. Miller. Litho Walsall)

1991 (4 July). 65th Birthday of Queen Elizabeth II. As T **255a** and similar horiz designs. Multicoloured. P 14.

1506	2r. Type **255a**	1·60	60
1507	5r. Queen with Queen Mother and Princess Margaret, 1973	2·75	1·75
1508	8r. Queen and Prince Philip in open carriage, 1986	3·25	3·00
1509	12r. Queen at Royal Estates Ball	3·50	3·75
1506/9 *Set of 4*		10·00	8·00

MS1510 68×90 mm. 25r. Separate photographs of Queen and Prince Philip .... 5·75 6·50

(Des D. Miller. Litho Walsall)

1991 (4 July). Tenth Wedding Anniv of Prince and Princess of Wales. As T **255a**. Multicoloured. P 14.

1511	1r. Prince and Princess skiing, 1986	1·00	20
1512	3r.50 Separate photographs of Prince, Princess and sons	2·00	1·10
1513	7r. Prince Henry in Christmas play and Prince William watching polo	2·50	2·00
1514	15r. Princess Diana at Ipswich, 1990, and Prince Charles playing polo	3·75	3·75
1511/14 *Set of 4*		8·25	6·50

MS1515 68×90 mm. 25r. Prince and Princess of Wales in Hungary, and Princes William and Henry going to school .... 6·25 6·50

256 Boy painting

257 Class C57 Steam Locomotive

(Litho Questa)

1991 (25 July). Hummel Figurines. T **256** and similar vert designs. Multicoloured. P 14.

1516	10l. Type **256**	15	15
1517	25l. Boy reading at table	20	20
1518	50l. Boy with school satchel	30	30
1519	2r. Girl with basket	70	70
1520	3r.50 Boy reading	1·00	1·00
1521	8r. Girl and young child reading	2·25	2·50
1522	10r. School girls	2·25	2·50
1523	25r. School boys	4·75	6·50
1516/23	*Set of 8*	10·50	12·50

MS1524 Two sheets, each 97×127 mm. (a) 5r. As No. 1519; 5r. As No. 1520; 5r. As No. 1521; (b) 8r. As No. 1522; (b) 8r. As Type **256**; 8r. As No. 1517; 8r. As No. 1518; 8r. As No. 1523 *Set of 2 sheets* .... 9·00 11·00

(Litho B.D.T.)

1991 (25 Aug). "Phila Nippon '91" International Stamp Exhibition, Tokyo. Japanese Steam Locomotives. T **257** and similar multicoloured designs. P 14.

1525	1l. Type **257**	50	20
1526	25l. Class 6250 locomotive, 1915 (*horiz*)	75	30
1527	1r. Class D51, locomotive, 1936	1·25	40
1528	3r.50 Class 8620 locomotive, 1914 (*horiz*)	2·00	1·25
1529	5r. Class 10 locomotive, 1889 (*horiz*)	2·25	1·75
1530	7r. Class C61 locomotive, 1947	2·50	2·75
1531	10r. Class 9600 locomotive, 1913 (*horiz*)	2·50	3·00
1532	12r. Class D52 locomotive, 1943 (*horiz*)	2·75	3·50
1525/32	*Set of 8*	13·00	12·00

MS1533 Two sheets, each 118×80 mm. (a) 20r. Class C56 locomotive 1935 (*horiz*). (b) 20r. Class 1080 locomotive, 1925 (*horiz*) *Set of 2 sheets* .... 8·00 9·00

Rf.3.50

(257a)

258 *Salamis temora* and *Vanda caerulea*

1991 (? Oct). Nos. 1111/2 surch locally as T **257a**.

1533a	3r.50 on 2r.60 (No. 1111)	35·00
	ab. Surch double	65·00
1533b	3r.50 on 2r.70 (No. 1112)	

The precise issue date of Nos. 1533a/b is unknown, but the earliest reported is 28 October 1991.

(Litho Questa)

1991 (2 Dec). Butterflies and Flowers. T **258** and similar horiz designs. Multicoloured. P 14.

1534	10l. Type **258**	40	40
1535	25l. *Meneris tulbaghia* and *Incarvillea younghusbandii*	55	30
1536	50l. *Polyommatus icarus* and *Campsis grandiflora*	75	40
1537	2r. *Donnas plexippus* and *Thunbergia grandiflora*	1·25	90
1538	3r.50 *Colias interior* and *Medinilla magnifica*	1·75	1·75
1539	5r. *Ascalapha ordorata* and *Meconopsis horridula*	2·00	2·00
1540	8r. *Papilio memnon* and *Dillenia obovata*	2·50	3·00
1541	10r. *Precis octavia* and *Thespesia populnea*	3·00	10·50
1534/41	*Set of 8*	10·50	10·50

MS1542 Two sheets, each 100×70 mm. (a) 20r. *Bombax ceiba* and *Phyciodes tharos*. (b) 20r. *Amauris niavius* and *Bombax insigne* *Set of 2 sheets* .... 10·00 12·00

259 "H-II" Rocket

260 Williams "FW-07"

(Des K. Gromell. Litho Questa)

1991 (11 Dec). Japanese Space Programme. T **259** and similar multicoloured designs. P 14.

1543	15l. Type **259**	50	30
1544	20l. Projected "H-II" orbiting plane	50	30
1545	2r. Satellite "GMS-5"	1·25	75
1546	3r.50 Satellite "MOMO-1"	1·60	1·40
1547	7r. Satellite "CS-3"	2·50	2·75
1548	10r. Satellite "BS-2a, 2b"	2·75	3·00
1549	12r. "H-1" Rocket (*vert*)	3·00	3·50
1550	15r. Space Flier unit and U.S. space shuttle	3·00	3·50
1543/50	*Set of 8*	13·50	14·00

MS1551 Two sheets. (a) 116×85 mm. 20r. Dish aerial, Katsura Tracking Station (*vert*). (b) 85×116 mm. 20r. "M-3SII" rocket (*vert*) *Set of 2 sheets* .... 13·00 13·00

(Litho B.D.T.)

1991 (28 Dec). Formula 1 Racing Cars. T **260** and similar horiz designs. Multicoloured. P 14.

1552	20l. Type **260**	30	20
1553	50l. Brabham/BMW "BT50" turbo	45	30
1554	1r. Williams/Honda "FW-11"	60	45
1555	3r.50 Ferrari "312 T3"	1·25	1·25
1556	5r. Lotus/Honda "99T"	1·75	1·75
1557	7r. Benetton/Ford "B188"	2·00	2·25
1558	10r. Tyrrell "P34" six-wheeler	2·25	2·50
1559	21r. Renault "RE-30B" turbo	4·00	5·00
1552/59	*Set of 8*	11·50	12·50

MS1560 Two sheets, each 84×56 mm. (a) 25r. Brabham/BMW "BT50" turbo (*different*). (b) 25r. Ferrari "F189" *Set of 2 sheets* .... 16·00 13·00

261 "Testa Rosso", 1957

262 Franklin D. Roosevelt

(Litho Questa)

1991 (28 Dec). Ferrari Cars. T **261** and similar horiz designs. Multicoloured. P 14.

1561	5r. Type **261**	2·00	2·00
	a. Sheetlet of 9. Nos. 1561/9	16·00	16·00
1562	5r. "275GTB", 1966	2·00	2·00
1563	5r. "Aspirarta", 1951	2·00	2·00
1564	5r. "Testarossa"	2·00	2·00
1565	5r. Enzo Ferrari	2·00	2·00
1566	5r. "Dino 246", 1958	2·00	2·00
1567	5r. "Type 375", 1952	2·00	2·00
1568	5r. Nigel Mansell's Formula 1 racing car	2·00	2·00
1569	5r. "312T", 1975	2·00	2·00
1561/69	*Set of 9*	16·00	16·00

Nos. 1561/9 were printed together, *se-tenant*, in sheetlets of nine (3×3).

(Des R. Jung. Litho Questa)

1991 (30 Dec). 50th Anniv of Japanese Attack on Pearl Harbor. American War Leaders. T **262** and similar horiz designs. Multicoloured. P 14½.

1570	3r.50 Type **262**	1·75	1·50
	a. Sheetlet of 10. Nos. 1570/9	16·00	13·50
1571	3r.50 Douglas MacArthur and map of Philippines	1·75	1·50
1572	3r.50 Chester Nimitz and Pacific island	1·75	1·50
1573	3r.50 Jonathan Wainwright and barbed wire	1·75	1·50
1574	3r.50 Ernest King and U.S.S. *Hornet* (aircraft carrier)	1·75	1·50
1575	3r.50 Claire Chennault and Curtiss P-40B Tomahawk II fighters	1·75	1·50
1576	3r.50 William Halsey and U.S.S. *Enterprise* (aircraft carrier)	1·75	1·50
1577	3r.50 Marc Mitscher and U.S.S. *Hornet* (aircraft carrier)	1·75	1·50
1578	3r.50 James Doolittle and North American B-25B Mitchell bomber	1·75	1·50
1579	3r.50 Raymond Spruance and Douglas SBD Dauntless dive bomber	1·75	1·50
1570/79	*Set of 10*	16·00	13·50

Nos. 1570/9 were printed together, *se-tenant*, in sheetlets of ten with the stamps arranged in two horizontal strips of five separated by a gutter showing Japanese fighters attacking Pearl Harbor and Admiral Isoroku Yamamoto.

263 Brandenburg Gate and Postcard commemorating Berlin Wall

(Des L. Fried (Nos. 1580, 1583, 1585, 1597, **MS**1599b/d), J. Iskowitz (Nos. 1581/2, 1584, 1586/7, 1589, 1593, 1598, **MS**1599a,f). W. Hanson (Nos. 1594/5, **MS**1599e,h), W. Wright (others). Litho Questa)

1992 (30 Jan). Anniversaries and Events. T **263** and similar multicoloured designs. P 14.

1580	20l. Type **263**	25	20
1581	50l. Schwarzenburg Palace	1·40	40
1582	1r. Spa at Baden	1·75	40
1583	1r.75 Berlin Wall and man holding child	50	50
1584	2r. Royal Palace, Berlin	2·50	1·00
1585	4r. Demonstrator and border guards	1·10	1·25
1586	5r. Viennese masonic seal	4·50	2·25
1587	6r. De Gaulle and Normandy landings, 1944 (*vert*)	2·50	2·25
1588	6r. Lilienthal's signature and *Flugzeug Nr. 16* .	2·50	2·25
1589	7r. St. Marx	4·25	2·75
1590	7r. Trans-Siberian Railway Class VL80T electric locomotive No. 1406 (*vert*)	4·00	2·75
1591	8r. Kurt Schwitters (artist) and Landes museum	2·50	2·75
1592	9r. Map of Switzerland and man in Uri traditional costume	3·50	3·00
1593	10r. De Gaulle in Madagascar, 1958	2·50	3·00
1594	10r. Scouts exploring coral reef	2·50	3·00
1595	11r. Scout salute and badge (*vert*)	2·50	3·00
1596	12r. Trans-Siberian Railway steam locomotive	4·50	3·75
1597	15r. Imperial German badges	2·50	3·75
1598	20r. Josepsplatz, Vienna	6·00	6·00
1580/98 *Set of 19*		45·00	40·00

MS1599 Eight sheets. (a) 76×116 mm. 15r. General de Gaulle during Second World War (vert). (b) 101×72 mm. 18r. Ancient German helmet. (c) 101×72 mm. 18r. 19th-century shako. (d) 101×72 mm. 18r. Helmet of 1939. (e) 90×117 mm. 18r. Postcard of Lord Baden–Powell carried by rocket, 1937 (brownish grey, black and magenta) (*vert*). (f) 75×104 mm. 20r. Bust of Mozart (*vert*). (g) 115×85 mm. 20r. Trans-Siberian Railway Class P36 steam locomotive stopped at signal (57×43 *mm*). (h) 117×90 mm. 20r. Czechoslovakia 1918 10r. "Scout Post" stamp (*vert*) Set of 8 sheets .... 45·00 50·00

Anniversaries and Events:—Nos. 1580, 1583, 1585, 1597, **MS**1599b/d, Bicentenary of Brandenburg Gate, Berlin; Nos. 1581/2, 1584, 1586, 1589, 1598, **MS**1599f, Death bicentenary of Mozart (1991) Nos. 1587, 1593, **MS**1599a, Birth bicentenary of Charles de Gaulle (French statesman) (1990); No. 1588, Centenary of Otto Lilienthal's first gliding experiments; Nos. 1590, 1596, **MS**1599g, Centenary of Trans-Siberian Railway; No. 1591, 750th anniv of Hannover; No. 1592, 70th anniv of Swiss Confederation; Nos. 1594/5, **MS**1599e,h, 17th World Scout Jamboree, Korea.

264 Mickey Mouse on Flying Carpet, Arabia

(Des Walt Disney Co. Litho B.D.T.)

1992 (4 Feb). Mickey's World Tour. T **264** and similar multicoloured designs showing Walt Disney cartoon characters in different countries. P 13.

1600	25l. Type **264**	45	20

1601	50l. Goofy and Big Ben, Great Britain	55	25
1602	1r. Mickey wearing clogs, Netherlands	75	35
1603	2r. Pluto eating pasta, Italy	1·25	75
1604	3r. Mickey and Donald doing Mexican hat dance	1·40	1·25
1605	3r.50 Mickey, Goofy and Donald as tiki, New Zealand	1·40	1·40
1606	5r. Goofy skiing in Austrian Alps	1·50	1·50
1607	7r. Mickey and city gate, Germany	1·75	2·00
1608	10r. Donald as samurai, Japan	2·00	2·25
1609	12r. Mickey as heroic statue, Russia	2·25	2·75
1610	15r. Mickey, Donald, Goofy and Pluto as German band	2·50	3·00
1600/10 *Set of 11*		14·00	14·00

MS1611 Three sheets, each 83×104 mm. (a) 25r. Donald chasing leprechaun, Ireland (*horiz*). (b) 25r. Baby kangaroo surprising Pluto, Australia. (c) 25r. Mickey and globe *Set of 3 sheets* .... 13·00 14·00

265 Whimbrel   **265a** Palm Trees on Beach

(Des D. Delouise. Litho B.D.T. (6r.50+50, 30r., 40r.) or Questa (others))

1992 (17 Feb)–98. Birds. T **265** and similar vert designs. Multicoloured. P 13 (6r.50+50l., 30r., 40r.) or 14½ (others).

1612	10l. Type **265**	60	1·00
1613	25l. Great Egret	70	60
1614	50l. Grey Heron	75	65
1615	2r. Shag	1·60	75
1616	3r.50 Roseate Tern	1·75	85
1617	5r. Greenshank	2·25	1·10
1617a	6r.50 +50l. Egyptian Vulture (1.1.94)	3·50	3·50
1618	8r. Hoopoe	2·75	2·50
1619	10r. Black-shouldered Kite	2·75	2·50
1620	25r. Scarlet Ibis	4·50	4·25
1620a	30r. Peregrine Falcon (1.1.94)	5·50	5·00
1620b	40r. Black Kite (1.1.94)	6·50	6·50
1621	50r. Grey Plover	6·50	7·50
1621a	100r. Common Shoveler (26.10.98)	20·00	20·00
1612/21a *Set of 14*		55·00	50·00

Nos. 1617a, 1620a/b and 1621a are larger, 23×32 mm.

(Des D. Miller. Litho Questa)

1992 (3 Mar). 40th Anniv of Queen Elizabeth II's Accession. Multicoloured. P 14.

1622	1r. Type **265a**	60	25
1623	3r.50 Path leading to jetty	2·00	1·00
1624	7r. Tropical plant	2·75	2·75
1625	10r. Palm trees on beach (*different*)	3·00	3·25
1622/25 *Set of 4*		7·50	6·50

MS1626 Two sheets each 74×97 mm. (a) 18r. Dhow. (b) 18r. Palm trees on beach (*different*) Set of 2 sheets .... 14·00 12·00

266 Powder-blue Surgeonfish

(Litho B.D.T.)

1992 (23 Mar). Fish. T **266** and similar horiz designs. Multicoloured. P 14.

1627	7l. Type **266**	30	20
1628	20l. Catalufa	40	25
1629	50l. Yellow-finned Tuna	55	30
1630	1r. Twin-spotted Snapper	75	35
1631	3r.50 Hawaiian Squirrelfish	1·50	1·25
1632	5r. Picasso Triggerfish	2·00	2·00
1633	8r. Bennett's Butterflyfish	2·25	2·50
1634	10r. Parrotfish	2·50	2·75
1635	12r. Coral Hind	2·75	3·00
1636	15r. Skipjack Tuna	2·75	3·00
1627/36 *Set of 10*		14·00	14·00

MS1637 Four sheets, each 116×76 mm. (a) 20r. Thread-finned Butterflyfish. (b) 20r. Oriental Sweetlips. (c) 20r. Two-banded Anemonefish ("Clownfish"). (d) 20r. Clown Triggerfish *Set of 4 sheets* .... 13·00 15·00

266a Minnie Mouse in Court of Lions

267 Coastguard Patrol Boats

(Des Walt Disney Co. Litho Questa)

1992 (15 Apr). International Stamp Exhibitions. Multicoloured designs as T **266a** showing Walt Disney cartoon characters. P 13½×14.

(a) "Granada '92", Spain. The Alhambra

1638	2r. Type **266a**	90	70
1639	5r. Goofy in Lions Fountain	1·75	1·75
1640	8r. Mickey Mouse at the Gate of Justice	2·25	2·75
1641	12r. Donald Duck serenading Daisy at the Vermilion Towers	2·75	3·50
1638/41	*Set of 4*	7·00	7·75

MS1642 127×102 mm. 25r. Goofy pushing Mickey in wheelbarrow ... 5·50 6·00

(b) "World Columbian Stamp Expo '92". Chicago Landmarks

1643	1r. Mickey meeting Jean Baptiste du Sable (founder)	1·00	40
1644	3r.50 Donald Duck at Old Chicago Post Office	2·00	1·25
1645	7r. Donald at Old Fort Dearborn	3·00	2·75
1646	15r. Goofy in Field Museum of Natural History	4·00	4·50
1643/46	*Set of 4*	9·00	8·00

MS1647 127×102 mm. 25r. Mickey and Minnie Mouse at Columbian Exposition, 1893 *(horiz).* P 14×13½ ... 5·50 6·00

On No. 1646 the design is wrongly captioned as the Science and Industry Museum.

(Litho Questa)

1992 (21 Apr). Centenary of National Security Service. T **267** and similar horiz designs. Multicoloured. P 14.

1648	3r.50 Type **267**	2·50	1·25
1649	5r. Infantry in training	2·50	1·75
1650	10r. Aakoatey fort	2·75	3·00
1651	15r. Fire Service	11·00	10·00
1648/51	*Set of 4*	17·00	14·50

MS1652 100×68 mm. 20r. Ceremonial procession, 1892 ... 7·00 9·00

268 Flowers of the United States of America

269 *Laetiporus sulphureus*

(Des W. Wright. Litho Questa)

1992 (26 Apr). National Flowers. T **268** and similar multicoloured designs. P 14½.

1653	25l. Type **268**	50	30
1654	50l. Australia	70	30
1655	2r. England	1·60	1·10
1656	3r.50 Brazil	2·00	1·50
1657	5r. Holland	2·25	2·00
1658	8r. France	2·50	3·00
1659	10r. Japan	2·75	3·00
1660	15r. Africa	3·50	4·50
1653/60	*Set of 8*	14·00	14·00

MS1661 Two sheets, each 114×85 mm. (a) 25r. *Plumieria rubra, Classia fistula* and *Eugenia malaccensis* (57×43 mm). (b) 25r. *Bauhinia variegata, Catharanthus roseus* and *Plumieria alba* (57×43 mm). P 14 *Set of 2 sheets* ... 9·00 10·00

(Litho Walsall)

1992 (14 May). Fungi. T **269** and similar vert designs. Multicoloured. P 14.

1662	10l. Type **269**	30	30
1663	25l. *Coprinus atramentarius*	40	30
1664	50l. *Ganoderma lucidum*	60	40
1665	3r.50 *Russula aurata*	1·25	1·00
1666	5r. *Gifola umbellata* ("*Polyporus umbellatus*")	1·75	1·75
1667	8r. *Suillus grevillei*	2·25	2·50
1668	10r. *Clavaria zollingeri*	2·50	2·50
1669	25r. *Boletus edulis*	5·00	6·00
1662/69	*Set of 8*	12·50	13·00

MS1670 Two sheets, each 100×70 mm. (a) 25r. *Marasmius oreades*; (b) 25r. *Pycnoporus cinnabarinus* ("*Trametes cinnabarina*") *Set of 2 sheets* ... 12·00 13·00

269a Pole Vault

270 Hurdling

(Litho Questa)

1992 (1 June–5 Oct). Olympic Games, Albertville and Barcelona. (1st issue). Multicoloured designs as T **269a**. P 14.

1671	10l. Type **269a**	20	10
1672	25l. Men's pommel horse *(horiz)*	25	15
1673	50l. Men's shot put	30	25
1674	1r. Men's horizontal bar *(horiz)*	35	30
1675	2r. Men's triple jump *(horiz)*	80	65
1676	3r.50 Table tennis	1·10	1·10
1677	5r. Two-man bobsled (5 Oct)	1·40	1·40
1678	7r. Freestyle wrestling *(horiz)*	1·75	2·00
1679	8r. Freestyle ski jump (5 Oct)	1·75	2·00
1680	9r. Baseball	2·00	2·25
1681	10r. Women's cross-country Nordic skiing (5 Oct)	2·00	2·25
1682	12r. Men's 200 metres backstroke *(horiz)*	2·00	2·25
1671/82	*Set of 12*	12·50	13·00

MS1683 Three sheets. (a) 100×70 mm. 25r. Decathlon *(horiz).* (b) 100×70 mm. 25r. Women's slalom skiing *(horiz)* (5 Oct). (c) 70×100 mm. 25r. Men's figure skating (5 Oct) *Set of 3 sheets* ... 12·00 13·00

(Litho Walsall)

1992 (1 June). Olympic Games, Barcelona (2nd issue). T **270** and similar vert designs. Multicoloured. P 14.

1684	10l. Type **270**	10	10
1685	1r. Boxing	30	30
1686	3r.50 Women's sprinting	1·00	90
1687	5r. Discus	1·50	1·25
1688	7r. Basketball	4·50	2·75
1689	10r. Long-distance running	2·50	2·75
1690	12r. Aerobic gymnastics	2·50	3·25
1691	20r. Fencing	3·25	4·50
1684/91	*Set of 8*	14·00	14·00

MS1692 Two sheets, each 70×100 mm. (a) 25r. Olympic symbol and national flags. (b) 25r. Olympic symbol and flame *Set of 2 sheets* ... 8·50 9·00

271 Deinonychus

271a New York Public Library

(Des D. Ben-Ami. Litho Questa)

1992 (15 Sept). "Genova '92" International Thematic Stamp Exhibition. Prehistoric Animals. T **271** and similar vert designs. Multicoloured. P 14.

1693	5l. Type **271**	40	20
1694	10l. Styracosaurus	40	20
1695	25l. Mamenchisaurus	50	30
1696	50l. Stenonychosaurus	60	30

1697	1r. Parasaurolophus	75	40
1698	1r.25 Scelidosaurus	85	50
1699	1r.75 Tyrannosaurus	1·10	55
1700	2r. Stegosaurus	1·25	60
1701	3r.50 Iguanodon	1·50	80
1702	4r. Anatosaurus	1·50	1·00
1703	5r. Monoclonius	1·60	1·10
1704	7r. Tenontosaurus	1·90	1·90
1705	8r. Brachiosaurus	1·90	1·90
1706	10r. Euoplocephalus	2·00	2·00
1707	25r. Triceratops	3·25	4·50
1708	50r. Apatosaurus	6·00	8·00
1693/1708 Set of 16		23·00	22·00

MS1709 Four sheets, each 116×85 mm. (a) 25r. Hadrosaur hatchling. (b) 25r. Iguanodon fighting Allosaurus. (c) 25r. Tyrannosaurus attacking Triceratops. (d) 25r. Brachiosaurus and Iguanodons *Set of 4 sheets*... 15·00 16·00

(Des Kerri Schiff. Litho Questa)

1992 (28 Oct). Postage Stamp Mega Event, New York. Sheet 100×70 mm. P 14.
MS1710 20r. **271a** multicoloured.................. 2·50 3·50

272 Destruction of LZ-129 *Hindenburg* (airship), 1937

273 Zubin Mehta (musical director)

(Des K. Grommell. Litho B.D.T.)

1992 (28 Oct). Mysteries of the Universe. T **272** and similar multicoloured designs, each in separate miniature sheet. P 14.
MS1711 Sixteen sheets, each 100×71 mm. (a) 25r. Type **272**. (b) 25r. Loch Ness Monster. (c) 25r. Crystal skull. (d) 25r. Space craft in Black Hole. (e) 25r. Ghosts (*vert*). (t) 25r. Flying saucer, 1947 (*vert*). (g) 25r. Bust of Plato (Atlantis). (h) 25r. U.F.O, 1973. (i) 25r. Crop circles. (j) 25r. Mil Mi-26 Russian helicopter at Chernobyl nuclear explosion. (k) 25r. Figure from Plain of Nazca. (l) 25r. Stonehenge (*vert*). (m) 25r. Yeti footprint (*vert*). (n) 25r. The Pyramid of Giza. (o) 25r. *Marie Celeste* (brigantine) (*vert*). (p) 25r. American Grumman TBF Avenger fighter aircraft (Bermuda Triangle) *Set of 16 sheets*... 55·00 55·00

(Litho B.D.T.)

1992 (9 Nov). 150th Anniv of New York Philharmonic Orchestra. Sheet 100×70 mm. P 14.
MS1712 **273** 20r. multicoloured.................. 6·00 6·00

274 Friedrich Schmiedl

275 Goofy in Father's Weekend, 1953

(Litho B.D.T.)

1992 (1 Dec). 90th Birth Anniv of Friedrich Schmiedl (rocket mail pioneer). Sheet 104×69 mm. P 14½×14.
MS1713 **274** 25r. multicoloured.................. 5·50 6·50

(Des Walt Disney Co. Litho Questa)

1992 (7 Dec). 60th Anniv of Goofy (Disney cartoon character). T **275** and similar multicoloured designs showing Goofy in various cartoon films. P 14×13½ (horiz) or 13½×14 (vert).

1714	10l. Type **275**	10	10
1715	50l. *Symphony Hour*, 1942	35	20
1716	75l. *Frank Duck Brings 'Em Back Alive*, 1946..	45	20
1717	1r. *Crazy with the Heat*, 1947	45	20
1718	2r. *The Big Wash*, 1948	70	60
1719	3r.50 *How to Ride a Horse*, 1950	1·25	1·25
1720	5r. *Two Gun Goofy*, 1952	1·50	1·50
1721	8r. *Saludos Amigos*, 1943 (*vert*)	2·00	2·25

1722	10r. *How to be a Detective*, 1952	2·00	2·25
1723	12r. *For Whom the Bulls Toil*, 1953	2·25	2·50
1724	15r. *Double Dribble*, 1946 (*vert*)	2·25	2·50
1714/24 Set of 11		12·00	12·00

MS1725 Three sheets, each 127×102 mm. (a) 20r. *Double Dribble*, 1946 (*different*) (*vert*). (b) 20r. *The Goofy Success Story*, 1955 (*vert*). (c) 20r. *Mickey and the Beanstalk*, 1947 *Set of 3 sheets*.... 10·00 10·50

276 Minnie Mouse in "Le Missioner" (Toulouse-Lautrec)

(Des Euro-Disney, Paris. Litho Cartor)

1992 (7 Dec). Opening of Euro-Disney Resort, France. T **276** and similar multicoloured designs showing Disney cartoon characters superimposed on Impressionist paintings. P 14×13½.

1726	5r. Type **276**	1·50	1·75
	a. Sheetlet of 9. Nos. 1726/34	12·00	14·00
1727	5r. Goofy in "The Card Players" (Cezanne)..	1·50	1·75
1728	5r. Mickey and Minnie Mouse in "The Cafe Terrace, Place du Forum" (Van Gogh).....	1·50	1·75
1729	5r. Mickey in "The Bridge at Langlois" (Van Gogh)	1·50	1·75
1730	5r. Goofy in "Chocolate Dancing" (Toulouse-Lautrec)	1·50	1·75
1731	5r. Mickey and Minnie in "The Seine at Asnieres" (Renoir)	1·50	1·75
1732	5r. Minnie in Ball at the Moulin Rouge" (Toulouse-Lautrec)	1·50	1·75
1733	5r. Mickey Mouse in "Wheatfield with Cypresses" (Van Gogh)	1·50	1·75
1734	5r. Minnie in "When will you Marry?" (Gauguin)	1·50	1·75
1726/34 Set of 9		12·00	14·00

MS1735 Four sheets. (a) 128×100 mm. 20r. Minnie as can-can dancer. P 14×13½. (b) 128×100 mm. 20r. Goofy as cyclist. (c) 100×128 mm. 20r. Mickey as artist. P 14×13½. (d) 100×128 mm. 20r. Donald as Frenchman (*vert*). P 13½×14 *Set of 4 sheets* 12·00 14·00
Nos. 1726/34 were printed together, *se-tenant*, in sheetlets of nine.

277 Rivers

278 Jurgen Klinsmann (Germany)

(Litho Questa)

1992 (30 Dec). South Asian Association for Regional Co-operation Year of the Environment. T **277** and similar horiz designs showing natural and polluted environments. Multicoloured. P 14.

1736	25l. Type **277**	15	10
1737	50l. Beaches	25	10
1738	5r. Oceans	80	1·00
1739	10r. Weather	1·50	2·25
1736/39 Set of 4		2·40	3·00

(Litho Questa)

1993 (7 Jan). World Cup Football Championship, U.S.A. (1994) (1st issue). T **278** and similar multicoloured designs showing German players and officials. P 14.

1740	10l. Type **278**	40	20
1741	25l. Pierre Littbarski	45	20
1742	50l. Lothar Matthaus	55	20
1743	1r. Rudi Voller	75	25
1744	2r. Thomas Hassler	1·25	60
1745	3r.50 Thomas Berthold	1·60	1·00
1746	4r. Jurgen Kohler	1·75	1·25
1747	5r. Berti Vogts	1·90	1·40
1748	6r. Bodo Illgner	2·25	2·25
1749	7r. Klaus Augenthaler	2·25	2·25

1750	8r. Franz Beckenbauer	2·25	2·25
1751	10r. Andreas Brehme	2·50	2·75
1752	12r. Guido Buchwald	2·50	3·25
1740/52	Set of 13	18·00	16·00

MS1753 Two sheets, each 103×73 mm. (a) 35r. German players celebrating (horiz). (b) 35r. Rudi Voller (horiz) Set of 2 sheets .... 13·00 14·00
See also Nos. 1990/MS1998 and 2089/MS2101.

279 German Navy Airship L-13 bombing London, 1914–18

280 Elvis Presley

(Des W. Wright and W. Hanson (Nos. 1754, 1766, MS1767a), W. Wright (others). Litho B.D.T.)

1993 (7 Jan). Anniversaries and Events. T **279** and similar horiz designs. Multicoloured. P. 14.

1754	1r. Type **279**	1·25	50
1755	3r.50 Radio telescope	70	1·00
1756	3r.50 Chancellor Adenauer and Pres De Gaulle	70	1·00
1757	6r. Indian Rhinoceros	6·00	2·50
1758	6r. Columbus and globe	3·25	2·00
1759	7r. Conference emblems	1·50	2·00
1760	8r. Green Seaturtle	1·75	2·00
1761	10r. America (yacht), 1851	1·75	2·25
1762	10r. Melvin Jones (founder) and emblem	1·75	2·25
1763	12r. Columbus landing on San Salvador	3·75	3·75
1764	15r. "Voyager I" approaching Saturn	6·00	6·00
1765	15r. Adenauer, N.A.T.O. flag and Lockheed F-1046 Starfighter aircraft	6·00	6·00
1766	20r. Graf Zeppelin over New York, 1929	6·00	6·00
1754/66	Set of 13	35·00	32·00

MS1767 Five sheets, each 111×80 mm. (a) 20r. Count Ferdinand von Zeppelin. (b) 20r. "Landsat" satellite. (c) 20r. Konrad Adenauer. (d) 20r. Scarlet Macaw. (e) 20r. Santa Maria Set of 5 sheets .... 25·00 30·00
Anniversaries and Events:—Nos. 1754, 1766, MS1767a, 75th death anniv of Count Ferdinand von Zeppelin; Nos. 1755, 1764, MS1767b, International Space Year; Nos. 1756. 1765, MS1767c, 25th death anniv of Konrad Adenauer; Nos. 1757, 1760, MS1767d, Earth Summit '92, Rio; Nos. 1758, 1763, MS1767e, 500th anniv of Discovery of America by Columbus; No. 1759, International Conference on Nutrition, Rome; No. 1761, Americas Cup Yachting Championship; No. 1762, 75th anniv of International Association of Lions Clubs.

(Des A. Nahigian. Litho Questa)

1993 (7 Jan). 15th Death Anniv of Elvis Presley (singer). T **280** and similar vert designs. Multicoloured. P. 14.

1768	3r.50 Type **280**	90	70
	a. Strip of 3. Nos. 1768/70	2·50	1·90
1769	3r.50 Elvis with guitar	90	70
1770	3r.50 Elvis with microphone	90	70
1768/70	Set of 3	2·50	1·90

Nos. 1768/70 were printed together, horizontally and vertically se-tenant, in sheetlets of nine (3×3).

L'ETUDE
FRAGONARD

280a "The Study" (Fragonard)

(Litho Walsall)

1993 (7 Jan). Bicentenary of the Louvre, Paris. Multicoloured. P. 12.

1771	8r. Type **280a**	95	1·10
	a. Sheetlet of 8. Nos. 1771/8	7·00	8·00
1772	8r. "Denis Diderot" (Fragonard)	95	1·10

1773	8r. "Marie-Mádélaine Guimard" (Fragonard)	95	1·10
1774	8r. "Inspiration" (Fragonard)	95	1·10
1775	8r. "Waterfalls, Tivoli" (Fragonard)	95	1·10
1776	8r. "The Music Lesson" (Fragonard)	95	1·10
1777	8r. "The Bolt" (Fragonard)	95	1·10
1778	8r. "Blind-man's Buff" (Fragonard)	95	1·10
1779	8r. "Self-portrait" (Corot)	95	1·10
	a. Sheetlet of 8. Nos. 1779/86	7·00	8·00
1780	8r. "Woman in Blue" (Corot)	95	1·10
1781	8r. "Woman with a Pearl" (Corot)	95	1·10
1782	8r. "Young Girl at her Toilet" (Corot)	95	1·10
1783	8r. "Haydee" (Corot)	95	1·10
1784	8r. "Chartres Cathedral" (Corot)	95	1·10
1785	8r. "The Belfry of Douai" (Corot)	95	1·10
1786	8r. "The Bridge of Mantes" (Corot)	95	1·10
1787	8r. "Madame Sériziat" (David)	95	1·10
	a. Sheetlet of 8. Nos. 1787/94	7·00	8·00
1788	8r. "Pierre Sériziat" (David)	95	1·10
1789	8r. "Madame De Verninac" (David)	95	1·10
1790	8r. "Madame Récamier" (David)	95	1·10
1791	8r. "Self-portrait" (David)	95	1·10
1792	8r. "General Bonaparte" (David)	95	1·10
1793	8r. "The Lictors bringing Brutus his Son's Body" (David) (left detail)	95	1·10
1794	8r. "The Lictors bringing Brutus his Son's Body" (David) (right detail)	95	1·10
1771/94	Set of 24	21·00	24·00

MS1795 Two sheets, each 100×70 mm. (a) 20r. "Gardens of the Villa D'Este, Tivoli" (Corot) (85×52 mm). (b) 20r. "Tiger Cub playing with its Mother" (Delacroix) (85×52 mm). P 14½ Set of 2 sheets .... 8·50 8·50
Nos. 1771/8, 1779/86 and 1787/94 were each printed together, se-tenant, in sheetlets of eight stamps and one centre label.

281 James Stewart and Marlene Dietrich (Destry Rides Again)

(Des P. Wolff and D. Lewis. Litho Questa)

1993 (18 Jan). Famous Western Films. T **281** and similar vert designs. Multicoloured. P 13½×14.

1796	5r. Type **281**	1·50	1·10
	a. Sheetlet of 8. Nos. 1796/1803	11·00	8·00
1797	5r. Gary Cooper (The Westerner)	1·50	1·10
1798	5r. Henry Fonda (My Darling Clementine)	1·50	1·10
1799	5r. Alan Ladd (Shane)	1·50	1·10
1800	5r. Kirk Douglas and Burt Lancaster (Gunfight at the O.K. Corral)	1·50	1·10
1801	5r. Steve McQueen (The Magnificent Seven)	1·50	1·10
1802	5r. Robert Redford and Paul Newman (Butch Cassidy and The Sundance Kid)	1·50	1·10
1803	5r. Jack Nicholson and Randy Quaid (The Missouri Breaks)	1·50	1·10
1796/1803	Set of 8	11·00	8·00

MS1804 Two sheets, each 134×120 mm. (a) 20r. John Wayne (The Searchers) (French poster). (b) 20r. Clint Eastwood (Pale Rider) (French poster) Set of 2 sheets .... 9·00 7·50
Nos. 1796/1803 were printed together, se-tenant, in sheetlets of eight.

Coronation Anniversary
1953-1993

281a Queen Elizabeth II at Coronation (photograph by Cecil Beaton)

(Des Kerri Schiff. Litho Questa)

1993 (2 June). 40th Anniv of Coronation. As T **281a** and similar vert designs. P 13½×14.

1805	3r.50 multicoloured	1·00	1·10
	a. Sheetlet of 8. Nos. 1805/8×2	9·50	11·00
1806	5r. multicoloured	1·25	1·40
1807	10r. indigo and black	1·50	1·75
1808	10r. indigo and black	1·50	1·75
1805/8	Set of 4	4·75	5·50

Designs:—No. 1805 Type **281a**; No. 1806 St. Edward's Crown; No. 1807, Guests in the Abbey; No. 1808, Queen Elizabeth II and Prince Philip.

Nos. 1805/8 were printed together in sheetlets of eight, containing two *se-tenant* blocks of four.

282 Blue Goatfish

283 Gull-billed Tern

(Des S. Barlowe. Litho Cartor)

1993 (30 June). Fish. T **282** and similar multicoloured designs. P 14×13½.

1809	3r.50 Type **282**	60	70
	a. Sheetlet of 12. Nos. 1809/20	6·50	7·50
1810	3r.50 Emperor Angelfish	60	70
1811	3r.50 Madagascar Butterflyfish	60	70
1812	3r.50 Regal Angelfish	60	70
1813	3r.50 Forceps Butterflyfish ("Longnose Butterflyfish")	60	70
1814	3r.50 Racoon Butterflyfish	60	70
1815	3r.50 Harlequin Filefish	60	70
1816	3r.50 Rectangle Triggerfish	60	70
1817	3r.50 Yellow-tailed Anemonefish	60	70
1818	3r.50 Clown Triggerftsh	60	70
1819	3r.50 Zebra Lionfish	60	70
1820	3r.50 Maldive Anemonefish ("Clown fish")	60	70
1821	3r.50 Black-faced Butterflyfish	60	70
	a. Sheetlet of 12. Nos. 1821/32	6·50	7·50
1822	3r.50 Bird Wrasse	60	70
1823	3r.50 Checkerboard Wrasse	60	70
1824	3r.50 Yellow-faced Angelfish	60	70
1825	3r.50 Masked Bannerfish	60	70
1826	3r.50 Thread-finned Butterflyfish	60	70
1827	3r.50 Picasso Triggerfish	60	70
1828	3r.50 Pennant Coralfish ("Pennantfish")	60	70
1829	3r.50 Coral Hind ("Grouper")	60	70
1830	3r.50 Black-backed Butterflyfish	60	70
1831	3r.50 Red-toothed Triggerfish	60	70
1832	3r.50 Melon Butterflyfish	60	70
1809/32	Set of 24	13·00	15·00

MS1833 Two sheets. (a) 69×96 mm. 25r. Klein's Butterflyfish (*vert*). (b) 96×69 mm. 25r. Brown Anemonefish (*vert*). P 12×13 *Set of 2 sheets* ... 8·00 · 8·50

Nos. 1809/20 and 1821/32 were printed together, *se-tenant*, in sheetlets of 12 with the backgrounds forming composite designs.

Nos. 1810, 1812 and 1824 are both inscribed "Anglefish" in error.

(Des S. Barlowe. Litho Cartor)

1993 (5 July). Birds. T **283** and similar multicoloured designs. P 14×13½ (horiz) or 13½×14 (vert).

1834	3r.50 Type **283**	65	70
	a. Sheetlet of 12. Nos. 1834/45	7·00	7·50
1835	3r.50 White-tailed Tropic Bird	65	70
1836	3r.50 Great Frigate Bird	65	70
1837	3r.50 Wilson's Petrel	65	70
1838	3r.50 White Tern	65	70
1839	3r.50 Brown Booby	65	70
1840	3r.50 Marsh Harrier	65	70
1841	3r.50 Common Noddy	65	70
1842	3r.50 Green Heron ("Little Heron")	65	70
1843	3r.50 Turnstone	65	70
1844	3r.50 Curlew	65	70
1845	3r.50 Crab Plover	65	70
1846	3r.50 Pallid Harrier (*vert*)	65	70
	a. Sheetlet of 12. Nos. 1846/57	7·00	7·50
1847	3r.50 Cattle Egret (*vert*)	65	70
1848	3r.50 Koel (*vert*)	65	70
1849	3r.50 Tree Pipit (*vert*)	65	70
1850	3r.50 Short-eared Owl (*vert*)	65	70
1851	3r.50 Common Kestrel ("European Kestrel") (*vert*)	65	70
1852	3r.50 Yellow Wagtail (*vert*)	65	70
1853	3r.50 Grey Heron ("Common Heron") (*vert*)	65	70
1854	3r.50 Black Bittern (*vert*)	65	70
1855	3r.50 Common Snipe (*vert*)	65	70
1856	3r.50 Little Egret (*vert*)	65	70
1857	3r.50 Little Stint (*vert*)	65	70
1834/57	Set of 24	14·00	15·00

MS1858 Two sheets, each 105×75 mm. (a) 25r. Caspian Tern. (b) 25r. Audubon's Shearwater P 13×12 *Set of 2 sheets* ... 8·50 · 9·00

Nos. 1834/45 and 1846/57 were printed together, *se-tenant*, in sheetlets of 12 with the backgrounds forming composite designs.

284 Precious Wentletrap (*Epitonium scalare*)

285 Sifaka Lemur

(Litho Questa)

1993 (15 July). Shells. T **284** and similar vert designs. Multicoloured. P 14.

1859	7l. Type **284**	30	30
1860	15l. Common Purple Janthina (*Janthina janthina*)	35	30
1861	50l. Asiatic Arabian Cowrie (*Cypraea arabica asiatica*)	45	30
1862	3r.50 Common or Major Harp (*Harpa major*)	1·50	1·00
1863	4r. Amplustre or Royal Paper Bubble (*Aplustrum amplustre*)	1·75	1·25
1864	5r. Sieve Cowrie (*Cypraea cribraria*)	1·75	1·40
1865	6r. Episcopal Mitre (*Mitra mitra*)	2·00	2·00
1866	7r. Camp Pitar Venus (*Lioconcha castrensis*)	2·00	2·25
1867	8r. Spotted or Eyed Auger (*Terebra guttata*)	2·25	2·50
1868	10r. Exposed Cowrie (*Cypraea succincta*)	2·50	2·50
1869	12r. Geographic Map Cowrie (*Cypraea mappa geographus*)	2·75	3·50
1870	20r. Bramble Murex (*Murex tribulus*)	3·50	4·50
1859/70	Set of 12	19·00	20·00

MS1871 Three sheets, each 104×75 mm. (a) 25r. Black-striped Triton (*Cymatium hepaticum*). (b) 25r. Scorpion Conch (*Lambis scorpio*). (c) 25r. Bull-mouth Helmet (*Cypraecassis rufa*) *Set of 3 sheets* ... 17·00 · 19·00

(Litho Questa)

1993 (20 July). Endangered Species. T **285** and similar vert designs. Multicoloured. P 14.

1872	7l. Type **285**	50	30
1873	10l. Snow Leopard	50	30
1874	15l. Numbat	50	30
1875	25l. Gorilla	90	40
1876	2r. Koala	1·10	70
1877	3r.50 Cheetah	1·25	1·10
1878	5r. Yellow-footed Rock Wallaby	1·40	1·40
1879	7r. Orang-Utan	2·25	2·25
1880	8r. Black Lemur	2·25	2·25
1881	10r. Black Rhinoceros	4·00	3·00
1882	15r. Humpback Whale	5·00	4·00
1883	20r. Mauritius Parakeet	5·50	4·50
1872/83	Set of 12	22·00	18·00

MS1884 Three sheets, each 104×75 mm. (a) 25r. Giant Panda. (b) 25r. Tiger. (c) 25r. Indian Elephant *Set of 3 sheets* ... 17·00 · 19·00

286 Symbolic Heads and Arrows

287 Early Astronomical Equipment

(Litho Questa)

1993 (25 July). Productivity Year. T **286** and similar vert design. Multicoloured. P 14.

1885	7r. Type **286**	1·25	1·40
1886	10r. Abstract	1·60	1·75

(Des Kerri Schiff (Nos. 1890, 1894, 1896, 1898, **MS**1899d/e). Litho Questa)

1993 (11 Oct). Anniversaries and Events. T **287** and similar multicoloured designs. P 14.

1887	3r.50 Type **287**	1·00	1·00
1888	3r.50 "Still Life with Pitcher and Apples" (Picasso)	1·00	1·00
1889	3r.50 "Zolte Raze" (Menasze Seiden-beurel)	1·00	1·00
1890	3r.50 Prince Naruhito and engagement photographs (*horiz*)	1·00	1·00
1891	5r. "Bowls and Jug" (Picasso)	1·25	1·25
1892	5r. Krysztofory Palace, Cracow	1·25	1·25
1893	8r. "Jabtka i Kotara" (Waclaw Borowski)	1·75	1·90
1894	8r. Marina Kiehl (Germany) (women's downhill skiing)	1·75	1·90
1895	10r. "Bowls of Fruit and Loaves on a Table" (Picasso)	1·90	2·00
1896	10r. Masaka Owada and engagement photographs (*horiz*)	1·90	2·00
1897	15r. American astronaut in space	2·75	3·00
1898	15r. Vegard Ulvang (Norway) (30km cross-country skiing)	2·75	3·00
1887/98	*Set of 12*	17·00	18·00

MS1899 Five sheets. (a) 105×75 mm. 20r. Copernicus. (b) 105×75 mm. 20r. "Green Still Life" (detail) (Picasso) (*horiz*). (c) 105×75 mm. 25r. "Pejzaz Moraki-Port z Doplywajacym Ststkiem" (detail) (Roman Sielski) (*horiz*). (d) 75×105 mm. 25r. Masako Owada. (e) 105×105 mm. 25r. Ice hockey goalkeeper *Set of 5 sheets*........ 21·00 23·00

Anniversaries and Events:—Nos. 1887, 1897, **MS**1899a, 450th death anniv of Copernicus (astronomer); Nos. 1888, 1891, 1895, **MS**1899b, 20th death anniv of Picasso (artist); Nos. 1889, 1892/3, **MS**1899c, "Polska '93" International Stamp Exhibition, Poznan; Nos. 1890, 1896, **MS**1899d, Marriage of Crown Prince Naruhito of Japan; Nos. 1894, 1898, **MS**1899e, Winter Olympic Games '94, Lillehammer.

288 *Limenitis procris* and *Mussaenda*

289 Airship LZ-127 *Graf Zeppelin* in Searchlights

(Des Tracy Pedersen. Litho B.D.T.)

1993 (25 Oct). Butterflies and Flowers. T **288** and similar multicoloured designs. P 14.

1900	7l. Type **288**	40	20
1901	20l. *Danaus limniace* and *Thevetia neriifolia*	55	20
1902	25l. *Amblypodia centaurus* and *Clitoria ternatea*	55	20
1903	50l. *Papilio crino* and *Crossandra infundibuliformis*	90	20
1904	5r. *Mycalesis patnia* and *Thespesia populnia*	2·00	1·40
1905	6r.50+50l. *Idea jasonia* and *Cassia glauca*	2·25	2·50
1906	7r. *Catopsilia pomona* and *Calotropis*	2·25	2·50
1907	10r. *Precis orithyia* and *Thunbergia grandiflora*	2·75	2·75
1908	12r. *Vanessa cardui* and *Caesalpinia pulcherrima*	3·00	3·50
1909	15r. *Papilio polymnestor* and *Nerium oleander*	3·25	3·75
1910	18r. *Cirrochroa thais* and *Vinca rosea*	3·50	4·00
1911	20r. *Pachliopta hector* and *Ixora coccinea*	3·50	4·00
1900/11	*Set of 12*	22·00	23·00

MS1912 Three sheets, each 105×72 mm. (a) 25r. *Cheritra freja* and *Bauhinia purpurea* (*vert*). (b) 25r. *Rohana parisatis* and *Plumeria acutifolia* (*vert*). (c) 25r. *Hebomoia glaucippe* and *Punica granatum* (*vert*) *Set of 3 sheets* .... 15·00 17·00

(Litho Walsall)

1993 (22 Nov). Aviation Anniversaries. T **289** and similar multicoloured designs. P 14.

1913	3r.50 Type **289**	2·00	65

1914	5r. Homing pigeon and message from Santa Catalina mail service, 1894	2·25	1·10
1915	10r. Eckener and airship LZ-27 *Graf Zeppelin*	2·75	2·50
1916	15r. Pilot's badge and loading Philadelphia-Washington mail, 1918	4·00	4·25
1917	20r. U.S.S. *Macon* (airship) and mooring mast, 1933	4·00	4·25
1913/17	*Set of 5*	13·50	11·50

MS1918 Two sheets. (a) 70×100 mm. 25r. Santos Dumont's airship Balloon No. 5 and Eiffel Tower. 1901. (b) 100×70 mm. 25r. Jean-Pierre Blanchard's balloon, 1793 (*vert*). *Set of 2 sheets* .... 9·00 9·00

Anniversaries:—Nos. 1913, 1915, 1917, **MS**1918a, 125th birth anniv of Hugo Eckener (airship pioneer); Nos. 1914, 1916, **MS**1918b, Bicent of First Airmail Flight.

290 Ford Model "T"

(Litho Questa)

1993 (22 Nov). Centenaries of Henry Ford's First Petrol Engine (Nos. 1919/30, **MS**1943a) and Karl Benz's First Four-wheeled Car (others). T **290** and similar horiz designs. P 14.

1919	3r.50 multicoloured	90	1·00
	a. Sheetlet of 12. Nos. 1919/30	9·50	10·50
1920	3r.50 multicoloured	90	1·00
1921	3r.50 black and reddish violet	90	1·00
1922	3r.50 multicoloured	90	1·00
1923	3r.50 multicoloured	90	1·00
1924	3r.50 multicoloured	90	1·00
1925	3r.50 multicoloured	90	1·00
1926	3r.50 multicoloured	90	1·00
1927	3r.50 multicoloured	90	1·00
1928	3r.50 multicoloured	90	1·00
1929	3r.50 multicoloured	90	1·00
1930	3r.50 black, light brown and reddish violet	90	1·00
1931	3r.50 multicoloured	90	1·00
	a. Sheetlet of 12. Nos. 1931/42	9·50	10·50
1932	3r.50 multicoloured	90	1·00
1933	3r.50 greenish black, black and reddish violet	90	1·00
1934	3r.50 multicoloured	90	1·00
1935	3r.50 multicoloured	90	1·00
1936	3r.50 multicoloured	90	1·00
1937	3r.50 multicoloured	90	1·00
1938	3r.50 multicoloured	90	1·00
1939	3r.50 multicoloured	90	1·00
1940	3r.50 multicoloured	90	1·00
1941	3r.50 multicoloured	90	1·00
1942	3r.50 black, light brown and reddish violet	90	1·00
1919/42	*Set of 24*	19·00	21·00

MS1943 Two sheets, each 100×70 mm. (a) 25r. multicoloured. (b) 25r. multicoloured *Set of 2 sheets* .... 9·00 10·00

Designs:—No. 1920, Henry Ford; No. 1921, Plans of first petrol engine; No. 1922, Ford "Probe GT", 1993; No. 1923, Front of Ford "Sportsman", 1947; No. 1924, Back of Ford "Sportsman"; No. 1925, Advertisement of 1915; No. 1926, Ford "Thunderbird", 1955; No. 1927, Ford logo; No. 1928 Ford "Edsel Citation", 1958; No. 1929, Ford half-ton pickup, 1941; No. 1930, Silhouette of early Ford car; No. 1931 Daimler-Benz "Straight 8", 1937; No. 1932, Karl Benz; No. 1933, Mercedes-Benz poster; No. 1934, Mercedes "38-250SS", 1929; No. 1935, Benz "Viktoria", 1893; No. 1936, Benz logo; No. 1937 Plan of Mercedes engine No. 1938, Mercedes-Benz "300SL Gullwing", 1952; No. 1939, Mercedes-Benz "SL", 1993; No. 1940 Front of Benz 4-cylinder car, 1906; No. 1941, Back of Benz 4-cylinder car and advertisement; No. 1942, Silhouette of early Benz car; No. **MS**1943a, Ford Model "Y", 1933; No. **MS**1943b, Mercedes "3005", 1955.

Nos. 1919/30 and 1931/42 were printed together, *se-tenant*, in sheetlets of 12 each forming a composite design.

291 Ivan, Sonia, Sasha and Peter in the Snow

(Des Rosemary DeFiglio. Litho Questa)

1993 (20 Dec). Peter and the Wolf. T **291** and similar horiz designs showing scenes from Walt Disney's cartoon film. Multicoloured. P 14×13½.

1944	7l. Type **291**	25	25
1945	15l. Grandpa and Peter	30	25
1946	20l. Peter on bridge	30	25
1947	25l. Yascha, Vladimir and Mischa	30	25
1948	50l. Sasha on lookout	45	30
1949	1r. The Wolf	60	35
1950	3r.50 Peter dreaming	70	80
	a. Sheetlet of 9. Nos. 1950/8	5·75	6·50
1951	3r.50 Peter taking gun	70	80
1952	3r.50 Peter with gun in snow	70	80
1953	3r.50 Sasha and Peter	70	80
1954	3r.50 Sonia and Peter	60	60
1955	3r.50 Peter with Ivan and Sasha	70	80
1956	3r.50 Ivan warning Peter of the Wolf	70	80
1957	3r.50 Ivan, Peter and Sasha in tree	70	80
1958	3r.50 Wolf below tree	70	80
1959	3r.50 Wolf and Sonia	70	80
	a. Sheetlet of 9. Nos. 1959/67	5·75	6·50
1960	3r.50 Sasha attacking the Wolf	70	80
1961	3r.50 Sasha walking into Wolf's mouth	70	80
1962	3r.50 Peter firing pop gun at Wolf	70	80
1963	3r.50 Wolf chasing Sonia	70	80
1964	3r.50 Ivan tying rope to Wolf's tail	70	80
1965	3r.50 Peter and Ivan hoisting Wolf	70	80
1966	3r.50 Sasha and the hunters	70	80
1967	3r.50 Ivan and Peter on Wolf hanging from tree	70	80
1944/67	Set of 24	13·00	15·00

MS1968 Two sheets. (a) 102×127 mm. 25r. Sonia as an angel. (b) 127×102 mm. 25r. Ivan looking proud
Set of 2 sheets ..... 8·00 8·50

Nos. 1950/8 and 1959/67 were printed together, *se-tenant*, in sheetlets of nine.

292 "Girl with a Broom" (Rembrandt)

(Des Kerri Schiff. Litho Cartor)

1994 (2 Feb). Famous Paintings by Rembrandt and Matisse. T **292** and similar multicoloured designs. P 13.

1969	50l. Type **292**	40	25
1970	2r. "Girl with Tulips" (Matisse)	90	70
1971	3r.50 "Young Girl at half-open Door" (Rembrandt)	1·25	1·10
1972	3r.50 "Portrait of Greta Moll" (Matisse)	1·25	1·10
1973	5r. "The Prophetess Hannah" (Rembrandt)	1·50	1·25
1974	6r.50 "The Idol" (Matisse)	1·75	1·75
1975	7r. "Woman with a Pink Flower" (Rembrandt)	1·75	1·75
1976	9r. "Mme Matisse in a Japanese Robe" (Matisse)	2·00	2·25
1977	10r. "Portrait of Mme Matisse" (Matisse)	2·00	2·25
1978	12r. "Lucretia" (Rembrandt)	2·25	2·50
1979	15r. "Lady with a Ostrich Feather Fan" (Rembrandt)	2·25	2·75
1980	15r. "The Woman with the Hat" (Matisse)	2·25	2·75
1969/80	Set of 12	17·00	18·00

MS1981 Three sheets. (a) 106×132 mm. 25r. "The Music-makers" (detail) (Rembrandt). (b) 132×106 mm. 25r. "Married Couple with Three Children" (detail) (Rembrandt) (horiz). (c) 132×106 mm. 25r. "The Painter's Family" (detail) (Matisse) *Set of 3 sheets* ..... 17·00 17·00

No. 1979 is inscribed "The Lady with an Ostich Feather Fan" in error.

293 Hong Kong 1983 $1 Space Museum Stamp and Moon-lantern Festival

(Des W. Hanson. Litho Questa)

1994 (18 Feb). "Hong Kong '94" International Stamp Exhibition (1st issue). T **293** and similar horiz design. Multicoloured. P 14.

1982	4r. Type **293**	65	80
	a. Horiz pair. Nos. 1982/3	1·25	1·60
1983	4r. Maldive Islands 1976 5r. "Viking" space mission stamp and Moon lantern Festival	65	80

Nos. 1982/3 were printed together, *se-tenant*, in horizontal pairs throughout the sheet with the centre part of each pair forming a composite design.

294 Vase

295 Windischmann (U.S.A.) and Giannini (Italy)

(Des Kerri Schiff. Litho Questa)

1994 (18 Feb). "Hong Kong '94" International Stamp Exhibition (2nd issue). Ching Dynasty Cloisonné Enamelware. T **294** and similar vert designs. Multicoloured. P 14.

1984	2r. Type **294**	90	85
	a. Sheetlet of 6. Nos. 1984/9	4·75	4·50
1985	2r. Flower holder	90	85
1986	2r. Elephant with vase on back	90	85
1987	2r. Tibetan style lama's teapot	90	85
1988	2r. Fo-Dog	90	45
1989	2r. Teapot with swing handle	90	85
1984/89	Set of 6	4·75	4·50

Nos. 1984/9 were printed, *se-tenant*, in sheetlets of six.

(Litho Questa)

1994 (28 Feb). World Cup Football Championship, U.S.A. (2nd issue). T **295** and similar multicoloured designs. P 14.

1990	7l. Type **295**	30	25
1991	20l. Carnevale (Italy) and Gascoigne (England)	50	25
1992	25l. England players congratulating Platt	50	25
1993	3r.50 Koeman (Holland) and Klinsmann (Germany)	1·25	80
1994	5r. Quinn (Ireland) and Maldini (Italy)	1·40	1·00
1995	7r. Lineker (England)	2·00	1·50
1996	15r. Hassam (Egypt) and Moran (Ireland)	3·00	3·50
1997	18r. Canniggia (Argentina)	3·25	3·50
1990/97	Set of 8	11·00	10·00

MS1998 Two sheets, each 103×73 mm. (a) 25r. Ogris (Austria). (b) 25r. Conejo (Costa Rica) (horiz) *Set of 2 sheets* ..... 13·00 12·00

296 Humpback Whale

297 Dome of the Rock, Jerusalem

(Litho Questa)

1994 (20 May). Centenary of Sierra Club (environmental protection society) (1992). Endangered Species. T **296** and similar multicoloured designs. P 14.

1999	6r.50 Type **296**	1·60	1·60
	a. Sheetlet of 6. Nos. 1999/2004	8·50	8·50
2000	6r.50 Ocelot crouched in grass	1·60	1·60
2001	6r.50 Ocelot sitting	1·60	1·60
2002	6r.50 Snow Monkey	1·60	1·60
2003	6r.50 Prairie Dog	1·60	1·60
2004	6r.50 Golden Lion Tamarin	1·60	1·60
2005	6r.50 Prairie Dog eating (*horiz*)	1·60	1·60
	a. Sheetlet of 6. Nos. 2005/10	8·50	8·50
2006	6r.50 Prairie Dog outside burrow (*horiz*)	1·60	1·60
2007	6r.50 Herd of Woodland Caribou (*horiz*)	1·60	1·60

2008	6r.50 Woodland Caribou facing left (horiz)	1·60	1·60
2009	6r.50 Woodland Caribou facing right (horiz) ..	1·60	1·60
2010	6r.50 Pair of Galapagos Penguins (horiz)	1·60	1·60
2011	6r.50 Galapagos Penguin facing right..............	1·60	1·60
	a. Sheetlet of 8. Nos. 2011/18........................	11·00	11·00
2012	6r.50 Galapagos Penguin looking straight ahead..	1·60	1·60
2013	6r.50 Bengal Tiger looking straight ahead	1·60	1·60
2014	6r.50 Bengal Tiger looking right.........................	1·60	1·60
2015	6r.50 Philippine Tarsier with tree trunk at left.	1·60	1·60
2016	6r.50 Philippine Tarsier with tree trunk at right	1·60	1·60
2017	6r.50 Head of Philippine Tarsier........................	1·60	1·60
2018	6r.50 Sierra Club Centennial emblem (black, buff and deep turquoise-green)...............	1·60	1·60
2019	6r.50 Golden Lion Tamarin between two branches (horiz).......................................	1·60	1·60
	a. Sheetlet of 8. Nos. 2019/26........................	11·00	11·00
2020	6r.50 Golden Lion Tamarin on tree trunk (horiz).	1·60	1·60
2021	6r.50 Tail fin of Humpback Whale and coastline (horiz).......................................	1·60	1·60
2022	6r.50 Tail fin of Humpback Whale at night (horiz)...	1·60	1·60
2023	6r.50 Bengal Tiger (horiz)...................................	1·60	1·60
2024	6r.50 Ocelot (horiz)...	1·60	1·60
2025	6r.50 Snow Monkey in water climbing out of pool (horiz)...	1·60	1·60
2026	6r.50 Snow Monkey swimming (horiz).............	1·60	1·60
1999/2026 Set of 28...		35·00	35·00

Nos. 1999/2004, 2005/10, 2011/18 and 2019/26 were each printed together, *se-tenant*, as two sheetlets of six (Nos. 1999/2010) or two sheetlets of eight (Nos. 2011/26).

(Litho Cartor)

1994 (10 June). Solidarity with the Palestinians. P 13½×14.

2027	**297**	8r. multicoloured	1·60	1·60

298 Elasmosaurus

299 Mallet Steam Locomotive, Indonesia

(Des L. Birmingham. Litho B.D.T.)

1994 (20 June). Prehistoric Animals. T **298** and similar multicoloured designs. P 14.

2028/59	25l., 50l., 1r., 3r.×24, 5r., 8r., 10r., 15r., 20r. Set of 32	30·00	28·00
MS2060 Two sheets, each 106×76 mm. (a) 25r. Gallimimus. (b) 25r. Plateosaurus (vert) Set of 2 sheets..		8·00	8·50

Nos. 2031/42 and 2043/54 were each printed together, *se-tenant*, in sheetlets of 12 forming composite designs. The species depicted are, in addition to Type **298**, Dilophosaurus, Avimimus, Dimorphodon, Megalosaurus, Kuehneosaurus, Dryosaurus, Kentrosaurus, Baraposaurus, Tenontosaurus, Elaphrosaurus, Maiasaura, Huayangosaurus, Rutiodon, Pianitzkysaurus, Quetzalcoatlus Daspletosaurus Pleurocoelus, Bary onyx, Pentaceratops, Kritosaurus, Microvenator, Nodosaurus Montanaceratops, Dromiceiomimus Dryptosaurus, Parkosaurus, Chasmosaurus, Edmontonia, Anatosaurus, Velociraptor and Spinosaurus.

(Des K. Gromell. Litho B.D.T.)

1994 (4 July). Railway Locomotives of Asia. T **299** and similar multicoloured designs. P 14.

2061	25l. Type **299**	20	20
2062	50l. Class C62 steam locomotive, Japan, 1948	25	20
2063	1r. Class D51 steam locomotive, Japan, 1936 (horiz)	30	20
2064	5r. Steam locomotive, India (horiz)........	90	90
2065	6r.50+50l. Class W steam locomotive, India (horiz)	1·25	1·50
	a. Sheetlet of 6. Nos. 2065/70...............	6·50	8·00
2066	6r.50+50l. Class C53 steam locomotive, Indonesia (horiz)	1·25	1·50
2067	6r.50+50l. Class C10 steam locomotive, Japan (horiz)	1·25	1·50
2068	6r.50+50l. Hanomag steam locomotive, India (horiz)	1·25	1·50
2069	6r.50+50l. Hikari express train, Japan (horiz) ..	1·25	1·50
2070	6r.50+50l. Class C55 steam locomotive, Japan, 1935 (horiz)	1·25	1·50
2071	8r. Class 485 electric locomotive, Japan (horiz)......................................	1·50	1·75
2072	10r. Class WP steam locomotive, India (horiz)..	1·75	2·00
2073	15r. Class RM steam locomotive, China (horiz)..	2·00	2·25
2074	20r. Class C57 steam locomotive, Japan, 1937...	2·25	2·50
2061/74 Set of 14..		15·00	17·00
MS2075 Two sheets, each 110×80 mm. (a) 25r. Steam locomotive pulling goods train, Indonesia (horiz). (b) 25r. class 8620 steam locomotive, Japan, 1914 (horiz) Set of 2 sheets...		9·00	9·50

Nos. 2065/70 were printed together, *se-tenant* in sheetlets of six. No. 2069 is inscribed "Hakari" in error.

MALDIVES ‌

300 Japanese Bobtail

(Litho Questa)

1994 (11 July). Cats. T **300** and similar multicoloured designs. P 14.

2076	7l. Type **300**	30	20
2077	20l. Siamese (vert)	45	20
2078	25l. Persian Longhair............................	45	20
2079	50l. Somali (vert)	55	20
2080	3r.50 Oriental Shorthair..........................	1·25	80
2081	5r. Burmese	1·50	1·00
2082	7r. Bombay carrying kitten.................	1·75	1·50
2083	10r. Turkish Van (vert)	1·75	1·75
2084	12r. Javanese (vert)	2·00	2·00
2085	15r. Singapura	2·25	2·75
2086	18r. Turkish Angora (vert)	2·50	3·25
2087	20r. Egyptian Mau (vert).......................	2·50	3·25
2076/87 Set of 12..		15·00	15·00
MS2088 Three sheets. (a) 70×100 mm. 25r. Birman (vert). (b) 70×100 mm. 25r. Karat (vert). (c) 100×70 mm. 25r. Abyssinian (vert) Set of 3 sheets.....		13·00	15·00

301 Franco Baresi (Italy) and Stuart McCall (Scotland) **302** Crew of "Apollo 11"

(Litho Questa)

1994 (4 Aug). World Cup Football Championship, U.S.A. (3rd issue). T **301** and similar multicoloured designs. P 14.

(a) Horiz designs

2089	10l. Type **301**	40	40
	a. Sheetlet of 6. Nos. 2089/94...............	5·50	5·50
2090	25l. Mick McCarthy (Ireland) and Gary Lineker (England).............................	50	50
2091	50l. J. Helt (Denmark) and R. Gordillo (Spain)..	50	50
2092	5r. Martin Vasquez (Spain) and Enzo Scifo (Italy).....................................	1·25	1·25
2093	10r. Championship emblem....................	1·60	1·60
2094	12r. Tomas Brolin (Sweden) and Gordon Durie (Scotland)..............................	1·75	1·75

(b) Vert designs

2095	6r.50 Bebeto (Brazil)...............................	1·25	1·25
	a. Sheetlet of 6. Nos. 2095/2100..........	6·75	6·75
2096	6r.50 Lothar Matthaus (Germany)	1·25	1·25
2097	6r.50 Diego Maradona (Argentina)	1·25	1·25
2098	6r.50 Stephane Chapuisat (Switzerland)....	1·25	1·25
2099	6r.50 George Hagi (Rumania)	1·25	1·25
2100	6r.50 Carlos Valderama (Colombia)..........	1·25	1·25
2089/100 Set of 12...		12·00	12·00
MS2101 100×70 mm. 10r. Egyptian players......................		4·25	4·25

Nos. 2089/94 and 2095/100 were each printed together, *se-tenant*, in sheetlets of six.

(Des W. Hanson. Litho B.D.T.)

1994 (8 Aug). 25th Anniv of First Moon Landing. T **302** and similar multicoloured designs. P 14.

2102	5r. Type **302**	1·00	1·00
	a. Sheetlet of 6. Nos. 2102/7	5·50	5·50
2103	5r. "Apollo 11" mission logo	1·00	1·00
2104	5r. Edwin Aldrin (astronaut) and *Eagle*	1·00	1·00

2105	5r. Crew of "Apollo 12"	1·00	1·00
2106	5r. "Apollo 12" mission logo	1·00	1·00
2107	5r. Alan Bean (astronaut) and equipment	1·00	1·00
2108	5r. Crew of "Apollo 16"	1·00	1·00
	a. Sheetlet of 6. Nos. 2108/13	5·50	5·50
2109	5r. "Apollo 16" mission logo	1·00	1·00
2110	5r. Astronauts with U.S. flag	1·00	1·00
2111	5r. Crew of "Apollo 17"	1·00	1·00
2112	5r. "Apollo 17" mission logo	1·00	1·00
2113	5r. Launch of "Apollo 17"	1·00	1·00
2102/13	Set of 12	11·00	11·00

MS2114 100×76 mm. 25r. Launch of Russian rocket
from Baikonur (vert) .... 4·00 4·75

Nos. 2102/7 and 2108/13 were printed together, se-tenant, in sheetlets of six.

303 Linford Christie
(Great Britain) (100
metres), 1992

304 U.S. Amphibious DUKW

(Des Kerri Schiff. Litho Questa)

1994 (8 Aug). Centenary of International Olympic Committee. Gold Medal Winners. T **303** and similar vert designs. Multicoloured. P 14.

2115	7r. Type **303**	1·50	1·25
2116	12r. Koji Gushiken (Japan) (gymnastics), 1984	1·75	2·00

MS2117 106×71 mm. 25r. George Hackl (Germany)
(single luge), 1994 .... 4·50 5·00

(Des J. Batchelor. Litho Questa)

1994 (8 Aug). 50th Anniv of D-Day. T **304** and similar horiz designs. Multicoloured. P 14.

2118	2r. Type **304**	75	30
2119	4r. Tank landing craft unloading at Sword Beach	1·25	60
2120	18r. Infantry landing craft at Omaha Beach	4·00	4·75
2118/20	Set of 3	5·50	5·00

MS2121 105×76 mm. 25r. Landing craft with
Canadian commandos .... 6·00 6·00

305 Duckpond, Suwan Folk
Village

306 U.S. "Voyager 2"
Satellite

(Des Kerri Schiff. Litho B.D.T. (3r.) or Questa (others))

1994 (8 Aug). "Philakorea '94" International Stamp Exhibition, Seoul. T **305** and similar multicoloured designs. P 13½×14 (Nos. 2123/30) or 14 (others).

2122	50l. Type **305**	50	30
2123	3r. Pear-shaped bottle	60	70
	a. Sheetlet of 8. Nos. 2123/30	4·25	5·00
2124	3r. Vase with dragon decoration	60	70
2125	3r. Vase with repaired lip	60	70
2126	3r. Stoneware vase with floral decoration	60	70
2127	3r. Celadon-glazed vase	60	70
2128	3r. Unglazed stone vase	60	70
2129	3r. Ritual water sprinkler	60	70
2130	3r. Long necked celadon-glazed vase	60	70
2131	3r.50 Yongduson Park	70	75
2132	20r. Ploughing with ox, Hahoe	3·50	4·50
2122/32	Set of 11	8·50	10·00

MS2133 70×102 mm. 25r. "Hunting" (detail from
eight-panel painted screen) (vert) .... 4·50 5·50

Nos. 2123/30, each 24×47 mm, were printed together, se-tenant, in sheetlets of eight.

(Des Outsiders Group. Litho Questa)

1994 (8 Aug). Space Exploration. T **306** and similar multicoloured designs. P 14.

2134	5r. Type **306**	1·50	1·25
	a. Sheetlet of 12. Nos. 2134/45	16·00	13·50
2135	5r. Russian "Sputnik" satellite	1·50	1·25
2136	5r. "Apollo-Soyuz" mission	1·50	1·25
2137	5r. "Apollo 10" on parachutes	1·50	1·25
2138	5r. Apollo 11" mission flag	1·50	1·25
2139	5r. Hubble space telescope	1·50	1·25
2140	5r. Edwin "Buzz" Aldrin (astronaut)	1·50	1·25
2141	5r. RCA lunar camera	1·50	1·25
2142	5r. Lunar Rover (space buggy)	1·50	1·25
2143	5r. Jim Irwin (astronaut)	1·50	1·25
2144	5r. "Apollo 12" lunar module	1·50	1·25
2145	5r. Astronaut holding equipment	1·50	1·25
2134/45	Set of 12	16·00	13·50

MS2146 Two sheets. (a) 70×100 mm. 25r. David Scott (astronaut) in open hatch of "Apollo 9" (b) 100×70 mm. 25r. Alan Shepherd Jr. (astronaut)
(horiz) Set of 2 sheets .... 13·00 12·00

Nos. 2134/45 were printed together, se-tenant, in sheetlets of 12 forming a composite design.

307 Mother, Child, Old Man and
Town Skyline

308 School Band

(Litho Questa)

1994 (24 Oct). United Nations Development Programme. T **307** and similar horiz design. Multicoloured. P 14.

2147	1r. Type **307**	25	10
2148	8r. Fisherman with son and island	1·60	2·25

(Litho Questa)

1994 (28 Nov). 50th Anniv of Aminiya School. Children's Paintings. T **308** and similar multicoloured designs. P 14.

2149	15l. Type **308**	15	10
2150	50l. Classroom	25	15
2151	1r. School emblem and hand holding book (vert)	35	15
2152	8r. School girls holding books (vert)	2·00	2·25
2153	10r. Sporting activities	2·00	2·25
2154	11r. School girls holding crown (vert)	2·00	2·75
2155	13r. Science lesson	2·25	2·75
2149/55	Set of 7	8·00	9·50

309 Boeing 747

(Des W. Wright. Litho B.D.T.)

1994 (31 Dec). 50th Anniv of International Civil Aviation Organization. T **309** and similar horiz designs. Multicoloured. P 14.

2156	50l. Type **309**	75	25
2157	1r. Hawker Siddeley ("de Havilland") Comet 4	1·00	25
2158	2r. Malé International Airport	1·60	55
2159	3r. Lockheed L.1649 Super Star	1·75	85
2160	8r. European Airbus	2·50	2·75
2161	10r. Dornier Do-228	2·50	2·75
2156/61	Set of 6	9·00	6·75

MS2162 100×70 mm. 25r. Concorde .... 5·00 6·00

310 Pintail ("Northern Pintail")

(Des Outsiders Group. Litho Questa)

1995 (27 Feb). Ducks. T **310** and similar multicoloured designs. P 14.

2163	5r. Type **310**	1·00	1·00
	a. Sheetlet of 9. Nos. 2163/71	8·00	8·00
2164	5r. Comb Duck	1·00	1·00
2165	5r. Ruddy Shelduck	1·00	1·00
2166	5r. Garganey	1·00	1·00
2167	5r. Indian Whistling Duck ("Lesser Whistling Duck")	1·00	1·00
2168	5r. Green-winged Teal	1·00	1·00
2169	5r. Fulvous Whistling Duck	1·00	1·00
2170	5r. Common Shoveler ("Northern Shoveler")	1·00	1·00
2171	5r. Cotton Pygmy Goose	1·00	1·00
2172	6r.50+50l. European Pochard (*vert*)	1·00	1·00
	a. Sheetlet of 9. Nos. 2172/80	8·00	8·00
2173	6r.50+50l. Mallard (*vert*)	1·00	1·00
2174	6r.50+50l. European Wigeon (*vert*)	1·00	1·00
2175	6r.50+50l. Common Shoveler ("Northern Shoveler") (*vert*)	1·00	1·00
2176	6r.50+50l. Pintail (*vert*)	1·00	1·00
2177	6r.50+50l. Garganey (*vert*)	1·00	1·00
2178	6r.50+50l. Tufted Duck (*vert*)	1·00	1·00
2179	6r.50+50l. Red-crested Pochard ("Ferruginous Duck") (*vert*)	1·00	1·00
2180	6r.50+50l. Ferruginous Duck ("Red crested Pochard") (*vert*)	1·00	1·00
2163/80	*Set of 18*	16·00	16·00

MS2181 Two sheets. (a) 100×71 mm. 25r. Spotbill Duck ("Garganey"). (b) 73×100 mm. 25r. Cotton Pygmy Goose (*vert*) *Set of 2 sheets* .... 7·50 8·50

Nos. 2163/71 and 2172/80 were printed together, *se-tenant*, in sheetlets of nine, each with enlarged top margin, forming composite designs.

311 Taj Mahal, India

(Litho Questa)

1995 (28 Feb). Famous Monuments of the World. T **311** and similar multicoloured designs. P 14.

2182	7l. Type **311**	50	25
2183	10l. Washington Monument, U.S.A	10	10
2184	15l. Mount Rushmore, U.S.A	10	10
2185	25l. Arc de Triomphe, Paris (*vert*)	10	10
2186	50l. Sphinx, Egypt (*vert*)	50	20
2187	5r. El Castillo, Toltec pyramid, Yucatan	85	1·00
2188	8r. Toltec statue, Tula, Mexico (*vert*)	1·25	2·00
2189	12r. Victory Column, Berlin (*vert*)	1·60	2·50
2182/89	*Set of 8*	4·50	5·50

MS2190 Two sheets, each 112×85 mm. (a) 25r. Easter Island statue (42×56 *mm*). (b) 25r. Stonehenge, Wiltshire (85×28 *mm*) *Set of 2 sheets* .... 7·50 8·50

312 Donald Duck driving Chariot

(Des Rosemary DeFiglio. Litho B.D.T.)

1995 (22 Mar). History of Wheeled Transport. T **312** and similar multicoloured designs showing scenes from Disney cartoon film Donald and the Wheel. P 13.

2191	3l. Type **312**	10	10
2192	4l. Donald with log	10	10
2193	5l. Donald driving Stephenson's *Rocket*	10	10
2194	10l. Donald pondering over circle (*vert*)	10	10
2195	20l. Donald in crashed car (*vert*)	10	10
2196	25l. Donald listening to early gramophone.	10	10
2197	5r. Donald on Mammoth	1·25	1·25
2198	20r. Donald pushing early car	3·75	4·75
2191/98	*Set of 8*	5·00	6·00

313 Donald Duck playing Saxophone

314 Islamic Centre, Malé

(Des Alvin White Studios. Litho B.D.T.)

1995 (22 Mar). 60th Birthday of Donald Duck. T **313** and similar multicoloured designs showing Walt Disney cartoon characters. P 13.

2199	5r. Type **313**	90	90
	a. Sheetlet of 8. Nos. 2199/2206	6·50	6·50
2200	5r. Moby Duck playing fiddle	90	90
2201	5r. Feathry Duck with banjo and drum	90	90
2202	5r. Daisy Duck playing harp	90	90
2203	5r. Gladstone Gander with clarinet	90	90
2204	5r. Huey, Dewey and Louie with bassoon..	90	90
2205	5r. Gus Goose playing flute	90	90
2206	5r. Prof. Ludwig von Drake playing trombone	90	90
2207	5r. Daisy picking flowers	90	90
	a. Sheetlet of 8. Nos. 2207/14	6·50	6·50
2208	5r. Donald with backpack	90	90
2209	5r. Grandma Duck with kitten	90	90
2210	5r. Gus Goose and pie	90	90
2211	5r. Gyro Gearloose in space	90	90
2212	5r. Huey, Dewey and Louie photographing porcupine	90	90
2213	5r. Prof Ludwig von Drake	90	90
2214	5r. Scrooge McDuck with money	90	90
2199/214	*Set of 16*	13·00	13·00

MS2215 Four sheets. (a) 108×130 mm. 25r. Donald playing banjo. (b) 133×108 mm. 25r. Donald posing for photo. (c) 108×130 mm. 25r. Donald conducting (*horiz*). (d) 102×121 mm. 25r. Huey, Dewey and Louie (*horiz*) *Set of 4 sheets* ...... 14·00 15·00

Nos. 2199/2206 and 2207/14 were printed together, *se-tenant*, in sheetlets of eight.

(Litho Questa)

1995 (1 May). Eid Greetings. T **314** and similar vert designs. Multicoloured. P 14.

2216	1r. Type **314**	15	15
2217	1r. Rose	15	15
2218	8r. Orchid	1·50	1·50
2219	10r. Orchid (*different*)	1·50	1·50
2216/19	*Set of 4*	3·00	3·00

315 Killer Whale

(Des K. Gromell. Litho Questa)

1995 (16 May). "Singapore '95" International Stamp Exhibition (1st issue). Whales, Dolphins and Porpoises. T **315** and similar horiz designs. Multicoloured. P 14.

2220	1r. Type **315**	40	30
2221	2r. Bottlenose Dolphins	45	35
2222	3r. Right Whale	60	70
	a. Sheetlet of 12. Nos. 2222/33	6·00	7·50
2223	3r. Pair of Killer Whales	60	70
2224	3r. Humpback Whale	60	70
2225	3r. Pair of Belugas	60	70
2226	3r. Narwhal	60	70
2227	3r. Head of Blue Whale	60	70
2228	3r. Bowhead Whale	60	70
2229	3r. Head of Fin Whale	60	70
2230	3r. Pair of Pilot Whales	60	70
2231	3r. Grey Whale	60	70
2232	3r. Sperm Whale	60	70
2233	3r. Pair of Goosebeaked Whales	60	70
2234	3r. Hourglass Dolphin	60	70
	a. Sheetlet of 12. Nos. 2234/45	6·50	7·50

2235	3r. Bottlenose Dolphin (*different*)	60	70
2236	3r. Dusky Dolphin	60	70
2237	3r. Spectacled Porpoise	60	70
2238	3r. Fraser's Dolphin	60	70
2239	3r. Camerson's Dolphin	60	70
2240	3r. Pair of Spinner Dolphins	60	70
2241	3r. Pair of Dulls Dolphins	60	70
2242	3r. Spotted Dolphin	60	70
2243	3r. Indus River Dolphin	60	70
2244	3r. Hector's Dolphin	60	70
2245	3r. Amazon River Dolphin	60	70
2246	8r. Humpback Whale and calf	1·25	1·50
2247	10r. Common Dolphin	1·40	1·60
2220/47 *Set of 28*		16·00	17·00

MS2248 Two sheets, each 100×70 mm. (a) 25r. Sperm Whale (*different*). (b) 25r. Pair of Hourglass Dolphins *Set of 2 sheets* .... 9·00 9·00

Nos. 2222/33 and 2234/45 were printed together, *se-tenant*, in sheetlets of 12.

See also Nos. 2302/**MS**2310.

316 Scout Camp and National Flag

317 Soviet Heavy Howitzer Battery

(Des B. Hargreaves. Litho Questa)

1995 (6 July). 18th World Scout Jamboree, Netherlands. T **316** and similar multicoloured designs. P 14.

2249	10r. Type **316**	1·75	2·00
	a. Horiz strip of 3. Nos. 2249/51	5·00	6·00
2250	12r. Campfire cooking	1·90	2·25
2251	15r. Scouts erecting tent	2·00	2·40
2249/51 *Set of 3*		5·00	6·00

MS2252 102×72 mm. 25r. Scouts around camp fire (vert) .... 3·50 4·00

Nos. 2249/51 were printed in sheets of nine containing three *se-tenant* horizontal strips, each forming a composite design.

(Des W. Wright. Litho Queata)

1995 (6 July). 50th Anniv of End of Second World War in Europe. T **317** and similar horiz designs. Multicoloured. P 14.

2253	5r. Type **317**	1·10	85
	a. Sheetlet of 8. Nos. 2253/60	8·00	6·00
2254	5r. Ruins of Berchtesgaden	1·10	85
2255	5r. Boeing B-17 Flying Fortress dropping food over the Netherlands	1·10	85
2256	5r. Soviet Ilyushin Il-1 bomber	1·10	85
2257	5r. Liberation of Belsen	1·10	85
2258	5r. Supermarine Spitfire and V-1 flying bomb	1·10	85
2259	5r. U.S. tanks advancing through Cologne	1·10	85
2260	5r. Reichstag in ruins	1·10	85
2253/60 *Set of 8*		8·00	6·00

MS2261 107×76 mm. 25r. Soviet and U.S. troops celebrating .... 3·50 4·00

Nos. 2253/60 were printed together, *se-tenant*, in sheetlets of eight with the stamps arranged in two horizonal strips of four separated by a gutter showing R.A.F. Lancasters over Dresden.

318 Asian Child and Dove

319 United Nations Emblem

(Des J. Iskowitz. Litho)

1995 (6 July). 50th Anniv of United Nations (1st issue). T **318** and similar vert designs. Multicoloured. P 14.

2262	6r.50+50l. Type **318**	90	1·25
	a. Horiz strip of 3. Nos. 2262/4	2·75	3·75
2263	8r. Globe and dove	1·00	1·40
2264	10r. African child and dove	1·10	1·50
2262/64 *Set of 3*		2·75	3·75

MS2265 72×102 mm. 25r. United Nations emblem and dove .... 2·75 3·75

Nos. 2262/4 were printed in sheets of nine containing three *se-tenant* horizontal strips, each forming a composite design.

(Litho Questa)

1995 (6 July). 50th Anniv of United Nations (2nd issue). T **319** and similar horiz designs. P 14.

2266	30l. black, bright blue and green	10	10
2267	8r. multicoloured	1·00	1·25
2268	11r. multicoloured	1·25	1·75
2269	13r. black, grey and rosine	1·60	2·25
2266/69 *Set of 4*		3·50	4·75

Designs:—8r. Symbolic women, flag and map; 11r. U.N. soldier and symbolic dove; 13r. Gun barrels, atomic explosion and bomb sight.

320 Asian Child eating Rice

321 Queen Elizabeth the Queen Mother

(Des J. Iskowitz. Litho)

1995 (6 July). 50th Anniv of Food and Agriculture Organization (1st issue). T **320** and similar multicoloured designs. P 14.

2270	6r.50+50l. Type **320**	1·00	1·25
	a. Horiz strip of 3. Nos. 2270/2	2·75	3·25
2271	8r. F.A.O. emblem	1·00	1·25
2272	10r. African mother and child	1·00	1·25
2270/72 *Set of 3*		2·75	3·25

MS2273 72×102 mm. 25r. African child and symbolic hand holding maize .... 5·00 6·00

Nos. 2270/2 were printed in sheets of nine containing three *se-tenant* horizontal strips.

See also Nos. 2311/12.

(Litho Questa)

1995 (6 July). 95th Birthday of Queen Elizabeth the Queen Mother. T **321** and similar vert designs. P 13½×14.

2274	5r. orange-brown, pale brown and black	1·00	1·10
	a. Sheetlet of 8. Nos. 2274/7×2	7·25	8·00
2275	5r. multicoloured	1·00	1·10
2276	5r. multicoloured	1·00	1·10
2277	5r. multicoloured	1·00	1·10
2274/77 *Set of 4*		3·50	4·00

MS2278 125×100 mm. 25r. multicoloured .... 6·00 6·00

Designs:—No. 2274, Queen Elizabeth the Queen Mother (pastel drawing); No. 2275, Without hat; No. 2276, At desk (oil painting); No. 2277, Type **321**; No. **MS**2278, Wearing lilac hat and dress.

Nos. 2274/7 were printed together in sheetlets of eight containing two *se-tenant* horizontal strips of four.

(Des J. Batchelor. Litho Questa)

1995 (6 July). 50th Anniv of End of Second World War in the Pacific. Horiz designs as T **317**. P 14.

2279	6r.50+50l. Grumman F6F-3 Hellcat aircraft	1·50	1·50
	a. Sheetlet of 6. Nos. 2279/84	8·00	8·00
2280	6r.50+50l. F4-U1 fighter aircraft attacking beach	1·50	1·50
2281	6r.50+50l. Douglas SBD Dauntless aircraft	1·50	1·50
2282	6r.50+50l. American troops in landing craft Guadalcanal	1·50	1·50
2283	6r.50+50l. U.S. marines in Alligator tanks	1·50	1·50
2284	6r.50+50l. U.S. landing ship	1·50	1·50
2279/84 *Set of 6*		8·00	8·00

MS2285 106×74 mm. 25r. F4-U1. fighter aircraft .... 4·00 4·50

Nos. 2279/84 were printed together, *se-tenant*, in sheetlets of six with the stamps arranged in two horizontal strips of three separated by a gutter showing U.S. marines in landing craft.

322 Students using Library

(Litho Questa)

1995 (12 July). 50th Anniversary of National Library. T **322** and similar horiz designs. Multicoloured. P 14.

2286	2r. Type **322**	25	25
2287	8r. Students using library (*different*)	1·00	1·50
MS2288	105×75 mm. 10r. Library entrance (100×70 mm). Imperf	1·40	1·60

323 Spur-thighed Tortoise

324 *Russula aurata* (fungi) and *Papilio demodocus* (butterfly)

(Des D. Burkhardt. Litho Questa)

1995 (22 Aug). Turtles and Tortoises. T **323** and similar horiz designs. Multicoloured. P 14.

2289	3r. Type **323**	70	80
	a. Sheetlet of 8. Nos. 2289/96	5·00	5·75
2290	3r. Aldabra Turtle	70	80
2291	3r. Loggerhead Turtle	70	80
2292	3r. Olive Ridley Turtle	70	80
2293	3r. Leatherback Turtle	70	80
2294	3r. Green Turtle	70	80
2295	3r. Atlantic Ridley Turtle	70	80
2296	3r. Hawksbill Turtle	70	80
2297	10r. Hawksbill Turtle on beach	1·50	1·75
	a. Vert strip of 4. Nos. 2297/2300	5·50	6·25
2298	10r. Pair of Hawksbill Turtles	1·50	1·75
2299	10r. Hawksbill Turtle climbing out of water.	1·50	1·75
2300	10r. Hawksbill Turtle swimming	1·50	1·75
2289/2300	*Set of 12*	10·50	12·00
MS2301	100×70 mm. 25r. Green Turtle	3·75	4·50

Nos. 2289/96 were printed together, *se-tenant*, in sheetlets of eight forming a composite design.

Nos. 2297/2300, which include the W.W.F. Panda emblem, were printed together in sheets of 12 (3×4) containing three vertical *se-tenant* strips.

(Des L. Nelson. Litho Questa)

1995 (18 Oct). "Singapore '95" International Stamp Exhibition (2nd issue). Butterflies and Fungi. T **324** and similar multicoloured designs. P 14.

2302	2r. Type **324**	75	75
	a. Sheetlet of 4. Nos. 2302/5	2·75	2·75
2303	2r. *Lepista saeva* and *Kallimoides rumia*	75	75
2304	2r. *Lepesto nuda* and *Hypolimnas salmacis*.	75	75
2305	2r. *Xerocomus subtomentosus* ("*Boletus subtomentosus*") and *Precis octavia*	75	75
2306	5r. *Gyroporus castaneus* and *Hypolimnas salmacis*	1·10	1·10
	a. Sheetlet of 4. Nos. 2306/9	4·75	4·75
2307	8r. *Gomphidius glutinosus* and *Papilio dardanus*	1·25	1·25
2308	10r. *Russula olivacea* and *Precis octavia*	1·40	1·40
2309	12r. *Boletus edulis* and *Prepona praeneste*	1·40	1·40
2302/9	*Set of 8*	7·25	7·25
MS2310	Two sheets, each 105×76 mm. (a) 25r. *Amanita muscaria* and *Kallimoides rumia* (vert). (b) 25r. *Boletus rhodoxanthus* and *Hypolimnas salmacis* (vert) *Set of 2 sheets*	8·00	8·00

Nos. 2302/5 and 2306/9 were each printed together, *se-tenant*, in sheetlets of four, forming composite designs.

No. 2304 is inscribed "Lapista" in error.

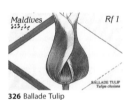

325 Planting Kaashi

326 Ballade Tulip

(Litho Questa)

1995 (2 Nov). 50th Anniv of Food and Agriculture Organization (2nd issue). T **325** and similar vert design. Multicoloured. P 14.

2311	7r. Type **325**	90	1·10
2312	8r. Fishing boat	1·10	1·25

(Des L. Fried. Litho Questa)

1995 (4 Dec). Flowers. T **326** and similar multicoloured designs. P 14.

2313	1r. Type **326**	25	15
2314	3r. White Mallow	60	50
2315	5r. Regale Trumpet Lily	1·10	1·00
2316	5r. *Dendrobium* "Waipahu Beauty"	1·10	1·00
	a. Sheetlet of 9. Nos. 2316/24	9·00	8·00
2317	5r. *Brassocattleya* "Jean Murray"	1·10	1·00
2318	5r. *Cymbidium* "Fort George"	1·10	1·00
2319	5r. *Paphiopedilum malipoense*	1·10	1·00
2320	5r. *Cycnoches chlorochilon*	1·10	1·00
2321	5r. *Rhyncholaelia digbgana*	1·10	1·00
2322	5r. *Lycaste deppei*	1·10	1·00
2323	5r. *Masdevallia constricta*	1·10	1·00
2324	5r. *Paphiopedilum* "Clair de Lune"	1·10	1·00
2325	7r. *Lilactime Dahlia*	1·25	1·25
2326	8r. Blue Ideal Iris	1·25	1·25
2327	10r. Red Crown Imperial	1·40	1·40
2313/27	*Set of 15*	14·00	13·00
MS2328	Two sheets, each 106×76 mm. (a) 25r. *Encyclia cochleata* (vert). (b) 25r. *Psychopsis kramerina* (vert) *Set of 2 sheets*	8·00	9·50

Nos. 2316/24 were printed together, *se-tenant*, in sheetlets of nine.

327 John Lennon with Microphone

328 Elvis Presley with Microphone

(Litho Questa)

1995 (8 Dec). 15th Death Anniv of John Lennon (musician). T **327** and similar vert designs. Multicoloured. P 14.

2329	5r. Type **327**	1·50	1·25
	a. Sheetlet of 6. Nos. 2329/34	8·00	6·50
2330	5r. With glasses and moustache	1·50	1·25
2331	5r. With guitar	1·50	1·25
2332	5r. With guitar and wearing glasses	1·50	1·25
2333	5r. Wearing sun glasses and red jacket	1·50	1·25
2334	5r. Wearing headphones	1·50	1·25
2329/34	*Set of 6*	8·00	6·50
MS2335	88×117 mm. 2, 3, 8, 10r. Different portraits of John Lennon	5·50	5·50
MS2336	102×72 mm. 25r. John Lennon performing	5·50	5·50

Nos. 2329/34 were printed together, *se-tenant*, in sheetlets of six.

(Des R. Martin. Litho Questa)

1995 (8 Dec). 60th Birth Anniv of Elvis Presley (entertainer). T **328** and similar multicoloured designs. P 13½×14.

2337	5r. Type **328**	90	80
	a. Sheetlet of 9. Nos. 2337/45	7·25	6·50
2338	5r. Wearing red jacket	90	80
2339	5r. Wearing blue jacket	90	80
2340	5r. With microphone and wearing blue jacket	90	80
2341	5r. In army uniform	90	80
2342	5r. Wearing yellow bow tie	90	80
2343	5r. In yellow shirt	90	80
2344	5r. In light blue shirt	90	80
2345	5r. Wearing red and white high-collared jacket	90	80
2337/45	*Set of 9*	7·25	6·50
MS2346	30×110 mm. 25r. Elvis Presley (horiz). P 14×13½	4·25	4·50

Nos. 2337/45 were printed together, *se-tenant*, in sheetlets of nine.

329 Johannes van der Waals (1919 Physics)

330 Rhythmic Gymnast and Japanese Fan

(Des R. Rundo. Litho Questa)

1995 (28 Dec). Centenary of Nobel Prize Trust Fund. T **329** and similar vert designs. Multicoloured. P 14.

2347/55	5r.×9 (Type **329** Charles Guillaume (1920 Physics); Sir James Chadwick (1935 Physics); Willem Einthoven (1924 Medicine); Henrik Dam (1943 Medicine); Sir Alexander Fleming (1945 Medicine); Hermann Muller (1946 Medicine); Rodney Porter (1972 Medicine); Werner Arber (1978 Medicine))		
	a. Sheetlet of 9. Nos. 2347/55	8·50	9·00
2356/64	5r.×9 (Niels Bohr (1922 Physics); Ben Mottelson (1975 Physics); Patrick White (1973 Literature); Elias Canetti (1981 Literature); Theodor Kocher (1909 Medicine); August Krogh (1920 Medicine); William Murphy (1934 Medicine); John Northrop (1946 Chemistry); Luis Leloir (1970 Chemistry))		
	a. Sheetlet of 9. Nos. 2356/64	8·50	9·00
2365/73	5r.×9 (Dag Hammarskjöld (1961 Peace); Alva Myrdal (1982 Peace); Archbishop Desmond Tutu (1984 Peace); Rudolf Eucken (1908 Literature); Aleksandr Solzhenitsyn (1970 Literature); Gabriel Marquez (1982 Literature); Chen Yang (1957 Physics); Karl Muller (1987 Physics); Melvin Schwartz (1988 Physics))		
	a. Sheetlet of 9. Nos. 2365/73	8·50	9·00
2374/82	5r.×9 (Robert Millikan (1923 Physics); Louis de Broglie (1929 Physics); Ernest Walton (1951 Physics); Richard Willstatter (1915 Chemistry); Lars Onsager (1968 Chemistry); Gerhard Herzberg (1971 Chemistry); William B. Yeats (1923 Literature); George Bernard Shaw (1925 Literature); Eugene O'Neill (1936 Literature))		
	a. Sheetlet of 9. Nos. 2374/82	8·50	9·00
2383/91	5r.×9 (Bernardo Houssay (1947 Medicine); Paul Muller (1948 Medicine); Walter Hess (1949 Medicine); Sir MacFarlane Burnet (1960 Medicine); Baruch Blumberg (1976 Medicine); Daniel Nathans (1978 Medicine); Glenn Seaborg (1951 Chemistry); Ilya Prigogine (1977 Chemistry); Kenichi Fukui (1981 Chemistry))		
	a. Sheetlet of 9. Nos. 2383/91	8·50	9·00
2392/400	5r.×9 (Carl Spitteler (1919 Literature); Henri Bergson (1927 Literature); Johannes Jensen (1944 Literature); Antoine-Henri Becquerel (1903 Physics); Sir William H. Bragg (1915 Physics); Sir William L. Bragg (1915 Physics); Frederik Bier (1908 Peace); Leon Bourgeois (1920 Peace); Karl Branting (1921 Peace))		
	a. Sheetlet of 9. Nos. 2392/2400	8·50	9·00
2347/2400	Set of 54	45·00	48·00

MS2401 Six sheets. (a) 80×110 mm. 25r. Konrad Bloch (1964 Medicine). (b) 80×110 mm. 25r. Samuel Beckett (1969 Literature). (c) 80×110 mm. 25r. Otto Wallach (1910 Chemistry). (d) 110×80 mm. 25r. Hideki Yukawa (1949 Physics). (e) 110×80 mm. 25r. Eisaku Sato (1974 Peace). (f) 110×80 mm. 25r. Robert Koch (1905 Medicine) *Set of 6 sheets* .... 17·00 20·00

Nos. 2347/55, 2356/64, 2365/73, 2374/82, 2383/91 and 2392/2400 were printed together, *se-tenant*, in sheetlets of nine.

(Des L. Fried. Litho Questa)

1996 (25 Jan). Olympic Games, Atlanta (1st issue). T **330** and similar multicoloured designs. P 14.

2402	1r. Type **330**	25	10
2403	3r. Archer and Moscow Olympics logo	50	35
2404	5r. Diver and Swedish flag	1·00	1·00
2405	5r. Canadian Maple Leaf	1·00	1·00
	a. Sheetlet of 9. Nos. 2405/13	8·00	8·00
2406	5r. Shot putting (Decathlon)	1·00	1·00
2407	5r. Moscow Olympic medal and ribbon	1·00	1·00
2408	5r. Fencer	1·00	1·00
2409	5r. Gold medal	1·00	1·00
2410	5r. Equestrian competitor	1·00	1·00
2411	5r. Sydney Opera House	1·00	1·00
2412	5r. Athlete on starting blocks	1·00	1·00
2413	5r. South Korean flag	1·00	1·00
2414	7r. High jumper and Tower Bridge, London	1·10	1·10
2415	10r. Athlete on starting blocks and Brandenburg Gate Germany	1·40	1·60
2416	12r. Hurdler and Amsterdam Olympic logo	1·60	1·90
2402/16	Set of 15	12·50	12·50

MS2417 Two sheets, each 113×80 mm. (a) 25r. Red Olympic Flame (*vert*). (b) 25r. Multicoloured Olympic Flame (*vert*) *Set of 2 sheets* .... 8·00 9·00

Nos. 2405/13 were printed together, *se-tenant*, in sheetlets of nine. See also Nos. 2469/**MS**2488.

331 "Self Portrait" (Degas)

(Litho Questa)

1996 (22 Apr). 125th Anniv of Metropolitan Museum of Art, New York. T **331** and similar multicoloured designs. P 13½×14.

2418/25	4r.×8 (Type **331**; "Andromache and Astyanax (Prud'hon); "René Grenier" (Toulouse-Lautrec); "The Banks of the Biévre near Bicêtre" (Rousseau); "The Repast of the Lion" (Rousseau); "Portrait of Yves Gobillard-Morisot" (Degas); "Sun flowers" (Van Gogh); "The Singer in Green" (Degas))		
	a. Sheetlet of 8. Nos. 2418/25	8·00	8·50
2426/33	4r.×8 ("Still Life" (Fantin-Latour); "Portrait of a Lady in Grey" (Degas); "Apples and Grapes" (Monet); "The Englishman" (Toulouse-Lautrec); "Cypresses" (Van Gogh); "Flowers in a Chinese Vase" (Redon); "The Gardener" (Seurat); "Large Sunflowers I" (Nolde))		
	a. Sheetlet of 8. Nos. 2426/33	8·00	8·50
2434/41	4r.×8 (All by Manet: "The Spanish Singer"; "Young Man in Costume of Maio"; "Mademoiselle Victorine"; "Peonies"; "Boating", "Woman with a Parrot", "George Moore"; "The Monet Family in their Garden")		
	a. Sheetlet of 8. Nos. 2434/41	8·00	8·50
2442/9	4r.×8 ("Goldfish" (Matisse); "Spanish Woman: Harmony in Blue" (Matisse); "Nasturtiums and the "Dance" IL" (Matisse); "The House behind Trees" (Braque); "Mada Primavesi" (Klimt); "Head of a Woman" (Picasso) "Woman in White" (Picasso), "Harlequin" (Picasso))		
	a. Sheetlet of 8. Nos. 2442/9	8·00	8·50
2418/49	Set of 32	29·00	30·00

MS2450 Four sheets, each 95×70 mm containing horiz designs, 81×53 mm. P 14. (a) 25r. "Northeaster" (Homer). (b) 25r. "The Fortune Teller" (De La Tour). (c) 25r. "Santo (Sanzio), Ritratto de Andrea Navagero a Agostino Beazzano" (Raphael). (d) 25r. "Portrait of a Woman" (Rubens) *Set of 4 sheets* .... 17·00 20·00

Nos. 2418/25, 2426/33, 2434/41 and 2442/9 were each printed together, *se-tenant*, in sheetlets of eight stamps and one centre label.

332 Mickey Mouse on Great Wall of China

(Des Walt Disney Company Asia Pacific Ltd. Litho Questa)

1996 (10 May). "CHINA '96" Ninth Asian International Stamp Exhibition, Peking. T **332** and similar multicoloured designs showing Walt Disney cartoon characters in China. P 14×13½ (horiz) or 13½×14 (vert).

2451	2r. Type **332**	80	80
	a. Sheetlet of 6. Nos. 2451/6	4·25	4·25
2452	2r. Pluto with temple guardian	80	80
2453	2r. Minnie Mouse with Pandas	80	80
2454	2r. Mickey windsurfing nearjunks	80	80
2455	2r. Goofy cleaning Grottoe statue	80	80
2456	2r. Donald and Daisy Duck at Marble Boat	80	80
2457	2r. Mickey with terracotta warriors	80	80
	a. Sheetlet of 6. Nos. 2457/62	4·25	4·25
2458	2r. Goofy with geese and masks	80	80
2459	2r. Donald and Goofy on traditional fishing boat	80	80
2460	2r. Mickey and Minnie in dragon boat	80	80
2461	2r. Donald at Peking opera	80	80
2462	2r. Mickey and Minnie in Chinese garden	80	80
2463	3r. Mickey and Minnie at the Ice Pagoda (*vert*)	1·00	1·00
	a. Sheetlet of 5. Nos. 2463/7	4·50	4·50
2464	3r. Donald and Mickey flying Chinese kites (*vert*)	1·00	1·00
2465	3r. Goofy playing anyiwu (*vert*)	1·00	1·00
2466	3r. Paper cutouts Mickey and Goofy (*vert*)	1·00	1·00
2467	3r. Donald and Mickey in dragon dance (*vert*)	1·00	1·00
2451/67	Set of 17	13·00	13·00

MS2468 Three sheets. (a) 108×133 mm. 5r. Mickey pointing. (b) 133×108 mm. 7r. Mickey and Minnie watching Moon. (c) 133×108 mm. 8r. Donald using chopsticks *Set of 3 sheets* .... 5·50 6·00

Nos. 2451/6, 2457/62 and 2463/7 were each printed together, *se-tenant*, in sheetlets of six (Nos. 2451/6, 2457/62) or five stamps and one label (Nos. 2463/7).

333 Stella Walsh (Poland) (100m sprint, 1932) on Medal

(Litho B.D.T.)

1996 (27 May). Olympic Games, Atlanta (2nd issue). Previous Gold Medal Winners. T **333** and similar multicoloured designs. P 14.

2469	1r. Type **333**	25	15
2470	3r. Emile Zatopek (Czechoslovakia) (10,000m running, 1952) and Olympic torch (*vert*)	50	35
2471	5r. Yanko Rousseu (Bulgaria) (lightweight, 1980) (*vert*)	85	85
	a. Sheetlet of 9. Nos. 2471/9	7·00	7·00
2472	5r. Peter Baczako (Hungary) (middle heavyweight, 1980) (*vert*)	85	85
2473	5r. Leonid Taranenko (Russia) (heavyweight, 1980) (*vert*)	85	85
2474	5r. Aleksandr Kurlovich (Russia) (heavyweight, 1988) (*vert*)	85	85
2475	5r. Assen Zlateu (Bulgaria) (middleweight, 1980) (*vert*)	85	85
2476	5r. Zang Guoqiang (China) (flyweight, 1984) (*vert*)	85	85
2477	5r. Yurik Vardanyan (Russia) (heavyweight, 1980) (*vert*)	85	85
2478	5r. Sultan Rakhmanov (Russia) (super heavyweight, 1980) (*vert*)	85	85
2479	5r. Vassily Alexeev (Russia) (super heavyweight, 1972) (*vert*)	85	85
2480	5r. Ethel Catherwood (Canada) (high jump, 1928) (*vert*)	85	85
	a. Sheetlet of 6. Nos. 2480/5	4·50	4·50
2481	5r. Mildred Didrikson (U.S.A.) (javelin, 1932) (*vert*)	85	85
2482	5r. Francina Blankers-Koen (Netherlands) (80m hurdles, 1948) (*vert*)	85	85
2483	5r. Tamara Press (Russia) (shot put, 1960)	85	85
2484	5r. Lia Manchu (Romania) (discus, 1968)	85	85
2485	5r. Rosa Mota (Portugal) (marathon, 1988)	85	85
2486	10r. Olga Fikotova (Czechoslovakia) (discus, 1956) on medal	1·40	1·60
2487	12r. Joan Benoit (U.S.A.) (marathon, 1984) on medal	1·60	1·90
2469/87	Set of 19	15·00	15·00

MS2488 Two sheets. (a) 76×106 mm. 25r. Naeem Suleymanoglu (Turkey) (weightlifting, 1988) (*vert*). (b) 105×75 mm. 25r. Irena Szewinska (Poland) (400m running, 1976) on medal *Set of 2 sheets* .... 8·50 9·00

Nos. 2471/9 (weightlifters) and Nos. 2480/5 (women's track and field as T **333**) were each printed together, *se-tenant*, in sheetlets of nine or six.

No. 2469 identifies the event as 10 metres in error.

Maldives مٍوٍۇۇٍ

Rf8

334 Queen Elizabeth II

(Litho Questa)

1996 (10 July). 70th Birthday of Queen Elizabeth II. T **334** and similar vert designs showing different photographs. Multicoloured. P 13½×14.

2489	8r. Type **334**	1·75	1·75
	a. Strip of 3. Nos. 2489/91	5·25	5·25
2490	8r. Wearing hat	1·75	1·75
2491	8r. At desk	1·75	1·75
2489/91	Set of 3	5·25	5·25

MS2492 125×103 mm. 25r. Queen Elizabeth and Queen Mother on Buckingham Palace Balcony .... 6·50 6·00

Nos. 2489/91 were printed together, *se-tenant*, in horizontal and vertical strips of three throughout sheets of nine.

335 African Child   **336** "Sputnik 1" Satellite

(Litho B.D.T. (No. 2495) or Questa (others))

1996 (10 July). 50th Anniv of U.N.I.C.E.F. T **335** and similar vert designs. Multicoloured. P 14.

2493	5r. Type **335**	75	55
2494	7r. European girl	1·00	1·25
2495	7r. Maldivian boy	1·00	1·25
2496	10r. Asian girl	1·40	1·50
2493/96	Set of 4	3·75	4·00

MS2497 114×74 mm. 25r. Baby with toy .... 3·50 4·50

1996 (10 July). Space Exploration. T **336** and similar multicoloured designs. Litho. P 14.

2498	6r. Type **336**	1·10	1·10
	a. Sheetlet of 6. Nos. 2498/2503	6·00	6·00
2499	6r. "Apollo 11" command module	1·10	1·10
2500	6r. "Skylab"	1·10	1·10
2501	6r. Astronaut Edward White walking in Space	1·10	1·10
2502	6r. "Mariner 9"	1·10	1·10
2503	6r. "Apollo" and "Soyuz" docking	1·10	1·10
2498/503	Set of 6	6·00	6·00

MS2504 104×74 mm. 25r. Launch of "Apollo 8" (*vert*) .. 4·50 5·00

Nos. 2498/2503 were printed together, *se-tenant*, in sheetlets of six, the background forming a composite design.

337 *Epiphora albida*

1996 (10 July). Butterflies. T **337** and similar multicoloured designs. Litho. P 14.

2505	7r. Type **337**		1·25	1·25
	a. Sheetlet of 6. Nos. 2505/10		6·75	6·75
2506	7r. *Satyrus dryas*		1·25	1·25
2507	7r. *Satyrus lena*		1·25	1·25
2508	7r. *Papilio tynderaeus*		1·25	1·25
2509	7r. *Urota suraka*		1·25	1·25
2510	7r. *Satyrus nercis*		1·25	1·25
2511	7r. *Papilio troilus* (vert)		1·25	1·25
	a. Sheetlet of 8. Nos. 2511/18		9·00	9·00
2512	7r. *Papilio cresphontes* (vert)		1·25	1·25
2513	7r. Lime Swallowtail caterpillar (vert)		1·25	1·25
2514	7r. *Cynthia virginiensis* (vert)		1·25	1·25
2515	7r. Monarch caterpillar (vert)		1·25	1·25
2516	7r. *Danaus plexippus* (vert)		1·25	1·25
2517	7r. Monarch caterpillar and pupa (vert)		1·25	1·25
2518	7r. *Chlosyne harrisii* (vert)		1·25	1·25
2519	7r. *Cymothoe coccinata* (vert)		1·25	1·25
	a. Sheetlet of 8. Nos. 2519/22×2		9·00	9·00
2520	7r. *Morpho rhetenor* (vert)		1·25	1·25
2521	7r. *Callicore lidwina* (vert)		1·25	1·25
2522	7r. *Heliconius erato reductimacula* (vert)		1·25	1·25
2505/22 *Set of 18*			20·00	20·00

MS2523 Two sheets, each 106×76 mm. (a) 25r. *Heliconius charitonius* (vert). (b) 25r. *Heliconius cydno* (vert) *Set of 2 sheets* .... 8·50 9·00

Nos. 2505/10, 2511/18 and 2519/22 were each printed together, se-tenant, in sheetlets of six or eight.

338 Amtrak F40H Diesel-electric Locomotive, U.S.A.

339 Bongo

1996 (2 Sept). Trains of the World. T **338** and similar horiz designs. Multicoloured. Litho. P 14.

2524	3r. Type **338**		80	80
	a. Sheetlet of 9. Nos. 2524/32		6·50	6·50
2525	3r. Stephenson's *Experiment*		80	80
2526	3r. Indian-Pacific Intercontinental, Australia		80	80
2527	3r. Stephenson's Killingworth type steam locomotive, 1815		80	80
2528	3r. George Stephenson		80	80
2529	3r. Stephenson's *Rocket*, 1829		80	80
2530	3r. High Speed Train 125, Great Britain, 1975		80	80
2531	3r. First rail passenger coach *Experiment*, 1825		80	80
2532	3r. Union Pacific Class U25B diesel locomotive (inscr "Tofac"), U.S.A.		80	80
2533	3r. Southern Pacific "Daylight" express, U.S.A., 1952		80	80
	a. Sheetlet of 9. Nos. 2533/41		6·50	6·50
2534	3r. Timothy Hackworth's *Sans Pareil*, 1829		80	80
2535	3r. Chicago and North Western diesel locomotive, USA		80	80
2536	3r. Richard Trevithick's *Pen-y-Darren* locomotive, 1804		80	80
2537	3r. Isambard Kingdom Brunel		80	80
2538	3r. Great Western locomotive, 1838		80	80
2539	3r. Vistadome observation car, Canada		80	80
2540	3r. Mohawk and Hudson Railroad *Experiment*, 1832		80	80
2541	3r. ICE high speed train, Germany		80	80
2542	3r. Electric container locomotive, Germany		80	80
	a. Sheetlet of 9. Nos. 2542/50		6·50	6·50
2543	3r. John Blenkinsop's rack locomotive, 1811		80	80
2544	3r. Diesel-electric locomotive, Western Australia		80	80
2545	3r. Timothy Hackworth's *Royal George*, 1827		80	80
2546	3r. Robert Stephenson		80	80
2547	3r. Trevithick's *Newcastle*		80	80
2548	3r. Deltic diesel-electric locomotive, Great Britain		80	80
2549	3r. Stockton and Darlington Railway locomotive No. 5 *Stockton*, 1826		80	80
2550	3r. Channel Tunnel "Le Shuttle" train		80	80
2524/50 *Set of 27*			19·00	19·00

MS2551 Three sheets, each 96×91 mm. (a) 25r. Peter Cooper's *Tom Thumb*, 1829. (b) 25r. John Jarvis's *De Witt Clinton*, 1831. (c) 25r. William Hudson's *The General* 1855 *Set of 3 sheets* .... 13·00 13·00

Nos. 2524/32, 2533/41 and 2542/50 were printed together, se-tenant, in sheetlets of nine.

No. 254 is inscribed "F4 OPH" in error.

1996 (9 Sept). Wildlife of the World. T **339** and similar multicoloured designs. Litho. P 14.

2552	5r. Type **339**		1·50	1·25
	a. Sheetlet of 8. Nos. 2552/9		11·00	9·00
2553	5r. Bushbuck		1·50	1·25
2554	5r. Namaqua Dove		1·50	1·25
2555	5r. Hoopoe		1·50	1·25
2556	5r. African Fish Eagle		1·50	1·25
2557	5r. Egyptian Goose		1·50	1·25
2558	5r. Saddle-bill Stork		1·50	1·25
2559	5r. Blue-breasted Kingfisher		1·50	1·25
2560	5r. Yellow Baboon		1·50	1·25
	a. Sheetlet of 8. Nos. 2560/7		11·00	9·00
2561	5r. Banded Duiker ("Zebra Duiker")		1·50	1·25
2562	5r. Yellow-backed Duiker		1·50	1·25
2563	5r. Pygmy Hippopotamus		1·50	1·25
2564	5r. Large-spotted Genet		1·50	1·25
2565	5r. African Spoonbill		1·50	1·25
2566	5r. White-faced Whistling Duck		1·50	1·25
2567	5r. Helmet Guineafowl		1·50	1·25
2568	7r. Cotton-headed Tamarin (horiz)		1·75	1·50
	a. Sheetlet of 9. Nos. 2568/76		13·00	12·00
2569	7r. European Bison (horiz)		1·75	1·50
2570	7r. Tiger (horiz)		1·75	1·50
2571	7r. Capercaillie (horiz)		1·75	1·50
2572	7r. Giant Panda (horiz)		1·75	1·50
2573	7r. *Trogonoptera brookiana* (butterfly) (horiz)		1·75	1·50
2574	7r. American Beaver (horiz)		1·75	1·50
2575	7r. *Leiopelma hamiltoni* (frog) (horiz)		1·75	1·50
2576	7r. Manatee (horiz)		1·75	1·50
2552/76 *Set of 25*			35·00	30·00

MS2577 106×76 mm. 25r. Chimpanzee (horiz) .... 4·50 5·00

Nos. 2552/9, 2560/7 and 2568/76 were each printed together, se-tenant, in sheetlets of eight or nine, the backgrounds forming composite designs.

No. 2553 is inscribed "BUSHBACK" in error.

340 Giant Panda

1996 (9 Sept). Endangered Species. T **340** and similar multicoloured designs. Litho. P 14.

2578	5r. Type **340**		1·50	1·25
	a. Sheetlet of 6. Nos. 2578/83		8·00	6·75
2579	5r. Indian Elephant		1·50	1·25
2580	5r. Arrow-poison Frog		1·50	1·25
2581	5r. Mandrill		1·50	1·25
2582	5r. Snow Leopard		1·50	1·25
2583	5r. California Condor		1·50	1·25
2584	5r. Whale-headed Stork ("Shoebill Stork")		1·50	1·25
	a. Sheetlet of 6. Nos. 2584/9		8·00	6·75
2585	5r. Red-billed Hornbill		1·50	1·25
2586	5r. Hippopotamus		1·50	1·25
2587	5r. Gorilla		1·50	1·25
2588	5r. Lion		1·50	1·25
2589	5r. South African Crowned Crane		1·50	1·25
2578/89 *Set of 12*			16·00	13·50

MS2590 Two sheets, each 110×80 mm. (a) 25r. Tiger (vert). (b) 25r. Leopard *Set of 2 sheets* .... 9·50 11·00

Nos. 2578/83 and 2584/9 were each printed together, se-tenant, in sheetlets of six.

341 Mickey Mouse climbing out of Puddle

(Des Alvin White Studio, Litho Questa)

1996 (2 Dec). Centenary of the Cinema. T **341** and similar horiz designs showing a series of cartoon frames from *The Little Whirlwind* (Nos. 2591/2607) and *Pluto and the Flypaper* (Nos. 2608/24). Multicoloured. P 14×13½.

2591	4r. Type **341**	1·25	1·25
	a. Sheetlet of 8. Nos. 2591/8 and 1 label..	9·00	9·00
2592	4r. Frame 2	1·25	1·25
2593	4r. Frame 3	1·25	1·25
2594	4r. Frame 4	1·25	1·25
2595	4r. Frame 5	1·25	1·25
2596	4r. Frame 6	1·25	1·25
2597	4r. Frame 7	1·25	1·25
2598	4r. Frame 8	1·25	1·25
2599	4r. Frame 9	1·25	1·25
	a. Sheetlet of 9. Nos. 2599/2607	10·00	10·00
2600	4r. Frame 10	1·25	1·25
2601	4r. Frame 11	1·25	1·25
2602	4r. Frame 12	1·25	1·25
2603	4r. Frame 13	1·25	1·25
2604	4r. Frame 14	1·25	1·25
2605	4r. Frame 15	1·25	1·25
2606	4r. Frame 16 (Mickey holding fish above head)	1·25	1·25
2607	4r. Frame 17 (Mickey throwing fish into pool)	1·25	1·25
2608	4r. Frame 1 (Pluto)	1·25	1·25
	a. Sheetlet of 8. Nos. 2608/15 and 1 label	9·00	9·00
2609	4r. Frame 2	1·25	1·25
2610	4r. Frame 3	1·25	1·25
2611	4r. Frame 4	1·25	1·25
2612	4r. Frame 5	1·25	1·25
2613	4r. Frame 6	1·25	1·25
2614	4r. Frame 7	1·25	1·25
2615	4r. Frame 8	1·25	1·25
2616	4r. Frame 9	1·25	1·25
	a. Sheetlet of 9. Nos. 2616/24	10·00	10·00
2617	4r. Frame 10	1·25	1·25
2618	4r. Frame 11	1·25	1·25
2619	4r. Frame 12	1·25	1·25
2620	4r. Frame 13	1·25	1·25
2621	4r. Frame 14	1·25	1·25
2622	4r. Frame 15	1·25	1·25
2623	4r. Frame 16	1·25	1·25
2624	4r. Frame 17	1·25	1·25
2591/624	*Set of 34*	38·00	38·00

MS2625 Two sheets, 111×131 mm. (a) 25r. Frame 18 (*The Little Whirlwind*). (b) 25r. Frame 18 (*Pluto and the Flypaper*) *Set of 2 sheets* ... 12·00 15·00

Nos. 2591/8, 2599/2607, 2608/15 and 2616/24 were printed together, *se-tenant*, in sheets of eight or nine. It is intended that the stamps should be separated and used as a flip book to produce a moving image.

342 Letter "O" with Chinese Character

343 California Condor

(Des M. Friedman. Litho Questa)

1997 (12 Feb). "HONG KONG '97" International Stamp Exhibition. T **342** and similar multicoloured designs. P 13½×14.

2626	5r. Letter "H" and Chinese couple	85	85
	a. Sheetlet of 8. Nos. 2626/33	6·00	6·00
2627	5r. Type **342**	85	85
2628	5r. Letter "N" and Chinese dragon	85	85
2629	5r. Letter "G" and carnival dragon	85	85
2630	5r. Letter "K" and modern office block	85	85
2631	5r. Letter "O" and Chinese character (*different*)	85	85
2632	5r. Letter "N" and Chinese fan cases	85	85
2633	5r. Letter "G" and Chinese junk	85	85
2626/33	*Set of 8*	6·00	6·00

MS2634 106×125 mm. 25r. "HONG KONG" as on Nos. 2626/33 (76×38 *mm*) ... 3·75 4·50

Nos. 2626/33 were printed together, *se-tenant*, in sheetlets of eight.

1997 (12 Feb). Birds of the World. T **343** and similar vert designs. Multicoloured. Litho. P 14.

2635	5r. Type **343**	1·00	1·00
	a. Sheetlet of 9. Nos. 2635/43	8·00	8·00
2636	5r. Audouin's Gull	1·00	1·00
2637	5r. Atlantic Puffin	1·00	1·00
2638	5r. Resplendent Quetzal	1·00	1·00
2639	5r. Puerto Rican Amazon	1·00	1·00
2640	5r. Lesser Bird of Paradise	1·00	1·00
2641	5r. Japanese Crested Ibis	1·00	1·00
2642	5r. Mauritius Kestrel	1·00	1·00
2643	5r. Kakapo	1·00	1·00
2635/43	*Set of 9*	8·00	8·00

MS2644 76×106 mm. 25r. Ivory-billed Woodpecker ..... 5·50 6·00

Nos. 2635/43 were printed together, *se-tenant*, in sheetlets of nine with the backgrounds forming a composite design.

344 Ye Qiabo (China) (women's 500/100m speed skating, 1992)

345 Crowned Solitary Eagle

(Litho Questa)

1997 (13 Mar). Winter Olympic Games, Nagano, Japan (1998). T **344** and similar vert designs. Multicoloured. P 14.

2645	2r. Type **344**	40	25
2646	3r. Leonhard Stock (Austria) (downhill skiing, 1980)	55	35
2647	5r. Hernia van Szabo-Planck (Austria) (figure skating, 1924)	85	85
	a. Sheetlet of 8. Nos. 2647/50×2	6·00	6·00
2648	5r. Katarina Witt (Germany) (figure skating, 1988)	85	85
2649	5r. Natalia Bestemianova and Andrei Bukin (Russia) (pairs ice dancing, 1988)	85	85
2650	5r. Jayne Torvill and Christopher Dean (Great Britain) (pairs ice dancing, 1984)	85	85
2651	8r. Bjorn Daehlie (Norway) (cross country skiing, 1992)	1·25	1·25
2652	12r. Wolfgang Hoppe (Germany) (bobsleigh, 1984)	1·75	2·00
2645/52	*Set of 8*	6·50	6·50

MS2653 Two sheets, each 76×106 mm. (a) 25r. Sonja Henie (Norway) (figure skating, 1924). (b) 25r. Andree Joly and Pierre Brunet (France) (pairs ice dancing, 1932) *Set of 2 sheets* ... 8·00 9·00

Nos. 2645/52 were printed together, *se-tenant*, in sheetlets of eight containing two of each design.

(Litho Questa)

1997 (20 Mar). Eagles. T **345** and similar multicoloured designs. P 14.

2654	1r. Type **345**	55	25
2655	2r. African Hawk Eagle (*horiz*)	75	35
2656	3r. Lesser Spotted Eagle	1·00	65
2657	5r. Steller's Sea Eagle	1·25	1·25
2658	5r. Bald Eagle attacking	1·25	1·25
	a. Sheetlet of 6. Nos. 2658/63	6·75	6·75
2659	5r. Bald Eagle on branch	1·25	1·25
2660	5r. Bald Eagle looking left	1·25	1·25
2661	5r. Bald Eagle looking right	1·25	1·25
2662	5r. Bald Eagle sitting on branch with leaves	1·25	1·25
2663	5r. Bald Eagle soaring	1·25	1·25
2664	8r. Spanish Imperial Eagle (*horiz*)	1·75	2·00
2665	10r. Harpy Eagle	1·75	2·00
2666	12r. Crested Serpent Eagle (*horiz*)	2·00	2·50
2654/66	*Set of 13*	15·00	15·00

MS2667 Two sheets. (a) 73×104 mm. 25r. Bald Eagle. (b) 104×73 mm. 25r. American Bald Eagle (*horiz*) *Set of 2 sheets* ... 9·00 10·00

Nos. 2658/63 were printed together, *se-tenant*, in sheetlets of six.

346 Blitzer Benz, 1911

347 Patris II, Greece (1926)

1997 (27 Mar). Classic Cars. T **346** and similar horiz designs. Multicoloured. Litho. P 14.

2668	5r. Type **346**	80	85
	a. Sheetlet of 6. Nos. 2668/73	4·25	4·50
2669	5r. Datsun, 1917	80	85
2670	5r. Auburn 8-120, 1929	80	85
2671	5r. Mercedes-Benz C280, 1996	80	85
2672	5r. Suzuki UR-1	80	85
2673	5r. Chrysler Atlantic	80	85
2674	5r. Mercedes-Benz 190SL, 1961	80	85
	a. Sheetlet of 6. Nos. 2674/9	4·25	4·50
2675	5r. Kwaishinha D.A.T., 1916	80	85
2676	5r. Rolls-Royce Roadster 20/25	80	85
2677	5r. Mercedes-Benz SLK, 1997	80	85
2678	5r. Toyota Camry, 1996	80	85
2679	5r. Jaguar MK 2, 1959	80	85
2668/79 Set of 12		8·50	9·00

MS2680 Two sheets, each 100×70 mm. (a) 25r. Volkswagen, 1939. (b) 25r. Mazda RX-01 Set of 2 sheets ... 7·50 8·50

Nos. 2668/73 and 2674/9 were each printed together, *se-tenant*, in sheetlets of six.

No. **MS**2680b is inscribed "MAZADA" in error.

(Des D. Miller. Litho Questa)

1997 (1 Apr). Passenger Ships. T **347** and similar multicoloured designs. P 14.

2681	1r. Type **347**	45	15
2682	2r. *Infanta Beatriz*, Spain (1928)	60	25
2683	3r. *Vasilefs Constantinos*, Greece (1914)	75	75
	a. Sheetlet of 9. Nos. 2683/91	6·00	6·00
2684	3r. *Cunene*, Portugal (1911)	75	75
2685	3r. *Selandia*, Denmark (1912)	75	75
2686	3r. *President Harding*, U.S.A. (1921)	75	75
2687	3r. *Ulster Monarch*, Great Britain (1929)	75	75
2688	3r. *Matsonia*, U.S.A. (1913)	75	75
2689	3r. *France*, France (1911)	75	75
2690	3r. *Campania*, Great Britain (1893)	75	75
2691	3r. *Klipfontein*, Holland (1922)	75	75
2692	3r. *Eridan*, France (1929)	75	75
	a. Sheetlet of 9. Nos. 2692/2700	6·00	6·00
2693	3r. *Mount Clinton*, U.S.A. (1921)	75	75
2694	3r. *Infanta Isabel*, Spain (1912)	75	75
2695	3r. *Suwa Maru*, Japan (1914)	75	75
2696	3r. *Yorkshire*, Great Britain (1920)	75	75
2697	3r. *Highland Chieftain*, Great Britain (1929)	75	75
2698	3r. *Sardinia*, Norway (1920)	75	75
2699	3r. *San Guglielmo*, Italy (1911)	75	75
2700	3r. *Avila*, Great Britain (1927)	75	75
2701	8r. *Stavangerfjord*, Norway (1918)	1·50	1·75
2702	12r. *Baloeran*, Netherlands (1929)	2·00	2·25
2681/702 Set of 22		17·00	17·00

MS2703 Four sheets. (a) 69×69 mm. 25r. *Mauritania*, Great Britain (1907). (b) 69×69 mm. 25r. *United States*, U.S.A. (1952). (c) 69×69 mm. 25r. *Queen Mary*, Great Britain (1930). (d) 91×76 mm. 25r. Royal Yacht *Britannia* and Chinese junk, Hong Kong (56×42 mm) Set of 4 sheets ... 18·00 18·00

Nos. 2683/91 and 2692/2700 were each printed together, *se-tenant*, in sheetlets of nine.

No. **MS**2703d is inscribed "BRITTANIA" in error.

348 Prayer Wheels, Lhasa

(Des M. Freedman and Dena Rubin. Litho Questa)

1997 (7 Apr). 50th Anniv of U.N.E.S.C.O. T **348** and similar multicoloured designs. P 14×13½ (horiz) or 13½×14 (vert).

2704	1r. Type **348**	20	15
2705	2r. Ruins of Roman Temple of Diana, Portugal (*horiz*)	30	25
2706	3r. Santa Maria Cathedral, Hildesheim, Germany (*horiz*)	45	35
2707	5r. Vivunga National Park, Zaire	75	75
	a. Sheetlet of 8. Nos. 2707/14 and central label	5·50	5·50
2708	5r. Valley of Mai Nature Reserve, Seychelles	75	75

2709	5r. Kandy, Sri Lanka	75	75
2710	5r. Taj Mahal, India	75	75
2711	5r. Istanbul, Turkey	75	75
2712	5r. Sana'a, Yemen	75	75
2713	5r. Bleinheim Palace, England	75	75
2714	5r. Grand Canyon National Park, U.S.A.	75	75
2715	5r. Tombs, Gondar, Ethiopia	75	75
	a. Sheetlets of 8. Nos. 2715/22 and central label	5·50	5·50
2716	5r. Bwindi National Park, Uganda	75	75
2717	5r. Bemaraha National Reserve, Madagascar	75	75
2718	5r. Buddhist ruins at Takht-I-Bahi, Pakistan	75	75
2719	5r. Anuradhapura, Sri Lanka	75	75
2720	5r. Cairo, Egypt	75	75
2721	5r. Ruins, Petra, Jordan	75	75
2722	5r. Volcano, Ujung Kulon National Park, Indonesia	75	75
2723	5r. Terrace, Mount Taishan, China	75	75
	a. Sheetlet of 8. Nos. 2723/30 and central label	5·50	5·50
2724	5r. Temple, Mount Taishan, China	75	75
2725	5r. Temple turret, Mount Taishan, China	75	75
2726	5r. Standing stones, Mount Taishan, China	75	75
2727	5r. Courtyard, Mount Taishan, China	75	75
2728	5r. Staircase, Mount Taishan, China	75	75
2729	5r. Terracotta Warriors, China	75	75
2730	5r. Head of Terracotta Warrior, China	75	75
2731	7r. Doorway, Abu Simbel, Egypt	90	95
2732	8r. Mandraki, Rhodes, Greece (*horiz*)	1·25	1·25
2733	8r. Agios Stefanos Monastery, Meteors, Greece (*horiz*)	1·25	1·25
	a. Sheetlet of 5. Nos. 2733/7 and label	5·50	5·50
2734	8r. Taj Mahal, India (*horiz*)	1·25	1·25
2735	8r. Cistercian Abbey of Fontenay, France (*horiz*)	1·25	1·25
2736	8r. Yarushima, Japan (*horiz*)	1·25	1·25
2737	8r. Cloisters, San Gonzalo Convent, Portugal (*horiz*)	1·25	1·25
2738	8r. Olympic National Park, U.S.A. (*horiz*)	1·25	1·25
	a. Sheetlet of 5. Nos. 2738/42 and label	5·50	5·50
2739	8r. Waterfall, Nahanni National Park, Canada (*horiz*)	1·25	1·25
2740	8r. Mountains, National Park, Argentina (*horiz*)	1·25	1·25
2741	8r. Bonfin Salvador Church, Brazil (*horiz*)	1·25	1·25
2742	8r. Convent of the Companions of Jesus, Morelia, Mexico (*horiz*)	1·25	1·25
2743	8r. Two-storey Temple, Horyu Temple, Japan (*horiz*)	1·25	1·25
	a. Sheetlet of 5. Nos. 2743/7 and label	5·50	5·50
2744	8r. Summer house, Horyu Temple, Japan (*horiz*)	1·25	1·25
2745	8r. Temple and cloister, Horyu Temple, Japan (*horiz*)	1·25	1·25
2746	8r. Single storey Temple, Horyu Temple, Japan (*horiz*)	1·25	1·25
2747	8r. Well, Horyu Temple, Japan (*horiz*)	1·25	1·25
2748	10r. Scandals Nature Reserve, France (*horiz*)	1·25	1·40
2749	12r. Temple on the Lake, China (*horiz*)	1·50	1·75
2704/49 Set of 46		35·00	42·00

MS2750 Four sheets, each 127×102 mm. (a) 25r. Fatehpur Sikri Monument, India (*horiz*). (b) 25r. Temple, Chengde, China (*horiz*). (c) 25r. Serengeti National Park, Tanzania (*horiz*). (d) 25r. Buddha, Anuradhapura, Sri Lanka (*horiz*) Set of 4 sheets ... 13·00 14·00

Nos. 2707/14, 2715/22 and 2723/30 were each printed together, *se-tenant*, in sheetlets of eight stamps with a central label and Nos. 2733/7, 2738/42 and 2743/7 in sheetlets of five stamps with a top left-hand corner label.

No. 2717 is inscribed "MADAGASCAR" and No. 2737 "COVENT", both in error.

349 White Doves and S.A.A.R.C. Logo

(Litho Security Printers (M), Malaysia)

1997 (12 May). Ninth South Asian Association for Regional Co-operation Summit, Malé. T **349** and similar horiz design. Multicoloured. P 13.

2751	3r. Type **349**	40	35
2752	5r. Flags of member countries	1·00	75

350 Queen Elizabeth II

(Litho Questa)

1997 (12 June). Golden Wedding of Queen Elizabeth and Prince Philip. T 350 and similar horiz designs. Multicoloured. P 14.

2753	5r. Type 350	1·00	1·00
	a. Sheetlet of 6. Nos. 2753/8	5·50	5·50
2754	5r. Royal coat of arms	1·00	1·00
2755	5r. Queen Elizabeth and Prince Philip at opening of Parliament	1·00	1·00
2756	5r. Queen Elizabeth and Prince Philip with Prince Charles, 1948	1·00	1·00
2757	5r. Buckingham Palace from the garden	1·00	1·00
2758	5r. Prince Philip	1·00	1·00
2753/58	Set of 6	5·50	5·50

MS2759 100×70 mm. 25r. Queen Elizabeth II.......... 4·00 4·50
Nos. 2753/8 were printed together, se-tenant, in sheetlets of six.

351 Early Indian Mail Messenger

(Des J. Iskowitz. Litho Questa)

1997 (12 June). "Pacific '97" International Stamp Exhibition, San Francisco. Death Centenary of Heinrich pan Stephan (founder of the U.P.U.). T 351 and similar horiz designs. P 14.

2760	2r. turquoise-green and black	55	60
	a. Sheetlet of 3. Nos. 2760/2	1·50	1·60
2761	2r. chestnut and black	55	60
2762	2r. violet	55	60
2760/2	Set of 3	1·50	1·60

Designs:—No. 2760, Type 351; No. 2761, Von Stephan and Mercury No. 2762, Autogyro, Washington.
Nos. 2760/2 were printed together, se-tenant, in sheetlets of three with enlarged right-hand margin.

352 "Dawn at Kanda Myojin Shrine"
353 Common Noddy

(Litho Questa)

1997 (12 June). Birth Bicentenary of Hiroshige (Japanese painter). "One Hundred Famous Views of Edo". T 352 and similar vert designs. Multicoloured. P 13½×14.

2763	8r. Type 352	1·25	1·25
	a. Sheetlet of 6. Nos. 2763/8	6·75	6·75
2764	8r. "Kiyomizu Hall and Shinobazu Pond at Ueno"	1·25	1·25
2765	8r. "Ueno Yamashita"	1·25	1·25
2766	8r. "Moon Pine, Ueno"	1·25	1·25
2767	8r. "Flower Pavilion, Dango Slope, Sendagi"	1·25	1·25
2768	8r. "Shitaya Hirokoji"	1·25	1·25
2763/68	Set of 6	6·75	6·75

MS2769 Two sheets each 102×127 mm. (a) 25r. "Hilltop View, Yushima Tenjin Shrine". (b) 25r. "Seido and Kanda River from Shohei Bridge" Set of 2 sheets .... 7·50 8·50
Nos. 2763/8 were printed together, se-tenant, in sheetlets of six.

(Des M. Lebouef. Litho B.D.T.)

1997 (17 June). Birds. T 353 and similar vert designs. Multicoloured. P 14.

2770	30l. Type 353	30	45
2771	1r. Spectacled Owl	75	40

2772	2r. Malay Fish Owl	1·25	65
2773	3r. Peregrine Falcon	1·50	1·00
2774	5r. Golden Eagle	1·50	1·10
2775	7r. Ruppell's Parrot	1·50	1·50
	a. Sheetlet of 6. Nos. 2775/80	8·00	8·00
2776	7r. Blue-headed Parrot	1·50	1·50
2777	7r. St. Vincent Amazon	1·50	1·50
2778	7r. Grey Parrot	1·50	1·50
2779	7r. Masked Lovebird	1·50	1·50
2780	7r. Sun Conure	1·50	1·50
2781	8r. Bateleur	1·50	1·50
2782	10r. Whiskered Tern with chicks	1·50	1·75
2783	10r. Common Caracara	1·50	1·75
2784	15r. Red-footed Booby	2·25	2·50
2770/84	Set of 15	19·00	18·00

MS2785 Two sheets, each 67×98 mm. (a) 25r. American Bald Eagle. (b) 25r. Secretary Bird Set of 2 sheets.......... 12·00 12·00
Nos. 2775/80 were printed together, se-tenant, in sheetlets of six.

354 Canarina eminii
355 Archaeopteryx

(Litho Questa)

1997 (24 June). Flowers. T 354 and similar multicoloured designs. P 14½×14 (vert) or 14×14½ (horiz).

2786	1r. Type 354	25	15
2787	2r. Delphinium macrocentron	40	25
2788	3r. Leucadendron discolor	55	40
2789	5r. Nymphaea caerulea	75	60
2790	7r. Rosa multiflora polyantha (20×23 mm)..	1·00	1·00
2791	8r. Bulbophyllum barbigerum	1·50	1·50
2792	8r. Acacia seyal (horiz)	1·50	1·50
	a. Sheetlet of 6. Nos. 2792/7	8·00	8·00
2793	8r. Gloriosa superba (horiz)	1·50	1·50
2794	8r. Gnidia subcordata (horiz)	1·50	1·50
2795	8r. Platycelyphium voense (horiz)	1·50	1·50
2796	8r. Aspilia mossambicensis (horiz)	1·50	1·50
2797	8r. Adenium obesum (horiz)	1·50	1·50
2798	12r. Hibiscus vitifolius	2·00	2·50
2786/98	Set of 13	14·00	14·00

MS2799 Two sheets, each 105×76 mm. (a) 25r. Aerangis rhodosticta (horiz). (b) 25r. Dichrostachys cinerea and two sailing boats (horiz) Set of 2 sheets .... 16·00 16·00
Nos. 2792/7 were printed together, se-tenant, in sheetlets of six with the backgrounds forming a composite design.

(Des. J. Ruff and M. Lebouef. Litho Questa)

1997 (20 Nov). Prehistoric Animals. Multicoloured. P 14.

(a) T 355 and similar horiz designs

2800	5r. Type 355	1·00	65
2801	7r. Diplodocus	1·10	1·10
	a. Sheetlet of 6. Nos. 2801/6	6·00	6·00
2802	7r. Tyrannosaurus rex	1·10	1·10
2803	7r. Pteranodon	1·10	1·10
2804	7r. Montanceratops	1·10	1·10
2805	7r. Dromaeosaurus	1·10	1·10
2806	7r. Oviraptor	1·10	1·10
2807	8r. Mosasaurus	1·10	1·10
2808	12r. Deinonychus	1·10	1·10
2809	15r. Triceratops	1·10	1·10

(b) Square designs, 31×31 mm

2810	7r. Troodon	1·10	1·10
	a. Sheetlet of 6. Nos. 2810/15	6·00	6·00
2811	7r. Brachiosaurus	1·10	1·10
2812	7r. Saltasaurus	1·10	1·10
2813	7r. Oviraptor	1·10	1·10
2814	7r. Parasaurolophus	1·10	1·10
2815	7r. Psittacosaurus	1·10	1·10
2816	7r. Triceratops	1·10	1·10
	a. Sheetlet of 6. Nos. 2816/21	6·00	6·00
2817	7r. Pachycephalosaurus	1·10	1·10
2818	7r. Iguanodon	1·10	1·10
2819	7r. Tyrannosaurus rex	1·10	1·10
2820	7r. Corythosaurus	1·10	1·10
2821	7r. Stegosaurus	1·10	1·10
2822	7r. Euophlocephalus	1·10	1·10
	a. Sheetlet of 6. Nos. 2822/7	6·00	6·00
2823	7r. Compsognathus	1·10	1·10
2824	7r. Herrerasaurus	1·10	1·10

2825	7r. Styracosaurus	1·10	1·10
2826	7r. Baryonyx	1·10	1·10
2827	7r. Lesothosaurus	1·10	1·10
2800/27 Set of 28		27·00	27·00

MS2828 Two sheets. (a) 99×79 mm. 25r. Tyrannosaurus rex (42×28 mm). (b) 73×104 mm. 25r. Archaeopteryx (31×31 mm) Set of 2 sheets.......... 20·00 20·00

Nos. 2801/6, 2810/15, 2816/21 and 2822/7 were each printed together, se-tenant, in sheetlets of six, with the backgrounds forming composite designs (Nos. 2801/6 and 2810/15) or with enlarged illustrated margins (Nos. 2816/21 and 2822/7).

355a Brazilian Team, 1994

(Litho Questa)

1997 (10 Dec). World Cup Football Championship, France. As T 355a and similar horiz designs. P 14×13½.

2829	1r. black	30	15
2830	2r. black	45	25
2831	3r. multicoloured	55	35
2832	3r.×8 (brownish black; brownish black; multicoloured; multicoloured; brownish black; multicoloured; brownish black; multicoloured)		
	a. Sheetlet of 8. Nos. 2832/9 and central label	3·75	4·00
2840/7	3r.×8 (multicoloured; multicoloured; brownish black; brownish black; multicoloured; brownish black; multicoloured; brownish black)		
	a. Sheetlet of 8. Nos. 2840/7 and central label	3·75	4·00
2848/55	3r.×8 (multicoloured; multicoloured; multicoloured; brownish black; brownish black; multicoloured; multicoloured; multicoloured)		
	a. Sheetlet of 8. Nos. 2848/55 and central label	3·75	4·00
2856	7r. black	1·10	1·10
2857	8r. black	1·40	1·40
2858	10r. multicoloured	1·50	1·60
2829/58 Set of 30		15·00	15·00

MS2859 Three sheets. (a) 103×128 mm. 25r. multicoloured. P 13½×14. (b) 103×128 mm. 25r. multicoloured. P 14×13½. (c) 128×103 mm. 25r. multicoloured. P 13½×14 Set of 3 sheets...................... 12·00 13·00

Designs: Horiz—No. 2829, Type 355a; No. 2830, German player, 1954; No. 2831, Maradona holding World Cup, 1986; No. 2832, Brazilian team, 1958; No. 2833, Luis Bellini, Brazil, 1958; No. 2834, Brazilian team, 1962; No. 2835, Carlos Alberto, Brazil, 1970; No. 2836, Mauro, Brazil, 1962; No. 2837, Brazilian team, 1970; No. 2838, Dunga, Brazil, 1994; No. 2839, Brazilian team, 1994; No. 2840, Paulo Rossi, Italy, 1982; No. 2841, Zoff and Gentile, Italy, 1982; No. 2842, Angelo Schavio, Italy; No. 2843, Italian team, 1934; No. 2844, Italian team with flag, 1934; No. 2845, Italian team, 1982; No. 2846, San Paolo Stadium, Italy; No. 2847, Italian team, 1938; No. 2848, English player with ball, 1966; No. 2849, Wembley Stadium, London; No. 2850, English player heading ball, 1966; No. 2851, English players celebrating, 1966; No. 2852, English and German players chasing ball, 1966; No. 2853, English player wearing No. 21 shirt, 1966; No. 2854, English team with Jules Rimet trophy, 1966; No. 2855 German player wearing No. 5 shirt, 1966; No. 2856, Argentine player holding trophy, 1978; No. 2857, English players with Jules Rimet trophy, 1966; No. 2858, Brazilian player with trophy, 1970; No. MS2859c, Klinsmann, Germany. Vert—No. MS2859a, Ronaldo, Brazil; No. MS2592b, Schmeichel, Denmark.

Nos. 2832/9, 2840/7 and 2848/55 were each printed together, se-tenant, in sheetlets of 8 stamps and a central label.

355b Diana Princess of Wales Laughing

356 Pres Nelson Mandela

(Litho Questa)

1998 (9 Feb). Diana, Princess of Wales Commemoration. As T 355b and similar vert designs. Multicoloured (except Nos. 2864, 2870, 2872, 2877 and MS2878b). P 13½.

2860	7r. Type 355b	80	85
	a. Sheetlet of 6. Nos. 2860/5	4·25	4·50
2861	7r. With Prince William and Prince Harry...	80	85
2862	7r. Carrying bouquets	80	85
2863	7r. In white evening dress	80	85
2864	7r. Wearing bowtie (chestnut and black)....	80	85
2865	7r. Wearing black jacket	80	85
2866	7r. With Indian child on lap	80	85
	a. Sheetlet of 6. Nos. 2866/71	4·25	4·50
2867	7r. Wearing blue evening dress	80	85
2868	7r. Wearing blue jacket and poppy	80	85
2869	7r. Wearing cream jacket	80	85
2870	7r. Wearing blouse and jacket (lake-brown and black)	80	85
2871	7r. Wearing red jacket	80	85
2872	7r. Wearing hat (new blue and black)	80	85
	a. Sheetlet of 6. Nos. 2872/7	4·25	4·50
2873	7r. Wearing red evening dress	80	85
2874	7r. With Sir Richard Attenborough	80	85
2875	7r. Wearing jeans and white shirt	80	85
2876	7r. Wearing white jacket	80	85
2877	7r. Carrying bouquet (orange-brown and black)	80	85
2860/77 Set of 18		12·50	13·50

MS2878 Three sheets. (a) 100×70 mm. 25r. On skilift. (b) 100×70 mm. 25r. Wearing polkadot dress (brown and black). (c) 70×100 mm. 25r. Wearing garland of flowers Set of 3 sheets.................. 12·00 13·00

Nos. 2860/5, 2866/71 and 2872/7 were each printed together, se-tenant, in sheetlets of six.

Two 50r. values embossed on gold foil also exist from limited printings.

(Des Zina Saunders. Litho Questa)

1998 (1 Mar). 80th Birthday of Nelson Mandela (President of South Africa). P 14.

2879	356	7r. multicoloured	1·75	1·40

357 Pres John F. Kennedy

(Des M. Bennett. Litho Questa)

1998 (1 Mar). Pres John F. Kennedy Commemoration. T 357 and similar vert portraits. Multicoloured: background colours given. P 13½×14.

2880	5r. deep turquoise-green (Type 357)	75	80
	a. Sheetlet of 9. Nos. 2880/8	6·00	6·50
2881	5r. turquoise-green	75	80
2882	5r. ochre (inscr at right)	75	80
2883	5r. pale lemon	75	80
2884	5r. bluish violet	75	80
2885	5r. violet-blue	75	80
2886	5r. lavender-grey	75	80
2887	5r. drab (inscr at left)	75	80
2888	5r. cobalt (value at bottom right)	75	80
2880/88 Set of 9		6·00	6·50

Nos. 2880/8 were printed together, se-tenant, in sheetlets of nine with enlarged illustrated right-hand margin.

358 Yakovlev Yak-18 (from 1947)

359 White American Shorthair

(Des W. Wright. Litho Questa)

1998 (1 Mar). Aircraft in Longest Continuous Production. T **358** and similar horiz designs. Multicoloured. P 14.

2889	5r. Type **358**	95	95
	a. Sheetlet of 9. Nos. 2889/97	7·75	7·75
2890	5r. Beechcraft Bonanza (from 1947)	95	95
2891	5r. Piper Cub (1937–82)	95	95
2892	5r. Tupolev Tu-95 (1954–90)	95	95
2893	5r. Lockheed C-130 Hercules (from 1954) ..	95	95
2894	5r. Piper PA-28 Cherokee (from 1961)	95	95
2895	5r. Mikoyan Gurevich MiG-21 (from 1959) .	95	95
2896	5r. Pilatus PC-6 Turbo Porter (from 1960)...	95	95
2897	5r. Antonov An-2 (from 1949)	95	95
2889/97 *Set of 9*		7·75	7·75
MS2898 120×90 mm. 25r. Boeing KC-135E (from 1956) (84×28 *mm*)		4·25	4·50

Nos. 2889/97 were printed together, *se-tenant*, in sheetlets of nine with enlarged margin at foot containing text.

(Des R. Martin. Litho Questa)

1998 (1 June). Cats. T **359** and similar multicoloured designs. P 14.

2899	5r. Type **359**	1·25	65
2900	7r. American Curl and Maine Coon (*horiz*)	1·25	1·25
	a. Sheetlet of 6. Nos. 2900/5	6·75	6·75
2901	7r. Maine Coon (*horiz*)	1·25	1·25
2902	7r. Siberian (*horiz*)	1·25	1·25
2903	7r. Somali (*horiz*)	1·25	1·25
2904	7r. European Burmese (*horiz*)	1·25	1·25
2905	7r. Nebelung (*horiz*)	1·25	1·25
2906	7r. Bicolor British Shorthair (*horiz*)	1·25	1·25
	a. Sheetlet of 6. Nos. 2906/11	6·75	6·75
2907	7r. Manx (*horiz*)	1·25	1·25
2908	7r. Tabby American Shorthair (*horiz*)	1·25	1·25
2909	7r. Silver Tabby Persian (*horiz*)	1·25	1·25
2910	7r. Oriental White (*horiz*)	1·25	1·25
2911	7r. Norwegian Forest Cat (*horiz*)	1·25	1·25
2912	8r. Sphynx Cat	1·10	1·10
2913	10r. Tabby American Shorthair	1·25	1·25
2914	12r. Scottish Fold	1·40	1·60
2899/914 *Set of 16*		17·00	17·00
MS2915 Two sheets, each 98×68 mm. (a) 30r. Norwegian Forest Cat. (b) 30r. Snowshoe *Set of 2 sheets*		8·50	9·00

Nos. 2900/5 and 2906/11 were each printed together, *se-tenant*, in sheetlets of six, forming composite designs.

360 Boeing 747-400

361 Captain Edward Smith's Cap

(Des S. Gardner. Litho Questa)

1998 (10 Aug). Aircraft. T **360** and similar horiz designs. Multicoloured. P 14.

2916	2r. Type **360**	65	30
2917	5r. CL-215 (flying boat)	1·00	1·00
	a. Sheetlet of 8. Nos. 2917/24	7·00	7·00
2918	5r. Orion	1·00	1·00
2919	5r. Yakolev Yak-54	1·00	1·00
2920	5r. Cessna sea plane	1·00	1·00
2921	5r. CL-215 (amphibian)	1·00	1·00
2922	5r. CL-215 SAR (amphibian)	1·00	1·00
2923	5r. Twin Otter	1·00	1·00
2924	5r. Rockwell Quail	1·00	1·00
2925	5r. F.S.W. fighter	1·00	1·00
	a. Sheetlet of 8. Nos. 2925/32	7·00	7·00
2926	5r. V-Jet II	1·00	1·00
2927	5r. Pilatus PC-12	1·00	1·00
2928	5r. Citation Exel	1·00	1·00
2929	5r. Stutz Bearcat	1·00	1·00
2930	5r. Cessna T-37 (B)	1·00	1·00
2931	5r. Peregrine Business Jet	1·00	1·00
2932	5r. Beech 58 Baron	1·00	1·00
2933	7r. Boeing 727	1·25	1·25
2934	8r. Boeing 747-400	1·25	1·25
2935	10r. Boeing 737	1·40	1·40
2916/35 *Set of 20*		18·00	18·00
MS2936 Two sheets, each 98×68 mm. (a) 25r. Beechcraft Model 18. (b) 25r. Falcon Jet *Set of 2 sheets*		9·00	10·00

Nos. 2917/24 and 2925/32 were each printed together, *se-tenant*, in sheetlets of eight.

(Des Zina Saunders. Litho Cartor)

1998 (27 Sept). *Titanic* Commemoration. T **361** and similar horiz designs. Multicoloured. P 14.

2937	7r. Type **361**	1·40	1·40
	a. Sheetlet of 6. Nos. 2937/42	7·50	7·50
2938	7r. Deck chair	1·40	1·40
2939	7r. Fifth Officer Harold Lowe's coat button	1·40	1·40
2940	7r. Lifeboat	1·40	1·40
2941	7r. *Titanic's* wheel	1·40	1·40
2942	7r. Passenger's lifejacket	1·40	1·40
2937/42 *Set of 6*		7·50	7·50
MS2943 110×85 mm. 25r. *Titanic* from newspaper picture		5·00	5·50

Nos. 2937/42 were printed together, *se-tenant*, in sheetlets of six with enlarged illustrated top margin.

362 Guava Tree

(Litho B.D.T.)

1998 (30 Nov). 20th Anniv of International Fund for Agriculture. T **362** and similar horiz designs. Multicoloured. P 14.

2944	1r. Type **362**	40	15
2945	5r. Selection of fruit	1·25	75
2946	7r. Fishing boat	1·50	1·50
2947	8r. Papaya Tree	1·50	1·75
2948	10r. Vegetable produce	1·75	2·00
2944/48 *Set of 5*		5·75	5·50

THREADFIN BUTTERFLY FISH (*Chaetodon auriga*)

363 Thread-finned Butterflyfish

(Des T. Wood. Litho Questa)

1998 (10 Dec). Fish. T **363** and similar horiz designs. Multicoloured. P 14.

2949	50l. Type **363**	20	30
2950	50l. Queen Angelfish	20	30
2951	1r. Oriental Sweetlips	30	15
2952	3r. Mandarin Fish	50	50
	a. Sheetlet of 9. Nos. 2952/60	4·00	4·00
2953	3r. Copper-banded Butterflyfish	50	50
2954	3r. Harlequin Tuskfish	50	50
2955	3r. Yellow-tailed Demoiselle	50	50
2956	3r. Wimplefish	50	50
2957	3r. Red Emperor Snapper	50	50
2958	3r. Clown Triggerfish	50	50
2959	3r. Common Clown	50	50
2960	3r. Palette Surgeonfish ("Regal Tang")	50	50
2961	5r. Emperor Angelfish	80	80
	a. Sheetlet of 9. Nos. 2961/9	6·75	6·75
2962	5r. Common Squirrelfish ("Diadem Squirrelfish")	80	80
2963	5r. Lemon-peel Angelfish	80	80
2964	5r. Powder-blue Surgeonfish	80	80
2965	5r. Moorish Idol	80	80
2966	5r. Bicolor Angelfish ("Bicolor Cherub")	80	80
2967	5r. Duboulay's Angelfish ("Scribbled Angelfish")	80	80
2968	5r. Two-banded Anemonefish	80	80
2969	5r. Yellow Tang	80	80
2970	7r. Red-tailed Surgeonfish ("Achilles Tang")	1·00	1·10
2971	7r. Bandit Angelfish	1·00	1·10
2972	8r. Hooded Butterflyfish ("Red-headed Butterflyfish")	1·10	1·25
2973	50r. Blue-striped Butterflyfish	5·50	6·50
2949/73 *Set of 25*		19·00	20·00
MS2974 Two sheets, each 110×85 mm. (a) 25r. Long-nosed Butterflyfish. (b) 25r. Porkfish *Set of 2 sheets* .		7·50	8·50

Nos. 2952/60 and 2961/9 were each printed together, *se-tenant*, in sheetlets of nine.

364 Baden-Powell inspecting Scouts, Amesbury, 1909

(Des J. Iskowitz. Litho Questa)

1998 (15 Dec). 19th World Scout Jamboree, Chile. T **364** and similar multicoloured designs. P 14.

2975	12r. Type **364**		1·75	2·00
	a. Sheetlet of 3. Nos. 2975/7		4·75	5·50
2976	12r. Sir Robert and Lady Baden-Powell with children 1927		1·75	2·00
2977	12r. Sir Robert Baden-Powell awarding merit badges, Chicago, 1926		1·75	2·00
2975/77 Set of 3			4·75	5·50

Nos. 2975/7 were printed together, *se-tenant*, in sheetlets of three with enlarged illustrated margins at top and right.

365 Diana, Princess of Wales

366 Triton Shell

(Des G. Eichorn. Litho Questa)

1998 (15 Dec). First Death Anniv of Diana, Princess of Wales. P 14½×14.

2978	**365**	10r. multicoloured	1·00	1·50
		a. Sheetlet of 6		5·00

No. 2978 was printed in sheetlets of six with an enlarged illustrated left margin.

1999 (1 Apr). International Year of the Ocean. Marine Life. T **366** and similar horiz designs. Multicoloured. Litho. P 14.

2979	25l. Type **366**		60	60
	a. Sheetlet of 6. Nos. 2979/82 and 2992/3.		5·75	5·75
2980	50l. Napoleon Wrasse		75	75
2981	1r. Whale Shark		1·00	1·00
2982	3r. Grey Reef Shark		1·25	1·25
2983	5r. Harp Seal		1·10	1·10
	a. Sheetlet of 9. Nos. 2983/91		9·00	9·00
2984	5r. Killer Whale		1·10	1·10
2985	5r. Sea Otter		1·10	1·10
2986	5r. Beluga		1·10	1·10
2987	5r. Narwhal		1·10	1·10
2988	5r. Walrus		1·10	1·10
2989	5r. Sea Lion		1·10	1·10
2990	5r. Humpback Salmon		1·10	1·10
2991	5r. Emperor Penguin		1·10	1·10
2992	7r. Blue Whale		1·75	1·75
2993	7r. Skipjack Tuna		1·10	1·10
	a. Sheetlet of 6. No. 2993×6		6·00	6·00
2994	8r. Ocean Sunfish		1·25	1·25
	a. Sheetlet of 4. Nos. 2994/7		4·50	4·50
2995	8r. Opalescent Squid		1·25	1·25
2996	8r. Electric Ray		1·25	1·25
2997	8r. Corded Neptune		1·25	1·25
2979/97 Set of 19			19·00	19·00
MS2998	Three sheets, each 110×85 mm. (a) 25r. Horseshoe Crab. (b) 25r. Blue Whale. (c) 25r. Triton shell *Set of 3 sheets*		11·00	12·00

Nos. 2979/82 and 2992/3 were printed together, *se-tenant*, in sheetlets of six. No. 2993 was also available in a sheetlet containing six examples of the one design. Nos. 2983/91 and 2994/7 were each printed together, *se-tenant*, in sheetlets of nine (Nos. 2983/91 with the backgrounds forming a composite design) or four (Nos. 2994/7).

367 Broderip's Cowrie

(Litho Questa)

1999 (1 Apr). Marine Life. T **367** and similar horiz designs. Multicoloured. P 14.

2999	30l. Type **367**		30	35
3000	1r. White Tern		1·25	40
3001	3r. Green Heron		1·75	1·10

3002	5r. Manta Ray		1·25	1·10
	a. Sheetlet of 9. Nos. 3002/10		10·00	9·00
3003	5r. Green Turtle		1·25	1·10
3004	5r. Spotted Dolphins		1·25	1·10
3005	5r. Moorish Idols		1·25	1·10
3006	5r. Threadfin Anthias		1·25	1·10
3007	5r. Goldbar Wrasse		1·25	1·10
3008	5r. Palette Surgeonfish		1·25	1·10
3009	5r. Three-spotted Angelfish		1·25	1·10
3010	5r. Oriental Sweetlips		1·25	1·10
3011	5r. Brown Booby		1·25	1·10
	a. Sheetlet of 9. Nos. 3011/19		10·00	9·00
3012	5r. Red-tailed Tropic Bird		1·25	1·10
3013	5r. Sooty Tern		1·25	1·10
3014	5r. Striped Dolphin		1·25	1·10
3015	5r. Spinner Dolphin		1·25	1·10
3016	5r. Crab Plover		1·25	1·10
3017	5r. Hawksbill Turtle		1·25	1·10
3018	5r. Indo-Pacific Sergeant		1·25	1·10
3019	5r. Yellow-finned Tuna		1·25	1·10
3020	7r. Blackflag Sandperch		1·25	1·25
3021	8r. Coral Hind		1·40	1·40
3022	10r. Olive Ridley Turtle		1·60	1·60
2999/3022 Set of 24			26·00	24·00
MS3023	Two sheets, each 110×85 mm. (a) 25r. Cinnamon Bittern. (b) 25r. Blue-faced Angelfish *Set of 2 sheets*		8·50	9·00

Nos. 3002/10 and 3011/19 were each printed together, *se-tenant*, in sheetlets of nine with the backgrounds forming composite designs.

368 Mickey Mouse

1999 (27 May). 70th Anniv of Mickey Mouse (Disney cartoon character). T **368** and similar multicoloured designs. Litho. P 13½×14.

3024/9	5r.×6 (Mickey Mouse: Type **368**; laughing; looking tired; frowning; smiling; winking)			
	a. Sheetlet of 6. Nos. 3024/9		5·50	5·50
3030/5	5r.×6 (Minnie Mouse: facing left and smiling; with eyes closed; with hand on head; looking surprised; smiling; looking cross)			
	a. Sheetlet of 6. Nos. 3030/5		5·50	5·50
3036/41	7r.×6 (Donald Duck: facing left and smiling; laughing; looking tired; looking cross; smiling; winking)			
	a. Sheetlet of 6. Nos. 3036/41		6·00	6·00
3042/7	7r.×6 (Daisy Duck: with half closed eyes; laughing; looking shocked; looking cross; looking forwards; with head on one side)			
	a. Sheetlet of 6. Nos. 3042/7		6·00	6·00
3048/53	7r.×6 (Goofy: facing right and smiling; with eyes close; with half closed eyes; looking shocked; looking puzzled; looking thoughtful)			
	a. Sheetlet of 6. Nos. 3048/53		6·00	6·00
3054/9	7r.×6 (Pluto: looking shocked; with eyes closed; smiling; scowling; with tongue out (orange background); with tongue out (green background))			
	a. Sheetlet of 6. Nos. 3054/9		6·00	6·00
3024/59 Set of 36			32·00	32·00
MS3060	Six sheets, each 127×102 mm. (a) 25r. Minnie Mouse wearing necklace. (b) 25r. Mickey with hand on head. (c) 25r. Mickey wearing baseball hat. (d) 25r. Mickey facing right (*horiz*). (e) 25r. Minnie looking left (includes label showing Mickey with bouquet). (f) 25r. Minnie drinking through straw. P 13½×14 (*vert*) or 14×13½ (*horiz*) *Set of 6 sheets*		23·00	23·00

Nos. 3024/9, 3030/5, 3036/41, 3042/7, 3048/53 and 3054/9 were each printed together, *se-tenant*, in sheetlets of six stamps, with enlarged illustrated margins.

369 Great Orange Tip

370 Scelidosaurus

(Des T. Wood. Litho Questa)

1999 (8 June). Butterflies. T **369** and similar multicoloured designs.
P 14.

3061	50l. Type **369**	15	25
3062	1r. Large Green Aporandria	25	20
3063	2r. Common Mormon	40	30
3064	3r. African Migrant	55	40
3065	5r. Common Pierrot	85	60
3066	7r. Crimson Tip (*vert*)	1·10	1·10
	a. Sheetlet of 6. Nos. 3066/71	6·00	6·00
3067	7r. Tawny Rajah (*vert*)	1·10	1·10
3068	7r. Leafwing Butterfly (*vert*)	1·10	1·10
3069	7r. Great Egg-fly (*vert*)	1·10	1·10
3070	7r. Blue Admiral (*vert*)	1·10	1·10
3071	7r. African Migrant (*vert*)	1·10	1·10
3072	7r. Common Red Flash (*vert*)	1·10	1·10
	a. Sheetlet of 6. Nos. 3072/7	6·00	6·00
3073	7r. Burmese Lascar (*vert*)	1·10	1·10
3074	7r. Common Perriot (*vert*)	1·10	1·10
3075	7r. Baron (*vert*)	1·10	1·10
3076	7r. Leaf Blue (*vert*)	1·10	1·10
3077	7r. Great Orange Tip (*vert*)	1·10	1·10
3078	10r. Giant Red-eye	1·25	1·60
3061/78	*Set of 18*	15·00	15·00

MS3079 Two sheets, each 70×100 mm. (a) 25r.
Crimson Tip. (b) 25r. Large Oak Blue *Set of 2 sheets*. 8·50 9·50
Nos. 3066/71 and 3072/7 were each printed together, *se-tenant*, in sheetlets of six with backgrounds forming composite designs.

(Des Spotlight Designs. Litho Questa)

1999 (22 June). Prehistoric Animals. T **370** and similar horiz designs.
Multicoloured. P 14.

3080	1r. Type **370**	25	15
3081	3r. Yansudaurus	45	40
3082	5r. Ornitholestes	85	70
3083	7r. Dimorphodon (*vert*)	1·10	1·10
	a. Sheetlet of 6. Nos. 3083/8	6·00	6·00
3084	7r. Rhamphorhynchus (*vert*)	1·10	1·10
3085	7r. Allosaurus (*vert*)	1·10	1·10
3086	7r. Leaellynasaura (*vert*)	1·10	1·10
3087	7r. Troodon (*vert*)	1·10	1·10
3088	7r. Syntarsus (*vert*)	1·10	1·10
3089	7r. Anchisaurus (*vert*)	1·10	1·10
	a. Sheetlet of 6. Nos. 3089/94	6·00	6·00
3090	7r. Pterenodon (*vert*)	1·10	1·10
3091	7r. Barosaurus (*vert*)	1·10	1·10
3092	7r. Iguanodon (*vert*)	1·10	1·10
3093	7r. Archaeopteryx (*vert*)	1·10	1·10
3094	7r. Ceratosaurus (*vert*)	1·10	1·10
3095	7r. Stegosaurus (*vert*)	1·10	1·10
	a. Sheetlet of 6. Nos. 3095/3100	6·00	6·00
3096	7r. Corythosaurus (*vert*)	1·10	1·10
3097	7r. Cetiosaurus (*vert*)	1·10	1·10
3098	7r. Avimimus (*vert*)	1·10	1·10
3099	7r. Styracosaurus (*vert*)	1·10	1·10
3100	7r. Massospondylus (*vert*)	1·10	1·10
3101	8r. Astrodon (*vert*)	1·10	1·25
3080/101	*Set of 22*	20·00	20·00

MS3102 Two sheets, each 116×81 mm. (a) 25r.
Megalosaurus (*vert*). (b) 25r. Brachiosaurus (*vert*)
Set of 2 sheets 7·50 8·00
Nos. 3083/8, 3089/94 and 3095/3100 were each printed together, *se-tenant*, in sheetlets of six, forming composite designs.

371 Express Locomotive, Egypt, 1856

371a King George VI and Queen Elizabeth, 1936

(Litho Questa)

1999 (26 Oct). Trains of the World. T **371** and similar horiz designs.
Multicoloured. P 14.

3103	50l. Type **371**	45	35
3104	1r. Channel Tunnel Le Shuttle, France, 1994	50	20
3105	2r. Gowan and Marx locomotive, U.S.A., 1839	70	30
3106	3r. TGV train, France, 1981	85	40
3107	5r. "As 6/6" electric locomotive, Switzerland, 1954	1·25	70
3108	7r. Stephenson's long-boilered locomotive, Great Britain, 1846 (red livery)	1·50	1·50
	a. Sheetlet of 6. Nos. 3108/13	8·00	8·00
3109	7r. *Cornwall*, Great Britain, 1847	1·50	1·50
3110	7r. First locomotive, Germany, 1848	1·50	1·50
3111	7r. *Great Western* locomotive, Great Britain, 1846	1·50	1·50
3112	7r. Standard Stephenson locomotive, France, 1837	1·50	1·50
3113	7r. *Meteor*, Great Britain, 1843	1·50	1·50
3114	7r. Class 4T diesel-electric locomotive, Great Britain, 1940–65	1·50	1·50
	a. Sheetlet of 6. Nos. 3114/19	8·00	8·00
3115	7r. Mainline diesel-electric locomotive No. 20101, Malaya, 1940–65	1·50	1·50
3116	7r. Class 7000 high-speed electric locomotive, France, 1949	1·50	1·50
3117	7r. Diesel hydraulic express locomotive, Thailand, 1940–65	1·50	1·50
3118	7r. Diesel hydraulic locomotive, Burma, 1940–65	1·50	1·50
3119	7r. "Hikari" super express train, Japan, 1940–65	1·50	1·50
3120	8r. Stephenson's long-boilered locomotive, Great Britain, 1846 (orange and green livery)	1·50	1·50
3121	10r. Philadelphia, Austria, 1838	1·50	1·50
3122	15r. S.E. and C. Railway Class E steam locomotive, Great Britain, 1940	2·00	2·25
3103/22	*Set of 20*	24·00	22·00

MS3123 Two sheets, each 110×85 mm. (a) 25r.
Passenger locomotive, France, 1846. (b) 25r.
Southern Railway Class *King Arthur*, steam
locomotive, Great Britain, 1940 *Set of 2 sheets* 11·00 12·00
Nos. 3108/13 and 3114/19 were each printed together, *se-tenant*, in sheetlets of six containing two horizontal strips of three.

(Litho Questa)

1999 (1 Dec). "Queen Elizabeth the Queen Mother's Century". Vert
designs as T **371a**. P 14.

3124	7r. black and gold	1·25	1·25
	a. Sheetlet of 4. Nos. 3124/7	4·50	4·50
3125	7r. black and gold	1·25	1·25
3126	7r. multicoloured	1·25	1·25
3127	7r. multicoloured	1·25	1·25
3124/27	*Set of 4*	4·50	4·50

MS3128 153×157 mm. 25r. multicoloured. P 13½×14. 5·00 5·00
Designs: Type **371a**; No. 3125, Queen Elizabeth, 1941; No. 3126, Queen Elizabeth in evening dress, 1960; No. 3127, Queen Mother at Ascot, 1981. (37×50 *mm*)—No. **MS**3128, Queen Mother in Garter robes.
Nos. 3124/7 were printed together, *se-tenant*, as a sheetlet of four stamps and a central label with inscribed and embossed margins. No. **MS**3128 also shows the Royal Arms embossed in gold.
A 50r. value embossed on gold foil also exists from a limited printing.

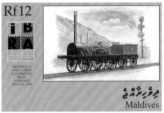

371b *Adler* (first German railway locomotive), 1833

(Litho Questa)

1999 (23 Dec). "iBRA '99" International Stamp Exhibition, Nuremberg.
Horiz designs as T **371b**. Multicoloured. P 14×14½.

3129	12r. Type **371b**	2·00	2·50
3130	15r. *Drache* (Henshell and Sohn's first locomotive), 1848	2·25	2·75

The captions on Nos. 3129/30 are transposed.

371c "Haunted House"

(Des R. Sauber. Litho Questa)

1999 (23 Dec). 150th Death Anniv of Katsushika Hokusai, (Japanese artist) Designs as T **371c**. Multicoloured (except No. 3133). P 14×13½.

3131	7r. Type **371c**	1·25	1·25
	a. Sheetlet of 6. Nos. 3131/6	6·75	6·75
3132	7r. "Juniso Shrine at Yotsuya"	1·25	1·25
3133	7r. Drawing of bird (blk, lt sage-grn and gold)	1·25	1·25
3134	7r. Drawing of two women	1·25	1·25
3135	7r. "Lover in the Snow"	1·25	1·25
3136	7r. "Mountain Tea House"	1·25	1·25
3137	7r. "A Coastal View"	1·25	1·25
	a. Sheetlet of 6. Nos. 3137/42	6·75	6·75
3138	7r. "Bath House by a Lake"	1·25	1·25
3139	7r. Drawing of a horse	1·25	1·25
3140	7r. Drawing of two birds on branch	1·25	1·25
3141	7r. "Evening Cool at Ryogoku"	1·25	1·25
3142	7r. "Girls boating"	1·25	1·25
3131/42	Set of 12	13·50	13·50

MS3143 Two sheets, each 100×70 mm. (a) 25r. "Girls gathering Spring Herbs" (vert). (b) 25r. "Scene in the Yoshiwara" (vert). P 13½×14 Set of 2 sheets ... 9·00 9·50

Nos. 3131/6 and 3137/42 were each printed together, se-tenant, in sheetlets of six.

371d Baby Boy and Young Mother

372 Standard Stephenson Railway Locomotive *Versailles*, 1837

(Litho Questa)

1999 (23 Dec). Tenth Anniv of United Nations Rights of the Child Convention. Vert designs as T **371d**. Multicoloured. P 14.

3144	10r. Type **371d**	1·60	2·00
	a. Sheetlet of 3. Nos. 3144/6	4·25	5·50
3145	10r. Young girl laughing	1·60	2·00
3146	10r. Three children	1·60	2·00
3144/46	Set of 3	4·25	5·50

MS3147 110×85 mm. 25r. Sir Peter Ustinov (Goodwill ambassador for U.N.I.C.E.F.) ... 4·00 4·75

(Litho Questa)

1999 (23 Dec). "PhilexFrance '99" International Stamp Exhibition, Paris. Railway Locomotives. Two sheets, each 106×81 mm, containing T **372** and similar horiz design. Multicoloured. P 14×13½.

MS3148 (a) 25r. Type **372**. (b) 25r. Stephenson long-boilered locomotive, 1841 Set of 2 sheets ... 8·50 9·50

373 Phobos and Demos (Martian Moons)

(Des B. Regal. Litho Questa)

2000 (24 Jan). Future Colonisation of Mars. T **373** and similar multicoloured designs. P 14.

3149	5r. Type **373**	1·25	1·10
	a. Sheetlet of 9. Nos. 3149/57	10·00	9·00
3150	5r. Improved Hubble Telescope	1·25	1·10

3151	5r. Passenger shuttle	1·25	1·10
3152	5r. Skyscrapers on Mars	1·25	1·10
3153	5r. Martian taxi	1·25	1·10
3154	5r. Martian landing facilities	1·25	1·10
3155	5r. Vegetation in Martian bio-sphere	1·25	1·10
3156	5r. Walking on Mars and bio-sphere	1·25	1·10
3157	5r. Mars rover	1·25	1·10
3158	5r. Russian Phobos 25 satellite	1·25	1·10
	a. Sheetlet of 9. Nos. 3158/66	10·00	9·00
3159	5r. Earth and Moon	1·25	1·10
3160	5r. Space shuttle leaving Earth	1·25	1·10
3161	5r. Lighthouse on Mars	1·25	1·10
3162	5r. Mars excursion space liner	1·25	1·10
3163	5r. Mars shuttle and skyscrapers	1·25	1·10
3164	5r. Viking Lander	1·25	1·10
3165	5r. Mars air and water purification plant	1·25	1·10
3166	5r. Family picnic on Mars	1·25	1·10
3149/66	Set of 18	20·00	18·00

MS3167 Two sheets, each 110×85 mm. (a) 25r. Astronaut with jet-pack; (b) 25r. Mars Set of 2 sheets ... 11·00 12·00

Nos. 3149/57 and 3158/66 were each printed together, se-tenant, in sheetlets of nine with the backgrounds forming composite designs and inscribed top margins.

374 Coconuts

(Litho Questa)

2000 (1 Feb). "Destination 2000 – Maldives" Tourism Campaign. T **374** and similar horiz designs. Multicoloured. P 14×13½.

3168	7r. Type **374**	2·00	2·00
	a. Sheetlet of 6. Nos. 3168/73	11·00	11·00
3169	7r. Shoal of Skipjack Tuna	2·00	2·00
3170	7r. Seaplane and traditional dhow	2·00	2·00
3171	7r. *Plumera alba*	2·00	2·00
3172	7r. Lionfish	2·00	2·00
3173	7r. Windsurfers	2·00	2·00
3168/73	Set of 6	11·00	11·00

Nos. 3168/73 were printed together, se-tenant, in sheetlets of six with an enlarged illustrated and inscribed left margin.

374a Eagle and American Declaration of Independence, 1776

375 Sun and Moon over Forest

(Des Dreamscape Studios. Litho Cartor)

2000 (14 Feb). New Millennium (1st issue). People and Events of 18th-Century (1750–1800). Multicoloured designs as T **374a**. P 12½.

3174	3r. Type **374a**	1·00	90
	a. Sheetlet of 17. Nos. 3174/90	15·00	13·50
3175	3r. Montgolfier brothers and first manned hot air balloon flight, 1783	1·00	90
3176	3r. Napoleon and mob (French Revolution, 1789)	1·00	90
3177	3r. James Watt and drawing of steam engine, 1769)	1·00	90
3178	3r. Wolfgang Amadeus Mozart (born 1756)	1·00	90
3179	3r. Front cover of *The Dream of the Red Chamber* (Chinese novel, published 1791).	1·00	90
3180	3r. Napoleon and Pyramid (conquest of Egypt, 1798)	1·00	90
3181	3r. Empress Catherine the Great of Russia and St. Petersburg, 1762	1·00	90
3182	3r. Joseph Priestley (discovery of oxygen, 1774)	1·00	90

3183	3r. Benjamin Franklin (publication of work on electricity, 1751)	1·00	90
3184	3r. Edward Jenner (development of smallpox vaccine, 1796)	1·00	90
3185	3r. Death of General Wolfe, 1759	1·00	90
3186	3r. "The Swing" (Jean Honors Fragonard), 1766	1·00	90
3187	3r. Ludwig von Beethoven (born 1770)	1·00	90
3188	3r. Marriage of Louis XVI of France and Marie Antoinette, 1770	1·00	90
3189	3r. Captain James Cook (exploration of Australia, 1770) (59×39 mm)	1·00	90
3190	3r. Luigi Gavani and frog (experiments into the effect of electricity on nerves and muscles, 1780)	1·00	90
3174/90 Set of 17		15·00	13·50

Nos. 3174/90 were printed together, *se-tenant*, in sheetlets of 17 including a central label (59×39 mm) and inscribed left margin.

The main design on No. 3184 may depict Sir William Jenner who undertook research into typhus.

On No. 3185 the uniforms are incorrectly shown as blue instead of red.

See also Nos. 3258/**MS**3264.

(Des Deborah Max. Litho B.D.T.)

2000 (8 Mar). Solar Eclipse (11 August 1999). T **375** and similar vert designs showing varying stages of eclipse as seen from Earth (Nos. 3191/6) or Space (Nos. 3197/3202). Multicoloured. P 14.

3191	7r. Type **375**	1·50	1·50
	a. Sheetlet of 6. Nos. 3191/6	8·00	8·00
3192	7r. "Second Contact"	1·50	1·50
3193	7r. "Totality"	1·50	1·50
3194	7r. "Third Contact"	1·50	1·50
3195	7r. "Fourth Contact"	1·50	1·50
3196	7r. Observatory	1·50	1·50
3197	7r. "First Contact"	1·50	1·50
	a. Sheetlet of 6. Nos. 3197/3202	8·00	8·00
3198	7r. "Second Contact"	1·50	1·50
3199	7r. "Totality"	1·50	1·50
3200	7r. "Third Contact"	1·50	1·50
3201	7r. "Fourth Contact"	1·50	1·50
3202	7r. Solar and Heliospheric Observatory	1·50	1·50
3191/202 Set of 12		16·00	16·00

Nos. 3191/6 and 3197/3202 were each printed together, *se-tenant*, in sheetlets of six with the backgrounds forming composite designs.

376 Red Lacewing

377 "Martin Rijckaert"

(Des S. Stines. Litho Cartor)

2000 (10 Apr). Butterflies of the Maldives. T **376** and similar horiz designs. Multicoloured. P 13½.

3203	5r. Type **376**	1·25	1·25
	a. Sheetlet of 9. Nos. 3203/11	10·00	10·00
3204	5r. Large Oak Blue	1·25	1·25
3205	5r. Yellow Coster	1·25	1·25
3206	5r. Great Orange-tip	1·25	1·25
3207	5r. Common Pierrot	1·25	1·25
3208	5r. Cruiser	1·25	1·25
3209	5r. Hedge Blue	1·25	1·25
3210	5r. Common Eggfly	1·25	1·25
3211	5r. Plain Tiger	1·25	1·25
3212	5r. Common Wall Butterfly	1·25	1·25
	a. Sheetlet of 9. Nos. 3212/20	10·00	10·00
3213	5r. Koh-i-Noor Butterfly	1·25	1·25
3214	5r. Painted Lady ("Indian Red Admiral")	1·25	1·25
3215	5r. Tawny Rajah	1·25	1·25
3216	5r. Blue Triangle	1·25	1·25
3217	5r. Orange Albatross	1·25	1·25
3218	5r. Common Rose Swallowtail	1·25	1·25
3219	5r. Jewelled Nawab	1·25	1·25
3220	5r. Striped Blue Crow	1·25	1·25
3203/20 Set of 18		20·00	20·00
MS3221 Two sheets (a) 85×110 mm. 25r. Large Tree Nymph. (b) 110×85 mm. 25r. Blue Pansy Set of 2 sheets		11·00	12·00

Nos. 3203/11 and 3212/20 were each printed together, *se-tenant*, in sheetlets of nine with the backgrounds forming composite designs.

No. 3219 is insribed "JEWELED NAWAB" in error.

(Litho Questa)

2000 (12 May). 400th Birth Anniv of Sir Anthony Van Dyck (Flemish painter). T **377** and similar multicoloured designs. P 13½×14.

3222	5r. Type **377**	1·60	1·60
	a. Sheetlet of 6. Nos. 3222/7	8·75	8·75
3223	5r. "Frans Snyders"	1·60	1·60
3224	5r. "Quentin Simons"	1·60	1·60
3225	5r. "Lucas van Uffel", 1632	1·60	1·60
3226	5r. "Nicolaes Rockox"	1·60	1·60
3227	5r. "Nicholas Lamier"	1·60	1·60
3228	5r. "Inigo Jones"	1·60	1·60
	a. Sheetlet of 6. Nos. 3228/33	8·75	8·75
3229	5r. "Lucas van Uffel", c. 1622–25	1·60	1·60
3230	5r. Detail of "MarFaretha de Vos, Wife of Frans Snyders	1·60	1·60
3231	5r. Peter Brueghel the Younger"	1·60	1·60
3232	5r. "Cornelis van der Geest"	1·60	1·60
3233	5r. "Francois Langlois as a Savoyard"	1·60	1·60
3234	5r. "Portrait of a Family"	1·60	1·60
	a. Sheetlet of 6. Nos. 3234/9	8·75	8·75
3235	5r. "Earl and Countess of Denby and Their Daughter"	1·60	1·60
3236	5r. Family Portrait"	1·60	1·60
3237	5r. "A Genoese Nobleman with his Children"	1·60	1·60
3238	5r. "Thomas Howard, Earl of Arundel, and His Grandson"	1·60	1·60
3239	5r. "La dama d'oro"	1·60	1·60
3222/39 Set of 18		25·00	25·00
MS3240 Six sheets. (a) 102×127 mm. 25r. "The Painter Jan de Wael and his Wife Gertrude de Jode". (b) 102×127 mm. 25r. "John, Count of Nassau-Siegen, and His Family". (c) 102×127 mm. 25r. "The Lomellini Family". (d) 102×127 mm. 25r. "Lucas and Cornelis de Wael". (e) 127×102 mm. 25r. "Sir Kenelm and Lady Digby with their two Eldest Sons". (f) 127×102 mm. 25r. "Sir Philip Herbert, 4th Earl of Pembroke, and His Family" (*horiz*). P 14×13½ Set of 6 sheets		27·00	29·00

Nos. 3222/7, 3228/33 and 3234/9 were each printed together, *se-tenant*, in sheetlets of six with illustrated margins.

No. 3230 is inscribed "Margaretha de Vos, Wife of Frans Snders" in error.

378 Japanese Railways "Shinkansen", High Speed Electric Train

379 Republic Monument

(Des. E. Nisbet. Litho Questa)

2000 (8 June). "The Stamp Show 2000" International Stamp Exhibition, London. Asian Railways. T **378** and similar horiz designs. Multicoloured. P 14.

3241	5r. Type **378**	1·50	85
3242	8r. Japanese Railways "Super Azusa", twelve-car train	1·75	1·75
3243	10r. Tobu Railway "Spacia", ten-car electric train, Japan	2·00	2·00
3244	10r. Shanghai-Nanking Railway passenger tank locomotive, China, 1909	2·00	2·00
	a. Sheetlet of 6. Nos. 3244/9	11·00	11·00
3245	10r. Shanghai-Nanking Railway "Imperial Yellow" express mail locomotive, China, 1910	2·00	2·00
3246	10r. Manchurian Railway "Pacific" locomotive, China, 1914	2·00	2·00
3247	10r. Hankow Line mixed traffic locomotive, China, 1934	2·00	2·00
3248	10r. Chinese National Railway freight locomotive 1949	2·00	2·00
3249	10r. Chinese National Railway mixed traffic locomotive, 1949	2·00	2·00
3250	10r. East Indian Railway passenger tank locomotive Fawn, 1856	2·00	2·00
	a. Sheetlet of 6. Nos. 3250/5	11·00	11·00
3251	10r. East Indian Railway express locomotive, 1893	2·00	2·00
3252	10r. Bengal-Nagpur Railway Atlantic Compound locomotive, India, 1909	2·00	2·00
3253	10r. Great Peninsular Railway passenger and mail locomotive, India, 1924	2·00	2·00
3254	10r. North Western Class X2 Pacific locomotive, India, 1932	2·00	2·00
3255	10r. Indian National Railway Class YP Pacific locomotive, India, 1949–70	2·00	2·00

3256	15r. Japanese Railway "Nozomi", high speed electric train	2·75	3·25
3241/56	Set of 16	29·00	29·00

MS3257 Two sheets, each 100×70 mm. (a) 25r. Indian National Railways Class WP locomotive (57×41 mm). (b) 25r. Chinese National Railway Class JS locomotive (57×41 mm) *Set of 2 sheets* .... 12·00 13·00
Nos. 3244/9 and 3250/5 were each printed together, *se-tenant*, in sheetlets of six with enlarged inscribed right-hand margins.

2000 (31 Aug). New Millennium (2nd issue). T **379** and similar horiz designs. Multicoloured. Litho. P 13.

3258	10l. Type **379**	15	30
3259	30l. Bodu Thakurufaanu Memorial Centre....	20	15
3260	1r. Modern medical facilities and new hostpital	75	15
3261	7r. Malé International Airport	1·60	2·00
3262	7r. Hukuru Miskiiy	1·60	2·00
3263	10r. Computer room, science lab and new school	1·75	2·00
3258/63	Set of 6	5·50	6·00

MS3264 Three sheets, each 106×77 mm. (a) 25r. Tourist resort and fish packing factory. (b) 25r. Islamic Centre. (c) 25r. People's Majlis (assembly) *Set of 3 sheets* .... 11·00 14·00

379a "Apollo 18" and "Soyuz 19" docking

380 George Stephenson and *Locomotion No. 1*, 1825

(Des B. Pevsner. Litho Questa)

2000 (13 Sept). 25th Anniv of "Apollo-Soyuz" Joint Project. Multicoloured designs as T **379a**. P 14.

3265	13r. Type **379a**	1·75	2·00
	a. Sheetlet of 3. Nos. 3265/7	4·75	5·50
3266	13r. "Soyuz 19"	1·75	2·00
3267	13r. "Apollo 18"	1·75	2·00
3265/67	Set of 3	4·75	5·50

MS3268 105×76 mm. 25r. "Soyuz 19" (*horiz*) .... 4·00 4·50
Nos. 3265/7 were printed together, *se-tenant*, in sheetlets of three with enlarged illustrated and inscribed margins.

(Des J. Iskowitz. Litho Questa)

2000 (13 Sept). 175th Anniv of Stockton and Darlington Line (first public railway). T **380** and similar horiz design. Multicoloured. P 14.

3269	10r. Type **380**	2·25	2·25
	a. Sheetlet of 2. Nos. 3269/70	4·50	4·50
3270	10r. William Hedley's *Puffing Billy* locomotive	2·25	2·25

Nos. 3269/70 were printed together, *se-tenant*, in sheetlets of two with enlarged illustrated and inscribed margins.

380a LZ-127 *Graf Zeppelin*, 1928

380b Suzanne Lenglen (French tennis player), 1920

(Des G. Capasso. Litho Questa)

2000 (13 Sept). Centenary of First Zeppelin Flight. Multicoloured designs as T **380a**. P 14.

3271	13r. Type **380a**	2·75	2·75
	a. Sheetlet of 3. Nos. 3271/3	7·50	7·50
3272	13r. LZ-130 *Graf Zeppelin* II, 1938	2·75	2·75
3273	13r. LZ-9 *Ersatz*, 1911	2·75	2·75
3271/73	Set of 3	7·50	7·50

MS3274 115×80 mm. 25r. LZ-88 (L-40), 1917 (37×50 mm) .... 5·50 6·00
Nos. 3271/3 were printed together, *se-tenant*, in sheetlets of three with enlarged illustrated and inscribed margins.
No. 3272 is inscribed "LZ-127" in error.

(Litho Questa)

2000 (13 Sept). Olympic Games, Sydney. Horiz designs as T **380b**. Multicoloured. P 14.

3275	10r. Type **380b**	2·25	2·25
	a. Sheetlet of 4. Nos. 3275/8	8·00	8·00
3276	10r. Fencing	2·25	2·25
3277	10r. Olympic Stadium, Tokyo, 1964, and Japanese flag	2·25	2·25
3278	10r. Ancient Greek long jumping	2·25	2·25
3275/78	Set of 4	8·00	8·00

Nos. 3275/8 were printed together, *se-tenant*, in sheetlets of four (2×2) with the horizontal rows separated by a gutter margin showing Sydney landmarks and athlete with Olympic torch.

381 White Tern

382 Dendrobium crepidatum

(Des T. Wood. Litho Questa)

2000 (13 Sept). Tropical Birds. T **381** and similar multicoloured designs. P 13½×14 (horiz) or 14×13½ (vert).

3279	15l. Type **381**	35	50
3280	25l. Brown Booby	40	50
3281	30l. White-collared Kingfisher (*vert*)	40	50
3282	1r. Black-winged Stilt (*vert*)	60	25
3283	10r. White-collared Kingfisher (*different*) (*vert*)	2·00	2·00
	a. Sheetlet of 6. Nos. 3283/8	11·00	11·00
3284	10r. Island Thrush (*vert*)	2·00	2·00
3285	10r. Red-tailed Tropic Bird (*vert*)	2·00	2·00
3286	10r. Peregrine Falcon (*vert*)	2·00	2·00
3287	10r. Night Heron (*vert*)	2·00	2·00
3288	10r. Great Egret (*vert*)	2·00	2·00
3289	10r. Great Frigate Bird	2·00	2·00
	a. Sheetlet of 6. Nos. 3289/94	11·00	11·00
3290	10r. Common Noddy	2·00	2·00
3291	10r. Common Tern	2·00	2·00
3292	10r. Red-footed Booby ("Sula Sula")	2·00	2·00
3293	10r. Sooty Tern	2·00	2·00
3294	10r. White-tailed Tropic Bird (*Phaethon lepturus*)	2·00	2·00
3295	13r. Ringed Plover	2·00	2·00
	a. Sheetlet of 6. Nos. 3295/3300	11·00	11·00
3296	13r. Turnstone	2·00	2·00
3297	13r. Great Australian Stone Plover ("Thicknee")	2·00	2·00
3298	13r. Black-bellied Plover	2·00	2·00
3299	13r. Crab Plover	2·00	2·00
3300	13r. Curlew	2·00	2·00
3279/300	Set of 22	35·00	35·00

MS3301 Two sheets, each 77×103 mm. (a) 25r. Great Cormorant (*vert*). (b) 25r. Cattle Egret (*vert*) *Set of 2 sheets* .... 12·00 13·00
Nos. 3283/8, 3289/4 and 3295/3300 were each printed together, *se-tenant*, in sheetlets of six, with the backgrounds forming composite designs.
No. 3294 is inscribed "Leturus" in error.

(Des R. Martin. Litho Questa)

2000 (13 Sept). Orchids. T **382** and similar vert designs. Multicoloured. P 14.

3302	50l. Type **382**	45	50
3303	1r. *Eulophia guineensis*	55	25
3304	2r.50 *Cymbidium finlaysonianum*	85	60
3305	3r.50 *Paphiopedilum drury*	1·00	75
3306	10r. *Angraecum germinyanum*	1·75	1·75
	a. Sheetlet of 6. Nos. 3306/11	9·50	9·50
3307	10r. *Phalaenopsis amabilis*	1·75	1·75
3308	10r. *Thrixspermum cantipeda*	1·75	1·75
3309	10r. *Phaius tankervilleae*	1·75	1·75
3310	10r. *Rhynchostylis gigantea*	1·75	1·75
3311	10r. *Papilionanthe teres*	1·75	1·75
3312	10r. *Aerides odorata*	1·75	1·75
	a. Sheetlet of 6. Nos. 3312/17	9·50	9·50
3313	10r. *Dendrobium chrysotoxum*	1·75	1·75
3314	10r. *Dendrobium anosmum*	1·75	1·75
3315	10r. *Calypso bulbosa*	1·75	1·75
3316	10r. *Paphiopedilum fairrieanum*	1·75	1·75
3317	10r. *Cynorkis fastigiata*	1·75	1·75
3302/17	Set of 16	21·00	21·00

MS3318 Two sheets, each 96×72 mm. (a) 25r. *Cymbidium dayanum.* (b) 25r. *Spathoglottis plicata Set of 2 sheets* .... 8·50   9·50

Nos. 3306/11 and 3312/17 were each printed together, *se-tenant*, in sheetlets of six with the backgrounds and margins forming composite designs.

383 Honda CB 750 Motorcycle, 1969

(Des B. Pevsner. Litho Questa)

2000 (30 Oct). A Century of Motorcycles. T **383** and similar horiz designs. Multicoloured. P 13½.

3319	7r. Type **383**	1·10	1·10
	a. Sheetlet of 6. Nos. 3319/24	6·00	6·00
3320	7r. Pioneer Harley Davidson, 1913	1·10	1·10
3321	7r. Bohmerland 1925	1·10	1·10
3322	7r. American Indian, 1910	1·10	1·10
3323	7r. Triumph Trophy 1200, 1993	1·10	1·10
3324	7r. Moto Guzzi 500S, 1928	1·10	1·10
3325	7r. Matchless, 1907	1·10	1·10
	a. Sheetlet of 6. Nos. 3325/30	6·00	6·00
3326	7r. Manch 4 1200 TTS, 1966	1·10	1·10
3327	7r. Lambretta LD-150, 1957	1·10	1·10
3328	7r. Yamaha XJP 1200, 1990's	1·10	1·10
3329	7r. Daimler, 1885	1·10	1·10
3330	7r. John Player Norton, 1950s-60's	1·10	1·10
3319/30	*Set of 12*	12·00	13·00

MS3331 Two sheets, each 62×46 mm. (a) 25r. Harley Davidson, 1950. (b) 25r. Electra Glide, 1960. P 13×13½ *Set of 2 sheets* .... 8·00   9·00

Nos. 3319/24 and 3325/30 were each printed together, *se-tenant*, in sheetlets of six with illustrated vertical or horizontal gutter margins.

384 Corn Lily   **385** Racoon Butterflyfish (*Chaetodon lunula*)

(Des L. Schwinger. Litho Questa)

2000 (15 Nov). Flowers of the Indian Ocean. T **384** and similar multicoloured designs. P 14.

3332	5r. Type **384**	1·00	1·00
	a. Sheetlet of 6. Nos. 3332/7	5·50	5·50
3333	5r. Clivia	1·00	1·00
3334	5r. Red Hot Poker	1·00	1·00
3335	5r. Crown of Thorns	1·00	1·00
3336	5r. Cape Daisy	1·00	1·00
3337	5r. Geranium	1·00	1·00
3338	5r. Fringed Hibiscus (*horiz*)	1·00	1·00
	a. Sheetlet of 6. Nos. 3338/43	5·50	5·50
3339	5r. Erica vestita (*horiz*)	1·00	1·00
3340	5r. Bird-of-Paradise Flower (*horiz*)	1·00	1·00
3341	5r. Peacock Orchid (*horiz*)	1·00	1·00
3342	5r. Mesembryanthemums (*horiz*)	1·00	1·00
3343	5r. African Violets (*horiz*)	1·00	1·00
3332/43	*Set of 12*	11·00	11·00

MS3344 Two sheets, each 112×80 mm. (a) 25r. Gladiolus, (b) 25r. Calla Lily (*horiz*) *Set of 2 sheets* ..... 8·50   9·50

Nos. 3332/7 and 3338/43 were each printed together, *se-tenant*, in sheetlets of six with the backgrounds and margins forming composite designs.

(Des Irene Lampe (Nos. 3369/74 and MS3375b), L. Birmingham (others). Litho Questa)

2000 (15 Nov). Marine Life of the Indian Ocean. T **385** and similar horiz designs. Multicoloured. P 14.

3345	5r. Type **385**	85	85
	a. Sheetlet of 8. Nos. 3345/52	6·00	6·00
3346	5r. Wrasse (*Stethojulis albovittata*)	85	85
3347	5r. Green Turtle	85	85
3348	5r. Jobfish	85	85
3349	5r. Damsel fish	85	85
3350	5r. Meyer's Butterflyfish (*Chaetodon meyeri*)	85	85
3351	5r. Wrasse (*Cirrhilabrus exquisitus*)	85	85
3352	5r. Maldive Anemonefish	85	85
3353	5r. Hind (*Cephalopholis* sp)	85	85
	a. Sheetlet of 8. Nos. 3353/60	6·00	6·00
3354	5r. Regal Angelfish (*Pygopolites diacanthus*) (red face value)	85	85
3355	5r. Forceps Butterflyfish (*Forcipiger flavissimus*)	85	85
3356	5r. Goatfish	85	85
3357	5r. Trumpet fish	85	85
3358	5r. Butterfly Perch (*Pseudanthias squamipinnis*)	85	85
3359	5r. Two-spined Angelfish (*Centropyge bispinosus*)	85	85
3360	5r. Sweetlips	85	85
3361	5r. Twin-spotted Wrasse (*Coris aygula*)	85	85
	a. Sheetlet of 8. Nos. 3361/8	6·00	6·00
3362	5r. Snapper	85	85
3363	5r. Sea Bass	85	85
3364	5r. Bennett's Butterflyfish (*Chaetodon bennetti*)	85	85
3365	5r. Pelagic Snapper	85	85
3366	5r. Cardinalfish	85	85
3367	5r. Six-barred Wrasse (*Thalassoma hardwicke*)	85	85
3368	5r. Surgeonfish	85	85
3369	5r. Longnosed Filefish	85	85
	a. Sheetlet of 6. Nos. 3369/74	4·50	4·50
3370	5r. Hawaiian Squirrelfish	85	85
3371	5r. Freckled Hawkfish	85	85
3372	5r. McCosker's Flasher Wrasse	85	85
3373	5r. Regal Angelfish (*Pygoplites diacanthus*) (white face value)	85	85
3374	5r. Angelfish (*Parseentzopyge venusta*)	85	85
3345/3374	*Set of 30*	22·00	22·00

MS3375 Four sheets, 106×76 mm (b) or 108×80 mm (others) (a) 25r. Moray Eel. (b) 25r. Yellow-bellied Hamlet (*Hypoplectrus aberrans*). (c) 25r. Yellow-banded Angelfish (*Pomacanthus maculosus*). (d) 25r. Spiny Butterflyfish (*Pygoplites diacanthus*) Set of 4 sheets .... 15·00   17·00

Nos. 3345/52, 3353/60, 3361/8 and 3369/74 were each printed together, *se-tenant*, in sheetlets of six or eight with the backgrounds forming composite designs.

On No. 3369 "Oxymoncanthus", on 3371 "Paracirrhites" is misspelled "Paraeirrhites" and 3374 is the Purple-mask Angelfish (*Centropyge venustus*), not as decribed.

385a "Nobleman with Golden Chain" (Tintoretto)

(Des D. Keren. Litho Walsall)

2000 (29 Nov). "Espana 2000" International Stamp Exhibition, Madrid. Paintings from the Prado Museum. As T **385a** and similar vert designs. Multicoloured. P 12.

3376	7r Type **385a**	1·25	1·25
	a. Sheetlet of 6. Nos. 3376/81	6·75	6·75
3377	7r. "Triumphal Arch" (Domenichino)	1·25	1·25
3378	7r. "Don Garzia de' Medici" (Bronzino)	1·25	1·25
3379	7r. Man from "Micer Marsilio and his Wife" (Lorenzo Lotto)	1·25	1·25
3380	7r. "The Infanta Maria Antonieta Fernanda" (Jacopo Amigoni)	1·25	1·25
3381	7r. Woman from "Micer Marsilio and his Wife"	1·25	1·25
3382	7r. "Self-portrait" (Albrecht Dürer)	1·25	1·25
	a. Sheetlet of 6. Nos. 3382/7	6·75	6·75
3383	7r. "Woman and her Daughter" (Adriaen van Cronenburg)	1·25	1·25
3384	7r. "Portrait of a Man" (Albrecht Dürer)	1·25	1·25
3385	7r. Wife and daughters from "The Artist and his Family" (Jacob Jordaens)	1·25	1·25
3386	7r. "Artemisia" (Rembrandt)	1·25	1·25

3387	7r. Man from "The Artist and his Family"....	1·25	1·25
3388	7r. "The Painter Andrea Sacchi (Carlo Maratta)	1·25	1·25
	a. Sheetlet of 6. Nos. 3388/93	6·75	6·75
3389	7r. Two Turks from "The Turkish Embassy to the Court of Naples" (Giuseppe Bonito)	1·25	1·25
3390	7r. "Charles Cecil Roberts" (Pompeo Girolamo Batoni)	1·25	1·25
3391	7r. "Francesco Albani" (Andrea Sacchi)	1·25	1·25
3392	7r. Three Turks from "The Turkish Embassy to the Court of Naples"	1·25	1·25
3393	7r. "Sir William Hamilton" (Pompeo Girolamo Batoni)	1·25	1·25
3394	7r. Women from "Achilles amongst the Daughters of Lycomedes" (Rubens and Van Dyck)	1·25	1·25
	a. Sheetlet of 6. Nos. 3394/9	6·75	6·75
3395	7r. Woman in red dress from "Achilles amongst the Daughters of Lycomedes"	1·25	1·25
3396	7r. Men from "Achilles amongst the Daughters of Lycomedes"	1·25	1·25
3397	7r. "The Duke of Lerma on Horseback" (Rubens)	1·25	1·25
3398	7r. "The Death of Seneca" (workshop of Rubens)	1·25	1·25
3399	7r. "Marie de' Medici" (Rubens)	1·25	1·25
3400	7r. "The Marquesa of Villafranca" (Goya)	1·25	1·25
	a. Sheetlet of 6. Nos. 3400/5	6·75	6·75
3401	7r. "Maria Ruthven" (Van Dyck)	1·25	1·25
3402	7r. "Cardinal-Infante Ferdinand" (Van Dyck)	1·25	1·25
3403	7r. "Prince Frederick Hendrick of Orange-Nassau" (Van Dyck)	1·25	1·25
3404	7r. Endymion Porter from "Self-portrait with Endymion Porter" (Van Dyck)	1·25	1·25
3405	7r. Van Dyck from "Self-portrait with Endymion Porter"	1·25	1·25
3406	7r. "King Philip V of Spain" (Hyacinthe Rigaud)	1·25	1·25
	a. Sheetlet of 6. Nos. 3406/11	6·75	6·75
3407	7r. "King Louis IV of France" (Hyacinthe Rigaud)	1·25	1·25
3408	7r. "Don Luis, Prince of Asturias" (Michel-Ange Houasse)	1·25	1·25
3409	7r. "Duke Emanuele II of Savoy with his Wife and Son" (Charles Dauphin)	1·25	1·25
3410	7r. "Kitchen Maid" (Charles-François Hutin)	1·25	1·25
3411	7r. "Hurdy-gurdy Player" (Georges de la Tour)	1·25	1·25
3376/3411	Set of 36	38·00	38·00

MS3412 Six sheets. (a) 110×90 mm. 25r. "The Devotion of Rudolf I" (Peter Paul Rubens and Jan Wildens) (*horiz*). (b) 110×90 mm. 25r. "The Artist and his Family" (Jacob Jordaens) (*horiz*). (c) 90×110 mm. 25r. "The Turkish Embassy to the Court of Naples" (Giuseppe Bonito). (d) 90×110 mm. 25r. "Camilla Gonzaga, Countess of San Segundo, with her Three Children (Parmigianino). (e) 90×110 mm. 25r. "Elizabeth of Valois" (Sofonisba Anguisciola). (f) 110×90 mm. 25r. "Duke Carlo Emanuele II of Savoy with his Wife and Son" (Charles Dauphin) *Set of 6 sheets* .... 26·00 28·00

Nos. 3376/81, 3382/7, 3388/93, 3394/9, 3400/5 and 3406/11 were each printed together, *se-tenant*, in sheetlets of six with inscribed margins.

386 Steam Locomotive *Hiawatha*, **387** Porsche 911S, 1966
1935

(Des M. Harper. Litho Questa)

2000 (30 Nov). Milestones in 20th-century Transport. T **386** and similar multicoloured designs. P 14.

3413	2r.50 Steam Locomotive *Papyrus*, 1934 (*vert*)	75	50
3414	3r. Type **386**	75	50
3415	5r. Thrust SSC rocket car, 1997	1·00	1·00
	a. Sheetlet of 6. Nos. 3415/20	5·50	5·50
3416	5r. Curtiss R3C-2 seaplane, 1925	1·00	1·00
3417	5r. Steam locomotive *Rocket*, 1829	1·00	1·00
3418	5r. TGV electric train, 1990, France	1·00	1·00
3419	5r. Steam locomotive *Mallard*, 1938	1·00	1·00
3420	5r. SNCF Class BB 9004 electric locomotive, 1955	1·00	1·00

3421	5r. Lockheed XP-80 aircraft, 1947	1·00	1·00
	a. Sheetlet of 6. Nos. 3421/6	5·50	5·50
3422	5r. Mikoyan MiG 23 Foxbat aircraft, 1965...	1·00	1·00
3423	5r. Hawker Tempest aircraft, 1943	1·00	1·00
3424	5r. *Bluebird* car, 1964	1·00	1·00
3425	5r. *Blue Flame* car, 1970	1·00	1·00
3426	5r. *Thrust 2* car, 1983	1·00	1·00
3427	12r. Supermarine SBG seaplane, 1931	2·00	2·25
3428	13r. MLX01 train, 1998	2·00	2·25
3413/28	Set of 16	16·00	16·00

MS3429 Two sheets. (a) 100×75 mm. 25r. Lockheed SR-71 Blackbird airplane, 1976 (*vert*). (b) 75×100 mm. 25r. Bell X-1 aircraft, 1947 *Set of 2 sheets* .... 10·00 11·00

Nos. 3415/20 and 3421/6 were each printed together, *se-tenant*, in sheetlets of six with the backgrounds forming composite designs.

(Des G. Capasso. Litho Questa)

2000 (30 Nov). "The World of Porsche." T **387** and similar horiz designs. Multicoloured. P 14.

3430	12r. Type **387**	1·75	2·00
	a. Sheetlet of 3. Nos. 3430/2	4·75	5·50
3431	12r. Model 959, 1988	1·75	2·00
3432	12r. Model 993 Carrera, 1995	1·75	2·00
3433	12r. Model 356 SC, 1963	1·75	2·00
	a. Sheetlet of 3. Nos. 3433/5	4·75	5·50
3434	12r. Model 911 Turbo, 1975	1·75	2·00
3435	12r. Contemporary model	1·75	2·00
3430/35	Set of 6	9·50	11·00

MS3436 110×85 mm. 25r. Model Boxter, 2000 (56×42 mm) .... 4·00 4·50

Nos. 3430/2 and 3433/5 were each printed together, *se-tenant*, in sheetlets of three with illustrated and inscribed margins.

388 Limited Edition Trans-Am, **389** Pierce-Arrow (1930)
1976

(Des G. Capasso. Litho Questa)

2000 (30 Nov). "The World of the Pontiac". T **388** and similar horiz designs. Multicoloured. P 14.

3437	12r. Type **388**	1·75	2·00
	a. Sheetlet of 3. Nos. 3437/9	4·75	5·50
3438	12r. Trans-Am, 1988	1·75	2·00
3439	12r. Trans-Am Coupe, 1988	1·75	2·00
3440	12r. Yellow Trans-Am, 1970–72	1·75	2·00
	a. Sheetlet of 3. Nos. 3440/2	4·75	5·50
3441	12r 25th Anniv Trans-Am, 1989	1·75	2·00
3442	12r. Trans-Am GT convertible, 1994	1·75	2·00
3437/42	Set of 6	9·50	11·00

MS3443 110×85 mm. 25r. Trans-Am model, 1999 (56×42 mm) .... 4·00 4·50

Nos. 3437/9 and 3440/2 were each printed together, *se-tenant*, in sheetlets of three with illustrated and inscribed margins.

(Des Artworks Studio. Litho Questa)

2000 (30 Nov). 20th-century Classic Cars. T **389** and similar horiz designs. Multicoloured. P 14.

3444	1r. Type **389**	40	15
3445	2r. Mercedes-Benz 540K (1938)	60	30
3446	7r. Auburn Convertible Sedan (1931)	1·40	1·40
	a. Sheetlet of 6. Nos. 3446/51	7·75	7·75
3447	7r. Mercedes SSKL (1931)	1·40	1·40
3448	7r. Packard Roadster (1929)	1·40	1·40
3449	7r. Chevrolet (1940)	1·40	1·40
3450	7r. Mercer (1915)	1·40	1·40
3451	7r. Packard Sedan (1941)	1·40	1·40
3452	7r. Chevrolet Roadster (1932)	1·40	1·40
	a. Sheetlet of 6. Nos. 3452/7	7·75	7·75
3453	7r. Cadillac Fleetwood Roadster (1929)	1·40	1·40
3454	7r. Bentley Speed Six (1928)	1·40	1·40
3455	7r. Cadillac Fleetwood (1930)	1·40	1·40
3456	7r. Ford Convertible (1936)	1·40	1·40
3457	7r. Hudson Phaeton (1929)	1·40	1·40
3458	8r. Duesenberg J (1934)	1·40	1·40
3459	10r. Bugatti Royale (1931)	1·50	1·75
3444/59	Set of 16	19·00	19·00

MS3460 Two sheets, each 106×81 mm. (a) 25r. Rolls Royce P-1 (1931). (b) 25r. Cord Brougham (1930) *Set of 2 sheets* .... 8·50 9·50

Nos. 3446/51 and 3452/7 were each printed together, *se-tenant*, in sheetlets of six with illustrated margins.

No. 3457 is inscribed "HUDSIN" in error.

Rf10
(389a)

Rf10
(389b)

2001. Surch locally as T **389a** or **389b**.

3460a	10r. on 7r. (as T **392**)	20·00	
	ab. Surch double	75·00	
3460b	10r. on 50r. (No 2973)	—	
	bb. Surch inverted	75·00	

390 *Cortinarius collinitus*

390a German commanders looking across English Channel

(Des T. Wood. Litho Questa)

2001 (2 Jan). Fungi. T **390** and similar vert designs. Multicoloured. P 14.

3461	30l. Type **390**	25	35
3462	50l. *Russula ochroleuca*	25	35
3463	2r. *Lepiota acutesquamosa*	60	30
3464	3r. *Hebeloma radicosum*	70	35
3465	7r. *Tricholoma aurantium*	1·10	1·10
	a. Sheetlet of 6. Nos. 3465/70	6·00	6·00
3466	7r. *Pholiota spectabilis*	1·10	1·10
3467	7r. *Russula caerulea*	1·10	1·10
3468	7r. *Amanita phalloides*	1·10	1·10
3469	7r. *Mycena strobilinoides*	1·10	1·10
3470	7r. *Boletus satanas*	1·10	1·10
3471	7r. *Amanita muscaria*	1·10	1·10
	a. Sheetlet of 6. Nos. 3471/6	6·00	6·00
3472	7r. *Mycena lilacifolia*	1·10	1·10
3473	7r. *Coprinus comatus*	1·10	1·10
3474	7r. *Morchella crassipes*	1·10	1·10
3475	7r. *Russula nigricans*	1·10	1·10
3476	7r. *Lepiota procera*	1·10	1·10
3477	13r. *Amanita echinocephala*	1·75	1·75
3478	15r. *Collybia iocephala*	1·90	1·90
3461/78 Set of 18		17·00	17·00

MS3479 Two sheets, each 112×82 mm. (a) 25r. *Tricholoma aurantium*. (b) 25r. *Lepiota procera*. Set of 2 sheets .... 8·00 9·00

Nos. 3465/70 and 3471/6 were each printed together, *se-tenant*, in sheetlets of six with inscribed margins.

(Des R. Rundo. Litho Questa)

2001 (2 Jan). 60th Anniv of Battle of Britain. As T **390a** and similar horiz designs. Multicoloured. P 14.

3480	5r. Type **390a**	1·60	1·40
	a. Sheetlet of 8. Nos. 3480/7	11·50	10·00
3481	5r. Armourers with German bomber	1·60	1·40
3482	5r. German Stuka dive-bombers	1·60	1·40
3483	5r. Bombing the British coast	1·60	1·40
3484	5r. German bomber over Greenwich	1·60	1·40
3485	5r. St. Paul's Cathedral surrounded by fire	1·60	1·40
3486	5r. British fighter from German bomber	1·60	1·40
3487	5r. Spitfire on fire	1·60	1·40
3488	5r. Prime Minister Winston Churchill	1·60	1·40
	a. Sheetlet of 8. Nos. 3488/95	11·50	10·00
3489	5r. British fighter pilots running to planes	1·60	1·40
3490	5r. RAF planes taking off	1·60	1·40
3491	5r. British fighters in formation	1·60	1·40
3492	5r. German bomber crashing	1·60	1·40
3493	5r. British fighters attacking	1·60	1·40
3494	5r. German bomber in sea	1·60	1·40
3495	5r. Remains of German bomber in flames	1·60	1·40
3480/95 Set of 16		23·00	20·00

MS3496 Two sheets, each 103×66 mm. (a) 25r. Hawker Hurricane. (b) 25r. Messerschmitt ME 109 Set of 2 sheets .... 15·00 15·00

Nos. 3480/7 and 3488/95 were printed together, *se-tenant*, in sheetlets of eight with the two horizontal *se-tenant* rows separated by a gutter margin showing scenes from the Battle of Britain.

390b Donkeys from "Donkey Ride on the Beach" (Isaac Lazarus Israêls)

(Litho Questa)

2001 (15 Jan). Bicentenary of Rijksmuseum, Amsterdam. Dutch Paintings. As T **390b** and similar vert designs. Multicoloured. P 13½×14.

3497	7r. Type **390b**	1·25	1·25
	a. Sheetlet of 6. Nos. 3497/3502	6·75	6·75
3498	7r. "The Paternal Admonition" (Gerard ter Borch)	1·25	1·25
3499	7r. "The Sick Woman" (Jan Havicksz Steen)	1·25	1·25
3500	7r. Girls from "Donkey Ride on the Beach".	1·25	1·25
3501	7r. "Pompejus Occo" (Dick Jacobsz)	1·25	1·25
3502	7r. "The Pantry" (Pieter de Hooch)	1·25	1·25
3503	7r. Woman in doorway from "The Little Street" (Johannes Vermeer)	1·25	1·25
	a. Sheetlet of 6. Nos. 3503/8	6·75	6·75
3504	7r. Woman with maid from "The Love Letter" (Johannes Vermeer)	1·25	1·25
3505	7r. "Woman in Blue Reading a Letter" (Johannes Vermeer)	1·25	1·25
3506	7r. Woman from "The Love Letter"	1·25	1·25
3507	7r. "The Milkmaid" (Johannes Vermeer)	1·25	1·25
3508	7r. Woman in alley from "The Little Street"	1·25	1·25
3509	7r. "Rembrandt's Mother" (Gerard Dou)	1·25	1·25
	a. Sheetlet of 6. Nos. 3509/14	6·75	6·75
3510	7r. "Girl dressed in Blue" (Johannes Verspronck)	1·25	1·25
3511	7r. "Old Woman at Prayer" (Nicolaes Maes)	1·25	1·25
3512	7r. "Feeding the Hungry" (De Meester van Alkmaar)	1·25	1·25
3513	7r. "The Threatened Swan" (Jan Asselyn)	1·25	1·25
3514	7r. "The Daydreamer" (Nicolaes Maes)	1·25	1·25
3515	7r. "The Holy Kinship" (Geertgen Tot Sint Jans)	1·25	1·25
	a. Sheetlet of 6. Nos. 3515/20	6·75	6·75
3516	7r. "Sir Thomas Gresham" (Anthonis Mor Vas Dashorst)	1·25	1·25
3517	7r. "Self portrait as St. Paul" (Rembrandt)	1·25	1·25
3518	7r. "Cleopatra's Banquet" (Gerard Lairesse).	1·25	1·25
3519	7r. "Flowers in a Glass" (Jan Brueghel the elder)	1·25	1·25
3520	7r. "Nicolaes Hasselaer" (Frans Hals)	1·25	1·25
3497/3520 Set of 24		26·00	26·00

MS3521 Four sheets. (a) 118×78 mm.25r. "The Syndics" (Rembrandt). (b) 88×118 mm. 25r. "Johannes Wtenbogaert" (Rembrandt). (c) 118×88 mm. 25r. "The Night Watch" (Rembrandt). (d) 118×88 mm. 25r. "Shipwreck on a Rocky Coast" (Wijnandus Johannes Nuyen) (*horiz*). P 13½×14 (*vert*) or 14×13½ (*horiz*) Set of 4 sheets .... 18·00 21·00

Nos. 3497/3502, 3503/8, 3509/14 and 3515/20 were printed together, *se-tenant*, in sheetlets of six with illustrated and inscribed margins.

391 *Windfall* (schooner), 1962

392 Roses

(Des L. Schwinger. Litho Questa)

2001 (12 Feb). Maritime Disasters. T **391** and similar horiz designs. Multicoloured. P 14.

3522	5r. Type **391**	1·25	1·25
	a. Sheetlet of 6. Nos. 3522/7	6·75	6·75
3523	5r. *Kobenhavn* (barque), 1928	1·25	1·25
3524	5r. *Pearl* (schooner), 1874	1·25	1·25
3525	5r. HMS *Bulwark* (battleship), 1914	1·25	1·25
3526	5r. *Patriot* (brig), 1812	1·25	1·25

3527	5r. *Lusitania* (liner), 1915	1·25	1·25
3528	5r. *Milton latrides* (coaster), 1970	1·25	1·25
	a. Sheetlet of 6. Nos. 3528/33	6·75	6·75
3529	5r. *Cyclops* (freighter), 1918	1·25	1·25
3530	5r. *Marine Sulphur Queen* (tanker), 1963	1·25	1·25
3531	5r. *Rosalie* (full-rigged ship), 1840	1·25	1·25
3532	5r. *Mary Celeste* (sail merchantman), 1872	1·25	1·25
3533	5r. *Atlanta* (brig), 1880	1·25	1·25
3522/33	Set of 12	13·00	13·00

MS3534 Two sheets, each 110×85 mm. (a) 25r. *L'Astrolabe and La Boussole* (La Perouse, 1789). (b) 25r. *Titanic* (liner), 1912 Set of 2 sheets .... 14·00 14·00

Nos. 3522/7 and 3528/33 were printed together, *se-tenant*, in sheetlets of six with the backgrounds forming composite designs.

No. 3530 is inscribed "SULPHER" and No. **MS**3534a "LA BAUSSOLE", both in error.

(Litho Questa)

2001 (1 Mar.). P 15×14.

| 3535 | **392** | 10r. multicoloured | 1·25 | 1·25 |

393 Interior of Dharumavantha Rasgefaanu Mosque

(Litho Questa)

2001 (9 July). 848th Anniv of Introduction of Islam to the Maldives. T **393** and similar horiz designs. Multicoloured (except Nos. 3537/8). P 14×13½.

3536	10r. Type **393**	1·40	1·60
	a. Sheetlet of 6. Nos. 3536/41	7·50	8·50
3537	10r. Plaque of Hukurumiskiiy (black and grey-olive)	1·40	1·60
3538	10r. Family studying the Holy Quran (black)	1·40	1·60
3539	10r. Class at Institute of Islamic Studies	1·40	1·60
3540	10r. Centre for the Holy Quran	1·40	1·60
3541	10r. Islamic Centre, Malé	1·40	1·60
3536/41	Set of 6	7·50	8·50

MS3542 116×90 mm. 25r. Tomb of Sultan Abul Barakaat .... 3·75 4·50

Nos. 3536/41 were each printed in sheetlets of six with illustrated left margins.

394 Emperor Angelfish

395 "Young Women in Mist"

395a Victoria as a young girl (face value bottom left)

(Litho Questa)

2001 (16 July). Fish. T **394** and similar horiz design. Multicoloured. P 14×15.

| 3543 | 10r. Type **394** | 2·25 | 2·25 |
| 3544 | 10r. Indian Ocean Lionfish (*Pterois miles*) | 2·25 | 2·25 |

(Litho Questa)

2001 (18 July). "Philanippon '01" International Stamp Exhibition, Tokyo. Japanese Art. T **395** and similar vert designs. Multicoloured. P 14.

3545	7r. Type **395**	1·00	1·10
	a. Sheetlet of 5. Nos. 3545/9	4·50	5·00
3546	7r. "Woman with Parasol"	1·00	1·10
3547	7r. "Courtesan"	1·00	1·10
3548	7r. "Comparison of Beauties"	1·00	1·10
3549	7r. "Barber"	1·00	1·10
3550	7r. Ichikawa Danjuro V in black robes (20×81 *mm*)	1·00	1·10
	a. Sheetlet of 5. Nos. 3550/4	4·50	5·00

3551	7r. Ichikawa Danjuro V in brown robes with sword (20×81 *mm*)	1·00	1·10
3552	7r. Ichikawa Danjuro V with arms folded (20×81 *mm*)	1·00	1·10
3553	7r. Ichikawa Danjuro V seated in brown robes (20×81 *mm*)	1·00	1·10
3554	7r. Otani Tomoeman I and Bando Mitsugaro I (53×81 *mm*)	1·00	1·10
3545/3554	Set of 10	9·00	10·00

MS3555 Two sheets each 88×124 mm. (a) 25r. "Courtesan Hinazuru" (Kitagawa Utamaro). (b) 25r. "Tsutsui Jomyo and the Priest Ichirai" (Torii Kiyomasu I). P 13½×14 Set of 2 sheets .... 8·00 9·00

Nos. 3545/9, which show paintings of women by Kitagawa Utamaro, and Nos. 3550/4, which show famous actors by Katsukawa Shunsho, were each printed together, *se-tenant*, in sheetlets of five, with inscribed margins.

(Des Irene Lampe. Litho Questa)

2001 (26 Aug). Death Centenary of Queen Victoria. As T **395a** and similar vert designs. Multicoloured. P 14.

3556	10r. Type **395a**	1·40	1·60
	a. Sheetlet of 4. Nos. 3556/9	5·00	5·75
3557	10r. Victoria in old age	1·40	1·60
3558	10r. Victoria as a young girl (face value top right)	1·40	1·60
3559	10r. Queen Victoria in mourning	1·40	1·60
3556/59	Set of 4	5·00	5·75

MS3560 125×87 mm. 25r. Young Queen Victoria in evening dress .... 3·75 4·25

Nos. 3556/9 were printed together, *se-tenant*, in sheetlets of four containing two vertical columns, separated by an illustrated gutter.

395b Mao as a teenager (chestnut background)

(Des E. Moreiro. Litho Questa)

2001 (26 Aug). 25th Death Anniv of Mao Tse-tung (Chinese leader). As T **395b** and similar vert designs. Multicoloured. P 13½×14.

3561	15r. Type **395b**	1·50	1·75
	a. Sheetlet of 3. Nos. 3561/3	4·00	4·75
3562	15r. Mao as leader of Communist Party in 1930s (bluish violet background)	1·50	1·75
3563	15r. Mao in 1940s (greenish grey background)	1·50	1·75
3561/63	Set of 3	4·00	4·75

MS3564 139×132 mm. 25r. Mao as leader of China in 1960s .... 3·50 4·00

Nos. 3561/3 were printed together, *se-tenant*, in sheetlets of three with enlarged illustrated margins.

395c Portrait in Garter robes after Annigoni

395d Alfred Piccaver (opera singer) as Duke of Mantua

(Des B. Pevsner. Litho Questa)

2001 (26 Aug). 75th Birthday of Queen Elizabeth II. As T **395c** and similar vert designs. Multicoloured. P 14.

3565	7r. Type **395c**	1·75	1·75
	a. Sheetlet of 5. Nos. 3565/70	9·50	9·50
3566	7r. Queen at Coronation	1·75	1·75
3567	7r. In evening gown and tiara	1·75	1·75
3568	7r. In uniform for Trooping the Colour	1·75	1·75

3569	7r. In Garter robes and hat	1·75	1·75
3570	7r. Queen wearing cloak of kiwi feathers...	1·75	1·75
3565/70 *Set of 6*		9·50	9·50
MS3571 112×138 mm. 25r. Young Queen Elizabeth		5·00	6·00

Nos. 3565/70 were printed together, *se-tenant*, in sheetlets of six with a further portrait in the left margin.

(Des R. Sauber. Litho Questa)

2001 (26 Aug). Death Centenary of Giuseppe Verdi (Italian composer). As T **395d** and similar vert designs. Multicoloured. P 14.

3572	10r. Type **395d**	2·50	2·25
	a. Sheetlet of 4. Nos. 3572/5	9·00	8·00
3573	10r. Heinrich's costume from "Rigoletto" (opera)	2·50	2·25
3574	10r. Cologne's costume from "Rigoletto"	2·50	2·25
3575	10r. Cornell MacNeil (opera singer) as Rigoletto	2·50	2·25
3572/75 *Set of 4*		9·00	8·00
MS3576 79×119 mm. 25r. Matteo Manvgerri (opera singer) as Rigoletto		7·00	7·00

Nos. 3572/5 were printed together, *se-tenant*, in sheetlets of four with an enlarged illustrated top margin.

396 Adolfo Pérez Esquivel (Peace Prize, 1980)

397 Mercedes-Benz W165 Racing Car, 1939

(Des R. Sauber. Litho Questa)

2001 (29 Sept). Centenary of Nobel Prizes. Prize Winners. T **396** and similar vert designs. Multicoloured. P 14.

3577	7r. Type **396**	85	90
	a. Sheetlet of 6. Nos. 3577/82	4·50	4·75
3578	7r. Mikhail Gorbachev (Peace, 1990)	85	90
3579	7r. Betty Williams (Peace, 1976)	85	90
3580	7r. Alfonso Garcia Robles (Peace, 1982)	85	90
3581	7r. Paul d'Estournelles de Constant (Peace, 1909)	85	90
3582	7r. Louis Renault (Peace, 1907)	85	90
3583	7r. Ernesto Moneta (Peace, 1907)	85	90
	a. Sheetlet of 6. Nos. 3583/8	4·50	4·75
3584	7r. Albert Luthuli (Peace, 1960)	85	90
3585	7r. Henri Dunant (Peace, 1901)	85	90
3586	7r. Albert Gobat (Peace, 1902)	85	90
3587	7r. Sean MacBride (Peace, 1974)	85	90
3588	7r. Elie Ducommun (Peace, 1902)	85	90
3589	7r. Simon Kuznets (Economics, 1971)	85	90
	a. Sheetlet of 5. Nos. 3589/93	4·00	4·00
3590	7r. Wassily Leontief (Economics, 1973)	85	90
3591	7r. Lawrence Klein (Economics, 1980)	85	90
3592	7r. Friedrich von Hayek (Economics, 1974)	85	90
3593	7r. Leonid Kantorovich (Economics, 1975)	85	90
3577/93 *Set of 17*		13·00	13·50
MS3594 Three sheets, each 108×127 mm. (a) 25r. Trygve Haavelmo (Economics, 1989). (b) 25r. Octavio Paz (Literature, 1990). (c) 25r. Vicente Aleixandre (Literature, 1977) *Set of 3 sheets*		11·00	14·00

Nos. 3577/82, 3583/8 and 3589/93 were each printed together, *se-tenant*, in sheetlets of six or five stamps plus a label showing the Nobel Museum, Sweden (Nos. 3589/93), each with a portrait of Alfred Nobel appearing in the enlarged top margin.

2001 (30 Oct). Centenary of Mercedes-Benz Cars. T **397** and similar horiz designs. Multicoloured. P 14.

3595	2r.50 Type **397**	45	35
3596	5r. 460 Nurburg Sport-roadster, 1928	85	65
3597	7r. 680S racing car, 1927	1·00	1·10
	a. Sheetlet of 6. Nos. 3597/3602	5·50	6·00
3598	7r. 150, 1934	1·00	1·10
3599	7r. 540K Roadster, 1936	1·00	1·10
3600	7r. 770 "GroBer Mercedes", 1932	1·00	1·10
3601	7r. 220SE, 1958	1·00	1·10
3602	7r. 500SL, 1990	1·00	1·10
3603	7r. 290, 1933	1·00	1·10
	a. Sheetlet of 6. Nos. 3603/8	5·50	6·00
3604	7r. Model 680S, 1927	1·00	1·10
3605	7r. 300SL Coupé, 1953	1·00	1·10
3606	7r. Benz Victoria, 1911	1·00	1·10
3607	7r. 280SL, 1968	1·00	1·10
3608	7r. W125 racing car, 1937	1·00	1·10

3609	8r. Boattail Speedster, 1938	1·10	1·25
3610	15r. "Blitzen Benz", 1909	1·60	1·75
3595/3610 *Set of 16*		14·50	15·00
MS3611 Two sheets, each 109×96 mm. (a) 25r. 370S, 1931. (b) 25r. 300SLR racing car, 1955 *Set of 2 sheets*		8·50	9·50

Nos. 3597/3602 and 3603/8 were each printed together, *se-tenant*, in sheetlets of six, with enlarged illustrated margins.

Nos. 3600 and 3606 are inscribed "GROBERMERCEDES" or "BENA", both in error.

398 Eusebio and Portuguese Flag

399 *Cymothoe lucasi*

(Des G. Bibby. Litho Walsall)

2001 (29 Nov). World Cup Football Championship, Japan and Korea (2002). T **398** and similar multicoloured designs. P 14.

3612	1r. Type **398**	20	15
3613	3r. Johan Cruyff and Dutch flag	45	35
3614	7r. Footballer and French flag	1·00	90
3615	10r. Footballer and Japanese flag	1·25	1·25
3616	12r. World Cup Stadium, Seoul, Korea (horiz)	1·50	1·75
3617	15r. Poster for first World Cup Championship, Uruguay, 1930	1·75	2·25
3612/17 *Set of 6*		5·50	6·00
MS3618 70×100 mm. 25r. Gerd Müller, 1974 World Cup Final (43×57 mm)		3·75	4·25

(Des Irene Lampe. Litho Questa)

2001 (26 Dec). Moths and Butterflies. T **399** and similar multicoloured designs. P 14.

3619	7r. Type **399**	90	95
	a. Sheetlet of 6. Nos. 3619/24	4·75	5·00
3620	7r. *Milionia grandis*	90	95
3621	7r. *Ornithoptera Croesus*	90	95
3622	7r. *Hyantis hodeva*	90	95
3623	7r. *Ammobiota festiva*	90	95
3624	7r. *Salamis temora*	90	95
3625	7r. *Zygaena occitanica*	90	95
	a. Sheetlet of 6. Nos. 3625/30	4·75	5·00
3626	7r. *Campylotes desgodinsi*	90	95
3627	7r. *Bhutanitis thaidina*	90	95
3628	7r. *Helicopsis endymion*	90	95
3629	7r. *Parnassius charitonius*	90	95
3630	7r. *Acaca ecucogiap*	90	95
3631	10r. *Papilio dardanus*	1·25	1·40
	a. Sheetlet of 4. Nos. 3631/4	4·50	5·00
3632	10r. *Baomisa hieroglyphica*	1·25	1·40
3633	10r. *Troides prattorum*	1·25	1·40
3634	10r. *Funonia rhadama*	1·25	1·40
3619/34 *Set of 16*		14·00	15·00
MS3635 Two sheets (a) 83×108 mm. 25r. *Hypolera cassotis.* (b) 108×83 mm. 25r. *Euphydryas maturna* (vert) *Set of 2 sheets*		9·50	10·00

Nos. 3619/24, 3625/30 and 3631/4 were each printed together, *se-tenant*, in sheetlets of six or four with enlarged illustrated margins.

Nos. 3621 and 3629 are inscribed "eroesus" or "charltonius", both in error.

400 John F. Kennedy in American Football Kit, 1927

401 Princess Diana wearing Pink Jacket

(Des J. Iskowitz. Litho Questa)

2001 (26 Dec). John F. Kennedy (American President) Commemoration. T **400** and similar vert designs. Multicoloured. P 14.

3636	5r. Type **400**	75	85
	a. Sheetlet of 6. Nos. 3636/41	4·00	4·50
3637	5r. John Kennedy at Harvard, 1935	75	85
3638	5r. As U.S. Navy officer, Solomon Islands, 1943	75	85
3639	5r. On wedding day, 1953	75	85
3640	5r. With brother, Robert, 1956	75	85
3641	5r. Presidential Inauguration, 1961	75	85
3642	5r. With First Secretary Nikita Khrushchev of U.S.S.R., 1961	75	85
	a. Sheetlet of 6. Nos. 3642/7	4·00	4·50
3643	5r. With Prime Minister Harold MacMillan of Great Britain	75	85
3644	5r. With Pres. Charles de Gaulle of France, 1961	75	85
3645	5r. With Prime Minister Jawaharlal Nehru of India, 1962	75	85
3646	5r. With Chancellor Konrad Adenauer of West Germany, 1963	75	85
3647	5r. With Martin Luther King (Civil Rights campaigner) 1963	75	85
3636/47 *Set of 12*		8·00	9·00

MS3648 Two sheets, each 82×112 mm. (a) 25r. John Kennedy. (b) 25r. With wife, Paris, 1961 *Set of 2 sheets* .... 8·00 9·00

Nos. 3636/41 and 3642/7 were each printed together, *se-tenant*, in sheetlets of six with the enlarged illustrated right margins showing a further portrait.

No. 3642 is inscribed "PRIMIER" in error.

(Des A. Pinchkhadze. Litho Questa)

2001 (26 Dec). 40th Birth Anniv of Diana, Princess of Wales. T **401** and similar vert designs. Multicoloured. P 14.

3649	10r. Type **401**	1·25	1·75
	a. Sheetlet of 4. Nos. 3649/52	4·50	6·00
3650	10r. In evening dress with tiara	1·25	1·75
3651	10r. Wearing matching yellow hat and coat	1·25	1·75
3652	10r. In beige dress	1·25	1·75
3649/52 *Set of 4*		4·50	6·00

MS3653 73×109 mm. 25r. Princess Diana wearing pearls .... 3·75 4·25

Nos. 3649/52 were printed together, *se-tenant*, in sheetlets of four with an enlarged illustrated left margin.

Rf5 **MALDÍVES**

402 "Running Horse" (Xu Beihong)

403 Swinhoe's Snipe

(Des Y. Lee. Litho Questa)

2001 (26 Dec). Chinese New Year ("Year of the Horse"). Paintings by Xu Beihong. T **402** and similar multicoloured designs. P 14.

3654	5r. Type **402**	1·50	1·50
	a. Sheetlet of 5. Nos. 3654/8	6·75	6·75
3655	5r. "Standing Horse" (from back, with head up)	1·50	1·50
3656	5r. "Running Horse" (*different*)	1·50	1·50
3657	5r. "Standing Horse" (with head down)	1·50	1·50
3658	5r. "Horse" (with head up, from front)	1·50	1·50
3654/58 *Set of 5*		6·75	6·75

MS3659 110×70 mm. 15r. Six Horses running (57×37 mm) .... 2·50 2·75

Nos. 3654/8 were printed together, *se-tenant*, in sheetlets of five with an enlarged inscribed top margin. P 14×14½.

(Des Jennifer Toombs. Litho B.D.T.)

2002 (8 Apr). Birds. T **403** and similar horiz designs. Multicoloured. P 14.

3660	1r. Type **403**	50	25
3661	2r. Oriental Honey Buzzard	75	40

3662	3r. Asian Koel	80	55
3663	5r. Red-throated Pipet	1·00	80
3664	5r. Cattle Egret	1·00	1·00
	a. Sheetlet of 6. Nos. 3664/9	5·50	5·50
3665	5r. Barn Swallow	1·00	1·00
3666	5r. Osprey	1·00	1·00
3667	5r. Green-backed Heron ("Little Heron")	1·00	1·00
3668	5r. Ruddy Turnstone	1·00	1·00
3669	5r. Sooty Tern	1·00	1·00
3670	5r. Lesser Noddy	1·00	1·00
	a. Sheetlet of 6. Nos. 3670/5	5·50	5·50
3671	5r. Roseate Tern	1·00	1·00
3672	5r. Great Frigate Bird ("Frigate Minor")	1·00	1·00
3673	5r. Black-shafted Tern ("Saunder's Tern")	1·00	1·00
3674	5r. White-bellied Storm Petrel	1·00	1·00
3675	5r. Red-footed Booby	1·00	1·00
3676	7r. Rose-ringed Parakeet	1·40	1·40
	a. Sheetlet of 6. Nos. 3676/81	7·50	7·50
3677	7r. Common Swift	1·40	1·40
3678	7r. Lesser Kestrel	1·40	1·40
3679	7r. Golden Oriole	1·40	1·40
3680	7r. Asian Paradise Flycatcher	1·40	1·40
3681	7r. Indian Roller	1·40	1·40
3682	7r. Pallid Harrier	1·40	1·40
	a. Sheetlet of 6. Nos. 3682/7	7·50	7·50
3683	7r. Grey Heron	1·40	1·40
3684	7r. Blue-tailed Bee-eater	1·40	1·40
3685	7r. White-breasted Water Hen	1·40	1·40
3686	7r. Cotton Teal ("Cotton Pygmy Goose")	1·40	1·40
3687	7r. Maldivian Pond Heron	1·40	1·40
3688	7r. Short-eared Owl	1·40	1·40
3689	10r. White Spoonbill ("Eurasian Spoonbill")	1·50	1·50
3690	12r. Pied Wheatear	1·75	2·00
3691	15r. Oriental Pratincole	2·25	2·75
3660/91 *Set of 32*		35·00	35·00

MS3692 Four sheets, each 114×57 mm. (a) 25r. White Tern. (b) 25r. Greater Flamingo. (c) 25r. Cinnamon Bittern. (d) 25r. White-tailed Tropicbird .... 32·00 30·00

Nos. 3664/9, 3670/5, 3676/81 and 3682/7 were each printed together, *se-tenant*, in sheetlets of six with the backgrounds forming composite designs which extend onto the inscribed margins.

Rf3 **Maldives**

404 Havana Brown

405 Queen Elizabeth with Princess Margaret

(Des B. Pevsner and R. Martin. Litho B.D.T.)

2002 (8 Apr). Cats. T **404** and similar multicoloured designs. P 14.

3693	3r. Type **404**	70	35
3694	5r. American Wirehair	1·00	60
3695	7r. Persian (*horiz*)	1·10	1·10
	a. Sheetlet of 6. Nos. 3695/3700	6·00	6·00
3696	7r. Exotic Shorthair (*horiz*)	1·10	1·10
3697	7r. Ragdoll (*horiz*)	1·10	1·10
3698	7r. Manx (*horiz*)	1·10	1·10
3699	7r. Tonkinese (*horiz*)	1·10	1·10
3700	7r. Scottish Fold (*horiz*)	1·10	1·10
3701	7r. British Blue	1·10	1·10
	a. Sheetlet of 6. Nos. 3701/6	6·00	6·00
3702	7r. Red Mackerel Manx	1·10	1·10
3703	7r. Scottish Fold	1·10	1·10
3704	7r. Somali	1·10	1·10
3705	7r. Balinese	1·10	1·10
3706	7r. Exotic Shorthair	1·10	1·10
3707	8r. Norwegian Forest Cat	1·10	1·25
3708	10r. Seal Point Siamese	1·25	1·60
3693/3708 *Set of 16*		15·00	15·00

MS3709 110×85 mm. 25r. Blue Mackerel Tabby Cornish Rex .... 4·00 4·50

Nos. 3695/3700 and 3701/6 were each printed together, *se-tenant*, in sheetlets of six each with enlarged illustrated side margins.

(Des D. Miller. Litho Questa)

2002 (22 Apr). Golden Jubilee. T **405** and similar square designs. Multicoloured. P 14½.

3710	10r. Type **405**	2·50	2·50
	a. Sheetlet of 4. Nos. 3710/13	9·00	9·00
3711	10r. Princess Elizabeth wearing white hat and coat	2·50	2·50

3712	10r. Queen Elizabeth in evening dress...........	2·50	2·50
3713	10r. Queen Elizabeth on visit to Canada.......	2·50	2·50
3710/13	*Set of 4*...	9·00	9·00

MS3714 76×108 mm. 25r. Paying homage, at
Coronation, 1953. P 14............................... 4·50 4·75

Nos. 3710/13 were printed together, *se-tenant*, in sheetlets of four, with an illustrated left margin.

406 Sivatherium   **406a** Ama Dablam, Nepal

(Litho Questa)

2002 (21 May). Prehistoric Animals. T **406** and similar multicoloured designs. P 14.

3715	7r. Type **406**...	1·50	1·50
	a. Sheetlet of 6. Nos. 3715/20......................	8·00	8·00
3716	7r. Flat-headed Peccary	1·50	1·50
3717	7r. Shasta Ground Sloth	1·50	1·50
3718	7r. Harlan's Ground Sloth	1·50	1·50
3719	7r. European Woolly Rhinoceros....................	1·50	1·50
3720	7r. Dwarf Pronghorn	1·50	1·50
3721	7r. Macrauchenia	1·50	1·50
	a. Sheetlet of 6. Nos. 3721/6	8·00	8·00
3722	7r. Glyptodon	1·50	1·50
3723	7r. Nesodon	1·50	1·50
3724	7r. Imperial Tapir and calf..............................	1·50	1·50
3725	7r. Short-faced Bear.......................................	1·50	1·50
3726	7r. Mastodon	1·50	1·50
3715/26	*Set of 12*...	16·00	16·00

MS3727 Two sheets, each 94×67 mm. (a) 25r. Sabre-
toothed Cat. (b) 25r. Mammoth *Set of 2 sheets*.......... 9·50 10·00

Nos. 3715/20 and 3721/6 were each printed together, *se-tenant*, in sheetlets of six with the backgrounds forming composite designs which extend onto the sheetlet margins.

Nos. 3722 and 3726 are inscribed "GlYPTODON" and "MAMMOTH", both in error.

(Des T. Wood. Litho Questa)

2002 (11 July). International Year of Mountains. As T **406a** and similar vert designs. Multicoloured.

3728	15r. Type **406a**...	1·75	2·25
	a. Sheetlet of 4. Nos. 3728/31	6·00	8·00
3729	15r. Mount Clements, USA...............................	1·75	2·25
3730	15r. Mount Artesonraju, Peru	1·75	2·25
3731	15r. Mount Cholatse, Nepal.............................	1·75	2·25
3728/31	*Set of 4*...	6·00	8·00

MS3732 96×65 mm. 25r. Mount Jefferson, U.S.A., and
balloon .... 3·75 4·25

Nos. 3728/31 were printed together, *se-tenant*, in sheetlets of four with an enlarged illustrated left margin.

407 Downhill Skiing   **407a** Buddhist pagoda, Thailand

(Litho Questa)

2002 (11 July). Winter Olympic Games, Salt Lake City. T **407** and similar vert designs. Multicoloured. P 13½.

3733	12r. Type **407**	1·75	2·00
3734	12r. Ski jumping...	1·75	2·00

MS3735 82×103 mm. Nos. 3733/4.......................... 3·75 4·25

(Des T. Wood. Litho Questa)

2002 (11 July). 20th World Scout Jamboree, Thailand. As T **407a** and similar vert designs. Multicoloured. P 14.

3736	15r. Type **407a**...	2·00	2·50
	a. Sheetlet of 3. Nos. 3736/8	5·50	6·50
3737	15r. Thai Scout (*vert*)......................................	2·00	2·50
3738	15r. Scout badges on Thai flag (*vert*)..............	2·00	2·50
3736/38	*Set of 3*...	5·50	6·50

MS3739 106×78 mm. 25r. Mountain-climbing badge
and knot diagrams .... 3·75 4·00

Nos. 3736/8 were printed together, *se-tenant*, in sheetlets of three with an enlarged illustrated right margin.

408 Ship, Aircraft and W.C.O. Logo

(Litho Questa)

2002 (11 July). 50th Anniv of World Customs Organization. Sheet 135×155 mm. P 13½.

MS3740 **408** 50r. multicoloured........................... 7·50 9·00

409 Elvis Presley

(Litho Questa)

2002 (7 Oct). 25th Death Anniv of Elvis Presley (American entertainer). P 13½×14.

3741	**409**	5r. multicoloured...	1·00	1·00
		a. Sheetlet of 9..		7·50

No. 3741 was printed in sheetlets of nine with an enlarged left margin repeating the stamp design portrait.

410 *Morpho menelaus*   **411** Torsten Frings (Germany)

(Des R. Rundo. Litho B.D.T.)

2002 (4 Nov). Flora and Fauna. T **410** and similar multicoloured designs. P 14.

3742	7r. Type **410**	1·50	1·50
	a. Sheetlet of 6. Nos. 3742/7	8·00	8·00
3743	7r. *Heliconius erato*	1·50	1·50
3744	7r. *Thecla coronata*	1·50	1·50
3745	7r. *Battus philenor*	1·50	1·50
3746	7r. *Ornithoptera priamus*	1·50	1·50
3747	7r. *Danaus gilippus berenice*	1·50	1·50
3748	7r. *Ipomoea tricolor* Morning Glory..............	1·50	1·50
	a. Sheetlet of 6. Nos. 3748/53	8·00	8·00
3749	7r. *Anemone coronaria* "Wedding Bell"........	1·50	1·50

3750	7r. *Narcissus* "Barrett Browning"	1·50	1·50
3751	7r. "Nigella Persian Jewel"	1·50	1·50
3752	7r. *Osteospermum* "Whirligig Pink"	1·50	1·50
3753	7r. "Iris Brown Lasso"	1·50	1·50
3754	7r. *Laelia gouldiana*	1·50	1·50
	a. Sheetlet of 6. Nos. 3754/9	8·00	8·00
3755	7r. *Cattleya* "Louise Georgiana"	1·50	1·50
3756	7r. *Laeliocattleya* "Christopher Gubler"	1·50	1·50
3757	7r. *Miltoniopsis* "Bert Field Crimson Glow"	1·50	1·50
3758	7r. *Lemboglossum bictoniense*	1·50	1·50
3759	7r. *Derosara* "Divine Victor"	1·50	1·50
3742/59 *Set of 18*		24·00	24·00

MS3760 Three sheets. (a) 72×50 mm. 25r. *Cymothoe lurida* (butterfly). (b) 66×45 mm. 25r. *Perennial Aster* "Little Pink Beauty". (c) 50×72 mm. 25r. *Angraecum veitchii* (vert) *Set of 3 sheets* ...... 10·00 11·00

Nos. 3742/7 (butterflies), 3748/53 (flowers) and 3754/9 (orchids) were each printed together, *se-tenant*, in sheetlets of six with the backgrounds forming composite designs that extend onto the sheetlet margins.

Nos. 3742 and 3748 are inscribed "*Menelus*" or "*Impomoea*", both in error.

(Litho Cartor)

2002 (12 Nov). World Cup Football Championship, Japan and South Korea. T **411** and similar vert designs. Multicoloured. P 13½.

3761	7r. Type **411**	1·00	1·00
	a. Sheetlet of 6. Nos. 3761/6	5·50	5·50
3762	7r. Roberto Carlos (Brazil)	1·00	1·00
3763	7r. Torsten Frings (Germany) (*different*)	1·00	1·00
3764	7r. Ronaldo (Brazil), with one finger raised	1·00	1·00
3765	7r. Oliver Neuville (Germany)	1·00	1·00
3766	7r. Ronaldo (Brazil), heading ball	1·00	1·00
3767	7r. Eul Yong Lee (South Korea) and Alpay Ozalan (Turkey)	1·00	1·00
	a. Sheetlet of 6. Nos. 3767/72	5·50	5·50
3768	7r. Myung Bo Hong (South Korea) and Hakan Sukur (Turkey)	1·00	1·00
3769	7r. Chong Gug Song (South Korea) and Emre Belozoglu (Turkey)	1·00	1·00
3770	7r. Chong Gug Song (South Korea) and Ergun Penbe (Turkey)	1·00	1·00
3771	7r. Ki Hyeon Seol (South Korea) and Ergun Penbe (Turkey)	1·00	1·00
3772	7r. Chong Gug Song (South Korea) and Hakan Unsal (Turkey)	1·00	1·00
3761/72 *Set of 12*		11·00	11·00

MS3773 Four sheets, each 82×82 mm. (a) 15r. Cafu (Brazil) and Oliver Neuville (Germany); 15r. World Cup Trophy. (b) 15r. Dietmar Hamann (Germany); 15r. Cafu (Brazil), holding Trophy. (c) 15r. Hakan Sukur (Turkey); 15r. Sang Chul Yoo (South Korea). (d) 15r. Ilhan Mansiz (Turkey); 15r. Young Pyo Lee (South Korea) *Set of 4 sheets* ...... 14·00 15·00

Nos. 3761/6 and 3767/72 were each printed together, *se-tenant*, in sheetlets of six with inscribed margins.

412 Hairdresser Bear   **413** Charles Lindbergh and *Spirit of St. Louis*

2002 (18 Nov). Centenary of the Teddy Bear. T **412** and similar vert designs. Multicoloured. P 14.

3774	8r. Type **412**	1·00	1·10
	a. Sheetlet of 4. Nos. 3774/7	3·50	4·00
3775	8r. Construction worker bear	1·00	1·10
3776	8r. Gardener bear	1·00	1·10
3777	8r. Chef bear	1·00	1·10
3778	12r. Nurse bear	1·40	1·50
	a. Sheetlet of 3. Nos. 3778/80	3·75	4·00
3779	12r. Doctor bear	1·40	1·50
3780	12r. Dentist bear	1·40	1·50
3781	12r. Bride ("MOTHER") bear	1·40	1·50
	a. Sheetlet of 3. Nos. 3781/3	3·75	4·00
3782	12r. Brother and sister bears	1·40	1·50
3783	12r. Groom ("FATHER") bear	1·40	1·50
3774/83 *Set of 10*		11·00	12·00

MS3784 Three sheets, each 110×105 mm. (a) 30r. Golfer bear. (b) 30r. Footballer bear. (c) 30r. Skier bear ("SNOW BOARDER") *Set of 3 sheets* ...... 11·00 12·00

Nos. 3774/7 (working bears), 3778/80 (healthy bears) and 3781/3 (family bears) were each printed together, *se-tenant*, in sheetlets of three or four die-cut in the shape of a teddy bear.

The miniature sheets of Nos. **MS**3784a/c are also die-cut in the shape of a teddy bear.

(Litho Questa)

2002 (2 Dec). 75th Anniv of First Solo Transatlantic Flight. T **413** and similar vert designs. Multicoloured. P 14.

3785	12r. Type **413**	2·50	2·50
	a. Sheetlet of 4. Nos. 3785/8	9·00	9·00
3786	12r. Lindbergh, in flying helmet, and *Spirit of St. Louis*	2·50	2·50
3787	12r. Lindbergh holding propeller	2·50	2·50
3788	12r. Lindbergh in overalls and *Spirit of St. Louis*	2·50	2·50
3789	12r. Donald Hall (designer)	2·50	2·50
	a. Sheetlet of 4. Nos. 3789/92	9·00	9·00
3790	12r. Charles Lindbergh (pilot)	2·50	2·50
3791	12r. Lindbergh under wing of *Spirit of St. Louis*	2·50	2·50
3792	12r. Lindbergh, Mahoney and Hall at Ryan Airlines	2·50	2·50
3785/92 *Set of 8*		18·00	18·00

Nos. 3785/8 and 3789/92 were each printed together, *se-tenant*, in sheetlets of four containing two vertical pairs separated by a large, illustrated gutter.

414 Princess Diana   **415** Joseph Kennedy with Sons Joseph Jr. and John, 1919

(Litho Questa)

2002 (2 Dec). Fifth Death Anniv of Diana, Princess of Wales. T **414** and similar vert design. Multicoloured. P 14.

3793	12r. Type **414**	1·75	2·00
	a. Sheetlet of 4	6·00	
3794	12r. In evening dress and tiara	1·75	2·00
	a. Sheetlet of 4	6·00	

Nos. 3793/4 were each printed in sheetlets of four with an additional portrait on an enlarged margin.

(Litho Questa)

2002 (2 Dec). Presidents John F. Kennedy and Ronald Reagan Commemoration. T **415** and similar vert designs. Multicoloured. P 14.

3795	7r. Type **415**	1·00	1·25
	a. Sheetlet of 6. Nos. 3795/3800	5·50	6·50
3796	7r. John F. Kennedy aged 11	1·00	1·25
3797	7r. Kennedy inspecting Boston waterfront, 1951	1·00	1·25
3798	7r. Kennedy in naval ensign uniform, 1941	1·00	1·25
3799	7r. With sister Kathleen in London, 1939	1·00	1·25
3800	7r. Talking to Eleanor Roosevelt, 1951	1·00	1·25
3801	12r. Ronald Reagan facing right	1·50	2·00
	a. Sheetlet of 4. Nos. 3801/2, each ×2	5·50	6·50
3802	12r. Ronald Reagan (full-face portrait)	1·50	2·00
3795/3802 *Set of 8*		8·00	9·50

Nos. 3795/3800 were printed together, *se-tenant*, as a sheetlet of six with the stamps arranged in two vertical strips of three separated by a wide gutter showing a further portrait.

Nos. 3801/2 were printed together, *se-tenant*, as a sheetlet of four containing two of each design in a horizontal strip with an enlarged top margin showing a further portrait.

416 Wedding of Princess Juliana and Prince Bernhard, 1937

(Litho Questa)

2002 (8 Dec). "Amphilex '02" International Stamp Exhibition, Amsterdam. Dutch Royal Family. T **416** and similar horiz designs. P 14.

3803	7r. blue-black and black	1·00	1·00
	a. Sheetlet of 6. Nos. 3803/8	5·50	5·50
3804	7r. chocolate and black	1·00	1·00
3805	7r. dull claret and black	1·00	1·00
3806	7r. olive-brown and black	1·00	1·00
3807	7r. slate-violet and black	1·00	1·00
3808	7r. sage-green and black	1·00	1·00
3809	7r. multicoloured	1·00	1·00
	a. Sheetlet of 6. Nos. 3809/14	5·50	5·50
3810	7r. agate and black	1·00	1·00
3811	7r. multicoloured	1·00	1·00
3812	7r. multicoloured	1·00	1·00
3813	7r. multicoloured	1·00	1·00
3814	7r. multicoloured	1·00	1·00
3803/14 Set of 12		11·00	11·00

Designs:—No. 3803, Type **416**; No. 3804, Princess Juliana and Prince Bernhard with baby Princess Beatrix, 1938; No. 3805, Princess Juliana with her daughters in Canada, 1940–45; No. 3806, Inauguration of Queen Juliana, 1948; No. 3807, Royal Family inspecting Zeeland floods, 1953; No. 3808, Queen Juliana and Prince Bernhard; No. 3809, "Princess Beatrix as a Baby" (Pauline Hille); No. 3810, "Princess Beatrix in Flying Helmet" (John Klinkenberg); No. 3811, "Princess Beatrix" (Beatrice Filius); No. 3812, "Princess Beatrix and Prince Claus" (Will Kellermann); No. 3813, "Queen Beatrix in Royal Robes" (Graswinkel); No. 3814, "Queen Beatrix" (Marjolijn Spreeuwenberg).

Nos. 3803/8 and 3809/14 were each printed together, *se-tenant*, in sheetlets of six containing two horizontal rows of three separated by a large illustrated gutter.

417 Flame Basslet

(Des A. Shafiu. Litho Questa)

2002 (24 Dec). Marine Life. T **417** and similar multicoloured designs. P 14 (horiz) or 11×13 (vert).

3815	10l. Type **417**	15	60
3816	15l. Teardrop Butterflyfish	20	60
3817	20l. White-tailed Damselfish ("Hambug Damselfish")	20	60
3818	25l. Bridled Tern (23×27 mm)	75	60
3819	50l. Clown Surgeonfish ("Blue-lined Surgeonfish")	35	30
3820	1r. Common Tern (23×27 mm)	1·25	30
3821	2r. Common Noddy (23×27 mm)	1·75	70
3822	2r.50 Yellow-breasted Wrasse	80	1·00
3823	2r.50 Blue Shark (23×27 mm)	80	1·00
3824	4r. Harlequin Filefish	1·00	1·00
3825	5r. Masked Unicornfish ("Orangespine Unicornfish")	1·00	1·00
3826	10r. Emperor Angelfish	1·75	1·75
3827	12r. Catalufa ("Bullseye")	2·00	2·25
3828	20r. Scalloped Hammerhead Shark (23×27 mm)	3·50	4·25
3815/28 Set of 14		14·00	14·50

No. 3822 is inscribed "wrass" in error.

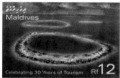

418 Atolls from the Air

(Litho Questa)

2002 (25 Dec). 30 Years of Maldives' Tourism Promotion. T **418** and similar horiz designs. Multicoloured. P 13½.

3829	12r. Type **418**	2·75	2·75
	a. Sheetlet of 4. Nos. 3829/32	10·00	10·00
3830	12r. Island beach	2·75	2·75
3831	12r. Surfing	2·75	2·75
3832	12r. Scuba diving	2·75	2·75
3829/32 Set of 4		10·00	10·00

Nos. 3829/32 were printed, as separate stamps, in sheetlets of four with enlarged vertical margins.

419 Decorated Drum

(Litho Questa)

2003 (31 Jan). 50th Anniv of National Museum. T **419** and similar horiz designs. Multicoloured. P 14.

3835	3r. Type **419**	50	40
3836	3r.50 Carved covered bowl	55	50
3837	6r.50 Ceremonial sunshade	1·00	85
3838	22r. Ceremonial headdress	3·50	5·00
3835/38 Set of 4		5·00	6·00

420 Popeye diving   **421** Father with Baby

(Litho Questa)

2003 (27 Jan). "Popeye" (cartoon character). T **420** and similar multicoloured designs showing summer sports. P 14.

3839	7r. Type **420**	85	95
	a. Sheetlet of 6. Nos. 3839/44	4·50	5·00
3840	7r. Surfing	85	95
3841	7r. Sailboarding	85	95
3842	7r. Baseball	85	95
3843	7r. Hurdling	85	95
3844	7r. Tennis	85	95
3839/44 Set of 6		4·50	5·00
MS3845	120×90 mm. 25r. Volleyball (*horiz*)	3·25	3·75

Nos. 3839/44 were printed together, *se-tenant*, in sheetlets of six with the backgrounds forming a composite design which extends on to the sheetlet margins.

(Litho B.D.T.)

2003 (31 Jan). U.N.I.C.E.F. "First Steps" Campaign. T **421** and similar vert designs. Multicoloured. P 14½×14.

3846	2r.50 Type **421**	60	35
3847	5r. Mother and baby	1·00	75
3848	20r. Campaign emblem	3·75	5·00
3846/48 Set of 3		4·75	5·50

422 *Cypraea caputserpentis* (Cowrie)   **423** David Brown

(Litho B.D.T.)

2003 (25 Mar). Sea Shells. T **422** and similar vert designs. Multicoloured. P 13½×13.

3849	10r. Type **422**	2·00	2·25
3850	10r. *Trachycardium orbita* (Cardita Clam)	2·00	2·25
3851	10r. *Architectonica perspectiva* (Sundial Shell)	2·00	2·25
3852	10r. *Conus capitaneus* (Corn Shell)	2·00	2·25
3849/52 Set of 4		7·25	8·00

2003 (7 Apr). "Columbia" Space Shuttle Commemoration. Sheet 184×145 mm, containing T **423** and similar vert designs showing crew members. Multicoloured. Litho. P 13½×13.
MS3853 7r. Type **423**; 7r. Commander Rick Husband; 7r. Laurel Clark; 7r. Kalpana Chawla; 7r. Michael Anderson; 7r. William McCool; 7r. Ilan Ramon............ 7·00 8·00

424 Queen wearing Polka Dot Jacket   **425** Prince William as Toddler

(Des R. Rundo. Litho B.D.T.)

2003 (12 May). 50th Anniv of Coronation. T **424** and similar vert designs. P 14.
MS3854 147×85 mm.15r. Type **424**; 15r. Queen after Coronation wearing Imperial State Crown; 15r. Queen wearing tiara (all black, blackish brown and grey-brown)... 7·50 8·50
MS3855 68×98 mm. 25r. Queen wearing tiara and blue sash (multicoloured)................................. 4·50 5·00

(Des R. Rundo. Litho B.D.T.)

2003 (26 May). 21st Birthday of Prince William. T **425** and similar vert designs. Multicoloured. P 14.
MS3856 148×78 mm. 15r. Type **425**; 15r. As teenager (looking forward); 15r. As teenager (looking right)... 7·50 8·00
MS3857 68×98 mm. 25r. As young boy, wearing school cap.. 4·50 5·00

426 "Painting"

(Litho B.D.T.)

2003 (17 June). 20th Death Anniv of Joan Miró (artist). T **426** and similar horiz designs. Multicoloured. P 14.
3858   3r. Type **426**... 55   35
3859   5r. "Hirondelle Amour"................................. 90   60
3860   10r. "Two Women"....................................... 1·50 1·60
3861   15r. "Women listening to Music".................. 2·00 2·50
3858/61 Set of 4... 4·50 4·50
MS3862 176×134 mm. 12r. "Woman and Birds"; 12r. "Nocturne"; 12r. "Morning Star"; 12r. "The Escape Ladder"... 6·50 7·50
MS3863 Two sheets, each 83×104 mm. (a) 25r. "Women encircled by the Flight of a Bird". (b) 25r. "Rhythmic Personages". Both imperf Set of 2 sheets... 7·00 8·00

427 "Jabach Altarpiece" (detail of drummer and piper)   **428** "The Actor Nakamura Sojuro as Mitsukuni" (detail) (Utagawa Yoshitaki)

(Litho B.D.T.)

2003 (17 June). 475th Death Anniv of Albrecht Dürer (artist). T **427** and similar multicoloured designs. P 14.
3864   3r. Type **427**... 55   45
3865   5r. "Portrait of a Young Man".................... 90   65
3866   7r. "Wire-drawing Mill" (horiz)................... 1·25 1·40
3867   10r. "Innsbruck from the North" (horiz) ...... 1·50 1·75
3864/67 Set of 4... 3·75 3·75
MS3868 174×157 mm. 12r. "Portrait of Jacob Muffel"; 12r. "Portrait of Hieronymus Holzschuher"; 12r. "Portrait of Johannes Kleburger"; 12r. "Self-portrait".......................... 6·50 7·50
MS3869 145×105 mm. 25r. "The Weiden Mill"................. 3·50 3·75

(Litho B.D.T.)

2003 (17 June). Japanese Art. Ghosts and Demons. T **428** and similar vert designs. Multicoloured. P 14.
3870   2r. Type **428**... 45   20
3871   5r. "The Actor Nakamura Sojuro as Mitsukuni" (detail of ghosts) (Utagawa Yoshitaki)... 90   65
3872   7r. "The Ghost of Kohada Koheiji" (Shunkosai Hokuei)................................. 1·10 1·00
3873   15r. "Ariwara no Narihira as Seigen" (Utagawa Kunisada)................................. 1·90 2·50
3870/73 Set of 4... 4·00 4·00
MS3874 149×145 mm. 10r. "The Ghost of Shikibunojo Mitsumune" (Utagawa Kunisada); 10r. "Fuwa Bansakui" (Tsukioka Yoshitoshi); 10r. "The Lantern Ghost of Oiwa" (Shunkosai Hokuei); 10r. "The Greedy Hag" (Tsukioka Yoshitoshi)................. 5·50 6·50
MS3875 116×86 mm. 25r. "The Spirit of Sakura Sogoro haunting Hotta Kozuke" (Utagawa Kuniyoshi)... 3·25 3·50

429 Maurice Garin (1903)   **430** Santos-Dumont Monoplane No. 20 Demoiselle on Ground, 1909

2003 (3 July). Centenary of Tour de France Cycle Race. T **429** and similar vert designs showing past winners. Multicoloured. Litho. P 13½.
MS3876 160×100 mm. 10r. Type **429**; 10r. Henri Cornet (1904); 10r. Louis Trousselier (1905); 10r. René Pottier (1906) .... 6·50 7·00
MS3877 160×100 mm. 10r. Lucien Petit-Breton on cycle (1907); 10r. Close up of Lucien Petit-Breton (1907); 10r. Francois Faber (1909); 10r. Octave Lapize (1910)....................................... 6·50 7·00
MS3878 160×100 mm. 10r. Eddy Merckx (1974); 10r. Bernard Thévenet (1975); 10r. Lucien van Impe (1976); 10r. Bernard Thévenet (1977) .... 6·50 7·00
MS3879 Three sheets, each 100×70 mm. (a) 25r. Start of first Tour De France at Le Réveil Matin café, Montgeron. (b) 25r. Henri Desgranges (editor of L'Auto). (c) 25r. Bernard Hinault (1979) Set of 3 sheets... 6·50 7·00

2003 (14 July). Centenary of Powered Flight. T **430** and similar horiz designs. Multicoloured. Litho. P 14.
MS3880 176×97 mm. 10r. Type **430**; 10r. Santos-Dumont monoplane No. 20 Demoiselle taking off, 1909; 10r. Voisin-Farman No. 1 biplane, 1908; 10r. Glenn Curtiss' Gold Bug, 1909.................... 7·50 8·00
MS3881 176×97 mm. 10r. Santos-Dumont's Airship No. 1; 10r. Santos-Dumont's Airship No. 4; 10r. Santos Dumont's Ballon No. 14 and 14 bis biplane, 1906; 10r. Santos-Dumont's Airship No. 16 .... 7·50 8·00
MS3882 Two sheets, each 105×75 mm. (a) 25r. Santos-Dumont's Ballon No. 6 circling Eiffel Tower, Paris, 1901. (b) 25r. Santos-Dumont's 14 bis biplane, 1906 Set of 2 sheets.................... 8·00 8·50

A 200r. stamp issued on 26 July 2003, embossed on gold foil and featuring a portrait of President Maumoon Abdul Gayoom to commemorate his 25 years of service, was available from a limited printing.

431 "Near Taormina, Scirocco" (1924)

2003 (4 Dec). Paul Klee (artist) Commemoration. T **431** and similar multicoloured designs. P 13½.
MS3883 162×135 mm. 10r. Type **431**; 10r. "Small Town Among the Rocks" (1932); 10r. "Still Life with Props" (1924); 10r. "North Room", (1932) .... 4·50 5·50
MS3884 70×103 mm. 25r. "Dame Demon" (1935) (vert) .... 3·25 3·50

432 Man Ice-skating

433 "Portrait of Jaime Sabartés" (1901)

2003 (4 Dec). 25th Death Anniv of Norman Rockwell (artist). T **432** and similar vert designs. Multicoloured. Litho. P 13½.
MS3885 10r. Type **432**; 10r. Man lying on back and boy with dog; 10r. Man and boy going fishing; 10r. Man and boy sweeping .... 4·50 5·50
MS3886 45×81 mm. 25r. Illustration for Hallmark Cards (1957). Imperf .... 3·50 3·75

2003 (4 Dec). 30th Death Anniv of Pablo Picasso (artist). T **433** and similar vert designs. Multicoloured. Litho. P 13½.
MS3887 133×167 mm. 10r. Type **433**; 10r. "Portrait of the Artist's Wife (Olga)" (1923); 10r. "Portrait of Olga" (1923); 10r. "Portrait of Jaime Sabartés" (1904) .... 8·00 8·00
MS3888 67×100 mm. 30r. "The Tragedy" (1903). Imperf .... 7·50 7·50

434 Ari Atoll

435 Goldtail Demoiselle

2003 (22 Dec). International Year of Freshwater. T **434** and similar vert designs. Multicoloured. Litho. P 14.
MS3889 147×85 mm. 15r. Type **434**; 15r. Running tap; 15r. Desalination plant, Malé .... 7·00 8·00
MS3890 96×66 mm. 25r. Community rain water tank .... 4·00 4·50

2003 (22 Dec). Marine Life. Sheet 147×105 mm containing T **435** and similar horiz designs. Multicoloured. P 14.
MS3891 4r. Type **435**; 4r. Queen Coris; 4r. Eight-banded Butterflyfish; 4r. Meyer's Butterflyfish; 4r. Exquisite Butterflyfish; 4r. Yellowstripe Snapper; 4r. Yellowback Anthias; 4r. Black-spotted Moray; 4r. Clown Anemonefish .... 6·00 6·50
The stamps in No. MS3891 were printed together, se-tenant, with the backgrounds forming a composite design.

436 Clown Triggerfish

(Litho B.D.T.)

2003 (22 Dec). Tropical Fish. T **436** and similar horiz designs. Multicoloured. P 14.
3892 1r. Type **436** 35 15
3893 7r. Sixspot Grouper .... 1·25 1·00
3894 10r. Long-nosed Butterflyfish .... 1·75 1·75
3895 15r. Longfin Bannerfish .... 2·50 3·00
3892/95 Set of 4 .... 5·25 5·50
MS3896 116×134 mm. 7r. Bluestreak Cleaner Wrasse; 7r. Threeband Demoiselle; 7r. Palette Surgeonfish; 7r. Emperor Snapper; 7r. Bicolor Angelfish; 7r. Picasso Triggerfish .... 6·50 7·50
MS3897 72×102 mm. 25r. Chevron Butterflyfish .... 4·50 5·00

(Litho B.D.T.)

2003 (22 Dec). Tropical Butterflies. Multicoloured designs as T **436**. P 14.
3898 3r. Yamfly (vert) 65 35
3899 5r. Striped Blue Crow (vert) .... 1·00 65
3900 8r. Indian Red Admiral (vert) .... 1·60 1·60
3901 15r. Great Eggfly (vert) .... 2·75 3·50
3898/3901 Set of 4 .... 5·50 5·50
MS3902 116×134 mm. 7r. Blue Triangle; 7r. Monarch; 7r. Broad-bordered Grass Yellow; 7r. Red Lacewing; 7r. African Migrant; 7r. Plain Tiger .... 6·50 7·50
MS3903 102×72 mm. 25r. Beak Butterfly (vert) .... 4·50 5·00

(Litho B.D.T.)

2003 (22 Dec). Birds. Horiz designs as T **436**. Multicoloured. P 14.
3904 15l. Great Frigate Bird 70 60
3905 20l. Ruddy Turnstone 70 60
3906 25l. Hoopoe 90 70
3907 1r. Cattle Egret .... 1·50 75
3904/7 Set of 4 .... 3·50 2·40
MS3908 116×134 mm. 7r. Red-billed Tropic Bird; 7r. Red-footed Booby; 7r. Common Tern; 7r. Caspian Tern; 7r. Western ("Common") Curlew; 7r. Grey ("Black-bellied") Plover .... 8·00 8·50
MS3909 72×102 mm. 25r. Grey Heron .... 5·50 6·00

(Litho B.D.T.)

2003 (22 Dec). Flowers. Multicoloured designs as T **436**. P 14.
3910 30l. Coelogyne asperata (vert) 30 25
3911 75l. Calanthe rosea (vert) 55 30
3912 2r. Eria javanica (vert) .... 1·25 70
3913 10r. Spathoglottis affinis (vert) .... 2·25 2·75
3910/13 Set of 4 .... 3·75 3·50
MS3914 116×134 mm. 7r. Strelitzia reginae; 7r. Anthurium andreanum; 7r. Alpinia purpurata; 7r. Dendrobium phalaenopsis; 7r. Vanda tricolor; 7r. Hibiscus rosa-sinensis .... 7·50 8·50
MS3915 72×102 mm. 25r. Ipomoea crassicaulis (vert) .... 5·00 5·50

437 "Landscape"

2004 (8 Mar). Hong Kong 2004 International Stamp Exhibition. 125th Birth Anniv of Gao Jian-fu (artist). T **437** and similar vert designs. Multicoloured. P 13½.
MS3916 170×149 mm. 7r. Type **437**; 7r. "Moon Night"; 7r. "Fox"; 7r. Chinese ink and colour on paper (spider and web); 7r. Chinese ink and colour on paper (girl); 7r. Chinese ink and colour on paper (man) .... 6·50 7·50
MS3917 108×129 mm. 12r. "Eagle"; 12r. "Sunset" .... 4·00 4·50

438 German Team (1974)

2004 (8 Mar). Centenary of FIFA (Fédération Internationale de Football Association). T **438** and similar horiz designs showing winning football teams. Multicoloured. Litho. P 13½.

3918	5r. Type **438**	85	85
3919	5r. Argentina (1978)	85	85
3920	5r. Italy (1982)	85	85
3921	5r. Argentina (1986)	85	85
3922	5r. Germany (1990)	85	85
3923	5r. Brazil (1994)	85	85
3924	5r. France (1998)	85	85
3925	5r. Brazil (2002)	85	85
3918/25	*Set of 8*	6·00	6·00

439 F-BVFD over Rio de Janeiro

2004 (8 Mar). Last Flight of Concorde (2003). T **439** and similar horiz designs. Multicoloured. Litho. P 13½.
MS3926 147×150 mm. 1r. Type **439**; 1r. F-BVFC over New York; 1r. F-BTSD over Honolulu; 1r. F-BTDS over Lisbon; 1r. F-BVFA over Washington; 1r. F-BVFD over Dakar; 1r. G-BOAC over Singapore; 1r. G-BOAA over Sydney; 1r. G-BOAD over Hong Kong; 1r. G-BOAD over Amsterdam; 1r. G-BOAE over Tokyo; 1r. G-BOAF over Madrid...... 4·00 4·00
MS3927 Three sheets, each 70×100 mm. (a) 25r. 204 G-BOAC against Union Jack. (b) 25r. 214 G-BOAG over London. (c) 25r. 214 G-BOAG against museum exhibits *Set of 3 sheets*...... 17·00 17·00

440 "Self Portrait" (Anthony van Dyck)

441 Major General Clarence Huebner

(Litho B.D.T.)

2004 (29 Mar). 300th Anniv of St. Petersburg. "Treasures of the Hermitage". T **440** and similar multicoloured designs. P 14.

3928	1r. Type **440**	25	15
3929	3r. "Self Portrait" (Michael Sweets)	55	40
3930	7r. "Anna Dalkeith, Countess of Morton" (Anthony van Dyck)	1·25	1·00
3931	12r. "Lady Anna Kirk" (Anthony van Dyck)	2·00	2·75
3928/31	*Set of 4*	3·50	3·75

MS3932 116×180 mm. 10r. "Portrait of Prince Alexander Kurakin" (Louis-Elisabeth Vigée-Lebrun); 10r. "Portrait of a Lady in Waiting to the Infanta Isabella" (Peter Paul Rubens); 10r. "Portrait of a Lady in Blue" (Thomas Gainsborough); 10r. "The Actor Pierre Jéliolte in the Role of Apollo" (Louis Tocqué)...... 6·50 7·00
MS3933 Two sheets, each 102×72 mm. (a) 25r. "A Scene from Corneille's Tragedy Le Comte d'Essex" (Nicolas Lancret) (*horiz*). (b) 25r. "The Stolen Kiss" (Jean-Honoré Fragonard) (*horiz*) *Set of 2 sheets*...... 7·50 8·50

2004 (19 May). 60th Anniv of D-Day Landings. Ten sheets containing T **441** and similar multicoloured designs. P 13½.
MS3934 Five sheets. (a) 137×117 mm. 6r. Type **441**; 6r. Brig. General Anthony McAuliffe; 6r. Major General Leonard Gerow; 6r. General Adolf Galland; 6r. Brig. General W. M. Hoge; 6r. Major General Sir Percy Hobart. (b) 127×127 mm. 6r. Rear Admiral Kirk; 6r. General Field Marshal Erwin Rommel; 6r. General George Marshall; 6r. General Jan Smuts; 6r. General Lieutenant Gunther Blumentritt; 6r. Major General J. Lawton Collins. (c) 138×137 mm. 6r. Winston Churchill; 6r. Admiral Sir Bertram Ramsey; 6r. Lieutenant General Dietrich Kraiss; 6r. Major General Richard Gale; 6r. General George Patton; 6r. Major General Maxwell Taylor. (d) 138×137 mm. 6r. General Dwight Eisenhower; 6r. Field Marshal Guenther von Kluge; 6r. Air Marshal Sir Trafford Leigh-Mallory; 6r. Field Marshal Walter Model; 6r. Field Marshal Gerd von Rundstedt; 6r. Sir Arthur Tedder. (e) 137×127 mm. 6r. Lieutenant General Omar Bradley (*horiz*); 6r. Rear Admiral Hall (*horiz*); 6r. Major General Huebner (*horiz*); 6r. Grossadmiral Karl Donitz (*horiz*); 6r. Rear Admiral Wilkes (*horiz*); 6r. Capt. Chauncey Camp (*horiz*) *Set of 5 sheets*...... 40·00 40·00
MS3935 Five sheets. (a) 68×98 mm. 30r. Rear Admiral Donald Moon. (b) 68×98 mm. 30r. Lieutenant General Sir Frederick Morgan. (c) 68×98 mm. 30r. General Henry Arnold. (d) 69×99 mm. 30r. General Sir Bernard Montgomery. (e) 98×68 mm. 30r. Rear Admiral Carlton Bryant (*horiz*) *Set of 5 sheets*...... 32·00 32·00

442 George Herman Ruth Jr

443 Firefly Class 2-2-2 GR1840

2004 (6 July). Centenary of Baseball World Series. T **442** and similar vert designs showing George Herman Ruth Jr. ("Babe Ruth"). Multicoloured. Litho. P 13½.

3936	3r. Type **442**	30	40
	a. Sheet. No. 3936×16	4·00	
3937/40	10r.×4 Swinging bat; Looking sombre; Carrying two bats; Looking left	3·75	4·25
	b. Sheetlet of 4. Nos. 3937/40	3·75	4·25

Nos. 3936 and 3937/40 were printed in sheetlets of 16 and four stamps respectively with illustrated margins.

2004 (6 July). Bicentenary of Steam Trains. T **443** and similar horiz designs. Multicoloured. P 13½.
MS3941 Six sheets. (a) 105×150 mm. 12r.×4, Type **443**; French 'Single' (1854); Medoc Class 2-4-0 Swiss (1857); German 4-4-0 (1893). (b) 105×150 mm. 12r.×4, Planet Class 2-2-0 (1830); American 4-4-0 (1855); *Newmar* (1846); Class 500 4-6-0 (1900). (c) 105×150 mm. 12r.×4, *Adler* 2-2-2 (1835); *Beuth* 2-2-2 (1843); *Northumbrian* 0-2-2 (1830); Class 4-6-2 (1901). (d) 150×105 mm.12r.×4, *The Evening Star*; *The Britannia*; *The George Stephenson*; Sudan Railways 310 2-8-2. (e) 150×105 mm. 12r.×4, East African Railways Garratt; Rhodesian Railways 12th Class; Class 2-6-2; Class 19d 4-8-2. (f) 150×105 mm. 12r.×4, Woodburning Beyer Garratt; Double-headed train over Kaaiman River; Garratt 4-8-2+2-8-2; Class 15 Garratt *Set of 6 sheets*...... 48·00 48·00
MS3942 Six sheets. (a) 100×70 mm. 30r. *Lord Nelson*. (b) 100×70 mm. 30r. *The American*. (c) 100×70 mm. 30r. *Flying Scotsman*. (d) 100×70 mm. 30r. *Vauxhall* 2-2-0 (1834). (e) 70×102 mm. 30r. *Claud Hamilton* Class 4-4-0. (f) 70×102 mm. 30r. Class P8 4-6-0 (1906) *Set of 6 sheets*...... 40·00 40·00

444 "Nègre Attaqué par un Jaguar"

2004 (6 July). 160th Birth Anniv of Henri Rousseau (French artist). T **444** and similar multicoloured designs. Litho. P 13½.

MS3943 127×127 mm. 10r.×4, Type **444**; "Paysage Exotique"; "La Cascade"; "Le Repas du Lion"................ 5·50   6·00
MS3944 75×92 mm. 25r. "Le Rêve" (detail). Imperf........ 4·00   4·50

445 "Conversation" (1909)

2004 (6 July). 50th Death Anniv of Henri Matisse (French artist). T **445** and similar multicoloured designs. Litho. P 13½.

MS3945 126×128 mm. 10r.×4, Type **445**; "Still Life with a Blue Tablecloth" (1909); "Seville Still Life II" (1910–11); "Woman before an Aquarium" (1921–23) .... 5·50   6·00
MS3946 62×93 mm. 25r. "Interior at Nice" (1921). Imperf .... 4·00   4·50

446 "The Endless Enigma" (1938)

2004 (6 July). Birth Centenary of Salvador Dali (Spanish artist). T **446** and similar horiz designs. Multicoloured. Litho. P 13½.

MS3947 126×127 mm. 10r.×4, Type **446**; "The Persistence of Memory (1931)"; "Soft Construction with Boiled Beans – Premonition of Civil War" (1936)"; "Still Life moving Fast" (1956) .... 5·50   6·00
MS3948 100×65 mm. 25r. "Figure on the Rocks" (1926). Imperf.. 4·00   4·50

447 "Still Life with Peppermint Bottle and Blue Rug" (1893–95)

2004 (6 July). 165th Birth Anniv of Paul Cézanne (French artist). T **447** and similar multicoloured designs. Litho. P 13½.

MS3949 127×127 mm. 10r.×4, Type **447**; "House in Provence" (1880); "Le Château Noir" (1900–04); "Basket of Apples" (1895) .... 7·00   7·50
MS3950 75×92 mm. 25r. "Boy in a Red Waistcoat leaning on his Elbow". Imperf................................ 5·50   6·00

448 Woman and Book

449 Marilyn Monroe

2004 (29 July). 176th Birth Anniv of Jules Verne (French writer). T **448** and similar horiz designs showing scenes from novels. Litho. P 13½.

MS3951 Five sheets, each 150×100 mm. (a) agate; lemon and bright scarlet; blackish lilac, lemon and bright scarlet; reddish-brown; lemon and bright scarlet; blackish green, lemon and bright scarlet. (b) steel-blue; lemon and bright scarlet; steel-blue, lemon and bright scarlet; blue-black; lemon and bright scarlet; blue-black, lemon and bright scarlet. (c) maroon; lemon and bright scarlet; bottle-green, lemon and bright scarlet; deep blue and bright scarlet; bottle-green and bright scarlet. (d) purple-brown, ultramarine and bright scarlet; multicoloured; deep purple and bright scarlet; deep rose-lilac and bright scarlet. (e) deep grey-green and bright scarlet; sepia and bright scarlet; deep grey-green, lemon and bright scarlet; deep reddish purple, lemon and bright scarlet Set of 5 sheets.. 42·00   42·00
MS3952 Five sheets, each 98×67 mm. (a) purple-brown and bright scarlet. (b) steel-blue and bright scarlet. (c) deep blue, lemon and bright scarlet. (d) blackish purple, lemon and bright scarlet. (e) reddish-brown, lemon and bright scarlet Set of 5 sheets.. 26·00   26·00

Designs—**MS**3951 (a) "Family without a Name" 12r.×4, Type **448**; Soldier; Battle scene on dockside; Men with rifles. (b) "The Lighthouse at the End of the World" 12r.×4, Crew on ship; Man on rocks and waves; Rocks on coastline; Man wearing hat and coastline. (c) "Michael Strogoff, Courier of the Czar" 12r.×4, Man held at gunpoint; Man and woman in tall grass; Two men and robed characters; Man and dog in flattened grass. (d) 12r.×4, "Archipelago on Fire"; "Clovis Dardentor"; "The Golden Volcano"; "Le Superbe Orénoque". (e) "César Cascabel" 12r.×4, Men in snow storm; Moustached man; Man caught in gust; Crowd reading poster. **MS**3952 (a) 25r. "The Survivors of the Chancellor". (b) 25r. "César Cascabel". (c) 25r. "The Lighthouse at the End of the World". (d) 25r. "Family without a Name". (e) 25r. "Keraban the Inflexible".

2004 (16 Aug). Marilyn Monroe (actress) Commemoration. Litho. P 13½.

3953   **449**   7r. multicoloured 70   80
    a. Sheetlet of 6. No. 3953×6 .... 3·50

No. 3953 was printed in sheetlets of six with illustrated margins.

450 Olympic Gold Medal, St Louis

(Litho B.D.T.)

2004 (30 Sept). Olympic Games, Athens. T **450** and similar multicoloured designs. P 14½.

3954   2r. Type **450** 40   25
3955   5r. Greek art... 75   60
3956   7r. Comte Jean de Beaumont .... 1·10   1·10
3957   12r. The pommel horse (horiz)...................... 1·75   2·50
3954/57 Set of 4.. 3·50   4·00

451 Fromia monilis

452 Silvertip Shark

2004 (4 Nov). Star Fish. T **451** and similar vert designs. Multicoloured. Litho. P 15×14.

3958   10r. Type **451** .... 2·00   2·25
3959   10r. Nardoa novaecaledoniae .... 2·00   2·25
3960   10r. Fromia monilis (rose red background) ... 2·00   2·25
3961   10r. Linckia laevigata .... 2·00   2·25
3958/61 Set of 4.. 7·25   8·00

2004 (4 Nov). Sharks. T **452** and similar horiz designs. Multicoloured. Litho. P 14.
MS3962 136×115 mm. 10r.×4, Type **452**; Silky Shark; Great White Shark; Gray Reef Shark.................................. 7·00 7·50
MS3963 96×65 mm. 25r. Starry Smoothhound............... 4·50 5·00

453 *Cethosia cydippe*

2004 (15 Dec). Butterflies. T **453** and similar multicoloured designs. Litho. P 14.
MS3964 180×111 mm. 10r.×4, Type **453**; *Amesia sanguiflua; Pericallia galactina; Limenitis dudu dudu* . 7·50 8·00
MS3965 98×68 mm. 25r. *Papilio demoleus malayanus* (*vert*) .... 4·75 5·25

454 *Eurypegasus draconis*

2004 (15 Dec). Endangered Species. *Eurypegasus draconis* (Little Dragonfish). T **454** and similar horiz designs. Multicoloured. Litho. P 14.
3966   7r. Type **454** .... 1·10 1·25
   a. Block of 4. Nos. 3966/9 .... 4·00 4·50
   b. Horiz strip of 4. Nos. 3966/9 .... 4·00 4·50
3967   7r. Orange *Eurypegasus draconis*.................. 1·10 1·25
3968   7r. White *Eurypegasus draconis*..................... 1·10 1·25
3969   7r. *Eurypegasus draconis* on sandy sea bed ... 1·10 1·25
3966/69 *Set of 4* .... 4·00 4·50
Nos. 3966/9 were each printed together, *se-tenant*, both in blocks of four in sheetlets of 12 and in two horizontal strips of four separated by an illustrated central gutter in sheetlets of eight.

455 *Eyelash Pit Viper*

2004 (15 Dec). Reptiles and Amphibians. T **455** and similar multicoloured designs. Litho. P 14.
MS3970 180×111 mm. 10r.×4, Type **455**; Basilisk Lizard; Calico Snake; Maki Frog .... 6·00 6·50
MS3971 66×96 mm. 25r. *Naja melanoleuca* (*vert*) .... 4·00 4·50

456 *Hygrocybe psittacina*

2004 (15 Dec). Mushrooms. T **456** and similar multicoloured designs. Litho. P 14.
MS3972 181×111 mm. 10r.×4, Type **456**; *Hygrocybe miniata; Aleuria aurantia; Thaxterogaster porphyreum* .... 6·50 7·00
MS3973 98×68 mm. 25r. *Galerina autumnalis* (*vert*)...... 4·25 4·75

457 Striped Dolphin

2004 (15 Dec). Dolphins. T **457** and similar horiz designs. Multicoloured. Litho. P 14.
MS3974 181×111 mm. 10r.×4, Type **457**; Amazon River Dolphin; Bottlenose Dolphin; Spinner Dolphin .... 6·00 6·50
MS3975 97×66 mm. 25r. Long-snouted Spinner Dolphin .... 4·00 4·50

458 Jupp Derwall   459 Deng Xiaoping

(Des M. Servin. Litho)

2005 (26 Jan). European Football Championship, 2004, Portugal. Commemoration of 1980 Cup Final between Germany and Belgium. T **458** and similar multicoloured designs. P 14.
MS3976 148×86 mm. 12r.×4, Type **458**; René Vandereycken; Horst Hrubesch; Estadio Olimpico..... 5·50 6·50
MS3977 97×86 mm. 25r. German team, 1980 (50×37 mm) .... 3·75 4·25

2005 (26 Jan). Birth Centenary (2004) of Deng Xiaoping (Chinese Leader, 1978–89). Sheet 96×67 mm. Litho. P 14.
MS3978 **459**   25r. multicoloured..................................... 3·25 3·75

460 Macroplata

2005 (26 Jan). Prehistoric Animals. T **460** and similar multicoloured designs. Litho. P 14.
MS3979 Four sheets, each 148×111 mm. (a) 10r.×4, Type **460**; Ichthyosaurus; Shonisaurus; Archelon. (b) 10r.×4 (*vert*), Pterodactyl; Cearadactylus; Pterosaur; Sordes. (c) 10r.×4 (*vert*), Deinonychus; Styracosaurus (from front); Ornitholestes; Euoplocephalus. (d) 10r.×4 (*vert*), Albertosaurus; Iguanodon; Deinonychus; Baryonyx *Set of 4 sheets* .. 27·00 28·00
MS3980 Four sheets, each 96×67 mm. (a) 25r. Muraeonosaurus. (b) 25r. Archaeopteryx. (c) 25r. Styracosaurus (from side). (d) 25r. Leptoceratops *Set of 4 sheets* .... 20·00 21·00

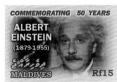

461 Albert Einstein

2005 (20 Sept). 50th Death Anniv of Albert Einstein (physicist). T **461** and similar multicoloured designs. Litho. P 13.
MS3981 110×135 mm. 15r.×4, Type **461**; Smiling; With pipe in mouth; With raised eyebrows.................. 8·50 8·50
MS3982 55×85 mm. 25r. Albert Einstein (*vert*)............... 5·50 5·50

462 Oscar (Brazil)

2005 (20 Sept). 75th Anniv of First World Cup Football Championship, Uruguay. T **462** and similar vert designs. Multicoloured. Litho. P 13½.

MS3983	175×130 mm. 15r.×3, Type **462**; Karl-Heinz Rummenigge (Germany); Oliver Kahn (Germany)......	6·50	7·50
MS3984	124×105 mm. 25r. Karlheinz Forster (Germany). P 12...	3·75	4·00

463 Chicago Skyline   464 Hans Christian Andersen (statue)

2005 (20 Sept). Centenary of Rotary International. T **463** and similar vert designs. Multicoloured. Litho. P 13.

MS3985	151×68 mm. 15r.×3, Type **463**; Skyline with Sears Tower; Skyline (*different*).............................	6·50	7·50
MS3986	102×67 mm. 25r. Telecommunications tower	4·00	4·50

The stamps of No. **MS**3985 form a composite design showing a panoramic view of Chicago's skyline.

2005 (20 Sept). Birth Bicentenary of Hans Christian Andersen (writer). T **464** and similar vert designs. Multicoloured. Litho. P 13.

MS3987	70×151 mm. 15r.×3, Type **464**; Hans Christian Andersen; Statue facing left	6·50	7·50
MS3988	71×101 mm. 25r. "The Little Mermaid".............	3·75	4·00

465 Admiral Cuthbert Collingwood   466 Elvis Presley, 1956

2005 (20 Sept). Bicentenary of the Battle of Trafalgar. T **465** and similar multicoloured designs. Litho. P 13.

3989	10r. Type **465**	2·50	2·50
	a. Sheetlet of 4. Nos. 3989/92	9·00	9·00
3990	10r. Napoleon Bonaparte	2·50	2·50
3991	10r. Admiral Lord Horatio Nelson....................	2·50	2·50
3992	10r. Captain Thomas Masterman Hardy.........	2·50	2·50
3989/92 *Set of 4*..		9·00	9·00
MS3993	99×70 mm. 25r. Ships engaged in battle.........	7·50	7·50

Nos. 3989/92 were printed together, se-tenant, in sheetlets of four stamps with an enlarged, illustrated left margin.

2005 (15 Nov). 70th Birth Anniv of Elvis Presley. T **466** and similar vert designs. Multicoloured. Litho. P 14×13½.

3994	7r. Type **466**	1·10	1·10
	a. Sheetlet of 6. Nos 3994/9	6·00	6·00
3995	7r. On Frank Sinatra Show, 1960	1·10	1·10
3996	7r. In 1962	1·10	1·10
3997	7r. Performing in Las Vegas, 1969.................	1·10	1·10

3998	7r. Arriving in Hawaii, 1973..............................	1·10	1·10
3999	7r. In concert, 1975	1·10	1·10
4000	7r. In "Love Me Tender", 1956.......................	1·10	1·10
	a. Sheetlet of 6. Nos. 4000/5	6·00	6·00
4001	7r. In "Loving You", 1957................................	1·10	1·10
4002	7r. In "King Creole", 1958..............................	1·10	1·10
4003	7r. Riding motorcycle in "Roustabout", 1964..	1·10	1·10
4004	7r. In "Double Trouble", 1967..........................	1·10	1·10
4005	7r. In "Live a Little, Love a Little", 1968	1·10	1·10
3994/4005 *Set of 12*..		12·00	12·00

Nos. 3994/9 and 4000/5 were each printed together, se-tenant, in sheetlets of six stamps with enlarged illustrated margins.

An 85r. gold stamp with an illustration showing Elvis Presley playing guitar was also issued, on 17 January 2006.

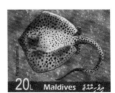

467 "Purple Bird" (Anna Badger)   468 Himantura uamak

2006 (24 Jan). "Kids-Did-It!" Designs. T **467** and similar vert designs showing children's paintings. Multicoloured. Litho. P 13½.

4006	10r. Type **467**	1·25	1·25
	a. Sheetlet of 4. Nos. 4006/9	4·50	4·50
4007	10r. "Parrots" (Nick Abrams)	1·25	1·25
4008	10r. "Pretty Bird" (Jessie Abrams)	1·25	1·25
4009	10r. "Royal Parrot" (Ashley Mondfrans)...........	1·25	1·25
4010	10r. "Orange Sunflower" (Brett Walker)..........	1·25	1·25
	a. Sheetlet of 4. Nos. 4010/13	4·50	4·50
4011	10r. "Red Flower Pot" (Jessica Shutt)............	1·25	1·25
4012	10r. "Flower Pot" (Nick Abrams)	1·25	1·25
4013	10r. "Blue Flower Vase" (Trevor Nielsen)........	1·25	1·25
4014	10r. "Bubbles" (Raquel Bobolia)	1·25	1·25
	a. Sheetlet of 4. Nos. 4014/17	4·50	4·50
4015	10r. "Bubble Fish" (Sarah Bowen)	1·25	1·25
4016	10r. "Lipfish" (Elsa Fleischer)	1·25	1·25
4017	10r. "Flounder" (Erica Malchowski)	1·25	1·25
4006/17 *Set of 12*		13·50	13·50

Nos. 4006/9, 4010/13 and 4014/17 were each printed together, se-tenant, in sheetlets of four stamps with enlarged illustrated right margins.

2006 (27 Feb). Rays. T **468** and similar horiz designs. Multicoloured. Litho. P 14×14½.

4018	20l. Type **468**	25	25
4019	1r. *Manta birostris*......................................	50	25
4020	2r. *Taeniura lymma*....................................	90	50
4021	20r. *Aetobatus narinari*.................................	4·00	4·50
4018/21 *Set of 4*..		5·00	5·00

Numbers have been left for additions to this set.

469 Emblem   470 Mozart

2006 (9 Mar). 20th Anniv of SAARC (South Asian Association for Regional Co-operation). Sheet 115×125 mm. Litho. P 13½×13.

MS4032	**469** 25r. multicoloured................................	4·25	5·50

2006 (29 June). 250th Birth Anniv of Wolfgang Amadeus Mozart (composer). T **470** and similar vert designs. Multicoloured. Litho. P 13.

4033	12r. Type **470**	2·75	2·75
	a. Sheetlet of 4. Nos. 4033/6	10·00	10·00
4034	12r. Portrait of Mozart (facing left)	2·75	2·75
4035	12r. Young Mozart	2·75	2·75
4036	12r. Bust of Mozart	2·75	2·75
4033/36 *Set of 4*..		10·00	10·00

Nos. 4033/6 were printed together, se-tenant, in sheetlets of four stamps with enlarged illustrated right margins.

471 Queen Elizabeth II and Pres. John F. Kennedy

2006 (30 June). 80th Birthday of Queen Elizabeth II. T **471** and similar vert designs. Multicoloured. Litho. P 14½.

4037	15r. Type **471**		2·50	2·50
	a. Sheetlet of 4. Nos. 4037/40		9·00	9·00
4038	15r. With Pres. Reagan, riding horses		2·50	2·50
4039	15r. Dancing with Pres. Ford		2·50	2·50
4040	15r. With Pres. Bush		2·50	2·50
4037/40 Set of 4			9·00	9·00
MS4041	126×126 mm. 25r. "Horse in a Field" (detail) (George Stubbs)		5·50	5·50

Nos. 4037/40 were printed together, *se-tenant*, in sheetlets of four stamps with enlarged illustrated margins.
The stamp within No. **MS**4041 is incorrectly inscribed "QUEEN ELIZABETH II".

472 Norway 1951 Winter Olympics 55ö+20ö Stamp

473 "100"

(Litho B.D.T.)

2006 (2 Aug). Winter Olympic Games, Turin. T **472** and similar multicoloured designs. Litho. P 14½.

4042	7r. Type **472**		1·25	1·10
4043	8r. Poster for Winter Olympic Games, Oslo, 1952 (*vert*)		1·50	1·50
4044	10r. Poster for Winter Olympic Games, Garmisch-Partenkirchen, Germany, 1936 (*vert*)		1·75	1·75
4045	12r. Germany 1935 Winter Olympics 6pf.+4pf. skating stamp (*vert*)		2·00	2·25
4042/45 Set of 5			6·00	6·00

2006 (12 Nov). Centenary of Postal Service in the Maldives. Sheet 135×175 mm. Litho. P 12½.

MS4046	**473** 12r. multicoloured		2·25	2·50

474 Elvis Presley

2006 (15 Nov). 50th Anniv of Purchase of Gracelands by Elvis Presley. T **474** and similar vert design. Multicoloured, background tint given. Litho. P 13½.

4047	12r. Type **474** (grey)		2·25	2·25
	a. Sheetlet of 4. Nos. 4047/50		8·00	8·00
4048	12r. Elvis Presley singing (brownish grey)		2·25	2·25
4049	12r. As No. 4048 (lavender-grey)		2·25	2·25

4050	12r. As Type **474** (greenish grey)		2·25	2·25
4047/50 Set of 4			8·00	8·00

Nos. 4047/50 were printed together, *se-tenant*, in sheetlets of four stamps with enlarged illustrated right margins.

475 International Airship Exhibition, Frankfurt, Germany, 1909

476 R-7 Missile (*Sputnik 1* launcher)

2006 (15 Nov). 50th Death Anniv of Ludwig Durr (Zeppelin engineer). T **475** and similar horiz designs. Multicoloured. Litho. P 13½.

4051	15r. Type **475**		2·50	2·50
	a. Sheetlet of 3. Nos. 4051/3		6·75	6·75
4052	15r. Hot air balloons at International Airship Exhibition, Frankfurt, 1909		2·50	2·50
4053	15r. Airship LZ-129 *Hindenburg*		2·50	2·50
4051/53 Set of 3			6·75	6·75

Nos. 4051/3 were printed together, *se-tenant*, in sheetlets of three stamps with enlarged illustrated right margins.

2006 (15 Nov). Space Anniversaries. T **476** and similar horiz designs. Multicoloured. Litho. P 13½.

(a) Sputniks 1, 2 and 3

4054	8r. Type **476**		1·75	1·75
	a. Sheetlet of 6. Nos. 4054/9		9·50	9·50
4055	8r. *Sputnik 1*		1·75	1·75
4056	8r. Inside *Sputnik 1*		1·75	1·75
4057	8r. *Sputnik 2*		1·75	1·75
4058	8r. *Sputnik 1* orbits over the Earth		1·75	1·75
4059	8r. *Sputnik 3*		1·75	1·75

(b) 20th Anniv of Giotto Comet Probe

4060	12r. Nucleus of Halley's Comet		2·25	2·25
	a. Sheetlet of 4. Nos. 4060/3		8·00	8·00
4061	12r. Halley's Comet		2·25	2·25
4062	12r. *Giotto* Space Probe and Halley's Comet		2·25	2·25
4063	12r. Image of Halley's Comet by *Giotto* Probe		2·25	2·25
4054/63 Set of 10			17·00	17·00
MS4064	150×100 mm. 12r.×4 *Calipso* Satellite; *CloudSat* Satellite; *Aqua* Satellite; *Aura* Satellite		8·00	9·00
MS4065	Two sheets, each 100×70 mm. (a) 25r. *Stardust* Satellite, 2004. (b) 25r. *Giotto* Comet Probe		8·00	9·00

Nos. 4054/9 and 4060/3 were each printed together, *se-tenant*, in sheetlets of six or four stamps with enlarged illustrated margins.
The stamps and margins of No. **MS**4064 form a composite design showing satellites above the Earth.

477 *Pomacanthus imperator*

478 Ragged-finned Lion Fish

2007 (8 Feb). Fish. T **477** and similar horiz designs. Multicoloured. Litho. P 13.

4066	10r. Type **477**		2·25	2·25
4067	10r. *Balistoides conspicillum*		2·25	2·25
4068	10r. *Chaetodon meyeri*		2·25	2·25
4069	10r. *Dascyllus arnanus*		2·25	2·25
4066/69 Set of 4			8·00	8·00

2007 (8 Feb). Fish of the Maldives. T **478** and similar horiz designs. Multicoloured. Litho. P 14.

4070	1r. Type **478**		35	20
4071	2r. Vlaming's Unicornfish		50	30
4072	10r. White-spotted Grouper		2·00	2·00
4073	10r. Bicolour Parrotfish		2·00	2·00
	a. Sheetlet of 4. Nos. 4073/6		7·25	7·25
4074	10r. Blue-barred Parrotfish		2·00	2·00
4075	10r. Bullethead Parrotfish		2·00	2·00
4076	10r. Dusky Parrotfish		2·00	2·00
4077	10r. Imperial Angelfish		2·00	2·00
	a. Sheetlet of 4. Nos. 4077/80		7·25	7·25
4078	10r. Clown Triggerfish		2·00	2·00
4079	10r. Black-saddled Coral Trout		2·00	2·00
4080	10r. Slender Grouper		2·00	2·00
4081	20r. Maldive Anemonefish		3·50	4·00

4070/81 Set of 12			20·00	20·00

MS4082 Three sheets, each 93×63 mm. (a) 30r. Picasso Triggerfish. (b) 30r. Blue-faced Angelfish. (c) 30r. Shadow Soldierfish *Set of 3 sheets* .... 12·00 13·00

Nos. 4073/6 and 4077/80 were each printed together, *se-tenant*, in sheetlets of six or four stamps with enlarged illustrated margins.

479 Bar-tailed Godwit

2007 (8 Feb). Migratory Birds of the Maldives. T **479** and similar multicoloured designs. Litho. P 14.

4083	1r. Type **479**	65	35
4084	2r. Black-headed Gull	1·10	75
4085	10r. Masked Booby (*vert*)	2·50	2·50
4086	10r. Common Swifts	2·50	2·50
	a. Sheetlet of 4. Nos. 4086/9	9·00	9·00
4087	10r. Sooty Tern	2·50	2·50
4088	10r. Yellow Wagtail	2·50	2·50
4089	10r. House Sparrow	2·50	2·50
4090	10r. Tufted Duck	2·50	2·50
	a. Sheetlet of 4. Nos. 4090/3	9·00	9·00
4091	10r. Caspian Tern	2·50	2·50
4092	10r. Southern Giant Petrel	2·50	2·50
4093	10r. Glossy Ibis	2·50	2·50
4094	20r. Kentish Plover	4·00	4·50
4083/94 Set of 12		25·00	25·00

MS4095 Three sheets. (a) 64×94 mm. 30r. Golden-throated Barbet (*vert*). (b) 94×64 mm. 30r. Purple Herons. (c) 64×94 mm. 30r. Osprey (*vert*) *Set of 3 sheets* .... 14·00 15·00

Nos. 4086/9 and 4090/3 were each printed together, *se-tenant*, in sheetlets of four stamps with enlarged illustrated margins.

480 *Dendrobium formosum*

481 *Ranunculus eschscholtzii*

2007 (8 Feb). Orchids of Asia. T **480** and similar multicoloured designs. Litho. P 14.

4096	1r. Type **480**	65	20
4097	2r. Bulbophyllum Elizabeth Ann	1·10	30
4098	10r. Dendrobium bigibbum	2·50	2·50
4099	10r. Cymbidium erythrostylum	2·50	2·50
	a. Sheetlet of 4. Nos. 4099/4102	9·00	9·00
4100	10r. Phaius humboldtii×Phaius tuberculosis ..	2·50	2·50
4101	10r. Dendrobium farmeri	2·50	2·50
4102	10r. Dendrobium junceum	2·50	2·50
4103	10r. Bulbophyllum lasiochilum	2·50	2·50
	a. Sheetlet of 4. Nos. 4103/6	9·00	9·00
4104	10r. Phaius Microburst	2·50	2·50
4105	10r. Coelogyne mooreana	2·50	2·50
4106	10r. Bulbophyllum nasseri	2·50	2·50
4107	20r. Spathoglottis gracilis	4·00	4·00
4096/4107 Set of 12		25·00	25·00

MS4108 Three sheets, each 66×97 mm. (a) 30r. Coelogyne cristata (*horiz*). (b) 30r. Dendrobium crocatum (*horiz*). (c) 30r. Bulbophyllum graveolens (*horiz*) .... 14·00 15·00

Nos. 4099/4102 and 4103/6 were each printed together, *se-tenant*, in sheetlets of four stamps with enlarged illustrated right margins.

2007 (8 Feb). Flowers of the World. T **481** and similar horiz designs. Multicoloured. Litho. P 14.

4109	1r. Type **481**	35	20
4110	2r. Ratibida columnaris	50	30
4111	10r. Mentzelia laevicaulis	2·00	2·00
4112	10r. Ipomopsis aggregate	2·00	2·00
	a. Sheetlet of 4. Nos. 4112/15	7·25	7·25
4113	10r. Rosa woodsii	2·00	2·00
4114	10r. Lewisia rediviva	2·00	2·00
4115	10r. Penstemon rydbergii	2·00	2·00

4116	10r. Machaeranthera tanacetifolia	2·00	2·00
	a. Sheetlet of 4. Nos. 4116/19	7·25	7·25
4117	10r. Aquilegia coerulea	2·00	2·00
4118	10r. Gentiana detonsa	2·00	2·00
4119	10r. Linum perenne	2·00	2·00
4120	20r. Clintonia uniflora	3·50	4·00
4109/20 Set of 12		20·00	20·00

MS4121 Three sheets, each 95×67 mm. (a) 30r. Encelia farinosa. (b) 30r. Epilobium angustifolium. (c) 30r. Ipomoea purpurea *Set of 3 sheets* .... 12·00 13·00

Nos. 4112/15 and 4116/19 were each printed together, *se-tenant*, in sheetlets of four stamps with enlarged illustrated margins.

482 Scout Badge

(Litho Cardon Enterprise)

2007 (21 Feb). Centenary of World Scouting. P 13½.

4122	**482**	15r. multicoloured	2·50	2·75

MS4123 110×80 mm. **482** 25r. pale new blue and bright reddish violet .... 3·75 4·00

No. 4122 was printed in sheetlets of three stamps with enlarged illustrated margins.

483 King Penguins

484 Diana, Princess of Wales

(Litho Cardon Enterprise)

2007 (1 May). International Polar Year. Penguins. T **483** and similar vert designs. Multicoloured. P 13½.

4124	12r. Type **483**	2·75	2·75
	a. Sheetlet of 6. Nos. 4124/9	15·00	15·00
4125	12r. King Penguin preening	2·75	2·75
4126	12r. King Penguin (bright yellow-green background)	2·75	2·75
4127	12r. Two King Penguin chicks	2·75	2·75
4128	12r. King Penguin chick with wings raised...	2·75	2·75
4129	12r. King Penguin chick huddled against adult	2·75	2·75
4124/29 Set of 6		15·00	15·00

MS4130 100×70 mm. 25r. African Penguin wearing party hat .... 6·00 6·00

Nos. 4124/9 were printed together, *se-tenant*, in sheetlets of six stamps with enlarged illustrated margins.

(Litho Cardon Enterprise)

2007 (12 Aug). Tenth Death Anniv of Diana, Princess of Wales. T **484** and similar vert designs. Multicoloured. P 13½.

4131	8r. Type **484**	1·40	1·40
	a. Sheetlet of 6. Nos. 4131/6	7·50	7·50
4132	8r. Wearing white hat and pearls	1·40	1·40
4133	8r. Wearing white hat and white coat with pinstripes	1·40	1·40
4134	8r. Wearing white hat and green dress with white pinstripes	1·40	1·40
4135	8r. Carrying bouquet, wearing white hat and white coat with pinstripes	1·40	1·40
4136	8r. Wearing grey jacket and grey and white hat	1·40	1·40
4131/36 Set of 6		7·50	7·50

MS4137 100×70 mm. 25r. Wearing black jacket with white lapels and white and black hat .... 4·50 4·75

Nos. 4131/6 were printed together, *se-tenant*, in sheetlets of six stamps with enlarged illustrated left margins.

485 Ferrari 312 T 4

(Litho Cardon Enterprise)

2007 (12 Aug). 60th Anniv of Ferrari. T **485** and similar horiz designs. Multicoloured. P 13½.

4138	8r. Type **485**	1·25	1·25
	a. Sheetlet of 8. Nos. 4138/45	9·00	9·00
4139	8r. 456 GT, 1992	1·25	1·25
4140	8r. 250 GT Berlinetta, 1959	1·25	1·25
4141	8r. F1 89, 1989	1·25	1·25
4142	8r. 456M GTA, 1998	1·25	1·25
4143	8r. 735 LM, 1955	1·25	1·25
4144	8r. DINO 308 GT4, 1973	1·25	1·25
4145	8r. F 200l, 2001	1·25	1·25
4138/45	Set of 8	9·00	9·00

Nos. 4138/45 were printed together, *se-tenant*, in sheetlets of eight stamps.

486 *Chaetodon triangulum*

2007 (9 Oct). Fish. T **486** and similar horiz designs. Multicoloured. Litho. P 13½.

4146	10l. Type **486**	15	25
4147	50l. *Chaetodon kleinii*	25	25
4148	12r. *Chaetodon trifasciatus*	2·25	2·25
4149	15r. *Chaetodon madagascariensis*	2·50	2·50
4150	20r. *Chaetodon lunula*	3·00	3·00
4146/50	Set of 5	7·50	7·50

487 Elvis Presley

488 Rie Mastenbroek (Netherlands) (swimming triple gold medallist)

2008 (8 Jan). 30th Death Anniv (2007) of Elvis Presley. T **487** and similar horiz designs. Multicoloured. Litho. P 13½.

4151	8r. Type **487**	1·40	1·40
	a. Sheetlet of 6. Nos. 4151/6	7·50	7·50
4152	8r. Wearing bright blue jacket, playing guitar	1·40	1·40
4153	8r. Wearing red jacket	1·40	1·40
4154	8r. Wearing grey collarless jacket and black shirt	1·40	1·40
4155	8r. Wearing blue shirt, singing	1·40	1·40
4156	8r. Wearing red shirt, holding microphone	1·40	1·40
4151/56	Set of 6	7·50	7·50

Nos. 4151/6 were printed together, *se-tenant*, in sheetlets of six stamps with enlarged illustrated margins.

2008 (8 Jan). Olympic Games, Beijing. T **488** and similar vert designs showing scenes from Olympic Games, Berlin, 1936. Multicoloured. Litho. P 13½.

4157	7r. Type **488**	1·40	1·40
	a. Horiz strip of 4. Nos. 4157/60	5·00	5·00
4158	7r. Poster for Olympic Games, Berlin, 1936	1·40	1·40
4159	7r. Jesse Owens (USA) (field and track quadruple gold medallist)	1·40	1·40
4160	7r. Jack Beresford (Great Britain) (double scull gold medallist)	1·40	1·40
4157/60	Set of 4	5·00	5·00
MS4161	177×101 mm. Nos. 4157/60	5·00	5·50

Nos. 4157/60 were printed together, *se-tenant*, as horizontal strips of four stamps in sheetlets of 16 (4×4).

489 Americas Cup Yachts

2008 (8 Jan). America's Cup Yachting Championship. T **489** and similar vert designs showing yachts. Multicoloured. Litho. P 13½.

4162	10r. Type **489**	1·50	1·75
	a. Strip of 4. Nos. 4162/5	7·50	8·50
4163	12r. Two yachts (green yacht in background)	1·75	2·00
4164	15r. Two yachts (*Prada* in foreground)	2·25	2·50
4165	20r. Two yachts (yellow yacht in foreground)	2·75	3·00
4162/65	Set of 4	7·50	8·50

Nos. 4162/5 were printed together, *se-tenant*, as horizontal and vertical strips of four stamps in sheets of 16 (4×4).

490 Emblem of First Scout Jamboree, Kuda Bandos, 1986

491 Rose in Ozone Layer and Pollutants

2008 (19 Feb). 50th Anniv of Scouting in the Maldives (5l. to 5r.) and Centenary of World Scouting (8r.). T **490** and similar horiz designs. Multicoloured. P 13½.

4166	5l. Type **490**	25	25
	a. Sheetlet of 8. Nos. 4166/73	3·00	3·00
4167	10l. Second Scout Jamboree, Kuda Bandos, 1988	30	30
4168	15l. Third Scout Jamboree, Huraa, 1990	35	35
4169	20l. Fourth National Scout Jamboree, Villingili, December 1992	35	35
4170	25l. Fifth National Scout Jamboree, Villingili, September 1993	35	35
4171	30l. Jamboree '98 badge	35	35
4172	95l. Scout Jamboree 2002	50	50
4173	5r. Eighth National (Golden Jubilee) Jamboree, Hulhumale, 15–19 April, 2007.	1·00	1·00
4166/73	Set of 8	3·00	3·00
MS4174	130×172 mm. 8r. Lord Baden-Powell	1·40	1·60

Nos. 4166/73 all show emblems. They were printed together, *se-tenant*, in sheetlets of eight stamps with enlarged illustrated margins.

2008 (10 Sept). International Day for the Preservation of the Ozone Layer. Sheet 177×127 mm containing T **491** and similar vert designs showing posters drawn by Maldivian students for International Ozone Day 2002. Multicoloured. Litho. P 12½.

MS4175	5r. Type **491**; 12r. Two people, trees and sea with fish in ozone bubble; 15r. People standing on globe holding up ozone layer; 18r. Four people standing on island holding up ozone layer	7·00	8·00

492 Elvis Presley

2008 (11 Sept). Elvis Presley Commemoration. T **492** and similar vert designs. Multicoloured. Litho. P 13½.

4176	8r. Type **492**	1·40	1·40
	a. Sheetlet of 6. Nos. 4176/81	7·50	7·50
4177	8r. With hand close-up in right foreground of picture	1·40	1·40
4178	8r. Wearing jumpsuit, shown in yellow with blue background	1·40	1·40
4179	8r. Holding microphone, lemon background	1·40	1·40
4180	8r. Wearing white	1·40	1·40
4181	8r. Wearing stetson, sitting on car bonnet	1·40	1·40
4176/81	Set of 6	7·50	7·50

Nos. 4176/81 were printed together, *se-tenant*, in sheetlets of six stamps with enlarged illustrated margins.

493 Sopwith F-1 Camel

2008 (11 Sept). 90th Anniv of the Royal Air Force. T **493** and similar horiz designs. Multicoloured. Litho. P 11½.

4182	12r. Type **493**	3·00	3·00
	a. Sheetlet of 4. Nos. 4182/5	11·00	11·00
4183	12r. Aerospatiale Puma HC1 helicopter	3·00	3·00
4184	12r. Wessex helicopter	3·00	3·00
4185	12r. Armstrong Whitworth Atlas seaplane	3·00	3·00
4182/85	Set of 4	11·00	11·00

Nos. 4182/5 were printed together, *se-tenant*, in sheetlets of four stamps with enlarged illustrated margins.

494 *Voyager II* and Uranus Rings   495 Troops in Trench

2008 (11 Sept). 50 Years of Space Exploration and Satellites. T **494** and similar vert designs. Multicoloured. Litho. P 13½.

4186	8r. Type **494**	1·25	1·25
	a. Sheetlet of 6. Nos. 4186/91	6·75	6·75
4187	8r. Titan 3E Centaur rocket launches *Voyager II*, 1977	1·25	1·25
4188	8r. *Voyager II* and Neptune's Great Dark Spot	1·25	1·25
4189	8r. *Voyager II* and Jupiter's Great Red Spot	1·25	1·25
4190	8r. Technician places *Voyager's* Gold Record	1·25	1·25
4191	8r. *Voyager II* and Saturn's Rings	1·25	1·25
4192	12r. *Sputnik I* in space, 1957	2·00	2·00
	a. Sheetlet. Nos. 4192/5	7·25	7·25
4193	12r. Components of *Sputnik I*	2·00	2·00
4194	12r. Technician and *Sputnik I*	2·00	2·00
4195	12r. *Sputnik I* above Moon	2·00	2·00
4196	12r. *Explorer I* atop launcher *Juno I*, 1958	2·00	2·00
	a. Sheetlet of 4. Nos. 4196/9	7·25	7·25
4197	12r. *Explorer I* and Planet Earth	2·00	2·00
4198	12r. *Explorer I* above Earth	2·00	2·00
4199	12r. Dr. James Van Allen and the Van Allen radiation belt	2·00	2·00
4200	12r. *Vanguard I* in orbit below Earth, 1953	2·00	2·00
	a. Sheetlet of 4. Nos. 4200/3	7·25	7·25
4201	12r. Two technicians with *Vanguard I*	2·00	2·00
4202	12r. *Vanguard I* satellite and rocket	2·00	2·00
4203	12r. *Vanguard I* above Earth	2·00	2·00
4204	12r. Spitzer Space Telescope (bright star in gas cloud at right)	2·00	2·00
	a. Sheetlet of 4. Nos. 4204/7	7·25	7·25
4205	12r. Spitzer Space Telescope (gas cloud only at foot and left of telescope)	2·00	2·00
4206	12r. Spitzer Space Telescope (bright stars in gas cloud below telescope)	2·00	2·00
4207	12r. Spitzer Space Telescope (with solar panels visible)	2·00	2·00
4186/4207	Set of 22	35·00	35·00

Nos. 4186/91, 4192/5, 4196/9, 4200/3 and 4204/7 were each printed together, *se-tenant*, in sheetlets of six or four stamps with enlarged illustrated margins.

2008 (11 Nov). 90th Anniv of the End of World War One. T **495** and similar multicoloured designs. Litho. P 11½.

MS4208	91×140 mm.12r.×4 Type **495**; Two soldiers looking out from trench (side view); Soldiers in trench (seen from back); ANZAC soldier carrying wounded comrade	8·00	8·50
MS4209	195×178 mm.12r.×4 Motorcycle despatch riders studying map; ANZAC troops ascending hill; Tank; Two soldiers looking out from trench (seen from back)	8·00	8·50

496 Pres. Barack Obama   497 Abraham Lincoln

2009 (20 Jan). Inauguration of President Barack Obama. T **496** and similar multicoloured designs. Litho. P 11½ or 13.

MS4210	165×140 mm.10r.×6 Type **496**; Pres. Obama facing right; Pres. Obama; Michelle Obama; Pres. Obama facing left; Michelle Obama clapping; Pres. Obama facing camera, smiling	9·00	10·00
MS4211	85×110 mm. 30r. Pres. Barack Obama and Michelle Obama (50×37 *mm*)	6·50	7·50

2009 (12 Feb). Birth Bicentenary of Abraham Lincoln (US President 1861–5). Sheet 136×175 mm containing T **497** and similar vert designs. Multicoloured. Litho. P 13.

MS4212	12r.×4 Type **497**; Seated by desk; Seated by desk, holding book; Abraham Lincoln (head turned to left)	6·00	7·00

498 Black-saddled Coralgrouper (*Plectropomus laevis*)

2009 (24 Sept). Fish. T **498** and similar horiz designs. Multicoloured. Litho. P 13.

4213	12r. Type **498**	2·25	2·25
4214	12r. Sixblotch Hind (*Cephalopholis sexmaculata*)	2·25	2·25
4215	12r. Foursaddle Grouper (*Epinephelus spilotoceps*)	2·25	2·25
4216	12r. Peacock Hind (*Cephalopholis argus*)	2·25	2·25
4213/16	Set of 4	8·00	8·00

499 Scotty (James Doohan)   500 Prince Harry at Official Naming of the British Garden

2009 (29 Sept). *Star Trek*. T **499** and similar multicoloured designs. Litho. P 13½.

MS4217	178×127 mm.12r.×4 Type **499**; Dr. McCoy (DeForest Kelly) (looking left); Captain Kirk (William Shatner); Mr. Spock (Leonard Nimoy) (in profile)	7·00	7·50
MS4218	127×178 mm.12r.×4 Fleet crew; Uhura (Nichelle Nichols); Mr. Spock (speaking); Dr. McCoy (all horiz)	7·00	7·50

2009 (29 Sept). Visit of Prince Harry to New York. Sheet 140×100 mm. Litho. P 11½.

MS4219 12r.×4 Type **500**; With little girl at World Trade Center site; Prince Harry speaking; Competing in Polo Classic .... 8·50   8·50

501 Marilyn Monroe

2009 (21 Oct). Marilyn Monroe Commemoration. Litho. P 12½.

MS4220 16r.×4 Type **501**; Sitting in open-top car; Wearing print blouse; Laying down (head and shoulders portrait).. 7·50   8·50

502 Crimson Rose   **503** Beluga Whale
(*Atrophaneura hector*)

2009 (21 Oct). Butterflies of Maldives. T **502** and similar multicoloured designs. Litho. P 12½ (4221/4) or 12 (**MS**4225/6).

4221	10l. Type **502**	25	40
4222	16r. Common Mormon (*Papilio polytes*).........	3·00	3·25
4223	18r. Common Jay (*Graphium dosun*)...............	3·25	3·50
4224	20r. Common Tiger (*Danaus genutia*).............	3·50	3·75
4221/24	*Set of 4*	9·00	10·00

MS4225 176×75 mm.12r.×4 Small Salmon Arab (*Colotis amata*); Lemon Pansy (*Junonia lemonias*); Tamil Yeoman (*Cirrochroa thais*); Dark Blue Tiger (*Tirumala septentrionis*) (all horiz)............................... 8·00   8·50

MS4226 100×70 mm.15r.×2 Common Jezebel (*Delias eucharis*); Common Gull (*Cepora nerissa*) .... 6·00   6·50

2009 (21 Oct). Whales. T **503** and similar multicoloured designs. Litho. P 12½ (4227/30) or 12 (**MS**4231).

4227	10l. Type **503**	25	40
4228	12r. Hector's Beaked Whale (*Mesoplodon hectori*).......................................	2·75	2·75
4229	16r. Beaked Whale (*Mesoplodon layardii*).......	3·25	3·50
4230	18r. Baird's Beaked Whale (*Berardius bairdii*)	3·50	3·75
4227/30	*Set of 4*	8·75	9·00

MS4231 150×110 mm. 12r.×6 Dwarf Sperm Whale (*Kogia sima*); Pygmy Sperm Whale (*Kogia breviceps*); Baird's Beaked Whale (*Berardius bairdii*); Sperm Whale (*Physeter catodon*); Shepherd's Beaked Whale (*Tasmacetus shepherdi*); Cuvier's Beaked Whale (*Ziphius cavirostris*) (all horiz)................................ 15·00   16·00

504 Y-5   **505** Melon-headed Whales

2009 (12 Nov). Centenary of Chinese Aviation and Aeropex 2009 Exhibition, Beijing. T **504** and similar horiz designs showing aircraft. Multicoloured. Litho. P 14.

MS4232 145×95 mm. 9r.×4 Type **504**; Y-7; Y-8; Y-12..... 6·00   6·50
MS4233 120×79 mm. 25r. MA60 (50×38 *mm*)................. 4·75   5·00

2009 (18 Nov). Endangered Species. Melon-headed Whale (*Peponocephala electra*). T **505** and similar horiz designs. Multicoloured. Litho. P 13½.

4234	8r. Type **505**	2·00	2·00
	a. Strip of 4. Nos. 4234/7...............	7·25	7·25
4235	8r. Melon-headed Whale...................	2·00	2·00
4236	8r. Four Whales.............................	2·00	2·00
4237	8r. Six whales...............................	2·00	2·00
4234/37	*Set of 4*	7·25	7·25

MS4238 112×165 mm. Nos. 4234/7, each ×2 .... 12·00   13·00

Nos. 4234/7 were printed together, *se-tenant*, as horizontal and vertical strips of four stamps in sheetlets of 16.

No. **MS**4238 contains two blocks of Nos. 4234/7 separated by an illustrated gutter.

506 *Copelandia bispora*   **507** *Apollo 11
Command Module*

2009 (18 Nov). Fungi. T **506** and similar vert designs. Multicoloured. Litho. P 11½.

MS4239 180×80 mm. 8r.×4 Type **506**; *Copelandia cyanescens*; *Psilocybe semilanceata*; *Volvariella vovvacea*........ 7·00   7·50
MS4240 120×110 mm. 8r.×6 Dark grey fungi; Two round-headed chestnut fungi; Yellow-brown fungi with prominent gills around edge of cap; White fungi with prominent gills; Dark chestnut fungi; Two bracket fungi.. 8·00   8·50

2009 (7 Oct). 40th Anniv of First Manned Landing on Moon. T **507** and similar multicoloured designs. Litho. P 13½.

MS4241 130×100 mm. 12r.×4 Type **507**; *Apollo 11*; Astronaut Neil Armstrong; *Apollo 11* Lunar Module. 7·00   7·50
MS4242 100×70 mm. 30r. Astronauts Michael Collins, Edwin E. Aldrin and Neil Armstrong (*horiz*)................. 5·50   6·00

508 *Nelumbo nucifera*   **508a** Tiger Symbol

2009 (9 Dec). Flowers. T **508** and similar horiz designs. Multicoloured. Litho. P 11½ (**MS**4243) or 11½×12 (others).

MS4243 150×110 mm. 10r.×6 Type **508**; *Rosa bracteata*; *Freycinetia cumingiana*; *Thespesia lampas*; *Plumeria champa*; *Plumeria cubensis* .... 9·00   10·00
MS4244 110×80 mm. 15r.×2 *Plumeria rubra*; *Hibiscus tilaceus*... 5·50   6·00
MS4245 110×80 mm. 15r.×2 *Lagerstroemia speciosa*; *Plumeria alba* .... 5·50   6·00

2010 (4 Jan). Chinese New Year. Year of the Tiger. Sheet 120×90 mm containing T **508a** and similar vert design. Multicoloured. Litho. P 12.

MS4245a 25r. Type **508a**; 25r. Tiger..................................... 6·00   7·00

508b Rat   **509** White-tailed Tropicbird
(*Phaethon lepturus*)

2010 (4 Jan). Chinese Lunar Calendar. 30th Anniv of Chinese Zodiac Stamps. Sheet 183×154 mm containing T **508b** and similar square designs. Multicoloured.

MS4245b 3r.×12 Type **508b**; Ox; Tiger; Rabbit; Dragon; Snake; Horse; Ram; Monkey; Rooster; Dog; Pig .... 7·00   7·00

2010 (22 June). Birds of the Maldives. T **509** and similar multicoloured designs. Litho. P 11½×12.

MS4246 170×106 mm. 8r.×6 Type **509**; Common Tern (*Sterna hirundo*); Bar-tailed Godwit (*Limosa lapponica*); Crab Plover (*Dromas ardeola*); Whimbrel (*Numenius phaeopus hudsonicus*); Black-winged Stilt (*Himantopus himantopus*)....................... 9·00   9·00
MS4247 100×70 mm. 30r. Asian Koel or Dhivel (*Eudynamys scolopacea*).. 7·00   7·00

510 *Conus abbas*   **511** Olive Ridley Turtle
                              (*Lepidochelys olivacea*)

2010 (22 June). Seashells of Maldives. T **510** and similar vert designs. Multicoloured. Litho. P 11½.

4248	10l. Type **510**	25	40
4249	12r. *Conus amadis*	1·75	1·75
4250	16r. *Conus bengalensis*	2·50	2·75
4251	18r. *Pinctada margaritifera*	3·00	3·25
4248/51	*Set of 4*	6·75	7·25

MS4252 150×100 mm. 15r.×4 *Harpa costata; Phalium fimbria; Zoila friendii friendii; Cypraeleucodon tenuidon.* P 12×11½ .... 9·00   9·50

2010 (22 June). Reptiles of the Maldives. Two sheets containing T **511** and similar horiz designs. Multicoloured. Litho. P 11½ (**MS**4253) or 11½×12 (**MS**4254).

MS4253 150×100 mm. 15r.×4 Type **511**; Good Sucker Lizard (*Calotes versicolor*); Indian Wolf Snake (*Lycodon aulicus*); Green Turtle (*Chelonia mydas*) .... 8·50   9·00

MS4254 100×70 mm. 15r. Common House Gecko (*Hemidactylus frenatus*); 15r. Loggerhead Turtle (*Caretta caretta gigas*) .... 5·50   6·00

512 Lyndon B. Johnson   **513** Elvis Presley as Ross Carpenter

2010 (22 June). 50th Anniv of Election of Pres. John F. Kennedy. Two sheets, each 129×100 mm, containing T **512** and similar vert designs. Multicoloured. P 13½.

MS4255 15r.×4 Type **512**; John F. Kennedy; Election campaign leaflets; Campaign badge .... 8·00   8·50

MS4256 15r.×4 President John F. Kennedy; 1955 Pulitzer Prize medal (won for book *Profiles in Courage*); Civil Rights Act, 1964; Peace Corps emblem (established by JFK, 1961) .... 8·00   8·50

2010 (22 June). Elvis Presley in Film *Girls! Girls! Girls!*, 1962. Four sheets containing T **513** and similar vert designs. Multicoloured. Litho. P 13½.

MS4257 90×125 mm. 25r. Type **513** .... 3·25   3·25

MS4258 125×90 mm. 25r. Wearing cap and mauve and white spotted pyjamas .... 3·25   3·25

MS4259 90×125 mm. 25r. Wearing white shirt, singing .... 3·25   3·25

MS4260 125×90 mm. 25r. Poster for *Girls! Girls! Girls!* .. 3·25   3·25

514 Brownies   **515** Girl standing in Corner
                         (Aisthathe Shamha nizam) (First)

2010 (22 June). Centenary of Girlguiding. T **514** and similar multicoloured designs. Litho. P 13×13½ (**MS**4261) or 13½×13 (**MS**4262) or 11½×12 (**MS**4263).

MS4261 150×100 mm. 16r.×4 Type **514**; Two guides; Guide rock climbing; Two guides jumping for joy .... 8·00   8·50

MS4262 71×100 mm. 30r. Brownie saluting (*vert*) .... 4·50   4·75

MS4263 124×240 mm. 12r. 'girls worldwide say 100 YEARS of changing lives'. 12r. '58 YEARS OF MALDIVES' (both 34×26 *mm*) .... 6·50   6·50

(Litho)

2010 (10 Dec). Human Rights Commission of the Maldives. Prevention of Child Abuse. Winning Entries in Children's Poster Drawing Competition. Two sheets, each 179×234 mm containing T **515** and similar multicoloured designs. P 13½.

MS4264 10l. Type **515**; 20l. Girl sitting on floor, silhouettes and 'Join your hands to protect us not to abuse us!!' (Shaulann Shafeeq) (Third); 95l. Man and crying woman and boy (Sameen Moosa) (Third); 5r. Children and 'we dont bully' in speech bubbles (Zaha Mohamed Ziyad) (Second) .... 1·50   1·50

MS4265 25l. Blindfolded girl and gagged girl ('Open Your eyes! And Break our silence') (Emau Ahmed Saleem) (Third); 50l. Three silhouettes (Rishwan Naseem) (Special Prize); 1r. Child's hand and 'THIS CHILD NEEDS HOPE' (Ahmed Nafiu) (Special Prize); 2r. Boy holding drawing and 'It Shouldn't HURT to be a CHILD' (Sam'aan Abdul Raheem) (Special Prize); 3r. Family and heart (Ummu Haanee Hussain) (First); 4r. Wounded girl (Fathimath Shaufa Easa) (Second); 6r. Girl and 'Stop Child Abuse' (Hussain Hazim) (Third); 7r. Child fallen from bed (Fathimath Afaaf Bushree) (Second) (*all vert*) .... 3·25   3·50

(Litho)

2015 (1 Feb). Holiday Resorts. Horiz designs. Multicoloured. P 13.

4266	15r. Kuredu Resort	1·75	1·75
4267	15r. Vilamendhoo Island Resort and Spa	1·75	1·75
4268	15r. Meeru Island Resort and Spa	1·75	1·75
4269	15r. Komandoo Island Resort and Spa	1·75	1·75
4270	15r. Veligandu Island Resort and Spa............	1·75	1·75
4266/70	*Set of 5*..	7·75	7·75

(Litho)

2015 (26 July). 50th Anniv of Independence. Horiz designs. Multicoloured. P 13.

4271	10r. Sailing boat...	1·50	1·50
4272	10r. Dancing at Independence celebrations	1·50	1·50
4273	15r. Island resort...	2·00	2·00
4274	15r. Anglers..	2·00	2·00
4275	25r. Independence Signing Ceremony...........	3·00	3·00
4276	25r. Planting palm tree.....................................	3·00	3·00
4271/6	*Set of 6*..	11·50	11·50

APPENDIX

The following stamps have been issued in excess of postal needs.

2012

40th Anniv of Diplomatic Relations between the Maldive Islands and People's Republic of China. 40r.×6

2013

Fauna of the Indian Ocean: Starfish of the Indian Ocean. 20r.×4; Seals of the Indian Ocean. 20r.×4; Dugongs of the Indian Ocean (*Dugong dugon*). 20r.×4; Whales of the Indian Ocean. 20r.×4; Fish of the Indian Ocean. 22r.×4; Dolphins of the Indian Ocean. 22r.×4; Birds of the Indian Ocean. 22r.×4; Seashells of the Indian Ocean. 22r.×4; Turtles of the Indian Ocean. 22r.×4; WWF. White-breasted Waterhen (*Amaurornis phoenicurus*). 22r.×4

Fauna and Flora of the Maldives: Saltwater Crocodile (*Crocodylus porosus*). 20r.×4; Lizards. 20r.×4; Water Birds. 20r.×4; Protected Marine Species. 20r.×4; Fruit Bats. 20r.×4; Birds of Prey. 22r.×4; Short-eared Owl (*Asio flammeus*). 22r.×4; Orchids. 22r.×4; Fish. 22r.×4; Tropical Butterflies. 22r.×4

70th Birth Anniv of Bobby Fisher (chess player). 20r.×4

Brasiliana 2013 International Philatelic Exhibition, Rio de Janeiro. Confederations Cup, Brazil, 2013. Football Players. 20r.×4

Marilyn Monroe. 20r.×4

150th Birth Anniv of Pierre de Coubertin. 20r.×4

Birth of Prince George of Cambridge. 20r.×4

95th Birthday of Nelson Mandela. 22r.×4

Elvis Presley. 22r.×4

40th Death Anniv of Pablo Picasso. 22r.×4

85th Death Anniv of Mahatma Gandhi. 22r.×4

50th Anniv of the First Woman in Space Valentina Tereshkova. 22r.×4

Formula 1 Race Cars. 20r.×4

The History of the Automobile. 20r.×4

Rescue Boats. 20r.×4

Yuri Gagarin. 20r.×4

Steam Trains. 20r.×4

High-speed Trains. 22r.×4

Seaplanes. 22r.×4

Space Tourism. 22r.×4

Fire Engines. 22r.×4

Concorde. 22r.×4

2014

20th Death Anniv of Ayrton Senna (racing driver). 20r.×4

110th Birth Anniv of Salvador Dali. 20r.×4

Tribute to Nelson Mandela. 20r.×4

40th Death Anniv of Charles Lindbergh (aviator). 20r.×4

90th Death Anniv of Giacomo Puccini (composer). 20r.×4

125th Birth Anniv of Charlie Chaplin (actor). 22r.×4

300th Birth Anniv of Christoph Willibald Gluck (composer). 22r.x4
80th Death Anniv of Marie Curie (chemist). 22r.x4
60th Death Anniv of Frida Kahlo (painter). 22r.x4
25th Death Anniv of Bette Davis (actress). 22r.x4
Masters of Impressionism (Paintings): Edouard Manet. 20r.x4;
    Edgar Degas. 20r.x4; Camille Pissarro. 20r.x4; Berthe Morisot. 20r.
    x4; Mary Cassatt. 20r.x4; 175th Birth Anniv of Paul Cézanne. 22r.
    x4; Pierre-Auguste Renoir. 22r.x4; Claude Monet. 22r.x4; American
    Impressionists. 22r.x4; Armand Guillaumin. 22r.x4
Fauna of the Indian Ocean: Crustaceans of the Indian Ocean. 22r.x4;
    Frogs of the Indian Ocean. 22r.x4; Octopus of the Indian Ocean. 20r.
    x4; Reptiles of the Indian Ocean. 20r.x4; Sharks of the Indian Ocean.
    20r.x4; Birds of Prey of the Indian Ocean. 22r.x4; Butterflies of the
    Indian Ocean. 22r.x4; Deep Water Creatures of the Indian Ocean. 22r.
    x4; Jellyfish of the Indian Ocean. 22r.x4;
Owls of the Indian Ocean. 22r.x4
70th Death Anniv of Wassily Kandinsky. 20r.x4
20th Anniv of Channel Tunnel. 20r.x4
60th Anniv of the Marilyn Monroe-Joe Di Maggio Marriage. 20r.x4
Centenary of the beginning of the First World War. 20r.x4
20th Anniv of Red List (Endangered Species). 20r.x4
Centenary of E. Marinella, Naples. 20r.x5
60th Anniv of Elvis Presley's First Single *That's All Right/Blue Moon of
    Kentucky.* 22r.x4
60th Death Anniv of Henri Matisse. 20r.x4
70th Death Anniv of Louis Renault. 20r.x4
70th Anniv of the Battle of the Bulge during the World War II. 22r.x4
China Art. Paintings of He Xiangning. 22r.x4
Greatest Flemish Painters: Pieter Brueghel the Elder and Younger. 20r.
    x4; Hans Memling. 22r.x4; Dieric Bouts. 20r.x4; Quentin Matsys. 20r.x4;
    Peter Paul Rubens. 20r.x4; Frans Hals. 22r.x4; Sir Anthony van Dyck.
    22r.x4; Jan van Eyck. 22r.x4; Rogier van der Weyden. 22r.x4
World Cup Football, Brazil (1st issue). 15r.x6
Greatest Cricket Players. 20r.x4
Greatest Chess Players. 20r.x4
Greatest Judo Fighters. 20r.x4
Rally Racing. 20r.x4
Winter Olympic Games, Sochi, Russia. 20r.x4
Horse Racing. 22r.x4
Greatest Table Tennis Players. 22r.x4
Greatest Golf Players. 22r.x4
50th Anniv of the title of World Champion Muhammad Ali. 22r.x4
250th Anniv of the Hermitage Museum, St. Petersburg, Russia. 20r.x4
450th Birth Anniv of Galileo Galilei. 20r.x4
World Cup Football, Brazil (2nd issue). 20r.x4
50th Anniv of Martin Luther King Jr.'s Nobel Prize. 20r.x4
Tenth Anniv of Cassini, a space exploration mission to Saturn. 20r.x3
SIDS 2014. Third International Conference on Small Island Developing
    States, Samoa. 22r.x4
110th Birth Anniv of Deng Xiaoping. 22r.x4
Spain's King Felipe VI. 22r.x4
85th Anniv of round-the-world flight by the *Graf Zeppelin.* 22r.x4
17th ASEAN Games, Incheon, South Korea. 22r.x4
Mushrooms. 20r.x4
Cats. 20r.x4
Butterflies. 20r.x4
Dolphins. 20r.x4
Turtles. 20r.x4
Minerals. 22r.x4
Orchids. 22r.x4
Dogs. 22r.x4
Dinosaurs. 22r.x4
Lighthouses. 22r.x4
Birds of the Maldives: Pigeons and Fruits. 20r.x4; Water Birds and Corals.
    20r.x4; Wading Birds and Insects. 20r.x4; Songbirds. 20r.x4; Pelicans.
    20r.x4; Owls and Mushrooms. 22r.x4; Birds of Prey. 22r.x4; Seabirds
    and Shells. 22r.x4; Terns and Lighthouses. 22r.x4; Bee-eaters and
    Orchids. 22r.x4

2015

Transport History: Motorcycles. 20r.x4; Pioneers of Aviation. 20r.x4;
    Special Transport. 20r.x4; Electric Transport. 20r.x4; Sled Dogs. 20r.x4;
    Horse-drawn Transport. 22r.x4; Invention of Trains. 22r.x4; Maritime
    Timeline. 22r.x4; Spaceships. 22r.x4; Submarines. 22r.x4
World War II. 70th Anniv of the Allied Landing in Normandy. 20r.x4
175th Birth Anniv of Pyotr Ilyich Tchaikovsky. 20r.x4
Nobel Prize Winners 2014. 20r.x4
Chinese New Year. Year of the Goat. 20r.x4
World War II. 70th Anniv of the Liberation of Paris. 22r.x4
Indian Mars Orbiter Mission. 22r.x4
135th Birth Anniv of Albert Einstein. 22.r.x4
75th Birth Anniv of John Lennon. 22r.x4
80th Birthday of Sophia Loren (actress). 22r.x4
40th Birthday of Tiger Woods (golfer). 22r.x4
Fauna of Indian Subcontinent: Owls. 20r.x4; Fish. 20r.x4; Parrots. 20r.x4;
    Snow Leopards. 20r.x4; Dolphins. 20r.x4; Butterflies. 22r.x4; Turtles. 22r.
    x4; Tigers. 22r.x4; Asian Elephants. 22r.x4; Rare Monkeys. 22r.x4
Post-Impressionism 1880-1910. Paintings: Paul Gauguin. 20r.x4; Henri
    de Toulouse-Lautrec. 20r.x4; Henri Rousseau. 20r.x4; Robert Antoine
    Pinchon. 20r.x4; Paul Signac. 20r.x4; Vincent van Gogh. 22r.x4;
    Paul Cézanne. 22r.x4; Odilon Redon. 22r.x4; Emile Bernard. 22r.x4;
    Georges Lemmen. 22r.x4
70th Anniv of the end of World War II. 20r.x4
Birth Centenary of Ingrid Bergman. 20r.x4
80th Birth Anniv of Elvis Presley. 20r.x4
25th Anniv of the Liberation of Nelson Mandela. 20r.x4

85th Birth Anniv of Buzz Aldrin (astronaut). 20r.x4
The World's Strongest Chess Players. 22r.x4
Birth Centenary of Frank Sinatra. 22r.x4
Bicentenary of the Battle of Waterloo. 22r.x4
245th Birth Anniv of Ludwig van Beethoven. 22r.x4
125th Birth Anniv of Boris Pasternak. 22r.x4
World of Sport: Cricket. 20r.x4; Tennis. 20r.x4; Baseball. 20r.x4; Cycling.
    20r.x4; Formula 1 (motor racing). 20r.x4; Table Tennis. 22r.x4; Rugby.
    22r.x4; Football. 22r.x4; Water Sports. 22r.x4; Golf. 22r.x4
Rescue and Working Dogs. 20r.x4
Domestic Fauna: Cats. 20r.x4
Birds of the World: Kingfishers. 20r.x4
Beauty of Flowers: Orchids. 20r.x4
Asian Fauna: Pandas (*Ailuropoda melanoleuca*). 20r.x4
Prehistoric Fauna: Dinosaurs. 22r.x4
Killer Whales (*Orcinus orca*). 22r.x4
Birds of Prey: Eagles. 22r.x4
Birds of the World. Owls. 22r.x4
Ocean Shapes: Shells. 22r.x4
New Horizons: Mission to Pluto in 2015. 20r.x4
Heroic Age of Antarctic Exploration. Centenary of the Endurance
    Expedition. 20r.x4
MonacoPhil International Philatelic Exhibition, Monaco. 105th Birth
    Anniv of Jacques-Yves Cousteau. 20r.x4
115th Anniv of the Flight of the Glider by the Wright Brothers. 20r.x4
50th Anniv of Porsche 912. 20r.x4
Vasco Da Gama. 22r.x4
Space Pioneers. 22r.x4
Rail Transport. High-speed Trains. 22r.x4
World War I. Centenary of the Invention of Gas Mask. 22r.x4
120th Death Anniv of Louis Pasteur. 22r.x4
Conservation Projects around the Globe: Asian Elephant in Asia.
    (*Elephas maximus maximus*). 20r.x4; Dolphins in Kenya. 20r.x4;
    Brown Bear in Romania. *Ursus arctos*. 20r.x4; Pandas in China.
    Ailuropoda melanoleuca. 20r.x4; Colobus Monkey in Africa. 20r.x4;
    Seal Protection in South Africa. *Arctocephalus pusillus*. 22r.x4; Sea
    Turtles. 22r.x4; Puma and Jaguar in South America. 22r.x4 Penguins in
    Africa. *Spheniscus demersus*. 22r.x4; Great White Shark. *Carcharodon
    carcharias*. 22r.x4
Paintings: Baroque. 17th-century. 20r.x4; Dutch Golden Age.
    17th-century. 20r.x4; Impressionism. 1860s-1880s. 20r.x4; Post
    Impressionism. 1880s-1910s. 20r.x4; Cubism. 1900s-1910s. 20r.x4;
    Renaissance. C. 1400-1600. 22r.x4; Romanticism. Mid 18th-century – mid
    19th-century. 22r.x4;
Realism. Mid 19th-century. 22r.x4; Symbolism. 1880s-1900s. 22r.x4;
    Surrealism. 1920-1960s. 22r.x4
Birth of Princess Charlotte of Cambridge. 20r.x4
330th Birth Anniv of George Frideric Handel. 20r.x4
25th Anniv of the Liberation of Nelson Mandela. 20r.x4
International Year of Light and Light-based Technologies. 20r.x4
Queen Elizabeth II Longest Reigning British Monarch. 20r.x4
175th Anniv of the Penny Black. 22r.x4
155th Anniv of the Pony Express. 22r.x4
Homage to Marilyn Monroe. 22r.x4
Scouting in Maldives 1963-2015. 22r.x4
105th Birth Anniv of Mother Teresa. 22r.x4
Baa Atoll UNESCO Biosphere Reserve. 5, 10, 25, 50r.
Fish of the Maldives. 20r.x12
Birds of the Indian Ocean: Birds of Prey. 20r.x4
Birds of the Maldives: Ducks. 20r.x4
Fish of the Maldives. Sharks. 20r.x4
Birds of the Maldives. Terns. 20r.x4
Birds of the Indian Ocean. Wading Birds. 22r.x4
Birds of the Indian Ocean. Seabirds. 22r.x4
Fish of the Maldives. 22r.x4
175th Death Anniv of Niccolo Paganini. 20r.x4
150th Death Anniv of Abraham Lincoln. 20r.x4
15th Anniv of the Tragedy of the Concorde. 20r.x4
Remembering Princess Diana. 22r.x4
Athletics World Championships, Beijing, China. 22r.x4
World War II. 70th Anniv of the Bombing of Dresden. 22r.x4
European Football Championship, France (2016). 22r.x4
65th Birthday of Narendra Modi (Prime Minister of India). 22r.x4
Rotary in Sri Lanka and Maldives. 22r.x4
50th Anniv of the First Spacewalks. 22r.x4

2016

WWF. Green Humphead Parrotfish (*Bolbometapon muricatum*). 22r.x4
Tall Ships. 20r.x4
Seaplanes. 20r.x4
Nobel Prize Winners 2015. 20r.x4
Discovery of liquid salty water on Mars. 20r.x4
The Apollo Missions. 20r.x4
British Trains. 22r.x4
Lighthouses. 2015 International Year of Light. 22r.x4
Fire Engines. 22r.x4
Maldivian Red Crescent. 22r.x4

Mauritius

GREAT BRITAIN STAMPS USED IN MAURITIUS. We no longer list the Great Britain stamps with obliteration "B 53" as there is no evidence that British stamps were available from the Mauritius Post Office.

See under SEYCHELLES for stamps of Mauritius used at Victoria with "B 64" cancellations between 1861 and 1890.

A similar "B 65" cancellation was used on the island of Rodrigues, a dependency of Mauritius, from 11 December 1861 onwards.

PRICES FOR STAMPS ON COVER TO 1945	
Nos. 1/5	from × 2
Nos. 6/9	from × 3
Nos. 10/15	from × 4
Nos. 16/25	from × 5
Nos. 26/9	from × 3
Nos. 30/1	—
Nos. 32/5	from × 4
Nos. 36/44	from × 5
Nos. 46/72	from × 3
Nos. 76/82	from × 5
Nos. 83/91	from × 6
Nos. 92/100	from × 4
Nos. 101/11	from × 3
Nos. 117/24	from × 8
Nos. 127/32	from × 7
No. 133	from × 4
Nos. 134/5	from × 10
No. 136	from × 8
Nos. 137/56	from × 6
Nos. 157/63	from × 5
Nos. 164/221	from × 3
No. 222	—
Nos. 223/41	from × 3
Nos. 242/4	from × 10
Nos. 245/8	from × 3
Nos. 249/63	from × 2
Nos. E1/2	from × 10
No. E3	from × 30
No. E4	—
No. E5	from × 10
No. E6	from × 25
Nos. D1/5	from × 40
Nos. R1/3	from × 15

CROWN COLONY

Nos. 1/25 and 36/44 were printed in Mauritius.

1 ("POST OFFICE")   **2** ("POST PAID")

(Engraved on copper by J. O. Barnard)

1847 (21 Sept). Head of Queen on groundwork of diagonal and perpendicular lines. Imperf.

1	1	1d. orange-red	—	£1300000
2		2d. deep blue	—	£1500000

A single plate contained one example of each value.

It is generally agreed that fifteen examples of No. 1 have survived (including two unused) and twelve of No. 2 (including four unused). Most are now in permanent museum collections.

NOTE. Our prices for early Mauritius are for stamps in very fine condition. Exceptional copies are worth more, poorer copies considerably less.

(Engraved on copper by J. O. Barnard)

1848 (June)–**59**. Imperf.

A. Earliest impressions. Design deep, sharp and clear. Diagonal lines predominate. Thick paper (Period of use: 1d. 1853–54, 2d. 1848–49)

3	2	1d. orange-vermilion/yellowish	£70000	£18000
4		2d. indigo-blue/grey to bluish	£65000	£26000
		a. "PENOE" for "PENCE" (R. 3/1)	£130000	£45000
5		2d. deep blue/grey to bluish	£65000	£26000
		a. "PENOE" for "PENCE" (R. 3/1)	£130000	£45000

B. Early impressions. Design sharp and clear but some lines slightly weakened. Paper not so thick, grey to yellowish white or bluish (Period of use: 1d. 1853–55, 2d. 1849–54)

6	2	1d. vermilion	£35000	£7500
7		1d. orange-vermilion	£35000	£7000
8		2d. blue	£38000	£9000
		a. "PENOE" for "PENCE" (R. 3/1)	£70000	£17000
9		2d. deep blue	£45000	£9500

C. Intermediate impressions. White patches appear where design has worn. Paper yellowish white, grey or bluish, of poorish quality (Period of use: 1d and 2d. 1854–57)

10	2	1d. bright vermilion	£23000	£3000
11		1d. dull vermilion	£23000	£3000
12		1d. red	£23000	£3000
13		2d. deep blue	£30000	£4250
14		2d. blue	£24000	£3500
		a. "PENOE" for "PENCE" (R. 3/1)..from	£42000	£8000
15		2d. light blue	£24000	£3500

D. Worn impressions. Much of design worn away but some diagonal lines distinct. Paper yellowish, grey or bluish, of poorish quality (Period of use: 1d. 1857–59, 2d. 1855–58)

16	2	1d. red/yellowish or grey	£8000	£950
17		1d. red-brown/yellowish or grey	£8000	£950
18		1d. red/bluish	£7500	£900
		a. Doubly printed		
19		1d. red-brown/bluish	£7500	£900
20		2d. blue (shades)/yellowish or grey	£10000	£1700
		a. "PENOE" for "PENCE" (R. 3/1)..from	—	£3500
21		2d. grey-blue/yellowish or grey	£11000	£1600
22		2d. blue (shades)/bluish	£10000	£1600
		a. Doubly printed		

E. Latest impressions. Almost none of design showing except part of Queen's head and frame. Paper yellowish, grey or bluish, of poorish quality (Period of use: 1d. 1859, 2d. 1856–58)

23	2	1d. red	£6500	£800
24		1d. red-brown	£6500	£800
25		2d. grey-blue/bluish	£8000	£1200
		a. "PENOE" for "PENCE" (R. 3/1)	£15000	£2250

Earliest known use of the 2d. value is on 19 June 1848, but the 1d. value is not known used before 27 September 1853.

There were separate plates for the 1d. and 2d. values, each of 12 (3×4).

3   **(4)**   **5**

(Eng G. Fairman. Recess P.B.)

1858*. Surch with T **4**. Imperf.

26	3	4d. green	£1800	£450

*Although originally gazetted for use from 8 April 1854, research into the archives indicates that No. 26 was not actually issued until 1858, when the stamps were mentioned in an ordinance of 30 April. The earliest dated postmark known is 27 March 1858.

PERKINS BACON "CANCELLED". For notes on these handstamps, showing "CANCELLED" between horizontal bars forming an oval, see Catalogue Introduction.

1858–62. No value expressed. Imperf.

27	3	(4d.) green	£450	£200
28		(6d.) vermilion	65·00	£120
29		(9d.) dull magenta (1859)	£900	£225
		a. Reissued as (1d.) value (11.62)	†	£170

Prepared for use but not issued

30	3	(No value), red-brown		27·00
31		(No value), blue (H/S "CANCELLED" in oval £13000)		10·00

Use of the dull magenta as a 1d. value can be confirmed by the presence of the "B 53" cancellation which was first introduced in 1861. Remainders of Nos. 30/1, overprinted "L.P.E. 1890" in red, were perforated at the London Philatelic Exhibition and sold as souvenirs.

(Recess P.B.)

1859–61. Imperf.

32	5	6d. blue (H/S "CANCELLED" in oval £15000)	£800	55·00
33		6d. dull purple-slate (1861)	40·00	65·00
34		1s. vermilion (H/S "CANCELLED" in oval £11000)	£3250	70·00
35		1s. yellow-green (1861)	£650	£150

The 1859 printings had the colours transposed by mistake.

| | 6 | 7 | 8 |

(Engraved on copper by J. Lapirot)

1859 (Mar–Nov). Imperf.

(a) Early impressions

| 36 | 6 | 2d. deep blue | £20000 | £3750 |
| 37 | | 2d. blue | £18000 | £3250 |

(b) Intermediate prints. Lines of background, etc, partly worn away (July)

| 38 | 6 | 2d. blue | £9500 | £1400 |

(c) Worn impressions, bluish paper (Oct)

| 39 | 6 | 2d. blue | £4750 | £900 |

(d) Retouched impression (Nov)

39a	6	2d. blue	†	—
		ab. "MAURITUIS" (R. 2/4)	†	£130000
		ac. "MAURITUS" (R. 3/1)	†	£130000

Nos. 36/9a were printed from a plate of 12 (4×3).
Research by Mr A. Rudge has established the existence of an initial state of the plate, before the lines were deepened to produce the "Early impression". Only one stamp from this state has so far been identified.
The plate became worn through use, and was eventually extensively re-engraved. Only two pairs (one on cover) have been recorded from this re-touched impression. The errors made in the re-engraving of the inscriptions probably resulted in it being withdrawn from use.

(1848 plate re-engraved by R. Sherwin)

1859 (Oct). Bluish paper. Imperf.

| 40 | 7 | 2d. deep blue | £225000 | £8000 |

The 1d. plate was also re-engraved, but was not put into use. Reprints in black were made in 1877 from both 1d. and 2d. re-engraved plates. Coloured autotype illustrations were prepared from these reprints and 600 were included in the R.P.S.L. handbook on *British Africa* in 1900. Further reprints in black were made in 1911 after the plates had been presented to the R.P.S.L. and defaced.

(Lithographed by L. A. Dardenne)

1859 (12 Dec). White laid paper. Imperf.

41	8	1d. deep red	£16000	£2500
41a		1d. red	£12000	£1700
42		1d. dull vermilion	£9500	£1400
43		2d. slate-blue	£10000	£1300
43a		2d. blue	£6000	£950
44		2d. pale blue	£5500	£850
		a. Heavy retouch on neck	—	£2000
		b. Retouched below "TWO"	—	£1200

The neck retouch shows a prominent curved white line running from the base of the chignon to the nape of the neck. No. 44b shows several diagonal lines in the margin below "TWO".

| | 9 | 10 |

(Typo D.L.R.)

1860 (7 Apr)–**63**. No wmk. P 14.

46	9	1d. purple-brown	£400	42·00
47		2d. blue	£425	55·00
48		4d. rose	£425	42·00
49		6d. green (1862)	£1000	£170
50		6d. slate (1863)	£400	£110
51		9d. dull purple	£190	42·00
52		1s. buff (1862)	£400	95·00
53		1s. green (1863)	£900	£200

(Recess P.B.)

1862. Intermediate perf 14 to 16.

54	5	6d. slate	40·00	£110
		a. Imperf between (horiz pair)	£8000	
55		1s. deep green	£2750	£325

(Typo D.L.R.)

1863–72. Wmk Crown CC. P 14.

56	9	1d. purple-brown	80·00	17·00
		w. Wmk inverted	95·00	40·00
		y. Wmk inverted and reversed		
57		1d. brown	£100	13·00
58		1d. bistre (1872)	£140	17·00

59		2d. pale blue	75·00	13·00
		a. Imperf (pair)	£1800	£2000
		w. Wmk inverted	£190	38·00
		x. Wmk reversed	—	£160
		y. Wmk inverted and reversed		
60		2d. bright blue	95·00	
61		3d. deep red	£170	45·00
61a		3d. dull red	90·00	21·00
		aw. Wmk inverted	£225	55·00
62		4d. rose	95·00	3·75
		w. Wmk inverted	£275	30·00
63		6d. dull violet	£425	50·00
		w. Wmk inverted		
		x. Wmk reversed		
		y. Wmk inverted and reversed	†	£200
64		6d. yellow-green (1865)	£325	16·00
65		6d. blue-green	£250	6·50
		w. Wmk inverted	£400	55·00
		y. Wmk inverted and reversed		
66		9d. yellow-green (1872)	£190	£400
		w. Wmk inverted		
67	10	10d. maroon (1872)	£375	60·00
		w. Wmk inverted		
68	9	1s. yellow	£375	30·00
		w. Wmk inverted	£550	75·00
69		1s. blue (1866)	£130	28·00
		w. Wmk inverted	—	85·00
		x. Wmk reversed	—	£275
70		1s. orange (1872)	£300	12·00
		w. Wmk inverted	£425	70·00
		x. Wmk reversed	—	£200
		y. Wmk inverted and reversed	†	£225
71		5s. rosy mauve	£275	55·00
		w. Wmk inverted	£500	£150
72		5s. bright mauve (1865)	£325	55·00
		w. Wmk inverted	£500	£140

Most values of the above set, including the 2d. bright blue, exist imperforate, but these are from proof sheets. The 2d. pale blue imperforate (No. 59a) was issued in error.

HALF PENNY ½ d

| HALF PENNY | HALF PENNY |
| (11) | (12) |

1876.

(a) Nos. 51 and 67 surch with T 11 locally

76	9	½d. on 9d. dull purple	26·00	24·00
		a. Surch inverted	£750	
		b. Surch double	—	£2250
77	10	½d. on 10d. maroon	4·75	29·00
		y. Wmk inverted and reversed		

(b) Prepared for use, but not issued. No. 51 surch with T 12

78	9	½d. on 9d. dull purple (R.)	£3250	
		a. "PRNNY"		
		b. Black surch	£4750	

| HALF PENNY | One Penny | One Shilling |
| (13) | (14) | (15) |

1877 (Apr–Dec). Nos. 62, 67 (colour changed) and 71/2 surch T **13** by D.L.R. or T **14/15** locally.

79	10	½d. on 10d. rose	12·00	50·00
		w. Wmk inverted	£120	
80	9	1d. on 4d. rose-carmine (6 Dec)	25·00	27·00
		w. Wmk inverted	£150	£110
81		1s. on 5s. rosy mauve (6 Dec)	£350	£120
		w. Wmk inverted	£550	£200
82		1s. on 5s. bright mauve (6 Dec)	£350	£150
		w. Wmk inverted		

(New Currency. 100 cents = 1 rupee)

"CANCELLED" OVERPRINTS. Following the change of currency in 1878 various issues with face values in sterling were overprinted "CANCELLED" in serifed type and sold as remainders. The stamps involved were Nos. 51, 56/62, 65, 67/8, 71/2, 76, 78/b, 79 and 81/2. Examples of such overprints on stamps between Nos. 51 and 72 are worth about the same as the prices quoted for used, on Nos. 78/b they are worth 5% of the unused price, on No. 79 65% and on Nos. 81/2 20%.

2 CENTS 2 Rs. 50 C.
| (16) | (17) |

1878 (3 Jan). Surch as T **16** or **17** (No. 91) by De La Rue. Wmk Crown CC. P 14.

83	**10**	2c. dull rose (lower label blank)	17·00	12·00
		w. Wmk inverted	£120	80·00
84	**9**	4c. on 1d. bistre	27·00	10·00
85		8c. on 2d. blue	85·00	4·25
		w. Wmk inverted		
86		13c. on 3d. orange-red	26·00	50·00
87		17c. on 4d. rose	£190	4·50
88		25c. on 6d. slate-blue	£275	8·00
89		38c. on 9d. pale violet	50·00	£100
90		50c. on 1s. green	90·00	5·50
		w. Wmk inverted		
91		2r.50 on 5s. bright mauve	22·00	26·00
83/91 *Set of 9*			£700	£200

	18		**19**		**20**
	21		**22**		**23**
	24		**25**		**26**

(Typo D.L.R.)

1879 (Mar)–**80**. Wmk Crown CC. P 14.

92	**18**	2c. Venetian red (1.80)	55·00	27·00
93	**19**	4c. orange	65·00	3·50
		w. Wmk inverted		
94	**20**	8c. blue (1.80)	40·00	4·00
		w. Wmk inverted	—	£160
95	**21**	13c. slate (1.80)	£180	£325
96	**22**	17c. rose (1.80)	95·00	10·00
		w. Wmk inverted	—	£200
97	**23**	25c. olive-yellow	£475	18·00
98	**24**	38c. bright purple (1.80)	£200	£375
99	**25**	50c. green (1.80)	6·50	5·50
		w. Wmk inverted		£160
100	**26**	2r.50 brown-purple (1.80)	55·00	80·00
92/100 *Set of 9*			£1000	£750

27

(Typo D.L.R.)

1883–94. Wmk Crown CA. P 14.

101	**18**	1c. pale violet (1893)	2·50	45
102		2c. Venetian red	40·00	7·00
103		2c. green (1885)	4·75	60
104	**19**	4c. orange	95·00	7·00
		w. Wmk inverted		
105		4c. carmine (1885)	5·50	1·00
		w. Wmk inverted	—	£130
		x. Wmk reversed	†	£275
106	**20**	8c. blue (1891)	5·00	1·50
		w. Wmk inverted		
		x. Wmk reversed	†	£275
107	**27**	15c. chestnut (1893)	9·00	1·25
		w. Wmk inverted	—	£160
108		15c. blue (1894)	12·00	1·50
109		16c. chestnut (1885)	12·00	2·75
110	**23**	25c. olive-yellow	14·00	4·00
		w. Wmk inverted	£400	£200
111	**25**	50c. orange (1887)	45·00	20·00
		w. Wmk inverted		
101/11 *Set of 11*			£225	42·00
101s, 103s, 105s, 107s/9s, 111s Optd "SPECIMEN" *Set of 7.*			£750	

16 CENTS **16 CENTS**
(28) (28a)

1883 (26 Feb). No. 96 surch with T **28/a** locally.

112	**22**	16c. on 17c. rose (surch T **28**–14½ mm long)	£170	55·00
		a. Surch double	†	£2750
		b. Horiz pair. Nos. 112/13	£850	£750
113		16c. on 17c. rose (surch T **28**–15½ mm long)	£180	55·00
		a. Surch double	—	£3000
114		16c. on 17c. rose (surch T **28a**)	£375	£140

These stamps were surcharged using two different settings, each of which produced three horizontal rows at a time.

The length of the surcharge in the first setting (Type **28**) is either 14½ mm or 15½ mm and these exist in horizontal *se-tenant* pairs.

In Type **28** the height of the surcharge is 3.25 mm. On the second setting (Type **28a**) the type differs, especially the numerals and "S", with the surcharge measuring 15-15½ mm long and 3 mm high.

SIXTEEN CENTS **2 CENTS** **2 CENTS**
(29) (30) (31)

1883 (14 July). Surch with T **29** by D.L.R. Wmk Crown CA. P 14.

115	**22**	16c. on 17c. rose	£110	2·25
		w. Wmk inverted		

1886 (11 May). No. 98 surch with T **30** locally.

116	**24**	2c. on 38c. bright purple	£160	45·00
		a. Without bar	—	£250
		b. Surch inverted	£1200	£950
		c. Surch double	£1300	

1887 (6 July). No. 95 surch with T **31** locally.

117	**21**	2c. on 13c. slate (R.)	75·00	£120
		a. Surch inverted	£275	£300
		b. Surch double	£850	£750
		c. Surch double, one on back of stamp	£950	
		d. Surch double, both inverted	†	£1600

TWO CENTS

TWO CENTS
(32) (33)

1891 (10–16 Sept). Nos. 88, 96, 98 and 105 surch locally as T **32** (Nos. 118/19, 121) or T **33** (No. 120).

118	**19**	2c. on 4c. carmine (No. 105) (12 Sept)	2·25	1·00
		a. Surch inverted	85·00	
		b. Surch double	90·00	85·00
		c. Surch double, one inverted	90·00	85·00
119	**22**	2c. on 17c. rose (No. 96) (16 Sept)	£140	£150
		a. Surch inverted	£550	£600
		b. Surch double	£900	£900
120	**9**	2c. on 38c. on 9d. pale violet (No. 89) (16 Sept)	16·00	8·00
		a. Surch inverted	£600	
		b. Surch double	£800	£800
		c. Surch double, one inverted	£190	£200
		w. Wmk inverted	†	£400
121	**24**	2c. on 38c. bright purple (No. 98)	12·00	16·00
		a. Surch inverted	£1300	
		b. Surch double	£250	£275
		c. Surch double, one inverted	£275	£300

Minor varieties are also known with portions of the surcharge missing, due to defective printing.

ONE CENT

ONE CENT
(34) (35)

1893 (1–7 Jan). Surch with T **34** by D.L.R. or T **35** locally. Wmk Crown CA. P 14.

123	**18**	1c. on 2c. pale violet	2·50	1·50
		s. Optd "SPECIMEN"	35·00	
124	**27**	1c. on 16c. chestnut (7 Jan)	3·25	4·50
		w. Wmk inverted	85·00	

36	**37**

(Typo D.L.R.)

1895–99. Wmk Crown CA. P 14.

127	**36**	1c. dull purple and ultramarine (8.7.97)	75	1·50

128		2c. dull purple and orange (8.7.97)	8·00	50
129		3c. dull purple and deep purple	70	50
130		4c. dull purple and emerald (8.7.97) ...	5·50	50
131		6c. green and rose-red (1899)	6·50	4·00
132		18c. green and ultramarine (8.7.97)	23·00	3·50
127/32 Set of 6			40·00	9·50
127s/32s Optd "SPECIMEN" Set of 6			£150	

(Des L. Duvergé. Typo D.L.R.)

1898 (15 Apr). Diamond Jubilee. Wmk CA over Crown (sideways). P 14.

133	**37**	36c. orange and ultramarine	14·00	27·00
		s. Optd "SPECIMEN"	55·00	

6
CENTS
(38)

15
CENTS
(39)

1899 (23–28 May). Nos. 132/3 surcharged with T **38/9** locally.

134	**36**	6c. on 18c. green and ultramarine (R.)	1·75	1·00
		a. Surch inverted	£700	£300
135	**37**	15c. on 36c. orange and ultramarine (B) (28 May)	3·50	1·75
		a. Bar of surch omitted	£475	

The space between "6" and "CENTS" varies from 2½ to 4½ mm.

40. Admiral Mahé de La Bourdonnais, Governor of Mauritius, 1735–46

(Recess D.L.R.)

1899 (13 Dec). Birth Bicentenary of La Bourdonnais. Wmk Crown CC. P 14.

136	**40**	15c. ultramarine	35·00	4·75
		s. Optd "SPECIMEN"	80·00	
		w. Wmk inverted	£180	

1900. No. 109 surch with T **41** locally.

137	**27**	4c. on 16c. chestnut	17·00	27·00

4
Cents
(41)

12
CENTS
(43)

42

(Typo D.L.R.)

1900–05. Ordinary paper. Wmk Crown CC (1r.) or Crown CA (others) (sideways on 2r.50, 5r.). P 14.

138	**36**	1c. grey and black (1901)	50	10
139		2c. dull purple and bright purple (4.01)..	1·00	20
140		3c. green and carmine/yellow (1902) ..	4·25	1·25
141		4c. purple and carmine/yellow	2·75	40
		w. Wmk inverted		
142		4c. grey-green and violet (1903)	2·75	2·00
		w. Wmk inverted		
143		4c. black and carmine/blue (14.10.04).	18·00	60
		w. Wmk inverted	27·00	17·00
144		5c. dull purple and bright purple/buff (8.10.02)	12·00	£100
145		5c. dull purple and black/buff (2.03) ...	2·50	2·50
146		6c. purple and carmine/red (1902)	4·75	80
		a. Wmk sideways	£2500	£2500
		w. Wmk inverted	32·00	20·00
147		8c. green and black (16.7.02)	4·50	15·00
148		12c. grey-black and carmine (16.7.02)	3·00	2·25
149		15c. green and orange	30·00	10·00
		w. Wmk inverted		
150		15c. black and blue/blue (1905)	65·00	1·25
151		25c. green and carmine/green (1902)....	30·00	50·00
		a. Chalk-surfaced paper	6·00	28·00
152		50c. dull green and deep green/yellow (1902)	17·00	75·00
153	**42**	1r. grey-black and carmine (1902)	65·00	55·00

		w. Wmk inverted	£140	£150
154		2r.50 green and black/blue (1902)	40·00	£160
155		5r. purple and carmine/red (1902)	£110	£180
138/55 Set of 18			£350	£550
138s/55s Optd "SPECIMEN" Set of 18			£425	

Examples of Nos. 144 and 151/5 are known showing a forged Port Louis postmark dated "SP 29 10".

1902. No. 132 surch with T **43**.

156	**36**	12c. on 18c. green and ultramarine	3·50	10·00

The bar cancelling the original value seems in some cases to be one thick bar and in others two thin ones.

Postage & Revenue.
(44)

1902 (7 July). Various stamps optd with T **44** locally.

157	**36**	4c. purple and carmine/yellow (No. 141)	2·50	20
158		6c. green and rose-red (No. 131)	2·75	2·75
159		15c. green and orange (No. 149)	8·50	1·25
160	**23**	25c. olive-yellow (No. 110)	9·00	3·25
161	**25**	50c. green (No. 99)	26·00	7·50
162	**26**	2r.50 brown-purple (No. 100)	£130	£225
157/62 Set of 6			£160	£225

Nos. 157/62 were overprinted to make surplus stocks of postage stamps available for revenue (fiscal) purposes also.

1902 (22 Sept). No. 133 surch as T **43**, but with longer bar.

163	**37**	12c. on 36c. orange and ultramarine	2·50	1·25
		a. Surch inverted	£800	£475

The note below No. 156 also applies to No. 163.
Forged double surcharge errors show a straight, instead of a curved, serif to the "1" of "12".

(Typo D.L.R.)

1904–07. Ordinary paper (2c., 4c., 6c.) or chalk-surfaced paper (others). Wmk Mult Crown CA. P 14.

164	**36**	1c. grey and black (1907)	8·00	4·50
165		2c. dull and bright purple (1905)	35·00	3·00
		a. Chalk-surfaced paper	32·00	1·75
166		3c. green and carmine/yellow	21·00	13·00
167		4c. black and carmine/blue	40·00	1·50
		a. Chalk-surfaced paper	16·00	10
168		6c. purple and carmine/red	25·00	30
		a. Chalk-surfaced paper	14·00	10
171		15c. black and blue/blue (1907)	4·00	35
174		50c. green and deep green/yellow	3·00	7·00
175	**42**	1r. grey-black and carmine (1907)	50·00	60·00
164/75 Set of 8			£130	75·00

Nos. 176 to 180 are vacant.

46

47

(Typo D.L.R.)

1910 (17 Jan). Ordinary paper (1c. to 15c.) or chalk-surfaced paper (25c. to 10r.). Wmk Mult Crown CA. P 14.

181	**46**	1c. black	3·00	30
		w. Wmk inverted	†	
182		2c. brown	2·75	10
		w. Wmk inverted	†	£150
183		3c. green	3·00	10
		a. "A" of "CA" missing from wmk	†	—
		w. Wmk inverted	50·00	
184		4c. pale yellow-green and carmine	4·00	10
		w. Wmk inverted	—	75·00
		y. Wmk inverted and reversed	†	£160
185	**47**	5c. grey and carmine	3·50	3·00
186	**46**	6c. carmine-red	7·00	20
		a. Pale red	11·00	2·50
		ab. "A" of "CA" missing from wmk	†	—
187		8c. orange	3·50	2·25
188	**47**	12c. greyish slate	4·25	2·75
189	**46**	15c. blue	19·00	20
190	**47**	25c. black and red/yellow	2·00	12·00
191		50c. dull purple and black	3·75	20·00
192		1r. black/green	21·00	15·00
193		2r.50 black and red/blue	29·00	75·00
194		5r. green and red/yellow	45·00	95·00
195		10r. green and red/green	£170	£300
181/95 Set of 15			£275	£475

181s/95s Optd "SPECIMEN" *Set of 15*.................................... £375
On Nos. 185, 191, 192, 193 and 194 the value labels are as in T **48**.

48	**49**

(Typo D.L.R.)

1913–22. Die I. Ordinary paper (5c., 12c.) or chalk-surfaced paper (others). Wmk Mult Crown CA. P 14.

196	**48**	5c. grey and carmine (1913)	4·00	4·25
		a. *Slate-grey and carmine*........................	12·00	12·00
198	**49**	12c. greyish slate (1914)............................	8·50	1·00
199		25c. black and red/*yellow* (1913)	50	1·40
		a. *White back* (1914)	3·25	22·00
		aw. Wmk inverted and reversed...............	65·00	
		b. *On orange-buff* (1920).......................	35·00	60·00
		c. *On pale yellow* (1921)	35·00	40·00
		cs. Optd "SPECIMEN"	55·00	
		cw. Wmk inverted	£180	
		d. Die II. *On pale yellow* (1921)	1·25	26·00
		ds. Optd "SPECIMEN".................................	50·00	
200	**48**	50c. dull purple and black (1920)	50·00	£130
201		1r. black/*blue-green* (olive back)		
		(1917)	9·00	23·00
		a. *On emerald* (olive back) (1921)........	14·00	55·00
		b. Die II. *On emerald* (emerald back)		
		(1921)	2·25	7·50
		bs. Optd "SPECIMEN"	50·00	
202		2r.50 black and red/*blue* (1916)	45·00	75·00
203		5r. green and red/*orange-buff* (1921) .	£150	£225
		a. *On pale yellow* (1921)	£130	£170
		b. Die II. *On pale yellow* (1922)	90·00	£190
204	**49**	10r. green and red/*green* (*blue-green*		
		back) (1913)	£110	£225
		a. *On blue-green* (olive back) (1919).....	£1100	
		b. *On emerald* (olive back) (1921)	£160	£225
		c. *On emerald* (emerald back) (1921)..	90·00	£200
		d. Die II. *On emerald* (emerald back)		
		(1922)	55·00	£190
		ds. Optd "SPECIMEN".................................	70·00	

196/204d *Set of 8*.. £225 £500
196s/202s, 203as, 204s Optd "SPECIMEN" *Set of 8*........... £300

Examples of Nos. 200/4d are known showing part strikes of the forged Port Louis postmark mentioned after Nos. 138/55.

49a

(Typo D.L.R.)

1921–26. Chalk-surfaced paper (50r). Wmk Mult Script CA. P 14.

205	**46**	1c. black...	1·00	1·00
		w. Wmk inverted.......................................	45·00	55·00
206		2c. brown...	1·00	10
		w. Wmk inverted.......................................	28·00	38·00
207		2c. purple/*yellow* (1926)......................	4·00	2·50
		w. Wmk inverted.......................................	28·00	38·00
208		3c. green (1926)....................................	4·50	4·00
209		4c. pale olive-green and carmine........	1·50	1·75
		x. Wmk reversed	£130	
210		4c. green (1922).....................................	1·00	10
		w. Wmk inverted.......................................	£100	
		x. Wmk reversed		
211		4c. brown (1926)	6·00	3·00
212		6c. carmine	12·00	6·50
		x. Wmk reversed	95·00	
213		6c. bright mauve (1922).......................	1·25	10
214		8c. orange (1925)..................................	2·25	26·00
215		10c. grey (1922)	2·00	3·25
216		10c. carmine-red (1926).........................	12·00	9·00
217		12c. carmine-red (1922).........................	1·50	40
218		12c. grey (1926)	1·75	6·00
219		15c. blue..	5·50	6·50
		ax. Wmk reversed	£120	£120
		b. *Cobalt* (1926).....................................	1·00	25
220		20c. blue (1922)	2·00	80
221		20c. purple (1926)..................................	8·50	17·00
222	**49a**	50r. dull purple and green (1924)	£950	£2750
		s. Optd "SPECIMEN"	£400	

205/21 *Set of 17* .... 55·00 75·00

205s/21s Optd "SPECIMEN" *Set of 17*...................................... £475

Normal   Open "C" (R. 9/6 of right pane)

A	B

Two types of duty plate in the 12c. In Type B the letters of "MAURITIUS" are larger; the extremities of the downstroke and the tail of the "2" are pointed, instead of square, and the "c" is larger.

(Typo D.L.R.)

1921–34. Die II. Chalk-surfaced paper (25c. to 10r.). Wmk Mult Script CA. P 14.

223	**49**	1c. black (1926).....................................	2·25	3·00
224		2c. brown (1926)	1·25	10
225		3c. green (1926)....................................	2·75	40
226		4c. sage-green and carmine (1926) ...	3·75	30
		a. Open "C"..	80·00	
		b. Die I (1932)...	19·00	60·00
		ba. Open "C"...	£190	
226c		4c. green (Die I) (1932)........................	15·00	45
		ca. Open "C"...	£180	
227	**48**	5c. grey and carmine (1922)	1·00	10
		a. Die I (1932)...	12·00	6·00
228	**49**	6c. sepia (1927).....................................	5·50	60
229		8c. orange (1926)..................................	3·25	18·00
230		10c. carmine-red (1926).........................	4·75	20
		a. Die I (1932)...	17·00	17·00
231		12c. grey (Type A) (1922)	1·40	25·00
232		12c. carmine-red (Type A) (1922).........	65	3·50
232a		12c. pale grey (Type A) (1926)...............	7·00	24·00
		as. Optd "SPECIMEN"	50·00	
232b		12c. grey (Type B) (1934).......................	21·00	20
233		15c. Prussian blue (1926)......................	4·75	20
234		20c. purple (1926)..................................	4·75	40
235		20c. Prussian blue (Die I) (1932)	10·00	2·75
		a. Die II (1934)..	29·00	40
236		25c. black and red/*pale yellow* (1922)....	1·00	15
		a. Die I (1932)...	10·00	70·00
237	**48**	50c. dull purple and black (1921)	7·50	4·50
238		1r. black/*emerald* (1924)	7·00	1·00
		a. Die I (1932)...	28·00	65·00
239		2r.50 black and red/*blue* (1922)	20·00	18·00
240		5r. green and red/*yellow* (1924).........	50·00	£100
241	**49**	10r. green and red/*emerald* (1924)........	£160	£375

223/41 *Set of 20* £275 £475
223s/41s Optd or Perf (Nos. 226cs, 235s) "SPECIMEN"
Set of 20.. £600

3
Cents

(50)	50a Windsor Castle

1925 (25 Nov.). Nos. 210, 217 and 220 surch locally as T **50**.

242	**46**	3c. on 4c. green............................	9·00	7·00
243		10c. on 12c. carmine-red	45	1·50
244		15c. on 20c. blue............................	60	1·50

242/4 *Set of 3* .... 9·00 9·00
242s/4s Optd "SPECIMEN" *Set of 3*...................... 95·00

Diagonal line by turret (Plate 2A R. 10/1 and 10/2)   Dot to left of chapel (Plate 2B R. 8/3)   Dot by flagstaff (Plate 4 R. 8/4)

1935 (6 May). Silver Jubilee. Wmk Mult Script CA. P 13½×14.

245	**50a**	5c. ultramarine and grey	50	10
		f. Diagonal line by turret	85·00	30·00
		g. Dot to left of chapel	£140	65·00
		h. Dot by flagstaff	£160	75·00
246		12c. green and indigo	4·50	10
		f. Diagonal line by turret	£150	50·00
		g. Dot to left of chapel	£350	80·00
247		20c. brown and deep blue	5·50	20
		f. Diagonal line by turret	£225	70·00
		g. Dot to left of chapel	£325	90·00
248		1r. slate and purple	29·00	50·00
		h. Dot by flagstaff	£400	£550
245/8 *Set of 4*			35·00	50·00
245s/8s Perf "SPECIMEN" *Set of 4*			£130	

50b King George VI and Queen Elizabeth   **51**

20c. Line through sword (R. 2/2)   **20c.** Line by sceptre (R. 5/3)

(Des D.L.R. Recess B.N.)

1937 (12 May). Coronation. Wmk Mult Script CA. P 11×11½.

249	**50b**	5c. violet	40	20
250		12c. scarlet	75	2·25
251		20c. bright blue	1·75	1·00
		a. Line through sword	90·00	50·00
		b. Line by sceptre	90·00	50·00
249/51 *Set of 3*			2·50	3·00
249s/51s Perf "SPECIMEN" *Set of 3*			£110	

Similar but less pronounced examples of the "Line by sceptre" occur on R. 5/2 and R. 5/6.

3c. Sliced "S" at right (R. 2/2, 3/2, right pane)   **3c.** Split frame (R. 7/6, right pane, Key Plate 1)

4c. Damaged "S" (R. 4/4, right pane).   **10c.** Sliced "S" at top (R. 4/1, left pane and R. 8/4, right pane)

20c., 2r.50 Broken frame under "A" of "MAURITIUS" (R. 9/3 left pane, Key Plate 2)   **25c.** "IJ" flaw (R. 3/6 of right pane)

1r. Battered "A" (R. 6/1 of right pane)

(Typo D.L.R.)

1938–49. T **51** and similar types. Chalk-surfaced paper (25c. to 10r.). Wmk Mult Script CA. P 14.

252		2c. olive-grey (9.3.38)	30	10
		a. Perf 15×14 (1942)	1·00	10
253		3c. reddish purple and scarlet (27.10.38)	2·00	2·00
		a. Sliced "S" at right	85·00	85·00
		b. Split frame	£200	
		c. *Reddish lilac and red* (4.43)	5·50	4·00
		ca. Sliced "S" at right	£225	£200
254		4c. dull green (26.2.38)	7·00	2·00
		a. Open "C"	£225	£120
		b. *Deep dull green* (4.43)	2·50	2·25
		ba. Open "C"	£150	£130
		bb. Damaged "S"	£250	
255		5c. slate-lilac (23.2.38)	17·00	85
		a. *Pale lilac (shades)* (4.43)	3·25	20
		b. Perf 15×14 (1942)	60·00	10
256		10c. rose-red (9.3.38)	2·75	30
		a. Sliced "S" at top	£170	48·00
		b. *Deep reddish rose (shades)* (4.43)	2·50	20
		ba. Sliced "S" at top	£160	38·00
		c. Perf 15×14. *Pale reddish rose* (1942)	42·00	2·75
		ca. Sliced "S" at top	£700	£150
257		12c. salmon (*shades*) (26.2.38)	1·00	20
		a. Perf 15×14 (1942)	55·00	1·25
258		20c. blue (26.2.38)	1·00	10
		a. Broken frame	£1000	£300
259		25c. brown-purple (2.3.38)	22·00	20
		a. "IJ" flaw	£600	65·00
		b. Ordinary paper (1942)	9·00	10
		ba. "IJ" flaw	£300	48·00
260		1r. grey-brown (2.3.38)	45·00	3·00
		a. Battered "A"	£900	£250
		b. Ordinary paper (1942)	20·00	1·75
		ba. Battered "A"	£650	£170
		c. *Drab* (4.49)	55·00	20·00
		ca. Battered "A"	£1000	£475
261		2r.50 pale violet (2.3.38)	60·00	30·00
		a. Ordinary paper (8.4.43)	42·00	28·00
		ab. Broken frame	£1500	£800
		b. *Slate-violet* (4.48)	70·00	50·00
262		5r. olive-green (2.3.38)	55·00	45·00
		a. Ordinary paper. *Sage-green* (8.4.43)	38·00	45·00
263		10r. reddish purple (*shades*) (2.3.38)	80·00	55·00
		a. Ordinary paper (8.4.43)	17·00	48·00
252/63a *Set of 12*			£120	£110
252s/63s Perf "SPECIMEN" *Set of 12*			£425	

Less pronounced examples of the "Sliced 'S'" variety on the 3c. occur in other positions the slice on the 10c. at R.4/1 also varies considerably. The prices for the listed varieties being for pronounced examples, as illustrated. The illustration of the "Battered 'A'" on the 1r. value shows the variety as it appears on issues between 1942 and 1949. On early printings of No. 260a the top of the "A" is normal.

The broken frame on the 2r.50 (No. 261ab) differs slightly from that on the 20c. but the distorted frame above "AU" is the same.

The stamps perf 15×14 were printed by Bradbury, Wilkinson from De La Rue plates and issued only in the colony in 1942. De La Rue printings of the 2c. to 20c. in 1943–45 were on thin, whiter paper. 1942–45 printings of the 25c. to 10r. were on unsurfaced paper.

51a Houses of Parliament, London   **52** 1d. "Post Office" Mauritius and King George VI

(Des and recess D.L.R.)

1946 (20 Nov). Victory. Wmk Mult Script CA. P 13½×14.

264	**51a**	5c. lilac	10	75
265		20c. blue	20	25
264s/5s Perf "SPECIMEN" *Set of 2*			95·00	

(Recess B.W.)

1948 (22 Mar). Centenary of First British Colonial Postage Stamp. Wmk Mult Script CA. P 11½×11.

266	**52**	5c. orange and magenta	10	50
267		12c. orange and green	15	25
268	–	20c. blue and light blue	15	10
269	–	1r. blue and red-brown	80	30
266/9 *Set of 4*			1·10	1·00
266s/9s Perf "SPECIMEN" *Set of 4*			£180	

Design:—20c., 1r. As T **52** but showing 2d. "Post Office" Mauritius.

52a King George
VI and Queen
Elizabeth

52b

(Des and photo Waterlow (T **52a**). Design recess, name typo B.W.
(T **52b**))

1948 (25 Oct). Royal Silver Wedding. Wmk Mult Script CA.
270	**52a**	5c. violet	10	10
271	**52b**	10r. magenta	17·00	42·00

52c Hermes, Globe and Forms
of Transport

52d Hemispheres, Jet-powered
Vickers Viking Airliner and
Steamer

52e Hermes and Globe

52f U.P.U. Monument

(Recess Waterlow (T **52c**, **52f**). Designs recess, name typo B.W.
(T **52d/e**))

1949 (10 Oct). 75th Anniv of U.P.U. Wmk Mult Script CA.
272	**52c**	12c. carmine	50	2·50
273	**52d**	20c. deep blue	2·25	2·50
274	**52e**	35c. purple	60	1·50
275	**52f**	1r. sepia	50	20
272/5	*Set of 4*		3·50	6·00

53 Labourdonnais Sugar
Factory

54 Grand Port

55 Aloe Plant

56 Tamarind Falls

57 Rempart Mountain

58 Transporting cane

59 Mauritius Dodo and
map

60 Legend of Paul
and Virginie

61 La Bourdonnais
Statue

62 Government House,
Reduit

63 Pieter Both
Mountain

64 Timor Deer

65 Port Louis

66 Beach scene

67 Arms of Mauritius

67a Queen
Elizabeth II

(Photo Harrison)

1950 (1 July). T **53/67**. Chalk-surfaced paper. Wmk Mult Script CA.
P 13½×14½ (horiz), 14½×13½ (vert).
276	**53**	1c. bright purple	10	50
277	**54**	2c. rose-carmine	15	10
278	**55**	3c. yellow-green	60	4·25
279	**56**	4c. green	20	3·00
280	**57**	5c. blue	15	10
281	**58**	10c. scarlet	30	75
282	**59**	12c. olive-green	1·50	3·00
283	**60**	20c. ultramarine	1·00	15
284	**61**	25c. brown-purple	2·50	40
285	**62**	35c. violet	40	10
		w. Wmk inverted	†	£3250
286	**63**	50c. emerald-green	2·75	50
287	**64**	1r. sepia	9·50	10
288	**65**	2r.50 orange	23·00	20·00
289	**66**	5r. red-brown	24·00	20·00
		w. Wmk inverted	†	£3250
290	**67**	10r. dull blue	17·00	45·00
276/290	*Set of 15*		75·00	85·00

The latitude is incorrectly shown on No. 282.

(Des and eng B.W. Recess D.L.R.)

1953 (2 June). Coronation. Wmk Mult Script CA. P 13½×13.
291	**67a**	10c. black and emerald	1·50	15

68 Tamarind Falls   **69** Historical Museum, Mahebourg

(Photo Harrison)

1953 (3 Nov)–**58**. Designs previously used for King George VI issue but with portrait of Queen Elizabeth II as in T **68/9**. Chalk-surfaced paper. Wmk Mult Script CA. P 13½×14½ (horiz) or 14½×13½ (vert).

293	**54**	2c. bright carmine (1.6.54)	10	10
294	**55**	3c. yellow-green (1.6.54)	30	40
295	**53**	4c. bright purple	10	1·00
		w. Wmk inverted	£110	
296	**57**	5c. Prussian blue (1.6.54)	10	10
297	**68**	10c. bluish green	20	10
		a. Yellowish green (9.2.55)	1·00	10
298	**69**	15c. scarlet	10	10
299	**61**	20c. brown-purple	15	20
		w. Wmk inverted	6·00	10·00
300	**60**	25c. bright ultramarine	1·50	10
		a. Bright blue (19.6 57)	7·50	75
301	**62**	35c. reddish violet	20	10
		w. Wmk inverted	£350	
302	**63**	50c. bright green	55	85
302a	**59**	60c. deep green (2.8.54)	10·00	10
		ab. Bronze-green (27.8.58)	14·00	10
303	**64**	1r. sepia	30	10
		a. Deep grey-brown (19.6.57)	4·50	65
		w. Wmk inverted	£400	
304	**65**	2r.50 orange (1.6.54)	14·00	9·00
305	**66**	5r. red-brown (1.6.54)	25·00	10·00
		a. Orange-brown (19.6.57)	60·00	16·00
306	**67**	10r. deep grey-blue (1.6.54)	14·00	2·00
293/306 Set of 15			60·00	21·00

Nos. 296 and 300 exist in coils, constructed from normal sheets.
See also Nos. 314/16.

70 Queen Elizabeth II and King George III (after Lawrence)

(Litho Enschedé)

1961 (11 Jan). 150th Anniv of British Post Office in Mauritius. W w **12**. P 13½×14.

307	**70**	10c. black and brown-red	10	10
		w. Wmk inverted	40·00	20·00
308		20c. ultramarine and light blue	30	50
		w. Wmk inverted	70·00	35·00
309		35c. black and yellow	40	50
310		1r. deep maroon and green	60	30
			£170	
307/10 Set of 4			1·25	1·25

70a Protein Foods   **70b** Red Cross Emblem

(Des M. Goaman. Photo Harrison)

1963 (4 June). Freedom from Hunger. W w **12**. P 14×14½.

311	**70a**	60c. reddish violet	40	10

(Des V. Whitely. Litho B.W.)

1963 (2 Sept). Red Cross Centenary. W w **12**. P 13½.

312	**70b**	10c. red and black	15	10
313		60c. red and blue	60	20

1963 (12 Nov)–**65**. As Nos. 297, 302ab and 304 but wmk w **12**.

314	**68**	10c. bluish green (1964)	15	10
		a. Yellowish green (21.1.65)	25	10

315	**59**	60c. bronze-green (28.5.64)	4·00	10
316	**65**	2r.50 orange	13·00	8·50
314/16 Set of 3			15·00	8·50

71 Bourbon White Eye

(Des D. M. Reid-Henry. Photo Harrison)

1965 (16 Mar). Horiz designs as T **71**. W w **12** (upright). Multicoloured; background colours given. P 14½×14.

317		2c. lemon	40	15
		a. Grey (leg) omitted	£375	
		w. Wmk inverted	18·00	
318		3c. brown	1·00	15
		a. Black (eye and beak) omitted	£450	
		w. Wmk inverted	70·00	
319		4c. light reddish purple	30	15
		a. Mauve-pink omitted*	80·00	
		b. Pale grey omitted	£350	
		c. Orange omitted	£450	
		w. Wmk inverted	8·00	7·50
320		5c. grey-brown	3·75	10
		w. Wmk inverted	£110	
321		10c. light grey-green	30	10
		w. Wmk inverted	14·00	
322		15c. pale grey	2·00	40
		a. Red (beak) omitted	£900	
		w. Wmk inverted	80·00	
323		20c. light yellow-bistre	2·00	10
		w. Wmk inverted	25·00	
324		25c. bluish grey	2·00	30
		w. Wmk inverted	11·00	
325		35c. greyish blue	3·75	10
		w. Wmk inverted	£130	
326		50c. light yellow-buff	50	40
		w. Wmk inverted	95·00	
327		60c. light greenish yellow	60	10
		w. Wmk inverted	1·50	75
328		1r. light yellow-olive	11·00	10
		a. Pale orange omitted	£325	
		b. Light grey (ground) omitted	£475	£475
329		2r.50 pale stone	5·00	9·50
330		5r. pale grey-blue	15·00	17·00
		a. Brown-red omitted	£450	£450
331		10r. pale bluish green	35·00	38·00
317/31 Set of 15			70·00	60·00

Designs:—3c. Rodriguez Fody; 4c. Mauritius Olive White Eye; 5c. Mascarene Paradise Flycatcher; 10c. Mauritius Fody; 15c. Mauritius Parakeet; 20c. Mauritius Greybird; 25c. Mauritius Kestrel; 35c. Pink Pigeon; 50c. Reunion Bulbul; 60c. Mauritius Blue Pigeon (extinct); 1r. Mauritius Dodo (extinct); 2r.50, Rodriguez Solitaire (extinct); 5r. Mauritius Red Rail (extinct); 10r. Broad-billed Parrot (extinct).

*On the 4c. the background is printed in two colours so that in No. 319a the background colour is similar to that of the 5c.

On No. 317a it is the deep grey which is missing, affecting the leg, beak and part of the branch. On No. 319c the missing orange affects the under breast of the bird, which appears much paler. On No. 328a the omission affects the legs and part of the body and on No. 330a the whole of the bird appears in the same colour as the legs.

The 50c. and 2r.50 exist with PVA gum as well as gum arabic.
Nos. 320 and 324 exist in coils, constructed from normal sheets.
See also Nos. 340/1 and 370/5.

71a I.T.U. Emblem

(Des M. Goaman. Litho Enschedé)

1965 (17 May). I.T.U. Centenary. W w **12**. P 11×11½.

332	**71a**	10c. red-orange and apple-green	20	10
333		60c. yellow and bluish violet	70	20

71b I.C.Y. Emblem

(Des V. Whiteley. Litho Harrison)

1965 (25 Oct). International Co-operation Year. W w **12**. P 14½.

334	**71b**	10c. reddish purple and turquoise-green.	15	10
335		60c. deep bluish green and lavender....	30	20

71c Sir Winston Churchill and St. Paul's Cathedral in Wartime

(Des Jennifer Toombs. Photo Harrison)

1966 (24 Jan). Churchill Commemoration. W w **12**. P 14.

336	**71c**	2c. new blue	10	3·50
		w. Wmk inverted	60·00	
337		10c. deep green	40	10
		w. Wmk inverted	45·00	
338		60c. brown	1·40	20
		w. Wmk inverted	17·00	
339		1r. bluish violet	1·50	20
336/9	Set of 4		3·00	3·50

1966–67. As Nos. 320, 325 but wmk w **12** sideways*.

340		5c. grey-brown (1966)	70	15
		w. Wmk Crown to right of CA	50·00	
341		35c. greyish blue (27.6.67)	30	15

*The normal sideways watermark shows Crown to left of CA, as seen from the back of the stamp.

No. 340 exists in coils, constructed from normal sheets.

72 "Education"

73 "Science"

74 "Culture"

(Des Jennifer Toombs. Litho Harrison)

1966 (1 Dec). 20th Anniv of U.N.E.S.C.O. W w **12** (sideways). P 14.

342	**72**	5c. slate-violet, red, yellow and orange	25	30
343	**73**	10c. orange-yellow, violet and deep olive	30	10
344	**74**	60c. black, bright purple and orange....	1·40	15
342/4	Set of 3		1·75	50

86 Red-tailed Tropic Bird

(Des D. M. Reid-Henry. Photo Harrison)

1967 (1 Sept). Self-Government. T **86** and similar horiz designs. Multicoloured. W w **12**. P 14½.

345		2c. Type **86**	25	2·75
		w. Wmk inverted	18·00	
346		10c. Rodriguez Brush Warbler	80	10
347		60c. Rose-ringed Parakeet (extinct)	85	10
348		1r. Grey-rumped Swiftlet	90	10
345/8	Set of 4		2·50	2·75

(90)

1967 (1 Dec). Self-Government. As Nos. 317/31 but wmk sideways* on Nos. 352/3 and 357. Optd with T **90**. P 14×14½.

349		2c. lemon	10	50
		w. Wmk inverted	15·00	
350		3c. brown	10	50
		w. Wmk inverted	20·00	
351		4c. light reddish purple	10	50
		a. Orange omitted	£325	
352		5c. grey-brown	10	10
353		10c. light grey-green	10	10
		w. Wmk Crown to right of CA	20·00	
354		15c. pale grey	10	30
355		20c. light yellow-bistre	15	10
		w. Wmk inverted	15·00	
356		25c. bluish grey	15	10
357		35c. greyish blue	20	10
		w. Wmk Crown to right of CA	£100	
358		50c. light yellow-buff	30	15
359		60c. light greenish yellow	30	10
		w. Wmk inverted	10·00	
360		1r. light yellow-olive	1·50	10
361		2r.50 pale stone	1·00	2·25
362		5r. pale grey-blue	6·00	3·25
363		10r. pale bluish green	10·00	15·00
349/63	Set of 15		18·00	21·00

*The normal sideways watermark shows Crown to the left of CA, as seen from the back of the stamp.

91 Flag of Mauritius **92** Arms and Mauritius Dodo Emblem

(Litho D.L.R.)

1968 (12 Mar). Independence. T **91/2**. P 13½×13.

364	**91**	2c. multicoloured	10	2·00
365	**92**	3c. multicoloured	20	2·00
366	**91**	15c. multicoloured	60	10
367	**92**	20c. multicoloured	60	10
368	**91**	60c. multicoloured	1·10	10
369	**92**	1r. multicoloured	1·10	10
364/9	Set of 6		3·25	4·00

1968 (12 July). As Nos. 317/18, 322/3 and 327/8 but background colours changed as below.

370		2c. olive-yellow	20	4·50
		a. Black printed double	£150	
		b. Grey printed double	£110	
371		3c. cobalt	1·75	8·50
		w. Wmk inverted	85·00	
372		15c. cinnamon	55	20
		a. Greenish blue omitted	£500	
373		20c. buff	3·50	4·00
374		60c. rose	1·50	1·25
		w. Wmk inverted	50·00	
375		1r. reddish purple	3·25	1·50
370/5	Set of 6		9·50	18·00

93 Dominique rescues Paul and Virginie

(Des V. Whiteley, from prints. Litho Format)

1968 (2 Dec). Bicentenary of Bernardin de St. Pierre's Visit to Mauritius. Multicoloured designs as T **93**. P 13½.

376		2c. Type **93**	10	1·25
377		15c. Paul and Virginie crossing the river	65	10
378		50c. Visit of La Bourdonnais to Madame de la Tour (horiz)	1·25	10
379		60c. Meeting of Paul and Virginie in Confidence (vert)	1·25	10
380		1r. Departure of Virginie for Europe (horiz)	1·25	20
381		2r.50 Bernardin de St. Pierre (vert)	1·75	3·75
376/81	Set of 6		5·50	5·00

99 Black-spotted Emperor

(Des J. Vinson (3c., 20c., 1r.) R. Granger Barrett (others). Photo Harrison)

1969 (12 Mar)–**73**. W w **12** (sideways* on 2, 3, 4, 5, 10, 15, 60 and 75c). Chalk-surfaced paper. P 14.

382	2c. multicoloured	10	2·75
	a. Pale green printed double**	£120	
383	3c. multicoloured	10	3·50
	w. Wmk Crown to right of CA	£150	
384	4c. multicoloured	2·50	4·50
	w. Wmk Crown to right of CA	22·00	
385	5c. multicoloured	30	10
386	10c. scarlet, black and flesh	2·00	10
	w. Wmk Crown to right of CA	27·00	
387	15c. ochre, black and cobalt	30	10
	w. Wmk Crown to right of CA	2·75	
388	20c. multicoloured	65	70
	a. Glazed ordinary paper (20.2.73)	45	13·00
389	25c. red, black and pale apple-green	30	3·75
	a. Glazed ordinary paper (22.1.71)	3·75	6·50
	aw. Wmk inverted	4·00	8·00
390	30c. multicoloured	1·50	1·75
	a. Glazed, ordinary paper (20.3.73)	8·00	18·00
391	35c. multicoloured	1·75	1·25
	a. Glazed ordinary paper (3.2.71)	1·00	3·50
	aw. Wmk inverted	2·50	
392	40c. multicoloured	35	1·25
	a. Glazed ordinary paper (20.2.73)	8·00	18·00
	aw. Wmk inverted	22·00	
393	50c. multicoloured	1·00	10
	a. Red omitted	£190	
	b. Glazed ordinary paper (22.1.71)	1·50	1·25
	ba. Red printed double		
	bw. Wmk inverted	1·50	20
394	60c. black, rose and ultramarine	1·50	10
395	75c. multicoloured	1·50	2·75
	w. Wmk Crown to right of CA	32·00	
396	1r. multicoloured	60	10
	a. Glazed ordinary paper (22.1.71)	2·25	15
	aw. Wmk inverted	95·00	
397	2r. 50 multicoloured	3·00	8·50
	a. Glazed ordinary paper (20.2.73)	2·00	18·00
398	5r. multicoloured	12·00	12·00
	a. Glazed ordinary paper (22.1.71)	12·00	3·50
	aw. Wmk inverted	55·00	
399	10r. multicoloured	2·50	4·75
	w. Wmk inverted (26.1.72)	1·50	1·50
382/99 *Set of 18*		27·00	40·00
388a/98a *Set of 9*		35·00	70·00

Designs:—3c. Red Reef Crab; 4c. Episcopal Mitre (*Mitra mitra*); 5c. Black-saddled Pufferfish ("Bourse"); 10c. Starfish; 15c. Sea Urchin; 20c. Fiddler Crab 25c. Spiny Shrimp; 30c. Single Harp Shells and Double Harp Shell; 35c. Common Paper Nautilus (*Argonauta argo*); 40c. Spanish Dancer (*Hexabranchus sanguineus*); 50c. Orange Spider Conch (*Lambis crocata*) and Violet Spider Conch (*Lambis violacea*); 60c. Blue Marlin; 75c. *Conus clytospira*; 1r. Dolphin (fish); 2r.50, Spiny Lobster; 5r. Ruby Snapper ("Sacre Chien Rouge"); 10r. Yellowedged Lyretail ("Croissant Queue Jaune").

*The normal sideways watermark shows Crown to left of CA, *as seen from the back of the stamp.*

**No. 382a occurs from a sheet on which a second printing of the pale green appears above the normal.

Nos. 385/6 and 389 exist in coils constructed from normal sheets.

This set was re-issued between 1972 and 1974 with watermark w **12** upright on 2c. to 15c., 60c. and 75c. and sideways on other values. Between 1974 and 1977 it was issued on Multiple Crown CA Diagonal watermark paper.

117 Gandhi as Law Student

(Des J. W. Litho Format)

1969 (1 July). Birth Centenary of Mahatma Gandhi. T **117** and similar vert designs. Multicoloured. W w **12**. P 13½.

400	2c. Type **117**	30	20
401	15c. Gandhi as stretcher-bearer during Zulu Revolt	65	10
402	50c. Gandhi as Satyagrahi in South Africa	80	50
403	60c. Gandhi at No. 10 Downing Street, London	80	10
404	1r. Gandhi in Mauritius, 1901	90	10
405	2r. 50 Gandhi, the "Apostle of Truth and Non-Violence"	2·00	2·00
400/5 *Set of 6*		5·00	2·75
MS406 153×153 mm. Nos. 400/5		11·00	8·00

124 Frangourinier Cane-crusher (18th-cent)

(Des V. Whiteley. Photo Enschedé)

1969 (22 Dec*). 150th Anniv of Telfair's Improvements to the Sugar Industry. T **124** and similar multicoloured designs. W w **12** (sideways on 2c. to 1r.), P 11½×11 (2r.50) or 11×11½ (others).

407	2c. Three-roller Vertical Mill	10	20
408	15c. Type **124**	10	10
409	60c. Beau Rivage Factory, 1867	10	10
410	1r. Mon Desert-Alma Factory, 1969	10	10
411	2r.50 Dr. Charles Telfair (*vert*)	25	1·25
407/11 *Set of 5*		60	1·60
MS412 159×88 mm. Nos. 407/11†. Wmk sideways. P 11×11½		1·50	2·25

*This was the local release date but the Crown Agents issued the stamps on 15 December.

†In the miniature sheet the 2r.50 is perf 11 at the top and imperf on the other three sides.

EXPO '70' OSAKA
(**128**)

129 Morne Plage, Mountain and Boeing 707

1970 (7 Apr). World Fair, Osaka. Nos. 394 and 396 optd with T **128** by Harrison & Sons.

413	60c. black, rose and ultramarine	10	10
	w. Wmk Crown to right of CA	70·00	
414	1r. multicoloured	20	20

(Des H. Rose. Litho G. Gehringer, Kaiserslautern, Germany)

1970 (2 May). Inauguration of Lufthansa Flight, Mauritius–Frankfurt. T **129** and similar multicoloured design. P 14.

415	25c. Type **129**	30	20
416	50c. Boeing 707 and Map (*vert*)	30	20

131 Lenin as a Student

133 2d. "Post Office" Mauritius and original Post Office

(Photo State Ptg Works, Moscow)

1970 (15 May). Birth Centenary of Lenin. T **131** and similar vert design. P 12×11½.

417	15c. blackish green and silver	10	10
418	75c. blackish brown and gold	20	20

Design:—75c. Lenin as Founder of U.S.S.R.

(Des and litho D.L.R.)

1970 (15 Oct). Port Louis, Old and New. T **133** and similar horiz designs. Multicoloured. W w **12** (sideways). P 14.

419	5c. Type **133**		20	10
420	15c. G.P.O. Building (built 1870)		20	10
421	50c. Mail Coach (c. 1870)		80	10
422	75c. Port Louis Harbour (1970)		95	25
423	2r.50 Arrival of Pierre A. de Suffren (1783)		1·00	2·00
419/23 *Set of 5*			2·75	2·25
MS424 165×95 mm. Nos. 419/23			4·75	8·50

138 U.N. Emblem and Symbols

(Des Jennifer Toombs. Litho Format)

1970 (24 Oct). 25th Anniv of United Nations. W w **12** (sideways). P 14½.

425	**138**	10c. multicoloured	10	10
426		60c. multicoloured	40	10

139 Rainbow over Waterfall

(Des R. Granger Barrett from local ideas (60c.), R. Granger Barrett from local ideas and adapted by N. Mossae (others). Litho Format)

1971 (12 Apr). Tourism. T **139** and similar horiz designs. Multicoloured. W w **12** (sideways*). P 14.

427	10c. Type **139**		25	10
428	15c. Trois Mamelles Mountains		25	10
	w. Wmk Crown to right of CA		18·00	
429	60c. Beach scene		35	10
430	2r.50 Marine life		50	1·50
427/30 *Set of 4*			1·25	1·50

*The normal sideways watermark shows Crown to left of CA, *as seen from the back of the stamp.*

Nos. 427/30 are inscribed on the reverse with details of tourist attractions in Mauritius.

140 "Crossroads" of Indian Ocean

(Des R. Granger Barrett (60c.) or V. Whiteley (others). Litho Harrison)

1971 (23 Oct). 25th Anniv of Plaisance Airport. T **140** and similar horiz designs. Multicoloured. W w **12** (sideways* on 15c.). P 14.

431	15c. Type **140**		45	10
	w. Wmk Crown to right of CA		32·00	
432	60c. Boeing 707 and Terminal Buildings		70	10
	w. Wmk inverted		2·75	
433	1r. Air hostesses on gangway		75	10
	w. Wmk inverted		3·25	90
434	2r.50 Farman F.190 Roland Garros airplane, Choisy Airfield, 1937		2·25	4·50
431/34 *Set of 4*			3·75	4·50

*The normal sideways watermark shows Crown to left of CA, *as seen from the back of the stamp.*

141 Princess Margaret Orthopaedic Centre

(Des and litho Harrison)

1971 (2 Nov). Third Commonwealth Medical Conference. T **141** and similar horiz design. Multicoloured. W w **12**. P 14×13½.

435	10c. Type **141**		10	10
	w. Wmk inverted		7·00	
436	75c. Operation Theatre in National Hospital		50	20

1972 (10 Jan)–**74**. As Nos. 382/99 but W w **12** upright (2, 3, 4, 5, 10, 15, 60, 75c.) or sideways* (others). Glazed, ordinary paper (2, 3, 5, 10, 15, 60, 75c.) or chalk-surfaced paper (others).

437	2c. multicoloured (20.2.73)		30	2·75
	a. Chalk-surfaced paper (13.6.74)		1·50	4·50
	aw. Wmk inverted		50·00	
438	3c. multicoloured (20.2.73)		4·25	5·50
	a. Chalk-surfaced paper (13.6.74)		40	3·50
439	4c. multicoloured (13.6.74)		9·50	11·00
440	5c. multicoloured		4·00	30
	aw. Wmk inverted		60	
	b. Chalk-surfaced paper (25.2.74)		30	10
441	10c. scarlet, black and flesh		4·25	30
	a. Chalk-surfaced paper (8.11.73)		9·00	2·00
	aw. Wmk inverted		26·00	
442	15c. ochre, black and cobalt (20.2.73)		1·00	90
	aw. Wmk inverted		50·00	
	b. Chalk-surfaced paper (25.2.74)		35	40
443	20c. multicoloured (8.11.73)		1·00	3·00
	c. Printed on the gummed side		60·00	
444	25c. red, black and apple-green (12.12.73)		35	4·00
	w. Wmk Crown to right of CA		50·00	
445	30c. multicoloured (8.11.73)		3·50	10·00
446	35c. multicoloured (8.11.73)		6·50	75
	a. Orange-brown omitted		£150	
	w. Wmk Crown to right of CA		14·00	
447	40c. multicoloured (8.11.73)		6·50	12·00
448	50c. multicoloured (12.12.73)		45	10
	a. Red omitted		£140	
	w. Wmk Crown to right of CA		38·00	30·00
449	60c. black, rose and ultramarine (20.2.73)		1·25	60
	aw. Wmk inverted		22·00	
	b. Chalk-surfaced paper (25.2.74)		65	10
	ba. Rose omitted		95·00	
450	75c. multicoloured (20.2.73)		1·75	13·00
	a. Chalk-surfaced paper (8.11.73)		3·00	1·25
451	1r. multicoloured (8.11.73)		1·25	30
452	2r.50 multicoloured (12.12.73)		2·00	4·50
453	5r. multicoloured (12.12.73)		2·00	2·00
	a. Greenish blue printed double		80·00	
	b. Greenish blue omitted		80·00	
454	10r. multicoloured (8.11.73)		5·00	8·00
437/54 *Set of 18*			42·00	55·00

*The normal sideways watermark shows Crown to left of CA, *as seen from the back of the stamp.*

Nos. 440b and 444 exist in coils, constructed from normal sheets.

142 Queen Elizabeth and Prince Philip

(Des and photo Harrison)

1972 (24 Mar). Royal Visit. T **142** and similar multicoloured design. W w **12**. P 14.

455	15c. Type **142**		15	10
456	2r.50 Queen Elizabeth II (*vert*)		2·00	2·00

143 Theatre Façade

(Des and litho Harrison)

1972 (26 June). 150th Anniversary of Port Louis Theatre. T **143** and similar horiz design. Multicoloured. W w **12**. P 14.

457	10c. Type **143**		10	10
	w. Wmk inverted		3·50	
458	1r. Theatre Auditorium		40	20
	w. Wmk inverted		7·00	

144 Pirate Dhow

(Des and litho Harrison)

1972 (17 Nov). Pirates and Privateers. T **144** and similar multicoloured designs. W w **12** (sideways on 60c. and 1r.). P 14½×14 (60c., 1r.) or 14×14½ (others).

459	15c. Type **144**	65	15
460	60c. Treasure chest (*vert*)	1·00	20
461	1r. Lemene and L'Hirondelle (*vert*)	1·25	20
462	2r.50 Robert Surcouf	4·50	8·00
459/62 *Set of 4*		6·75	8·00

145 Mauritius University   **146** Map and Hands

(Des and litho Harrison)

1973 (10 Apr). Fifth Anniv of Independence. T **145** and similar horiz designs. Multicoloured. W w **12** (sideways*). P 14.

463	15c. Type **145**	10	10
	w. Wmk Crown to right of CA	38·00	
464	60c. Tea Development	15	15
465	1r. Bank of Mauritius	15	15
463/65 *Set of 3*		30	30

*The normal sideways watermark shows Crown to left of CA, *as seen from the back of the stamp*.

(Des and litho Harrison)

1973 (25 Apr). O.C.A.M.* Conference. T **146** and similar multicoloured design. W w **12** (sideways on 10c.†). P 14½×14 (10c.) or 14×14½ (2r.50).

466	10c. O.C.A.M. emblem (*horiz*)	10	10
	w. Wmk Crown to left of CA	65·00	
467	2r.50 Type **146**	40	45

*O.C.A.M. = Organisation Commune Africaine Malgache et Mauricierme.

† The normal sideways watermark shows Crown to right of CA, *as seen from the back of the stamp.*

147 W.H.O. Emblem

(Des and litho Harrison)

1973 (20 Nov). 25th Anniv of W.H.O. W w **12**. P 14.

468	**147**	1r. multicoloured	10	10
		a. Wmk sideways	20	10

148 Meteorological Station, Vacoas

(Des and litho Harrison)

1973 (27 Nov). I.M.O./W.M.O. Centenary. W w **12** (sideways). P 14.

469	**148**	75c. multicoloured	30	70

149 Capture of the *Kent*, 1800

(Des and litho Harrison)

1974 (21 Mar). Birth Bicent of Robert Surcouf (privateer). W w **12** (sideways). P 14.

470	**149**	60c. multicoloured	50	85

150 P. Commerson   **151** Cow being Milked
(naturalist)

(Des and litho Harrison)

1974 (18 Apr). Death Bicent of Philibert Cornmerson (1973). W w **12**. P 14½.

471	**150**	2r.50 multicoloured	30	40

(Des and litho Harrison)

1974 (23 Oct). Eighth F.A.O. Regional Conference for Africa, Mauritius. W w **12** (sideways). P 14.

472	**151**	60c. multicoloured	20	20

152 Mail Train

(Des and litho Harrison)

1974 (4 Dec). Centenary of Universal Postal Union. T **152** and similar horiz design. Multicoloured. W w **12**. P 14.

473	15c. Type **152**	40	15
474	1r. New G.P.O., Port Louis	40	20

(Des and litho Harrison)

1975 (1 Jan)–**77**. As Nos. 382/99 but W w **14** (sideways* on 2 to 15c., 60c. and 75c.). Chalk-surfaced paper.

475	2c. multicoloured (16.8.77)	9·00	2·50
476	3c. multicoloured (16.8.77)	9·00	2·50
	w. Wmk Crown to right of CA	40·00	
477	4c. multicoloured (16.8.77)	10·00	3·00
478	5c. multicoloured (19.3.75)	1·50	40
	w. Wmk Crown to right of CA	7·50	
479	15c. ochre, black and cobalt (21.1.75)	2·25	1·50
	w. Wmk Crown to right of CA	9·00	
480	20c. multicoloured (19.3.76)	1·25	45
	a. Grey (background) omitted	£275	
481	25c. red, black and apple-green (19.3.75)	1·00	9·00
482	30c. multicoloured (21.1.75)	60	8·00
	a. Yellow omitted	£150	
483	35c. multicoloured (19.3.76)	1·75	15
	a. Orange-brown omitted	95·00	
484	40c. multicoloured (19.3.76)	1·00	60
485	50c. multicoloured (19.3.76)	1·00	10
	w. Wmk inverted	26·00	
486	60c. black, rose and ultramarine (16.8.77)	8·00	25
487	75c. multicoloured (19.4.77)	1·25	1·50
488	1r. multicoloured (19.3.76)	1·00	20
	a. Deep bluish green (fin and tail markings) omitted	£275	
489	2r.50 multicoloured (16.8.77)	28·00	4·00
	w. Wmk inverted	30·00	
490	5r. multicoloured (21.1.75)	4·00	16·00
	w. Wmk inverted	£100	
491	10r. multicoloured (21.1.75)	4·50	10·00
475/91 *Set of 17*		75·00	55·00

*The normal sideways watermark shows Crown to left of CA, *as seen from the back of the stamp.*

153 "Cottage Life" (F. Leroy)

(Des and litho Harrison)

1975 (6 Mar). Aspects of Mauritian Life. T **153** and similar multicoloured designs showing paintings. W w **14** (sideways* on 15c., 60c. and 2r.50). P 14.

493	15c. Type **153**	20	10
	w. Wmk Crown to right of CA	50·00	
494	60c. "Milk Seller" (A. Richard) (perf)	35	10
	a. Brown and stone (ornaments and frame) double		
495	1r. "Entrance of Port Louis Market" (Thuillier)	35	10
496	2r.50 "Washerwoman" (Max Boullee) (vert)	90	80
	w. Wmk Crown to right of CA	4·25	
493/96 Set of 4		1·60	85

*The normal sideways watermark shows Crown to left of CA, as seen from the back of the stamp.

154 Mace across Map

(Des Harrison. Litho Questa)

1975 (21 Nov). French-speaking Parliamentary Assemblies Conference. Port Louis. W w **14** (sideways). P 14.

497	**154**	75c. multicoloured	30	1·25

155 Woman with Lamp ("The Light of the World")

(Des A. H. Abdoolah; adapted Harrison. Litho Questa)

1975 (5 Dec). International Women's Year. W w **14** (sideways). P 14½.

498	**155**	2r.50 multicoloured	35	2·00

156 Parched Landscape

(Des Harrison (50c.), J.W. Ltd (60c.) Litho Questa)

1976 (26 Feb). Drought in Africa. T **156** and similar design. Multicoloured. W w **14** (sideways on 50c.). P 14.

499	50c. Type **156**	15	30
500	60c. Map of Africa and carcass (vert)	15	30

157 Pierre Loti, 1953–70

(Des J. W. Litho Questa)

1976 (2 July). Mail Carriers to Mauritius. T **157** and similar horiz designs. Multicoloured. W w **14** (sideways*). P 14½×14.

501	10c. Type **157**	70	10
502	15c. Secunder, 1907	95	10
	w. Wmk Crown to right of CA	50·00	
503	50c. Hindoostan, 1842	1·60	15
504	60c. St. Geran, 1740	1·75	15

505	2r.50 Maën, 1638	4·00	7·50
501/5 Set of 5		8·00	7·50
MS506 115×138 mm. Nos. 501/5		10·00	13·00

*The normal sideways watermark shows Crown to left of CA, as seen from the back of the stamp.

158 "The Flame of Hindi carried across the Seas"

(Des N. Nagalingum (Type **158**), C. R. Prakashi and R. B. Kailash (1r.20); adapted J. W. Litho Questa)

1976 (28 Aug). Second World Hindi Convention. T **158** and similar horiz design. Multicoloured. W w **14** (sideways). P 14.

507	10c. Type **158**	10	10
508	75c. Type **158**	10	30
509	1r.20 Hindi script	20	1·25
507/9 Set of 3		30	1·50

159 Conference Logo and Map of Mauritius

160 King Priest and Breastplate

(Des J. W. Litho Questa)

1976 (22 Sept). 22nd Commonwealth Parliamentary Association Conference. T **159** and similar vert design. Multicoloured. W w **14**. P 14.

510	1r. Type **159**	40	10
511	2r.50 Conference logo	60	2·00

(Des J. W. Litho Walsall)

1976 (15 Dec). Moenjodaro Excavations, Pakistan. T **160** and similar vert designs. Multicoloured. W w **14**. P 14.

512	60c. Type **160**	50	10
513	1r. House with well and goblet	65	10
514	2r.50 Terracotta figurine and necklace	1·75	1·00
512/14 Set of 3		2·50	1·10

161 Sega Scene

(Des BG Studio. Litho J. W.)

1977 (20 Jan). Second World Black and African Festival of Arts and Culture, Nigeria. W w **14** (sideways). P 13.

515	**161**	1r. multicoloured	30	15

162 The Queen with Sceptre and Rod

163 Hugonia tomentosa

(Des L. Curtis. Litho Harrison)

1977 (7 Feb). Silver Jubilee. T **162** and similar vert designs. Multicoloured. W w **14** (sideways). P 14½×14.

516	50c. The Queen at Mauritius Legislative Assembly, 1972...........................	15	10
517	75c. Type **162**	20	10
518	5r. Presentation of Sceptre and Rod............	55	75
516/18	Set of 3	80	75

(Des Jennifer Toombs. Litho Questa)

1977 (22 Sept). Indigenous Flowers. T **163** and similar multicoloured signs. W w **14** (sideways on 20c. and 1r.50). P 14.

519	20c. Type **163**	25	10
520	1r. *Ochna Mauritiana* (*vert*)...............	45	10
521	1r.50 *Dombeya acutangula*	60	20
522	5r. *Trochetia blackburniana* (*vert*)......	1·25	1·50
519/22	Set of 4	2·25	1·75
MS523	130×130 mm. Nos. 519/22. Wmk sideways	4·25	8·00

164 de Havilland DHC–6 Twin Otter 200/300

165 Portuguese Map of Mauritius, 1519

(Des A. Theobald. Litho Questa)

1977 (31 Oct). Inaugural International Flight of Air Mauritius. T **184** and similar horiz designs. Multicoloured. W w **14** (sideways*). P 14½×14.

524	25c. Type **184**	60	10
	w. Wmk Crown to right of CA................	3·50	
525	50c. de Havilland DHC–6 Twin Otter 200/300 and Air Mauritius emblem........	80	10
	w. Wmk Crown to right of CA................	3·75	
526	75c. Piper PA-31 Navajo and Boeing 747-100	95	20
	w. Wmk Crown to right of CA................	4·00	
527	5r. Boeing 707	3·00	3·75
	w. Wmk Crown to right of CA................	12·00	
524/7	Set of 4	4·75	3·75
MS528	110×152 mm. Nos. 524/7	9·00	9·00

*The normal sideways watermark shows Crown to left of CA, *as seen from back of the stamp.*

(Des Harrison. Litho J. W.)

1978 (12 Mar)–**86**. Designs as T **165** in light brown, chestnut and black (25r.) or multicoloured (others). W w **14** (sideways* on horiz designs). P 13½.

A. Without imprint note

529A	10c. Type **165**	50	1·50
530A	15c. Dutch Occupation, 1638–1710 (*horiz*) ...	1·50	2·75
531A	20c. Van Keulen's map, c. 1700 (*horiz*)	80	2·75
	w. Wmk Crown to left of CA..................	30·00	
532A	25c. Settlement on Rodrigues, 1691	60	2·00
	w. Wmk inverted.................................	4·50	
533A	35c. French charter, 1715..........................	30	1·50
	w. Wmk inverted.................................	15·00	
534A	50c. Construction of Port Louis, c. 1736 (*horiz*)..	50	75
535A	60c. Pierre Poivre, c. 1767........................	60	2·75
536A	70c. Benin's map, 1763 (*horiz*)...................	2·75	4·00
537A	75c. First coinage	3·00	3·00
538A	90c. Battle of Grand Port, 1810 (*horiz*)...........	4·00	4·25
539A	1r. British landing, 1810 (*horiz*)...............	60	50
540A	1r.20 Government House, c. 1840 (*horiz*)........	1·75	4·00
541A	1r.25 Lady Gomm's ball, 1847......................	1·50	40
542A	1r.50 Indian immigration, 1835 (*horiz*)............	1·00	2·75
543A	2r. Race course, c. 1870 (*horiz*)...............	60	70
	w. Wmk Crown to left of CA..................	4·25	
544A	3r. Place d'Armes, c. 1880 (*horiz*).............	60	50
545A	5r. Royal Visit postcard, 1901 (*horiz*).........	60	1·75
	w. Wmk Crown to left of CA..................	30·00	
546A	10r. Royal College, 1914 (*horiz*)................	1·50	1·00
547A	15r. Unfurling Mauritian flag, 1968................	1·50	3·00
548A	25r. First Mauritian Prime Minister and Governor-General (*horiz*)................	2·50	3·25
529A/48A	Set of 20..	24·00	35·00

B. With imprint date at foot

529B	10c. Type **165** (11.84)...........................	1·75	1·25

532B	25c. Settlement on Rodrigues, 1691 (11.84)..	1·75	40
533B	35c. French charter, 1715 (1.84)................	1·00	20
534B	50c. Construction of Port Louis, c. 1736 (*horiz*) (11.84).............	1·25	20
537B	75c. First coinage, 1794 (15.6.83)	1·75	4·25
539B	1r. British landing, 1810 (*horiz*) (4.85).......	2·50	20
541B	1r.25 Lady Gomm's ball, 1847 (15.6.83)	1·75	20
543B	2r. Race course, c. 1870 (*horiz*) (15.6.83)	1·25	40
545B	5r. Royal Visit postcard, 1901 (*horiz*) (8.6.86)...	8·50	12·00
529B/45B	Set of 9...	19·00	17·00

*The normal sideways watermark shows Crown to right of CA, *as seen from the back of the stamp.*

Imprint dates: "1983" Nos. 533B, 537B, 541B, 543B; "1985", Nos. 529B, 532B/4B, 537B, 539B, 541B, 543B, 545B.

For 35c. as No. 533B, but perforated 14½ see No. 737 and for values watermarked w **16** see Nos. 740/57.

Nos. 533B and 543B are known imperforate but it is not believed that they were issued in this form.

166 Mauritius Dodo

167 Problem of Infection, World War I

(Des Jennifer Toombs. Litho Questa)

1978 (21 Apr). 25th Anniv of Coronation. T **166** and similar vert designs. P 15.

549	3r. grey-blue black and new blue	25	45
	a. Sheetlet of 6. Nos. 549/51, each×2	1·25	2·50
550	3r. multicoloured	25	45
551	3r. grey-blue, black and new blue	25	45
549/51	Set of 3	65	1·25

Designs:—No. 549, Antelope of Bohun; 550 Queen Elizabeth II.

Nos. 549/51 were printed together in small sheets of six, containing two *se-tenant* strips of three with horizontal gutter margin between.

(Des Jennifer Toombs. Litho Enschedé)

1978 (3 Aug). 50th Anniv of Discovery of Penicillin. T **167** and similar horiz designs. W w **14** (sideways). P 13½×14.

552	20c. multicoloured	85	10
553	1r. multicoloured	1·75	75
554	1r.50 black, olive-bistre and deep bluish green	2·50	1·40
555	5r. multicoloured	3·25	6·00
552/5	Set of 4	7·50	7·00
MS556	150×90 mm. Nos. 552/5............................	10·00	12·00

Designs:—1r. First mould-growth, 1928; 1r.50, *Penicillium chrysogenum* ("notatum"); 5r. Sir Alexander Fleming.

168 *Papilio manlius* (butterfly)

169 Ornate Table

(Des G. Drummond. Litho Walsall)

1978 (21 Sept). Endangered Species. T **168** and similar horiz designs. Multicoloured. W w **14** (sideways). P 13½×14.

557	20c. Type **168**	2·00	50
558	1r. Geckos.....................................	1·00	10
559	1r.50 Greater Mascarene Flying Fox	1·25	1·00
560	5r. Mauritius Kestrel	14·00	9·50
557/60	Set of 4	16·00	10·00
MS561	154×148 mm. Nos. 557/60..........................	50·00	18·00

(Des C. Abbott. Litho Questa)

1978 (21 Dec). Bicentenary of Reconstruction of Chateau Le Réduit. T **169** and similar vert designs. Multicoloured. W w **14**. P 14½×14.

562	15c. Type **169**	10	10
563	75c. Chateau Le Réduit	10	10
564	3r. Le Réduit gardens	40	45
562/4	Set of 3	50	50

170 Whitcomb Diesel Locomotive 65 H.P., 1949

(Des G. Hutchins. Litho Questa)

1979 (1 Feb). Railway Locomotives. T **170** and similar horiz designs. Multicoloured. W w **14** (sideways). P 14½.

565	20c. Type **170**	20	10
566	1r. *Sir William*, 1922	40	10
567	1r.50 Kitson type, 1930	60	45
568	2r. Garratt type, 1927	75	85
565/8 *Set of 4*		1·60	6·00
MS569 128×128 mm. Nos. 565/8		3·25	4·50

171 Father Laval and Crucifix

172 Astronaut descending from Lunar Module

(Des J. W. Litho Questa)

1979 (30 Apr). Beatification of Father Laval (missionary). T **171** and similar multicoloured designs. W w **14** (sideways on 5r.). P 14.

570	20c. Type **171**	15	10
571	1r.50 Father Laval	40	10
572	5r. Father Laval's tomb (*horiz*)	85	1·50
570/2 *Set of 3*		1·25	1·50
MS573 150×96 mm. Nos. 570/2 (wmk upright)		2·75	3·50

(Manufactured by Walsall)

1979 (20 July). Tenth Anniv of Moon Landing. T **172** and similar vert designs. Multicoloured. Imperf×roul 5*. Self-adhesive.

574	20c. Type **172**	40	60
	a. Booklet pane. Nos. 574/6	5·50	
	b. Booklet pane. Nos. 574/5, each×3	3·00	
575	3r. Astronaut performing experiment on Moon	70	1·40
576	5r. Astronaut on Moon	5·00	8·50
574/6 *Set of 3*		5·50	9·50

*Nos. 574/6 are separated by various combinations of rotary knife (giving a straight edge) and roulette.
Nos. 574/6 were only issued in 17r.80 stamp booklets.

173 Great Britain 1855 4d. Stamp and Sir Rowland Hill

174 Young Child being Vaccinated

(Des J. W. Litho Questa)

1979 (27 Aug). Death Centenary of Sir Rowland Hill. T **173** and similar vert designs showing stamps and Sir Rowland Hill. Multicoloured. W w **14**. P 14.

577	25c. Type **173**	10	10
578	2r. 1954 60c. definitive	70	55
579	5r. 1847 1d. "POST OFFICE"	1·25	1·75
577/79 *Set of 3*		1·90	2·25
MS580 120×89 mm. 3r. 1847 2d. "POST OFFICE"		1·75	2·00

(Des V. Whiteley Studio. Litho Questa)

1979 (11 Oct). International Year of the Child. T **174** and similar designs in black, ultramarine and bright blue (1r.) or multicoloured (others). W w **14** (sideways on 15, 25c., 1r.50, and 3r.). P 14½×14.

581	15c. Type **174**	10	10
582	25c. Children playing	10	10
583	1r. I.Y.C. emblem (*vert*)	20	10
584	1r.50 Girls in chemistry laboratory	40	35
585	3r. Boy operating lathe	70	1·10
581/85 *Set of 5*		1·25	1·50

175 The Lienard Obelisk

176 *Emirne* (French steam packet)

(Des L. Curtis. Litho Questa)

1980 (24 Jan). Pamplemousses Botanical Gardens. T **175** and similar horiz designs. Multicoloured. W w **14** (sideways*). P 14×14½.

586	20c. Type **175**	15	10
587	25c. Poivre Avenue	15	10
	w. Wmk Crown to right of CA	28·00	
588	1r. Varieties of Vacoas	30	10
589	2r. Giant Water Lilies	60	60
590	5r. Mon Plaisir (mansion)	1·00	3·50
586/90 *Set of 5*		2·00	4·00
MS591 152×105 mm. Nos. 586/90		3·50	5·50

*The normal watermark shows Crown to left of CA, *as seen from the back of the stamp.*

(Des J.W. Litho Walsall)

1980 (6 May). "London 1980" International Stamp Exhibition. Mail-carrying Ships. T **176** and similar horiz designs. Multicoloured. W w **14** (sideways*). P 14½×14.

592	25c. Type **176**	35	10
	w. Wmk Crown to right of CA	11·00	
593	1r. *Boissevain* (cargo liner)	55	10
594	2r. *La Boudeuse* (Bougainville)	75	70
595	5r. *Sea Breeze* (English clipper)	1·00	2·75
592/95 *Set of 4*		2·40	3·25

*The normal sideways watermark shows Crown to left of CA, *as seen from the back of the stamp.*

177 Blind Person Basket-making

178 Prime Minister Sir Seewoosagur Ramgoolam

(Des J. W. Litho Harrison)

1980 (27 June). Birth Centenary of Helen Keller (campaigner for the handicapped). T **177** and similar vert designs. Multicoloured. W w **14**. P 14.

596	25c. Type **177**	20	10
597	1r. Deaf child under instruction	45	10
598	2r.50 Helen reading braille	70	35
599	5r. Helen at graduation, 1904	1·25	1·25
596/99 *Set of 4*		2·40	1·60

(Des Walsall. Litho and gold foil embossed Questa)

1980 (18 Sept). 80th Birthday and 40th Year in Parliament of Prime Minister Sir Seewoosagur Ramgoolam. W w **14**. P 13½.

600	**178**	15r. multicoloured	1·50	2·50

No. 600 was printed in sheets of four stamps.

179 Headquarters, Mauritius Institute

(Des BG Studio. Litho J. W.)

1980 (1 Oct). Centenary of Mauritius, Institute. T **178** and similar horiz. designs. Multicoloured. W w **14** (sideways). P 13.

601	25c. Type **179**	15	10
602	2r. Rare copy of *Veda*	50	20
603	2r.50 Glory of India Cone shell	65	25
604	5r. "Le Torrent" (painting by Harpignies)	85	1·50
601/4 *Set of 4*		2·00	1·90

180 *Hibiscus liliiflorus*

181 Beau-Basain/ Rose Hill

(Des Jennifer Toombs. Litho Questa)

1981 (15 Jan). Flowers. T **180** and similar vert designs. Multicoloured. W w **14**. P 14.

605	25c. Type **180**	20	10
606	2r. *Erythrospermum monticolum*	70	65
607	2r.50 *Chasalia boryana*	75	1·25
608	5r. *Hibiscus columnaris*	1·25	3·25
605/8 *Set of 4*		2·50	4·50

(Des L. Curtis. Litho J. W.)

1981 (10 Apr). Coats of Arms of Mauritius Towns. T **181** and similar vert designs. Multicoloured. W w **14**. P 13½×13.

609	25c. Type **181**	10	10
610	1r.50 Curepipe	30	25
611	2r. Quatre-Bornes	35	30
612	2r.50 Vacoas/Phoenix	40	50
613	5r. Port Louis	70	1·40
609/13 *Set of 5*		1·75	2·25
MS614 130×130 mm. Nos. 609/13. P 14		2·25	6·50
w. Wmk inverted		£150	

182 Prince Charles as Colonel-in-Chief, Royal Regiment of Wales

183 Emmanuel Anquetil and Guy Rosemont

(Des J. W. Litho Questa)

1981 (22 July). Royal Wedding. T **182** and similar vert designs. Multicoloured. W w **14**. P 14.

615	25c. Wedding bouquet from Mauritius	10	10
616	2r.50 Type **182**	40	15
617	10r. Prince Charles and Lady Diana Spencer	80	90
615/17 *Set of 3*		1·10	1·00

(Des G. Vasarhelyi. Litho Questa)

1981 (27 Aug). Famous Politicians and Physician (5r.). T **183** and similar horiz designs. W w **14** (sideways). P 14½.

618	20c. black and carmine	10	10
619	25c. black and lemon	10	10
620	1r.25 black and emerald	30	50
621	1r.50 black and rose-red	35	25
622	2r. black and ultramarine	45	30
623	2r.50 black and orange-brown	50	90
624	5r. black and turquoise-blue	2·00	2·75
618/24 *Set of 7*		3·50	4·25

Designs:—25c. Remy Ollier and Sookdeo Bissoondoyal; 1r.25, Maurice Curé and Barthélemy Ohsan; 1r.50, Sir Guy Forget and Renganaden Seeneevassen; 2r. Sir Abdul Razak Mohamed and Jules Koenig; 2r.50, Abdoollatiff Mahomed Osman and Dazzi Rams (Pandit Sahadeo); 5r. Sir Thomas Lewis and electrocardiogram.

184 Drummer and Piper

(Des Jennifer Toombs. Litho Format)

1981 (16 Sept). Religion and Culture. T **184** and similar multicoloured designs. W w **14** (sideways on 20c. and 5r.). P 14×13½ (20c.), 13½×14 (2r.) or 13½ (5r.).

625	20c. Type **184**	10	10
626	2r. Swami Sivananda (*vert*)	1·25	1·25
627	5r. Chinese Pagoda	1·50	3·75
625/7 *Set of 3*		2·50	4·50

The 20c. value commemorates the World Tamil Culture Conference (1980).

185 "Skills"

186 Kaaba (sacred shrine Great Mosque of Mecca)

(Des BG Studio. Litho Questa)

1981 (15 Oct). 25th Anniv of Duke of Edinburgh Award Scheme. T **185** and similar vert designs. Multicoloured. W w **14**. P 14.

628	25c. Type **185**	10	10
629	1r.25 "Service"	10	10
	w. Wmk inverted	14·00	
630	5r. "Expeditions"	30	30
631	10r. Duke of Edinburgh	50	70
628/31 *Set of 4*		80	1·00

(Des Jennifer Toombs. Litho Questa)

1981 (26 Nov). Moslem Year 1400AD. Commemoration. T **186** and similar vert designs. Multicoloured. W w **14**. P 14½×14.

632	25c. Type **186**	30	10
633	2r. Mecca	80	80
634	5r. Mecca and Kaaba	1·40	2·75
632/4 *Set of 3*		2·25	3·25

187 Scout Emblem

(Des C. Abbott. Litho Walsall)

1982 (22 Feb). 75th Anniv of Boy Scout Movement and 70th Anniv of Scouting in Mauritius. T **187** and similar horiz designs. W w **14** (sideways). P 14×14½.

635	25c. deep lilac and light green	10	10
636	2r. deep brown and brown-ochre	35	30
637	5r. deep green and yellow-olive	65	80
638	10r. deep green and new blue	1·00	1·75
635/38 *Set of 4*		1·90	2·50

Designs:—2r. Lord Baden-Powell and Baden-Powell House; 5r. Grand Howl; 10r. Ascent of Pieter Both.

188 Charles Darwin

(Des L. Curtis. Litho Questa)

1982 (19 Apr). 150th Anniv of Charles Darwin's Voyage. T **188** and similar horiz designs. Multicoloured. W w **14** (sideways). P 14.

639	25c. Type **188**	20	10
	a. Yellow (background to side panels) omitted	£700	£700
640	2r. Darwin's telescope	50	45
641	2r.50 Darwin's elephant ride	1·25	75
642	10r. H.M.S. *Beagle* beached for repairs	1·50	3·00
639/42 *Set of 4*		3·00	3·75

189 Bride and Groom at Buckingham Palace

190 Prince and Princess of Wales with Prince William

(Des Jennifer Toombs. Litho J. W.)

1982 (1 July). 21st Birthday of Princess of Wales. T **189** and similar vert designs. Multicoloured. W w **14**. P 13.

643	25c. Mauritius coat of arms	10	10
644	2r.50 Princess Diana in Chesterfield, November 1981	40	45
645	5r. Type **189**	60	90
646	10r. Formal portrait	1·75	2·50
643/46 *Set of 4*		2·50	3·50

(Des Harrison. Litho Walsall)

1982 (22 Sept). Birth of Prince William of Wales. W w **14** (sideways). P 14×14½.

647	**190**	2r.50 multicoloured	1·25	65

191 Bois Fandamane Plant

192 Arms and Flag of Mauritius

(Des Harrison. Litho Format)

1982 (15 Dec). Centenary of Robert Koch's Discovery of Tubercle Bacillus. T **191** and similar vert designs. Multicoloured. W w **14**. P 14.

648	25c. Type **191**	30	10
649	1r.25 Central market, Port Louis	60	40
650	2r. Bois Banane plant	70	75
651	5r. Platte de Lizard plant	80	2·50
652	10r. Dr. Robert Koch	1·25	4·00
648/52 *Set of 5*		3·25	7·00

(Des and litho J. W.)

1983 (14 Mar). Commonwealth Day. T **192** and similar horiz designs. Multicoloured. W w **14** (sideways). P 13.

653	25c. Type **192**	10	10
654	2r.50 Satellite view of Mauritius	20	30
655	5r. Harvesting sugar cane	30	75
656	10r. Port Louis harbour	95	1·50
653/56 *Set of 4*		1·40	2·40

193 Early Wall-mounted Telephone

194 Map of Namibia

(Des G. Vasarhelyi. Litho Format)

1983 (24 June). World Communications Year. T **193** and similar multicoloured designs. W w **14** (sideways on 1r.25 and 10r.). P 14.

657	25c. Type **193**	15	10
658	1r.25 Early telegraph apparatus (*horiz*)	45	20
659	2r. Earth satellite station	55	50
660	10r. First hot-air balloon in Mauritius, 1784 (*horiz*)	95	2·75
657/60 *Set of 4*		1·90	3·25

(Des J. W. Litho Questa)

1983 (26 Aug). Namibia Day. T **194** and similar vert designs. Multicoloured. W w **14**. P 14.

661	25c. Type **194**	60	10
662	2r.50 Hands breaking chains	1·50	75
663	5r. Family and settlement	2·00	2·25
664	10r. Diamond mining	5·50	3·75
661/64 *Set of 4*		8·75	6·00

195 Fish Trap

196 Swami Dayananda

(Des Walsall. Litho Format)

1983 (25 Sept). Fishery Resources. T **185** and similar multicoloured designs. W w **14** (sideways on 1r. and 10r.). P 14.

665	25c. Type **195**	15	10
666	1r. Fishing boat (*horiz*)	30	15
667	5r. Game fishing	55	2·50
668	10r. Octopus drying (*horiz*)	80	4·00
665/68 *Set of 4*		1·60	6·00

(Des A. Theobald. Litho Questa)

1983 (3 Nov). Death Centenary of Swami Dayananda. T **186** and similar vert designs. Multicoloured. W w **14**. P 14.

669	25c. Type **186**	15	10
670	35c. Last meeting with father	15	10
671	2r. Receiving religious instruction	60	65
672	5r. Swami demonstrating strength	90	2·75
673	10r. At a religious gathering	1·25	4·25
669/73 *Set of 5*		2·75	7·00

197 Adolf von Plevitz

(Des L. Curtis. Litho Harrison)

1983 (8 Dec). 125th Anniv of the Arrival in Mauritius of Adolf von Plevitz (social reformer). T **197** and similar horiz designs. Multicoloured. W w **14** (sideways). P 14×14½.

674	25c. Type **197**	20	10
675	1r.25 La Laura Government school	60	30
676	5r. Von Plevitz addressing 1872 Commission of Enquiry	1·40	3·00
677	10r. Von Plevitz with Indian farm workers	2·00	4·50
674/77 *Set of 4*		3·75	7·00

198 Courtship Chase

199 Wreck of S.S. *Tayeb*

(Des N. Arlott. Litho Format)

1984 (26 Mar). Mauritius Kestrel. T **188** and similar multicoloured designs. W w **14** (sideways on 25c. and 2r.50). P 14.

678	25c. Type **188**	85	30
679	2r. Kestrel in tree (*vert*)	2·00	1·25
680	2r.50 Young Kestrel	2·25	2·25
681	10r. Head (*vert*)	3·25	8·50
678/81 *Set of 4*		7·50	11·00

(Des M. Joyce. Litho Questa)

1984 (23 May). 250th Anniv of "Lloyds List" (newspaper). T **199** and similar vert designs. Multicoloured. W w **14**. P 14½×14.

682	25c. Type **199**	30	10
683	1r. S.S. *Taher*	95	15
684	5r. East Indiaman *Triton*	2·50	2·75
685	10r. M.S. *Astor*	3·00	6·50
682/85 *Set of 4*		6·00	8·50

200 Blue Latan Palm

201 Slave Girl

(Des Jennifer Toombs. Litho Format)

1984 (23 July). Palm Trees. T **200** and similar vert designs. Multicoloured. W w **14**. P 14½.

686	25c. Type **200**	10	10
687	50c. *Hyophorbe vaughanii*	20	20
688	2r.50 *Tectiphiala ferox*	1·50	1·75
689	5r. Round Island Bottle-palm	2·25	3·50
690	10r. *Hyophorbe amaricaulis*	3·50	7·00
686/90 *Set of 5*		6·75	11·00

(Des C. Abbott. Litho Walsall)

1984 (20 Aug). 150th Anniv of the Abolition of Slavery and of the Introduction of Indian Immigrants. T **201** and similar designs. W w **14** (sideways on 2r., 10r.). P 14½.

691	26c. deep rose-lilac, rose-lilac and bistre	15	10
692	1r. deep rose-lilac and bistre	70	10
693	2r. deep rose-lilac and rose-lilac	1·50	1·00
694	10r. deep rose-lilac and rose-lilac	7·00	11·00
691/94 *Set of 4*		8·50	11·00

Designs: Vert—1r. Slave market. Horiz—2r. Indian immigrant family; 10r. Arrival of Indian immigrants.

202 75th Anniversary Production of *Faust* and Leoville L'Homme

203 The Queen Mother on Clarence House Balcony, 1980

(Des Walsall. Litho Questa)

1984 (10 Sept). Centenary of Alliance Francaise (cultural organization). T **202** and similar horiz designs. Multicoloured. W w **14** (sideways). P 14½×14.

695	25c. Type **202**	20	10
696	1r.25 Prize-giving ceremony and Aunauth Beejadbur	70	50

697	5r. First headquarters and Hector Clarenc..	2·00	3·00
698	10r. Lion Mountain and Labourdonnais	2·50	5·50
695/8 *Set of 4*		4·75	8·00

(Des A. Theobald (15r.), C. Abbott (others). Litho Questa)

1986 (7 June). Life and Times of Queen Elizabeth the Queen Mother. T **203** and similar vert designs. Multicoloured. W w **16**. P 14½×14.

699	25c. The Queen Mother in 1926	60	10
700	2r. With Princess Margaret at Trooping the Colour	1·50	45
701	5r. Type **203**	1·60	1·75
702	10r. With Prince Henry at his christening (from photo by Lord Snowdon)	1·90	4·25
699/702 *Set of 4*		5·00	6·00
MS703 91×73 mm. 15r. Reopening the Stratford Canal, 1964. Wmk sideways		6·50	5·50

204 High Jumping

205 Adult and Fledgling Pink Pigeons

(Des Joan Thompson. Litho Walsall)

1985 (24 Aug). Second Indian Ocean Islands Games. T **204** and similar vert designs. Multicoloured. W w **14**. P 14½.

704	25c. Type **204**	40	10
705	50c. Javelin-throwing	70	30
706	1r.25 Cycling	5·00	2·25
707	10r. Wind surfing	8·50	15·00
704/7 *Set of 4*		13·00	16·00

(Des N. Arlott. Litho Walsall)

1985 (2 Sept). Endangered Species. Pink Pigeon. T **205** and similar vert designs. Multicoloured. W w **16**. P 14.

708	25c. Type **205**	3·75	50
709	2r. Pink Pigeon displaying at nest	9·00	2·00
710	2r.50 On nest	9·50	4·00
711	5r. Pair preening	13·00	16·00
708/11 *Set of 4*		32·00	20·00

206 Caverne Patates, Rodrigues

(Des D. Miller. Litho Walsall)

1985 (27 Sept). Tenth Anniv of World Tourism Organization T **206** and similar horiz designs. Multicoloured. W w **16** (sideways). P 14½.

712	25c. Type **206**	50	10
713	35c. Coloured soils, Chamarel	50	40
714	5r. Serpent Island	5·00	5·50
715	10r. Coin de Mire Island	7·00	11·00
712/15 *Set of 4*		11·50	15·00

207 Old Town Hall, Port Louis

(Des Jennifer Toombs. Litho J. W.)

1985 (22 Nov). 250th Anniv of Port Louis. T **207** and similar horiz designs. Multicoloured. W w **16** (sideways). P 13×13½.

716	25c. Type **207**	20	10
717	1r. Al-Aqsa Mosque (180th anniv)	1·75	10
718	2r.50 Vase and trees (250th anniv of settlement of Tamil-speaking Indians)	1·50	2·00
719	10r. Port Louis Harbour	7·50	13·00
716/19 *Set of 4*		9·75	13·50

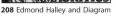

208 Edmond Halley and Diagram

208a Princess Elizabeth wearing badge of Grenadier Guards, 1942

(Des D. Hartley. Litho Walsall)

1986 (21 Feb). Appearance of Halley's Comet. T **208** and similar horiz designs. Multicoloured. W w **16** (sideways). P 14.

720	25c. Type **208**	65	10
721	1r.25 Halley's Comet (1682) and Newton's Reflector	1·50	50
722	3r. Halley's Comet passing Earth	2·00	2·25
723	10r. *Giotto* spacecraft	4·00	9·00
720/23 *Set of 4*		7·25	10·50

(Des A. Theobald. Litho Harrison)

1986 (21 Apr). 60th Birthday of Queen Elizabeth II. Multicoloured. W w **16**. P 14½×14.

724	25c. Type **208a**	15	10
725	75c. Investiture of Prince of Wales, 1969	20	10
726	2r. With Prime Minister of Mauritius, 1972	30	25
727	3r. In Germany, 1978	45	40
728	15r. At Crown Agents Head Office, London, 1983	1·25	2·00
7242/8 *Set of 5*		2·10	2·50

209 Maize (World Food Day)

210 *Cryptopus elatus*

(Des O. Bell. Litho Walsall)

1986 (25 July). International Events. T **209** and similar vert designs. Multicoloured. W w **16**. P 14.

729	25c. Type **209**	10	10
	w. Wmk inverted	29·00	
730	1r. African Regional Industrial Property Organization emblem (Tenth anniv)	30	10
731	1r.25 International Peace Year emblem	65	50
732	10r. Footballer and Mauritius Football Association emblem (World Cup Football Championship, Mexico)	4·00	10·00
729/32 *Set of 4*		4·50	10·00

(Des Harrison. Litho Walsall)

1986 (3 Oct). Orchids. T **210** and similar vert designs. Multicoloured. W w **16**. P 14½×14.

733	25c. Type **210**	50	10
734	2r. *Jumellea recta*	1·25	45
735	2r.50 *Angraecum mauritianum*	1·40	75
736	10r. *Bulbophyllum Longiorum*	2·25	5·50
733/36 *Set of 4*		5·00	6·00

1986 (1 Nov). As No. 533B but printed litho by Questa. "1986" imprint date. P 14½.

737	35c. French charter, 1715	7·00	3·75

Nos. 738/9 are vacant.

(Litho Questa)

1987 (11 Jan)–**89**. As Nos. 531/2 534, 543/5 and 548 but W w **16** (sideways on horiz designs). Imprint date. P 14½.

740	20c. Van Keulen's map, c. 1700 (*horiz*)	3·50	3·00
741	25c. Settlement on Rodriguez, 1691	3·50	1·75
743	50c. Construction of Port Louis, c. 1736 (*horiz*) (16.1.89)	3·00	1·50
752	2r. Race course, c. 1870 (*horiz*)	3·00	30
753	3r. Place d'Armes, c. 1880 (*horiz*) (18.1.89)	6·00	4·00
754	5r. Royal Visit postcard, 1901 (*horiz*) (16.1.89)	8·50	6·00

757	25r. First Mauritian Governor-General and Prime Minister (*horiz*) (16.1.89)	11·00	12·00
740/57 *Set of 7*		35·00	26·00

Imprint dates: "1987", Nos. 740/1, 752; "1989", Nos. 743, 752/3, 754, 757. Nos. 742, 744–751, 755/6 are vacant.

The watermark shows the crown to left of CA, *as seen from the back of the stamp.*

211 Hesketh Bell Bridge

(Des D. Hartley. Litho Format)

1987 (22 May). Mauritius Bridges. T **211** and similar horiz designs. Multicoloured. W w **16** (sideways). P 14½.

758	25c. Type **211**	35	10
759	50c. Sir Colville Deverell Bridge	50	20
760	2r.50 Cavendish Bridge	90	75
761	5r. Tamarin Bridge	1·10	2·00
762	10r. Grand River North West Bridge	1·25	2·50
758/62 *Set of 5*		3·75	5·00

212 Supreme Court, Port Louis

213 Dodo Mascot

(Des N. Shewring. Litho Walsall)

1987 (2 June). Bicentenary of the Mauritius Bar. T **212** and similar horiz designs. Multicoloured. W w **16** (sideways). P 14×14½.

763	25c. Type **212**	10	10
764	1r. District Court, Flacq	40	10
765	1r.25 Statue of Justice	50	20
766	10r. Barristers of 1787 and 1987	2·00	2·50
763/66 *Set of 4*		2·75	2·50

(Des O. Bell. Litho Format)

1987 (5 Sept). International Festival of the Sea. T **213** and similar multicoloured designs. W w **16** (sideways on 25c., 5r.). P 14×14½ (vert) or 14½×14 (horiz).

767	25c. Type **213**	70	20
768	1r.50 Yacht regatta (*horiz*)	2·25	1·00
769	3r. Water skiing (*horiz*)	3·25	3·75
770	5r. *Svanen* (barquentine)	3·75	8·00
767/70 *Set of 4*		9·25	11·50

214 Toys

215 Maison Ouvrière (Int Year of Shelter for the Homeless)

(Des G. Vasarhelyi. Litho Walsall)

1987 (30 Oct). Industrialisation. T **214** and similar horiz designs. Multicoloured. W w **14** (sideways). P 14.

771	20c. Type **214**	10	10
772	35c. Spinning factory	10	10
773	1r. Rattan furniture	10	10
774	2r.50 Spectacle factory	85	80
775	10r. Stone carving	2·50	3·00
771/75 *Set of 5*		3·25	3·50

(Des D. Miller. Litho Walsall)

1987 (30 Dec). Art and Architecture. T **215** and similar horiz designs. W w **16** (sideways). P 14×14½.

776	25c. multicoloured	15	10
777	1r. black and brownish grey	20	10
778	1r.25 multicoloured	45	40
779	2r. multicoloured	75	70

780	5r. multicoloured	1·50	2·75
776/80	Set of 5	2·75	3·50

Designs:—1r. "Paul et Virginie" (lithograph); 1r.25, Château de Rosnay; 9r. "Vielle" Ferme" (Boulle); 5r. "Trois Mamelles".

216 University of Mauritius

(Des A. Theobald. Litho B.D.T.)

1988 (11 Mar). 20th Anniv of Independence. T **216** and similar horiz designs Multicoloured. W w **14** (sideways). P 13½.

781	25c. Type **216**	10	10
782	75c. Anniversary gymnastic display	20	10
783	2r.50 Hurdlers and aerial view of Sir Maurice Rault Stadium	70	55
784	5r. Air Mauritius aircraft at Sir Seewoosagur Ramgoolam International Airport	1·40	1·60
785	10r. Governor-General Sir Veerasamy-Ringadoo and Prime Minister Aneerood Jugnauth	2·25	3·00
781/85	Set of 5	4·25	4·75

217 Breast Feeding | 218 Modern Bank Building

(Des D. Ashby. Litho B.D.T.)

1988 (1 July). 40th Anniv of World Health Organization. T **217** and similar vert designs. Multicoloured. W w **14**. P 13½.

786	20c. Type **217**	15	10
787	2r. Baby under vaccination umbrella and germ droplets	1·25	70
788	3r. Nutritious food	1·40	1·25
789	10r. W.H.O. logo	2·75	3·75
786/89	Set of 4	5·00	5·25

(Des N. Shewring (25r.). Litho B.D.T.)

1988 (1 Sept). 150th Anniv of Mauritius Commercial Bank Ltd. T **218** and similar multicoloured designs. W w **14** (sideways on 1, 25r.). P 13½.

790	25c. black, blue-green and new blue	10	10
791	1r. black and brown-lake	20	10
792	1r.25 multicoloured	40	30
793	25r. multicoloured	6·50	8·50
790/93	Set of 4	6·50	8·50

Designs: Horiz—1r. Mauritius Commercial Bank, 1897; 25r. 15 dollar bank note of 1838. Vert—1r.25, Bank arms.

219 Olympic Rings and Athlete

(Des P. Broadbent. Litho B.D.T.)

1988 (1 Oct). Olympic Games, Seoul. T **219** and similar horiz designs. Multicoloured. W w **14** (sideways). P 14.

794	25c. Type **219**	10	10
795	35c. Wrestling	15	15
796	1r.50 Long distance running	75	60
797	10r. Swimming	2·50	4·25
794/97	Set of 4	3·25	4·50

220 Nature Park

(Des D. Miller. Litho Harrison (40c. (No. 809), 3r., 4r. (No. 804A), 6r. (No. 806A), 10r. (to 1997)), D.L.R. (6r. (No. 806B), 10r. (from 1998)) or B.D.T. (others))

1989 (11 Mar)–**98**. Protection of the Environment. T **220** and similar multicoloured designs. P 14.

*I. W w **14** (sideways on horiz designs).*

A. Without imprint date

798A	15c. View beneath the sea (29.11.90)	40	1·50
802A	1r.50 Whimbrel (29.11.90)	1·00	1·50
803A	3r. Marine life	30	30
804A	4r. Fern Tree (vert)	40	40
805A	6r. Ecological scenery (vert)	60	50
807A	25r. Migratory birds and map (vert) (29.11.90)	2·50	3·25
798A/807A	Set of 6	4·75	6·75

B. With imprint date

798B	15c. View beneath the sea (26.7.94)	1·50	1·25
799B	20c. As 15c. (19.3.96)	1·00	2·00
800B	30c. Greenshank (15.8.95)	3·00	2·50
801B	40c. Type **220** (19.2.91)	20	60
801cB	60c. As 50c. (19.3.96)	20	1·00
804B	4r. Fern Tree (vert) (20.9.94*)	30	35
804aB	5r. Rivière du Poste estuary (26.10.98*)	40	1·00
805B	6r. Ecological scenery (vert) (29.12.98*)	45	1·25
806B	10r. Phelsuma ornata (gecko) on plant (vert)	1·00	2·00
806aB	15r. Benares waves (12.10.98*)	1·50	3·25
807B	25r. Migratory birds and map (vert) (28.4.98*)	7·00	5·50
798B/807B	Set of 11	15·00	19·00

*II. W w **16** (sideways on horiz designs)*

A. Without imprint date

808A	30c. Greenshank (29.11.90)	1·50	1·00
809A	40c. Type **220**	50	50
810A	50c. Round Island (vert) (4.10.91)	20	1·00
811A	75c. Bassin Blanc (4.10.91)	20	1·25
812A	1r. Mangrove (vert) (29.11.90)	20	10
813A	2r. Le Morne (4.10.91)	30	20
814A	5r. Riviere du Poste estuary (4.10.91)	60	50
815A	10r. Phelsuma ornata (gecko) on plant (vert)	80	70
816A	15r. Benares waves (4.10.91)	2·00	2·25
808A/16A	Set of 9	5·75	6·75

B. With imprint date

812B	1r. Mangrove (vert) (10.11.98)	30	60
817B	25r. Migratory birds and map (vert) (6.2.96)	3·00	4·00

*Local date of issue.

Imprint dates: "1991", No. 801B; "1993" No. 801B; "1994" Nos. 798B, 801B, 804B; "1995", Nos. 798B, 800B, 806B; "1996", Nos. 799B, 801cB, 817B "1997", Nos. 801B, 801cB, 806B, 817B; "1998", Nos. 804B/7B, 812B.

221 La Tour Sumeire, Port Louis | 222 Cardinal Jean

(Des A. Theobald. Litho B.D.T.)

1989 (14 July). Bicentenary of the French Revolution. T **221** and similar vert designs. W w **14**. P 14.

818	30c. black, emerald and pale greenish yellow.	15	10
819	1r. black, orange-brown and cinnamon	35	10
820	8r. multicoloured	2·50	2·75
821	15r. multicoloured	3·25	4·50
818/21	Set of 4	5·75	6·75

Designs:—1r. Salle de Spectacle du Jardin; 8r. Portrait of Comte de Malartic; 15r. Bicentenary logo.

(Des L. Curtis. Litho B.D.T.)

1989 (13 Oct). Visit of Pope John Paul II. T **222** and similar vert designs. Multicoloured. W w **14**. P 14×13½.

822	30c. Type **222**	30	10
823	40c. Pope John Paul II and Prime Minister Jugnauth, Vatican 1988	1·50	25
824	3r. Mère Marie Magdeleine de la Croix and Chapelle des Filles de Marie, Port Louis, 1864	1·50	1·25
825	6r. St. Francois d'Assise Church Pamplemousses	2·25	2·75
826	10r. Pope John Paul II	8·00	9·00
822/26 Set of 5		12·00	12·00

223 Nehru ceremonial uniform

(Des K. Clarkson. Litho B.D.T.)

1989 (14 Nov). Birth Centenary of Jawaharlal Nehru (Indian statesman). T **223** and similar horiz designs. Multicoloured. W w **16** (sideways). P 14.

827	40c. Type **223**	1·75	25
828	1r.50 Nehru with daughter, Indira, and grandsons	3·00	1·00
829	3r. Nehru and Gandhi	6·00	3·50
830	4r. Nehru with Presidents Nasser and Tito.	3·75	3·50
831	10r. Nehru with children	7·50	12·00
827/31 Set of 5		20·00	18·00

224 Cane cutting

225 Industrial Estate

(Des D. Miller. Litho B.D.T.)

1990 (10 Jan). 350th Anniv of Introduction of Sugar Cane to Mauritius. T **224** and similar horiz designs. Multicoloured. W w **16** (sideways). P 13½.

832	30c. Type **224**	15	10
833	40c. Sugar factory, 1867	20	10
834	1r. Mechanical loading of cane	40	10
835	25r. Modern sugar factory	11·00	15·00
832/35 Set of 4		11·00	15·00

(Des L. Curtis. Litho B.D.T.)

1990 (29 Mar). 60th Birthday of Prime Minister Sir Aneerood Jugnauth. T **225** and similar horiz designs. Multicoloured. W w **14** (sideways). P 13½.

836	35c. Type **225**	15	10
837	40c. Sir Aneerood Jugnauth at desk	15	10
838	1r.50 Mauritius Stock Exchange symbol	55	30
839	4r. Jugnauth with Governor-General Sir Seewoosagur Ramgoolam	1·75	2·25
840	10r. Jugnauth greeting Pope John Paul II	16·00	16·00
836/40 Set of 5		17·00	17·00

226 Desjardins (naturalist) (150th death anniv)

227 Letters from Alphabets

(Des D. Miller. Litho B.D.T.)

1990 (5 July). Anniversaries. T **226** and similar multicoloured designs. W w **14** (sideways on 35c., 8r.). P 14.

841	30c. Type **226**	30	10

842	35c. Logo on TV screen (25th anniv of Mauritius Broadcasting Corporation) (horiz)	30	10
843	6r. Line Barracks (now Police Headquarters) (250th anniv)	5·00	5·00
844	8r. Town Hall, Curepipe (centenary of municipality) (horiz)	3·50	6·00
841/44 Set of 4		8·25	10·00

(Des G. Vasarhelyi. Litho B.D.T.)

1990 (28 Sept). International Literacy Year. T **227** and similar horiz designs. Multicoloured. W w **14** (sideways). P 14.

845	30c. Type **227**	30	10
846	1r. Blind child reading Braille	2·50	15
847	3r. Open book and globe	3·50	2·25
848	10r. Book showing world map with quill pen	13·00	15·00
845/48 Set of 4		17·00	16·00

227a Queen Elizabeth II   **228** City Hall, Port Louis (25th anniv of City status)

(Des D. Miller. Litho Questa)

1991 (17 June). 65th Birthday of Queen Elizabeth II and 70th Birthday of Prince Philip. Multicoloured. W w **16** (sideways). P 14½×14.

849	8r. Type **227a**	1·75	2·75
	a. Horiz pair. Nos. 849/50 separated by label	3·50	5·50
850	8r. Prince Philip in Grenadier Guards ceremonial uniform	1·75	2·75

Nos. 849/50 were printed together, se-tenant, in sheetlets of ten (2×5) with designs alternating and the vertical rows separated by inscribed labels.

(Des G. Vasarhelyi. Litho Questa)

1991 (18 Aug). Anniversaries and Events. T **228** and similar multicoloured designs. W w **14** (sideways on 40c., 10r.). P 14.

851	40c. Type **228**	10	10
852	4r. Colonel Draper (race course founder) (150th death anniv) (vert)	1·75	2·00
853	6r. Joseph Barnard (engraver) and "POST PAID" 2d. stamp (175th birth anniv) (vert)	2·00	2·75
854	10r. Supermarine Spitfire Mauritius II (50th anniv of Second World War)	4·50	8·00
851/54 Set of 4		7·50	11·50

229 Euploea euphon   **230** Green Turtle, Tromelin

(Des I. Loe. Litho Walsall)

1991 (15 Nov). "Phila Nippon '91" International Stamp Exhibition, Tokyo. Butterflies. T **229** and similar horiz designs. W w **14** (sideways). P 14×14½.

855	40c. Type **229**	60	20
856	3r. Hypolimnas misippus (female)	1·90	1·00
857	8r. Papilo manlius	3·50	4·50
858	10r. Hypolimnas misippus (male)	3·50	4·75
855/58 Set of 4		8·50	9·50

(Des G. Vasarhelyi. Litho Walsall)

1991 (13 Dec). Indian Ocean Islands. T **230** and similar horiz designs. Multicoloured. W w **14** (sideways). P 14.

859	40c. Type **230**	50	20
860	1r. Glossy Ibis, Agalega	1·50	40
861	2r. Takamaka flowers, Chagos Archipelago	1·60	1·10
862	15r. Violet Spider Conch (Lambis violacea) sea shell, St. Brandon	7·00	12·00
859/62 Set of 4		9·50	12·50

231 Pres. Veerasamy Ringadon and President's Residence

(Des G. Vasarhelyi. Litho Walsall)

1992 (12 Mar). Proclamation of Republic. T **231** and similar horiz designs. W w **14** (sideways). P 13½×14.

863	40c. Type **231**	10	10
864	4r. Prime Minister Anerood Jugnauth and Government House	1·00	1·25
865	8r. Children and rainbow	2·25	4·50
866	10r. Presidential flag	10·00	10·00
863/66	*Set of 4*	12·00	14·00

232 Ticolo (mascot)   **233** Bouquet (25th anniv of Fleurir Maurice)

(Des G. Vasarhelyi. Litho B.D.T.)

1992 (25 June). Eighth African Athletics Championships, Port Louis. T **232** and similar multicoloured designs. W w **14** (sideways). P 13½×14.

867	40c. Type **232**	10	10
868	4r. Sir Anerood Juganauth Stadium (*horiz*)	75	1·25
869	5r. High jumping (*horiz*)	90	1·40
870	6r. Championships emblem	1·25	1·90
867/70	*Set of 4*	2·75	4·25

(Des D. Miller. Litho B.D.T.)

1992 (13 Aug). Local Events and Anniversaries. T **233** and similar multicoloured designs. W w **14** (sideways on 2, 3, 15r.). P 13½.

871	40c. Type **233**	15	10
872	1r. Swami Krishnanandji Maharaj (25th anniv of arrival)	60	10
873	2r. Boy with dog (humane education) (*horiz*)	2·00	75
874	3r. Commission Headquarters (Tenth anniv of Indian Ocean Commission) (*horiz*)	1·40	1·00
875	15r. Radio telescope antenna, Bras d'Eau (project inauguration) (*horiz*)	4·75	9·50
871/75	*Set of 5*	8·00	10·00

234 Bank of Mauritius Headquarters   **235** Housing Development

(Des D. Miller. Litho Walsall)

1992 (29 Oct). 25th Anniv of Bank of Mauritius. T **234** and similar multicoloured designs. W w **14** (sideways on horiz designs). P 14½.

876	40c. Type **234**	10	10
877	4r. Dodo gold coin (*horiz*)	2·25	1·10
878	8r. First bank note issue (*horiz*)	3·25	3·75
879	15r. Graph of foreign exchange reserves, 1967–92 (*horiz*)	5·50	9·50
876/79	*Set of 4*	10·00	13·00

(Des G. Vasarhelyi. Litho B.D.T.)

1993 (12 Mar). 25th Anniv of National Day. T **235** and similar vert designs. Multicoloured. W w **14**. P 15×14.

880	30c. Type **235**	10	10
881	40c. Gross domestic product graph on computer screen	10	10
882	3r. National colours on map of Mauritius	40	60
883	4r. Ballot box	45	75
884	15r. Grand Commander's insignia for Order of Star and Key of the Indian Ocean	2·00	5·00
880/84	*Set of 5*	2·75	6·00

236 Bell 206B Jet Ranger Helicopter

(Des N. Shewring. Litho B.D.T.)

1993 (14 June). 25th Anniv of Air Mauritius Ltd. T **236** and similar horiz designs. Multicoloured. W w **14** (sideways). P 14.

885	40c. Type **236**	1·25	30
886	3r. Boeing 747SP	1·75	1·25
887	4r. Aerospatiale/Aeritalia ATR 42	2·00	1·75
888	10r. Boeing 767-200ER	5·00	7·50
885/8	*Set of 4*	9·00	9·50
MS889	150×91 mm. Nos. 885/8	11·00	13·00

40cs ═══

(237)

1993 (15 Sept). No. 811A surch with T **237**.

890	40c. on 75c. Bassin Blanc	1·75	60

238 French Royal Charter, 1715, and Act of Capitulation, 1810   **239** Scotia (cable ship) and Map of Cable Route

(Des D. Miller. Litho B.D.T.)

1993 (16 Oct). Fifth Summit of French-speaking Nations. T **238** and similar vert designs. Multicoloured. W w **14**. P 14.

891	1r. Type **238**	90	10
892	5r. Road signs	3·00	2·50
893	6r. Code Napoleon	3·00	3·25
894	7r. Early Mauritius newspapers	3·00	3·50
891/94	*Set of 4*	9·00	8·50

(Des N. Shewring. Litho Cartor)

1993 (25 Nov). Centenary of Telecommunications. T **239** and similar horiz designs. Multicoloured. W w **14** (sideways). P 13.

895	40c. Type **239**	1·25	30
896	3r. Morse key and code	1·75	1·00
897	4r. Signal Mountain Earth station	2·00	1·75
898	8r. Communications satellite	3·25	6·50
895/98	*Set of 4*	7·50	8·50

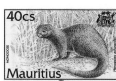

240 Indian Mongoose   **241** Dr. Edouard Brown-Sequard (physiologist) (death cent)

(Des A. Robinson. Litho Questa)

1994 (9 Mar). Mammals. T **240** and similar horiz designs. Multicoloured. W w **16** (sideways). P 14½.

899	40c. Type **240**	40	10
900	2r. Indian Black-naped Hare	1·25	40
901	8r. Pair of Crab-eating Macaque	3·25	4·00
902	10r. Adult and infant Common Tenrec	3·50	4·50
899/902 *Set of 4*		7·50	8·00

(Des N. Shewring. Litho B.D.T.)

1994 (16 June). Anniversaries and Events. T **241** and similar vert designs. Multicoloured. W w **14.** P 14.

903	40c. Type **241**	15	10
904	4r. Family in silhouette (International Year of the Family)	45	55
905	8r. World Cup and map of U.S.A. (World Cup Football Championship, U.S.A.)	1·50	2·25
906	10r. Control tower, SSR International Airport (50th anniv of Civil Aviation Organization)	1·75	2·75
903/6 *Set of 4*		3·50	5·00

242 *St. Géran* leaving L'Orient for Isle de France, 1744

(Des Jennifer Toombs. Litho Questa)

1994 (18 Aug). 250th Anniv of Wreck of *St. Géran* (sailing packet). T **242** and similar multicoloured designs. W w **16** (sideways). P 14.

907	40c. Type **242**	55	10
908	5r. In rough seas off Isle de France	1·40	80
909	6r. Bell and main mast	1·40	1·50
910	10r. Artifacts from wreck	1·90	3·75
907/10 *Set of 4*		4·75	5·50
MS911 119×89 mm. 15r. *St. Géran* leaving L'Orient (*vert*)		5·50	6·50

243 Ring-a-ring-a-roses **244** Nutmeg

(Des G. Vasarhelyi. Litho B.D.T.)

1994 (25 Oct). Children's Games and Pastimes. T **243** and similar horiz designs showing children's paintings. Multicoloured. W w **14** (sideways). P 13½.

912	30c. Type **243**	10	10
913	40c. Skipping and ball games	10	10
914	8r. Water sports	1·40	2·25
915	10r. Blind man's buff	1·40	2·25
912/15 *Set of 4*		2·75	4·25

(Des I. Loe. Litho Enschedé)

1995 (10 Mar). Spices. T **244** and similar vert designs. Multicoloured. W w **14.** P 13×14½.

916	40c. Type **244**	15	10
917	4r. Coriander	1·00	75
918	5r. Cloves	1·10	85
919	10r. Cardamom	2·00	3·00
916/19 *Set of 4*		3·75	4·25

244a H.M.S. *Mauritius* (cruiser)

(Des A. Theobald. Litho B.D.T.)

1995 (8 May). 50th Anniv of End of Second World War. Multicoloured. W w **14** (sideways). P 13½.

920	5r. Type **244a**	2·00	2·50
921	5r. Mauritian soldiers and map of North Africa	2·00	2·50
922	5r. Consolidated PBY-5 Catalina flying boat, Tombeau Bay	2·00	2·50
920/22 *Set of 3*		5·50	6·75

245 Mare Longue Reservoir **246** Ile Plate Lighthouse

(Des A. Theobald. Litho B.D.T.)

1995 (8 May). Anniversaries. T **245** and similar horiz designs. Multicoloured. W w **14** (sideways). P 13½.

923	40c. Type **245** (50th anniv of construction)	15	10
924	4r. Mahebourg to Curepipe road (bicentenary of construction)	1·25	1·40
925	10r. Buildings on fire (centenary of Great Fire of Port Louis)	2·75	4·00
923/25 *Set of 3*		3·75	5·00

(Des N. Shewring. Litho Enschedé)

1995 (28 Aug). Lighthouses. T **246** and similar vert designs. Multicoloured. W w **14.** P 13×14½.

926	30c. Type **246**	1·00	30
927	40c. Pointe aux Caves	1·00	30
928	8r. Ile aux Fouquets	3·25	4·25
929	10r. Pointe aux Canonniers	3·75	4·50
926/29 *Set of 4*		8·00	8·50
MS930 130×100 mm. Nos. 926/9		11·00	11·00

247 Symbolic Children under U.N.I.C.E.F. Umbrella **248** C.O.M.E.S.A Emblem

(Des E. Nisbet. Litho B.D.T.)

1995 (24 Oct). 50th Anniv of United Nations. T **247** and similar horiz designs. Multicoloured. W w **14** (sideways). P 13½.

931	40c. Type **247**	20	10
932	4r. Hard hat and building construction (I.L.O.)	65	55
933	8r. Satellite picture of cyclone (W.M.O.)	1·40	1·75
934	10r. Bread and grain (F.A.O)	1·60	1·90
931/35 *Set of 4*		3·50	3·75

(Des E. Nisbet. Litho Cartor)

1995 (8 Dec). Inauguration of Common Market for Eastern and Southern Africa. W w **14.** P 13×13½.

935	**248**	60c. black and rose	25	10
936		4r. black and cobalt	75	60
937		8r. black and lemon	1·25	1·75
938		10r. black and bright emerald	1·60	2·00
935/38 *Set of 4*			3·50	4·00

249 *Pachystyla bicolor*

(Des I. Loe. Litho Cartor)

1996 (11 Mar). Snails. T **249** and similar horiz designs. Multicoloured. W w **14** (sideways). P 14×13½.

939	60c. Type **249**	20	10
940	4r. *Gonidomus pagodus*	75	65
941	5r. *Harmogenanina implicate*	75	75
942	10r. *Trapidophora eugeniae*	1·25	2·25
939/42 *Set of 4*		2·75	3·25

250 Boxing

(Des R. Walton. Litho B.D.T.)

1996 (26 June). Centenary of Modern Olympic Games. T **250** and similar horiz designs. Multicoloured. W w **16** (sideways). P 13½.

943	60c. Type **250**	10	10
944	4r. Badminton	60	50
945	5r. Basketball	1·25	1·00
946	10r. Table tennis	1·40	2·25
943/46 *Set of 4*		3·00	3·50

251 *Zambezia* (freighter)

(Des J. Batchelor. Litho B.D.T.)

1996 (30 Sept). Ships. T **261** and similar horiz designs. Multicoloured. W w **14** (sideways). P 14.

947	60c. Type **251**	45	10
948	4r. *Sir Jules* (coastal freighter)	1·10	70
949	6r. *Mauritius* (cargo liner)	1·40	1·25
950	10r. *Mauritius Pride* (container ship)	1·90	3·00
947/50 *Set of 4*		4·25	4·50
MS951 125×91 mm. Nos. 947/50		4·25	6·00

252 Posting a Letter

(Des D. Miller. Litho B.D.T.)

1996 (2 Dec). 150th Anniv of the Post Office Ordinance. T **252** and similar horiz designs. Multicoloured. W w **16** (sideways). P 13½.

952	60c. Type **252**	20	10
953	4r. "B53" duplex postmark	60	55
954	5r. Modern mobile post office	85	75
955	10r. Carriole (19th-century horse-drawn postal carriage)	1·75	2·50
952/55 *Set of 4*		3·00	3·50

253 Vavang

254 Governor Mahé de la Bourdonnais and Map

(Des I. Loe. Litho Cartor)

1997 (10 Mar). Fruits. T **253** and similar vert designs. Multicoloured. W w **14**. P 13×13½.

956	60c. Type **253**	15	10
957	4r. Pom Zako	60	55
958	5r. Zambos	75	70
959	10r. Sapot Negro	1·40	2·25
956/59 *Set of 4*		2·50	3·25

(Des G. Vasarhelyi. Litho B.D.T.)

1997 (9 June). Aspects of Mauritius History. T **254** and similar horiz designs. Multicoloured. W w **14** (sideways). P 13½.

960	60c. Type **254**	1·25	30
961	1r. La Perouse and map of Pacific	1·75	30
962	4r. Governor Sir William Gomm and Lady Gomm's Ball, 1847	1·75	1·25
963	6r. George Clark discovering skeleton of dodo, 1865	2·25	2·00
964	10r. Professor Brian Abel-Smith and Social Policies report of 1960	1·75	4·00
960/64 *Set of 5*		8·00	7·00

255 1d. "POST OFFICE" Mauritius

(Des D. Miller. Litho B.D.T.)

1997 (22 Sept). 150th Anniv of "POST OFFICE" Stamps. T **255** and similar horiz designs. Multicoloured. W w **14** (sideways). P 13½.

965	60c. Type **255**	55	30
	a. Sheetlet of 12. Nos. 965×7 and 966×5..	7·75	
	b. Booklet pane of 10 with margins all round	3·75	
966	4r.2d. "POST OFFICE" Mauritius	1·25	1·25
	a. Booklet pane of 10 with margins all round	9·00	
967	5r. "POST OFFICE" 1d. and 2d. on gold background	2·00	2·25
	a. Booklet pane of 10 with margins all round	13·00	
968	10r. "POST OFFICE" 2d. and 1d. on silver background	3·25	4·75
	a. Booklet pane of 10 with margins all round	22·00	
965/68 *Set of 4*		6·25	7·75
MS969 127×90 mm. 20r. "POST OFFICE" stamps on cover to Bordeaux		5·50	6·50

Nos. 965/8 were issued in separate sheets, but Nos. 965/6 also exist as a sheetlet of 12 (3×4), containing seven 60c. and five 4r.

256 Wheelwright

(Des N. Shewring. Litho Walsall)

1997 (1 Dec). Small Businesses. T **266** and similar horiz designs. Multicoloured. W w **14** (sideways). P 14½.

970	60c. Type **256**	15	10
971	4r. Laundryman	60	55
972	5r. Shipwright	1·50	90
973	15r. Quarryman	4·00	5·50
970/73 *Set of 4*		5·50	6·25

257 *Phelsuma guentheri* (gecko)

(Des W. Oliver. Litho B.D.T.)

1998 (11 Mar). Geckos. T **257** and similar horiz designs. Multicoloured. W w **14** (sideways). P 13½.

974	1r. Type **257**	35	10
975	6r. *Nactus serpensinsula durrelli*	1·00	1·00
976	7r. *Nactus coindemirensis*	1·25	1·75
977	8r. *Phelsuma edwardnewtonii*	1·25	1·75
974/77 *Set of 4*		3·50	4·25

258 Steam Train on Viaduct

259 President Nelson Mandela

263 Governor Mahé de la Bourdonnais on 15c. Stamp of 1899

(Litho B.D.T.)

1998 (15 June). Inland Transport. T **258** and similar horiz designs. Multicoloured. W w **14** (sideways). P 13½.

978	40c. Type **258**	50	20
979	5r. Early lorry	1·00	70
980	6r. Bus in town street	1·25	1·10
981	10r. Sailing barge at wharf	1·75	3·00
978/81 *Set of 4*		4·00	4·50

(Litho Walsall)

1998 (10 Sept). State Visit of President Nelson Mandela of South Africa. W w **16**. P 14½.

982	**259**	25r. multicoloured	3·00	4·00

(Litho Cartor)

1999 (11 Feb). 300th Birth Anniv of Governor Mahé de la Bourdonnais. W w **14** (sideways). P 13×13½.

996	**263**	7r. deep ultramarine, black and bright crimson	1·60	1·90

264 *Clerodendron laciniatum*

(Des Lynn Chadwick. Litho B.D.T.)

1999 (10 Mar). Local Plants. T **264** and similar horiz design. Multicoloured. W w **14** (sideways). P 13½.

997	1r. Type **264**	25	10
998	2r. *Senecio lamarckianus*	40	20
999	5r. *Cyliadrocline commersonii*	80	75
1000	9r. *Psiadia pollicina*	1·25	2·50
997/1000 *Set of 4*		2·40	3·00

260 Count Maurice of Nassau and Dutch Landing

(Des A. Theobald. Litho Enschedé)

1998 (18 Sept). 400th Anniv of Dutch Landing on Mauritius. T **260** and similar horiz designs. W w **14** (sideways). P 13½.

983	50c. Type **260**	65	30
984	1r. Fort Frederik Hendrikand sugar cane	65	30
985	7r. Dutch map of Mauritius (1670)	2·75	2·75
986	8r. Diagram of landing	2·75	2·75
983/86 *Set of 4*		6·00	5·50
MS987 105×80 mm. 25r. Two Dutch ships		4·75	6·00

265 "The Washerwomen" (Hervé Masson)

(Des N. Shewring. Litho Enschedé)

1999 (18 June). Mauritius through Local Artists' Eyes. T **265** and similar horiz designs. Multicoloured. W w **14** (sideways). P 14×15.

1001	1r. Type **265**	25	10
1002	3r. "The Casino" (Gaetan de Roanay)	65	60
1003	4r. "The Four Elements" (Andrée Poilly)	75	75
1004	6r. "Going to Mass" (Xavier Le Juge de Segrais)	1·10	1·75
1001/4 *Set of 4*		2·50	2·75

261 Cascade Balfour

(Des N. Shewring. Litho B.D.T.)

1998 (16 Nov). Waterfalls. T **261** and similar multicoloured designs. W w **16** (sideways on 1, 5r.). P 13½.

988	1r. Type **261**	55	10
989	5r. Rochester Falls	1·40	80
990	6r. Cascade G.R.S.E. (*vert*)	1·60	1·25
991	10r. 500ft. Cascade (*vert*)	3·00	4·50
988/91 *Set of 4*		6·00	6·00

262 Plan of Le Réduit

(Des D. Miller. Litho Questa)

1998 (14 Dec). 250th Anniv of Château Le Réduit. T **262** or similar horiz designs. Multicoloured. W w **14** (sideways). P 14½.

992	1r. Type **262**	30	10
993	4r. "Le Château du Réduit, 1814" (P. Thuillier)	75	65
994	5r. "Le Réduit, 1998" (Hassen Edun)	85	80
995	15r. Commemorative monument	2·50	4·00
992/95 *Set of 4*		4·00	5·00

266 Old Chimney, Alma

267 Mosquito and Sprayer (Eradication of Malaria)

(Des N. Shewring. Litho Questa)

1999 (17 Sept). Old Sugar Mill Chimneys. T **266** and similar vert designs. Multicoloured. W w **16**. P 14½.

1005	1r. Type **266**	25	10
1006	2r. Antoinette	50	20
1007	5r. Belle Mare	90	90
1008	7r. Grande Rosalie	1·25	2·00
1005/8 *Set of 4*		2·50	2·75
MS1009 132×100 mm. Nos. 1005/8. W w **14**		2·75	3·25

(Des N. Shewring (2r.), O. Bell (others). Litho Cartor)

1999 (7 Dec). 20th-century Achievements. T **267** and similar horiz designs. Multicoloured. W w **14** (sideways). P 13½×13.

1010	1r. Type **267**	45	10
1011	2r. Judge's robes, silhouette and airliner (emancipation of women)	1·00	30
1012	5r. Conference room (international conference centre)	1·00	1·00
1013	9r. Spoons full of sugar (development of sugar industry)	2·00	3·00
1010/13	Set of 4	4·00	4·00

268 Crest

(Litho Enschedé)

2000 (25 Jan). 150th Anniv of Mauritius Chamber of Commerce and Industry. T **268** and similar triangular designs. Multicoloured. W w **14** (sideways). P 13½.

1014	1r. Type **268**	50	25
1015	2r. Unity, Vision and Service logos	75	40
1016	7r. Francis Channell (First Secretary, 1860–72)	1·75	2·25
1017	15r. Louis Lechelle (First President, 1850)	2·75	5·50
1014/17	Set of 4	5·25	7·50

269 *Crotopus striga* (beetle)

(Des R. Watton. Litho Questa)

2000 (29 Mar). Beetles. T **269** and similar horiz designs. Multicoloured. W w **14** (sideways). P 14½.

1018	1r. Type **269**	25	10
1019	2r. *Cratopus armatus*	35	15
1020	3r. *Cratopus chrysochlorus*	55	40
1021	15r. *Cratopus nigrogranatus*	2·25	3·00
1018/21	Set of 4	3·00	3·25
MS1022	130×100 mm. Nos. 1018/21	3·50	4·00

270 Handball

(Des A. Robinson. Litho Questa)

2000 (28 June). Olympic Games, Sydney. T **270** and similar horiz designs. Multicoloured. W w **14** (sideways). P 14½.

1023	1r. Type **270**	25	10
1024	2r. Archery	50	15
1025	5r. Sailing	85	75
1026	15r. Judo	2·00	3·00
1023/26	Set of 4	3·25	3·50

271 Sir Seewoosagur Ramgoolam greeting Mother Teresa, 1984

(Des R. Watton. Litho Cartor)

2000 (18 Sept). Birth Centenary of Sir Seewoosagur Ramgoolam (former Prime Minister). T **271** and similar multicoloured designs. W w **14** (sideways on 1r.) P 13½×13 (1r.) or 13×13½ (others).

1027	1r. Type **271**	1·25	30

1028	2r. Election as member of Legislative Council, 1948 (*vert*)	35	15
1029	5r. As a student, 1926 (*vert*)	80	70
1030	15r. As Prime Minister, 1968 (*vert*)	2·00	3·25
1027/30	Set of 4	4·00	4·00

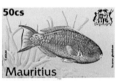

272 *Scarus ghobba*

(Des A. Robinson. Litho Questa)

2000 (9 Oct). Fish. T **272** and similar horiz designs. Multicoloured. W w **14** (sideways). P 14½.

1031	50c. Type **272**	35	75
1032	1r. *Cephalopholis sonneroti*	45	10
1033	2r. *Naso breuirostris*	65	15
1034	3r. *Lethrinus nebulosus*	80	15
1035	4r. *Centropyge debelius*	1·00	20
1036	5r. *Amphiprion chrysogaster*	1·00	25
1037	6r. *Foroipiger flauissimus*	1·25	35
1038	7r. *Acanthurus leucosternon*	1·25	50
1039	8r. *Pterois Volitans*	1·40	60
1040	10r. *Siderea grisea*	1·50	85
1041	15r. *Carcharhinus wheeleri*	2·00	2·50
1042	25r. *Istiophrous platypterus*	2·50	3·75
1031/42	Set of 12	12·50	9·00

MS1043 Three sheets, each 132×102 mm. (a) Nos. 1031/3 and 1042. (b) Nos. 1035 and 1038/40. (c) Nos. 1034, 1036/7 and 1041 *Set of 3 sheets* .... 7·50 9·00
For 10r. perf 13½, see No. 1174.

273 Affan Tank Wen   **274** Finished Pullover

(Des R. Hutchins. Litho Questa)

2000 (13 Dec). Famous Mauritians. T **273** and similar vert designs. Multicoloured. W w **14**. P 14½.

1044	1r. Type **273**	30	10
1045	5r. Alphonse Ravatoni	75	50
1046	7r. Dr. Idrice Goumany	1·10	1·25
1047	9r. Anjalay Coopen	1·40	1·75
1044/47	Set of 4	3·25	3·25

(Des A. Robinson. Litho Questa)

2001 (10 Jan). Textile Industry. T **274** and similar horiz designs. Multicoloured. W w **14** (sideways). P 14½.

1048	1r. Type **274**	40	10
1049	3r. Computer-aided machinery	75	50
1050	6r. T-shirt folding	1·40	1·10
1051	10r. Embroidery machine	1·90	2·50
1048/51	Set of 4	4·00	3·75

275 African Slave and Indian Indentured Labourer   **276** *Foetidia mauritiana*

(Des G. Vasarhelyi. Litho Questa)

2001 (1 Feb). Anti-Slavery and Indentured Labour Campaign Commemoration. W w **14**. P 14×13½.

1052	**275**	7r. multicoloured	1·60	2·00

(Des Jennifer Toombs. Litho B.D.T.)

2001 (21 Mar). Trees. T **276** and similar horiz designs. Multicoloured. W w **14** (sideways). P 13½×14.

1053	1r. Type **276**	40	10
1054	3r. *Diospyros tessellaria*	85	30
1055	5r. *Sideroxylon puberulum*	1·25	85
1056	15r. *Gastonia mauritiana*	2·75	4·00
1053/56 *Set of 4*		4·75	4·75

277 *Géographe* and *Naturaliste* (French corvettes)

(Des A. Theobald. Litho Questa)

2001 (13 June). Bicentenary of Baudin's Expedition to New Holland (Australia). T **277** and similar multicoloured designs. W w **14** (sideways on horiz designs). P 14.

1057	1r. Type **277**	55	25
1058	4r. Capt. Nicholas Baudin and map of voyage	1·25	55
1059	6r. Mascarene Martin (bird)	1·50	1·25
1060	10r. M. F. Peron and title page of book (*vert*)	1·75	2·75
1057/60 *Set of 4*		4·50	4·25

278 Hotel School

(Des N. Shewring. Litho Enschedé)

2001 (Sept). Mauritius Economic Achievements during the 20th-Century. T **278** and similar horiz designs. Multicoloured. W w **14** (sideways). P 13½.

1061	2r. Type **278**	40	15
1062	3r. Steel bar milling	50	30
1063	6r. Solar energy panels, Agalega	1·00	1·00
1064	10r. Indian Ocean Rim Association for Regional Co-operation	1·75	2·75
1061/64 *Set of 4*		3·25	3·75

279 Gandhi on Mauritius Stamp of 1969

280 De-husking Coconuts

(Litho B.D.T.)

2001 (2 Oct). Centenary of Gandhi's Visit to Mauritius. W w **14**. P 15×14.

1065	**279**	15r. multicoloured	2·75	3·25

(Des R. Watton. Litho B.D.T.)

2001 (5 Dec). Coconut Industry. T **280** and similar multicoloured designs. W w **14** (sideways on horiz designs). P 13½.

1066	1r. Type **280**	35	10
1067	5r. Shelling coconuts (*horiz*)	90	55
1068	6r. Drying copra (*horiz*)	1·10	1·00
1069	10r. Extracting coconut oil	2·00	2·75
1066/69 *Set of 4*		4·00	4·00

281 New Container Port

(Des N. Shewring. Litho B.D.T.)

2002 (12 Mar). Tenth Anniv of Republic. T **281** and similar horiz designs. Multicoloured. W w **14** (sideways). P 13½.

1070	1r. Type **281**	60	20
1071	4r. Symbols of Mauritius stock exchange	70	55
1072	5r. New reservoir under construction	90	90
1073	9r. Motorway junction	2·00	2·50
1070/73 *Set of 4*		3·75	3·75

282 *Abricta brunnea*　　　**283** Map by Alberto Cantino, 1502

(Des I. Loe. Litho B.D.T.)

2002 (12 June). Cicadas. T **282** and similar vert designs. Multicoloured. W w **14**. P 13½.

1074	1r. Type **282**	30	15
1075	6r. *Fractuosella darwini*	85	75
1076	7r. *Distantada thomaseti*	95	1·10
1077	8r. *Dinarobia claudeae*	1·10	1·40
1074/7 *Set of 4*		3·00	3·00
MS1078 130×100 mm. Nos. 1074/7		3·25	4·00

(Des G. Vasarhelyi. Litho B.D.T.)

2002 (18 Sept). 16th-century Maps of the South-west Indian Ocean. T **283** and similar horiz designs. Multicoloured. W w **14** (sideways). P 13½.

1079	1r. Type **283**	60	20
1080	3r. Map by Jorge Reinel, 1520	1·25	65
1081	4r. Map by Diogo Ribeiro	1·25	1·00
1082	10r. Map by Gerard Mercator, 1569	2·50	2·75
1079/82 *Set of 4*		5·00	4·25

284 Constellation of Orion

285 African Growth and Opportunity Act Logo

(Des N. Shewring. Litho Questa)

2002 (18 Dec). Constellations. T **284** and similar vert designs. Multicoloured. W w **14**. P 14½.

1083	1r. Type **284**	40	15
	w. Wmk inverted		
1084	7r. Sagittarius	1·00	90
1085	8r. Scorpius	1·10	1·25
1086	9r. Southern Cross	1·25	1·75
	w. Wmk inverted	2·00	
1083/86 *Set of 4*		3·25	3·50

(Litho Questa)

2003 (15 Jan). Second United States/Sub-Saharan Africa Trade and Economic Co-operation Forum. T **285** and similar square design. W w **14** (sideways). P 14½.

1087	**285**	1r. deep vermilion, ultramarine and lemon	25	10
1088		25r. deep vermilion, ultramarine and turquoise-blue	2·75	3·50

286 Echo Parakeet Chick

287 Trochetia boutoniana

(Des A. Robinson. Litho B.D.T.)

2003 (19 Mar). Endangered Species. Echo Parakeet. T **286** and similar vert designs. Multicoloured. W w **14**. P 13½.

1089	1r. Type **286**	65	25
1090	2r. Fledgling	1·00	50
1091	5r. Female parakeet	1·50	1·25
1092	15r. Male parakeet	2·50	3·25
1089/92 Set of 4		5·00	4·75

(Des Rosie Sanders. Litho Enschedé)

2003 (18 June). Trochetias. T **287** and similar vert designs. Multicoloured. W w **14**. P 13½.

1093	1r. Type **287**	30	10
1094	4r. Trochetia uniflora	75	40
1095	7r. Trochetia triflora	1·25	1·50
1096	9r. Trochetia parviflora	1·50	2·50
1093/96 Set of 4		3·50	4·00

288 Dolphin Emblem (Sixth Indian Ocean Games, Mauritius)

(Des D. Miller. Litho B.D.T.)

2003 (20 Aug). Anniversaries and Events. T **288** and similar horiz designs. Multicoloured. W w **14** (sideways). P 13½.

1097	2r. Type **288**	50	20
1098	6r. Crop in field and emblem (150th anniv of Mauritius Chamber of Agriculture)	1·00	80
1099	9r. Journal of voyage of Bonne-Esperance (250th anniv of visit of Abbé de la Caille)	1·60	2·25
1100	10r. Sugar cane and emblem (50th anniv of Mauritius Sugar Industry Research Institute)	1·60	2·25
1097/1100 Set of 4		4·25	5·00

289 Batterie de la Pointe du Diable

(Des A. Theobald. Litho B.D.T.)

2003 (10 Dec). Fortifications. T **289** and similar horiz designs. Multicoloured. P 13½.

1101	2r. Type **289**	40	20
1102	5r. Donjon St. Louis	80	60
1103	6r. Martello Tower	1·00	1·00
1104	12r. Fort Adelaide	1·75	2·75
1101/4 Set of 4		3·50	4·00

290 Emblem

291 Le Pouce

(Des D. Miller. Litho B.D.T.)

2004 (16 Feb). 20th Anniv of the Indian Ocean Commission. W w **14**. P 13½.

1105	**290**	10r. multicoloured	1·60	2·00

(Des D. Miller. Litho D.L.R.)

2004 (11 Mar). Mountains. T **291** and similar horiz designs. Multicoloured. W w **14** (sideways). P 14½.

1106	2r. Type **291**	30	15
1107	7r. Corps de Garde	1·00	80
1108	8r. Le Chat et La Souris	1·10	80
1109	25r. Piton du Milieu	3·00	5·50
1106/9 Set of 4		5·00	6·50

292 Tinman

(Des A. Robinson. Litho B.D.T.)

2004 (30 June). Traditional Trades. T **292** and similar horiz designs. Multicoloured. W w **14** (sideways). P 13½.

1110	2r. Type **292**	30	15
1111	7r. Shoe maker	90	80
1112	9r. Blacksmith	1·40	1·40
1113	15r. Basket maker	2·00	3·25
1110/13 Set of 4		4·00	5·00

293 Work Station, Emblem and SADC Head Quarters

(Litho B.D.T.)

2004 (16 Aug). 24th Southern African Development Community Summit. T **293** and similar horiz design. Multicoloured. W w **14** (sideways). P 13½.

1114	2r. Type **293**	30	30
1115	50r. As Type **293** but with "24th SADC Summit" in bright purple banner	4·50	6·00

294 Plaine Corail Airport

(Des N. Shewring. Litho B.D.T.)

2004 (12 Oct). Rodrigues Regional Assembly. T **294** and similar horiz designs. Multicoloured. W w **14** (sideways). P 13½.

1116	2r. Type **294**	50	20
1117	7r. Eco Tourism	1·25	1·75
1118	8r. Agricultural products	1·25	1·75
1119	10r. Coat of Arms	1·40	2·00
1116/19 Set of 4		4·00	5·00

295 Anthurium andreanum var acropolis

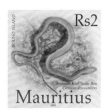

296 Juvenile Keel Scale Boa

(Des I. Loe. Litho Enschedé)

2004 (1 Dec). *Anthurium* Species. T **295** and similar square designs. Multicoloured. W w **14** (sideways). P 13½.

1120	2r. Type **295**	30	15
1121	8r. *Anthurium andreanum var tropical*...........	1·10	1·00
1122	10r. *Anthurium andreanum var paradisio*	1·40	1·40
1123	25r. *Anthurium andreanum var fantasia*........	3·00	4·75
1120/23	*Set of 4*...........	5·25	6·50

(Des A. Robinson. Litho B.D.T.)

2005 (18 Mar). Round Island. T **296** and similar square designs. Multicoloured. W w **14** (inverted). P 13½.

1124	2r. Type **296**...........	40	15
1125	8r. Hurricane Palm...........	1·10	1·10
1126	9r. Round Island Petrel...........	2·00	1·75
1127	25r. Mazambron...........	3·25	5·50
1125/27	*Set of 4*...........	6·00	7·75

297 Counter Services

(Des R. Watton. Litho B.D.T.)

2005 (14 July). Postal Services. T **297** and similar square designs. Multicoloured. W w **14** (sideways). P 13½.

1128	2r. Type **297**...........	40	10
1129	7r. Mail sorting...........	1·25	1·00
1130	8r. Mail distribution...........	1·50	1·50
1131	10r. Mail transfer...........	1·75	2·25
1128/31	*Set of 4*...........	4·50	4·25

298 Vagrant Depot

299 100 Gun Ship

(Des N. Shewring. Litho B.D.T.)

2005 (9 Oct). Stone Buildings. T **298** and similar horiz designs. Multicoloured. W w **14** (sideways). P 13½.

1132	2r. Type **298**...........	25	10
1133	7r. Postal Museum, Port Louis...........	80	85
1134	16r. Carnegie Library, Curepipe...........	2·25	3·50
1132/34	*Set of 3*...........	3·00	4·00

(Litho B.D.T.)

2005 (20 Dec). Model Ships. T **299** and similar multicoloured designs. W w **14**. P 14×13½.

1135	7r. Type **299**...........	90	60
1136	8r. Sampan...........	1·00	85
1137	9r. Roman galley...........	1·10	1·10
1138	16r. Drakkur...........	2·25	3·50
1135/38	*Set of 4*...........	4·75	5·50
MS1139	129×98 mm. 25r. Prow of drakkur with figurehead (*horiz*). P 13½×14...........	3·25	4·00

300 The Market

301 Prof. Basdeo Bissoondoyal

(Litho B.D.T.)

2006 (14 Feb). Bicentenary of Mahebourg. T **300** and similar multicoloured designs. W w **14** (sideways). P 13½×14.

1140	2r. Type **300**...........	35	10
1141	7r. Regattas...........	1·00	75
1142	8r. Le Lavoir...........	1·25	1·00
1143	16r. Pointe des Régates...........	2·25	3·50
1140/43	*Set of 4*...........	4·25	4·75
MS1144	137×87 mm. 16r. François Mahé de la Bourdonnais (Governor 1735–46) (*vert*); 16r. Charles Decaën (Governor, 1803–10) (*vert*). Wmk inverted. P 14×13½...........	4·50	5·50

(Des N. Ratty. Litho Cartor)

2006 (15 Apr). Birth Centenary of Professor Basdeo Bissoondoyal (Indo-Mauritian scholar, writer and social reformer). W w **14**. P 14.

1145	**301** 10r. multicoloured...........	1·60	2·00

302 Indian Mynah (biological control of locusts), 1763

303 *Cardisoma carnifex* (Tourloulou Crab)

(Des N. Ratty. Litho B.D.T.)

2006 (5 June). Ecology. T **302** and similar horiz designs. Multicoloured. W w **14** (sideways). P 13½.

1146	2r. Type **302**...........	1·00	30
1147	8r. Fish and artificial reef (fish repopulation), 1980...........	1·25	1·00
1148	10r. Terraces (erosion control), Rodrigues, 1958...........	1·75	1·60
1149	25r. Giant tortoises (first captive breeding programme), 1881...........	4·50	5·50
1146/49	*Set of 4*...........	7·75	7·75

2006 (9 Oct). Non Marine Crabs. T **303** and similar horiz designs. Multicoloured. W w **14** (inverted). P 13½.

1150	2r. Type **303**...........	45	15
1151	7r. *Geograpsus grayi* (Land Crab)...........	1·10	90
1152	8r. *Varuna litterata* (Freshwater Crab)...........	1·25	1·25
1153	25r. *Birgus latro* (Coconut Crab)...........	3·00	3·50
1150/53	*Set of 4*...........	5·25	5·25

304 Sapsiwaye

305 *Acropora rodriguensis*

(Des N. Shewring. Litho B.D.T.)

2006 (7 Dec). Traditional Children's Games. T **304** and similar multicoloured designs. W w **14** (sideways on horiz designs). P 13½.

1154	5r. Type **304**...........	60	40
1155	10r. Marbles (*horiz*)...........	1·00	1·00
1156	15r. Hop scotch (*horiz*)...........	1·50	2·00
1157	25r. Kite flying...........	2·40	3·00
1154/57	*Set of 4*...........	5·00	5·75

(Des Nurveen Ratty. Litho B.D.T.)

2007 (30 Apr). Corals. T **305** and similar horiz designs. Multicoloured. W w **14** (sideways). P 13½.

1158	3r. Type **305**...........	40	25
1159	5r. *Dendronephthya* sp.........	50	35
1160	10r. *Ctenella chagius*...........	90	80
1161	15r. *Porites lobata*...........	1·40	1·60
1162	22r. *Acropora clathrata*...........	1·75	2·50
1163	25r. *Tubastrea coccinea*...........	1·90	2·50
1158/63	*Set of 6*...........	6·25	7·25

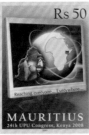

306 Drawing from Journal of the *Gelderland*, 1601

307 Computer Screen showing Globe and Postman

(Des Nurveen Ratty. Litho Cartor)

2007 (25 June). Dodo (*Raphus cucullatus*). T **306** and similar multicoloured designs. W w **14**. P 13½.

1164	5r. Type **306**	1·00	55
1165	10r. Pen drawing by Adrian Van de Venne, 1626	1·50	90
1166	15r. Painting published by Harrison, 1798	2·00	2·00
1167	25r. Chromolithograph by J. W. Frohawk, 1905	2·75	3·50
	w. Wmk inverted	20·00	
1164/67 *Set of 4*		6·50	6·25

MS1168 122×90 mm. 25r. Painting by Julian Pender Hulme, 2001 (28×45 *mm*). Wmk inverted. P 13×13½ .... 13·00 13·00

(Des Nurveen Ratty. Litho Lowe-Martin, Canada)

2007 (9 Oct). 24th UPU Congress, Nairobi. W w **14** (inverted). P 13×12½.

1169	**307**	50r. multicoloured	3·25	4·25

308 Ministers and Arms of Colony, 1957

(Des Nurveen Ratty. Litho B.D.T.)

2007 (4–27 Dec). Anniversaries and Events. T **308** and similar multicoloured designs. W w **14** (sideways on 5r., 25r.). P 13½.

1170	5r. Type **308** (50th anniv of Ministerial System)	75	50
	a. As Type **308** but inscr 'A. M' Osman at bottom right (27.12.07)	75	50
1171	10r. Statue of Manilall Doctor (centenary of arrival) (*vert*)	1·40	1·00
1172	15r. Scout camp and badge (centenary of scouting) (*vert*)	2·00	2·00
1173	25r. Port Louis Observatory (175th anniv of first meteorological observatory)	3·00	3·50
1170a/73 *Set of 4*		6·50	6·25

No. 1170 showed the incorrect portrait in the lower right corner and was inscribed 'A.H. Osman'. It was withdrawn from sale on 8 December and replaced by the corrected version, No. 1170a, inscribed 'A.M. Osman' on 27 December.

(Litho B.D.T.)

2008 (28 May). As No. 1040. W w **14** (sideways). P 13½.

1174	10r. *Siderea grisea*	1·50	1·25

309 Bernardin de St. Pierre, 1737–1814 (*Paul et Virginie*)

310 *Myonima obovata*

(Litho B.D.T.)

2008 (8 Dec). Mauritius in World Literature. T **309** and similar vert designs showing authors. Multicoloured. W w **18**. P 13½.

1175	5r. Type **309**	60	30
1176	10r. Alexandre Dumas, 1802–70 (*Georges*)	1·00	70
1177	15r. Charles Baudelaire, 1821–67 (sonnet *A une Dame Créole*)	1·60	1·75
1178	22r. Mark Twain, 1835–1910 (*Following the Equator*)	2·25	2·50
1179	25r. Joseph Conrad, 1857–1924 (*A Smile of Fortune*)	2·25	2·50
1175/79 *Set of 5*		7·00	7·00

(Des Nurveen Ratty. Litho B.D.T.)

2009 (9 Apr). Indigenous Flowers of Mauritius. T **310** and similar vert designs. Multicoloured. W w **18**. P 13½.

1180	3r. Type **310**	20	10
1181	4r. *Cylindrocline lorencei*	25	15
1182	5r. *Crinum mauritianum*	30	20
1183	6r. *Elaeocarpus bojeri*	35	20
1184	7r. *Bremeria landia*	35	20
1185	8r. *Distephanus populifolius*	45	35
1186	9r. *Gaertnera longifolia* var. *longifolia*	45	35
1187	10r. *Dombeya acutangula* var. *rosea*	65	40
1188	15r. *Aphloia theiformis*	90	60
1189	22r. *Barleria observatrix*	1·40	90
1190	25r. *Roussea simplex*	1·60	1·20
1191	50r. *Hibiscus fragilis*	3·00	2·50
1180/91 *Set of 12*		9·00	6·50

Imprint dates: 7r. 2009, 2010 or 2015; 8r., 15r., 25r. 2009 or 2010; others; 2009.

311 *Cylindraspis peltastes*

(Litho B.D.T.)

2009 (16 July). Extinct Mauritian Giant Tortoises. T **311** and similar multicoloured designs. W w **18** (sideways on 5, 15r.). P 13½.

1192	5r. Type **311**	60	30
1193	10r. *Cylindraspis vosmaeri* (*vert*)	1·00	70
1194	15r. *Cylindraspis inepta*	1·60	1·75
1195	25r. *Cylindraspis triserrata* (*vert*)	2·50	3·25
1192/95 *Set of 4*		5·25	5·50

MS1196 117×72 mm. 50r. *Cylindraspis peltastes* grazing. Wmk sideways .... 4·00 5·00

312 Brand Mauritius Logo

2009 (9 Oct). Branding Mauritius. T **312** and similar horiz design. Multicoloured. Litho. W w **18** (sideways). P 13½×13.

1197	7r. Type **312**	50	65
	a. Vert pair. Nos. 1197/8	1·00	1·25
1198	7r. Pieter Both Mountain	50	65

Nos. 1197/8 were printed together, *se-tenant*, in vertical pairs throughout the sheets.

313 Dragons

(Litho B.D.T.)

2009 (30 Nov). Anniversaries and Events. T **313** and similar multicoloured designs. W w **18** (sideways on horiz designs). P 13½.

1199	7r. Type **313** (Centenary (2008) of Chinese Chamber of Commerce, Mauritius)	65	30
1200	14r. Dr. K. Hazareesingh (writer) (birth centenary) (*vert*)	1·25	1·00
1201	20r. Document and map of 1809 (bicentenary of capture of Rodrigues Island by the British)	2·00	2·50
1202	– 21r. T. Callychurn (birth centenary) (*vert*)	2·00	2·50
1199/1202 *Set of 4*		5·50	5·75

313a Player, Football, Mauritius
Flag and Zakumi Mascot

(Des Anja Denker. Litho Enschedé)

2010 (9 Apr). Third Joint Issue of Southern Africa Postal Operators Association Members. World Cup Football Championship, South Africa. T **313a** and similar circular designs, each showing Zakumi mascot, different silhouettes of players on football and the national flag of a member country. Multicoloured. P 13½.

1202a	7r. Type **313a**	4·50	4·00

MS1202b 181×160 mm. 7r.×9 Namibia; South Africa; Zimbabwe; Malawi; Swaziland; Botswana; As
No. 1202a; Lesotho; Zambia.............................. 25·00 25·00

No. 1202a and the stamps within **MS**1202b were each perforated in a circle contained within an outer perforated square.

No. 1202a has a matt gold background but stamps from **MS**1202b have a shiny gold background. Similar designs were issued by Botswana, Lesotho, Malawi, Namibia, South Africa, Swaziland, Zambia and Zimbabwe.

314 Al-Idrissi

315 Mauritius 1847
2d. Blue

(Des Nitish Peechen. Litho B.D.T.)

2010 (5 Aug). Al-Idrissi (geographer and cartographer) Commemoration. W w **18**. P 13½.

1203	**314**	27r. multicoloured	2·25 2·75

(Des Nitish Peechen. Litho B.D.T.)

2010 (20 Aug). Expo 2010, Shanghai, China. W w **18**. P 13½.

1204	**315**	30r. deep violet-blue and vermilion	2·25	2·75

316 Battle of Grand Port, 1810

(Des Nitish Peechen. Litho B.D.T.)

2010 (28 Aug). Bicentenary of the Battle of Grand Port. T **316** and similar horiz design. Multicoloured. W w **18** (sideways). P 13½.

1205	14r. Type **316**	1·25	1·25
1206	21r. Map of Ile de la Passe	2·00	2·50

317 Sir Seewoosagur Ramgoolam

(Litho and embossed Cartor)

2010 (18 Sept). Sir Seewoosagur Ramgoolam ('Father of the Nation') Commemoration. W w **18**. P 13½.

1207	**317**	100r. multicoloured	6·75 8·00

The centre of No. 1207 is embossed in 22 carat gold.

318 'Acte de
Capitulation'

319 The Steps at
Aapravasi Ghat

2010 (3 Dec). Bicentenary of the British Conquest of Isle de France. T **318** and similar multicoloured design. Litho. W w **18** (sideways on 7r.). P 13½.

1208	2r. Type **318**	50	25
1209	7r. British troops on road to Port Louis, 1810 (horiz)	1·00	1·25

(Des Nitish Peechen. Litho B.D.T.)

2011 (18 Apr). Mauritius in World Heritage. T **319** and similar multicoloured designs. W w **18** (sideways on horiz designs and **MS**1214). P 13½.

1210	7r. Type **319**	60	35
1211	14r. Le Morne (The Mountain) (horiz)	1·10	1·00
1212	15r. The Monument, Le Morne (horiz)	1·25	1·40
1213	25r. The hospital kitchen, Aapravasi Ghat	2·00	2·75
1210/13 Set of 4		4·50	5·00
MS1214 120×100 mm. Nos. 1210/13		4·50	5·00

320 19th-century Census Form

(Des Nitish Peechen. Litho B.D.T.)

2011 (30 June). Anniversaries and Events. T **320** and similar multicoloured designs. P 13×13½ (horiz) or 13½×13 (vert).

1215	7r. Type **320** (Population Census 2011)	60	30
1216	14r. Sir Moilin Jean Ah Chuen (industrialist) (birth centenary) (vert)	1·10	1·00
1217	21r. Dr. Maurice Curé (founder of Mauritius Labour Party) (125th birth anniv) (vert)	1·60	2·25
1218	25r. Aerial view of Médine sugar factory (centenary of the Médine sugar estates)	2·00	2·75
1215/1218 Set of 4		4·75	5·75

321 Map of Rodrigues and
Telescope

(Des Nitish Peechen. Litho B.D.T.)

2011 (8 Sept). Commemorative Events. T **321** and similar horiz designs. Multicoloured. W w **18** (sideways). P 13½.

1219	11r. Type **321** (250th anniv of the observation of the transit of Venus from Rodrigues)	1·00	1·25
1220	12r. Laboratory (International Year of Chemistry)	1·00	1·25
1221	17r. Forest (International Year of Forests)	1·40	1·75
1219/21 Set of 3		3·00	3·75

322 Emblem   **323** Post Office, La Criée

(Des Nitish Peechen. Litho B.D.T.)

2011 (9 Oct). HIV/AIDS Awareness. 30th Anniv of Discovery of HIV/
AIDS Virus. W w **18**. P 13½.
1222 **322** 7r. multicoloured .... 1·75 1·25

(Des Nitish Peechen. Litho B.D.T.)

2011 (9 Oct). 150th Anniv of Post Office in Rodrigues. W w **18**
(sideways). P 13½.
1223 **323** 21r. multicoloured .... 2·50 2·50

324 Tea Leaves   **325** Grand Port District Port

(Des Nitish Peechen. Litho B.D.T.)

2011 (19 Dec). Tea Industry. T **324** and similar multicoloured designs.
W w **18** (sideways on horiz designs). P 13½.
1224 7r. Type **324** 60 40
1225 8r. Tea picking (*horiz*) 80 50
1226 15r. Leaf tea and tea bags (*horiz*)................... 1·10 1·25
1227 25r. Pouring cup of tea .... 1·75 2·25
1224/27 Set of 4 .... 3·75 2·75

(Des Nitish Peechen. Litho Cartor)

2012 (4 Apr). Law Day. T **325** and similar multicoloured designs.
W w **18** (sideways on horiz designs). P 13.
1228 7r. Type **325** 60 40
1229 8r. Interior of Court of Justice 80 50
1230 15r. Sir Michel Rivalland (Chief Justice
        1967–70) (*vert*) .... 1·10 75
1231 20r. The Gavel .... 1·60 2·25
1228/1231 Set of 4 .... 3·50 3·50

326 Racing

(Litho B.D.T.)

2012 (25 June). Bicentenary of Mauritius Turf Club. T **326** and similar
multicoloured designs. W w **18** (sideways on horiz designs and
MS1236). P 13½.
1232 7r. Type **326** 60 40
1233 10r. Aerial view of racetrack Champ de Mars ..... 1·00 70
1234 14r. Grandstand, 1917................................. 1·10 75
1235 21r. Insignia of Mauritius Turf Club (*vert*)...... 1·60 2·25
1232/1235 Set of 4 .... 3·75 3·50
MS1236 117×73 mm. 50r. The Paddock............................ 3·50 4·00

327 Old and New Custom House

(Litho B.D.T.)

2012 (10 Sept). Customs Department in Mauritius. T **327** and similar
multicoloured designs. W w **18** (sideways on 7, 8, 25r.). P 13½.
1237 7r. Type **327** 60 40
1238 8r. Customs officers scanning packages...... 80 50
1239 20r. Canine Unit sniffer dog and handler
        checking packages (*vert*)........................... 1·60 1·90
1240 25r. Marine Unit .... 1·75 2·25
1237/1240 Set of 4... 4·25 4·50

328 Emblem   **329** Marcel Cabon
                    (1912–72, writer,
                    journalist and poet)

(Litho B.D.T.)

2012 (9 Oct). Anniversaries and Events. T **328** and similar horiz
designs. Multicoloured. W w **18** (sideways). P 13½.
1241 6r. Type **328** (International Year of
        Co-operatives) 50 35
1242 14r. Flags of Mauritius and People's
        Republic of China (40th anniv of
        Diplomatic Relations) .... 1·00 90
1243 21r. Emblem (centenary of scouting in
        Mauritius) .... 1·60 1·90
1241/1243 Set of 3 .... 2·75 2·75

(Des Neshvin Ramasawmy. Litho B.D.T.)

2012 (12 Nov). Eminent Personalities. T **329** and similar vert design.
Multicoloured. W w **18**. P 13½.
1244 6r. Type **329** 50 35
1245 10r. Goolam Mahomed Dawjee Atchia
        (1890–1966, politician) .... 1·10 1·25

330 Foot Messenger, 1772

(Des Nurveen Ratty. Litho Cartor)

2012 (21 Dec). 240th Anniv of Postal Services in Mauritius. T **330**
and similar multicoloured designs. W w **18** (sideways). P 13×12½
(1246/50) or 13½ (**MS**1251).
1246 7r. Type **330** 60 65
      a. Horiz strip of 5. Nos. 1246/50..................
1247 7r. Packet mail landing, 1915....................... 60 65
1248 7r. Express letter messenger, 1930 .... 60 65
1249 7r. Inland mail arrival, 1935 .... 60 65
1250 7r. Delivery of mail bags by van, 2012........ 60 65
1246/1250 Set of 5... 2·75 3·00
MS1251 140×100 mm. 25r. Mauritius 1847 1d. red
stamp and copper plate; 25r. Mauritius 1847
2d. deep blue stamp and copper plate (both
42×28 mm).. 3·50 3·75
Nos. 1246/50 were printed together, *se-tenant*, as horizontal strips
of five stamps in sheets of 20.

331 Prison de Belle Mare

(Litho B.D.T.)

2013 (18 Apr). Sites and Monuments. T **331** and similar horiz designs. Multicoloured. W w **18** (sideways). P 13½.

1252	5r. Type **331**	50	35
1253	9r. Château de Bel Ombre	90	75
1254	10r. IBL Building–Bowen Square	1·10	1·00
1255	18r. Le Batelage	1·40	1·75
1252/1255	*Set of 4*	3·50	3·50

332 Solar Energy ('Maurice Ile Durable')

333 Hurricane Palm (*Hyophorbe amaricaulis*)

334 Hervé Masson (1919–90, painter)

(Litho B.D.T.)

2013 (30 May). Anniversaries and Events. T **332** and similar vert designs. Multicoloured. W w **18**. P 13½.

1256	2r. Type **332**	20	10
1257	3r. Red Cross emblem and Henri Dunant (founder) (150th anniv of the Red Cross)	30	20
1258	6r. Wind Energy ('Maurice Ile Durable')	50	35
1259	18r. Emblem (63rd FIFA Congress, Pailles, Mauritius)	1·40	1·90
1256/1259	*Set of 4*	2·25	2·25

(Litho B.D.T.)

2013 (30 Aug). Fauna and Flora. T **333** and similar vert designs. Multicoloured. W w **18**. P 13½.

1260	3r. Type **333**	30	20
1261	10r. Orchid (*Oeoniella polystachys*), Bras D'Eau National Park	1·10	75
1262	18r. Mascarene Swallow (*Phedina borbonica*), Bras d'Eau National Park	1·40	1·90
1260/1262	*Set of 3*	2·50	2·75

(Litho B.D.T.)

2013 (11 Dec). Eminent Personalities. T **334** and similar vert design. Multicoloured. W w **18**. P 13½.

1263	9r. Type **334**	90	70
1264	26r. Prof. Alexander de Smith (1922–74, Constitutional Commissioner for Mauritius in 1960s)	1·75	2·25

335 Dragonfly

336 Pere Laval (French Catholic priest and missionary, 150th death anniv)

(Litho B.D.T.)

2014 (28 Mar). Fauna and Flora. T **335** and similar multicoloured designs. W w **18** (sideways on horiz designs). P 13½.

1265	7r. Type **335**	60	50
1266	14r. Roussette de Rodrigues (Rodrigues Flying Fox)	1·25	1·00
1267	25r. Pignon d'Inde (Physic Nut) (*vert*)	2·10	2·75
1265/1267	*Set of 3*	3·50	3·75

(Litho B.D.T.)

2014 (28 May). Anniversaries and Events. T **336** and similar vert designs. Multicoloured. W w **18**. P 13½.

1268	8r. Type **336**	70	60

1269	14r. Children standing in cupped hands (Tenth anniv of the creation of the Ombudsperson for Children's Office)	1·25	1·25
1270	15r. Reverend Jean Joseph Lebrun (bicent of arrival in Mauritius)	1·25	1·25
1271	25r. Mobile phones (25 Years of the introduction of mobile phones to Mauritius)	2·10	2·40
1268/1271	*Set of 4*	4·75	4·75

337 Green Turtle

(Des Claude Perchat. Litho Phil@poste, France)

2014 (9 Oct). Green Turtle. P 13.

1272	**337**	14r. multicoloured	1·25	1·25

Stamps in similar designs were issued on the same day by Comores, France, French Southern and Antarctic Territories, Madagascar and Seychelles. A miniature sheet was also issued containing one Green Turtle stamp from each of the six countries.

338 Canal Dayot

(Litho B.D.T.)

2015 (5 June). Disaster Risk Reduction. W w **18** (sideways). P 13½.

1273	**338**	17r. multicoloured	1·60	1·60

339 Emblem

(Litho B.D.T.)

2015 (1 Aug). Ninth Indian Ocean Island Games, Réunion Island. W w **18** (sideways). P 13½.

1274	**339**	17r. multicoloured	1·60	1·60

340 Corvette *Le Chasseur* (Guillaume Dufresne d'Arsel) off Mont du Rempart, Mauritius, 20 September 1715

341 National Archives

(Des Franck Bonnet. Litho Phil@poste, France)

2015 (25 Sept). 300th Anniv of the French Landing in Mauritius. P 13.

1275	**340**	17r. multicoloured	1·75	1·75

(Litho Lowe-Martin Group)

2015 (27 Nov). Bicentenary of the National Archives. W w **18**. P 13.

1276	**341**	10r. multicoloured	1·00	1·00

STAMP BOOKLETS

1953 (10 Oct). Black on white cover. Stapled.
SB1   5r. booklet containing four 5c., eight 10c. and 50c. (Nos. 280, 286, 291) in blocks of 4 and one pane of 4 air mail labels £225

1954 (23 Sept). Black on white or grey cover. Stapled.
SB2   5r. booklet containing four 5c., eight 10c. and 50c. (Nos. 296/7, 302) in blocks of 4 and one pane of 4 air mail labels .... 40·00

1955. Black on grey cover. Stapled.
SB3   5r. booklet containing four 5c., eight 10c. and 50c. (Nos. 296, 297a, 302) in block of 4 and one pane of 4 air mail labels .... 50·00

1977 (?). Black on buff cover. Stapled.
SB3a   10r. booklet containing 5c., 20c., 50c., 75c. and 1r. (Nos. 478, 480, 485 and 486/7) each in blocks of four ....

1979 (20 July). Tenth Anniv of Moon Landing. Multicoloured cover, 165×92 mm, showing astronauts on front and Lunar Module above Moon on back. Stitched.
SB4   17r.80 booklet containing se-tenant panes of 3 or 6 (Nos. 574a/b) .... 8·00

B **1** Port Louis Post Office (*Illustration reduced.
Actual size 125×71 mm*)

1997 (22 Sept). 150th Anniv of "POST OFFICE" Stamps. Covers as Type B **1**. Panes attached by selvedge.
SB5   6r. booklet containing pane of ten 60c. (No. 965b) .... 3·75
SB6   40r. booklet containing pane of ten 4r. (No. 966a).. 9·00
SB7   50r. booklet containing pane of ten 5r. (No. 967a).... 13·00
SB8   100r. booklet containing pane of ten 10r. (No. 968a) .... 22·00

EXPRESS DELIVERY STAMPS

EXPRESS DELIVERY 15c.
(E **1**)

EXPRESS DELIVERY (INLAND) 15c.
(E **2**)

EXPRESS DELIVERY (INLAND) 15 c.
(E **3**)

EXPRESS DELIVERY (INLAND) 15 c
(E **4**)

Type E **2**. "(INLAND)" was inserted at a second printing on stamps already surcharged with Type E **1** (No. E1).
Type E **3**. New setting made at one printing. More space above and below "(INLAND)".
Type E **4**. New setting with smaller "15c" and no stop.

1903 (10 Aug)–**04**. No. 136 surch locally in red.

E1	E **1**	15c. on 15c. ultramarine	18·00	42·00
E2	E **2**	15c. on 15c. ultramarine (28.3.04)	65·00	£100
		a. "A" inverted	£1700	£1300
		b. "(INLAND)" inverted	†	£3500
E3	E **3**	15c. on 15c. ultramarine (4.04)	12·00	4·00
		a. Surch inverted	£1300	£850
		aw. Surch and wmk inverted	—	£1100
		b. Surch double, both inverted	£1900	£1900

		c. Imperf between (vert pair)	£8000	
		w. Wmk inverted		
		x. Wmk reversed		
E4	E **4**	15c. on 15c. ultramarine (1904)	£850	£800
		a. Surch inverted	—	£1900
		b. Surch double	—	£3500
		c. Surch double, both inverted	—	£5000
		d. "c" omitted	—	£2500

(FOREIGN) EXPRESS DELIVERY 18 CENTS
(E **5**)

1904. T **42** (without value in label), surch with Type E **5** locally. Wmk Crown CC. P 14.

E5	18c. green	4·50	38·00
	a. Exclamation mark for "I" in "FOREIGN"	£750	

1904. T **42** (without value in label) surch with Type E **3** locally.

E6	15c. grey-green (R.)	24·00	7·50
	a. Surch inverted	£1000	£900
	b. Surch double	£750	£750
	c. Surch double, one "LNIAND"	£850	£800

POSTAGE DUE STAMPS

D **1**

(Typo Waterlow)
1933–54. Wmk Mult Script CA. P 15×14.

D1	D **1**	2c. black	1·25	50
D2		4c. violet	50	65
D3		6c. scarlet	60	80
D4		10c. green	70	2·75
D5		20c. bright blue	70	3·00
D6		50c. deep magenta (1.3.54)	55	19·00
D7		1r. orange (1.3.54)	70	17·00
D1/7 *Set of 7*			4·50	40·00
D1s/5s Perf "SPECIMEN" *Set of 5*			£120	

(Typo D.L.R.)
1966–72. Chalk-surfaced paper. Wmk w **12**. P 13½×14 (2c.) or 15×14 (others).

D8	D **1**	2c. black (11.7.67)	3·00	5·00
D9		4c. slate-lilac (7.1.69)	1·75	8·00
D10		6c. red-orange (7.1.69)	6·50	30·00
		a. Perf 13½×14	23·00	65·00
D11		10c. yellow-green (16.2.67)	30	2·00
D12		20c. blue (3.1.66)	2·25	7·00
		a. Deep blue (7.1.69)	2·25	17·00
D13		50c. deep magenta (7.1.69)	1·00	15·00
		a. Magenta (10.1.72)	2·00	16·00
D8/13 *Set of 6*			13·00	60·00

POSTAGE DUE 10c
D **2**

1982 (25 Oct). Nos. 530A/1A, 535A, 540A, 542A and 547A optd. as Type D **2** by J. W. Dunn Printers Ltd.

D14		10c. on 15c. Dutch Occupation, 1638–1710.	20	30
D15		20c. on 20c. Van Keulen a map, circa 1700...	30	30
D16		50c. on 60c. Pierre Poivre, circa 1767	30	30
D17		1r. on 1r.20 Government House, circa 1840	40	30
D18		1r.50 on 1r.50 Indian immigration, 1835	50	75
D19		5r. on 15r. Unfurling Mauritian flag, 1968 ..	1·00	2·00
D14/19 *Set of 6*			2·40	3·50

FISCALS USED FOR POSTAGE

INLAND REVENUE (F 1)   INLAND (F 2)   REVENUE F 3

1889. T **19**, wmk Crown CA, optd. P 14.

R1	F **1**	4c. carmine	32·00	7·50
R2	F **2**	4c. lilac	10·00	13·00

(Typo D.L.R.)

1896. Wmk Crown CA. P 14.

R3	F **3**	4c. dull purple	50·00	70·00

Seychelles

Seychelles was administered as a dependency of Mauritius from 1810 until 1903, although separate stamp issues were provided from April 1890 onwards.

The first post office was opened, at Victoria on Mahé, on 11 December 1861 and the stamps of Mauritius were used there until 1890. No further post offices were opened until 1901.

Z 1

Stamps of MAURITIUS cancelled with Type Z **1**.

1859–61.
Z2	6d. blue (No. 32)	£900
Z3	6d. dull purple-slate (No. 33)	£2250
Z4	1s. vermilion (No. 34)	£1400

1860–63. (Nos. 46/53).
Z5	1d. purple-brown	£225
Z6	2d. blue	£275
Z7	4d. rose	£250
Z8	6d. green	£1000
Z9	6d. slate	£650
Z10	9d. dull purple	£120
Z11	1s. buff	£325
Z12	1s. green	£800

1862.
Z13	6d. slate (No. 54)	£800

1863–72. (Nos. 56/72).
Z14	1d. purple-brown	£130
Z14a	1d. brown	£110
Z15	1d. bistre	£120
Z16	2d. pale blue	£130
Z17	2d. bright blue	£130
Z18	3d. deep red	£160
Z19	3d. dull red	95·00
Z20	4d. rose	48·00
Z21	6d. dull violet	£250
Z22	6d. yellow-green	£110
Z23	6d. blue-green	80·00
Z24	9d. yellow-green	£1800
Z25	10d. maroon	£325
Z26	1s. yellow	£110
Z27	1s. blue	£325
Z28	1s. orange	£110
Z29	5s. rosy mauve	£950
Z30	5s. bright mauve	£950

1876. (Nos. 76/7).
Z31	½d. on 9d. dull purple	£325
Z32	½d. on 10d. maroon	£300

1877. (Nos. 79/82).
Z33	½d. on 10d. rose	£650
Z34	1d. on 4d. rose-carmine	
Z35	1s. on 5s. rosy mauve	
Z36	1s. on 5s. bright mauve	

1878. (Nos. 83/91).
Z37	2c. dull rose (lower label blank)	£100
Z38	4c. on 1d. bistre	£375
Z39	8c. on 2d. blue	40·00
Z40	13c. on 3d. orange-red	£120
Z41	17c. on 4d. rose	40·00
Z42	25c. on 6d. slate-blue	£120
Z43	38c. on 9d. pale violet	£600
Z44	50c. on 1s. green	£120
Z45	2r.50 on 5s. bright mauve	£500

1879–80. (Nos. 92/100).
Z46	2c. Venetian red	£130
Z47	4c. orange	£130
Z48	8c. blue	40·00
Z49	13c. slate	£1500
Z50	17c. rose	95·00
Z51	25c. olive-yellow	£200
Z52	38c. bright purple	£1800
Z53	50c. green	£850
Z54	2r.50 brown-purple	£850

1883–90.
Z55	2c. Venetian red (No. 102)	£100
Z56	2c. green (No. 103)	£200
Z57	4c. orange (No. 104)	70·00
Z58	4c. carmine (No. 105)	95·00
Z59	16c. chestnut (No. 109)	55·00
Z60	25c. olive-yellow (No. 110)	£110
Z61	50c. orange (No. 111)	£950

1883.
Z62	16c. on 17c. rose (No. 112)	£120

1883.
Z63	16c. on 17c. rose (No. 115)	48·00

1885.
Z64	2c. on 38c. bright purple (No. 116)	

1887.
Z65	2c. on 13c. slate (No. 117)	

POSTAL FISCAL

1889.
ZR1	4c. lilac (No. R2)	£1800

Mauritius stamps are occasionally found cancelled with the "SEYCHELLES" cds. Examples are known dated between 25 and 29 February 1884 when it seems that Type Z **1** may have been mislaid (*Price from* £500).

We no longer list the G.B. 1862 6d. lilac with this obliteration as there is no evidence that the stamps of Great Britain were sold by the Victoria post office.

PRICES FOR STAMPS ON COVER TO 1945	
Nos. 1/8	*from* × 20
Nos. 9/24	*from* × 30
No. 25	*from* × 10
No. 26	*from* × 20
No. 27	*from* × 10
Nos. 28/32	*from* × 20
No. 33	*from* × 5
No. 34	*from* × 30
Nos. 35/6	—
Nos. 37/40	*from* × 40
Nos. 41/2	*from* × 25
Nos. 43/5	*from* × 10
Nos. 46/50	*from* × 30
Nos. 51/4	*from* × 10
Nos. 55/6	—
Nos. 57/9	*from* × 10
Nos. 60/7	*from* × 20
Nos. 68/70	—
Nos. 71/81	*from* × 10
Nos. 82/131	*from* × 5
Nos. 132/4	*from* × 10
Nos. 135/49	*from* × 3

(Currency: 100 cents = 1 Mauritius, later Seychelles rupee)

DEPENDENCY OF MAURITIUS

PRINTERS. Nos. 1 to 123 were typographed by De La Rue & Co.

1

Die I

Die II

In Die I there are lines of shading in the middle compartment of the diadem which are absent from Die II.

Normal   Malformed "S"   Repaired "S"

The malformed "S" occurs on R. 7/3 of the left pane from Key Plate 2. It is believed that the repair to it took place in mid-1898. Both states may occur on other stamps in Types **1** and **4**. Stamps subsequently printed from Key Plate 3 showed the "S" normal.

1890 (5 Apr)–**92**. Wmk Crown CA. P 14.

(i) Die I

1	**1**	2c. green and carmine	8·00	20·00
2		4c. carmine and green	48·00	20·00
3		8c. brown-purple and blue	17·00	3·50
4		10c. ultramarine and brown	17·00	40·00
5		13c. grey and black	6·00	20·00
6		16c. chestnut and blue	15·00	4·25
7		48c. ochre and green	26·00	10·00
8		96c. mauve and carmine	70·00	48·00
1/8 *Set of 8*			£190	£150
1s/8s Optd "SPECIMEN" *Set of 8*			£225	

(ii) Die II (1892)

9	**1**	2c. green and rosine	2·50	1·00
10		4c. carmine and green	2·50	1·75
11		8c. brown-purple and ultramarine	16·00	1·75
12		10c. bright ultramarine and brown	16·00	3·25
13		13c. grey and black	7·50	2·00
14		16c. chestnut and ultramarine	45·00	11·00
		a. Malformed "S"		
9/14 *Set of 6*			80·00	9·00

The 10c. Die I also exists in ultramarine and chestnut, but has so far only been found with "SPECIMEN" overprint (*Price* £800).

3 cents (2)   **18 CENTS** (3)   **1R.** 4

1893 (1 Jan). Surch locally as T **2**.

15		3c. on 4c. (No. 10)	1·10	1·50
		a. Surch inverted	£300	£375
		b. Surch double	£475	
		c. Surch omitted (in horiz pair with normal)	£14000	
16		12c. on 16c. (No. 6)	7·00	8·50
		a. Surch inverted	£500	
		b. Surch double	£15000	£9000
17		12c. on 16c. (No. 14)	21·00	2·50
		a. Surch double	£4500	£4500
		b. Surch omitted (in pair with normal)		
18		15c. on 16c. (No. 6)	15·00	13·00
		a. Surch inverted	£325	£300
		b. Surch double	£1300	£1300
19		15c. on 16c. (No. 14)	26·00	3·00
		a. Surch inverted	£900	£1000
		b. Surch double	£700	£750
		c. Surch triple	£4500	
20		45c. on 48c. (No. 7)	35·00	7·50
21		90c. on 96c. (No. 8)	70·00	50·00
		a. Wide "O" (3½ *mm* wide instead of 3 *mm*) (R. 1/1, 2/1 of setting)	£400	£375
15/21 *Set of 7*			£150	75·00

Nos. 15/21 were each produced from settings of 30.

Nos. 15, 16, 18, 19 and 20 exist with "cents" omitted and with "cents" above value due to misplacement of the surcharge.

Some examples of No. 15b occur in the same sheet as No. 15c with the double surcharge on stamps from the last vertical row of the left pane and the surcharge omitted on stamps from the last vertical row of the right pane.

Most examples of the inverted surcharge error No. 16a were officially defaced with a red vertical ink line (*Price* £200, *unused*). Similarly examples of No. 19a exist defaced with a horizontal ink line (*Price* £400, *unused*).

1893 (Nov). New values. Die II. Wmk Crown CA. P 14.

22	**1**	3c. dull purple and orange	1·50	50
23		12c. sepia and green	2·50	1·00
24		15c. sage-green and lilac	9·00	2·00
25		45c. brown and carmine	25·00	35·00
22/5 *Set of 4*			35·00	35·00
22s/5s Optd "SPECIMEN" *Set of 4*			95·00	

1896 (1 Aug). No. 25 surch locally as T **3**.

26	**1**	18c. on 45c. brown and carmine	10·00	3·50
		a. Surch double	£1500	£1500
		b. Surch triple	£2250	
27		36c. on 45c. brown and carmine	10·00	60·00
		a. Surch double	£1800	
26s/7s Optd "SPECIMEN" *Set of 2*			70·00	

1897–1900. Colours changed and new values. Die II. Wmk Crown CA. P 14.

28	**1**	2c. orange-brown and green (1900)	2·00	3·00
		a. Repaired "S"	£350	£375
29		6c. carmine (1900)	3·75	50
		a. Repaired "S"	£450	£300
30		15c. ultramarine (1900)	11·00	8·00
		a. Repaired "S"	£550	£400
31		18c. ultramarine	13·00	1·50
32		36c. brown and carmine	48·00	7·50
33	**4**	75c. yellow and violet (1900)	55·00	70·00
		a. Repaired "S"	£650	£850
34		1r. bright mauve and deep red	15·00	8·00
35		1r.50 grey and carmine (1900)	85·00	95·00
		a. Repaired "S"	£800	£1000
36		2r.25 bright mauve and green (1900)	£110	85·00
		a. Repaired "S"	£1000	
28/36 *Set of 9*			£300	£250
28s/36s Optd "SPECIMEN" *Set of 9*			£275	

3 cents (5)   **6 cents** (5a)

1901 (21 June–Sept). Surch locally with T **5** or **5a**.

37		3c. on 10c. bright ultramarine and brown (No. 12) (9.01)	3·25	75
		a. Surch double	£900	
		b. Surch triple	£3250	
38		3c. on 16c. chestnut and ultramarine (No. 14) (8.01)	6·50	9·00
		a. Surch inverted	£700	£700
		b. Surch double	£500	£550
		c. "3 cents" omitted	£550	£550
		d. Malformed "S"	£275	£425
39		3c. on 36c. brown and carmine (No. 32)	2·00	80
		a. Surch double	£750	£850
		b. "3 cents" omitted	£650	£700
40		6c. on 8c. brown-purple and ultramarine (No. 11) (7.01)	6·50	3·50
		a. Surch inverted	£650	£750
37/40 *Set of 4*			16·00	12·50
37s/40s H/S "Specimen" (No. 37) or "SPECIMEN" *Set of 4*			£110	

1902 (June). Surch locally as T **5**.

41	**1**	2c. on 4c. carmine and green (No. 10)	4·75	2·75
42	**4**	30c. on 75c. yellow and violet (No. 33)	2·75	7·00
		a. Narrow "0" in "30" (R. 3/6, 5/2-4)	9·00	48·00
		b. Repaired "S"	£350	£550
43		30c. on 1r. bright mauve and deep red (No. 34)	19·00	50·00
		a. Narrow "0" in "30" (R. 3/6, 5/2-4)	40·00	£120
		b. Surch double	£1500	
44		45c. on 1r. bright mauve and deep red (No. 34)	9·00	50·00
45		45c. on 2r.25 bright mauve and green (No. 36)	50·00	£110
		a. Narrow "5" in "45" (R. 4/1)	£200	£375
		b. Repaired "S"	£750	£1200
41/5 *Set of 5*			75·00	£200
41s/5s Optd "Specimen" *Set of 5*			£140	

6   7   **3 cents** (8)

Dented frame (R. 1/6 of left pane)

1903 (26 May). Wmk Crown CA. P 14.

46	**6**	2c. chestnut and green	1·75	2·00
		a. Dented frame	£160	£190
47		3c. dull green	1·00	1·25
		a. Dented frame	£140	£170
48		6c. carmine	3·25	1·25
		a. Dented frame	£275	£170
49		12c. olive-sepia and dull green	5·00	2·50
		a. Dented frame	£325	£250
50		15c. ultramarine	6·50	3·00
		a. Dented frame	£375	£250
51		18c. sage-green and carmine	4·25	5·50
		a. Dented frame	£325	£400
52		30c. violet and dull green	8·50	18·00
		a. Dented frame	£400	£650
53		45c. brown and carmine	7·00	18·00
		a. Dented frame	£425	£650
		w. Wmk inverted	£500	£650
54	**7**	75c. yellow and violet	10·00	32·00
		a. Dented frame	£550	
55		1r.50 black and carmine	55·00	70·00
		a. Dented frame	£950	£1100
56		2r.25 purple and green	50·00	90·00
		a. Dented frame	£1000	£1400
46/56 *Set of 11*			£130	£225
46s/56s Optd "SPECIMEN" *Set of 11*			£225	

1903. Surch locally with T **8**.

57	**6**	3c. on 15c. ultramarine (3.7)	1·00	3·50
		a. Dented frame	£275	£325
58		3c. on 18c. sage-green and carmine (2.9)	2·75	48·00
		a. Dented frame	£400	£1000
59		3c. on 45c. brown and carmine (21.7)	3·00	4·00
		a. Dented frame	£350	£350
57/9 *Set of 3*			6·00	50·00
57s/9s H/S "Specimen" *Set of 3*			90·00	

CROWN COLONY

The Seychelles became a Separate Crown Colony by Letters Patent dated 31 August 1903.

1906. Wmk Mult Crown CA. P 14.

60	**6**	2c. chestnut and green	1·50	4·25
		a. Dented frame	£130	£225
61		3c. dull green	1·50	1·50
		a. Dented frame	£150	£170
62		6c. carmine	2·00	80
		a. Dented frame	£180	£130
63		12c. olive-sepia and dull green	3·00	3·25
		a. Dented frame	£275	£300
64		15c. ultramarine	3·00	2·00
		a. Dented frame	£275	£200
65		18c. sage-green and carmine	3·00	6·50
		a. Dented frame	£300	£400
66		30c. violet and dull green	6·00	8·00
		a. Dented frame	£350	£450
67		45c. brown and carmine	3·75	13·00
		a. Dented frame	£425	£500
68	**7**	75c. yellow and violet	8·50	55·00
		a. Dented frame	£550	
69		1r.50 black and carmine	60·00	65·00
		a. Dented frame	£950	£950
70		2r.25 purple and green	55·00	65·00
		a. Dented frame	£950	£1000
60/70 *Set of 11*			£130	£200

9   **10**   Split "A" (R. 8/3 of left pane)

1912 (Apr)–**16**. Wmk Mult Crown CA. P 14.

71	**9**	2c. chestnut and green	1·00	8·50
		a. Split "A"	£130	£300
72		3c. green	6·00	60
		a. Split "A"	£275	£130
73		6c. Carmine-red (6.13)	4·25	2·75
		a. Aniline-carmine (1916)	13·00	4·50
		b. Split "A"	£325	£170

74		12c. olive-sepia and dull green (1.13)	1·50	6·50
		a. Split "A"	£180	£325
75		15c. ultramarine	4·75	2·50
		a. Split "A"	£325	£180
76		18c. sage-green and carmine (1.13)	3·25	12·00
		a. Split "A"	£225	£425
77		30c. violet and green (1.13)	13·00	2·75
		a. Split "A"	£375	£190
78		45c. brown and carmine (1.13)	2·75	50·00
		a. Split "A"	£275	
79	**10**	75c. yellow and violet (1.13)	2·75	6·50
		a. Split "A"	£300	£400
80		1r.50 black and carmine (1.13)	11·00	1·00
		a. Split "A"	£475	£150
81		2r.25 deep magenta and green (*shades*) (1.13)	75·00	2·75
		a. Split "A"	£1100	£250
71/81 *Set of 11*			£110	85·00
71s/81s Optd "SPECIMEN" *Set of 11*			£250	

11   **12**   **13**

1917–22. Die I. Chalk-surfaced paper (18c. to 5r.). Wmk Mult Crown CA. P 14.

82	**11**	2c. chestnut and green	50	2·75
83		3c. green	2·00	1·25
84	**12**	5c. deep brown (1920)	4·25	13·00
85	**11**	6c. carmine	4·50	1·00
		a. Rose (1919)	12·00	2·50
86		12c. grey (1919)	2·50	1·75
87		15c. ultramarine	1·75	1·50
88		18c. purple/yellow (1919)	4·50	48·00
		a. On orange-buff (1920)	17·00	60·00
		b. On buff (1920)		
		c. Die II. On pale yellow (1922)	4·00	27·00
89	**13**	25c. black and red/buff (1920)	4·00	50·00
		a. On orange buff (1920)	40·00	75·00
		b. Die II. On pale yellow (1922)	5·00	18·00
90	**11**	30c. dull purple and olive (1918)	1·50	15·00
91		45c. dull purple and orange (1919)	3·50	48·00
92	**13**	50c. dull purple and black (1920)	12·00	60·00
93		75c. black/blue-green (olive back) (1918)	2·00	28·00
		a. Die II. On emerald back (1922)	1·40	24·00
94		1r. dull purple and red (1920)	22·00	70·00
95		1r.50 reddish purple and blue/blue (1918)	9·00	55·00
		a. Die II. Blue-purple and blue/blue (1922)	22·00	32·00
96		2r.25 yellow-green and violet (1918)	50·00	£160
97		5r. green and blue (1920)	£140	£275
82/97 *Set of 16*			£225	£650
82s/97s Optd "SPECIMEN" *Set of 16*			£325	

Examples of most values are known showing postmarks. These include part strikes of Seychelles postmarks dated "24 AP 93" and "AU 6 1903", and Victoria postmarks dated "NO 27" or "MY 6 35".

1921–32. Die II. Chalk-surfaced paper (18c. and 25c. to 5r.). Wmk Mult Script CA. P 14.

98	**11**	2c. chestnut and green	25	15
99		3c. green	1·75	15
100		3c. black (1922)	1·00	30
101		4c. green (1922)	1·00	2·50
102		4c. sage-green and carmine (1928)	6·50	20·00
103	**12**	5c. deep brown	75	5·50
104	**11**	6c. carmine	4·50	9·00
		w. Wmk inverted	£250	
105		6c. deep mauve (1922)	1·50	10
106	**13**	9c. red (1927)	3·75	4·25
107	**11**	12c. grey (1922)	2·75	20
		a. Die I (1932)	30·00	65
108		12c. carmine-red (1922)	2·00	30
110		15c. bright blue	2·00	65·00
111		15c. yellow (1922)	1·00	2·75
112		18c. purple/pale yellow (1925)	2·50	20·00
113	**13**	20c. bright blue (1922)	1·50	35
		a. Dull blue (1924)	8·50	55
114		25c. black and red/pale yellow (1925)	2·75	27·00
115	**11**	30c. dull purple and olive	1·25	15·00
		w. Wmk inverted		
116		45c. dull purple and orange	1·25	6·00
117	**13**	50c. dull purple and black	2·50	2·25
118		75c. black/emerald (1924)	8·00	22·00
119		1r. dull purple and red	28·00	18·00
		a. Die I (1932)	12·00	35·00
121		1r.50 black and blue/blue (1924)	16·00	22·00
122		2r.25 yellow-green and violet	20·00	14·00
123		5r. yellow-green and blue	£120	£170

98/123 *Set of* 24 .... £190   £375
98s/123s Optd "SPECIMEN" *Set of* 24.......................................   £400
    The 3c. green and 12c. grey (Die II) were reissued in 1927. "SPECIMEN" overprints on these printings are 15.5×1.75 mm instead of the 14.5×2.5 mm of the original issue. (*Price*, 3c. £550, 12c. £100).
    Examples of most values are known showing the forged postmarks mentioned above.

Extra flagstaff (Plate "1" R. 9/11)   Short extra flagstaff (Plate "2" R. 2/1)

Lightning conductor (Plate "3" R. 2/5)   Flagstaff on right-hand turret (Plate "5" R. 7/1)   Double flagstaff (Plate "6" R. 5/2)

1935 (6 May). Silver Jubilee. As T **50a** of Mauritius, but ptd by B.W. P 11×12.

128		6c. ultramarine and grey-black	1·25	2·50
		a. Extra flagstaff	£250	£425
		b. Short extra flagstaff	£275	£400
		c. Lightning conductor	£375	
		d. Flagstaff on right-hand turret	£425	£450
		e. Double flagstaff	£475	£500
129		12c. green and indigo	4·75	1·50
		a. Extra flagstaff	£3500	£3750
		b. Short extra flagstaff	£450	£300
		c. Lightning conductor	£2500	
		d. Flagstaff on right-hand turret	£700	£700
		e. Double flagstaff	£700	£700
130		20c. brown and deep blue	3·50	5·50
		a. Extra flagstaff	£400	£500
		b. Short extra flagstaff	£325	
		c. Lightning conductor	£500	£550
		d. Flagstaff on right-hand turret	£550	£650
		e. Double flagstaff	£600	
131		1r. slate and purple	7·50	30·00
		a. Extra flagstaff	£225	£425
		b. Short extra flagstaff	£425	£650
		c. Lightning conductor	£325	£500
		d. Flagstaff on right-hand turret	£650	
		e. Double flagstaff	£650	
128/31 *Set of* 4			15·00	35·00
128s/31s Perf "SPECIMEN" *Set of* 4			£170	

Examples are known showing forged Victoria "B MY 6 35" postmarks.

1937 (12 May). Coronation. As T **50b** of Mauritius. P 11×11½.

132		6c. sage-green	1·00	15
133		12c. orange	1·00	50
134		20c. blue	1·00	1·00
132/4 *Set of* 3			2·75	1·50
132s/4s Perf "SPECIMEN" *Set of* 3			£110	

14 Coco-de-mer Palm   **15** Giant Tortoise   **16** Fishing Pirogue

"Handkerchief" on oar flaw (R. 6/2)

(Photo Harrison)

1938 (1 Jan)–**49**. Wmk Mult Script CA. Chalk-surfaced paper. P 14½×13½ (vert) or 13½×14½ (horiz).

135	**14**	2c. purple-brown (10.2.38)	1·50	40
		a. Ordinary paper (18.11.42)	30	1·75
136	**15**	3c. green	12·00	2·75
136a		3c. orange (8.8.41)	1·25	1·00
		ab. Ordinary paper (18.11.42)	55	1·50
137	**16**	6c. orange	17·00	3·50
137a		6c. greyish green (8.8.41)	6·00	1·25
		aw. Wmk inverted	£1500	
		b. Ordinary paper. *Green* (18.11.42)	2·50	2·25
		c. Green (5.4.49)	18·00	1·25
138	**14**	9c. scarlet (10.2.38)	18·00	4·00
138a		9c. grey-blue (8.8.41)	38·00	40
		ab. Ordinary paper (18.11.42)	25·00	1·50
		ac. Ordinary paper. *Dull blue* (19.11.45)	8·00	3·25
		ad. Dull blue (5.4.49)	28·00	6·00
		aw. Wmk inverted	£4500	
139	**15**	12c. reddish violet	50·00	1·25
139a		15c. brown-carmine (8.8.41)	28·00	40
		ab. Ordinary paper. *Brown-red* (18.11.42)	9·50	4·75
139c	**14**	18c. carmine-lake (8.8.41)	14·00	60
		ca. Ordinary paper (18.11.42)	9·00	3·50
		cb. Rose-carmine (5.4.49)	38·00	16·00
140	**16**	20c. blue	45·00	6·00
140a		20c. brown-ochre (8.8.41)	26·00	65
		ab. "Handkerchief" flaw	£550	£160
		b. Ordinary paper (18.11.42)	3·25	3·00
		ba. "Handkerchief" flaw	£275	£180
141	**14**	25c. brown-ochre	50·00	14·00
142	**15**	30c. carmine (10.2.38)	50·00	11·00
142a		30c. blue (8.8.41)	45·00	50
		ab. Ordinary paper (18.11.42)	2·50	6·50
143	**16**	45c. chocolate (10.2.38)	38·00	4·25
		a. Ordinary paper. *Purple-brown* (18.11.42)	5·00	3·00
		b. Purple-brown (5.4.49)	42·00	20·00
144	**14**	50c. deep reddish violet (10.2.38)	20·00	60
		a. Ordinary paper (18.11.42)	1·75	3·25
144b		50c. bright lilac (13.6.49)	5·50	4·00
145	**15**	75c. slate-blue (10.2.38)	85·00	50·00
145a		75c. deep slate-lilac (8.8.41)	27·00	9·00
		ab. Ordinary paper (18.11.42)	4·25	9·00
146	**16**	1r. yellow-green (10.2.38)	£150	90·00
146a		1r. grey-black (8.8.41)	70·00	6·00
		ab. Ordinary paper (18.11.42)	6·00	7·50
147	**14**	1r.50 ultramarine (10.2.38)	48·00	8·50
		a. Ordinary paper (18.11.42)	8·50	18·00
		aw. Wmk inverted	£4500	
148	**15**	2r.25 olive (10.2.38)	75·00	18·00
		a. Ordinary paper (18.11.42)	32·00	40·00
149	**16**	5r. red (10.2.38)	32·00	16·00
		a. Ordinary paper (18.11.42)	35·00	48·00
135/49 *Set of* 25			£550	£225
135s/49s (*ex* 50c. bright lilac) Perf "SPECIMEN" *Set of* 24			£850	

    Examples of most values are known showing forged Victoria postmarks dated "NO 27", "SP 17 41", "DE 12 41", "SP 14 42", "DE 21 42" or "NO 16 43".

Lamp on mast flaw (R. 1/5)

1946 (23 Sept). Victory. As T **51a** of Mauritius.

150	9c. light blue		10	10
151	30c. deep blue		30	20
	a. Lamp on mast flaw		50·00	42·00
150s/1s Perf "SPECIMEN" Set of 2			95·00	

Line by crown (R. 1/3)

1948 (5 Nov). Royal Silver Wedding. As T **52a/b** of Mauritius.

152	9c. ultramarine		15	60
	a. Line by crown		48·00	65·00
153	5r. carmine		15·00	48·00

Examples are known showing forged Victoria "C 11 NOV 48" postmarks.

1949 (10 Oct). 75th Anniv of U.P.U. As T **52c/f** of Mauritius but inscribed "SEYCHELLES" in recess.

154	18c. bright reddish purple		20	25
155	50c. purple		1·75	3·25
156	1r. grey		50	40
157	2r.25 olive		35	1·25
154/7 Set of 4			2·50	4·75

17 Sailfish   **18** Map of Indian Ocean

(Photo Harrison)

1952 (3 Mar). Various designs as T **14/16** but with new portrait and crown as in T **17/18**. Chalk-surfaced paper. Wmk Mult Script CA. P 14½×13½ (vert) or 13½×14½ (horiz).

158	**17**	2c. lilac	75	70
		a. Error. Crown missing, W **9a**	£850	
		b. Error. St. Edward's Crown, W **9b**	£140	£190
159	**15**	3c. orange	1·25	30
		a. Error. Crown missing, W **9a**	£650	£700
		b. Error. St. Edward's Crown, W **9b**	£180	£180
160	**14**	9c. chalky blue	60	1·75
		a. Error. Crown missing, W **9a**	£1400	
		b. Error. St. Edward's Crown, W **9b**	£375	£500
161	**16**	15c. deep yellow-green	50	1·00
		a. Error. Crown missing, W **9a**	£900	
		b. Error. St. Edward's Crown, W **9b**	£325	£400
162	**18**	18c. carmine-lake	1·75	20
		a. Error. Crown missing, W **9a**	£1300	
		b. Error. St. Edward's Crown, W **9b**	£375	£425
163	**16**	20c. orange-yellow	3·00	1·50
		a. Error. Crown missing, W **9a**	£1400	£1200
		b. Error. St. Edward's Crown, W **9b**	£450	£600
164	**15**	25c. vermilion	70	3·50
		a. Error. Crown missing, W **9a**	£1700	
		b. Error. St. Edward's Crown, W **9b**	£450	
165	**17**	40c. ultramarine	1·25	2·75
		a. Error. Crown missing, W **9a**	£1800	
		b. Error. St. Edward's Crown, W **9b**	£800	
166	**16**	45c. purple-brown	2·00	30
		a. Error. Crown missing, W **9a**	£2000	
		b. Error. St. Edward's Crown, W **9b**	£475	£475
167	**14**	50c. reddish violet	1·50	1·75
		a. Error. Crown missing, W **9a**	£1700	£1700
		b. Error. St. Edward's Crown, W **9b**	£600	£700
168	**18**	1r. grey-black	6·50	4·50
		a. Error. Crown missing, W **9a**	£4250	
		b. Error. St. Edward's Crown, W **9b**	£1400	
169	**14**	1r.50 blue	14·00	18·00
		b. Error. St. Edward's Crown, W **9b**	£3500	
170	**15**	2r.25 brown-olive	19·00	21·00
		b. Error. St. Edward's Crown, W **9b**	£1600	
171	**18**	5r. red	21·00	22·00
		b. Error. St. Edward's Crown, W **9b**	£1100	
172	**17**	10r. green	28·00	50·00
158/72 Set of 15			90·00	£110

See *Introduction* re the watermark errors.

1953 (2 June). Coronation. As T **67a** of Mauritius.

173	9c. black and deep bright blue		60	70

19 Sailfish   **20** Seychelles Flying Fox

(Photo Harrison)

1954 (1 Feb)–**61**. Designs previously used for King George VI issue, but with portrait of Queen Elizabeth II, as in T **19** and T **20**. Chalk-surfaced paper. Wmk Mult Script CA. P 14½×13½ (vert) or 13½×14½ (horiz).

174	**19**	2c. lilac	10	10
175	**15**	3c. orange	10	10
175a	**20**	5c. violet (25.10.57)	2·75	30
176	**14**	9c. chalky blue	10	10
176a		10c. chalky blue (15.9.56)	1·00	2·25
		ab. Blue (11.7.61)	13·00	5·50
177	**16**	15c. deep yellow-green	2·50	30
178	**18**	18c. crimson	30	10
179	**16**	20c. orange-yellow	1·50	20
180	**15**	25c. vermilion	2·25	1·00
180a	**18**	35c. crimson (15.9.56)	6·50	1·75
181	**19**	40c. ultramarine	1·00	25
182	**16**	45c. purple-brown	20	15
183	**14**	50c. reddish violet	30	80
183a	**16**	70c. purple-brown (15.9.56)	6·50	2·25
184	**18**	1r. grey-black	1·75	40
185	**14**	1r.50 blue	11·00	15·00
186	**15**	2r.25 brown-olive	9·50	10·00
187	**18**	5r. red	18·00	9·00
188	**19**	10r. green	28·00	18·00
174/88 Set of 19			80·00	55·00

21 "La Pierre de Possession"   **(22)**

(Photo Harrison)

1956 (15 Nov). Bicentenary of "La Pierre de Possession". Wmk Mult Script CA. P 14½×13½.

189	**21**	40c. ultramarine	20	15
190		1r. black	30	20

e 191   **e** 191a   **s** 191   **s** 191b   **c** 191   **c** 191c

1957 (16 Sept). No. 182 surch with T **22**.

191	5c. on 45c. purple-brown		15	10
	a. Italic "e"		14·00	14·00
	b. Italic "s"		6·00	6·50
	c. Italic "c"		3·75	3·75
	d. Thick bars omitted		£1100	
	e. Surch double		£550	

There were two settings of this surcharge. The first setting contained No. 191a on R. 3/1, No. 191b on R. 5/3, No. 191c on R. 6/1 and 9/2, and No. 191d on R. 5/2. Nos. 191a and 191d did not occur on the second setting which shows No. 191b on R. 1/4, and No. 191c on R. 5/1 and R. 10/4.

23 Mauritius 6d. Stamp with Seychelles "B 64" Cancellation

(Recess: cancellation typo B.W.)

1961 (11 Dec). Centenary of First Seychelles Post Office. W w **12**. P 11½.

193	**23**	10c. blue, black and purple	25	10
194		35c. blue, black and myrtle-green	40	10
195		2r.25 blue, black and orange-brown	70	45
193/5 Set of 3			1·25	50

24 Black Parrot   **29** Anse Royale Bay   **40** Colony's Badge

(Des V. Whiteley. Photo Harrison)

1962 (21 Feb)–**68**. T **24**, **29**, **40** and similar designs. W w **12** (upright). P 13½×14½ (horiz designs and 10r.) or 14½×13½ (others).

196	5c. multicoloured	3·25	10
197	10c. multicoloured	1·50	10
198	15c. multicoloured	30	10
199	20c. multicoloured	1·75	10
200	25c. multicoloured	50	10
200a	30c. multicoloured (15.7.68)	8·50	6·00
201	35c. multicoloured	1·75	1·50
202	40c. multicoloured	20	1·50
203	45c. multicoloured (1.8.66)	3·50	5·00
204	50c. multicoloured	40	25
205	70c. ultramarine and light blue	7·00	3·00
206	75c. multicoloured (1.8.66)	2·75	4·25
207	1r. multicoloured	1·00	10
208	1r.50 multicoloured	5·50	6·50
209	2r.25 multicoloured	5·50	11·00
210	3r.50 multicoloured	2·25	6·50
211	5r. multicoloured	8·50	2·50
212	10r. multicoloured	16·00	4·00
196/212	Set of 18	60·00	45·00

Designs: Vert (as T **24**)—10c. Vanilla vine; 15c. Fisherman; 20c. Denis Island lighthouse; 25c. Clock Tower, Victoria; 50c. Cascade Church; 70c. Sailfish; 75c. Coco-de-Mer palm. Horiz (as T **29**)—30c., 35c. Anse Royale Bay; 40c. Government House; 45c. Fishing pirogue; 1r. Cinnamon; 1r.50, Copra; 2r.25, Map; 3r.50, Land settlement; 5r. Regina Mundi Convent.

The 1r. exists with PVA gum as well as gum arabic, but the 30c. exists with PVA gum only.

See also Nos. 233/7.

For stamps of the above issue overprinted "B.I.O.T." see under British Indian Ocean Territory.

1963 (4 June). Freedom from Hunger. As T **70a** of Mauritius.

213	70c. reddish violet	60	25

1963 (16 Sept). Red Cross Centenary. As T **70b** of Mauritius.

214	10c. red and black	25	10
215	75c. red and blue	75	1·50

(41)   **41a** Footballer's Legs, Ball and Jules Rimet Cup

1965 (15 Apr). Nos. 201 and 205 surch as T **41**.

216	45c. on 35c. multicoloured	15	15
217	75c. on 70c. ultramarine and light blue	35	15

1965 (1 June). I.T.U. Centenary. As T **71a** of Mauritius.

218	5c. orange and ultramarine	10	10
219	1r.50 mauve and apple-green	50	25

1965 (25 Oct). International Co-operation Year. As T **71b** of Mauritius.

220	5c. reddish purple and turquoise-green	15	10
221	40c. deep bluish green and lavender	35	30

1966 (24 Jan). Churchill Commemoration. As T **71c** of Mauritius.

222	5c. new blue	15	75
223	15c. deep green	45	10
224	75c. brown	1·25	45
225	1r.50 bluish violet	1·40	4·00
222/5	Set of 4	3·00	4·75

(Des V. Whiteley. Litho Harrison)

1966 (1 July). World Cup Football Championship.

226	**41a** 15c. violet, yellow-green, lake and yellow-brown	20	25
	a. "50 c GRENADA" on front of stamp	£375	
227	1r. chocolate, blue-green, lake and yellow-brown	35	40

No. 226a shows a positive offset of the Grenada duty plate from the blanket on the front and a negative offset on the reverse.

41b W.H.O. Building   **42** Seychelles Flying Fox

Des M. Goaman. Litho Harrison.

1966 (20 Sept). Inauguration of W.H.O. Headquarters, Geneva.

228	**41b** 20c. black, yellow-green and light blue	20	10
229	50c. black, light purple and yellow-brown	40	20

1966 (1 Dec). 20th Anniv of U.N.E.S.C.O. As Nos. 342/4 of Mauritius.

230	15c. slate-violet, red, yellow and orange	20	10
231	1r. orange-yellow, violet and deep olive	35	1·00
232	5r. black, bright purple and orange	80	1·00
230/2	Set of 3	1·25	1·00

1967–69. As Nos. 196/7, 204 and new values as T **42** but wmk w **12** (sideways).

233	5c. multicoloured (7.2.67)	35	2·50
234	10c. multicoloured (4.6.68)	30	15
235	50c. multicoloured (13.5.69)	1·75	3·75
236	60c. red, blue and blackish brown (15.7.68)	1·75	45
237	85c. ultramarine and light blue (as No. 205) (15.7.68)	1·00	40
233/7	Set of 5	4·50	6·50

The 10c. exists with PVA gum as well as gum arabic, but the 50c. to 85c. exist with PVA gum only.

UNIVERSAL ADULT SUFFRAGE 1967

(43)   **44** Money Cowrie, Mole Cowrie and Tiger Cowrie

1967 (18 Sept). Universal Adult Suffrage. As Nos. 198 and 206, but W w **12** (sideways), and Nos. 203 and 210 (wmk upright), optd with T **43**.

238	15c. multicoloured	10	10
	a. Opt double	£425	
239	45c. multicoloured	10	10
240	75c. multicoloured	10	10
241	3r.50 multicoloured	20	50
238/41	Set of 4	30	65

(Des V. Whiteley. Photo Harrison)

1967 (4 Dec). International Tourist Year. T **44** and similar horiz designs. Multicoloured. W w **12**. P 14×13.

242	15c. Type **44**	20	10
243	40c. Beech Cone, Textile or Cloth of Gold Cone and Virgin Cone	25	10
244	1r. Arthritic Spider Conch	35	10
245	2r.25 Subulate Auger and Trumpet Triton Shells	60	1·25
242/5	Set of 4	1·25	1·25

(48)   **49** Farmer with Wife and Children at Sunset

1968 (16 Apr). Nos. 202/3 and as No. 206 surch as T **48** (30c.) or with "CENTS" added, and three bars (others). W w **12** (sideways on No. 248)

246	30c. on 40c. multicoloured	15	50
247	60c. on 45c. multicoloured	20	30
248	85c. on 75c. multicoloured	20	30
246/8	Set of 3	50	1·00

(Des Mary Hayward. Litho Harrison)

1968 (2 Sept). Human Rights Year. W w **12**. P 14½×13½.

249	**49**	20c. multicoloured	10	10
250		50c. multicoloured	10	10
251		85c. multicoloured	10	10
252		2r.25 multicoloured	25	1·60
249/52		*Set of 4*	40	1·60

50 Expedition landing at Anse Possession   **54** Apollo Launch

(Des Mary Hayward. Litho and die-stamped Harrison)

1968 (30 Dec). Bicentenary of First Landing on Praslin. T **50** and similar multicoloured designs. W w **12** (sideways on 50c., 85c.). P 14.

253		20c. Type **50**	35	10
254		50c. French warships at anchor (*vert*)	40	15
255		85c. Coco-de-Mer and Black Parrot (*vert*)	90	25
256		2r.25 French warships under sail	90	3·25
253/6		*Set of 4*	2·25	3·25

(Des V. Whiteley. Litho Format)

1969 (9 Sept). First Man on the Moon. T **54** and similar horiz designs. Multicoloured. W w **12** (sideways on horiz designs). P 13½.

257		5c. Type **54**	10	50
258		20c. Module leaving Mother-ship for Moon	15	10
259		50c. Astronauts and Space Module on Moon	20	15
260		85c. Tracking station	25	15
261		2r.25 Moon craters with Earth on the "Horizon"	45	1·60
257/61		*Set of 5*	1·00	2·25

59 Picault's Landing, 1742   **60** Badge of Seychelles

(Des Mary Hayward. Litho Enschedé)

1969 (3 Nov)–**75**. Horiz designs as T **59**/**60**. Multicoloured. W w **12** (sideways*). Slightly toned paper. P 13×12½.

262		5c. Type **59**	10	10
	w.	Wmk Crown to right of CA	2·75	
263		10c. U.S. satellite-tracking station	10	10
	a.	Whiter paper (8.3.73)	70	75
264		15c. *Königsberg I* (German cruiser) at Aldabra, 1914	3·00	2·00
	a.	Whiter paper (8.3.73)	5·50	9·00
265		20c. Fleet re-fuelling off St. Anne, 1939–45..	1·75	10
	a.	Whiter paper (13.6.74)	1·25	2·00
266		25c. Exiled Ashanti King Prempeh	20	10
	a.	Whiter paper (8.3.73)	65	2·75
267		30c. Laying Stone of Possession, 1756	1·00	80
268		40c. As 30c. (11.12.72)	3·25	1·25
	a.	Whiter paper (13.6.74)	1·60	1·60
269		50c. Pirates and treasure	30	15
	a.	Whiter paper (13.6.74)	1·50	1·75
270		60c. Corsairs attacking merchantman	1·00	1·50
271		65c. As 60c. (11.12.72)	6·00	8·00
	aw.	Wmk Crown to left of CA	6·00	
	b.	Whiter paper (13.8.75)	6·50	9·50
272		85c. Impression of proposed airport	3·50	85
273		95c. As 85c. (11.12.72)	6·50	4·25
	a.	Whiter paper (13.6.74)	6·50	3·25
	aw.	Wmk Crown to left of CA		
274		1r. French Governor capitulating to British naval officer, 1794	35	15
	a.	Whiter paper (8.3.73)	1·00	1·25
275		1r.50 H.M.S. *Sybille* (frigate) and *Chiffone* (French frigate) in battle, 1801	1·75	2·00

	a.	Whiter paper (8.3.73)	3·50	10·00
276		3r.50 Visit of the Duke of Edinburgh, 1956	1·00	2·25
	a.	Whiter paper (13.8.75)	3·75	16·00
277		5r. Chevalier Queau de Quincy	1·00	2·75
278		10r. Indian Ocean chart, 1574	2·75	8·00
279		15r. Type **60**	4·00	14·00
262/79		*Set of 18*	28·00	48·00
263a/76a		*Set of 11*	29·00	50·00

*The normal sideways watermark shows Crown to right of CA on the 40, 65 and 95c. and to left of CA on the others, *as seen from the back of the stamp*.

The stamps on the whiter paper are highly glazed, producing shade variations and are easily distinguishable from the original printings on toned paper.

74 White Terns, French Warship and Island

(Des A. Smith; adapted V. Whiteley. Litho D.L.R.)

1970 (27 Apr). Bicentenary of First Settlement, St. Anne Island. T **74** and similar horiz designs. Multicoloured. W w **12** (sideways). P 14.

280		20c. Type **74**	1·40	10
281		50c. Spot-finned Flyingfish, ship and island.	45	10
282		85c. Compass and chart	45	10
283		3r.50 Anchor on sea-bed	70	1·50
280/3		*Set of 4*	2·75	1·60

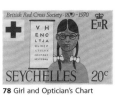 

78 Girl and Optician's Chart   **79** Pitcher Plant

(Des A. Smith. Litho Questa)

1970 (4 Aug). Centenary of British Red Cross. T **78** and similar multicoloured designs. W w **12** (sideways on horiz designs). P 14.

284		20c. Type **78**	30	10
285		50c. Baby, scales and milk bottles	30	10
286		85c. Woman with child and umbrella (*vert*).	30	10
287		3r.50 Red Cross local H.Q. building	1·25	2·75
284/7		*Set of 4*	2·00	2·75

(Des G. Drummond. Litho J. W.)

1970 (29 Dec). Flowers. T **79** and similar vert designs. Multicoloured. W w **12**. P 14.

288		20c. Type **79**	25	15
289		50c. Wild Vanilla	30	15
290		85c. Tropic-Bird Orchid	80	30
291		3r.50 Vare Hibiscus	1·00	2·25
288/91		*Set of 4*	2·10	2·50
MS292		81×133 mm. Nos. 288/91. Wmk inverted ..	2·75	13·00

80 Seychelles "On the Map"

(Des and litho J. W.)

1971 (18 May). "Putting Seychelles on the Map". Sheet 152×101 mm. W w **12** (sideways). P 13 ½.

MS293	**80**	5r. multicoloured	1·75	9·00

81 Piper PA-31 Navajo

82 Santa Claus delivering Gifts (Jean-Claude Waye Hive)

86 Fireworks Display

87 Giant Tortoise and Sailfish

(Des V. Whiteley. Litho Questa)

1972 (18 Sept). "Festival '72". T **86** and similar multicoloured designs. W w **12** (sideways* on 10 and 25c.). P 14.

315	10c. Type **86**		10	10
	w. Wmk Crown to right of CA	9·00		
316	15c. Pirogue race (horiz)		10	10
317	25c. Floats and costumes		10	10
318	5r. Water skiing (horiz)		60	1·25
315/18	Set of 4		65	1·40

*The normal sideways watermark shows Crown to left of CA, *as seen from the back of the stamp.*

(Des (from photograph by D. Groves) and photo Harrison)

1972 (20 Nov). Royal Silver Wedding. Multicoloured; background colour given. W w **12**. P 14×14½.

319	**87**	95c. turquoise-blue	15	10
320		1r.50 red-brown	15	10
		w. Wmk inverted	1·75	

(Des and litho J. W.)

1971 (28 June). Airport Completion. T **81** and similar multicoloured designs showing aircraft. W w **12** (sideways on horiz designs). P 14×14½ (5, 20 and 60c.) or 14½ (others).

294	5c. Type **81**		30	50
295	20c. Westland Wessex HAS-1 helicopter		65	10
296	50c. Consolidated PBY-5A Catalina amphibian (horiz)		70	10
297	60c. Grumman SA-16 Albatross		75	10
298	85e. Short S.26 "G" Class flying boat *Golden Hind* (horiz)		80	10
299	3r.50 Supermarine Walrus Mk 1 amphibian (horiz)		2·25	3·50
294/99	Set of 6		5·00	4·00

(Des Jennifer Toombs. Litho A. & M.)

1971 (12 Oct). Christmas. Drawings by local children. T **82** and similar horiz designs. Multicoloured. W w **12** (sideways*). P 13½.

300	10c. Type **82**		10	10
	w. Wmk Crown to left of CA	50		
301	15c. Santa Claus seated on turtle (Edison Thérésine)		10	10
	w. Wmk Crown to left of CA	50		
302	3r.50 Santa Claus landing on island (Isabelle Tirant)		40	2·25
300/2	Set of 3		50	2·25

*The normal sideways watermark shows Crown to right of CA, *as seen from the back of the stamp.*

87a Princess Anne and Captain Mark Philips

88 Seychelles Squirrelfish

(Des PAD Studio. Litho Questa)

1973 (14 Nov). Royal Wedding.

321	**87a**	95c. ochre	10	10
322		1r.50 dull deep blue	10	10

(Des G. Drummond. Litho Questa)

1974 (5 Mar). Fish. T **88** and similar horiz designs. Multicoloured. W w **12**. P 14½×14.

323	20c. Type **88**		25	15
324	50c. Harlequin Filefish		35	15
325	95c. Pennant Coralfish ("Papillon")		40	40
326	1r.50 Oriental Sweetlips ("Peau d'ane canal")		85	2·50
323/26	Set of 4		1·60	2·75

(83)   **(84)**

85 Seychelles Brush Warbler

ROYAL VISIT 1972

1971 (21 Dec). Nos. 267, 270 and 272 surch in grey as T **83**.

303	40c. on 30c. Laying Stone of Possession, 1756		30	55
304	65c. on 60c. Corsairs attacking merchantman		40	75
305	95c. on 85c. Impression of proposed airport		45	1·00
303/5	Set of 3		1·00	2·10

1972 (20 Mar). Royal Visit. Nos. 265 and 277 optd with T **84**.

306	20c. Fleet re-fuelling off St. Anne, 1939–45		15	20
307	5r. Chevalier Queau de Quincy (Gold)		1·00	3·00

(Des R. Gillmor. Litho Questa)

1972 (24 July). Rare Seychelles Birds. T **85** and similar vert designs. Multicoloured. W w **12** (sideways*). P 13½.

308	5c. Type **85**		60	70
309	20c. Bare-legged Scops Owl		2·25	70
310	50c. Seychelles Blue Pigeon		2·25	70
	w. Wmk Crown to right of CA	22·00		
311	65c. Seychelles Magpie Robin		2·75	75
312	95c. Seychelles Paradise Flycatcher		3·00	2·50
313	3r.50 Seychelles Kestrel		8·00	12·00
308/13	Set of 6		17·00	16·00
MS314	144×162 mm. Nos. 308/13		22·00	28·00
	w. Wmk Crown to right of CA	£200		

*The normal sideways watermark shows Crown to left of CA, *as seen from the back of the stamp.*

89 Globe and Letter

(Des Sylvia Goaman. Litho Enschedé)

1974 (9 Oct). Centenary of Universal Postal Union. T **89** and similar horiz designs. Multicoloured. W w **12** (sideways*). P 12½×12.

327	20c. Type **89**		10	10
	w. Wmk Crown to right of CA	29·00		
328	50c. Globe and radio beacon		20	10
329	95c. Globe and postmark		35	40
330	1r.50 Emblems within "UPU"		50	1·25
327/30	Set of 4		1·00	1·75

*The normal sideways watermark shows Crown to left of CA, *as seen from the back of the stamp.*

90 Sir Winston Churchill

(Des G. Vasarhelyi. Litho Questa)

1974 (30 Nov). Birth Centenary of Sir Winston Churchill. T **90** and similar horiz design. Multicoloured. W w **12**. P 14.

331	95c. Type **90**	20	20
332	1r.50 Profile portrait	35	80
MS333	81×109 mm. Nos. 331/2	60	1·75
	w. Wmk inverted	£250	

VISIT OF Q.E. II

(91)

INTERNAL SELF-GOVERNMENT OCTOBER 1975

(92)

1975 (8 Feb). Visit of R.M.S. "Queen Elizabeth II". Nos. 265a, 269a, 273a and 275a optd with T **91**.

334	20c. Fleet re-fuelling off St. Anne, 1939–45	15	15
335	50c. Pirates and treasure	20	20
336	95c. Impression of proposed airport (Sil)	25	40
337	1r.50 H.M.S. Sybille (frigate) and Chiffone (French frigate) in battle, 1801	35	1·75
334/37	Set of 4	85	2·25

1975 (1 Oct). Internal Self-Government. Nos. 265a, 271b, 274a, and 276a optd with T **92** in gold, by Enschedé.

338	20c. Fleet re-fuelling off St. Anne, 1939–45	15	15
339	65c. Corsairs attacking merchantman	25	30
340	1r. French Governor capitulating to British naval officer, 1794	30	35
341	3r.50 Visit of Duke of Edinburgh, 1956	75	2·50
338/41	Set of 4	1·25	3·00

93 Queen Elizabeth I

94 Map of Praslin and Postmark

(Des C. Abbott. Litho Walsall)

1975 (15 Dec). International Women's Year. T **93** and similar vert designs. Multicoloured. W w **14** (inverted). P 13½.

342	10c. Type **93**	10	50
343	15c. Gladys Aylward	10	50
344	20c. Elizabeth Fry	10	10
345	25c. Emmeline Pankhurst	10	10
346	65c. Florence Nightingale	25	20
347	1r. Amy Johnson	40	35
348	1r.50 Joan of Arc	50	1·50
349	3r.50 Eleanor Roosevelt	70	3·50
342/49	Set of 8	1·90	6·00

(Des J. W. Litho Questa)

1976 (30 Mar). Rural Posts. T **94** and similar vert designs showing maps and postmarks. Multicoloured. W w 14. P 14.

350	20c. Type **94**	20	10
351	65c. La Digue	30	20
352	1r. Mahé with Victoria postmark	35	25
353	1r.50 Mahé with Anse Royale postmark	55	2·00
350/53	Set of 4	1·25	2·25
MS354	166×127 mm. Nos. 350/3	1·50	3·00

95 First Landing, 1609 (inset portrait of Premier James Mancham)

96 Flags of Seychelles and U.S.A.

(Des G. Drummond. Litho J. W.)

1976 (29 June). Independence. T **95** and similar vert designs. Multicoloured. W w **12** (sideways). P 13½.

355	20c. Type **95**	15	15
356	25c. The Possession Stone	15	15
357	40c. First settlers, 1770	15	15
358	75c. Chevalier Queau de Quincy	15	60
359	1r. Sir Bickham Sweet-Escott	15	20
360	1r.25 Legislative Building	20	1·00
361	1r.50 Seychelles badge	20	1·00
362	3r.50 Seychelles flag	80	2·25
355/62	Set of 8	1·75	5·00

(Des and litho J. W.)

1976 (12 July). Seychelles Independence and American Independence Bicentenary. T **96** and similar horiz design. Multicoloured. W w **12** (sideways). P 13½.

363	1r. Type **96**	30	15
364	10r. Statehouses of Seychelles and Philadelphia	70	3·00

97 Swimming

(Des J. W. Litho Questa)

1976 (26 July). Olympic Games, Montreal. T **97** and similar horiz designs. W w **14** (sideways). P 14.

365	20c. ultramarine, cobalt and sepia	10	10
366	65c. bottle-green, apple-green and grey-black	35	10
367	1r. chestnut, blue-green and grey-black	35	10
368	3r.50 crimson, rose and grey-black	50	2·75
365/68	Set of 4	1·10	2·75

Designs:—65c. Hockey; 1r. Basketball; 3r.50, Football.

98 Seychelles Paradise Flycatcher

Independence 1976

(99)

(Des Mrs. R. Fennessy. Litho Questa)

1976 (8 Nov)–**77**. Fourth Pan-African Ornithological Congress, Seychelles. T **98** and similar multicoloured designs. W w **14** (sideways on Nos. 370/1). Ordinary paper. P 14.

369	20c. Type **98**	40	20
	a. Chalk-surfaced paper (7.3.77)	40	20
370	1r.25 Seychelles Sunbird (horiz)	90	1·00
	a. Chalk-surfaced paper (7.3.77)	90	1·00
371	1r.50 Seychelles Brown White Eye (horiz)	1·00	1·50
	a. Chalk-surfaced paper (7.3.77)	1·00	1·25
372	5r. Black Parrot	1·75	4·50
	a. Chalk-surfaced paper (7.3.77)	1·75	5·50
369/72	Set of 4	3·50	6·25

369a/72a *Set of 4*		3·50	6·25
MS373 161×109 mm. Nos. 369/72		5·00	9·00
a. 5r. value in miniature sheet imperf		£1000	

1976 (22 Nov). Independence. Nos. 265a, 269, 271b, 273a, 274a, 276a and 277/9 optd with T **99** (No. 271 additionally surch). W w **12** (sideways*).

374	20c. Fleet re-fuelling off St. Anne, 1939–45..		70	2·50
375	50c. Pirates and treasure		60	2·50
376	95c. Impression of proposed airport		2·25	2·25
	a. Opt inverted		£100	
	w. Wmk Crown to right of CA		2·25	
377	1r. French Governor capitulating to British naval officer, 1794		55	2·25
378	3r.50 Visit of Duke of Edinburgh, 1956		2·75	4·50
	a. Opt inverted		£100	
	b. On No. 276		3·50	4·00
	ba. Opt inverted		£120	
379	5r. Chevalier Queau de Quincy		1·75	7·50
380	10r. Indian Ocean chart, 1574		2·50	12·00
381	15r. Type **60**		2·75	12·00
382	25r. on 65c. Corsairs attacking merchantman		3·00	16·00
374/82 *Set of 9*			15·00	55·00

*The normal sideways watermark shows Crown to left of CA, *as seen from the back of the stamp.*

100 Inauguration of George Washington

(Des Jennifer Toombs. Litho Questa)

1976 (21 Dec). Bicentenary of American Revolution. T **100** and similar horiz designs. P 14×13½.

383	1c. crimson and light rose		10	10
384	2c. violet and light lilac		10	10
385	3c. bright blue and azure		10	10
386	4c. chestnut and light yellow		10	10
387	5c. emerald and light yellow-green		10	10
388	1r.50 sepia and cinnamon		30	35
389	3r.50 dp turquoise-blue and pale blue-green		35	70
390	5r. chestnut and light yellow		40	80
391	10r. chalky blue and azure		65	1·50
383/91 *Set of 9*			1·75	3·25
MS392 141×141 mm. 25r. plum and magenta			2·00	6·50

Designs:—2c. Jefferson and Louisiana Purchase; 3c. William Seward and Alaska Purchase; 4c. Pony Express, 1860; 5c. Lincoln's Emancipation Proclamation; 1r.50 Transcontinental Railroad, 1869; 3r.50 Wright Brothers flight, 1903; 5r. Henry Ford's assembly-line, 1913; 10r. J. F. Kennedy and 1969 Moonlanding; 25r. Signing Independence Declaration, 1776.

101 Silhouette of the Islands   **102** Cruiser *Aurora* and Flag

(Des G. Hutchins (Nos. 395/8), J.W. (others). Litho Questa)

1977 (5 Sept). Silver Jubilee. T **101** and similar multicoloured designs. W w **14** (sideways* on 20 and 40c., 5 and 10r.). P 14.

393	20c. Type **101**		10	10
	w. Wmk Crown to right of CA		£120	
394	40c. Silhouette (*different*)		10	10
395	50c. The Orb (*vert*)		10	10
396	1r. St. Edward's Crown (*vert*)		10	10
397	1r.25 Ampulla and Spoon (*vert*)		10	15
398	1r.50 Sceptre with Cross (*vert*)		10	15
399	5r. Silhouette (*different*)		25	30
400	10r. Silhouette (*different*)		45	60
393/400 *Set of 8*			1·00	1·25

MS401 133×135 mm. 20c., 50c., 1r., 10r. all wmk sideways		55	1·40
w. Wmk Crown to right of CA		£250	

*The normal sideways watermark shows Crown to left of CA, *as seen from the back of the stamp.*

(Litho State Printing Works, Moscow)

1977 (7 Nov). 60th Anniv of Russian October Revolution. P 12×12½.

402	**102**	1r.50 multicoloured	55	30
MS403 101×129 mm. No. 402			80	1·10

103 Coral Scene

(Des G. Drummond. Litho Walsall (40c., 1r., 1r.25, 1r.50), J. W. or Questa (25c. (No. 408B)), J. W. (others))

1977 (10 Nov)–**84**. Multicoloured designs as T **103**. Rupee values show "Re" or "Rs". W w **14** (sideways on 10, 20, 50 and 75c.). P 14½×14 (40c., 1r., 1r.25, 1r.50), 13 (5, 10, 15, 20r.) or 14 (others).

A. No imprint

404A	5c. Reef fish (10.4.78)		30	2·00
405A	10c. Hawksbill Turtle (6.2.78)		50	10
406A	15c. Coco-de-Mer (10.4.78)		30	1·50
407A	20c. Wild Vanilla Orchid (6.2.78)		1·50	10
408A	25c. *Hypolimnas misippus* (butterfly) (10.4.78)		1·50	1·75
409A	40c. Type **103**		40	10
410A	50c. Giant Tortoise (6.2.78)		30	10
411A	75c. Crayfish (6.2.78)		40	10
412A	1r. Madagascar Red Fody		1·25	10
413A	1r.25 White Tern		1·25	20
414A	1r.50 Seychelles Flying Fox		1·00	20
415A	3r.50 Green Gecko (10.4.78)		75	3·25
416A	5r. Octopus (6.2.78)		1·50	40
417A	10r. Tiger Cowrie (*Cypraea tigris*) (10.4.78)....		1·50	2·50
418A	15r. Pitcher Plant (10.4.78)		1·50	2·50
419A	20r. Coat of arms (6.2.78)		1·50	2·50
404A/19A *Set of 16*			14·00	15·00

B. With imprint date at foot

405B	10c. Hawksbill Turtle (14.3.80)		20	10
406B	15c. Coco-de-Mer (14.3.80)		20	15
407B	20c. Wild Vanilla Orchid (5.84)		4·00	4·50
408B	25c. *Hypolimnas misippus* (butterfly) (14.3.80)		2·25	2·50
409B	40c. Type **103** (14.3.80)		20	10
410B	50c. Giant Tortoise (14.3.80)		40	10
411B	75c. Crayfish (14.3.80)		50	30
412B	1r. Madagascar Red Fody (14.3.80)		8·00	75
	w. Wmk inverted		8·50	
414B	1r.50 Seychelles Flying Fox (14.3.80)		2·00	50
405B/14B *Set of 9*			16·00	8·00

The 40c., 1r., 1r.25 and 1r.50 values are horizontal designs, 31×27 mm; the 5, 10, 15 and 20r. are vertical, 28×36 mm; the others are horizontal, 29×25 mm.

Imprint dates: "1979", Nos. 405B/6B, 408B/14B; "1981", No. 409B; "1982", Nos. 405B/9B; "1988", No. 408B (Questa).

For rupee values showing face value as "R" see Nos. 487/94. For 10c. and 50c. with watermark w **14** (upright) and printed by Questa see Nos. 718 and 722. A printing of the 25c. by Questa on the same date has the same perforation and watermark as J. W. printings of No. 408B.

For 50c. and 3r. (inscr "Rs") with watermark w **16** and printed by Questa see Nos. 732/8.

104 St. Roch Roman Catholic Church, Bel Ombre

(Des G. Drummond. Litho Walsall)

1977 (5 Dec). Christmas. T **104** and similar horiz designs. Multicoloured. W w **14** (sideways). P 13½×14.

420	20c. Type **104**		10	10
421	1r. Anglican cathedral, Victoria		10	10
422	1r.50 Roman Catholic cathedral, Victoria		15	10
423	5r. St. Mark's Anglican church, Praslin		30	45
420/23 *Set of 4*			50	55

105 Liberation Day ringed on Calendar

106 Stamp Portraits of Edward VII, George V and George VI

(Des local artists; adapted L. Curtis. Litho Questa)

1978 (5 June). Liberation Day. T **105** and similar vert designs. Multicoloured. W w **14**. P 14×13½.

424	40c. Type **105**	10	10
425	1r.25 Hands holding bayonet, torch and flag	15	10
426	1r.50 Fisherman and farmer	15	15
427	5r. Soldiers and rejoicing people	35	40
424/27 *Set of 4*		60	60

(Des G. Drummond. Litho Questa)

1978 (21 Aug). 25th Anniv of Coronation. T **106** and similar vert designs. Multicoloured. W w **14**. P 14.

428	40c. Type **106**	10	10
429	1r.50 Victoria and Elizabeth II	15	10
430	3r. Queen Victoria Monument	25	25
431	5r. Queen's Building, Victoria	35	35
428/31 *Set of 4*		75	65
MS432 87×129 mm. Nos. 428/31		75	85

107 Gardenia

(Des G. Hutchins. Litho Questa)

1978 (16 Oct). Wildlife. T **107** and similar horiz designs. Multicoloured. W w **14** (sideways). P 13½×14.

433	40c. Type **107**	15	10
434	1r.25 Seychelles Magpie Robin	1·25	50
435	1r.50 Seychelles Paradise Flycatcher	1·25	50
436	5r. Green Turtle	75	1·10
433/36 *Set of 4*		3·00	2·00

108 Possession Stone

109 Seychelles Fody

(Des G. Hutchins. Litho Questa)

1978 (15 Dec). Bicentenary of Victoria. T **108** and similar horiz designs. Multicoloured. W w **14** (sideways). P 13½×14.

437	20c. Type **108**	10	10
438	1r.25 Plan of 1782 "L'Etablissement"	15	15
439	1r.50 Clock Tower	15	15
440	5r. Bust of Pierre Poivre	40	75
437/40 *Set of 4*		65	1·00

(Des G. Drummond. Litho Questa)

1979 (27 Feb). Birds (1st series). T **109** and similar vert designs. Multicoloured. W w **14**. P 14.

441	2r. Type **109**	55	50
	a. Horiz strip of 5. Nos. 441/5	2·50	2·25
442	2r. Green Heron	55	50
443	2r. Thick-billed Bulbul	55	50
444	2r. Seychelles Cave Swiftlet	55	50
445	2r. Grey-headed Lovebird	55	50
441/45 *Set of 5*		2·50	2·25

Nos. 441/5 were printed together, *se-tenant*, in horizontal strips of five throughout the sheet.

See also Nos. 463/7, 500/4 and 523/7.

110 Patrice Lumumba

111 1978 5r. Liberation Day Commemorative and Sir Rowland Hill

(Des G. Vasarhelyi. Litho Questa)

1979 (5 June). African Liberation Heroes. T **110** and similar vert designs. W w **14**. P 14×14½.

446	40c. black, deep violet and lilac	10	10
447	2r. black, blue and pale blue	20	25
448	2r.25 black, reddish brown and orange-brn...	20	30
449	5r. black, bronze-green and dull green	45	1·25
446/49 *Set of 4*		80	1·60

Designs:—2r. Kwame Nkrumah; 2r.25, Dr. Eduardo Mondlane; 5r. Amílcar Cabral.

(Des J.W. Litho Questa)

1979 (27 Aug). Death Centenary of Sir Rowland Hill. T **111** and similar vert designs showing stamps and Sir Rowland Hill. Multicoloured. W w **14**. P 14.

450	40c. Type **111**	10	10
451	2r.25 1972 50c. Rare Birds commemorative ...	25	70
452	3r. 1962 50c. definitive	35	95
450/52 *Set of 3*		60	1·60
MS453 112×88 mm. 5r. 1892 4c. definitive. Wmk inverted		50	55

112 Child with Book

113 The Herald Angel

(Des BG Studio. Litho Questa)

1979 (26 Oct). International Year of the Child. T **112** and similar multicoloured designs. W w **14** (sideways on 40c. and 2r.25). P 14½.

454	40c. Type **112**	10	10
455	2r.25 Children of different races	15	30
456	3r. Young child with ball (*vert*)	20	50
457	5r. Girl with glove-puppet (*vert*)	35	70
454/57 *Set of 4*		70	1·40

Nos. 454/7 were each printed in sheets including two *se-tenant* stamp-size labels.

(Des J. Cooter. Litho Walsall)

1979 (3 Dec). Christmas. T **113** and similar multicoloured designs. W w **14** (sideways on 3r.). P 14½×14 (3r.) or 14×14½ (others).

458	20c. Type **113**	10	10
459	2r.25 The Virgin and Child	30	40
460	3r. The Three Kings (*horiz*)	40	60
458/60 *Set of 3*		65	1·00
MS461 87×75 mm. 5r. The Flight into Egypt (*horiz*) (wmk sideways). P 14½×14		50	70

R.1.10

(114)

1979 (7 Dec). As Nos. 415 but with "1979" imprint date, surch with T **114**.

462	1r.10 on 3r.50 Green Gecko	30	50

115 Seychelles Kestrel

117 Sprinting

116 10 Rupees Banknote

(Des G. Drummond. Litho Questa)

1980 (29 Feb). Birds (2nd series). Seychelles Kestrel. T **115** and similar vert designs. Multicoloured. W w **14** (inverted). P 14.

463	2r. Type **115**	80	60
	a. Horiz strip of 5. Nos. 463/7	3·50	2·75
	aw. Wmk upright	80·00	
464	2r. Pair of Seychelles Kestrels	80	60
465	2r. Seychelles Kestrel with eggs	80	60
466	2r. Seychelles Kestrel on nest with chick	80	60
467	2r. Seychelles Kestrel chicks in nest	80	60
463/67	Set of 5	3·50	2·75

Nos. 463/7 were printed together, se-tenant, in horizontal strips of five throughout the sheet.

(Des B. Grout. Litho Questa)

1980 (18 Apr). "London 1980" International Stamp Exhibition. New Currency. T **116** and similar multicoloured designs showing banknotes. W w **14** (sideways on 40c. and 1r.50). P 14.

468	40c. Type **116**	15	10
469	1r.50 25 rupees	30	15
470	2r.25 50 rupees (vert)	40	25
471	5r. 100 rupees (vert)	80	75
468/71	Set of 4	1·50	1·10
MS472	119×102 mm. Nos. 468/71 (wmk sideways)	2·00	1·60

(Des J. W. Litho Questa)

1980 (13 June). Olympic Games, Moscow. T **117** and similar vert designs. Multicoloured. W w **14**. P 14×14½.

473	40c. Type **117**	10	10
474	2r.25 Weightlifting	20	20
475	3r. Boxing	30	30
476	5r. Sailing	60	50
473/76	Set of 4	1·10	1·00
MS477	90×121 mm. Nos. 473/6	1·40	2·25

118 Boeing 747-200

119 Female Palm

(Des A. Theobald. Litho Questa)

1980 (22 Aug). International Tourism Conference, Manila. T **118** and similar horiz designs. Multicoloured. W w **14** (sideways). P 14.

478	40c. Type **118**	10	10
479	2r.25 Bus	25	30
480	3r. Cruise liner	35	40
481	5r. La Belle Coralline (tourist launch)	55	65
478/81	Set of 4	1·10	1·25

(Des L. Curtis. Litho Harrison)

1980 (14 Nov). Coco-de-Mer (palms). T **119** and similar vert designs. Multicoloured. W w **14**. P 14.

482	40c. Type **119**	10	10
483	2r.25 Male Palm	25	20
484	3r. Artefacts	40	35
485	5r. Fisherman's gourd	55	55
482/85	Set of 4	1·10	1·00
MS486	82×140 mm. Nos. 482/5	1·60	1·60
	w. Wmk inverted	£200	

1981 (9 Jan)–**91**. As Nos. 412/14, 415 (but new value) and 416/19 all with face values redrawn to show "R" instead of "Re" or "Rs" and imprint date at foot. Chalk-surfaced paper.

487	1r. Madagascar Red Fody	1·00	60
	a. Ordinary paper (11.86)	1·75	80
488	1r.10 Green Gecko	70	1·00
489	1r.25 White Tern	2·75	1·75
490	1r.50 Seychelles Flying Fox	50	75
	a. Ordinary paper (11.91)	3·50	3·00
491	5r. Octopus	1·25	1·40
492	10r. Tiger Cowrie (Cypraea tigris)	3·75	3·50
493	15r. Pitcher Plant	4·25	4·50
494	20r. Coat of arms	5·00	6·00
487/94	Set of 8	17·00	18·00

Imprint dates: "1980", Nos. 487/94; "1981", No. 490; "1982", Nos. 487, 490; "1985", No. 491; "1986", No. 487a; "1988", No. 487; "1990", No. 487a; "1991", Nos. 487a, 490a.

For 1r.25, 3r. and 5r. watermarked w **16** see Nos. 735/8.

120 Vasco da Gama's Sao Gabriel, 1497

121 Male White Tern

(Des J. W. Litho Format)

1981 (27 Feb). Ships. T **120** and similar horiz designs. Multicoloured. W w **14** (sideways). P 14½×14.

495	40c. Type **120**	15	10
496	2r.25 Mascarenhas' caravel, 1505	50	55
497	3r.50 Darwin's H.M.S. Beagle, 1831	55	70
498	5r. Queen Elizabeth 2 (liner), 1968	60	1·00
495/98	Set of 4	1·60	2·10
MS499	141×91 mm. Nos. 495/98	1·50	3·50

(Des G. Drummond. Litho Questa)

1981 (10 Apr). Birds (3rd series). White Tern. T **121** and similar vert designs. Multicoloured. W w **14**. P 14.

500	2r. Type **121**	1·00	65
	a. Horiz strip of 5. Nos. 500/4	4·50	3·00
501	2r. Pair of White Terns	1·00	65
502	2r. Female White Tern	1·00	65
503	2r. Female White Tern on nest, and egg	1·00	65
504	2r. White Tern and chick	1·00	65
500/4	Set of 5	4·50	3·00

Nos. 500/4 were printed together, se-tenant, in horizontal strips of five throughout the sheet.

121a Victoria and Albert I

121b Prince Charles and Lady Diana Spencer

(Des D. Shults. Litho Questa)

1981 (23 June–16 Nov). Royal Wedding. Multicoloured.

(a) W w **15**. *P 14*

505	1r.50 Type **121a**	15	25
	a. Sheetlet of 7. No. 505×6 and No. 506	1·25	
506	1r.50 Type **121b**	65	75
507	5r. *Cleveland*	35	60
	a. Sheetlet of 7. No. 507×6 and No. 508	3·00	
508	5r. As No. 506	1·25	2·50
509	10r. *Britannia*	60	1·50
	aw. Wmk inverted	14·00	
	b. Sheetlet of 7. No. 509×6 and No. 510	4·50	
	bw. Wmk inverted	£120	
510	10r. As No. 506	1·75	3·00
	aw. Wmk inverted	50·00	
505/10 *Set of 6*		4·25	7·75
MS511 120×109 mm. 7r.50, As No. 506. Wmk sideways. P 12 (16 Nov)		1·00	1·00

(b) Booklet stamps. No wmk. P 12 (16 Nov)

512	1r.50 As No. 505	20	50
	a. Booklet pane. No. 512×4 with margins all round	80	
513	5r. As No. 508	1·25	2·00
	a. Booklet pane. No. 513×2 with margins all round	2·50	

Nos. 505/10 were printed in sheetlets of seven stamps of the same face value, each containing six of the "Royal Yacht" design and one of the larger design showing Prince Charles and Lady Diana.

Nos. 512/13 come from 22r. stamp booklets.

122 Britten Norman Islander   **123** Seychelles Flying Foxes in Flight

(Litho Harrison)

1981 (27 July). Tenth Anniv of Opening of Seychelles International Airport. Aircraft T **122** and similar horiz designs. Multicoloured. W w **14** (sideways*). P 14½.

514	40c. Type **122**	15	10
515	2r.25 Britten Norman "long nose" Trislander	40	45
	w. Wmk Crown to right of CA	13·00	
516	3r.50 Vickers Super VC-10 airliner	60	70
517	5r. Boeing 747-100 airliner	75	1·00
514/17 *Set of 4*		1·75	2·00

*The normal sideways watermark shows Crown to left of CA, *as seen from the back of the stamp.*

(Litho Format)

1981 (9 Oct). Seychelles Flying Fox (Roussette). T **123** and similar vert designs. Multicoloured. W w **14**. P 14.

518	40c. Type **123**	10	10
519	2r.25 Flying Fox eating	25	35
520	3r. Flying Fox climbing across tree branch	35	55
521	5r. Flying Fox hanging from tree branch	45	80
518/21 *Set of 4*		1·00	1·60
MS522 95×130 mm. Nos. 518/21		1·50	3·75

124 Chinese Little Bittern (male)   **125** Silhouette Island and La Digue

(Des G. Drummond. Litho Questa)

1982 (4 Feb). Birds (4th series). Chinese Little Bittern. T **124** and similar vert designs. Multicoloured. W w **14**. P 14.

523	3r. Type **124**	2·00	1·50
	a. Horiz strip of 5. Nos. 523/7	9·00	6·75
524	3r. Chinese Little Bittern (female)	2·00	1·50
525	3r. Hen on nest	2·00	1·50
526	3r. Nest and eggs	2·00	1·50
527	3r. Hen with chicks	2·00	1·50
523/27 *Set of 5*		9·00	6·75

Nos. 523/7 were printed together, *se-tenant*, in horizontal strips of five throughout the sheet.

(Des J. Cooter. Litho Format)

1982 (22 Apr). Modern Maps. T **125** and similar vert designs. Multicoloured. W w **14**. P 14½.

528	40c. Type **125**	15	10
529	1r.50 Denis and Bird Islands	20	25
530	2r.75 Praslin	30	65
531	7r. Mahé	50	2·25
528/31 *Set of 4*		1·10	2·75
MS532 92×128 mm. Nos. 528/31		1·10	5·00

126 "Education"

(Des PAD Studio. Litho Harrison)

1982 (5 June). Fifth Anniv of Liberation. T **126** and similar horiz designs. Multicoloured. W w **14** (sideways). P 14.

533	40c. Type **126**	10	10
534	1r.75 "Health"	25	25
535	2r.75 "Agriculture"	30	45
536	7r. "Construction"	80	1·40
533/36 *Set of 4*		1·25	2·00
MS537 128×120 mm. Nos. 533/6. P 14½		2·25	6·50

127 Tourist Board Emblem

(Des and litho Harrison)

1982 (1 Sept). Tourism. T **127** and similar horiz designs. Multicoloured. W w **14** (sideways). P 14.

538	1r.75 Type **127**	20	35
539	1r.75 Northolme Hotel	20	35
540	1r.75 Reef Hotel	20	35
541	1r.75 Barbarous Beach Hotel	20	35
542	1r.75 Coral Strand Hotel	20	35
543	1r.75 Beau Vallon Bay Hotel	20	35
544	1r.75 Fisherman's Cove Hotel	20	35
545	1r.75 Mahé Beach Hotel	20	35
538/45 *Set of 8*		1·40	2·50

128 Tata Bus

(Des C. Abbott. Litho Harrison)

1982 (18 Nov). Land Transport. T **128** and similar horiz designs. Multicoloured. W w **14** (sideways). P 14.

546	20c. Type **128**	10	10
547	1r.75 Mini-moke	20	30
548	2r.75 Ox-cart	25	65
549	7r. Truck	80	2·75
546/49 *Set of 4*		1·25	3·50

129 Radio Seychelles Control Room

(Des A. Theobald. Litho Questa)

1983 (25 Feb). World Communications Year. T **129** and similar horiz designs. Multicoloured. W w **14** (sideways). P 14.

550	40c. Type **129**	10	10
551	2r.75 Satellite Earth Station	30	60
552	3r.50 Radio Seychelles Television control room	45	90
553	5r. Postal services sorting office	60	1·75
550/53	Set of 4	1·25	3·00

130 Agricultural Experimental Station

(Des L. Curtis. Litho Questa)

1983 (14 Mar). Commonwealth Day. T **130** and similar horiz designs. Multicoloured. W w **14** (sideways). P 14.

554	40c. Type **130**	10	10
555	2r.75 Food processing plant	25	40
556	3r.50 Unloading fish catch	40	60
557	7r. Seychelles flag	65	1·40
554/57	Set of 4	1·25	2·25

131 Denis Island Lighthouse

132 *Royal Vauxhall Balloon, 1836*

(Des Harrison. Litho Format)

1983 (14 July). Famous Landmarks. T **131** and similar horiz designs. Multicoloured. W w **14** (sideways). P 14×13½.

558	40c. Type **131**	10	10
559	2r.75 Victoria Hospital	30	45
560	3r.50 Supreme Court	35	65
561	7r. State House	55	1·40
558/61	Set of 4	1·10	2·25
MS562	110×98 mm. Nos. 558/61	2·75	7·00

(Des A. Theobald. Litho Harrison)

1983 (15 Sept). Bicentenary of Manned Flight. T **132** and similar horiz designs. Multicoloured. W w **14** (sideways). P 14.

563	40c. Type **132**	15	10
564	1r.75 de Havilland DH.50J	30	30
565	2r.75 Grumman SA-16 Albatross flying boat	35	55
566	7r. Swearingen Merlin IIIA	55	1·75
563/66	Set of 4	1·25	2·40

133 Douglas DC-10-30 Aircraft

134 Swamp Plant and Moorhen

(Des Park Advertising. Litho Walsall)

1983 (26 Oct). First International Flight of Air Seychelles. W w **14** (sideways). P 14.

567	**133** 2r. multicoloured	1·75	2·00

(Des L. Curtis. Litho Questa)

1983 (17 Nov). Centenary of Visit to Seychelles by Marianne North (botanic artist). T **134** and similar vert designs. Multicoloured. W w **14**. P 14.

568	40c. Type **134**	35	10
569	1r.75 *Wormia flagellaria*	50	30
570	2r.75 Asiatic Pancratium	60	75
571	7r. Pitcher Plant	1·10	2·50
568/71	Set of 4	2·25	3·25
MS572	90×121 mm. Nos. 568/71	2·75	6·50

50c **(135)**

1983 (28 Dec). Nos. 505/10 surch as T **135**.

573	50c. on 1r.50 *Victoria and Albert I*	15	30
	a. Sheetlet of 7. No. 573×6 and No. 574	1·10	
	b. Albino surch	32·00	
	c. Surch double, one albino	35·00	
	d. Surch double, one inverted	55·00	
	e. Surch double, one in 2r.25 value	45·00	
574	50c. on 1r.50 Prince Charles and Lady Diana Spencer	40	1·50
	b. Albino surch	75·00	
	c. Surch double, one albino	85·00	
	d. Surch double, one inverted	£130	
	e. Surch double, one in 2r.25 value	£110	
575	2r.25 on 5r. *Cleveland*	45	70
	a. Sheetlet of 7. No. 575×6 and No. 576	3·25	
576	2r.25 on 5r. As No. 574	1·25	3·00
577	3r.75 on 10r. *Britannia*	75	1·10
	a. Sheetlet of 7. No. 577×6 and No. 578	5·50	
	b. Albino surch	30·00	
	c. Surch double	75·00	
578	3r.75 on 10r. As No. 574	1·60	3·50
	b. Albino surch	65·00	
	c. Surch double	£225	
573/78	Set of 6	4·25	9·00

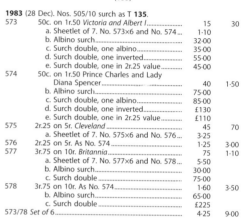

136 Coconut Vessel

137 Victoria Port

(Des Jennifer Toombs. Litho Format)

1984 (29 Feb). Traditional Handicrafts. T **136** and similar horiz designs. Multicoloured. W w **14** (sideways). P 14.

579	50c. Type **136**	15	10
580	2r. Scarf and doll	30	70
581	3r. Coconut-fibre roses	35	1·00
582	10r. Carved fishing boat and doll	90	4·50
579/82	Set of 4	1·50	5·75

(Des C. Collins. Litho Questa)

1984 (21 May). 250th Anniv of "*Lloyd's List*" (newspaper). T **137** and similar vert designs. Multicoloured. W w **14**. P 14½×14.

583	50c. Type **137**	25	10
584	2r. *Boissevain* (cargo liner)	65	55
585	3r. *Sun Viking* (liner)	90	90
586	10r. Loss of R.F.A. *Ennerdale II* (tanker)	2·40	3·50
583/86	Set of 4	3·75	4·50

138 Old S.P.U.P. Office

(Des D. Miller. Litho B.D.T.)

1984 (2 June). 20th Anniv of Seychelles People's United Party. T **138** and similar multicoloured designs. W w **14** (sideways on 50c., 3r.). P 14.

587	50c. Type **138**	10	10
588	2r. Liberation statue (vert)	25	50
589	3r. New S.P.U.P. office	35	85
590	10r. President René (vert)	1·00	4·00
587/90 Set of 4		1·50	5·00

139 1949 U.P.U. 2r.25 Stamp

(Des M. Joyce. Litho Harrison)

1984 (18 June). Universal Postal Union Congress, Hamburg. Sheet 70×85 mm. W w **14** (sideways). P 14½.

MS591	**139** 5r. yellow-olive, flesh and black	1·40	2·50

140 Long Jumping

(Des L. Curtis. Litho Questa)

1984 (28 July). Olympic Games, Los Angeles. T **140** and similar horiz designs. W w **14** (sideways). P 14.

592	50c. Type **140**	10	10
593	2r. Boxing	40	45
594	3r. Swimming	60	75
595	10r. Weightlifting	1·75	2·50
592/95 Set of 4		2·50	3·50
MS596 100×100 mm. Nos. 592/5		3·00	5·50

141 Sub-aqua Diving

142 Humpback Whale

(Des A. Theobald. Litho Questa)

1984 (24 Sept). Water Sports. T **141** and similar horiz designs. Multicoloured. W w **14** (sideways). P 14.

597	50c. Type **141**	30	10
598	2r. Paraskiing	90	45
599	3r. Sailing	1·00	75
600	10r. Water-skiing	2·40	2·50
597/600 Set of 4		4·25	3·50

(Des A. Jardine. Litho Questa)

1984 (19 Nov). Whale Conservation. T **142** and similar horiz designs. Multicoloured. W w **14** (sideways). P 14.

601	50c. Type **142**	1·50	20
602	2r. Sperm Whale	2·75	1·75
603	3r. Black Right Whale	3·00	2·50
604	10r. Blue Whale	6·00	9·00
601/4 Set of 4		12·00	12·00

143 Two Bare-legged Scops Owls in Tree

144 Giant Tortoises

(Des I. Lewington. Litho Walsall)

1985 (11 Mar). Birth Bicentenary of John J. Audubon (ornithologist). Bare-legged Scops Owl. T **143** and similar vert designs. Multicoloured. W w **14**. P 14.

605	50c. Type **143**	2·00	50
606	2r. Owl on branch	3·00	2·25
	w. Wmk inverted	†	£500
607	3r. Owl in flight	3·00	2·75
608	10r. Owl on ground	6·00	8·50
605/8 Set of 4		12·50	12·50

(Des D. Miller. Litho Format)

1985 (15 Mar). "Expo '85" World Fair, Japan. T **144** and similar vert designs. Multicoloured. W w **14**. P 14.

609	50c. Type **144**	70	30
610	2r. White Terns	2·00	1·75
611	3r. Windsurfing	2·00	2·25
612	5r. Coco-de-Mer	2·00	5·00
609/12 Set of 4		6·00	8·50
MS613 130×80 mm. Nos. 609/12		9·00	11·00

For these designs without "Expo '85" inscription see No. **MS**650.

145 The Queen Mother with Princess Anne and Prince Andrew, 1970

146 Boxing

(Des A. Theobald (10r.), C. Abbott (others). Litho Questa)

1985 (7 June). Life and Times of Queen Elizabeth the Queen Mother. T **145** and similar vert designs. Multicoloured. W w **16**. P 14½×14.

614	50c. The Queen Mother in 1930	25	10
615	2r. Type **145**	60	50
616	3r. On her 75th Birthday	80	75
617	5r. With Prince Henry at his christening (from photo by Lord Snowdon)	1·10	1·50
614/17 Set of 4		2·50	2·50
MS618 91×73 mm. 10r. Arriving at Blenheim Palace by Westland Wessex helicopter. Wmk sideways		3·00	3·25

(Des O. Bell. Litho Questa)

1985 (24 Aug). Second Indian Ocean Islands Games. T **146** and similar horiz designs. Multicoloured. W w **14** (sideways). P 14.

619	50c. Type **146**	15	10
620	2r. Football	55	50
621	3r. Swimming	75	75
622	10r. Windsurfing	2·40	2·75
619/22 Set of 4		3·50	3·50

1985 (1 Nov). Acquisition of First Air Seychelles "Airbus". As No. 413A, but additionally inscribed "AIR SEYCHELLES FIRST AIRBUS". "1985" imprint date.

623	1r.25 White Tern	3·25	2·75

147 Agriculture Students

148 Ford "Model T" (1919)

(Des Joan Thompson. Litho Questa)

1985 (28 Nov). International Youth Year. T **147** and similar vert designs. Multicoloured. W w **16**. P 14.

624	50c. Type **147**	10	10
625	2r. Construction students building wall	55	50
626	3r. Carpentry students	70	1·00
627	10r. Science students	2·25	5·00
624/27 Set of 4		3·25	6·00

SEYCHELLES

(Des J. W. Litho Questa)

1985 (18 Dec). Vintage Cars. T **148** and similar horiz designs. Multicoloured. W w **16** (sideways). P 14.

628	50c. Type **148**	60	20
629	2r. Austin "Seven" (1922)	1·50	1·00
630	3r. Morris "Oxford" (1924)	1·60	1·75
631	10r. Humber "Coupé" (1929)	2·50	6·50
628/31	Set of 4	5·50	8·50

149 Five Foot Transit Instrument

150 Ballerina

(Des Harrison. Litho Format)

1986 (28 Feb). Appearance of Halley's Comet. T **149** and similar vert designs. Multicoloured. W w **16**. P 14.

632	50c. Type **149**	40	10
633	2r. Eight foot quadrant	85	70
634	3r. Comet's orbit	85	95
635	10r. Edmond Halley	1·25	3·00
632/35	Set of 4	3·00	4·25

(Des C. Abbott. Litho Format)

1986 (4 Apr). Visit of Ballet du Louvre Company. "Giselle". T **150** and similar vert designs. Multicoloured. W w **16**. P 13½.

636	2r. Type **150**	50	75
637	3r. Male dancer	60	1·50
MS638	80×90 mm. 10r. Pas de deux	1·40	2·40

(Des A. Theobald. Litho Questa)

1986 (21 Apr). 60th Birthday of Queen Elizabeth II. Vert designs as T **208a** of Mauritius. Multicoloured. W w **16**. P 14½×14.

639	50c. Wedding photograph, 1947	10	10
640	1r.25 At State Opening of Parliament, 1982	25	35
641	2r. Queen accepting bouquet, Seychelles, 1972	30	50
642	3r. On board Royal Yacht *Britannia*, Qatar, 1979	40	75
643	5r. At Crown Agents Head Office, London, 1983	60	1·25
639/43	Set of 5	1·40	2·75

151 Ferry to La Digue

(Des G. Drummond. Litho Questa)

1986 (22 May). "Ameripex '86" International Stamp Exhibition, Chicago. Inter-island Communications. T **151** and similar multicoloured designs. W w **16** (sideways on 50c, 7r.). P 14.

644	50c. Type **151**	60	10
645	2r. Telephone kiosk (*vert*)	1·25	70
646	3r. Post Office counter, Victoria (*vert*)	1·40	1·10
647	7r. Air Seychelles Britten Norman "short nose" Trislander aircraft	4·00	3·50
644/47	Set of 4	6·50	5·00

152 Crests of Seychelles and Knights of Malta

152a Prince Andrew and Miss Sarah Ferguson

(Des Jennifer Toombs. Litho Format)

1986 (7 June). Seychelles Knights of Malta Day. W w **16** (sideways). P 14.

648	**152** 5r. multicoloured	1·10	1·60
MS649	101×81 mm. No. 648	2·75	4·00

1986 (12 July). Seychelles Philatelic Exhibition, Tokyo. Miniature sheet, 130×80 mm, containing stamps as Nos. 609/12, but without 'Expo 85' inscription and emblem. W w **16**. P 14.

MS650	As Nos. 609/12	1·75	3·00

(Des D. Miller. Litho Questa)

1986 (23 July). Royal Wedding. Multicoloured. W w **16**. P 14.

651	2r. Type **152a**	35	50
652	10r. Prince Andrew boarding Wessex helicopter, 1983	1·40	3·00

LAZOURNEN ENTERNASYONAL KREOL
(**153**)

1986 (28 Oct). International Creole Day. No. 487a optd with T **153**. "1986" imprint date.

653	1r. Madagascar Red Fody	2·75	3·00

154 Pope John Paul at Seychelles Airport

155 *Melanitis leda*

(Des L. Curtis. Litho Questa)

1986 (1 Dec). Visit of Pope John Paul II. T **154** and similar vert designs, each showing Pope and Seychelles scene. Multicoloured. W w **16**. P 14½×14.

654	50c. Type **154**	75	30
655	2r. Catholic Cathedral, Victoria	2·00	1·25
656	3r. Baie Lazare Parish Church	2·50	2·25
657	10r. Aerial view of People's Stadium	4·25	8·50
654/57	Set of 4	8·50	11·00
MS658	95×106 mm. Nos. 654/7. Wmk inverted	11·00	13·00

(Des R. Lewington. Litho Questa)

1987 (18 Feb). Butterflies. T **155** and similar horiz designs. Multicoloured. W w **16** (sideways). P 14½.

659	1r. Type **155**	1·00	30
660	2r. *Phalanta philiberti*	1·60	1·25
661	3r. *Danaus chrysippus*	1·90	2·25
662	10r. *Euploea mitra*	3·75	8·50
659/62	Set of 4	7·50	11·00

156 Royal Oak Scallop (*Cryptopecten pallium*)

157 Statue of Liberation

(Des Josephine Martin. Litho Walsall)

1987 (7 May). Seashells. T **156** and similar vert designs. Multicoloured. W w **14**. P 14½×14.

663	1r. Type **156**	1·25	30
664	2r. Golden Thorny Oyster (*Spondylus versicolor*)	2·00	1·00
665	3r. Ventral or Single Harp (*Harps ventricosa*) and Ornate Pitar Venus (*Lioconcha ornata*)	2·25	1·60
666	10r. Silver Conch (*Strombus lentiginosus*)	5·50	8·00
663/66	Set of 4	10·00	10·00

(Des Harrison. Litho Format)

1987 (5 June). Tenth Anniv of Liberation. T **157** and similar multicoloured designs. W w **16** (sideways on 2r., 3r.). P 14.

667	1r. Type **157**	20	25
668	2r. Seychelles Hospital (*horiz*)	35	50
669	3r. Orphanage Village (*horiz*)	45	75
670	10r. Proposed Sailfish Monument	1·00	2·50
667/70	Set of 4	1·75	3·50

158 Seychelles Savings Bank, Praslin

(Des A. Theobald. Litho Format)

1987 (25 June). Centenary of Banking in Seychelles. T **158** and similar horiz designs. W w **16** (sideways). P 14.

671	1r. bronze-green and sage-green	20	25
672	2r. bistre-brown and salmon	35	50
673	10r. royal blue and cobalt	1·00	2·50
671/73	Set of 3	1·40	3·00

Designs:—2r. Development Bank; 10r. Central Bank.

40TH WEDDING ANNIVERSARY
(158a)

1987 (9 Dec). Royal Ruby Wedding. Nos. 639/43 optd with T **158a** in silver.

674	50c. Wedding photograph, 1947	15	15
	a. Opt inverted	75·00	
675	1r.25 At State Opening of Parliament, 1982	25	65
676	2r. Queen accepting bouquet, Seychelles, 1972	30	65
677	3r. On board Royal Yacht *Britannia*, Qatar, 1979	40	1·10
678	5r. At Crown Agents Head Office, London, 1983	60	2·00
674/78	Set of 5	1·50	4·00

159 Tuna-canning Factory

(Des O. Bell. Litho B.D.T.)

1987 (11 Dec). Seychelles Fishing Industry. T **159** and similar diamond-shaped-designs. Multicoloured. W w **16**. P 14.

679	50c. Type **159**	15	15
680	2r. Trawler	45	55
681	3r. Weighing catch	70	1·00
682	10r. Unloading net	2·25	3·50
	w. Wmk inverted	40·00	
679/82	Set of 4	3·25	4·75

160 Water Sports

161 Young Turtles making for Sea

(Des Jennifer Toombs. Litho Questa)

1988 (9 Feb). Tourism. T **160** and similar horiz designs, each showing beach hotel. Multicoloured. W w **16** (sideways). P 14½.

683	1r. Type **160**	65	25
684	2r. Speedboat and yachts	1·00	65
685	3r. Yacht at anchor	1·60	1·40
686	10r. Hotel at night	3·50	6·50
683/86	Set of 4	6·00	8·00

(Des Doreen McGuinness. Litho Questa)

1988 (22 Apr). The Green Turtle. T **161** and similar vert designs. Multicoloured. W w **14**. P 14½×14.

687	2r. Type **161**	1·50	2·00
	a. Vert pair. Nos. 687/8	3·00	4·00

688	2r. Young turtles hatching	1·50	2·00
689	3r. Female turtle leaving sea	1·75	2·25
	a. Vert pair. Nos. 689/90	3·50	4·50
690	3r. Female laying eggs	1·75	2·25
687/90	Set of 4	6·00	7·75

Nos. 687/8 and 689/90 were each printed together, *se-tenant*, in vertical pairs throughout the sheets, each pair forming a composite design.

162 Shot Put

162a Leadenhall Street, 1928

(Des O. Bell. Litho Walsall)

1988 (29 July). Olympic Games, Seoul. T **162** and similar vert designs. Multicoloured. W w **16**. P 14½.

691	1r. Type **162**	30	25
692	2r. Type **162**	55	90
	a. Horiz strip of 5. Nos. 692/6	2·50	4·00
693	2r. High jump	55	90
694	2r. Gold medal winner on podium	55	90
695	2r. Athletics	55	90
696	2r. Javelin	55	90
697	3r. As No. 694	60	90
698	4r. As No. 695	80	1·10
699	5r. As No. 696	1·00	1·25
691/99	Set of 9	4·75	7·00
MS700	121×52 mm. 10r. Tennis. W w **14** (sideways*)	4·00	6·50
	w. Wmk Crown to right of CA	65·00	

*The normal sideways watermark shows Crown to left of CA, *as seen from the back of the stamp*.

Nos. 691, 693 and 697/9 were each printed in sheets of 50 of one design. No. 693 also exists from sheets containing Nos. 692/6 printed together, *se-tenant*, in horizontal strips of five.

(Des D. Miller (1r.), L. Curtis and D. Miller (2r.), E. Nisbet and D. Miller (3r.), S. Noon and D. Miller (10r.). Litho Questa)

1988 (30 Sept). 300th Anniv of Lloyd's of London. Multicoloured. W w **16** (sideways on 2, 3r.). P 14.

701	1r. Type **162a**	60	25
702	2r. *Cinq Juin* (travelling post office) (*horiz*)	1·60	75
703	3r. *Queen Elizabeth 2* (liner) (*horiz*)	3·00	1·50
704	10r. Loss of LZ-129 *Hindenburg* (airship), 1937	6·00	5·00
701/4	Set of 4	10·00	6·75

163 Police Motorcyclists

164 Father Christmas with Basket of Presents

(Des A. Theobald. Litho Questa)

1988 (25 Nov). First Anniv of Defence Forces Day. T **163** and similar horiz designs. Multicoloured. W w **14** (sideways). P 14.

705	1r. Type **163**	2·75	50
706	2r. Hindustan Aircraft Chetak helicopter	4·00	2·25
707	3r. *Andromanche* (patrol boat)	4·00	2·75
708	10r. BRDM armoured car	7·50	10·00
705/8	Set of 4	16·00	14·00

(Des S. Hoareau (50c.), R. Leste (2r.), F. Anacoura (3r.), A. McGaw (10r.), adapted N. Harvey. Litho B.D.T.)

1988 (1 Dec). Christmas. T **164** and similar vert designs. Multicoloured. W w **14**. P 13½.

709	50c. Type **164**	15	10
710	2r. Bird and gourd filled with presents	60	70
711	3r. Father Christmas basket weaving	80	90
712	10r. Christmas bauble and palm tree	2·25	5·00
709/12	Set of 4	3·25	6·00

165 *Dendrobium* sp.   **166** India 1976 25p. Nehru Stamp

(Des Annette Robinson. Litho Questa)

1988 (21 Dec). Orchids (1st series). T **165** and similar multicoloured designs. W w **16** (sideways on 2, 10r.). P 14.

713	1r. Type **165**	1·25	25
714	2r. *Arachnis* hybrid (horiz)	1·75	70
715	3r. *Vanda caerulea*	2·00	1·25
716	10r. *Dendrobium phalaenopsis* (horiz)	4·00	6·50
713/16	Set of 4	8·00	7·75

See also Nos. 767/70 and 795/8.

(Litho Questa)

1988 (30 Dec). As Nos. 405B and 410B, but W w **14** (upright). "1988" imprint date. P 14.

718	10c. Hawksbill Turtle	1·50	1·25
722	50c. Giant Tortoise	2·00	1·50

A new Questa printing of the 25c. was issued on the same date. It has the same watermark and perforation as No. 408B.

(Des O. Bell. Litho B.D.T.)

1989 (30 Mar). Birth Centenary of Jawaharlal Nehru (Indian statesman). T **166** and similar horiz design, each showing flags of Seychelles and India. Multicoloured. W w **16** (sideways). P 13½.

724	2r. Type **166**	1·25	50
725	10r. Jawaharlal Nehru	3·25	5·50

(Litho Walsall (1r.25), Questa (others))

1989 (1 May)–**91**. As Nos. 410, 415 (but new value), 489 and 491, but W w **16**. Chalk-surfaced paper (1r.25). Imprint date at foot. P 14½×14 (1r.25) 14×14½ (5r.) or 14 (others).

732	50c. Giant Tortoise (11.91)	2·75	3·00
735	1r.25 White Tern	2·75	2·75
736	3r. Green Gecko (as No. 415) (11.91)	6·50	7·00
738	5r. Octopus (1.91)	3·50	5·50
732/38	Set of 4	14·00	16·00

Imprint dates: "1989", No. 735; "1990", No. 738; "1991", Nos. 732, 736.

167 Pres. René addressing Rally at Old Party Office   **167a** Lift off "Saturn 5" Rocket

(Des D. Miller. Litho Walsall)

1989 (5 June). 25th Anniv of Seychelles People's United Party. T **167** and similar vert designs. Multicoloured. W w **16**. P 14.

742	1r. Type **167**	25	25
743	2r. Women with Party flags and Maison du People	60	50
744	3r. President René making speech and Torch of Freedom	70	80
745	10r. President René, Party flag and Torch of Freedom	2·25	5·00
742/45	Set of 4	3·50	6·00

(Des A. Theobald (10r.), D. Miller (others). Litho Questa)

1989 (20 July). 20th Anniv of First Manned Landing on Moon. Multicoloured. W w **16** (sideways on 2, 3r.). P 14×13½ (1, 5r.) or 14 (others).

746	1r. Type **167a**	55	25
747	2r. Crew of "Apollo 15" (30×30 *mm*)	85	75
748	3r. "Apollo 15" emblem (30×30 *mm*)	1·10	1·10

749	5r. James Irwin saluting U.S. flag on Moon	1·75	2·25
746/49	Set of 4	3·75	4·00
MS750	100×83 mm. 10r. Aldrin alighting from "Apollo 11" on Moon. P 14×13½	5·00	6·50

168 British Red Cross Ambulance, Franco-Prussian War, 1870   **169** Black Parrot and Map of Praslin

(Des A. Theobald. Litho Questa)

1989 (12 Sept). 125th Anniv of International Red Cross. T **168** and similar horiz designs. W w **16** (sideways). P 14½.

751	1r. black and orange-vermilion	3·00	35
752	2r. black, light green and orange-vermilion	3·25	1·50
753	3r. black and orange-vermilion	3·75	2·50
754	10r. black and orange-vermilion	10·00	12·00
751/54	Set of 4	18·00	16·00

Designs:—2r. *Liberty* (hospital ship), 1914–18; 3r. Sunbeam "Standard" army ambulance, 1914–18; 10r. "White Train" (hospital train), South Africa, 1899–1902.

(Des I. Lee. Litho Questa)

1989 (16 Oct). Island Birds. T **169** and similar vert designs. Multicoloured. W w **16**. P 14½×14.

755	50c. Type **169**	2·50	55
756	2r. Sooty Tern and Ile aux Vaches	3·50	1·75
757	3r. Seychelles Magpie Robin and Frégate	4·25	3·00
758	5r. Roseate Tern and Aride	4·75	7·50
755/58	Set of 4	13·50	11·50
MS759	83×109 mm. Nos. 755/8	14·00	15·00

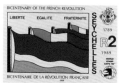

170 Flags of Seychelles and France

(Adapted D. Miller from local artwork. Litho B.D.T.)

1989 (17 Nov). Bicentenary of French Revolution and "World Stamp Expo '89", International Stamp Exhibition, Washington. T **170** and similar horiz designs. W w **16** (sideways). P 14.

760	2r. multicoloured	3·50	1·50
761	5r. black, new blue and scarlet	4·00	6·00
MS762	78×100 mm. 10r. multicoloured	5·00	7·00

Designs:—5r. Storming the Bastille, Paris, 1789; 10r. Reading Revolutionary proclamation, Seychelles, 1791.

171 Beau Vallon School   **172** *Disperis tripetaloides*

(Des L. Curtis. Litho B.D.T.)

1989 (29 Dec). 25th Anniv of African Development Bank. T **171** and similar multicoloured designs. W w **16** (sideways on 1, 2r.). P 14.

763	1r. Type **171**	45	25
764	2r. Seychelles Fishing Authority Headquarters	80	1·00
765	3r. *Variola* (fishing boat) (vert)	2·75	2·50
766	10r. *Deneb* (fishing boat) (vert)	6·50	10·00
763/66	Set of 4	9·50	12·50

(Des N. Shewring. Litho Questa)

1990 (26 Jan). Orchids (2nd series). T **172** and similar vert designs. Multicoloured. W w **16**. P 14.

767	1r. Type **172**	2·50	50
768	2r. *Vanilla phalaenopsis*	3·00	1·50
769	3r. *Angraecum eburneum* subsp *superbum* .	3·50	2·50
770	10r. *Polystachya concreta*	7·00	11·00
767/70 *Set of 4*		15·00	14·00

173 Seychelles 1903 2c. and Great Britain 1880 1½d. Stamps

174 Fumiyo Sako

(Des D. Miller. Litho Security Printers (M), Malaysia)

1990 (3 May). "Stamp World London 90" International Stamp Exhibition. T **173** and similar horiz designs each showing stamps. Multicoloured. W w **14** (sideways). P 12½.

771	1r. Type **173**	75	25
772	2r. Seychelles 1917 25c. and G.B. 1873 1s...	1·25	1·25
773	3r. Seychelles 1917 2c. and G.B. 1874 6d. ..	1·75	2·25
774	5r. Seychelles 1890 2c. and G.B. 1841 1d. red-brown	2·50	4·50
771/74 *Set of 4*		5·75	7·50
MS775 88×60 mm. 10r. Seychelles 1961 Post Office Centenary 2r.25 and G.B. 1840 Penny Black. Wmk upright		11·00	12·00

(Des D. Miller. Litho B.D.T.)

1990 (8 June). "EXPO 90" International Garden and Greenery Exhibition, Osaka. T **174** and similar vert designs. Multicoloured. W w **14**. P 14.

776	2r. Type **174**	1·75	1·00
777	3r. Male and female Coco-de-Mer palms....	2·00	1·50
778	5r. Pitcher Plant and Aldabra Lily..........	3·00	3·50
779	7r. Arms of Seychelles and Gardenia...........	3·75	6·00
776/79 *Set of 4*		9·50	11·00
MS780 130×85 mm. Nos. 776/9. Wmk inverted............		8·50	11·00

175 Air Seychelles Boeing 767-200ER over Island

176 Adult Class

(Des D. Miller. Litho Questa)

1990 (27 July). Air Seychelles "Boeing 767-200ER" World Record-breaking Flight (1989). W w **16**. P 14×14½.

781	**175** 3r. multicoloured	4·25	4·00

No. 781 was printed in sheetlets of ten, containing two horizontal strips of five, separated by a central gutter showing a map of the flight route from Grand Rapids, U.S.A. to the Seychelles.

(Des D. Miller. Litho Questa)

1990 (4 Aug). 90th Birthday of Queen Elizabeth the Queen Mother. Vert designs as T **18a** (2r.) or **18b** (10r.) of British Indian Ocean Territory. W w **16**. P 14×15 (2r.) or 14½ (10r.).

782	2r. multicoloured	1·00	75
783	10r. brownish black and violet	2·50	4·50

Designs:—2r. Queen Elizabeth in Coronation robes, 1937; 10r. Queen Elizabeth visiting Lord Roberts Workshops, 1947.

(Des G. Vasarhelyi. Litho Questa)

1990 (8 Sept). International Literacy Year. T **176** and similar vert designs. Multicoloured. W w **14**. P 14.

784	1r. Type **176**	75	25
785	2r. Reading a letter	1·50	1·25

786	3r. Following written instructions	2·00	2·00
787	10r. Typewriter, calculator and crossword......	5·00	8·50
784/87 *Set of 4*		8·50	11·00

177 Sega Dancers   **178** Beach

(Des Jennifer Toombs. Litho Cartor)

1990 (27 Oct). Kreol Festival. Sega Dancing. T **177** and similar vert designs. Multicoloured. W w **14**. P 13½×14.

788	2r. Type **177**	2·50	2·75
	a. Horiz strip of 5. Nos. 788/92	11·50	12·50
789	2r. Dancing couple (girl in yellow dress).....	2·50	2·75
790	2r. Female Sega dancer	2·50	2·75
791	2r. Dancing couple (girl in floral pattern skirt)	2·50	2·75
792	2r. Dancing couple (girl in red patterned skirt)	2·50	2·75
788/92 *Set of 5*		11·50	12·50

Nos. 788/92 were printed together, *se-tenant*, in horizontal strips of five throughout the sheet.

(Des D. Miller. Litho Questa)

1990 (10 Dec). First Indian Ocean Regional Seminar on Petroleum Exploration. T **178** and similar horiz design. Multicoloured. W w **16** (sideways). P 14½.

793	3r. Type **178**	1·75	1·50
794	10r. Geological map	5·75	7·50

(Des N. Shewring. Litho Questa)

1991 (1 Feb). Orchids (3rd series). Vert designs as T **172**. Multicoloured. W w **16**. P 14.

795	1r. *Bulbophyllum intertextum*	1·75	45
796	2r. *Agrostophyllum occidentale*	2·25	1·75
797	3r. *Vanilla planifolia*	2·50	2·50
798	10r. *Malaxis seyehellarum*	6·00	7·50
795/98 *Set of 4*		11·00	11·00

(Des D. Miller. Litho Questa)

1991 (17 June). 65th Birthday of Queen Elizabeth II and 70th Birthday of Prince Philip. Vert designs as T **227a** of Mauritius. Multicoloured. W w **16** (sideways). P 14½×14.

799	4r. Queen in evening dress	1·60	2·25
	a. Horiz pair. Nos. 799/800 separated by label	3·00	4·50
800	4r. Prince Philip in academic robes	1·60	2·25

Nos. 799/800 were printed in a similar sheet format to Nos. 849/50 of Mauritius.

179 *Precis rhadama*

180 "The Holy Virgin, Joseph, The Holy Child and St. John" (S. Vouillemont after Raphael)

(Des I. Lee. Litho Walsall)

1991 (15 Nov). "Phila Nippon '91" International Stamp Exhibition, Tokyo. Butterflies. T **179** and similar horiz designs. W w **14** (sideways). P 14×14½.

801	1r.50 Type **179**	2·00	85
802	3r. *Lampides boeticus*	2·50	2·25
803	3r.50 *Zizeeria knysna*	2·75	2·50
804	10r. *Phalanta phalantha*	7·25	7·50
801/4 *Set of 4*		13·00	12·00
MS805 78×81 mm. 10r. *Eagris sabadius*		7·00	7·50

(Des D. Miller. Litho B.D.T.)

1991 (2 Dec). Christmas. Woodcuts. T **180** and similar vert designs. W w **16**. P 13½×14.

806	50c. black, brown-ochre and bright crimson	50	15
807	1r. black, brown-ochre and myrtle-green...	90	25
808	2r. black, brown-ochre and blue	1·75	1·10
809	7r. black, brown-ochre & deep violet-blue.	4·50	7·50
806/9	Set of 4	7·00	8·00

Designs:—1r. "The Holy Virgin, the Child and Angel" (A. Bloating after Van Dyck); 2r. "The Holy Family, St. John and St. Anna" (L. Vorsterman after Rubens); 7r. "The Holy Family, Angel and St. Cathrin" (C. Bloemaert).

180a Seychelles Coastline

181 Seychelles Brush Warbler

(Des D. Miller. Litho Questa (5r.), Walsall (others))

1992 (6 Feb). 40th Anniv of Queen Elizabeth II's Accession. Multicoloured. W w **14** (sideways). P 14.

810	1r. Type **180a**	55	25
811	1r.50 Clock Tower, Victoria	65	40
812	3r. Victoria harbour	1·10	1·50
813	3r.50 Three portraits of Queen Elizabeth	1·25	1·75
814	5r. Queen Elizabeth II	1·40	2·75
810/14	Set of 5	4·50	6·00

(Des I. Lee. Litho B.D.T.)

1993 (1 Mar)–**2000**. Flora and Fauna. T **181** and similar multicoloured designs. W w **14** (sideways* on horiz designs). With imprint date. P 13½.

815	10c. Type **181**	2·00	1·50
	w. Wmk Crown to left of CA (1.7.96)	2·50	2·00
816	25c. Bronze Gecko (vert)	1·25	45
817	50c. Seychelles Tree Frog	1·25	40
	w. Wmk Crown to left of CA (1.7.96)	1·75	1·00
818	1r. Seychelles Splendid Palm (vert)	1·00	25
819	1r.50 Seychelles Skink (vert)	1·50	80
820	2r. Giant Tenebrioniid Beetle	1·25	45
	w. Wmk Crown to left of CA (1.7.96)	1·75	1·00
821	3r. Seychelles Sunbird	2·75	1·25
	w. Wmk Crown to left of CA (18.7.2000)	4·75	2·25
822	3r.50 Seychelles Killifish	1·50	1·00
823	4r. Seychelles Magpie Robin	3·25	1·75
824	5r. Seychelles Vanilla (plant) (vert)	2·00	1·75
825	10r. Tiger Chameleon	3·75	3·00
826	15r. Coca-de-Mer (vert)	4·75	6·00
827	25r. Seychelles Paradise Flycatcher (vert)	13·00	13·00
828	50r. Giant Tortoise	17·00	25·00
815/28	Set of 14	50·00	50·00

*The normal sideways watermark shows Crown to right of CA, as seen from the back of the stamp.

Imprint dates: "1993", Nos. 815/28; "1994", Nos. 818, 824/5, 827/8; "1996", Nos. 815w, 816, 817w, 820w, 826; "1998", No. 821; "2000", Nos. 815w, 817w, 818/19, 821w, 822.

182 Archbishop George Carey and Anglican Cathedral, Victoria

183 Athletics

(Des G. Vasarhelyi. Litho Cartor)

1993 (8 June). First Visit of an Archbishop of Canterbury to Seychelles. T **182** and similar horiz design. Multicoloured. W w **14** (sideways). P 13½.

834	3r. Type **182**	2·50	1·50
835	10r. Archbishop Corey with Air France Boeing 747-400 and Air Seychelles Boeing 737-200 airliners	6·00	8·50

(Des S. Noon. Litho Walsall)

1993 (21 Aug). Fourth Indian Ocean Island Games. T **183** and similar vert designs. Multicoloured. W w **14**. P 14½×14.

836	1r.50 Type **183**	65	55
837	3r. Football	1·25	1·00
838	3r.50 Cycling	2·00	1·75
839	10r. Sailing	3·25	6·00
836/39	Set of 4	6·50	9·50

184 *Scotia* (cable ship) off Victoria, 1893

(Des C. Abbott. Litho Cartor)

1993 (12 Nov). Centenary of Telecommunications. T **184** and similar horiz designs. Multicoloured. W w **14** (sideways). P 13.

840	1r. Type **184**	1·75	60
841	3r. Eastern Telegraph Co office, Victoria, 1904	2·50	1·75
842	4r. HF Transmitting Station, 1971	2·75	3·00
843	10r. New Telecoms House, Victoria, 1993	5·00	7·50
840/43	Set of 4	11·00	11·50

(185)

1994 (18 Feb). "Hong Kong '94" International Stamp Exhibition. Nos. 62, 64 and 66/7 of Zil Elwannyen Sesel surch as T **185**.

844	1r. on 2r.10 Souimanga Sunbird	50	30
845	1r.50 on 2r.75 Sacred Ibis	75	60
846	3r.50 on 7r. Seychelles Kestrel (vert)	1·60	2·25
847	10r. on 15r. Comoro Blue Pigeon (vert)	3·00	5·00
844/47	Set of 4	5·25	7·50

186 *Eurema floricola*

187 Lady Elizabeth Bowes-Lyon

(Des I. Lee. Litho Walsall)

1994 (16 Aug). Butterflies. T **186** and similar horiz designs. Multicoloured. W w **16** (sideways). P 14×14½.

848	1r.50 Type **186**	1·75	75
849	3r. *Coeliades forestan*	2·50	2·00
850	3r.50 *Borbo borbonica*	2·75	2·75
851	10r. *Zizula hylax*	5·50	7·50
848/51	Set of 4	11·00	11·50

(Des Jennifer Toombs. Litho B.D.T.)

1995 (26 Sept). 95th Birthday of Queen Elizabeth the Queen Mother. T **187** and similar vert designs. Multicoloured. W w **14**. P 14.

852	1r.50 Type **187**	75	40
853	3r. Duchess of York on wedding day, 1923	1·40	1·00
854	3r.50 Queen Elizabeth	1·60	1·40
855	10r. Queen Elizabeth the Queen Mother	3·50	6·50
852/55	Set of 4	6·50	8·50

188 Female Seychelles Paradise Flycatcher feeding Chick

189 Swimming

(Des N. Shewring. Litho B.D.T.)

1996 (12 July). Endangered Species. Seychelles Paradise Flycatcher. T **188** and similar vert designs. Multicoloured. W w **16**. P 14.

856	1r. Type **188**	70	95
	a. Strip of 4. Nos. 856/9	2·50	3·25
857	1r. Male bird in flight	70	95
858	1r. Female bird on branch	70	95
859	1r. Male bird on branch	70	95
85/59	*Set of 4*	2·50	3·25
MS860	60×53 mm. 10r. Pair on branch	5·00	6·50

In addition to normal sheets of each value Nos. 856/9 were also available in sheets of 16 with the stamps horizontally and vertically *se-tenant*.

(Des R. Walton. Litho Walsall)

1996 (15 July). Centenary of Modern Olympic Games. T **189** and similar vert designs. Multicoloured. W w **16**. P 14.

861	50c. Type **189**	40	20
862	1r.50 Running	60	45
863	3r. Sailing	1·00	1·50
864	5r. Boxing	1·60	3·00
861/64	*Set of 4*	3·25	4·75

190 Archbishop Makarios at Table

191 Comoro Blue Pigeon

(Litho Walsall)

1996 (19 Aug). 40th Anniv of Exile of Archbishop Makarios of Cyprus to Seychelles. T **190** and similar vert design. Multicoloured. W w **14**. P 14.

865	3r. Type **190**	1·50	1·00
866	10r. Archbishop Makarios in priest's robes	3·25	6·00

(Des N. Arlott. Litho Questa)

1996 (11 Nov). Birds. T **191** and similar vert designs. Multicoloured. W w **14**. P 14½.

867	3r. Type **191**	1·50	1·75
	a. Horiz pair. Nos. 867/8	3·00	3·50
868	3r. Seychelles Blue Pigeon	1·50	1·75
869	3r. Souimanga Sunbird	1·50	1·75
	a. Horiz pair. Nos. 869/70	3·00	3·50
870	3r. Seychelles Sunbird	1·50	1·75
871	3r. Red-headed Fody	1·50	1·75
	a. Horiz pair. Nos. 871/2	3·00	3·50
872	3r. Seychelles Fody	1·50	1·75
873	3r. Madagascar White Eye	1·50	1·75
	a. Horiz pair. Nos. 873/4	3·00	3·50
874	3r. Seychelles White Eye	1·50	1·75
867/74	*Set of 8*	10·00	11·50

Nos. 867/8, 869/70, 871/2 and 873/4 were each printed together, *se-tenant*, in horizontal pairs throughout the sheets with the background of each pair forming a composite design showing a regional map.

R1.50

(192)

1997 (12 Feb). "HONG KONG '97" International Stamp Exhibition. No. 226 of Zil Elwannyen Sesel surch with T **192**.

875	1r.50 on 2r. Western Reef Heron ("Dimorphic Little Egret")	2·50	2·50

(Des N. Shewring (No. **MS**882), D. Miller (others). Litho Questa (No. **MS**882), Cartor (others))

1997 (20 Nov). Golden Wedding of Queen Elizabeth and Prince Philip. Multicoloured designs as T **32a** of British Indian Ocean Territory. W w **14**. P 13.

876	1r. Queen Elizabeth wearing red and white suit	65	90
	a. Horiz pair. Nos. 876/7	1·25	1·75
877	1r. Prince Philip driving carriage	65	90
878	1r.50 Prince Philip	75	1·10
	a. Horiz pair. Nos. 878/9	1·50	2·25
879	1r.50 Queen Elizabeth with horse	75	1·10
880	3r. Prince Charles and Princess Anne on horseback	1·40	1·75
	a. Horiz pair. Nos. 880/1	2·75	3·50
881	3r. Prince Philip and Queen Elizabeth	1·40	1·75
876/81	*Set of 6*	5·00	6·75
MS882	110×70 mm. 10r. Queen Elizabeth and Prince Philip in landau (*horiz*). Wmk sideways. P 14½	4·00	4·50

Nos. 876/7, 878/9 and 880/1 were each printed together, *se-tenant*, in horizontal pairs throughout the sheets with the backgrounds forming composite designs.

(Des D. Miller. Litho Questa)

1998 (31 Mar). Diana, Princess of Wales Commemoration. Sheet, 145×70 mm, containing vert designs as T **33a** of British Indian Ocean Territory. Multicoloured. W w **14** (sideways). P 14½×14.

MS883 3r. Wearing red jacket, 1992; 3r. Wearing floral dress, 1981; 3r. Wearing blue and black jacket, 1993; 3r. Wearing white dress, Nepal 1993 (*sold at* 12r.+2r. charity premium) ... 2·00 3·50

193 Powderblue Surgeonfish

194 *Vierge du Cap* (galleon), 1721

(Litho Walsall)

1998 (30 Nov). International Year of the Ocean. T **193** and similar multicoloured designs. W w **14** (sideways). P 14.

884	3r. Type **193**	90	1·25
	a. Horiz strip of 6. Nos. 884/9	5·50	6·75
885	3r. Shoal of Soldierfish	90	1·25
886	3r. Lionfish	90	1·25
887	3r. School of fish	90	1·25
888	3r. Coral	90	1·25
889	3r. Turtle	90	1·25
884/89	*Set of 6*	5·50	6·75

Nos. 884/9 were printed together, *se-tenant*, as horizontal strips of six throughout the sheet.

(Des J. Batchelor. Litho Questa)

1999 (19 Mar). 18th-century Ships. T **194** and similar multicoloured designs. W w **16** (sideways). P 14.

890	1r.50 Type **194**	80	35
891	3r. *L'Elizabeth* (corvette), 1741	1·60	1·00
892	3r.50 *Curieuse* (sloop), 1768	1·60	1·75
893	10r. *La Flèche* (frigate), 1801	3·25	5·50
890/93	*Set of 4*	6·50	7·75
MS894	105×70 mm. 20r. *Le Cheval Marin* (French merchantman), 1774 (*vert*)	7·00	9·00

No. **MS**894 also includes the "Australia '99" World Stamp Exhibition, Melbourne, emblem on the sheet margin.

195 Royal Couple on steps of Chapel Royal, Windsor

196 Cathedral of the Immaculate Conception

(Des D. Miller. Litho Cartor)

1999 (1 Sept). Royal Wedding. T **195** and similar vert design. Multicoloured. W w **14**. P 13½.

895	3r. Type **195**	1·25	75
896	15r. In landau	4·75	7·00

(Litho Questa)

1999 (14 Dec). New Millennium. T **196** and similar horiz designs. Multicoloured. W w **14** (sideways). P 14½.

897	1r. Type **196**	60	30
898	1r.50 Fairy Tern at sunrise	2·00	1·25
899	2r.50 Dolphin and island	2·00	1·50
900	10r. Comet over beach	4·25	6·50
897/900 Set of 4		8·00	8·50

197 Lady Elizabeth Bowes-Lyon

198 Arrival of Jacobin Deportees (Bicentenary)

(Litho Questa)

2000 (4 Aug). Queen Elizabeth the Queen Mother's 100th Birthday. T **197** and similar vert designs. W w **14**. P 14½×14.

901	3r. multicoloured	1·40	70
902	5r. black and light brown	1·90	1·75
903	7r. black and lilac	2·50	3·25
904	10r. multicoloured	3·00	4·00
901/4 Set of 4		8·00	8·75

Designs:—5r. Queen Elizabeth in East End of London during Second World War; 7r. Visiting Seychelles with King George VI and Princess Elizabeth; 10r. Wearing blue hat and outfit.

(Des N. Shewring. Litho B.D.T.)

2001 (25 July). Milestones in Seychelles History. T **198** and similar multicoloured designs. W w **14** (sideways on horiz designs). P 14.

905	1r. Type **198**	65	30
906	1r.50 Victoria (160th anniv as capital)	75	40
907	3r. Father Léon des Avanchers (150th anniv of arrival)	1·40	1·00
908	3r.50 Victoria Fountain (centenary) (vert)	1·40	1·25
909	5r. Botanical Gardens (centenary)	2·00	2·50
910	10r. Independence monument (25th anniv) (vert)	2·75	4·50
905/10 Set of 6		8·00	9·00

199 Ruddy Shelduck

(Des T. Disley (No. **MS**915) or J. Pointer (others). Litho Questa)

2001 (4 Oct). BirdLife World Bird Festival. Migrant Ducks and Bare-legged Scops-owl (No. **MS**915). T **199** and similar multicoloured designs. W w **16** (sideways). P 14.

911	3r. Type **199**	2·25	2·25
912	3r. White-faced Whistling Duck	2·25	2·25
913	3r. Common Shoveler ("Northern Shoveler")	2·25	2·25
914	3r. Garganey	2·25	2·25

911/14 Set of 4		8·00	8·00

MS915 171×78 mm. 3r. Scops-owl in flight (35×30 mm); 3r. In tree trunk (35×30 mm); 3r. Young bird on branch (30×35 mm); 3r. Adult bird on perch (30×35 mm); 3r. Fledgling on branch (35×30 mm). P 14½ | 11·00 | 11·00

(Des A. Robinson. Litho Questa)

2002 (5 Aug). Queen Elizabeth the Queen Mother Commemoration. Sheet, 145×70 mm, containing vert designs as T **46a** of British Indian Ocean Territory. W w **14** (sideways). P 14½×14.

MS916 5r. blackish brown, gold and black; 10r. multicoloured | 4·75 | 6·00

Designs:—5r. Lady Elizabeth Bowes-Lyon, 1923; 10r. Queen Mother on her birthday, 1986.

200 Seychelles Frog

(Des J. Pointer. Litho Questa)

2003 (3 Feb). Endangered Species. Frogs. T **200** and similar horiz designs. Multicoloured. W w **14** (sideways). P 14.

917	1r. Type **200**	75	85
918	1r. Palm Frog	75	85
919	1r. Thomasset's Frog	75	85
920	1r. Gardiner's Frog	75	85
917/20 Set of 4		2·75	3·00

MS921 65×65 mm. 20r. Seychelles Tree Frog. Wmk upright | 7·50 | 9·50

201 Seychelles Blenny   (**203**)

(Des A. Robinson. Litho B.D.T.)

2003 (3 Nov)–05. Marine Life. T **201** and similar horiz designs. Multicoloured. W w **14** (sideways). P 14.

922	10c. Type **201**	40	1·00
923	25c. African Pygmy Angelfish (3.10.05)	1·00	1·50
924	50c. Seychelles Anemonefish	60	40
925	1r. Indian Butterflyfish	1·00	25
926	1r.50 Goldbar Wrasse	1·25	35
927	2r. Picasso Triggerfish (3.10.05)	2·00	70
928	3r. Seychelles Squirrelfish	1·50	1·00
929	3r.50 Palette Surgeonfish (3.10.05)	2·50	1·00
930	4r. Longfin Batfish (3.10.05)	3·00	1·50
931	5r. Green-beaked Parrotfish ("Greenthroat Parrotfish")	3·00	1·75
932	10r. Masked Moray (3.10.05)	5·50	3·25
933	15r. Lyretail Grouper (3.10.05)	7·50	8·50
934	25r. Emperor Snapper (3.10.05)	11·00	12·00
935	50r. Whale Shark	17·00	23·00
922/35 Set of 14		50·00	50·00

See also Nos. 986/96.

(Des D. Miller. Litho B.D.T.)

2004 (16 Feb). 20th Anniv of the Indian Ocean Commission. As T **290** of Mauritius. W w **14**. P 13½.

936	10r. multicoloured	4·75	6·00

(Des I. Loe. Litho B.D.T.)

2004 (1 July). Flora and Fauna. Nos. 819, 821 and 824/8 surch as T **203**.

937	1r. on 1r.50 Seychelles Skink ("2000" imprint date) (vert)	1·00	30
938	2r. on 3r. Seychelles Sunbird ("2000" imprint date)	1·50	65
939	3r.50 on 5r. Seychelles Vanilla ("1994" imprint date) (vert)	2·25	2·25
940	3r.50 on 10r. Tiger Chameleon ("1994" imprint date)	2·25	2·25
941	3r.50 on 15r. Coco-de-Mer ("1996" imprint date) (vert)	2·25	2·25
942	4r. on 25r. Paradise Flycatcher ("1994" imprint date) (vert)	2·50	2·50
943	4r. on 50r. Giant Tortoise ("1994" imprint date")	2·50	2·50
937/43 Set of 7		13·00	11·50

203a Pope John Paul II

204 Archbishop Makarios in Exile, 1956

205 Possession Stone (250th anniv of naming of Seychelles)

(Des A. Robinson. Litho B.D.T.)

2005 (18 Aug). Pope John Paul II Commemoration. Vert design as T **203a** W w **14** (inverted). P 14.

944	5r. multicoloured	1·75	2·00
	a. Sheetlet of 8	12·50	

No. 944 was printed in sheetlets of eight stamps with an enlarged, illustrated right margin.

(Des A. Robinson. Litho B.D.T.)

2006 (28 June). 50th Anniv of Exile of Archbishop Makarios of Cyprus to the Seychelles. T **204** and similar vert design. Multicoloured. W w **14**. P 14.

945	3r.50 Type **204**	1·75	1·50
946	15r. Archbishop Makarios	4·75	6·00

(Des D. Miller. Litho Enschedé)

2006 (28 June). 30th Anniv of Independence. T **205** and similar vert designs. Multicoloured. W w **14**. P 14.

947	50c. Type **205**	35	25
948	1r. National flag and national flags of 1977–96 and 1976	80	30
949	1r.50 Vallée de Mai, Praslin (World Heritage Site)	90	45
950	2r. School children	1·00	65
951	3r.50 Jacob Marie (musician) with bonm (musical arc)	1·75	1·50
952	4r. *Seychelles Progress* (tanker)	2·00	2·00
953	15r. "Selebre Sesel" emblem	4·25	7·00
947/53 *Set of 7*		10·00	11·00

206 *Solanum aldabrensis*

207 Kayaking

(Des Derek Miller. Litho Lowe-Martin, Canada)

2007 (19 Nov). 25th Anniv of Aldabra as a World Heritage Site. T **206** and similar square designs. Multicoloured. W w **14** (sideways). P 12½x13.

954	2r. Type **206**	1·25	1·10
955	3r.50 Dugong	1·75	1·75
956	10r. Giant Tortoise	4·00	5·50
954/56 *Set of 3*		6·25	7·50

(Des Richard Allen. Litho B.D.T.)

2008 (30 Apr). Olympic Games, Beijing. T **207** and similar square designs. Multicoloured. W w **14** (sideways). P 13½.

957	1r. Type **207**	60	30
958	1r.50 Swimming	85	85
959	2r. Sailing	95	1·10
960	3r.50 Javelin throwing	1·50	2·25
957/60 *Set of 4*		3·50	4·00

208 Pair of Aldabra Drongos

(Des Andrew Robinson. Litho B.D.T.)

2008 (1 Oct). Endangered Species. Aldabra Drongo (*Dicrurus aldabranus*) and Aldabra Red-headed Fody (*Foudia eminentissima aldabrana*). T **208** and similar horiz designs. Multicoloured. W w **14** (sideways). P 14.

961	1r. Type **208**	75	90
	a. Strip of 4. Nos. 961/4	2·75	3·25
962	1r. Pair of Aldabra Red-headed Fodies (in tree with foliage, looking to left)	75	90
963	1r. Pair of Aldabra Red-headed Fodies (on bare branch, looking to right)	75	90
964	1r. Pair of Aldabra Drongos (left hand bird facing forwards)	75	90
961/64 *Set of 4*		2·75	3·25
MS965 84×60 mm. 20r. Aldabra Red-headed Fody and Aldabra Drongo		12·00	12·00

Nos. 961/4 were printed together, *se-tenant*, as horizontal and vertical strips of four stamps in sheetlets of 16, and also in separate sheets of 50 (2 panes of 25).

209 Ferdinand Magellan

209a X1 being loaded under Superfortress, 1951

(Des John Batchelor (**MS**972). Litho B.D.T.)

2009 (25 May). Seafaring and Exploration. T **209** and similar vert designs. Multicoloured. W w **18**. P 14.

966	1r.50 Type **209**	30	30
967	3r.50 Sir Martin Frobisher	1·75	1·60
968	6r.50 Sir Francis Drake	2·75	3·00
969	8r. Henry Hudson	3·00	3·50
970	15r. Abel Tasman	5·75	7·00
971	27r. Sir John Franklin	9·25	13·00
966/71 *Set of 6*		20·00	25·00
MS972 110×70 mm. 7r. *Ascension* (East Indiaman), 1609 (400th anniv of first European landing on the Seychelles)		4·25	4·50

Nos. 966/71 were each printed in sheetlets of six stamps with enlarged illustrated margins.

(Litho Lowe-Martin)

2009 (20 July). International Year of Astronomy. 40th Anniv of First Moon Landing. T **209a** and similar horiz designs. Multicoloured. W w **18** (sideways). P 13.

973	3r.50 Type **209a**	1·75	1·60
974	7r. Lunar Landing Research Vehicle, 1964	3·25	3·50
975	8r. *Apollo 11* Launch Site, 1969	3·75	4·00
976	13r. Space Transportation System 86, 1997	5·25	6·50
977	20r. Soyuz TMA-13 rolls out to Launch Pad, 2008	6·75	9·00
973/77 *Set of 5*		19·00	22·00
MS978 100×80 mm. 24r. *An American Success Story* (astronaut John Young) (Alan Bean) (39×59 *mm*). Wmk upright		12·00	14·00

Nos. 973/77 were printed in separate sheetlets of six stamps with enlarged illustrated margins.

(Litho B.D.T.)

2010 (5 July). As Nos. 929/35 and new values (6r.50, 7r., 8r., 100r.). W w **18** (sideways). P 14.

986	3r.50 Palette Surgeonfish	1·25	80
987	4r. Longfin Batfish	1·40	1·25
988	5r. Green-beaked Parrotfish ('Greenthroat Parrotfish')	1·60	1·60
989	6r.50 Queen Coris	1·75	1·75
990	7r. White-lined Goatfish	2·10	2·10
991	8r. Three-spot Angelfish	2·20	2·50
992	10r. Masked Moray	3·00	3·00
993	15r. Lyretail Grouper	4·25	4·75
994	25r. Emperor Snapper	7·50	9·00
995	50r. Whale Shark	14·00	16·00
996	100r. Coral Grouper	25·00	27·00
986/96 *Set of 11*		60·00	65·00

Nos. 979/85 are left for possible additions to this definitive series.

210 Duke and Duchess of
Cambridge waving from
State Landau

(Litho B.D.T.)

2011 (1 Aug). Royal Wedding. T **210** and similar multicoloured
designs. W w **18** (sideways on horiz designs). P 14.
997		3r.50 Type **210**	1·75	1·50
998		4r. Duke and Duchess of Cambridge kissing on Buckingham Palace balcony (*vert*)	2·00	1·75
999		7r. Duke and Duchess of Cambridge waving from Buckingham Palace balcony (*vert*)	3·25	3·25
1000		25c. Duke and Duchess of Cambridge at Westminster Abbey after wedding ceremony (*vert*)	9·50	11·00
997/1000 *Set of 4*			15·00	16·00

211 State House, Victoria

(Des Andrew Robinson. Litho B.D.T.)

2011 (11 Nov). Centenary of the State House of Seychelles, Victoria.
W w **18** (sideways). P 14.
1001	**211**	3r.50 multicoloured	1·75	2·00

212 New Post Office, Victoria,
2011

(Litho B.D.T.)

2011 (11 Nov). 150th Anniv of the Seychelles Post Office. T **212** and
similar horiz design. Multicoloured. W w **18** (sideways). P 14.
1002		3r.50 Type **212**	2·25	2·00
1003		7r. The Old Post Office, Victoria, 1900s	4·00	4·50

213 Green Turtle

(Des Claude Perchat. Litho Phil@poste, France)

2014 (9 Oct). Green Turtle. P 13.
1004	**213**	50r. multicoloured	14·00	15·00

Stamps in similar designs were issued on the same day by Comores,
France, French Southern and Antarctic Territories, Madagascar and
Mauritius. A miniature sheet was also issued containing one Green
Turtle stamp from each of the six countries.

STAMP BOOKLETS

1979 (25 Apr). Deep green on green (No. SB1), deep blue on blue
(No. SB2) or black printed (No. SB3) covers, 120×75 mm, showing
Seychelles arms. Stapled.
SB1	5r. booklet containing four 20c. and 25c. and eight 40c. (Nos. 407/9) in blocks of 4	14·00	

SB2	10r. booklet containing four 50c., 75c. and 1r.25 (Nos. 410/11, 413) in pairs	4·00	
SB3	20r. booklet containing four 1r.50 and 3r.50 (Nos. 402, 415) in pairs	11·00	

1979 (26 Oct). Red (No. SB4) or blue (No. SB5) printed covers,
118×78 mm, showing Seychelles arms. Stamps attached by
selvedge.
SB4	15r. booklet containing 10c., 15c., 1r.50 and 2r. (Nos. 405/6, 414, 447), each in block of 4	8·00	
SB5	15r. booklet containing four 25c., 1r.25 and 2r. (Nos. 408, 413, 441/2 or 444/5) in blocks of 4, and two 3r. (No. 452) in pair	12·00	

1980 (29 Feb). 75th Anniv of Rotary International (No. SB6) and
Centenary of Visit of General Gordon (No. SB7). Orange (No. SB6)
or black (No. SB7) printed covers, 120×79 mm. Stamps attached
by selvedge.
SB6	15r. booklet containing four 15c., 1r. and 1r.10 on 3r.50, and two 3r. (Nos. 406, 412, 460, 462) in pairs	9·00	
SB7	20r. booklet containing 75c., 2r. and 2r.25 (Nos. 411, 441/2 or 444/5, 459, each in block of 4	9·00	

1980 (28 Nov). Black on orange (No. SB8) or black printed (No. SB9)
covers, 123×80 mm, showing Clock Tower, Central Victoria.
Stamps attached by selvedge.
SB8	15r. booklet containing four 40c., 1r. and 1r.25 (Nos. 409B, 412B, 413) in blocks of 4 and four 1r.10 on 3r.50 (No. 462) in pairs	15·00	
SB9	20r. booklet containing 1r.25, 1r.50 and 2r.25 (Nos. 413, 414B, 474), each in block of 4	11·00	

1981 (27 Feb). Ships. Multicoloured cover, 160×93 mm. Stapled.
SB10	35r.15 booklet containing 40c. (No. 495) in block of 10, 5r. (No. 498) in strip of 4 and No. **MS**499	7·50	

1981 (16 Nov). Royal Wedding. Multicoloured cover, 105×65 mm,
showing *The Victoria and Albert I*. Stitched.
SB11	22r. booklet containing eight 1r.50 in panes of four (No. 512a) and 5r. in pane of two (No. 513a)	3·25	

1998 (30 Nov). International Year of the Ocean. Folded multicoloured
card cover, 91×70 mm, showing marine life. Stamps attached by
selvedge.
SB12	36r. booklet containing Nos. 884/9, each×2	11·00	

POSTAGE DUE STAMPS

D **1**

(Frame recess, value typo B.W.)

1951 (1 Mar). Wmk Mult Script CA. P 11½.
D1	D **1**	2c. scarlet and carmine	80	1·50
D2		3c. scarlet and green	3·50	1·50
D3		6c. scarlet and bistre	2·25	1·25
D4		9c. scarlet and orange	2·50	1·25
D5		15c. scarlet and violet	2·25	12·00
D6		18c. scarlet and blue	2·25	13·00
D7		20c. scarlet and brown	2·25	13·00
D8		30c. scarlet and claret	2·25	8·50
D1/8 *Set of 8*			16·00	48·00

1964 (7 July)–**65**. As 1951 but W w **12**.
D9	D **1**	2c. scarlet and carmine	2·50	15·00
D10		3c. scarlet and green (14.9.65)	1·25	17·00

(Litho Walsall)

1980 (29 Feb). Design as Type D **1** but redrawn, size 18×22 mm.
W w **14** (sideways). P 14.
D11		5c. rosine and magenta	15	1·00
D12		10c. rosine and deep blue-green	15	1·00
D13		15c. rosine and bistre	20	1·00
D14		20c. rosine and orange-brown	20	1·00
D15		25c. rosine and bright violet	20	1·00
D16		75c. rosine and maroon	30	1·00
D17		80c. rosine and deep grey-blue	30	1·00
D18		1r. rosine and deep reddish purple	30	1·00
D11/18 *Set of 8*			1·60	8·00

ZIL ELWANNYEN SESEL
(SEYCHELLES OUTER ISLANDS)

I. Inscr "ZIL ELOIGNE SESEL"

For use from Aldabra, Coetivy, Farquhar and the Amirante Islands, served by the M.V. *Cinq-Juin* travelling post office, and also valid for postage in Seychelles.

1 Reef Fish   **2** Cinq Juin

1980 (20 June)–**81**. Designs as Nos. 404/11 (with imprint) and 487/94 of Seychelles but inscr. "ZIL ELOIGNE SESEL" as in T **1**. W w **14** (sideways on 10, 20, 50, 75c.). P 14½×14 (40c., 1r., 1r.25, 1r.50), 13½ (5, 10, 15, 20r.) or 14 (others).

1	5c. Type **1**	15	75
2	10c. Hawksbill Turtle	15	75
3	15c. Coco-de-Mer	15	75
4	20c. Wild Vanilla	20	75
5	25c. *Hypolimnas misippus* (butterfly)	1·00	75
6	40c. Coral scene	30	75
7	50c. Giant Tortoise	30	60
8	75c. Crayfish	35	60
9	1r. Madagascar Red Fody	1·25	1·00
10	1r.10 Green Gecko	40	1·00
11	1r.25 White Tern	1·50	70
12	1r.50 Seychelles Flying Fox	45	70
	w. Wmk inverted	1·75	
13	5r. Octopus	70	1·00
	a. Perf 13 (1981)	65	1·50
14	10r. Tiger Cowrie (*Cypraea tigris*)	80	1·50
	a. Perf 13 (1981)	80	2·50
15	15r. Pitcher Plant	80	3·00
	a. Perf 13 (1981)	1·10	2·50
16	20r. Seychelles coat of arms	80	3·25
	a. Perf 13 (1981)	1·40	3·75
1/16 *Set of 16*		8·00	16·00

Imprint dates: "1980", Nos. 1/16; "1981", Nos. 1/12, 13a/16a.

(Des L. Curtis. Litho Walsall)

1980 (24 Oct). Establishment of Travelling Post Office. T **2** and similar horiz designs. Multicoloured. W w **14** (sideways). P 14.

17	1r.50 Type **2**	20	20
18	2r.10 Hand-stamping covers	25	25
19	5r. Map of Zil Eloigne Sesel	40	40
17/19 *Set of 3*		75	75

Nos. 17/19 were printed in sheets including two *se-tenant* stamp-size labels.

The original version of No. 19 incorrectly showed the Agalega Islands as Seychelles territory. A corrected version was prepared prior to issue and stamps in the first type were intended for destruction. Mint examples and some used on first day covers are known, originating from supplies sent to some philatelic bureau standing order customers in error. Such stamps are not listed as they were not available from Seychelles post offices or valid for postage.

3 Yellow-finned Tuna

(Des G. Drummond. Litho Rosenbaum Bros, Vienna)

1980 (28 Nov). Marine Life. T **3** and similar horiz designs. Multicoloured. W w **14**. P 14.

20	1r.50 Type **3**	15	20
	w. Wmk inverted	27·00	
21	2r.10 Blue Marlin	20	35
	w. Wmk inverted	32·00	
22	5r. Sperm Whale	50	70
	w. Wmk inverted	27·00	
20/22 *Set of 13*		75	1·10

Nos. 20/2 were printed in sheets including two *se-tenant* stamp-size labels.

(Des D. Shults. Litho Questa)

1981 (23 June–16 Nov). Royal Wedding. Horiz designs as T **121a/b** of Seychelles. Multicoloured.

(a) W w **16**. P 14

23	40c. *Royal Escape*	10	10
	aw. Wmk inverted	15·00	
	b. Sheetlet of 7. No. 23×6 and No 24	90	
	bw. Wmk inverted	£120	
24	40c. Prince Charles and Lady Diana Spencer	40	55
	aw. Wmk inverted	50·00	
25	5r. *Victoria and Albert II*	35	40
	a. Sheetlet of 7. No. 25×6 and No. 26	3·00	
26	5r. As No. 24	1·25	1·75
27	10r. *Britannia*	60	85
	a. Sheetlet of 7. No. 27×6 and No. 28	4·50	
28	10r. As No. 24	1·50	3·25
23/38 *Set of 6*		3·75	6·25
MS29 120×109 mm. 7r.50, As No. 24. Wmk sideways. P 12 (16 Nov)		1·10	1·50

(b) Booklet stamps. No wmk. P 12 (16 Nov)

30	40c. As No. 23	35	75
	a. Booklet pane. No. 30×4 with margins all round	1·25	
31	5r. As No. 26	1·00	1·75
	a. Booklet pane. No. 31×2 with margins all round	2·00	

Nos. 23/8 were printed in sheetlets of seven stamps of the same face value, each containing six of the "Royal Yacht" design and one of the larger design showing Prince Charles and Lady Diana.

Nos. 30/1 come from 13r.20 stamp booklets.

4 Wright's Skink   **5** Cinq Juin ("Communications")

(Des and litho Walsall)

1981 (11 Dec). Wildlife (1st series). T **4** and similar horiz. designs. Multicoloured. W w **14** (sideways). P 14.

32	1r.40 Type **4**	15	15
33	2r.25 Tree Frog	20	20
34	5r. Robber Crab	40	40
32/34 *Set of 3*		65	65

See also Nos. 45/7.

(Des L. Curtis. Litho Harrison)

1982 (11 Mar). Island Development. Ships. T **5** and similar horiz designs. W w **14**. P 14×14½.

35	1r.75 black and orange	35	30
	w. Wmk inverted	35·00	
36	2r.10 black and turquoise-blue	40	45
	w. Wmk inverted	3·50	
37	5r. black and bright scarlet	50	60
35/37 *Set of 3*		1·10	1·25

Designs:—2r.10, Junon ("fisheries protection"); 5r. *Diamond M. Dragon* (drilling ship).

II. Inscr "ZIL ELWAGNE SESEL"

6 Paulette

(Des L. Curtis. Litho Harrison)

1982 (22 July). Local Mail Vessels. T **6** and similar horiz designs. Multicoloured. W w **14** (sideways). P 14.

38	40c. Type **6**	35	45
39	1r.75 Janette	40	80
40	2r.75 Lady Esme	50	95
41	3r.50 Cinq Juin	50	1·00
38/41 *Set of 4*		1·60	2·75

7 Birds flying over Island   **8** Red Land Crab

(Des Harrison. Litho Format)

1982 (19 Nov). Aldabra, World Heritage Site. T **7** and similar horiz designs. Multicoloured. W w **14** (sideways). P 14.

42	40c. Type **7**	30	15
43	2r.75 Map of the atoll	45	35
44	7r. Giant Tortoises	50	75
42/44	*Set of 3*	1·10	1·10

(Des G. Drummond. Litho Questa)

1983 (25 Feb). Wildlife (2nd series). T **8** and similar horiz designs. Multicoloured. W w **14** (sideways). P 14×14½.

45	1r.75 Type **8**	35	40
46	2r.75 Black Terrapin	45	55
47	7r. Madagascar Green Gecko	90	1·25
45/47	*Set of 3*	1·50	2·00

9 Map of Poivre Island and Ile du Sud   **10** Aldabra Warbler

(Des J. Cooler. Litho Format)

1983 (27 Apr). Island Maps. T **9** and similar vert designs. Multicoloured. W w **14**. P 14.

48	40c. Type **9**	20	40
49	1r.50 Île des Roches	30	55
50	2r.75 Astove Island	40	80
51	7r. Coëtivy Island	50	1·60
48/51	*Set of 4*	1·25	3·00
MS52	93×129 mm. Nos. 48/51	1·75	3·00

(Des G. Drummond. Litho Harrison)

1983 (13 July). Birds. T **10** and similar multicoloured designs. W w **14** (sideways on 5c. to 2r.75). "1983" imprint date. P 14½.

53	5c. Type **10**	40	60
54	10c. Zebra Dove ("Barred Ground Dove")	1·00	60
55	15c. Madagascar Nightjar	30	40
56	20c. Madagascar Cisticola ("Malagasy Grass Warbler")	30	40
57	25c. Madagascar White Eye	60	60
58	40c. Mascarene Fody	30	40
59	50c. White-throated Rail	5·50	60
60	75c. Black Bulbul	40	60
61	2r. Western Reef Heron ("Dimorphic Little Egret")	2·00	1·25
62	2r.10 Souimanga Sunbird	50	1·00
63	2r.50 Madagascar Turtle Dove	1·00	65
64	2r.75 Sacred Ibis	70	75
65	3r.50 Black Coucal (*vert*)	1·00	1·10
66	7r. Seychelles Kestrel (*vert*)	3·00	1·90
67	15r. Comoro Blue Pigeon (*vert*)	3·00	5·00
68	20r. Greater Flamingo (*vert*)	3·00	5·50
53/68	*Set of 16*	21·00	19·00

For 5c., 10c., 25c., 50c. and 2r. values in these designs, but inscribed "Zil Elwannyen Sesel", see Nos. 100/7, 165/73 and 226.

11 Windsurfing   **12** Map of Aldabra and Commemorative Postmark

(Des G. Wilby. Litho Questa)

1983 (27 Sept). Tourism. T **11** and similar horiz designs. Multicoloured. W w **14** (sideways). P 14.

69	50c. Type **11**	10	10
70	2r. Hotel	25	25
71	3r. View of beach	30	35
72	10r. Islands at sunset	75	1·75
69/72	*Set of 4*	1·25	2·10

1983 (16–28 Dec). Nos. 23/8 surch as T **135** of Seychelles.

73	30c. on 40c. *Royal Escape*	25	25
	a. Sheetlet of 7. No. 73×6 and No. 74	1·75	
	b. Surch double	50·00	
	c. Error. Surch 50c (as Seychelles No. 573)	60·00	
74	30c. on 40c. Prince Charles and Lady Diana Spencer	50	60
	b. Surch double	£130	
	c. Error. Surch 50c (as Seychelles No. 574)	£140	
75	2r. on 5r. *Victoria and Albert II* (28.12.83)	70	70
	a. Sheetlet of 7. No. 75×6 and No. 76	5·00	
	b. Albino surch	40·00	
	c. Surch double	75·00	
76	2r. on 5r. As No. 74 (28.12.83)	1·25	1·75
	b. Albino surch	65·00	
	c. Surch double	£200	
77	3r. on 10r. *Britannia* (28.12.83)	85	85
	a. Sheetlet of 7. No. 77×6 and No. 78	6·00	
78	3r. on 10r. As No. 74 (28.12.83)	1·60	2·50
73/78	*Set of 6*	4·75	6·00

(Des L. Curtis. Litho Questa)

1984 (30 Mar). Re-opening of Aldabra Post Office. T **12** and similar horiz designs. Multicoloured. W w **14** (sideways). P 14.

79	50c. Type **12**	15	30
80	2r.75 White-throated Rail	60	1·10
81	3r. Giant Tortoise	60	1·25
82	10r. Red-footed Booby	2·25	3·50
79/82	*Set of 4*	3·25	5·50

13 Fishing from Launch

(Des L. Curtis. Litho Walsall)

1984 (31 May). Game Fishing. T **13** and similar multicoloured designs. W w **14** (sideways on 50c., 10r.). P 14.

83	50c. Type **13**	15	30
84	2r. Hooked fish (*vert*)	45	75
85	3r. Weighing catch (*vert*)	60	1·00
86	10r. Fishing from boat (*different*)	2·00	3·00
83/86	*Set of 4*	2·75	4·50

14 Giant Hermit Crab   **15** Constellation of "Orion"

(Des G. Drummond. Litho Format)

1984 (24 Aug). Crabs. T **14** and similar horiz designs. Multicoloured. W w **14** (sideways). P 14½.

87	50c. Type **14**	25	40
88	2r. Fiddler Crabs	55	1·10
89	3r. Sand Crab	65	1·50
90	10r. Spotted Pebble Crab	1·40	4·25
87/90	*Set of 4*	2·50	6·50

(Des A. Theobald. Litho Format)

1984 (16 Oct). The Night Sky. T **15** and similar vert designs. Multicoloured. W w **14**. P 14.

91	50c. Type **15**	25	15
92	2r. "Cygnus"	50	55
93	3r. "Virgo"	60	80
94	10r. "Scorpio"	1·40	2·25
91/94	*Set of 4*	2·50	3·25

III. Inscr "ZIL ELWANNYEN SESEL"

16 *Lenzites elegans*

17 The Queen Mother attending Royal Opera House, Covent Garden

(Des G. Drummond. Litho Walsall)

1985 (31 Jan). Fungi. T **16** and similar vert designs. Multicoloured. W w **14**. P 14.

95	50c. Type **16**	60	85
96	2r. *Xylaria telfairei*	1·25	1·50
	w. Wmk inverted	£180	
97	3r. *Lentinus sajor-caju*	1·25	1·50
98	10r. *Hexagonia tennis*	2·25	3·00
95/98 *Set of 4*		4·75	6·00

(Litho Harrison)

1985 (1 May)–**87**. As Nos. 54, 57, 59 and 61 but inscr "Zil Elwannyen Sesel". W w **14** (sideways). P 14½.

100	10c. Zebra Dove ("Barred Ground Dove")	2·75	2·25
103	25c. Madagascar White Eye	3·50	1·50
105	50c. White-throated Rail (1.7.87)	4·00	1·60
107	2r. Western Reef Heron ("Dimorphic Little Egret")	4·00	3·75
100/7 *Set of 4*		13·00	8·25

Imprint dates: "1985", Nos. 100, 103, 107; "1987", Nos. 100, 105.

For 10c., 50c. and 2r. values watermarked w **16** (sideways) see Nos. 165/73 and 226.

(Des A. Theobald (10r.), C. Abbott (others). Litho Questa)

1985 (7 June). Life and Times of Queen Elizabeth the Queen Mother. T **17** and similar vert designs. Multicoloured. W w **16**. P 14½×14.

115	1r. The Queen Mother, 1936 (from photo by Dorothy Wilding)	20	25
	w. Wmk inverted	1·25	
116	2r. With Princess Anne at Ascot, 1974	35	50
	w. Wmk inverted	65	
117	3r. Type **17**	45	70
	w. Wmk inverted	14·00	
118	5r. With Prince Henry at his christening (from photo by Lord Snowdon)	60	1·25
115/18 *Set of 4*		1·40	2·40
MS119	91×73 mm. 10r. In a launch, Venice, 1985. Wmk sideways	1·50	2·75

18 Giant Tortoise

(Des. G. Vasarhelyi. Litho J. W.)

1985 (27 Sept). Giant Tortoises of Aldabra (1st series). T **18** and similar horiz designs. Multicoloured. W w **16** (sideways). P 14.

120	50c. Type **18**	3·25	1·25
121	75c. Giant Tortoises at stream	3·50	1·40
122	1r. Giant Tortoises on grassland	3·75	1·60
123	2r. Giant Tortoise (side view)	4·75	2·25
120/23 *Set of 4*		14·00	6·00
MS124	70×60 mm. 10r. Two Giant Tortoises. P 13×13½	16·00	15·00

For stamps as Nos. 120/3, but without circular inscription around W.W.F. emblem, see Nos. 153/6.

19 Phoenician Trading Ship (600 B.C.)

20 *Acropora palifera* and *Tubastraea coccinea*

(Des N. Shewring. Litho Format)

1985 (25 Oct). Famous Visitors. T **19** and similar horiz designs. Multicoloured. W w **14** (sideways). P 14.

125	50c. Type **19**	80	80
126	2r. Hugh Scott and H.M.S. *Sealark*	1·50	2·00
127	10r. Vasco da Gama and *Sao Gabriel*, 1502	2·50	4·50
125/27 *Set of 3*		4·25	6·50

Hugh Scott, described as Sir Hugh Scott on the stamp, visited the Islands in 1908, as stated, but not abroad HMS *Sealark*, which carried the 1905 expedition.

(Des A. Theobald. Litho Questa)

1986 (21 Apr). 60th Birthday of Queen Elizabeth II. Vert designs as T **208a** of Mauritius. Multicoloured. W w **16**. P 14½×14.

128	75c. Princess Elizabeth at Chester, 1951	15	25
129	1r. Queen and Duke of Edinburgh at Falklands Service, St. Paul's Cathedral, 1985	15	25
130	1r.50 At Order of St. Michael and St. George service, St. Paul's Cathedral, 1968	25	40
131	3r.75 In Mexico, 1975	40	90
132	5r. At Crown Agents Head Office, London, 1983	45	1·25
128/32 *Set of 5*		1·25	2·75

(Des D. Miller. Litho Questa)

1986 (23 July). Royal Wedding. Square designs as T **152a** of Seychelles. Multicoloured. W w **16**. P 14.

133	3r. Prince Andrew and Miss Sarah Ferguson on Buckingham Palace balcony	45	75
134	7r. Prince Andrew in naval uniform	65	1·75

(Des I. Loe. Litho Harrison)

1986 (17 Sept). Coral Formations. T **20** and similar vert designs. Multicoloured. W w **16**. P 14.

135	2r. Type **20**	1·75	1·75
	a. Horiz strip of 5. Nos. 135/9	8·00	8·00
136	2r. *Echinopora lamellosa* and *Favia pallida*	1·75	1·75
137	2r. *Sarcophyton* sp. and *Porites lutea*	1·75	1·75
138	2r. *Goniopora* sp. and *Goniastrea retiformis*	1·75	1·75
139	2r. *Tubipora musica* and *Fungia fungites*	1·75	1·75
135/9 *Set of 5*		8·00	8·00

Nos. 135/9 were printed together, *se-tenant*, in horizontal strips of five throughout the sheet, forming a composite design.

21 *Hibiscus tiliaceus*

22 Teardrop Butterflyfish and Lined Butterflyfish

(Des Annette Robinson. Litho Walsall)

1986 (12 Nov). Flora. T **21** and similar vert designs. Multicoloured. W w **16**. P 14.

140	50c. Type **21**	35	30
141	2r. *Crinum angustum*	1·60	1·50
142	3r. *Phaius tetragonus*	2·25	2·00
143	10r. *Rothmannia annae*	3·75	4·00
140/43 *Set of 4*		7·00	7·00

(Des G. Drummond. Litho Questa)

1987 (26 Mar). Coral Reef Fish. T **22** and similar vert designs. Multicoloured. W w **16**. P 14.

144	2r. Type **22**	1·10	1·40
	a. Horiz strip of 5. Nos. 144/8	5·00	6·00
145	2r. Knifejaw	1·10	1·40
146	2r. Narrow-banded Batfish	1·10	1·40
147	2r. Ringed Sergeant	1·10	1·40
148	2r. Lined Butterflyfish and Meyer's Butterflyfish	1·10	1·40
144/48	Set of 5	5·00	6·00

Nos. 144/8 were printed together, *se-tenant*, in horizontal strips of five throughout the sheet, forming a composite design.

23 Coconut   **24** "Vallée de Mai"
(Christine Harter)

(Des R. Gorringe. Litho Walsall)

1987 (26 Aug). Trees. T **23** and similar vert designs. Multicoloured. W w **16**. P 14½.

149	1r. Type **23**	80	85
150	2r. Mangrove	1·40	1·75
151	3r. Pandanus Palm	2·00	2·50
152	5r. Indian Almond	3·00	3·75
149/152	Set of 4	6·50	8·00

(Des G. Vasarhelyi. Litho Questa)

1987 (9 Sept). Giant Tortoises of Aldabra (2nd series). Designs as Nos. 120/3, but without circular inscr around W.W.F. emblem. Multicoloured. W w **16** (sideways). P 14.

153	50c. As Type **18**	3·00	2·00
154	75c. Giant Tortoises at stream	4·00	2·75
155	1r. Giant Tortoises on grassland	4·50	3·75
156	2r. Giant Tortoise (side view)	5·50	5·00
153/56	Set of 4	15·00	12·00

1987 (9 Dec). Royal Ruby Wedding. Nos. 128/32 optd with T **158a** of Seychelles in silver.

157	75c. Princess Elizabeth at Chester, 1951	25	20
158	1r. Queen and Duke of Edinburgh at Falklands Service, St. Paul's Cathedral, 1985	30	25
159	1r.50 At Order of St. Michael and St. George service, St. Paul's Cathedral, 1968	40	40
160	3r.75 In Mexico, 1975	60	90
161	5r. At Crown Agents Head Office, London, 1983	70	1·25
157/61	Set of 5	2·00	2·75

(Des D. Miller. Litho Questa)

1987 (16 Dec). Tourism. T **24** and similar vert designs. Multicoloured. W w **16**. P 14.

162	3r. Type **24**	3·25	3·25
	a. Horiz strip of 3. Nos. 162/4	8·75	8·75
163	3r. Ferns	3·25	3·25
164	3r. Bamboo	3·25	3·25
162/64	Set of 3	8·75	8·75

Nos. 162/4 were printed together, *se-tenant*, in horizontal strips of three throughout the sheet, forming the complete picture.

(Litho Harrison)

1988 (1 July–24 Nov). As No. 53, but inscr "Zil Elwannyen Sesel", and Nos. 100, 105 and 107, all W w **16** (sideways). "1988" imprint date. P 14½.

165	5c. Type **10** (24.11)	2·75	2·50
166	10c. Zebra Dove ("Barred Ground Dove") (24.11)	2·75	2·50
171	50c. White-throated Rail (24.11)	2·75	3·00
173	2r. Western Reef Heron ("Dimorphic Little Egret")	5·50	6·00
165/73	Set of 4	12·00	12·50

For 2r. printed by Walsall and perforated 14×14½ see No. 226.

25 *Yanga seychellensis* (beetle)

(Des I. Lee. Litho Walsall)

1988 (28 July). Insects. T **25** and similar horiz designs. Multicoloured. W w **14** (sideways). P 14.

180	1r. Type **25**	1·25	1·00
181	2r. *Belenois aldabrensis* (butterfly)	2·00	1·60
182	3r. *Polyspilota seychelliana* (mantid)	2·25	2·25
183	5r. *Polposipus herculeanus* (beetle)	2·75	3·00
180/83	Set of 4	7·50	7·00

26 Olympic Rings

(Des Joan Thompson. Litho Format)

1988 (31 Aug). Olympic Games, Seoul. Sheet 99×73 mm. W w **16** (sideways). P 14.

MS184	**26** 10r. multicoloured	4·00	3·00

(Des D. Miller (1r.), E. Nisbet and D. Miller (2r.), O. Bell and D. Miller (3r.), A. Theabald and D. Miller (5r.). Litho Walsall)

1988 (28 Oct). 300th Anniv of Lloyd's of London. Multicoloured designs as T **162a** of Seychelles. W w **14** (sideways on 2, 3r.). P 14.

185	1r. Modern Lloyd's Building, London	70	65
186	2r. *Retriever* (cable ship) (*horiz*)	1·50	1·50
187	3r. *Chantel* (fishing boat) (*horiz*)	2·00	1·50
188	5r. Wreck of *Torrey Canyon* (tanker), Cornwall, 1967	2·75	1·75
185/88	Set of 4	6·25	4·50

27 "Father Christmas landing with Presents" (Jean-Claude Boniface)

(Adapted G. Vasarhelyi, Litho Questa)

1988 (18 Nov). Christmas. Children's Paintings. T **27** and similar multicoloured designs. W w **16** (sideways on 1, 5r.). P 13½×14 (horiz) or 14×13½ (vert).

189	1r. Type **27**	35	40
190	2r. "Church" (Francois Barra) (*vert*)	60	80
191	3r. "Father Christmas flying on Bird" (Wizy Ernesta) (*vert*)	85	1·25
192	5r. "Father Christmas in Sleigh over Island" (Federic Lang)	1·40	2·00
189/92	Set of 4	2·75	4·00

(Des A. Theobald (10r.), D. Miller (others). Litho Questa)

1989 (20 July). 20th Anniv of First Manned landing on Moon. Multicoloured designs as T **167a** of Seychelles. W w **16** (sideways on 2, 3r.). P 14×13½ (1, 5r.) or 14 (others).

193	1r. Firing Room, Launch Control Centre	2·00	1·50
194	2r. Crews of "Apollo-Soyuz" mission (30×30 *mm*)	2·50	2·25
195	3r. "Apollo-Soyuz" emblem (30×30 *mm*)	2·75	3·00
196	5r. "Apollo" and "Soyuz" docking in space	3·75	4·50
193/96	Set of 4	10·00	10·00
MS197	82×100 mm. 10r. Recovery of "Apollo 11". P 14×13½	12·00	14·00

28 Dumb Cane   **29** Tec-Tec Broth

(Des Lynn Chadwick, Litho Questa)

1989 (9 Oct). Poisonous Plants (1st series). T **28** and similar horiz designs. Multicoloured. W w **16** (sideways). P 14.

198	1r. Type **28**	2·50	1·75
199	2r. Star of Bethlehem	3·00	2·75
200	3r. Indian Liquorice	3·25	3·25
201	5r. Black Nightshade	4·25	4·75
198/201	Set of 4	12·00	11·50

See also Nos. 214/17.

(Des O. Bell. Litho B.D.T.)

1989 (18 Dec). Creole Cooking. T **29** and similar vert designs. Multicoloured. W w **16**. P 14.

202	1r. Type **29**	1·50	1·50
203	2r. Pilaff á la Seychelloise	2·00	2·25
204	3r. Mullet grilled in banana leaves	2·25	2·50
205	5r. Daube	3·25	3·75
202/5	Set of 4	8·00	9·00
MS206	125×80 mm. Nos. 202/5	12·00	14·00

Stamps from No. **MS**206 have the white margin omitted on one or both vertical sides.

30 1980 Marine Life 5r. Stamp

(Des D. Miller. Litho Security Printers (M), Malaysia)

1990 (3 May). "Stamp World London 90" International Stamp Exhibition. T **30** and similar horiz designs showing stamps. Multicoloured. (sideways). W w **14** P 12½.

207	1r. Type **30**	2·25	1·75
208	2r. 1980 5r. definitive	2·75	2·50
209	3r. 1983 2r.75 definitive	3·00	3·00
210	5r. 1981 Wildlife 5r.	4·00	4·50
207/10	Set of 4	11·00	10·50
MS211	124×84 mm. Nos. 207/10. Wmk upright	12·00	14·00

(Des D. Miller. Litho Questa)

1990 (4 Aug). 90th Birthday of Queen Elizabeth the Queen Mother. Vert designs as T **18a** (2r.) or **18b** (10r.) of British Indian Ocean Territory. W w **16**. P 14×15 (2r.) or 14½ (10r.).

212	2r. multicoloured	1·50	2·00
213	10r. black and orange-brown	2·50	4·50

Designs:—2r. Duchess of York with baby Princess Elizabeth, 1926; 10r. King George VI and Queen Elizabeth visiting bombed district, London, 1940.

(Des Lynn Chadwick. Litho Security Printers (M), Malaysia)

1990 (5 Nov). Poisonous Plants (2nd series). Horiz designs as T **28**. Multicoloured. W w **14** (sideways). P 12½.

214	1r. Ordeal Plant	1·75	1·75
215	2r. Thorn Apple	2·25	2·50
216	3r. Strychnine Tree	2·50	2·75
217	5r. Bwa Zasmen	3·50	4·00
214/17	Set of 4	9·00	10·00

(Litho Walsall)

1991 (1 Jan). As No. 173, but different printer. W w **16** (sideways). "1990" imprint date. P 14×14½.

226	2r. Western Reef Heron ("Dimorphic Little Egret")	3·50	3·25

(Des D. Miller. Litho Questa)

1991 (17 June). 65th Birthday of Queen Elizabeth II and 70th Birthday of Prince Philip. Vert designs as T **227a** of Mauritius. Multicoloured. W w **16** (sideways). P 14½×14.

234	4r. Queen Elizabeth II	1·90	2·25
	a. Horiz pair. Nos. 234/5 separated by label	3·75	4·50

235	4r. Prince Philip	1·90	2·25

Nos. 234/5 were printed in a similar sheet format to Nos. 366/7 of Kiribati.

31 *St. Abbs* (full-rigged ship), 1860   **32** *Lomatopyllum aldabrense* (plant)

(Des J. Batchelor. Litho Walsall)

1991 (28 Oct). Shipwrecks. T **31** and similar horiz designs. Multicoloured. W w **14** (sideways). P 14.

236	1r.50 Type **31**	2·50	2·00
237	3r. *Norden* (barque), 1862	3·00	2·50
238	3r.50 *Clan Mackay* (freighter), 1894	3·25	2·75
239	10r. *Glenlyon* (freighter), 1905	7·00	7·50
236/9	Set of 4	14·00	13·00

(Des D. Miller. Litho Questa (5r.), Walsall (others))

1992 (6 Feb). 40th Anniv of Queen Elizabeth II's Accession. Horiz designs as T **180a** of Seychelles. Multicoloured. W w **14** (sideways). P 14.

240	1r. Beach	65	75
241	1r.50 Aerial view of Desroches	75	1·00
242	3r. Tree-covered coastline	1·25	1·50
243	3r.50 Three portraits of Queen Elizabeth II	1·25	1·60
244	5r. Queen Elizabeth II	1·40	1·75
240/4	Set of 5	4·75	6·00

(Des D. Miller. Litho Questa)

1992 (19 Nov). Tenth Anniv of Aldabra as a World Heritage Site. T **32** and similar vert designs. Multicoloured. W w **14**. P 14½×14.

245	1r.50 Type **32**	2·00	2·00
246	3r. White-throated Rail	5·50	3·75
247	3r.50 Robber Crab	3·00	3·75
248	10r. Aldabra Drongo	10·00	11·50
245/8	Set of 4	18·00	19·00

STAMP BOOKLETS

1980 (28 Nov). Black on yellow cover, 126×80 mm, showing map of Zil Elwannyen Sesel. Stamps attached by selvedge.

SB1	25r. booklet containing 40c., 1r. and 1r.10 (Nos. 6, 9/10), each in block of 4, and three 5r. (No. 13) in pair and single	14·00

1981 (16 Nov). Royal Wedding. Multicoloured cover, 105×65 mm, showing the *Royal Escape*. Stitched.

SB2	13r.20 booklet containing eight 40c. in panes of 4 (No. 30a) and two 5r. in pane of 2 (No. 31a)	4·00

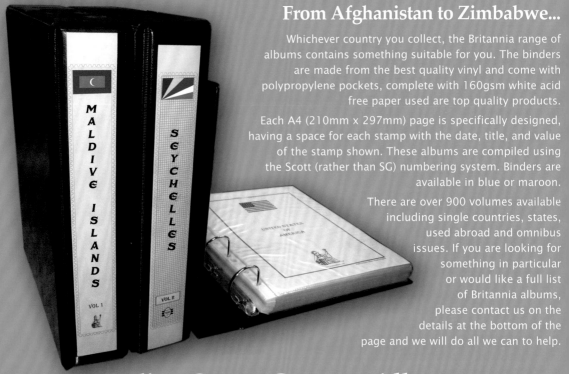

Est 1856
STANLEY GIBBONS

Dear Catalogue User,

As a collector and Stanley Gibbons catalogue user for many years myself, I am only too aware of the need to provide you with the information you seek in an accurate, timely and easily accessible manner. Naturally, I have my own views on where changes could be made, but one thing I learned long ago is that we all have different opinions and requirements.

I would therefore be most grateful if you would complete the form overleaf and return it to me. Please contact Lorraine Holcombe (lholcombe@stanleygibbons.com) if you would like to be emailed the questionnaire.

Very many thanks for your help.

Yours sincerely,

Hugh Jefferies,
Editor.

Hugh Jefferies (Catalogue Editor)
Catalogue Questionnaire Responses
Stanley Gibbons Limited
7 Parkside, Ringwood
Hampshire BH24 3SH
United Kingdom

Questionnaire

2016 Indian Ocean

1. Level of detail

   Do you feel that the level of detail in this catalogue is:
   a. too specialised   O
   b. about right   O
   c. inadequate   O

2. Frequency of issue

   How often would you purchase a new edition of this catalogue?
   a. Annually   O
   b. Every two years   O
   c. Every three to five years   O
   d. Less frequently   O

3. Design and Quality

   How would you describe the layout and appearance of this catalogue?
   a. Excellent   O
   b. Good   O
   c. Adequate   O
   d. Poor   O

4. How important to you are the prices given in the catalogue:
   a. Important   O
   b. Quite important   O
   c. Of little interest   O
   d. Of no interest   O

5. Would you be interested in an online version of this catalogue?
   a. Yes   O
   b. No   O

6. Do you like the new format?
   a. Yes   O
   b. No   O

7. What changes would you suggest to improve the catalogue? E.g. Which other indices would you like to see included?

   ....
   ....
   ....
   ....

8. Which other Stanley Gibbons Catalogues do you buy?

   ....
   ....
   ....
   ....

9. Would you like us to let you know when the next edition of this catalogue is due to be published?
   a. Yes   O
   b. No   O

   If so please give your contact details below.
   Name: ....
   Address:..
   ....
   ....
   ....
   Email: ....
   Telephone:...

10. Which other Stanley Gibbons Catalogues are you interested in?
    a. ....
    b. ....
    c. ....

Many thanks for your comments.

Please complete and return it to: Hugh Jefferies (Catalogue Editor)
Stanley Gibbons Limited, 7 Parkside, Ringwood, Hampshire BH24 3SH, United Kingdom
or email: lholcombe@stanleygibbons.com to request a soft copy

Stanley Gibbons

399 Strand

Unsure how to progress your collection?

Visit 399 Strand to get advice from our experienced and knowledgeable staff. They will help you choose the stamps and philatelic accessories that will enhance and develop your collection. They will also offer guidance on techniques for the care and storage of your stamps and covers.

We have a superb range of stamps albums and philatelic accessories.

We strive to cater for every need a collector might have, and if we don't have the exact item you need, we will recommend an equivalent or an alternative.

Come in, browse our range and choose what's best for you.

Before you commit to a particular album, take the time to talk to our staff who will help you weigh up the pros and cons before you make your decision. We are always happy to demonstrate anything we sell from tweezers to Frank Godden luxury albums.

Everything for the philatelic collector.

Just down the road from the Savoy Hotel, two minutes from Charing Cross Tube station

For more information, please contact Stephen Bowyer on:
Tel. +44 (0)207 557 4436 or sbowyer@stanleygibbons.com
399 Strand opening hours   **Mon-Fri 9am-5.30pm   Sat 9:30am-5.30pm   Sun Closed**

Est 1856
STANLEY GIBBONS

Stanley Gibbons Limited
399 Strand, London, WC2R 0LX
+44 (0)20 7557 4444
www.stanleygibbons.com

Indian Ocean Order Form

YOUR ORDER

Stanley Gibbons account number ☐ ☐ ☐ ☐ ☐ ☐

Condition (mint/UM/ used)	Country	SG No.	Description	Price	Office use only
			POSTAGE & PACKING	£3.60	
			TOTAL		

The lowest price charged for individual stamps or sets purchased from Stanley Gibbons Ltd, is £1.

Payment & address details

Name

Address (We cannot deliver to PO Boxes)

Postcode

Tel No.

Email

PLEASE NOTE Overseas customers MUST quote a telephone number or the order cannot be dispatched. Please complete ALL sections of this form to allow us to process the order.

☐ Cheque (made payable to Stanley Gibbons)

☐ I authorise you to charge my

☐ Mastercard ☐ Visa ☐ Diners ☐ Amex ☐ Maestro

Card No. ☐☐☐☐☐☐☐☐☐☐☐☐☐☐☐☐☐☐☐ (Maestro only)

Valid from ☐☐☐☐ Expiry date ☐☐☐☐ Issue No. (Maestro only) ☐☐ CVC No. (4 if Amex) ☐☐☐☐

CVC No. is the last three digits on the back of your card (4 if Amex)

Signature

Date

4 EASY WAYS TO ORDER

Post to
Lesley Mourne,
Stamp Mail Order
Department, Stanley
Gibbons Ltd, 399
Strand, London,
WC2R 0LX, England

Call
020 7836 8444
+44 (0)20 7836 8444

Fax
020 7557 4499
+44 (0)20 7557 4499

Click
lmourne@
stanleygibbons.com

How to Choose an Auction?

When I was in my teens I attended my
1st auction which, frankly, I found intimidating –
now, a few years (!) further on, with so few stamp
shops, buying stamps at auction has become an
essential tool of the collector's armoury … so
here are a few tips of what to look for …
and here's the reason why to do it now:

Collectors buy stamps from dealers
Dealers buy stamps from auctions
Therefore Collectors benefit buying from auction too …

So How to Choose an Auction ?

Check/Keep these Key Questions to ask: Features to Look for…

Name of Auction: UNIVERSAL PHILATELIC AUCTIONS		Name of Auction: (Insert Here) ?	
IMPORTANT BIDDER CHECKLIST			
	U P A 1st £55 WINNINGS FREE	✓	*Introductory Offer …. ?*	☐
1	NO Buyer's Premium ?	✓		☐
2	NO Risk ?	✓		☐
3	ALL Lots Guaranteed ?	✓		☐
4	Reducing Estimate System ?	✓		☐
5	Lots £10 to £100,000 ?	✓		☐
6	Describers: 295 years Total Experience?	✓		☐
7	Massive Philatelic Choice ? (20,000+/- lot auctions)	✓		☐
8	£1.5 to £2 Million Auctions ?	✓		☐
9	Prices Realised (transparency) ?	✓		☐
10	FREE highest quality catalogues ? (to New Clients & Regular Clients)	✓		☐
11	6,000+/- Catalogues Distributed Worldwide?	✓		☐
12	FREE On-line Catalogue ?	✓		☐
13	'Keyword' Searchable on-line ?.	✓		☐
14	3,000+ 300/600 DPI photos ?	✓		☐
15	Colour-corrected 300/600 DPI images ?	✓		☐
16	1,900+/- Different Bidders in each auction?	✓		☐
17	90%+/- Bidders Successful ?	✓		☐
18	Low Bid Steps ?	✓		☐
19	Conventional Bidding NO charge ?	✓		☐
20	Electronic Bidding NO charge ?	✓		☐
21	'Live' bidding NO charge ?	✓		☐
22	Limit Bidders accepted NO charge ?	✓		☐
23	Payment Instalments NO charge ?	✓		☐
24	NO Credit Card Charges ?	✓		☐
25	NO Paypal Charges ?	✓		☐
26	NO on-line bidding charges ? (Eg. TheSaleRoom.com)	✓		☐
27	No charge for scans ? (Reasonable requests)			☐
28	NO charge photocopies ? (Reasonable requests)			☐
29	FREE Expert Condition Reports			☐
30	Low Delivery Charges ?	✓		☐
31	Free Delivery Insurance ?	✓		☐
32	Generous *NO Quibble Refund Policy* ?.	✓		☐
33	Reduced UNSOLD LOTS SERVICE ?	✓		☐
34	Expert, Welcoming Friendly Service ?	✓		☐
35	Andrew's *FREE* '**TIPS OF THE TRADE**'	✓		☐

NEW
POST-FREE
UPA
Loyalty
Bonus

SPACE FOR NOTES:
C O M P A R I S O N

£55 1st Winnings Free ?
No buyer's premium ?
All lots guaranteed ?
Unique reducing
Estimate system ?
Loyalty Post Free ?

Indian Ocean
included ✓

**❝This is
My Promise
to YOU❞**

Request UPA Catalogue? ☐   Request Catalogue? ☐
Thank you, You're literally requesting The Collectors' Secret Weapon so